Visionary Women

Visionary Women

Ecstatic Prophecy in
Seventeenth-Century England

Phyllis Mack

UNIVERSITY OF CALIFORNIA PRESS
Berkeley · *Los Angeles* · *Oxford*

Portions of Chapters 1, 2, and 3 were published in an earlier form in the following articles:

"Women as Prophets during the English Civil War," *Feminist Studies* 8 (1982).

"The Female Prophet and her Audience: Class and Gender in the World Turned Upside Down," in *Reviving the English Revolution,* edited by Geoff Eley and William Hunt, Verso, 1988.

"Prophecy and Politics in Seventeenth-Century England," in *Witnesses for Change: Quaker Women over Three Centuries,* edited by Elizabeth Potts Brown and Susan Stuard, Rutgers University Press, 1989.

University of California Press
Berkeley and Los Angeles, California

University of California Press, Ltd.
Oxford, England

© 1992 by
The Regents of the University of California

Library of Congress Cataloging-in-Publication Data

Mack, Phyllis.
    Visionary Women : ecstatic prophecy in seventeenth-century England / Phyllis Mack.
      p.   cm.
    Includes bibliographical references and index.
    ISBN 0-520-07845-4 (alk. paper)
    1. Women, Quaker—England—History—17th century. 2. Prophecy (Christianity)—History—17th century. 3. Spirituality—Society of Friends—History—17th century. 4. Spirituality—England—History—17th century. I. Title.
IN PROCESS (ONLINE)
289.6'42'082—dc20   91-39580

Printed in the United States of America
9 8 7 6 5 4 3 2 1

The paper used in this publication meets the minimum requirements of American National Standard for Information Sciences—Permanence of Paper for Printed Library Materials, ANSI Z39.48-1984. ∞

For Tory

Contents

Acknowledgments

Several friends and colleagues have read and commented on portions of this study, while others have allowed me to read their own unpublished work and otherwise assisted my research. Thanks to Rudolph Bell, Edwin Bronner, Esther Cope, Patricia Crawford, Miriam Garber, John Gillis, Philip Greven, Carla Hesse, Suzanne Lebsock, Mark Robertson, Rachel Weil, and especially Margaret Hunt. Thanks also to Kenneth Carroll, for unstinting encouragement and good cheer, and to Joan Scott, Ruth Bloch, Sarah Hanley, and the other members of the Gender Seminar at the Institute for Advanced Study, Princeton (1985–86).

The staffs of several libraries have been extremely helpful and encouraging. I particularly want to thank Malcolm Thomas and the staff of the Library of the Society of Friends in London, and Edwin Bronner, Elizabeth Potts Brown, and the staff of the Quaker Collection at Haverford College Library. Thanks also to the staffs at the British Library, Bodleian Library, and Preston Public Record Office in England and to the Folger, Princeton University, Swarthmore College, and Union Theological Seminary libraries in the United States.

Many of the ideas in this book were developed as lectures at Amherst College, Barnard College, Boston College, Dartmouth College, Ithaca College, Haverford College, Rutgers University, the University of London, U.C.L.A., Massachusetts Institute of Technology, Yale University, and the Quaker Meeting of Cambridge, Massachusetts. I thank those institutions and audiences for their patronage and their stimulating questions. This study was also written with the assistance of the Rutgers

University Research Council, the Rockefeller Foundation, Haverford College (which awarded me a T. Wistar Brown fellowship in 1982), and the Institute for Advanced Study, Princeton, which provided a luxurious and stimulating environment in which to work in 1985–86. As readers for the University of California Press, Irene Brown and Jean Soderlund made invaluable contributions to the finished manuscript. My editors, Sheila Levine, David Severtson, and Mary Lamprech, have been immensely helpful and encouraging during the long process of completion and revision.

Both as a student of the Society of Friends (or Quakers), and as a struggling single parent, I am daily made aware of the importance of friendship in sustaining and enriching my own life. For their humor, hospitality, intellectual stimulation, and emotional support, I would like to thank Renée and Matthew Baigell, Maxine Berg and John Robertson, Scott Campbell, Gwen and Carmen Cerasoli, Ann Fagan and Gabor Vermes, Jane Fremon, Ziva Galili, Dee Garrison, Judy Gerson, Ruth and Rob Goldston, Deborah Hertz and Martin Bunzl, Margaret Hunt, Peg Jacob, Coppelia Kahn and Avi Wortis, Lisa and Alex Kent, Maureen McCarthy, Ann Markuson, Ruth Perry, Terry Poe, Marilyn, Phil, and Ari Rabinowitz and Sara Budin, Joanna Regulska and Anne Marie Poniz, Marea and Mark Robertson, Susan Shrepfer and Ed Ortiz, Carol, Neil, Laura, and Rachel Weinstein.

I dedicate this book to my beloved daughter, Tory, who has always helped me to find what is best in the world and in myself.

Abbreviations Used
in the Footnotes

BQ   William C. Braithwaite, *The Beginnings of Quakerism* (Cambridge, 1955)

Besse   Joseph Besse, *A Collection of the Sufferings of the People Called Quakers* (London, 1753)

DBR   *Biographical Dictionary of British Radicals in the Seventeenth Century*, ed. Richard L. Greaves and Robert Zaller (Brighton, 1982–84)

DQB   Dictionary of Quaker Biography, typescript, Haverford College Library and Library of the Society of Friends, London

EQW   *Early Quaker Writings, 1650–1700*, ed. Hugh Barbour and Arthur O. Roberts (Grand Rapids, 1973)

FL   *The Friends Library* (Philadelphia, 1842)

FPT   *The First Publishers of Truth*, ed. Norman Penney (London, 1907)

GBS   Great Book of Sufferings, MS, Library of the Society of Friends, London

JFHS   *Journal of the Friends Historical Society*

PP   *Piety Promoted, in a Collection of Dying Sayings of Many of the People Called Quakers*, 4 vols. (Philadelphia, 1854)

PWP   *The Papers of William Penn,* ed. Mary Maples Dunn and
           Richard S. Dunn (Philadelphia, 1981–)

QH   *Quaker History*

QPE   Hugh Barbour, *The Quakers in Puritan England* (New Haven
           and London, 1964)

SM   Swarthmore Manuscripts

SPQ   William C. Braithwaite, *The Second Period of Quakerism*
           (York, 1979)

Author's Note

In most quotations from seventeenth-century sources, archaisms such as "ye" and "yt" have been replaced with their modern alternatives, and modern spellings have been used to replace abbreviations and other orthographic conventions peculiar to the century or to particular authors. Otherwise, spelling and punctuation have been retained as they are in the sources.

Quakers called March "1st month," April "2d month," and so on. I have altered the Quaker system of dates to conform to modern practice. Thus, "1st month" becomes March, and so on.

In citations to manuscript sources, an effort has been made to impose consistency on volume and folio numbers, even though archival institutions will often catalog different manuscripts according to different conventions. A citation such as 1/123 refers to volume 1, folio 123. The abbreviations "fol." or "fols." are used whenever folio numbers do not follow a volume number. In references to the Swarthmore Manuscripts, parenthetical numerals such as (II, 235) refer to transcript number. Otherwise, citations follow the practices of the archival institutions.

This is not ink and paper, or words, which the worst of men, or the devil may read or talk of; but it is spirit, life, and power, killing and making alive; as a fire in the bosom.

Rebeckah Travers, For Those That
Meet to Worship . . . , *1659*

Introduction

I am come to bid thee come down, thou painted beast.
  Jane Ashburner to the rector of Aldingham, 1655

The woman who spoke (or rather screamed) those words called herself a "Friend," a member of a religious society whose adherents repudiated all outward distinctions of wealth, rank, and political power and affirmed the existence of a pure divine light in the heart of every human being. The Anglican priest whom she attacked called her a "Quaker," one of a group of religious fanatics who shouted, quaked, prophesied, and otherwise attempted to undermine the precarious social order of mid-seventeenth-century England. Gathered by George Fox during the early 1650s, the Society of Friends, or Quakers, originated in the remote rural counties of Cumberland, Lancashire, and Yorkshire. Their missionaries moved south to evangelize London and the southern counties in 1654 and then traveled even farther afield, preaching to audiences in New England, the Atlantic colonies, the Caribbean, even to Catholics and Moslems on the island of Malta and in Turkey. The Quakers were only one of many such groups to appear during the two decades of the English Civil War and Interregnum. Yet they were by far the most successful, attracting some sixty thousand members by 1660, the year King Charles II was restored to the throne. The Quakers were also the most receptive to the spiritual authority of women. Of the nearly three hundred visionary women who wrote and prophesied during that early period, over two hundred belonged to the Society of Friends.

During the movement's first decades, Quakers urged and enacted their experience of salvation in a highly public arena—in streets, marketplaces, churches, fields, and prisons—and they did this through flam-

1

boyant public gestures: symbolic signs, charismatic preaching, and martyrdom. By the final years of the century, after decades of systematic persecution by the restored monarchical government, Quakers were attempting to become part of the social and political mainstream. Their public behavior, now subjected to the moral discipline of recognized elders and ministers, became sober and restrained. Sermons and published writings, scrutinized by the Quakers' own Morning Meeting for censorship, took the form of calls for unity and renewed self-discipline rather than imprecations against society or predictions of God's reward or vengeance. Women as prophets retired behind the closed doors of the meeting house, while larger, centralized meetings for business were attended only by men. Instead of publishing polemical broadsides sold on streetcorners, men and women published testimonies detailing the achievements, final illnesses, and apotheoses of Quakers who died in bed.

The observer who seeks to understand Jane Ashburner's challenge to the rector of Aldingham finds an array of ready-made tools or lenses that might be used to bring that interaction between the woman and the priest into focus. The sociologist Max Weber would recognize the prophet's heightened emotionalism as characteristic of an "ideal type" of charismatic sect, which would later transform itself into another "ideal type" of bureaucratic church.[1] The anthropologist Victor Turner would place the woman at one end of a similar continuum: a movement of liminality or community evolving into a movement that was structured and hierarchical.[2] The feminist critic Elaine Hobby would recognize in women's visionary speech and writing the desire for self-expression in a wider public arena, while the poststructuralists Christina Berg and Philippa Berry would celebrate a uniquely feminine grammar, a flamboyant intrusion into the linguistic hegemony of the dominant male culture.[3]

1. Max Weber, *From Max Weber: Essays in Sociology*, trans. H. H. Gerth and C. Wright Mills (London: Oxford University Press, 1991), 51–55, 246ff., 294ff.
2. Victor Turner, *The Ritual Process: Structure and Anti-Structure* (Ithaca, N.Y.: Cornell University Press, 1977). "It is as though there are . . . two major 'models' for human interrelatedness. . . . The first is of society as a structured, differentiated, and often hierarchical system of politico-legal-economic positions. . . . The second, which emerges recognizably in the liminal period, is of society as an unstructured . . . and relatively undifferentiated *comitatus*, community, or even communion of equal individuals" (96).
3. Elaine Hobby, *Virtue of Necessity: English Women's Writing, 1649–88* (London: Virago Press, 1988), 27. Christina Berg and Philippa Berry, "Spiritual Whoredom: An Essay on Female Prophets in the Seventeenth Century," in *1642: Literature and Power in the Seventeenth Century*, ed. Francis Barker et al. (Colchester: University of Essex

The historian Philip Greven, writing from the perspective of post-Freudian psychology, would designate the woman as a self-punishing, compulsive, "evangelical" personality type and her descendants, those virtuous and respectable Friends so much admired by Voltaire, as "moderates."[4] The historian Christopher Hill, writing from a Marxist perspective, would subsume the category of "woman" within that of class and would interpret the prophet's attack on the enrobed Anglican priest as one aspect of a wider and more significant dynamic of class conflict.[5] Thus, depending on her (or his) own theoretical and political predispositions, the modern observer might view the woman prophet of the seventeenth century as a symbol of undiluted, charismatic energy; as a proto-feminist embarked on a meteoric public career; as the struggling victim of a repressive childhood; or, perhaps, as one of a reserve army of female spiritual labor, brought in to affirm egalitarian principles and accomplish dangerous ascetic practices and missionary work during a period of radical social change and laid off when these activities were no longer timely.

In picking up and handling these tools of analysis, some of them both dazzling and daunting to the nonexpert, historians of gender might view themselves as restorers of a venerable painting or tapestry, illuminating individual figures that had formerly been visible only in shadow, revealing still other shadows and depths, perhaps even other outlines and colors, and clarifying and enhancing the overall design. However, it soon becomes evident that this focus on gender, far from clarifying the existing design, has begun to obscure the painting's outlines and muddy the colors.

The Quaker prophets of the Civil War period did perceive and value their community as a movement of antistructure, energized not by laws or fixed programs but by charismatic preaching and a theology of universal love. They further understood that, in struggling to preserve the energy of the original visionary leaders in a later period of retrench-

---

Press, 1981). Berg and Berry characterize the Interregnum as "a brief moment—that of the 1640s and 1650s—wherein a small handfull of prophetesses actually represented their own sexuality within a discussive medium where an explicitly political content was subsumed within a highly personalized mode of expression. . . . In these utterances, the assumption of gender . . . is implicitly refused, to be replaced by a peculiarly androgynous mode of speech which is tremendously threatening" (38,52).

4. Philip Greven, *The Protestant Temperament: Patterns of Child-Rearing, Religious Experience, and the Self in Early America* (New York: Alfred A. Knopf, 1980).

5. Christopher Hill, *The World Turned Upside Down: Radical Ideas during the English Revolution* (New York: Viking Press, 1972).

ment, they were swimming against the tide of their own movement. Yet Quaker women prophets were never simply vessels of charismatic energy. On the contrary, they organized a system of charity, a communications network, care of prisoners, safe houses, and negotiations with magistrates, all of which distinguished Quakers from other more truly anarchic groups and helped to keep the movement alive through decades of persecution. Indeed, women who became prophets, Quaker and non-Quaker, turn out to be nothing more nor less than good citizens. We will find them paying taxes, raising families, manufacturing stockings, holding meetings, testifying in court, maintaining their farms and shops, and carrying their spinning wheels into prison. Their experiences suggest that models of liminality and structure are most meaningful when we restrict our field of vision to strictly formal structures and modes of authority; yet it was precisely *because* women had no formal authority as ordained ministers or magistrates that their activities were so effective in shaping and sustaining the Quakers' charismatic movement in its formative years.

The prophets of the Civil War period, many of them laborers, farmers, or artisans, understood their condemnation of an engorged clergy and aristocracy as both spiritual and social protest. And since women were commonly identified with the poor and deprived, both in Christian tradition and in popular and legal language, one would expect that those radical movements that championed the poor and deprived would also champion the increased authority of women. Yet we will see that those sects that were most radical in challenging traditional social and economic relationships were least likely to be attentive to the needs and rights of oppressed people who were female. Conversely, those women who were most conscious of their authority as females, Quaker and non-Quaker, were also those middle and upper class women who had the least affinity with the plight of the laboring classes. This suggests that there may have been at least two kinds of radicalism in seventeenth-century England and that they were actually at odds.

Religious visionaries frequently referred to their own strict upbringings as factors in shaping their intense desire for moral purity. Yet the psycho-historian's typologies of "moderate" and "evangelical" obscure the different emotional qualities of male and female spirituality. Quaker women portrayed their conversions as less dramatic reversals of status and as a less devastating sacrifice of all ties to home, all hope of parental love, than men did. Subsequently, women prophets were less insistent on their absolute freedom to separate from family and to travel and preach wherever the spirit might lead them. The language and behavior of visionary women, Quaker and non-Quaker, were also less emotional, less pretentious, and less unbalanced than those of men. Does women's more modulated experience of conversion and prophecy, an experience that prevailed in medieval society as well as in seventeenth-century England, imply that girls enjoyed a less repressive upbringing than boys did? Or does it imply, as Caroline Walker Bynum suggests, that adult women had less independent status to lose than men did?[6] Until we know a great deal more about child-rearing practices in relation to boys and girls at different social levels, we must remain agnostics on the precise relation of their childhood experiences to their adult behavior.

Women as prophets enjoyed virtually the only taste of public authority they would ever know. Some of them used that authority to write and publish their own works, to organize separate women's meetings, or to challenge the greater authority of the male leaders. Yet the assumption that visionary women were pursuing a covert strategy of self-assertion ignores the very real problem of agency for seventeenth-century religious actors. For the ground of women's authority as spiritual leaders was their achievement of complete self-transcendence, surely a very different subjective experience from that of the modern social activist or career woman. This suggests not that women as prophets were devoid of personal ambition but that they had a different, more complex view of the self and of the meaning of personal success.

It appears, in short, that the historian's attentiveness to the issue of gender is likely to raise more questions than it answers. It suggests that issues of class and gender have intersected in very different ways at different historical moments, forcing us to broaden our definition of the term "radical." It suggests (as many others have already observed) that the private actions of ordinary individuals have affected larger social and political movements as profoundly as the deeds of great and famous men, forcing us to broaden our definition of the term "politics." Finally, it focuses our attention on the volatile relationship between symbols and stereotypes of gender on the one hand and the thinking and behavior of real human beings on the other, leading us to revise our understanding of the complex terms "masculine" and "feminine."

Our study of seventeenth-century visionaries also points to a funda-

6. Caroline Walker Bynum, "Women's Stories, Women's Symbols: A Critique of Victor Turner's Theory of Liminality," in *Fragmentation and Redemption: Essays on Gender and the Human Body in Medieval Religion* (New York: Zone Books, 1991), 27–51, esp. 37–43.

mental issue in the history of religion—that of the nature of spirituality itself. The problem becomes clear when we examine a set of theoretical tools that are specifically designed to reveal the historical nature of belief systems and subjective experience—the theories of poststructuralism.

The poststructuralist seeks to dissolve the categories and polarities created by language.[7] Rather than shape and prod the stuff of human experience into meaningful, transcendent patterns, the task of the historian or literary critic is to unpack or deconstruct those patterns, to expose the ways in which human relationships, desires, and self-perceptions are constantly generated by the individual in interaction with culture. Human nature, says the poststructuralist, is never a constant, for even apparently elemental human needs and emotions—hunger, physical pain, mother love, sexuality—have no fixed shape, no solidity at all, apart from the cultural values or discourses that both mirror and alter the individual's perception of self.

I suspect that many seventeenth-century people would have found poststructuralist theory more easily digestible than many modern people do. As Michel Foucault and others have shown us, the internalization of social roles as inherent personality traits was only gradually and unevenly achieved during the age of the Victorians, while seventeenth-century men and women lived in a more formalized and public cultural environment.[8] For them, the decision whether to stand or sit, to become a farmer or a minister, to marry or to remain celibate, to nurse and caress an infant or to send it away, all were seen to depend more on family position, social convention, or public policy—on an almost tangible web of social and political relationships—than on individual impulse. For those men and women, a phrase like "gender roles" would have meant precisely what it said; the adoption of the social roles or conventions of masculine or feminine behavior. And the existence of those fixed conventions, whose character was trumpeted from pulpits, thrones, and parliaments, not only gave a kind of theatricality to the actions of men and women; it implied that roles could be switched. Hence the rituals of reversal and the practice of cross-dressing in the theater, on the street,

7. Mary Poovey, "Feminism and Deconstruction," *Feminist Studies* 14, no. 1 (Spring 1988): 51–65.

8. Michel Foucault, *Discipline and Punish: The Birth of the Prison*, trans. Alan Sheridan (New York: Pantheon Books, 1977); *The History of Sexuality*, vol. 1, *An Introduction*, trans. Robert Hurley (New York: Pantheon Books, 1978). See also Denise Riley, *Am I That Name? Feminism and the Category of "Women" in History* (Minneapolis: University of Minnesota Press, 1988), on the internalization of gender differences.

and in the village square, all of which were central to the festive life of contemporaries and were invested with a meaning very different from similar practices in our own culture.

Theories of poststructuralism are especially provocative, and especially problematic, for the historian of religion because the prayer and inner discipline of the women and men we will study were attempts to do nothing less than to deconstruct the self. In hundreds of published tracts, private letters, accounts of dreams, and autobiographical journals, Quakers and others recorded their attempts to apply the acid of self-criticism, fasting, and incessant prayer to their own bodies and personalities; to dissolve the habits, passions, gestures, and little secret sins that made them who they were; to expose themselves as creatures without status, without intelligence, without gender; to become blank. "I am as a white paper book without any line or sentence," wrote one Friend.[9]

What distinguished Quakers and others from the modern poststructuralist, of course, was their belief that beneath the individual self, which they called "the flesh," was an irreducible, eternal essence, which they called "the soul." "The flesh," wrote the Welsh Puritan Morgan Llwyd,

> is everything under the sun that is outside the inner man. Whatever is transient and not eternal—that is flesh. Man's senses are flesh, as well as the pleasures of the world. Playfulness in old and young is flesh. . . . Time and all that is limited by it is flesh. . . . The honour of great men and the snobbishness of small men are flesh. Flesh is all that the natural man can see, and hear, and get, and absorb.[10]

The woman or man who had erased the self, or flesh, and exposed the soul—that piece of God, as Quakers thought—was believed to speak a new, authentic language. The prayers and prophecies of such a person did not merely echo and distort reality, as ordinary language does, but were themselves reality: "This is not ink and paper, or words . . . but it is spirit, life, and power."[11] In short, the element that most separates

9. Richard Farnsworth to George Fox and Margaret Fell, no. 12, 1654, SM 3/51 (II, 64).

10. *Gweithiau Morgan Llwyd*, 1:219–20, quoted in R. Tudor Jones, "The Healing Herb and the Rose of Love: The Piety of Two Welsh Puritans," in *Reformation Conformity and Dissent: Essays in Honour of Geoffrey Nuttall*, ed. R. Buick Knox (London: Epworth Press, 1977), 166.

11. Rebeckah Travers, *For Those That Meet to Worship at the Steeplehouse, Called John Evangelist in London* (London, 1659), MSS vol. 81/8, Library of the Society of Friends, London.

modern observers from seventeenth-century religious visionaries is the
simple but profound fact that they believed in the soul and we, in our
scholarly roles as social scientists, historians, or literary critics, do not.
Having penetrated behind the false solidity of titles, personalities, *men-
talités*, even their own biology, they felt themselves to be gazing on
reality, while the modern scholar sees only a void. Yet the visionary's
attempt to heal the self through a radical denial of self can appear to us
only in its narrowest and most superficial aspect, as a form of ambition,
frustration, or even madness, unless we grant that for them acts of
self-negation were like tearing away a curtain in order to penetrate to
something else behind it, still to be revealed.

Having affirmed the centrality of the prophet's spiritual concerns—
having, as it were, pleaded for the soul as a category of historical
analysis—one must ask how the religious visionary's preoccupation
with the health of the soul affected his or her own subjective awareness.
We tend to imagine such a person as an isolated, introspective, and
ascetic figure. Yet the thrust of the visionary's energy was to make
something *universal* of her personal experience, to identify her own
particular insights with those expressed by biblical figures or the members of a religious congregation. The formal salutations and biblical
paraphrases in private letters and journals are therefore as revealing to
the historian as are the shreds of personal information they contain. The
visionary's sense of enhanced perception was also intensely *physical*. Her
negation of her material body did not open the way to the sensational,
out-of-the-body experiences of the modern occultist nor to the extreme
self-loathing of the medieval ascetic. Rather, she felt her body to be
flooded by a divine essence that she experienced variously as a loss of
control (as in the Quakers' shaking or quaking) or as the mystic's rush
of energy streaming from inside the self. Finally, the visionary's experience was profoundly *social*. Her enlightened condition did not imply
detachment from the world but connectedness with humanity and nature: a "unity with the creation," as George Fox said. Society made
individuals; salvation made bonding.

Each of these elements may be illustrated by a single religious text, the
diary of Ann Bathurst, a respectable, middle-aged widow and a member
of the mystical Philadelphian Society, which was active in London during
the 1690s. In 1679 Bathurst recorded a self-induced vision:

> I desired that one of my children might come up, and she came a little after:
> and then another of them, . . . then all my children one after another: and as
> they came up, I remembered two little children, which died one at fourteen

weeks, the other at fourteen days' end, and immediately as soon as I began to desire it, they came like two bright sparks.[12]

The text tells us that, contrary to the assumption of many historians, a woman might cherish the memory of her dead children even when she lost them as infants. It also tells us what a religious woman might make of that feeling. In a vision recorded four months later, Bathurst experienced intense physical ecstasy, feeling the locus of her own spiritual power in her womb. "Then I feared not the Enemy: and I had a light that shined from my stomach like a sun. . . . This was the first time I received, or knew I had, *the flame*."[13] Two months afterward, on a night when she was visited by Christ and God the Father, "then they opened my stomach, . . . and went into my stomach, and closed it up again. . . . O the joy! that I had gotten my God, my saviour and redeemer, sitting in me, as on a throne of refiner's fire."[14] In yet another vision eight years later, Bathurst extended her personal experience to encompass her wider spiritual community, becoming an intercessor for several male and female friends, who brought their own dead children to her to suckle and to receive the benefit of her prayers.[15]

The observer who seeks to understand the seventeenth-century religious visionary finds a group of women and men whose sensibilities ultimately elude the tools of the modern scholar. How, then, can our limited knowledge of their experiences be useful? Most obviously, we can trace a direct line from the earliest Quaker women leaders to the nineteenth-century movements of abolition and women's suffrage and to twentieth-century feminism and peace activism. Indeed, the history of Quakerism during its first fifty years not only establishes part of the heritage of modern feminism; it foreshadows some of the movement's deepest problems.

The earliest Quakers were radical and democratic not only because they appreciated the particular qualities of women as helpmeets or "mothers in Israel" but because they perceived the attributes of men and women to be fluid and interchangeable. The letters and visionary texts

    12. Diary of Ann Bathurst, Rawlinson Manuscripts D. 1262/13, March 17, 1679, Bodleian Library, Oxford.
    13. Ibid., fols. 32–33, July 26, 1679.
    14. Ibid., fol. 48, September 10, 1679.
    15. Ibid., fols. 300–1, May 27 and June 1, 1687.

written by the first female prophets are often indistinguishable from those written by men. Indeed, a few women prophets actually announced to their audiences that they *were* men; having transcended the social identities that dictated that they remain subject to their fathers and husbands, they claimed the right, with other genderless souls, to stand and speak at the very altar of the church and before the very doors of Parliament. This was a remarkably creative act, yet it did not liberate women from the constraints of a traditional gendered discourse. As prophets seeking to reinterpret rather than deny their own religious heritage, as public actors attempting to enlighten their audiences rather than simply attack them, women used not an unfamiliar, invented language but a traditional male language. Moreover, it is unlikely that anyone listening to those early prophets would have been moved to reevaluate negative female symbols and stereotypes; on the contrary, women as prophets relied on those very symbols (the Anglican priest as the "whore of Babylon," the luxurious trappings of the church as "menstrous rags") in order to discredit their antagonists.

By contrast, Quaker women ministers of the second generation based their public authority not only on their conviction of being "in the light" but on their competence and integrity as daughters, as mothers, and as heads of families. *Their* written texts are easily distinguishable from those of male Friends. Rather than emphasize the role of reason in the activities of worship and meditation, as male writers now did, women stressed the principles of universal love and personal virtue, principles they frequently depicted in mystical, highly feminine imagery. Their most intense spiritual experiences were attained not in the great open-air gatherings of earlier days but within the closed circles of their own women's meetings. The price women paid for this new autonomy was a dilution of the physical intensity of their earlier ecstatic experiences and a greater separation from those women who did not share their resources or family statuses. Their dignity as women was linked not only to a new appreciation of "feminine" qualities but to an emphasis on the specifically bourgeois qualities of moderation, competence in business and in the home, and personal self-control.

Thus, the history of Quaker women's achievements should not lead us to romanticize the family as a setting for women's creativity, nor should it be taken as a call for a new deconstruction of gender roles. It *can* remind us that there are modes of perception, of bodily awareness, and of human interaction that are beyond our ken but not necessarily beyond our capacity. It also allows us to contemplate a set of internal conflicts that have parallels in the concerns of today and presumably tomorrow, for modern feminists are certainly torn between a desire to cast away every vestige of women's traditional sphere of experience and a desire to salvage, even to celebrate, parts of that experience. Thus do we find our own voices echoing the prayers and arguments—and screams—of these remote seventeenth-century visionaries as we move to embrace our own political and spiritual struggles.

PART ONE

Feminine Symbolism and Female Prophecy: Gender and Knowledge in the World Turned Upside Down

CHAPTER ONE

Woman, Nature, and Spirit

And the tongue is a fire. The tongue is an unrighteous world
among our members, staining the whole body, setting on
fire the cycle of nature, and set on fire by hell. . . . No
human being can tame the tongue—a restless evil, full of
deadly poison. . . . From the same mouth come blessing and
cursing.

James 3:6–10

INTRODUCTION

Lady Eleanor Davies, whose lifetime saw the death of Queen Elizabeth
and the beheading of King Charles I, was the wealthy daughter of an earl,
wife of the attorney general for Ireland, mistress of a great estate, and
the mother of two children; she was also a prophet. One morning in
1625, she was awakened in the gallery of her manor house in Berkshire
by the voice of the prophet Daniel, "speaking as through a trumpet."
"Nineteen years and a half to the Judgment," intoned the voice, "and
you as the meek Virgin." From that moment until her death twenty-seven
years later, Lady Eleanor never looked back.[1]

Noting that her own maiden name of Audeley lent itself to a highly
significant anagram, "Eleanor Audelie: reveale o Daniel," she proceeded
to address the Archbishop of Canterbury with a written statement of
advice on international politics.[2] He was unimpressed and returned it to
her husband, who threw it into the fire. She retaliated by predicting that
Sir Davies would die within three years, which he did, in just half that
time (in 1626), after she began wearing mourning for him at dinner.

1. Lady Eleanor, *The Everlasting Gospel* (1649), 4. See Esther S. Cope, "Dame
Eleanor Davies, Never Soe Mad a Ladie?" *Huntingdon Library Quarterly*, 50, no. 2
(Spring 1987): 133–44; Theodore Spencer, "The History of an Unfortunate Lady,"
Harvard Studies and Notes in Philology and Literature 20 (1938): 43–59. Eleanor Davies
was born in about 1590. My thanks to Professor Cope for allowing me to read her
unpublished manuscript on Lady Eleanor's life, "*Dame Eleanor Davies, Never Soe Mad
a Ladie?*" forthcoming by the University of Michigan Press.
2. Lady Eleanor, *A Warning to the Dragon and All His Angels* (1625), 1.

Emboldened by this apparent vindication of her powers, she began circulating about the court, where her advice was requested by the royal family on matters relating to the queen's fertility. She soon acquired a national reputation as a prophet, her reputation further enhanced by her correct prediction of the death in 1628 of the Duke of Buckingham.

Lady Eleanor's troubles began when she decided to publish her political writings. In 1633, on the pretext of accompanying her husband to a continental spa, she traveled to Holland, where she brought out a tract, published at her own expense, comparing King Charles I to the biblical tyrant Belshazzar. She was promptly arrested, fined the enormous sum of three thousand pounds (which was never paid), and imprisoned for two years. The magistrates also burned her books, judging that she was dangerous because she had presumed to penetrate arcane biblical texts, "which much unbeseemed her sex," and because she had acquired the reputation of a "cunning woman" among the common people.[3] (One magistrate, clearly convinced she was insane, invented a new anagram, "Dame Eleanor Davies: never soe mad a ladie," which titillated the courtroom.) Lady Eleanor responded by imposing her own sentence on Archbishop Laud, a prediction of his death within the month. Confined in the gatehouse of Westminster, she petitioned the House of Commons for better treatment, demanded a formal apology from King Charles, and during a full moon received a visit from an angel, who rested on her bed for an hour and left a scent from his glove, "all oiled with ambergreece."[4] She was released from prison in 1635, and some months later she appeared in a church in Lichfield, sat in the bishop's throne, declared herself primate and metropolitan, and poured a kettle full of hot tar and wheat paste on the church hangings, calling it "holy water." This time (1637) she was condemned as a lunatic and committed to the asylum of Bedlam, whose inmates were visited by sightseers on weekend excursions.[5]

Released from Bedlam (and another imprisonment in the tower) in 1639, Lady Eleanor spent the rest of her life composing apocalyptic, antigovernment tracts that were handed personally to members of Par-

3. Eleanor Davies, *The Blasphemous Charge against Her* (London, 1649), quoted in Christina Berg and Philippa Berry, "Spiritual Whoredom: An Essay on Female Prophets in the Seventeenth Century," in *1642: Literature and Power in the Seventeenth Century*, ed. Francis Barker et al. (Colchester: University of Essex, 1981), 46.

4. Eleanor Davies, *Ezekiel the Prophet Explained* (1647), 5–6, quoted in Cope, "Dame Eleanor Davies," III.

5. Eleanor [Davies], *Bethlehem Signifying the House of Bread* . . . (1625), 5. Cope, "Dame Eleanor Davies," 134. Lady Eleanor lived separately but received the sacrament with other inmates (House of Lords Record Office, Main Papers, Sept. 22, 1647).

liament, which she may have visited almost daily during the 1640s. In 1639 she predicted that London would be destroyed by fire, and fires shortly broke out. In 1645 Archbishop Laud was executed, which confirmed, for her, the approaching end of the nineteen-and-a-half years before the Last Judgment. When Charles I was executed in 1649, yet another of her prophecies come true, her reputation revived, and she acquired a number of ardent disciples, one of whom wrote flowery introductions to her works. Her last prediction was of a second flood, to occur in 1656, but she did not live to see whether she had been right. Lady Eleanor died in 1652 and was buried with honor in the family chapel.

When a seventeenth-century Englishman was confronted by the shocking spectacle of a woman who prophesied in public, what did he see and hear? "A woman clothed with the sun," "a base slut," "a Jezebel," "a Jesuit," "a silly old woman," "a goat rough and hairy," "a woman to make your heart to tremble," "an old trot." There was enormous variation in the tone of contemporary responses to the speech and writing of visionary women, from the satirical sniping of playwrights like Ben Jonson and Thomas Heywood and the authors of astrological almanacs, to the ponderous introspection of Puritan spiritual treatises, to the purple prose of some mystical philosophers. There was also great variation in the reaction of these observers toward individual women, from sycophantic veneration, to cynical amusement, to outright sadism.

Surely one of the most bizarre elements of Lady Eleanor's very bizarre story is the fluidity of her public identity—the ease and rapidity with which contemporaries changed their perceptions of her from prophet, to witch, to lunatic, to prophet again. Part of the reason for this volatility must lie with Lady Eleanor's own extremely volatile personality, which inspired one of her early adversaries to heights of invective: "I will spend no more term time upon thee Hecate, Medusa, legion, clovenfooted Gorgon. Yet if I meet thee . . . assure thy self, I will kick thee and scratch a minced pie for a dog from thy ill kept filthy dunghill arse."[6] Her notoriety was increased by her ability to command sustained public attention by virtue of her wealth and social position and by the notorious

6. Mr. Brookes letter to the Ladie Davies written Anno 1622, SP14/130/135, Conway Papers, London Public Record Office. The diatribe concerned a lawsuit between Lady Eleanor and Mr. Brooke's wife. My thanks to Esther Cope for the transcript.

and eccentric behavior of other members of her family. (Her brother Mervin was executed for sodomy and as an accessory to the rape of his wife by a page. Another brother, Ferdinando, was, in her words, "a perverted papist." Her first husband, Sir John Davies, was widely known for his tempestuous disposition. Her second husband, Sir Archibald Douglas, who claimed to be a bastard son of King James I, was pronounced incurably insane when he uttered prophecies, hid himself in his bedclothes, and attacked a witness with his hands and teeth.)[7]

A more fundamental reason for the fluidity of Lady Eleanor's public persona lies not in the temperament of the real woman, nor in those of the individuals around her, but in the images and stereotypes *about* women that pervaded the culture in which she lived and that helped to mold that temperament into a shape her audiences understood. "As with language," writes historian Carlo Ginzburg, "culture offers to the individual a horizon of latent possibilities—a flexible and invisible cage in which he can exercise his own conditional liberty."[8] The following two chapters describe the cage of symbols and stereotypes that conditioned the public expression of visionary women during the period of the English Civil War, while chapter 3 describes the prophets of the 1640s from the perspective of the visionary herself.

RELIGIOUS METAPHOR AND THE FEMALE NATURE

Woman to man is either a god or a wolf.
John Webster, The White Devil

Images of womanhood have always been a fundamental element of Christian tradition. We are all acquainted with the figures of Eve and the Virgin Mary and with the symbol of the church as the bride of Christ. Protestants in seventeenth-century England and America had jettisoned the traditional feminine cults of Mary and the saints, but the traditional feminine qualities of humility, receptivity, and emotionalism remained appropriate to express their spiritual values. When they spoke of the absolute nullity of human virtue in relation to divine love and judg-

    7. House of Lords Record Office, Main Papers, January 29, 1641, discussed in Cope, "*Dame Eleanor Davies*," 82–83. On her brother's execution, Cynthia Herrup, "The Patriarch at Home: The Trial of the Earl of Castlehaven for Rape and Sodomy," typescript, Duke University, Dept. of History. Lady Eleanor married Douglas in 1627.
    8. Carlo Ginzburg, *The Cheese and the Worms: The Cosmos of a Sixteenth-Century Miller,* trans. John and Ann Tedeschi (Baltimore: Johns Hopkins University Press, 1980), xxi.

ment, that human nullity or spiritual nakedness was often see
nine. Thus, the Puritan Thomas Shephard equated the vanity
goodness with female corruption: "When the soul sees that a
teousness is a menstruous cloth, polluted with sin . . . it beg.... .. .. .,
out, How can I stand or appear before him with such continual pollutions."[9]

The existential experiences of sin and salvation were also expressed
in gendered imagery. In sermons, tracts, and spiritual diaries, the damned
soul was a selfish whore or a monster mother or a sow sprawling in the
mud with her piglets, while the soul that was saved was a nursing mother
or a bride eager for intimate union with the bridegroom. God was not
only a father and husband; he was a hen spreading her wings over her
baby chicks, and his words were milk, sucked in by believers as they
meditated on their Bibles or the minister's sermon. "It is said," wrote
Increase Mather, quoting from the biblical Song of Songs, "We have a
little sister that has no breasts, what shall we do for her? So there are little
places . . . in *New England*, that have no breasts, no ministers from whom
they may receive the sincere milk of the Word."[10]

One of the chief characteristics of this feminine religious symbolism was its mutability. Thus, a woman might be identified with the
moon,

> the lady of great beauty, the mistress of rain and waters, the giver of riches,
> the nurse of mankind, the governor of all states, kind, merciful, protecting
> men by sea and land, mitigating all tempests of fortune, dispensing with
> fate, nourishing all things growing on the earth, . . . restraining the rage of
> goblins.[11]

9. Thomas Shephard, *The Sound Believer*, quoted in David Leverenz, *The Language of Puritan Feeling: An Exploration in Literature, Psychology, and Social History*
(New Brunswick, N.J.: Rutgers University Press, 1980), 155.

10. Increase Mather, *David Serving His Generation*, quoted in Leverenz, *Language*,
1. See also Donald Maltz, "The Bride of Christ Is Filled with His Spirit," in *Women in
Ritual and Symbolic Roles*, ed. Julia Hoch-Smith and Anita Spring (New York and
London: Plenum Press, 1978), 27–44. On the image of God as mother elsewhere in
Europe, and in earlier periods, see Carolyn Walker Bynum, *Jesus as Mother: Studies in the
Spirituality of the High Middle Ages* (Berkeley: University of California Press, 1982),
110–69; Piero Camporesi, *The Incorruptible Flesh: Bodily Mutation and Mortification in
Religion and Folklore*, trans. Tania Croft-Murray (Cambridge and New York: Cam-
bridge University Press, 1988), 27.

11. Cornelius Agrippa, *Occult Philosophy*, trans. J. F. (1651), Book 2, 336, quoted
in Katherine Mary Briggs, *Pale Hecate's Team: An Examination of the Beliefs on Witchcraft and Magic among Shakespeare's Contemporaries and His Immediate Successors*
(London: Routledge and Kegan Paul, 1962), 80–81. For a general discussion of the
mutability of feminine spiritual symbolism, see Hoch-Smith and Spring, eds., *Women in
Ritual and Symbolic Roles*, 1–11.

Or she might as easily be identified with the lowest elements of the great Chain of Being, the ooze of animal appetite and putrefaction. "Women are like curst dogs," warns a character in John Webster's *The White Devil;* "civility keeps them tied all daytime, but they are let loose at midnight, then they do most good or most mischief."[12]

What was the meaning of the feminine imagery used to express so many facets of the spiritual experience of English Protestants, whether vigilant Puritans, complacent Anglicans, or ecstatic Ranters? How could a single symbolic archetype give such clear shape both to the still contentedness of the limpid soul at peace with God and to the aggression and bestiality of the weak human sinner? And how are we to understand the meaning of feminine spiritual symbolism in relation to the perception and behavior of individual women and men?

To a seventeenth-century Englishman, an image or metaphor of womanhood meant both less and more than it does to the modern reader. Less, because the Renaissance was an age of paradox, when the contemplation of truth and beauty in opposites was a central theme of rhetorical expression. Thus, an exposition of the virtues and vices of Mary and Eve might well have been intended as an intellectual or aesthetic exercise, more akin to Clément Marot's matched poems "The Beautiful Breast" and "The Ugly Breast" than to serious polemic; literary misogynists were not ipso facto woman haters.[13] More, because the enterprise of many seventeenth-century writers went far beyond that of the mere poet or scholar. They were seekers after God's own face, which was hidden behind the eyes and voices of the ministers and visionaries who spoke to them in increasingly unexpected contexts.[14]

12. John Webster, *The White Devil* (San Francisco: Chandler Publishing Co., 1961), 10.

13. Linda Woodbridge, *Women and the English Renaissance: Literature and the Nature of Womankind, 1540–1620* (Urbana and Chicago: University of Illinois Press, 1984), 5, 8. Woodbridge cites Spenser's *The Faerie Queene* as an example of this use of paradoxical feminine imagery (119–20). See also Rosalie Colie, *Paradoxica Epidemica: The Renaissance Tradition of Paradox* (Princeton: Princeton University Press, 1966). For the debate on women's character, see Katherine Usher Henderson and Barbara F. McManus, eds., *Half Humankind: Contexts and Texts of the Controversy about Women in England, 1540–1640* (Urbana and Chicago: University of Illinois Press, 1985).

14. For discussions of the meaning of symbolism in early modern culture, see Peter Burke, *Popular Culture in Early Modern Europe* (New York: Harper and Row, 1978), 170–73; E. H. Gombrich, *Symbolic Images: Studies in the Art of the Renaissance* (London: Phaidon, 1972; distributed by Praeger), 165, 178, 180–81; Michael Hunter, *John Aubrey and the Realm of Learning* (New York: Science History Publications, 1975), 127. All three writers emphasize the difficulty of determining the extent to which symbols were taken as personifications of real beings.

Catholics and early Protestants believed that the presence of God in the wine and wafer of the communion table was not symbolic but real. "It is the greatest idiocy," wrote Luther, "to say 'the bread means or is a symbol of the body he gave for us, and the chalice or wine is a symbol of the blood he shed for us.'"

> Christ's humanity is on the right hand of God and now also in all and over all things in the manner of the divine right hand, but you won't chew or slurp him like the cabbage or soup on your table unless he wills it. He has now become incomprehensible; you can't touch him even if he is in your bread— unless, that is, he binds himself to you and summons you to a special table with his word and with his word points out to you the bread you should eat. This he does in the Last Supper.[15]

Many radical Protestants, who had long denied the validity of consubstantiation or the "real presence" in the sense Luther gave the term, believed, nevertheless, in the real appearance or presence of God in human individuals and events. And this real presence was not tied to the ritual of a church or the hierarchy of a priesthood. It permeated the secret consciousness of the devout, illiterate worshiper as well as the public discourse of the educated minister. Thus, the prophet's statement, "I am Daniel," was not intended to be understood merely as descriptive metaphor ("I am [like] Daniel"), any more than the consecrated wafer was to be seen as bearing a mere resemblance or remembrance of God's flesh. It might mean, as it did for Quakers, that God inhabited the new prophet in exactly the same way as the biblical Daniel had been inhabited. It might even mean, as it did for followers of the prophet Lodowijk Muggleton, that their leader was to be seen as a physical reincarnation of a concrete biblical figure.

Of course an observer might conclude, as some did of Lady Eleanor, that a statement like "I am Daniel" was either misguided or insane. In most cases, however, critics rejected the visionary not because they denied the theoretical possibility of divine intervention in human history but because they believed either that the age of prophecy had ended with the coming of Christ or that the individual confronting them was an inappropriate vehicle for God's voice. Likewise, sceptics denigrated witchcraft not because they found the notion of diabolical possession

15. Martin Luther, "Vom Abendmahl Christi, Bekenntnis" (1528), quoted in Kristin Eldyss Sorensen Zapalac, "In His Image and Likeness": Political Iconography and Religious Change in Regensburg, 1500–1600 (Ithaca, N.Y., and London: Cornell University Press, 1990), 39. Das diese Wort Christi (1527), quoted in Zapalac, "In His Image," 39.

intrinsically ridiculous; what *was* ridiculous was the notion that Satan's magisterial presence would actually become manifest through the persona of a silly old woman. Thus, a parliamentary paper of 1645 included an editorial belittling the importance of witchcraft accusations: "But whence is it that devils should choose to be conversant with silly women that know not their right hands from their left, is the great wonder." The physician Reginald Scot stated as the purpose of his scientific treatise against witchcraft practices, "first, that the glory and power of God be not so abridged and abased, as to be thrust into the hand or lip of a lewd old woman; whereby the work of the Creator should be attributed to the power of a creature."[16]

The meaning of religious metaphor to seventeenth-century writers and actors was also different because their understanding of the relationship between mind and body was different. In this respect, contemporary thinking more closely resembled that of a modern neurologist than that of a modern layperson. For both groups, mental processes are defined in terms of physical processes, and emotions and insights are identifiable by concrete physical changes (the neurologist might say hormonal, they would have said humoral). Seventeenth-century Protestants were far removed, in their own estimation, from those superstitious Catholics who knelt before the encased body parts of saints as containers of powerful heavenly distillations or from the nuns and monks who dissected holy corpses oozing aromatic sap, discovering minute crosses or thorns embedded in the depths of the gall bladder, liver, or heart.[17] Yet Puritans and Anglicans did hold to the allied belief that the individual's spiritual state was reflected in the texture, moisture, and aroma of his or her own flesh. The condition of the body was thus a sign, visible both to oneself and to others, of the spiritual condition of the soul beneath the skin. In a letter to his friend Anne Conway, the Cambridge Platonist Henry More conjectured that a certain patient was cured neither by the power of the devil nor by miracle,

> but by a power partly natural and partly devotional . . . [because] the blood and spirits of this party [i.e., the healer] is become sanitive and healing, by long temperance and devotion . . . nature being so hugely advanced and

16. *Moderate Intelligencer*, September 4–11, 1645, quoted in Wallace Notestein, *A History of Witchcraft in England from 1558 to 1718* (1911; reprint, New York: Russell and Russell, 1965), 179–80. Reginald Scot, *The Discoverie of Witchcraft* (1584), quoted in Sydney Anglo, ed., *The Damned Art: Essays in the Literature of Witchcraft* (London: Routledge and Kegan Paul, 1977), 108.

17. Camporesi, *The Incorruptible Flesh*, 3–5.

perfectly concocted, that his blood and spirits are a true elixir, and therefore he laying his hand upon diseased persons, his spirits run out of his own body into the party diseased, and actuate and purify the blood and spirits of the diseased party, which I conceive they do with more efficacy, if he add devotion to his laying on of his hands, for that sets his spirits afloat the more copiously and animates them the more strongly.[18]

Far from posing a clear dichotomy between mind and body, seventeenth-century men and women *felt* certain kinds of knowledge. They described their own spirituality not as an ethereal, disembodied state but as polymorphous, subterranean energy, more akin to the power Freud ascribed to sex than it was to the diluted piety of an eighteenth-century pillar of the church. Thus, the metaphor of woman as vessel conveyed a literal as well as a literary meaning, for the woman's body was understood to be a potentially explosive device, the carrier of an inflammable spiritual essence. But whereas the visionary's protean energy had been transmuted by the real presence of God into pure spiritual ecstasy, the energy of the witch had been transmuted by Satanic influence into pure bestial malice or lust. "Nature hath put a fierceness into the female because of the impotency thereof," wrote the Puritan Daniel Rogers, "therefore the she bear [and] the lioness, are the most raging, and cruel. But grace makes that natural impotency of the woman, turn impotency for God."[19]

Clearly, the pervasiveness of feminine spiritual imagery does not automatically imply that all women saw themselves, or were perceived by others, as virginal handmaids or polluted whores. It does appear, however, that when a woman like Eleanor Davies assumed unconventional forms of spiritual authority—when she chastised those in power or published her visionary pronouncements on the state of the nation— she expressed herself in terms of a repertoire of images that formed a shared language between herself and her audience. Unable to justify her authority in terms of her own individual capacities (women being denied that kind of public forum), she invited her audience to contemplate her as the literal embodiment of a feminine archetype: God's secretary, vessel, handmaid, or bride, as she variously described herself. Her audience, in turn, responded to her largely in terms of her metaphoric

18. Henry More to Anne Conway, Grantham, June 7, 1654, reprinted in Marjorie Hope Nicholson, ed., *Conway Letters: The Correspondence of Ann, Viscountess Conway, Henry More, and Their Friends, 1642–1684* (New Haven: Yale University Press, 1930), no. 57.

19. D[aniel] R[ogers], *Matrimoniall Honour* . . . (London, 1642), 309.

qualities, as if they, the auditors, were readers and the prophet was herself a living text.

WOMEN'S NATURE

Contemporary beliefs about the fluidity of the feminine archetype derived from the more general belief, expressed in the writings of philosophers, doctors, playwrights, and ministers as well as in the pamphlets and broadsides of astrologers and religious sectarians, in the fluidity or mutability of real women. The image of the female personality that emerges from these various genres of popular and learned culture might best be described as amphibious. As civilized beings—on land, so to speak—women were portrayed as members of a particular class and upholders of cultural values, just as men were. Yet women were also portrayed as liminal creatures inhabiting a no-man's-land of natural and spiritual forces that had nothing to do with culture. Whereas a man's identity was chiefly determined by his place in the social hierarchy, which was part of a universal hierarchy, or Chain of Being, a woman's nature was thought to have no fixed identity or place. Outwardly ordinary, a woman was thought to have an inner essence or imagination that could careen over the widest emotional and spiritual landscape, all the way to a union with God and an identification with cosmic wisdom or, in the other spiritual direction, to suicidal insanity or possession by demons. As one proverb put it, "Women are in churches, saints: abroad, angels: at home, devils: at windows, sirens: at doors, [mag]pies: and in gardens, goats."[20]

Thus, if man, nature's great piece of work, stood poised on a point between the animals and the angels, woman seemed constantly to waver between both extremes. Eulogized as paragons of moral sensitivity in Puritan marriage tracts, conduct books, or elegies for pious matrons, women were labeled as beasts in the language of that same literature and in the ritual of popular custom. Thus, the ideal wife of one popular conduct book "submits herself with quietness, cheerfully, even as a well-broken horse turns at the least check of the rider's bridle, readily

20. Tertullian, *De cultu feminarum*, I.I.2, quoted in Peter.Brown, *The Body and Society: Men, Women, and Sexual Renunciation in Early Christianity* (New York: Columbia University Press, 1988), 153. M. P. Tilley, *A Dictionary of the Proverbs in England in the Sixteenth and Seventeenth Centuries* (Ann Arbor: University of Michigan Press, 1950), W702. On the instability of the female subject in English Renaissance literature and culture, see Catherine Belsey, *The Subject of Tragedy: Identity and Difference in Renaissance Drama* (London and New York: Methuen, 1985), Part 2.

going and standing as he wishes that sits upon her back."[21] C
women were compared to sows; bridles were put into the
scolds, or they were strapped into "cucking stools" and dunkeu
the water; it was not unheard of for unwanted wives to be sold in the
marketplace with halters around their necks.[22] One reason for the
witch's traditional affinity with animals, both as familiars and as victims,
was undoubtedly the perception that her pact with the devil meant the
triumph of animal appetite over reason or morality, a victory that was
easier to achieve with women than with men, given the relative power
of appetite over reason in the female constitution.[23]

Contemporaries argued that the fluidity of women was a biological
fact as well as a psychological and spiritual condition.[24] A woman's
body was believed to be more wet and spongy than a man's, making her
more lustful, irrational, and emotional. *Lustful,* because women's
spongy bodies could not readily expel bad humors and needed regular

21. William Whately, *A Bride-Bush* (London, 1617), 43, quoted in Peter Stallybrass, "Patriarchal Territories: The Body Enclosed," in *Rewriting the Renaissance: The Discourses of Sexual Difference in Early Modern Europe,* ed. Margaret W. Ferguson, Maureen Quilligan, and Nancy J. Vickers (Chicago and London: University of Chicago Press, 1986), 126.

22. Barry Reay, ed., *Popular Culture in Seventeenth-Century England* (London and Sydney: Croom Helm, 1985), 10; Lyle Koehler, *A Search for Power: The "Weaker Sex" in Seventeenth-Century New England* (Urbana, Chicago, and London: University of Illinois Press, 1980), 43, 307; Keith Thomas, *Man and the Natural World: A History of the Modern Sensibility* (New York: Pantheon Books, 1983), 43, 45. In New England the usual insult for men was "dog," implying someone who was craven or dependent, while "sow" or "pig" was commonly applied to women; pigs, raised only for slaughter, were "unclean, dependent, exploited by men for their own benefit, and controlled by Satan" (Robert St. George, "Heated Speech and Literacy in Seventeenth-Century New England," in *Seventeenth-Century New England,* ed. David D. Hall and David Grayson Allen, The Colonial Society of Massachusetts, vol. 63 [Charlottesville: University Press of Virginia, 1984], 290–91). On the cucking stool, used to punish scolds, see John Webster Spargo, *Judicial Folklore in England, Illustrated by the Cucking-Stool* (Durham, N.C.: Duke University Press, 1944).

23. For a theoretical discussion of cultural inversion in relation to witches and animals, see Stuart Clark, "Inversion, Misrule, and the Meaning of Witchcraft," *Past and Present* 87 (1980): 120. Many authors noted women's capacities to become masculine or animal-like. See Thomas Heywood, *The Exemplary Lives and Memorable Acts of Nine of the Most Worthy Women of the World* (London, 1640), on Deborah (5–19), Elpheda (132–50), and Bundeca (70–92).

24. For medical theory of women's biology, see Audrey Eccles, *Obstetrics and Gynecology in Tudor and Stuart England* (Kent, Ohio: Kent State University Press, 1982), Chap. 4, "The Female Reproductive System"; Hilda Smith, "Gynecology and Ideology in Seventeenth-Century England," in *Liberating Women's History: Theoretical and Critical Essays,* ed. Berenice A. Carroll (Urbana, Chicago, and London: University of Illinois Press, 1976), 97–115; Thomas Laqueur, "Orgasm, Generation, and the Politics of Reproductive Biology," in *The Making of the Modern Body: Sexuality and Society in the Nineteenth Century,* ed. Catherine Gallagher and Thomas Laqueur (Berkeley: University of California Press, 1987), 8–16.

sex in order to stay well ventilated and healthy. "A woman's honesty is penned up in a very little room," advised the author of *Poor Robin's Visions*; "it is confined only from her apron-strings downward."[25] *Irrational*, because the brain required a hot, dry (i.e., masculine) medium in order to effectively carry on its work; newborn babies were sprinkled with saltwater to dry out their brains and strengthen their wit.[26] The Puritan Richard Baxter counseled husbands to be patient toward "wives who, . . . by a natural passionate weakness, or by melancholy, or crazedness, are willfull. . . . Your passion and sourness to a person that cannot cure her own unpleasing carriage, is a more inexcusable fault and folly than hers, who hath not the power of reason as you have."[27] *Emotional*, because feelings were generated by the heart and by the motion of bodily fluids (blood, bile, phlegm, tears), not the soul or the brain. Not only did bodily fluids move according to the rhythm of the individual's emotional states; they actually contained the body's emotional energy, so that contact with the bodily fluids of another person might, in certain circumstances, place one under that person's occult influence. Weeping thus had sacramental significance as a tangible sign of an inward repentant grace, so that the words of the visionary Sarah Wight were more efficacious for being uttered through tears. Urine was another carrier of the individual's emotional essence, so that in Wales a man might signify his love for a woman by urinating on her dress. Semen was the locus of male sexual feeling, so that John Wilmot, Earl of Rochester, could imagine his whole conscious self transmuted into sperm:

> O that I now cou'd, by some chymic art,
> To sperm convert my vitals and my heart,
> That at one thrust I might my soul translate,
> And in the womb myself regenerate:
> There steep'd in lust, nine months I wou'd remain;
> Then boldly—my passage out again.[28]

Women, being generally more moist than men, were therefore more moody, passionate, impulsive, and emotionally powerful. "For . . . it may

25. William Winstanley, *Poor Robin's Visions* . . . (London, 1677), 128.

26. Smith, "Gynecology," 103.

27. Richard Baxter, "The Cure of Melancholy and Overmuch Sorrow," in *The Practical Works of Richard Baxter*, ed. William Orme (London, 1838), 274

28. John Wilmot, Earl of Rochester, "The Wish." On Sarah Wight's tears, see Barbara Ritter Dailey, "The Visitation of Sara Wight: Holy Carnival and the Revolution of the Saints in Civil War London," *Church History* 55 (1986): 440. On urine, see John Gillis, *For Better, for Worse: British Marriages, 1600 to the Present* (New York: Oxford University Press, 1985), 122, 126. This practice, undoubtedly dating to a much earlier period, was recorded in the nineteenth century.

be said of women in general," wrote the popular author Thomas Heywood, "that they are spare in their answers and peremptory in their demands and purposes, that their affections are still in the extremes; either so passionate, as by no counsel to be redressed; or so counterfeit, as to be by no man believed."[29] While the Earl of Rochester saw his transformation into sperm as a purely imaginative act, women actually succumbed to the coursing of their own bodily fluids, for menstruating women were believed to be especially prone to hysteria or extremes of emotion, an ailment known to contemporaries as "the mother."[30]

The sponginess and porosity of the female physiology not only made a woman more emotionally volatile and energetic; it also meant that she might experience difficulty in separating her powers of rational observation from her emotional or biological impulses. Since there was no strong inner scaffolding, no reliable central core or conscience, her mind was easily permeated not only by outside influences but by her own strong inner drives. Thus, a feeling of anger might seep involuntarily into the soul and pollute her religious ideals; heretical beliefs might seep into her bowels and engender lust. Hence the need for the policing of fathers, husbands, and ministers, for a few indiscreet words in a sermon or religious tract could lead to sexual infidelity, heresy, even murder, as they did in the case of Margaret Vincent, hanged in 1616 for killing her two small children. As one pamphleteer recounted the event, Vincent was a gentlewoman "of good parentage, . . . good education, graced with good parts from her youth . . . [with] modest and seemly carriage, . . . witty and of a ripe understanding." Happy as Eve in Eden, virtuous and rich, her woman's brain proved to be as dangerous as a nuclear weapon in the paws of a wild animal, for one day some "close papists" conversed with the lady and drew her into heresy, whereupon she decided that it would be a virtue to murder her two ungodly children, aged five and ten, whom she strangled with her garter. This "sweet lamb" became "a tigerous mother . . . more cruel than the viper, the envenomed serpent, the snake, or any beast whatsoever."[31] Another prominent gentlewoman, Joan

---

29. Richard Baxter wrote that melancholy "is much more frequently the disease of women than of men" ("The Cure of Melancholy," 273–74).

30. Edward Jordan, *A Briefe Discourse of a Disease Called the Suffocation of the Mother* (London, 1603). Jordan discounted the reality of diabolical possession; in his view, "extraordinary" female outbursts in the midst of lengthy sermons, as well as symptoms of delusion and insensibility, were actually the results of the mother. Menstruation and the want of a husband, as well as strong emotion, were particularly aggravating to this disease. As an antidote, Jordan advised prayer and fasting.

31. "A *Pitiless Mother* That Most Unnaturally at One Time Murdered Two of Her Own Children . . ." (London, 1616), reprinted in *Half Humankind*, ed. Henderson and

Drake, was described as a lovely, intelligent, cheerful creature, with a
"nimble quick sparrow-hawk eye." She succumbed, however, to a mood
of cynicism and atheistic despair after a childbirth botched by an in-
competent midwife, being

> ever after troubled with fumes and scurvy vapors mounting up unto her head,
> which bred in her . . . a continual headache . . . together with somewhat like
> unto a fire continually burning at her stomach, which no physic could remove,
> or was not God's pleasure it should; the which drew her towards a more
> constant constitution of sadness and distemper.[32]

Failing to "outface" this onslaught of depression by strength of character, she began shrieking in her bed that she would be damned to hell,
swallowing pins and stealing knives with which to kill herself, shaking
off the ministers who attempted to encourage her "as a great mastiff
turns off many small currs, laughing at them," finally threatening to beat
one of them over the head with a bedpost.[33]

As the authors of these women's stories repeatedly remind us, men
could observe the "otherness" of women not only in the extreme behavior of prophets, witches, or whores but in the preoccupations and
daily activities of respectable sisters, wives, and neighbors. The social
chasm that divided the fine lady and the fishwife was obvious and
important to contemporaries, but while the fine lady enjoyed greater
status and protection than her peers she was, if anything, even more
susceptible to the perils of her own female nature than the fishwife.
According to one medical expert,

> labour keepeth the body sound, and leaveth [working women] no leisure for
> melancholy musings: whereas, in London, and great towns, abundance of
> women that never sweat with bodily work, but live in idleness, . . . are
> miserable objects, continually vexed, and near distraction with discontent,
> and a restless mind.[34]

McManus, 361–68. A similar story of female piety run rampant told of the wife of an
honest tradesman who cut off her child's head rather than have it christened in the Church
of England (*Bloody News from Dover* . . . [London, 1647]). The same feminine traits are
described and condemned in Joseph Swetnam, *The Arraignment of Lewd, Idle, Froward,
and Unconstant Women* . . . (London, 1615), reprinted in *Half Humankind*, ed. Henderson and McManus, 189–217.

    32. R. Bishop, *Trodden Down Strength, by the . . . God of Strength. Or Mrs. Drake
Revived* (London, 1647), 7, 10–11.

    33. Ibid., 12, 15–16, 27, 30–31.

    34. Baxter, "The Cure of Melancholy," 273–74. In a sermon preached in London,
Thomas Master said, "A high place and honourable employment is not always successful,
especially if it encounter Minds weak and feminine: for some, like a too warm Sun, it
melts" (*The Virgin Mary. A Sermon Preach'd in St. Mary's College (Vulgo New-College)*

While a woman's breeding and deportment were crucial in reflecting and transmitting the status of her family, underneath her clothes and manners a middle or upper class woman was often portrayed as having potentially more in common with a peasant woman or a prostitute than with the men in her own household. Thus, the author of *Poor Robin's Almanac* would remark of the Quakers, "These zealous people make no distinction of persons, . . . yet though *Joan* be as good as my Lady in the dark, Madam by daylight deserves some reverance."[35]

It is not surprising that contemporaries tended to define the male character in terms of the individual's position in the class structure, while women were defined in terms of underlying, occult qualitis hat were irrelevant to their social position. In their own everyday experience, these writers could not help but observe that virtually every sort of woman—from the aristocrat practicing surgery or dispensing medicines on her estate, to the local white witch or midwife, to the "searchers" (poor old women hired to examine dead bodies in times of plague)—engaged in healing, assisted in childbirth, and comforted the dying, activities that were always awesome, frequently terrifying, and often involved the use of magic.[36] Indeed, black magic was sometimes the sole recourse of women attempting to mitigate the brutality of

---

Oxon, March the 25th, 1641 [London, 1710]). On the same phenomenon in Italy, see Camporesi, *The Incorruptible Flesh*, 82.

35. *Poor Robin. 1664. An Almanac after a New Fashion* (London, 1664), n.p. For a discussion of class and gender, see Sara Heller Mendelson, *The Mental World of Stuart Women: Three Studies* (Amherst: University of Massachusetts Press, 1987), Introduction. Mendelson stresses women's similarity of experience across class lines. Education for girls and boys after age seven was very different, but it was similar for all women; even aristocratic women were semiliterate. See also Burke, *Popular Culture*, 24, 49.

36. On women's work, similar across class lines, see Mendelson, *The Mental World of Stuart Women*, 8ff., 99. On women's medical practices, see Lucinda McCray Beier, "In Sickness and in Health: A Seventeenth-Century Family's Experience," in *Patients and Practitioners: Lay Perceptions of Medicine in Pre-Industrial Society*, ed. Roy Porter (Cambridge: Cambridge University Press, 1985), 118–21. Women who were summoned to attend a childbirth were called "gossips" (Adrian Wilson, "Participant or patient? Seventeenth-Century Childbirth from the Mother's Point of View," in *Patients and Practitioners*, ed. Porter, 134). Carol F. Karlsen also stresses the responsibility of all women for duties involving knowledge of healing, herbal medicines, assistance at births, and so on, all of which were directly related to witchcraft accusations (*The Devil in the Shape of a Woman: Witchcraft in Colonial New England* [New York and London: W. W. Norton and Co., 1987], 142). Charles Webster cites the role of gentlewomen who dispensed medicine to neighbors as charity (*The Great Instauration: Science, Medicine, and Reform, 1626–1660* [New York: Holmes and Meier Publishers, 1976], 255.) On searchers, see Thomas Rogers Forbes, *Chronicle from Aldgate: Life and Death in Shakespeare's London* (New Haven and London: Yale University Press, 1971), 96–98, 121–22. There were also the witch doctors, poor women who examined suspects for witches' marks (Notestein, *A History of Witchcraft*, 258).

their domestic environment. After John Spinkes, a London physician, punched his wife Elizabeth in the face, beat her with a horse whip, and locked her up in a lunatic asylum in order to force her to yield up part of her estate, she conspired with a local fortune teller to bewitch him, using a potion made of his urine, a cat's heart, and bull's blood stuck with pins.[37]

The common scold, the witch, the prophet, and the fine lady also shared a reliance on the power of words, rather than pens or swords, to make their wishes and ideas felt in a culture where the instrumental power of lustful or angry words or "heated speech" was perceived to be far greater than it is today.

> The tongue was considered a "witch," a "practiser of poisonings," a "box of poison," a murderer that cuts "like a *rasor*," "the first corrupting Instrument," the "unruliest member" that "defiles the whole body," an arrow, a hammer, a sword, a traitor, a "common pickpurse," and a "notorious robber." Speech itself was thought *"harder to be tamed . . . than a strong city is to be conquered."* . . . Speaking of cursers, . . . [an] English divine said it seemed "as if their throats were Hell itself."[38]

"It is proper," observed one treatise on wifely duty, "that not only arms but indeed also the speech of women never be made public; for the speech of a noble woman can be no less dangerous than the nakedness of the limbs."[39] This conflating of the acts of speech, greed, and sex was reflected in the negative image of the female religious zealot as a prostitute sprawled on her back:

> Yet of all *WHORES* there is no *WHORE* to a holy *WHORE*, . . . when she turns up the white of her eye, and the black of her tail when she falls flat on her back, according as the spirit moves her. The fire of her zeal kindles such a flame, that the Devil cannot withstand her. Besides she can fit a man with such a cloak for her knavery she can cover her lust with religion.[40]

37. Case of Spinkes vs. Spinkes, MS. DL/C/154 and DL/C/632, Greater London Council Record Office, recounted in Margaret Hunt, "Wife Beating, Domesticity, and Women's Independence in Early Eighteenth-Century London," forthcoming in *Gender and History*, 1992. Elizabeth Spinkes later testified "that she knew she should not be saved and she did not care what she did soe she might be revenged of him."

38. St. George, "Heated Speech," 280–83. On the moral dangers of the tongue, see Spargo, *Judicial Folklore*, 114ff.

39. Barbaro, *On Wifely Duties*, quoted in Stallybrass, "Patriarchal Territories," 127.

40. I. H., *A Strange Wonder or a Wonder in a Woman . . .* (London, 1642). In the play *The Dutch Courtesan*, by John Maston (1605), the whore is allied with the Family of Love (William C. Johnson, "The Family of Love in Stuart Literature: A Chronology of Name-Crossed Lovers," *Journal of Medieval and Renaissance Studies* 7 [1977]: 99–100).

An English street ballad of the 1640s made the same point more succinctly: "No venemous snake stings like a woman's tongue."[41] Women, words, Eve, the serpent: all alike, all bad.

Perhaps it was the volatility and supposed instrumental power of women's speech that induced such profound popular mistrust of women's cleverness. The archetypal symbol of destructive female intelligence was Eve, who used her brains and tongue to entice Adam into sin, as the Puritan Anne Hutchinson used her wit and eloquence to entice her neighbors in the Massachusetts Bay Colony into heresy in 1636.[42] Indeed, many writers asserted that the mere presence of an active female brain, embedded in an untrustworthy female body, was the sign of a tendency to lasciviousness or witchcraft. As one astrologer described the characteristics of those born under the sign Sagittarius, the male possesses

> a good wit, and a sharp. . . . Likewise touching the disposition of the mind, he shall be gentle, faithful, meek, liberal, mixed with stubbornness, by reason whereof he shall be of great authority, gentle, kind . . . and a great banquetor. . . . He shall be very ingenious, witty, artificial, sober, grave . . . and careful of his affairs: he shall be subtle and very wary about his doings so that he will not disclose his secrets to any man.

The female Sagittarius will also be intelligent: "And touching the disposition of the mind, she shall be very much given to arts of magic, and to witchcraft, and by reason of the subtlety of her wit, she shall put the same arts in practice. She shall be very curt, careful, merciful, childbearing and a great liar."[43] Unlike the male intelligence, which sustains the world of affairs, or culture, by predominating over the senses, the female intelligence—wily, duplicitous, and above all ruled by appetite— had the inbuilt potential to create disorder, to be an enemy to culture.

41. St. George, "Heated Speech," 293.
42. In Milton's *Paradise Lost,* Eve's pursuit of knowledge is associated with popular symbols of witchcraft, while in her renovation through marriage to Adam, she became an obedient wife (Linda Draper Henson, "The Witch in Eve: Milton's Use of Witchcraft in *Paradise Lost,*" in *Milton Reconsidered: Essays in Honor of Arthur E. Barker,* ed. John Karl Franson, Salzburg Studies in English Literature, Elizabethan and Renaissance Studies, no. 49 [Salzburg: Institut für Englische Sprache und Literatur, Universität Salzburg, 1976], and M. A. N. Radizinowicz, "Eve and Delila: Renovation and the Hardening of the Heart," in *Reason and the Imagination: Studies in the History of Ideas, 1600–1800,* ed. J. A. Mazzeo [New York: Columbia University Press, 1962], 155–81.)
43. William Wade, *Arcandam, or Alcandrin* . . . (London, 1652). In Thomas Heywood's *History of Women,* the eighth book treated of "Women everie way Learned; of Poetesses, . . . Witches, . . . Orators" (*Gunaikeion, or Nine Bookes of Various History concerninge Women* . . . [London, 1624], 369, 373).

John Winthrop, governor of Massachusetts, accused Jane Hawkins of consorting with the devil because she had knowledge of fertility potions and fell into trances, during which she spoke in Latin. Another woman, the contentious Anne Hibbens, was hanged as a witch in 1656 for, as one minister remarked, having "more wit than her neighbors." The ministers attending Mrs. Joan Drake described her glib use of scriptural argument as diabolical; "she replied nimbly and strongly, using to purpose all, or much of the Devil's rhetoric taught her against her self; yea and alleged many Scriptures, which she had never read, but only as tumbling and tossing over the Bible . . . to find places against her self"[44]

Given these perceptions of the actual physical power and potential danger of women's speech, it is not surprising that the successful female prophet was invariably described, paradoxically, as dumb; "dumb" meaning both stupid and mute, empty of everything but God. This notion was derived from the classical tradition of the *vates,* the visionary as an empty receptacle for divine inspiration. It also derived from the ancient Christian tradition of paradox, whereby God was compared to the lowest things in order to heighten the sense of divine mystery, as well as reflecting the doctrine that the last shall be first.[45] Thus, Arise Evans, who edited the visions of Elinor Channel for publication in 1653, emphasized her catatonic behavior as she wandered through the London streets, harrassed by jeering onlookers, searching for someone to listen to her message: "Now this woman was very sensible and profound in what she spake to me, as she said, when she is dumb, all her senses are taken up, and then the matter which troubles her mind, is dictated and made plain to her by the spirit of God; and when she comes to herself, she has it by heart."[46] The astrologer William Lilly recounted another story of a poor dumb woman summoned before King James I. As the king displayed portraits of himself, Queen Anne, and several other nobles, the woman accurately predicted when each of them would die; "and for manifestation of her sense and meaning, experience tells us how active

44. Koehler, *Search for Power,* 218–19. William Hubbard, *A General History of New England, from the Discovery to 1680* (1848), 574, quoted in Johan Winsser, "Mary Dyer and the 'Monster' Story," QH 79, no. 1 (Spring 1990): 22. Bishop, *Trodden Down Strength,* 22.

45. Colie, *Paradoxica Epidemica,* 24–26. On the paradox of strength in weakness applied to women, see Ian Maclean, *Woman Triumphant: Feminism in French Literature, 1610–1652* (Oxford: Clarendon Press, 1977), 21–22.

46. Elinor Channel, *A Message from God, by a Dumb Woman to His Highness the Lord Protector,* ed. Arise Evans, (London, 1653), 7.

and intelligent your dumb people are, so that they will almost apprehend any thing by signs."[47]

The characterization of the female visionary as an empty vessel reflected an attitude that was far more complicated than simple misogyny, for the defects of rationality and the attuned intuition of visionary women were actually viewed with respect, even envy, by those philosophers who felt alienated from God by their compulsive, prideful reliance on the power of their own reason. Indeed, in this respect all women had a clear spiritual advantage over men, for the static resulting from their weak and intermittent surges of intellectual energy was less likely to interfere with their capacity to act as receptors for the divine, spiritual energy emanating from heaven. The twelve ministers attempting to rescue the soul of Mrs. Joan Drake, who suffered for nearly a decade from the conviction that she was damned, were certainly sexist in their ridiculing of her prowess in quoting scripture and in their insistence that her erudition could only be the result of Satanic influence. Yet their genuine concern for her *soul*, as opposed to her mind, was surely reflective of more than a desire for the patronage of her aristocratic family. Moreover, the ministers acknowledged her final epiphany as having far transcended the spiritual condition that they themselves had attained by their own theology and erudition. Indeed, the eminent Thomas Hooker, one of Mrs. Drake's counselors during an early stage of his career, came to view her experience as paradigmatic of the believer's inward preparation and ultimate spiritual triumph.[48] Similarly, the editor George Garden was not being contemptuous when, at the very end of the century, he introduced the Belgian prophet Antonia Bourignon to the British reading public by describing her as vacuous:

And as her writings were not the result of study and human learning, so neither were they the result of meditation and human reasoning. *We* must

47. William Lilly, *A Prophecy of the White King: And Dreadfull Dead-men Explaned* (London, 1644), 3, 4–5.

48. George Huntston Williams, "Called by Thy Name, Leave Us Not: The Case of Mrs. Joan Drake, A Formative Episode in the Pastoral Career of Thomas Hooker in England," *Harvard Library Bulletin* 16 (1968): 111–128, 278–300. See also the account of John Ley, who counseled Mrs. Jane Ratcliffe during and after her conversion. Comparing her godliness to his own, he wrote "great heat of devotion if with little light of information in the lady (but in her truly there was both light and heat in a remarkable degree) may make them blessed, while great light of learning and little heat of zeal in the clergy may render them wretched" (Ley, *A Pattern of Piety on the Religious Life and Death of . . . Mrs. Jane Ratcliffe . . .* [London, 1640,] 65, quoted in Peter Lake, "Feminine Piety and Personal Potency: The 'Emancipation' of Mrs. Jane Ratcliffe," *The Seventeenth Century* 2 (1987): 150.

think before we write, . . . we must blot out, and mend, and add to our first draughts. But when she put pen to paper she wrote as fast as her hand could guide the pen. . . . In her conversations with God she used neither ideas nor meditations; but was in an admirable vacuity of all desire of knowing either this or that; having no will of her own.[49]

The ultimate manifestation of the prophet as a passive and entirely purified receptacle of divine energy was the maiden who preached prone, holding forth from a sickbed, or one who actually surmounted the death of the body, returning briefly from the grave with a message from the underworld. The motif of most popular accounts of such visionaries, published in cheap popular format by relatives, ministers, and magistrates, was not the mythic hero or shaman's lonely adventure of self-transcendence; it was illness and self-annihilation, derived from the tradition of the *ars moriendi* literature of the Middle Ages. Thus, the adolescent Sarah Wight hovered between life and death as she preached to assembled guests, while a typical pamphlet told of a poor, pious countryman's daughter in Nottinghamshire who excelled in goodness and simplicity. Having inexplicably died and been made ready for burial, she suddenly woke up, asked her mother for meat, ate and digested the food, and delivered her message from the beyond: "O People full of contempt, despising one another, some for riches, some for beauty, others for wisdom, . . . whereas before God, we are all alike with him, poor and rich, . . . therefore repent." Warning her audience to beware of the Whore of Babylon (in this case the papists), she finally subsided into the permanent condition of a pious corpse.[50] The spiritual degradation of Mrs. Joan Drake had begun with the stomach ailments and headache following upon a botched childbirth. Her spiritual epiphany was marked, at her own insistence, by her burial in a white dress, sign of her body's restoration to a state of enclosed virginity and dedication to a heavenly bridegroom at the very moment of its physical dissolution.[51]

49. George Garden, *Apology for M. Antonia Bourignon* (London, 1699), 41.
50. "The Wonderfull Workes of God Shewed, by a Prophecie of a Poore Country-mans Daughter in Nottingham-shire, November Last, 1641" (London, 1641), n. p. On the similar experience of Martha Hatfield in 1652, see Alfred Cohen, "Prophecy and Madness: Women Visionaries during the Puritan Revolution," *Journal of Psychohistory* 11 (1984): 419–20. On the link between illness and visionary behavior see Michael MacDonald, *Mystical Bedlam: Madness, Anxiety, and Healing in Seventeenth-Century England* (Cambridge: Cambridge University Press, 1981). MacDonald cites numerous cases of women treated for melancholy who thought they had spoken with God or with demons.
51. Bishop, *Trodden Down Strength*, 141.

MOTHER AND CHILD

"But where's the use of talking to a woman with
babbies?" continued Bartle. "She's got no conscience,
no conscience—it's all run to milk."
                    George Elliott, Adam Bede

Because contemporaries believed in the fundamental sameness of all
women's souls and bodies, regardless of the differences in outward
social attributes, it was but a series of infinitesimal steps from the figure
of the gossiping grandmother to the scold to the witch, or from the
pious matron to the prophet.[52] In fact, the most potent image of
woman's spiritual marginality was not the deviant witch brewing
potions or stroking her familiars but the ordinary mother. From the
onset of her pregnancy a woman was believed to enter a liminal and
potentially dangerous spiritual condition, for the process of gestation,
which doctors viewed as the fermentation of corrupt matter within the
womb, placed her outside the pale of strictly human culture.[53] Some
believed that she was safe against demons, while others thought she
was reduced to the condition of an animal. Roger Williams, the
founder of Rhode Island, observed that the act of childbirth had "the
filthiness and stink of nature," while a Puritan interpreted the biblical
Isaac's birth as supernatural, being lifted by God from Sara's dead
womb, in contrast to that of Ishmael, the exiled son, whose birth was
merely natural.[54] A pregnant woman was also believed to possess
intensified emotional energy and imagination. Her cravings, which
might be powerful enough to cause a miscarriage, were so legendary
that a man obsessed by a particularly strong craving was said to be
"with child."[55] Indeed, her essence had become so porous that the
mere objects of her sight could permeate her body and distort the fetus.
One man was said to walk with a stagger because his mother had

52. On the blurring of distinctions between the human being and the witch in
contemporary folklore, see Briggs, *Pale Hecate's Team,* 178.
53. Camporesi, *The Incorruptible Flesh,* 156–57. Keith Thomas, *Religion and the
Decline of Magic* (New York: Scribner's, 1971), 228.
54. Roger Williams, *George Fox Digg'd,* Appendix, quoted in Koehler, *Search for
Power,* 307. See also Leverenz, *Language,* 119.
55. The diarist Samuel Pepys wrote on May 14, 1660: "I sent my boy, who like
myself, is with child to see any strange thing." Pepys is quoted in Angus McLaren,
*Reproductive Rituals: Perceptions of Fertility in Britain from the Sixteenth Century to the
Nineteenth Century* (London and New York: Methuen, 1984), 169 n. 102.

caught sight of a drunken man while pregnant, while the sudden sight of a hare was said to cause a harelip.[56]

New mothers were treated as both more inhuman and more deeply pious than ordinary people. English Protestants continued to practice the old custom of churching, in which the mother participated in a religious ritual before reentering the human community: kneeling at the communion table, praying with the minister, and paying a thank offering to the church. Some Puritans attacked the practice as a remnant of Catholic superstition, objecting to the obligatory white veil worn by the mother (reminiscent of that worn by penitents) and to the implication of the woman's ritual impurity (she could not take communion until she had been churched); indeed, it was believed by some that where an unchurched mother walked the grass would not grow.[57] Yet Puritans also acknowledged the authentic piety of mothers whose first long look at death in childbirth had turned their souls to God. Richard Sibbes believed that women "bring others into this world with danger of their own, therefore they are forced to a nearer communion with God, because so many children as they bring forth, they are in peril of their lives."[58] Nursing mothers (and most mothers *did* nurse in seventeenth-century England) were perceived to be as powerful as they were comforting. Their milk was thought to be literally healing for adults as well as children; those with certain diseases were advised to nurse and those with sore eyes to have milk expressed directly into them. Babies sucked in their mother's principles, both good and bad, along with their milk, which was "really" mother's blood turned white. It was said that as King Charles I wanted his children to become Protestants, he "would not let them suck of a Roman Catholic nurse."[59]

56. Patricia Crawford, "'The Sucking Child': Adult Attitudes to Child Care in the First Year of Life in Seventeenth-Century England," *Continuity and Change* 1 (1986): 27. See also Patricia Crawford, "The Construction and Experience of Maternity in Seventeenth-Century England," in *Women as Mothers in Pre-Industrial England: Essays in Memory of Dorothy McClaren*, ed. Valerie Fildes (London and New York: Routledge, 1990), 6–7.

57. Thomas, *Religion and the Decline of Magic*, 39; Dorothy Ludlow, "'Arise and Be Doing': English Preaching Women, 1640–1660," Ph.D. diss., Indiana University, 1978, 56ff. In 1552 the minister Hugh Latimer recounted the case of a pregnant woman, imprisoned for infanticide, who was terrified of being executed before she was churched, or "purified" (Stephen Greenblatt, *Shakespearean Negotiations: The Circulation of Social Energy in Renaissance England* [Berkeley and Los Angeles: University of California Press, 1988], 129–30).

58. Richard Sibbes, *The Riches of Mercie* (1638), quoted in Leverenz, *Language*, 84.

59. On the virtues of mother's milk, see Dorothy McLaren, "Marital Fertility and Lactation, 1570–1720," in *Women in English Society, 1500–1800*, ed. Mary Prior (London and New York: Methuen, 1985), 29, 33. The prescription of mother's milk,

If even a normal childbirth was seen as a spiritually loaded event, the
death of an infant might well be spiritually catastrophic, because the
exhausted mother was instructed to interpret the death as punishment
for her own sinfulness. The valiant Elizabeth Gouge, wife of the author
of the widely read *Of Domesticall Duties*, died quietly after the birth of
her thirteenth child, inspiring a minister to preach that her end was an
"honour," that she died in her "calling," as a "soldier" in "battle," even
as "a preacher in the pulpit." Biblical women who died in childbirth, said
the minister, died as saints, and so too "did this pious matron."[60]
Stubborn Mary Onion, however, being an ambitious and worldly person, refused to give herself up to the pain of her delivery as punishment
for Eve's original sin, but when her first child was born dead she realized
that she had "neglected her spiritual good for a little worldly trash." She
died a few hours later, convinced that she was damned.[61] Women were
blamed (and sometimes blamed themselves) for the deaths of their infants because they copulated while nursing, because they opposed the
medical practice of bleeding sick babies, or because they simply loved
their children too much. When Sarah Henry's only son died of smallpox,
she was deeply shaken but comforted herself with the reflection that she
could not be blamed, since neither she nor her husband had been over-
fond of the child, "notwithstanding we had five daughters before." When
Mary Parsons confessed to charges of witchcraft, she explained her
diabolical seduction by saying

> she had lost a child and was exceedingly discontented at it and longed; *Oh
> that she might see her child again!* And at last the Devil in likeness of her child
> came to her bed side and talked with her, and asked to come into the bed to
> her, and she received it into the bed . . . and so entered into covenant with
> Satan and became a witch.[62]

---

especially from one who nurses a male child, is a strong part of the pharmacopoeia of
Galen. Only wealthy women used wet nurses, and even then many "godly women"
nursed their babies (Crawford, "'The Sucking Child,'" 31–32).

60. Nicholas Guy, *Pieties Pillar: Or a Sermon Preached at the Funeral of Mistresse
Elizabeth Gouge . . .* (London, 1626) 45, 49–52, quoted in Margaret George, *Women in
the First Capitalist Society: Experiences in Seventeenth-Century England* (Urbana and
Chicago: University of Illinois Press, 1988), 146.

61. Koehler, *Search for Power*, 57. See also the discussion of Mary, Countess of
Warwick, in Mendelson, *The Mental World of Stuart Women*, Chap. 2. On despair after
childbirth see MacDonald, *Mystical Bedlam*, 133–34; Crawford, "'The Sucking Child,'"
27. On the ritual of the deathbed scene in Puritan practice, see Andrew Wear, "Puritan
Perceptions of Illness in Seventeenth-Century England," in *Patients and Practitioners*, ed.
Porter, 64–66.

62. Quoted in Karlsen, *Devil*, 22.

In her despair she further confessed to the murder of one of her two dead children and was convicted of infanticide by the Massachusetts General Court.

Upper class women may have been especially vulnerable to the hazards of childbirth and the agony of infant mortality because of the added pressure on them to produce heirs. During the Tudor period, the experience of enduring ten, fifteen, or twenty births occurred most often among these elite women, who were also told that their labors would be more difficult and presumably more spiritually dangerous than those of a poor peasant.[63] The diary of Mary, Countess of Warwick, contains this entry, written in 1667:

> May the 16. I kept it a private fast being the day three year upon which my son died. . . . [I] had . . . large meditations upon the sickness and death of my only child . . . his sick bed expressions . . . how god was pleased to waken him. . . . Then I began to consider what sins I had committed that should cause God to call them to remembrance and slay my son.[64]

A century after the period of this study, a young Quaker woman named Mary Knowles composed a poem, "Written in the Terrors of Approaching Childbirth":

> Say thou Almighty Power that rulest above
> Must I through pain Unutterable prove
> How great the Sin of our first Mother's fall
> Whose dire presumption overwhelmed us all . . .
> Oh yes I ought Be contrite then my Soul
> Nor quit the Bleeding Saviour at the Tree
> Enduring all that gives full Victory
> Till with his Holy Lord he mounts on high
> Where Morning Stars together Sing and Angels shout for joy.

Mary Knowles's baby was born on July 20, 1768, and died the following day.[65]

A woman who gave birth to a deformed child found herself in an especially precarious moral position, because the baby's ugliness, which

63. Barbara J. Harris, "Property, Power, and Personal Relations: Elite Mothers and Sons in Yorkist and Early Tudor England," *Signs: Journal of Women in Culture and Society* 15 (1990):613.
64. Quoted in Mendelson, *The Mental World of Stuart Women*, 91.
65. Portfolio, Manuscripts, 6/158, Library of the Society of Friends, London. This may be the Mary Knowles who later disputed with Dr. Samuel Johnson (DQB, "Knowles"). See also McLaren, "Marital Fertility and Lactation," 22.

contemporaries saw as subhuman and animal-like, might be interpreted as a sign of the mother's own moral, social, and spiritual degradation as well as a divine message about the state of the world. Learned opinion emphasized the dominance of the father's role in procreation, both in biological terms (the male seed was thought to determine the child's character) and in social and economic terms (lawful paternity determined inheritance). Nevertheless, a prime explanation for the birth of a deformed child was that, despite all this male input, as it were, a woman's volatile imagination, infused by evil forces, was sufficient to transform the fetus into a monster; or the monster might be the result of her wanton, unnatural behavior in sitting astride her husband during intercourse; or the woman might simply be the unwitting vehicle for the expression of cosmic wrath for the sins of the nation.[66]

The power and ambiguity of these maternal associations became even weightier when they were brought to bear on the minister or visionary's role as a conduit of spiritual forces and on the worshiper's own spiritual helplessness. It often seemed, in fact, that while the father's relationship to the family was the paradigm for contemporary *political* thinking, the paradigm for the experience of spiritual striving and ultimate union with God was the relationship between the mother and her infant child. The labor of childbirth was the archetypal metaphor for the agony of spiritual transformation. Witnesses of the visionary transports of John and Mary Pordage claimed to have heard deafening cries of a woman in labor coming from Pordage's rectory, cries that signaled the mystical trans-

---

66. McLaren, *Reproductive Rituals*, 17–25. See also Koehler, *Search for Power*, 179–84. Some believed that both parents' sinfulness caused the birth of a deformed child, but the weight and experience of sin still lay more heavily on the woman because she endured the ordeal of labor, which was held to be punishment for Eve's sin (Sara Heller Mendelson, "Stuart Women's Diaries and Occasional Memoirs," in *Women in English Society, 1500–1800*, ed. Prior, 196). Elizabeth Waister was called a "poisoned whore," to whom God would send a stillborn or deformed child (Miranda Chaytor, "Household and Kinship: Ryton in the Late Sixteenth and Early Seventeenth Centuries," *History Workshop* 10 [1980]: 26). Other popular accounts of monstrous births and the moral message associated with them are reprinted in Hyder Edward Rollins, *The Pack of Autolycus, or Strange and Terrible News . . . 1624–1693* (1927; reprint, Cambridge, Mass.: Harvard University Press, 1969), nos. 14, 23, 31, 32. In 1643 a Puritan triumphantly recorded the birth of a monstrous child to two Popish parents, a judgment on the grandmother, who some years earlier, in derision toward the victims of Archbishop Laud, had named her three cats "Bastwick," "Burton," and "Prynne" (Eccles, *Obstetrics and Gynecology*, 46–47). See also G. V., "An Account of a Child Born at Furbick in Darbyshire, the 19th of January 1694, with a Top-knot & Rowle on Its Head, of Several Colours. With a Seasonable Caution against Pride" (London, 1694). See also Crawford, "'The Sucking Child,'" 27; Katherine Spark and Lorraine Daston, "Unnatural Conceptions: The Study of Monsters in France and England," *Past and Present* 92 (1981): 20–54; Thomas, *Man and the Natural World*, 39, 47–48; Gombrich, *Symbolic Images*, 180.

formation of their entire spiritual family.[67] The Puritan John Cotton portrayed the human sinner as an infant lying in its own excrement, washed and caressed by God's maternal love:

> Women, if they were not mothers, would not take such homely offices up, as to cleanse their children from their filth; why if God were not of the like affection to us, he would not cleanse us from our filthiness, . . . it is with us as it is with young infants that would lie in their defilements, if their mothers did not make them clean, and so would we even wallow in the defilements of sin, if God did not cleanse us.[68]

Samuel Willard declared, "The whole world is a sucking infant depending on the breasts of divine Providence."[69]

But the mother also pushes off the child, as Massachusetts governor John Winthrop saw to his terror when he was converted: "I became as a weaned child. I knew I was worthy of nothing for I knew I could do nothing for my self."[70] Quaker leader Margaret Fell would be a loving and judging mother figure to countless male and female Quakers: "A nursing mother thou art who feeds the hungry with good things, but the fat with judgment, who kills and slays the living and raises the dead. . . . Power in heaven and earth is given unto thee, thou glorious daughter of Sion."[71] The same blend of power and sustenance was conveyed by Edmund Spenser in *The Faerie Queene*, where Charissa, or Christian Charity, was depicted as a nursing mother of infinite capacities:

> A woman in her freshest age,
> Of wondrous beauty, and of bountie rare, . . .
> Her necke and breasts were ever open bare,
> That ay thereof her babes might sucke their fill; . . .

67. John Pordage, *Innocencie Appearing, through the Dark Mists of Pretended Guilt* (London, 1654), 10–19, 28–31, discussed in Nigel Smith, *Perfection Proclaimed: Language and Literature in Radical Religion* (Oxford: Clarendon Press, 1989), 208.

68. John Cotton, *A Practical Commentary . . . (on) John, 1st Epistle* (London, 1656), 40–41, quoted in Laurel Thatcher Ulrich, *Good Wives: Image and Reality in the Lives of Women in Northern New England, 1650–1750* (New York and Toronto: Oxford University Press, 1983), 124. On child-rearing and spirituality see Leverenz, *Language*, and Philip Greven, *The Protestant Temperament: Patterns of Child-Rearing, Religious Experience, and the Self in Early America* (New York: Alfred A. Knopf, 1977). Leverenz contrasts the leniency and affection expressed by mothers to small children and the severity of the father later on, resulting in a conception of God that synthesized the extremes of nurturer and judge. Greven cites the identification in Puritan culture of infancy and femininity; boys and girls were dressed alike and treated alike in the early years of life (22ff.).

69. Cotton Mather, *A Father Departing . . .* (Boston, 1723), 22–23, quoted in Leverenz, *Language*, 1, 119, 124–45.

70. Quoted in Ulrich, *Good Wives*, 142.

71. Thomas Holme to Margaret Fell, Chester Castle, August 28, 1655, SM, 1/197 (II, 355).

> A multitude of babes about her hong,
> Playing their sports, that joyd her to behold,
> Whom still she fed, whiles they were weake and young,
> But thrust them forth still, as they wexéd old: . . .
> And taking by the hand that Faeries sonne [the knight],
> Gan him instruct in every good behest,
> Of love, and righteousnesse, and well to donne,
> And wrath, and hatred warély to shonne.[72]

A cruder version of the same ambiguous maternal figure was depicted in the first Faust book published in England, in 1592. In all Faust's wanderings with Mephistopheles, the sight that most appalls him is the statue of the Brazen Virgin in Breslau: Bad children are brought by their mothers to the Virgin, who stands on a bridge over a mill. As the child kisses the statue, the arms close and crush the child, who is then dropped into the mill where it is cut into pieces and carried away by the river.[73]

If devout women and men became sucking infants in their relationship to God, if ministers and visionaries "gave birth" to holy words or miraculous acts or secreted them like mother's milk, the same was true of evil opinions or malicious acts. These too were portrayed as births, but as monstrous births, and their authors as monster mothers or witches, giving suck to demons or familiar spirits, even destroying their own children.[74] The arch villain in *The Faerie Queene* is Night, the offspring of Chaos and the mother of the monster Duessa, or mutability, a witch who excels at assuming false shapes, with breasts exuding "filthy matter" to feed her own monster children. Just so did the magistrates of Essex view Mary Adams, a pious young woman of respectable family who converted from sect to sect, finally becoming convinced that she was pregnant with the Holy Ghost. She gave birth to a dead, deformed child in prison after a labor lasting eight days. Confronted with the child, whom she could not bear to look at, she asked the jailer for a knife to

72. Edmund Spenser, *The Faerie Queene*, in *Edmund Spenser's Poetry*, ed. Hugh Maclean, 2d ed. (New York and London: W. W. Norton, 1982), 117.

73. William Rose, ed., *The Historie of the Damnable Life, and Deserved Death of Doctor John Faustus and the Second Report of Faustus, Containing His Appearances and the Deeds of Wagner* (1592; reprint, London, n.d.), 137–38.

74. The dynamic of witchcraft prosecutions almost exactly paralleled that of the crime of infanticide. Many infanticidal cases involved unwed mothers who, like witches, lived on the margins of society and carried an aura of sexual license: Both crimes involved concealment, both were directed against children, and both became objects of royal prosecution at about the same time (Peter C. Hoffer and N. E. H. Hull, *Murdering Mothers: Infanticide in England and New England, 1558–1803*, Linden Studies in Anglo-American Legal History [New York and London: New York University Press, 1981], 28, 55–56).

cut her nails and, in her despair, disemboweled herself. The account was
published and signed by ten town officials, who saw the monstrous birth
as proof that she had given birth to a devil.[75] (If Mary Adams had
managed to attract a more sympathetic audience, they might well have
interpreted the birth as a sign that she was set apart by God. The editors
of the works of the Belgian prophet Antonia Bourignon emphasized her
own monstrous birth, with hair growing down over her face and a
harelip, because it made her both abhorrent to her earthly mother and
spiritually unique, singled out for God the Mother's deeper love: "When
she came into this world, her mother thought she had borne a monster,
because her whole forehead was covered with black hair even to her
eyes, and her upper lip was fastened to her nose, and so her mouth stood
open . . . and [her mother] could not love her. . . . God then drew her
powerfully to himself."[76]

The antinomian midwife and prophet Anne Hutchinson was accused
of giving birth to thirty monsters after she was expelled from Massachusetts for holding meetings and preaching heretical doctrines. John
Winthrop, the governor of the colony, wrote gloatingly of the event:

> Mistress Hutchinson being big with child, and growing towards the time of
> her labor . . . she brought forth not one . . . but 30 monstrous births or
> thereabouts, at once; some of them bigger, some lesser, some of one shape,
> some of another; few of any perfect shape, none at all of them (as far as I could
> ever learn) of human shape . . . (and) look as she had vented mishapen
> opinions, so she must bring forth deformed monsters; and as about 30
> opinions in number, so many monsters.[77]

As Hutchinson left the meeting house after her public condemnation, a
single friend stood up, took her hand, and accompanied her from the
room. When a stranger asked who the friend might be he was told that
"it was the woman who had the monster." She was Mary Dyer, wife of
a millener and prominent local citizen, whom Hutchinson had assisted
in childbed that same year. Because the stillborn infant girl was severely

75. *An Account of Mary Adams, The Ranters Monster* (London, 1652). The theme
of demons nursing was common in witchcraft literature. See, for example, "The Wonderful Discovery of the Witchcrafts of Margaret and Philippa Flower" (London, 1619),
reprinted in *Half Humankind*, ed. Henderson and McManus, 369–79.

76. Garden, *Apology*, 264.

77. John Winthrop, *A Short Story of the Rise, Reign, and Ruine of the Antinomians,
Familists and Libertines* (Preface by Thomas Welde), quoted in *The Antinomian Contro-
versy, 1636–1638*, ed. David D. Hall (Middletown, Conn.: Wesleyan University Press,
1968), 214. See also Amy Schrager Lang, *Prophetic Woman: Anne Hutchinson and the
Problem of Dissent in the Literature of New England* (Berkeley: University of California
Press, 1987), 52–71.

deformed, she was secretly buried in the forest and exhumed five months
later by Winthrop and a posse of ministers, who interpreted the birth as
proof of Dyer's own deformed spirit as an antinomian heretic. A quarter
of a century later, the Reverend John Eliot still trembled at the memory:

> I now write . . . to answer that desire of Mr. [Richard] Baxter . . . about the
> monster. . . . Let him understand, this thing is exceedingly true and certain
> (against all gainsayings of men that desire to blind truth). The monster was
> born in my time whiles I was in N[ew] England . . . Mrs. Dyer (a great
> fomenting of those horrid opinions being the mother). . . . There being none
> present but some women of her own stamp, it was hushed up and suddenly
> buried . . . a most hideous creat[ure], a woman, a fish, a bird, & and beast
> all woven together. . . . [I write] with prayers to the father of all mercy to look
> down upon us in these sad times, and support us under all our fears.[78]

More clearly than evidence extracted under torture, these monstrous
births "proved" either that the women's very essences or imaginations
had become depraved when they embraced heretical doctrines or that
their true essences were evil from the beginning but had been masked by
their respectable social position and behavior.

If John Winthrop ever read *The Faerie Queene*, he might have seen
a glorified image of himself in the Red Cross Knight, standing up to the
figure of Error as a monster mother—elemental nature incarnate—who
spewed out her creatures (or opinions) and then devoured them. Winthrop reproved Anne Hutchinson's sons for not reining in their mother
and called them "vipers . . . [who] eat through the very bowels of your
mother, to her ruin."[79] In similar language, Spenser's monster mother

> lay upon the durtie ground,
> Her huge long taile her den all overspred,
> . . . Of her there bred
> A thousand yong ones, which she dayly fed,
> Sucking upon her poisonous dugs, each one
> Of sundry shapes, yet all ill favoréd: . . .

78. Rev. John Eliot to Thomas Brooks, London, May 19, 1660, reprinted in
Winsser, "Mary Dyer and the 'Monster' Story," 30–31. See also Karlsen, *Devil*, 16–17.
Hutchinson moved to Rhode Island, where she was killed in an Indian raid. Dyer, her
husband, and her one surviving child returned to London, where she later converted to
Quakerism and where she also may have read the tale of Mary Dyer's monster, printed
in numerous tracts in England and America during the 1640s. Mary Gadbury, who lived
with William Franklin as the spouse of Christ, claimed she was pregnant with a spiritual
birth; her critics said she had given birth to a dragon (Humphrey Ellis, *Pseudochristus*
[London, 1650], 22).
79. "Trial of A. Hutchinson before Boston Church," quoted in Koehler, *Search for
Power*, 226.

> The same so sore annoyéd the knight,
> That welnigh chokéd with the deadly stinke,
> His forces faile, ne can no longer fight.
> Whose corage when the feend perceived to shrinke,
> She poured forth out of her hellish sinke
> Her fruitfull curséd spawne of serpents small,
> Deforméd monsters, fowle, and black as inke,
> Which swarming all about his legs did crall,
> And him encombred sore, but could not hurt at all.[80]

If the Quaker leader James Nayler ever read Spenser's poem (which is much less likely), he might have identified less with the courage of the Red Cross Knight than with his weakness. After a female prophet called Martha Simmonds challenged his authority by screaming in his face, reducing him to helpless catatonia or spiritual babyhood, at least two male Quakers wrote of her as "Martha your miserable mother," and "Martha Simmonds who is called your mother."[81]

Ultimately, all these ambiguities of motherhood resolved themselves into one central image: the great cosmic womb of nature. Here was the source of the "genital moisture" of the first creation (personified, according to the Cambridge Platonist Henry More, as water nymphs). Here too was the death of the civilized, individual ego and of the care and tenderness of ordinary maternal feeling. So wrote the Ranter Abiezer Coppe:

> All my strength, my forces were utterly routed, my house I dwelt in fired; my father and mother forsook me, the wife of my bosom loathed me, mine old name was rotted, perished; and I was utterly plagued, consumed, damned, rammed, and sunk into nothing, into the bowels of the still Eternity (my mother's womb) out of which I came naked, and whetherto I returned again naked.[82]

80. Spenser, *The Faerie Queene*, in *Edmund Spenser's Poetry*, ed Maclean, 10, 11. Linda Paige discusses monster mothers in relation to nature goddesses in "Mothers of Paradox: Edmund Spenser's Monster Mothers in *The Faerie Queene*," typescript, University of Tennessee, Department of English, 1986.

81. Kenneth L. Carroll, "John Perrot: Early Quaker Schismatic," JFHS Suppl. 33 (1971): 10. George Fox wrote to Nayler about "Martha who is called your Mother" (Ralph Farmer, *Sathan Enthron'd in His Chair of Pestilence, or Quakerism in Its Exaltation* [London, 1657], 9).

82. Abiezer Coppe, *A Fiery Flying Roll*, quoted in Owen Watkins, *The Puritan Experiment: Studies in Spiritual Autobiography* (New York: Schocken Press, 1972), 146. Henry More, *Defence of the Philosophick Cabbala* (London, 1662), 77, quoted in Désirée Hirst, *Hidden Riches: Traditional Symbolism from the Renaissance to Blake* (New York: Barnes and Noble, 1964), 160.

CHAPTER TWO

Male and Female Power: Visionary Women and the Social Order

When ladies ride abroad with waxed boots, and men thresh
with their cloaks on; when the pot freezes in the
chimney-corner, and puss sits with her arse to the fire; when
women go abroad and fetch home wood, and men sit at
home by the fire side and burn it; when the icicles hang at
people's noses, and women cannot catch them a heat with
scolding; when all these signs come to pass, you may be
confident of cold weather.

     Poor Robin. 1664. An Almanack after a New Fashion

INTRODUCTION

The readers who attempted to decipher the arcane prophecies of Eleanor
Davies lived in at least two mental worlds, each with its own set of
assumptions about the symbolic associations of the words "male" and
"female" and about the qualities and behavior appropriate to real men
and women. The kind of power associated with the social and political
sphere, which was at least formally dominated by men, was power
exercised in daylight: self-willed, rational, organized, and generally obvious. The kind of power associated with the *spiritual* realm, in which
women often predominated, was, we have seen, power of a very different
sort. Spiritual power infused and energized the body, it was polymorphous and morally ambiguous, either godly or demonic.

    The polarity of reason and spirituality should not be taken to reflect
a difference between mind and body or between secular society and
religion. The opposition was rather between the world of culture, or the
ideally static and hierarchical social order, and that of a natural universe
pulsating with occult spiritual forces. "As Christ then has a body mys-

tical," wrote John Bunyan in a tract opposing women's separate meeting for worship,

> so he has a body politic, congregations modelled by the skill that his ministers have in his word . . . and the preserving of his glory in the world. . . . In *this* church, order and discipline, for the nourishing up of the true mystical body of Christ, has been placed from the foundation of the world. Wherefore in *this*, laws, and statutes, and government is to be looked after, and given heed unto. . . . Now, where there is order and government by laws and statutes, there must, of necessity, be also a distinction of sex, degrees, and age.[1]

In this sense, both negative and positive feminine symbols (the Whore of Babylon or the Woman in the Wilderness, representing the true church) pointed to a dimension of experience that was foreign to the culture of male clergymen and magistrates. Faced with a concrete embodiment of female spirituality, whether Satanic witch or pious visionary, an observer might have perceived a being completely wild: the witch, most obviously, as an emblem of social deviance and an instrument of infernal malice and the prophet as an uncivilized being in harmony with natural creation, just as Adam and Eve lived in harmony with nature before the Fall. Or the observer might have perceived a being who mediated between the worlds of culture and nature: a virtuous maiden lying in her own bed, using (more or less) coherent language as she preached to visitors, and a spiritual creature from another world— catatonic, lawless, inhuman.[2]

We can appreciate the fundamental difference between perceptions of male and female power by comparing popular accounts of witches with contemporary Faust legends, both of which depicted characters who sold their souls to the devil for personal gain. In the case of witches, over ninety percent of whom were women, the devil was said to approach his victim in the shape of a man or animal familiar, who converted her not by rational argument but by full physical penetration. Once inside her body, the devil actually permeated and changed her essence, as evidenced by the witches' marks or teats that appeared on her body. As a powerful

1. John Bunyan, *A Case of Conscience Resolved* . . . (1683), in *The Complete Works of John Bunyan, Author of "The Pilgrim's Progress,"* 4 vols., ed. Henry Stebbing (Hildesheim and New York: Georg Olms Verlag and Johnson Reprint Corp., 1970), 417.

2. The typology of gender in relation to concepts of nature and culture was developed by Sherry Ortner, "Is Female to Male as Nature Is to Culture?" in *Women, Culture, and Society*, ed. Michelle Z. Rosaldo and Louise Lamphere (Stanford: Stanford University Press, 1974). For a fuller discussion of this typology in relation to women as prophets, see Phyllis Mack, "Feminine Behavior and Radical Action: Franciscans, Quakers, and the Followers of Gandhi," *Signs: Journal of Women in Culture and Society* 11 (1986): 457–77.

agent of *maleficium,* she could then hurt others by a mere glance or even by her breath. The witch Margaret Johnson of Lancashire, whose confession was recorded in 1634, described her seduction thusly: While she sat at home in a mood of anger and depression, the devil appeared to her in the shape of a man in a black silk suit, offering to supply all her wants in exchange for her soul and to give her the power to kill man or beast whenever she desired. She agreed, and he defiled her by an act of "wicked uncleanness." Later she attended a sabbat at which she saw some witches grander than the rest who had no breasts at all but sharp bones for the devil to prick and raise blood, fashioning a pap or dug from which he might suck. (Margaret Johnson and three other witches were brought to London and examined by five physicians and ten female obstetricians, acting under the direction of William Harvey, discoverer of the circulation of the blood. They found "two things which might be called teats" on her body.)[3] During Anne Bodenham's trial for witchcraft in 1653, a servant who had consulted the cunning woman lamented her damned condition to the interrogator:

> Oh very damnable, very wretched; this hand of mine writ my name in the Devil's book, this finger of mine was pricked, here is yet the hole that was made, and with my blood I wrote my own damnation. . . . The Devil came, oh! in a terrible shape to me, entered within me, and there he lies, swelling in my body, gnawing at my heart, tearing my bowels within me, and there is no hope, but one time or other will tear me all in pieces. . . . I am not able to bear his beating and tearing me, he will kill me, there is no hope, I can scarce breathe already.[4]

In Faust stories the protagonist, usually a man, also made a pact with the devil for personal gain, above all the desire for knowledge and carnal pleasure. In popular Faust chapbooks, farces, plays, and puppet shows performed in England, the "hero" was depicted as both playful and intellectually curious. After long, entertaining conversations with an intelligent and charismatic Satan, he collected his reward: "Taking to him the wings of an eagle, [he] thought to fly over the whole world, and to know the secrets of heaven and earth."[5] His ambition to become an

3. *The Examination and Voluntary Confession of Margaret Johnson of Marsden* . . . abridged in C. L'Estrange Ewen, *Witchcraft and Demonianism* (London: Heath, Cranton, 1933), 248–50.

4. Edmund Bower, *Doctor Lamb Revived, or, Witchcraft Condemn'd in Anne Bodenham* (London, 1653), 17–18.

5. William Rose, ed., *The Historie of the Damnable Life, and Deserved Death of Doctor John Faustus and the Second Report of Faustus, Containing His Appearances and the Deeds of Wagner* (1592; reprint, London, n.d.), 67.

astronomer, an astrologer, and a calendar maker was more reminiscent
of the heroic quest of Prometheus than of the sinister practices of the
cunning woman, and his joys were not the bloodthirsty and perverted
ones of witches, who copulated with demons and murdered animals and
children, but the perfectly human ones of playing practical jokes on the
pope and sleeping with Helen of Troy. Inevitably, after having the time
of his life and suffering occasional pangs of remorse, Faust died a grue-
some death, his brains splattered against the walls of his room. Thus was
Faust portrayed as a curious, self-centered, even heroic, if gullible figure,
not a monster. His character was stronger and more active than that of
the witch, since his identity was less malleable than hers, yet also weaker,
since his pact with the devil ultimately killed him.[6] Faust was a man who
engaged in occult practices in order to penetrate the mysteries of nature.
The penetrated witch *became* nature; she herself was the mystery.

   An actual Faust story, cited in the Middlesex Sessions Rolls during the
reign of Charles I, was that of Thomas Browne, charged with selling his
soul to an evil spirit in return for a regular payment of a thousand pounds
"of current English money," protection from danger for forty-one years,
and a pleasing wife; a grand jury left it to another jury to decide if Browne
had played Dr. Faustus in Christopher Marlowe's play.[7] During the Civil
War period, male sectarian prophets were also viewed as Faust figures,
prideful and ambitious seekers after forbidden knowledge and authority,
while female sectarians were frequently depicted as witch figures, ani-
malistic creatures who were never seen to think but whose bodies secreted polluted substances as false notions. One diatribe against the
Brownist sect described a meeting similar to a witches' sabbat and a witty
young gentlewoman who was seduced by the minister. At first pensive
and sad, she suddenly began to vomit, scratch, and bite, crying, "I am
damned, I am damned," and was saved only by a miracle. Another attack
on the Brownists described an oracle who received her inspiration

---

   6. For a typical Faust-type story, see Samuel Clarke, *A Mirrour or Looking-Glasse
Both for Saints, and Sinners*, 2d ed. (London, 1654), 92–93, quoted in David D. Hall, "A
World of Wonders: The Mentality of the Supernatural in Seventeenth-Century New
England," in *Seventeenth-Century New England*, ed. David D. Hall and David Grayson
Allen, The Colonial Society of Massachusetts, vol. 63 (Charlottesville: University Press of
Virginia, 1984), 246. See also Keith Thomas, *Religion and the Decline of Magic* (New
York: Scribner's, 1971), 473–74; Leonard Forster, *The Man Who Wanted to Know
Everything* (London: University of London, Institute of Germanic Studies, 1981); Frances
A. Yates, *The Occult Philosophy in the Elizabethan Age* (London, Boston, and Henley:
Routledge and Kegan Paul, 1979), 115–25.
   7. John Cordy Jeaffreson, ed., *Middlesex County Records*, vol. 3, *Indictments,
Recognizances, Coroners' Inquisitions-Post-Mortem . . . 1 Charles I to 18 Charles II*
(London: County Record Society, 1888), xi, 88.

"namely not by her mouth only, but her belly being swollen, and sitting upon the sacred stool . . . then came the stinking oracle from und. or out of the stool below."[8] Mary White, who listened to the preaching of the Quaker Edward Burrough, "sometimes blared like a calf and sometimes did clasp her Legs about her Neck" and afterward brought charges of witchcraft against the Quakers. In New England, both male and female Quaker missionaries would be prosecuted by the Puritan authorities for their bad opinions, but only female prophets would be examined for marks of witchcraft.[9]

Contemporaries understood, to a far greater degree than some modern observers recognize, that individual men and women might assume the attributes of both male and female power. Male priests and rulers possessed sacred as well as rational authority, such as the king's reputed ability to heal by touch, while women were both practical and reasonable in their exercise of household government. The flexibility of gender roles was also affected by the status hierarchy; thus, the behavior of a male courtier or servant was functionally feminine in relation to his female superior, while the wife who ran a business or defended a castle in the absence of her husband was functionally masculine in relation to her apprentices or dependents.

Perhaps more than any other arena of social activity, the practice of religion offered the individual temporary liberation from rigid gender roles, for while the Protestant church was governed, analyzed, and defended by men, these same men allowed themselves a high degree of feminine expressiveness when, as worshipers, they assumed the role of loving spouse and supplicant before a masculine God. So the Leveler leader John Lilburne affirmed, "and this I counted my wedding day in which I was married to the Lord Jesus Christ; for now I know he loves me in that he bestowed so rich apparel this day upon me."[10] Conversely, women, who kept an enforced silence in matters of secular politics, might

8. *The Brownist Haeresies Confuted . . .* (1641). John Paget, *An Arrow against the Separation of the Brownists* (Amsterdam, 1618), 53. On male prophets, see Thomas, *Religion and the Decline of Magic*, 135ff.

9. *Quakers Are Inchanters, and Dangerous Seducers Appearing in Their Inchantment of One Mary White at Wickham-skeyth in Suffolk* (London, 1655), quoted in William York Tindall, *John Bunyan, Mechanick Preacher* (New York: Russell and Russell, 1964), 222.

10. John Lilburne, *A Work of the Beast* (1638), 8, quoted in Paul Christianson, *Reformers and Babylon: English Apocalyptic Visions from the Reformation to the Eve of the Civil War* (Toronto and Buffalo: University of Toronto Press, 1978), 170.

ɔf both men and women when they composed treatises
y or on their own spiritual travail. Thus, religious
ie individual moments of social as well as spiritual
; the worshiper to express a sensibility and authority
:cessible to him or her in secular life. It was therefore
..any dangerous practice, for it sanctioned a fluidity of self-
perception that, if allowed to interfere with the ordered functioning of
the hierarchies of state, church, and family, might render those hierarchies effectively null and void.

SPIRITUAL POWER AND SOCIAL STRUCTURE

If this [crossdressing] be not barbarous, make the rude
Scythian, the untamed *Moor,* the naked *Indian,* or the
wild *Irish,* Lords and Rulers of well governed Cities.
Hic Mulier: Or, The Man-Woman, *1620*

The interpretation of spiritual or occult energy, however bizarre its
manifestation and however reclusive the prophet, mystic, or hermit in
question, had always been linked to perceptions about the visionary's
relationship to the social structure itself. Visionary or occult behavior
was interpreted not by universal standards of reason or common sense
but by an individual, such as a priest, with the moral authority to
determine whether the spiritual source of the vision or prodigious action
was divine or diabolical. Or the behavior might emanate from someone
whose exalted position in the Chain of Being guaranteed that the source
was divine, as in the case of the king's touch. In the societies of late
medieval and Renaissance Europe, where the authority of the ruler was
as much sacred as it was political or administrative, occult energy might
thus have a positive (and usually conservative) social function as a source
of power available to bolster political and ecclesiastical hierarchies.

In Catholic countries, the church attempted to mediate the spiritual
authority of female visionaries through male confessors. The interro-
gations of these women and the investigations preceding canonization
focused heavily on the orthodoxy of the visions in question as well as on
the humility and obedience of the visionary herself.[11] In Protestant

11. On Catholic visionaries, see Elizabeth Petroff, *Consolation of the Blessed* (New York: Alta Gaia Society, 1979); Donald Weinstein and Rudolph M. Bell, *Saints and Society: The Two Worlds of Western Christendom, 1000–1700* (Chicago: University of Chicago Press, 1982).

England there were fewer means of channeling the behavior of the visionary to conform to the interests and values of the larger society or, rather, the dominant groups within the larger society. There was also a more acute sense of the power of spiritual forces to invade the individual human soul, forced to hold its own without the protective buffer of Roman Catholic ritual. In one English town the annual procession of St. George and the dragon was altered after the Reformation, the procession now being held with the dragon but without St. George.[12]

In the relatively stable years of the Elizabethan period, it was still possible to distinguish holy behavior, or sanctity, from criminal behavior, or diabolism, by reference to the political and social hierarchies. The queen's reputed ability to heal by touch did not place her in the same social or spiritual category as the village cunning woman, although both had occult curative powers. The aristocratic lady's function as a dispenser of herbal medicines on her estate did not quite place *her* in the same category as the local white witch, although their activities were also similar.[13] In this social environment, there was nothing necessarily sinister about the occult feats of individual female prophets. Indeed, many writers viewed feminine spiritual symbolism, embodied in the female visionary, in a positively benign light, as entirely appropriate to express their visions of an ultimate reconciliation of contending religious groups, an apocalypse resulting not from God the father's implacable judgment but from the goddess Sophia's love and intuitive wisdom. The politics of reconciliation and its accompanying feminine associations reached its apogee under Queen Elizabeth, when there evolved a highly sophisticated tradition of positive feminine symbolism around the figure of the queen and her coterie of alchemists and astrologers. Elizabeth was compared to the biblical prophet Deborah, Judith, Esther, the queen of Sheba, and the Virgin Mary. The entire edifice of Spenser's *The Faerie Queene* was infused and decorated not only with grotesque monster mothers but with feminine images of the spiritual and moral virtues of wisdom, courage, conciliation, and benign magic, all ultimately referring to a real female ruler.[14]

12. Peter Burke, *Popular Culture in Early Modern Europe* (New York and London: Harper and Row, 1978), 216.

13. Thomas, *Religion and the Decline of Magic*, Chaps. 2 and 3.

14. Robin Headlam Wells, *Spenser's "Faerie Queene" and the Cult of Elizabeth* (London and Totowa, N.J.: Barnes and Noble Books, 1983), 19; Frances Yates, *Astraea: The Imperial Theme in the Sixteenth Century* (Harmondsworth: Routledge and Kegan Paul, 1977), Part 2, "The Tudor Imperial Reform"; Peter Stallybrass, "Patriarchal Territories: The Body Enclosed," in *Rewriting the Renaissance: The Discourses of Sexual*

This benign attitude toward the arts of the magician or natural philosopher, and toward the feminine imagery of Elizabethan pageantry and
literature, became less tenable in the society of prerevolutionary England,
where women in general were perceived as more visible and more aggressive than before and where fears about increasing social dislocation
were frequently articulated as criticism of women's independence and
their co-optation of the dress and behavior normally reserved for men.[15]
One of those most disturbed about women's new assertiveness and the
blurring of gender boundaries was the eminent witch hunter King James
I. In a letter of 1620, one London gentleman reported:

> Yesterday the bishop of London called together all his clergy about this town,
> and told them he had express commandment from the King to will them to
> inveigh vehemently against the insolency of our women, and their wearing of
> broad brimmed hats, pointed doublets, their hair cut short or shorn, and some
> of them stilettos or poniards . . . adding withall that if pulpit admonitions will
> not reform them he would proceed by another course; the truth is the world
> is very much out of order.[16]

Two weeks later he reported an escalation of misogynist propaganda:

> Our pulpits ring continually of the insolence and impudence of women, and
> to help the matter forward the players have likewise taken them to task, and
> so too the ballads and ballad-singers, so that they can come nowhere but their
> ears tingle; and if all this will not serve, the King threatens to fall upon their
> husbands, parents or friends that have or should have power over them, and
> make them pay for it.[17]

Popular discussion of women's cross-dressing culminated in the publication in 1620 of two pamphlets, *Hic Mulier: Or, The Man-Woman* and
a humorous rejoinder, *Haec-Vir: Or The Womanish-Man*, which defended women's rights to exhibit the masculine virtues of courage and
self-control as well as masculine dress:

> But you say we are barbarous and shameless and cast off all softness, to run
> wild through a wilderness of opinions. . . . Because I stand not with my hands

Difference in Early Modern Europe, ed. Margaret W. Ferguson, Maureen Quilligan, and
Nancy J. Vickers (Chicago and London: University of Chicago Press, 1986), 129–33.

15. Mary Beth Rose, *The Expense of Spirit: Love and Sexuality in English Renais-
sance Drama* (Ithaca, N.Y., and London: Cornell University Press, 1988), 47, 66–72.
Jean E. Howard, "Crossdressing, the Theatre, and Gender Struggle in Early Modern
England," *Shakespeare Quarterly* 39 (1988): 418–40.

16. John Chamberlain to Sir D. Carleton, January 25, 1620, quoted in Rose, *Expense of Spirit*, 69–70.

17. John Chamberlain to Sir D. Carleton, February 12, 1620, quoted in Rose,
Expense of Spirit, 70.

on my belly . . . that am not dumb when wantons court me, as if ass-like I were ready for all burdens; or because I weep not when injury grips me, like a worried deer in the fangs of many curs, am I therefore barbarous or shameless?[18]

Moll Cutpurse, the villainous heroine of one popular London play, was sympathetically modeled on a real brawling, singing, smoking, bawdy woman named Mary Frith, who dressed as a man and dealt in stolen goods.[19] Not only did numbers of women engage in cross-dressing and other flamboyant or underworld activities; other, quite ordinary women (and men) loudly objected to a sermon by William Gouge, in which he approved of the law denying a married woman the right to own property. "I remember," Gouge later wrote, "that when these Domestical Duties were first uttered out of the pulpit, much exception was taken against the application of a wife's subjection to the restraining of her from disposing the common goods of the family without, or against her husband's consent." He also marveled at the fact that "many wives . . . think themselves every way as good as their husbands, and no way inferior to them."[20]

Women had also begun to resist the ceremony of churching (described in chapter 1) as a slur on their virtue and respectability, sometimes by physically assaulting the priest. When Joan Whitup, in Essex, was admonished for appearing at the altar without a white veil but in her own hat, as well as sitting in her own pew instead of the churching bench, she retorted, "none but whores did wear veils and . . . a harlot or a whore was the inventor of it, or that first wore a veil."[21] Thousands of women petitioned Parliament for the redress of economic and political griev-

18. "Hic-Mulier"; Or, the Man-Woman . . . (1620), reprinted in Half Humankind: Contexts and Texts of the Controversy about Women in England, 1540–1640, ed. Katherine Usher Henderson and Barbara F. McManus (Urbana and Chicago: University of Illinois Press, 1985), 265–76. "Haec-Vir"; Or, The Womanish Man . . . (1620), reprinted in Half Humankind, ed. Henderson and McManus, 278–89, esp. 284.

19. The play was The Roaring Girl by Thomas Middleton and Thomas Dekker (1608–11). For a discussion of the Hic-Mulier controversy, see Rose, Expense of Spirit, 71ff. Rose emphasizes the author's concern that women obscure differences in rank by cross-dressing. "Like death and disease . . . the female in male attire served as a leveler" (74). On cross-dressing see Howard, "Crossdressing, the Theatre, and Gender Struggle."

20. William Gouge, Of Domesticall Duties (1634), 3–4, 273, quoted in Linda Woodbridge, Women and the English Renaissance: Literature and the Nature of Womankind, 1540–1620 (Urbana and Chicago: University of Illinois Press, 1984), 129, 130.

21. William Hale, A Series of Precedents and Proceedings in Criminal Causes Extending from the Year 1475 to 1640 (London, 1847), 237 (April 23, 1614), quoted in Dorothy P. Ludlow, "'Arise and Be Doing': English 'Preaching' Women, 1640–1660," Ph.D. diss., Indiana University, 1978, 60. On churching, see also pages 56–62.

ances; in 1649, a group of Leveler women protested the imprisonment
of their men, insisting that they themselves were "assured of their creation in the image of God, and of an interest in Christ equal unto men,
as also of a proportionable share in the freedoms of this commonwealth."[22] There is also evidence that women's economic activities in
midwifery, dairy farming, and small trades were becoming more visible
in some areas of the country and that, in those very areas, rituals
expressing sexual hostility were more prominent.[23] In the skimmington,
or riding, a man (often dressed as a woman) rode backwards on a horse
accompanied by the rough music of clanging pots and pans, all of this
cacaphony intended to ridicule the woman who wore the breeches—who
beat, badgered, or cuckolded her husband.[24]

22. Quoted in Margaret George, *Women in the First Capitalist Society: Experiences
in Seventeenth-Century England* (Urbana and Chicago: University of Illinois Press, 1988),
65–66. On petitioning Parliament, see Ellen McArthur, "Women Petitoners and the Long
Parliament," *English Historical Review* 29 (1909): 698–709.

23. On dairy farming, see David Underdown, "The Taming of the Scold: The
Enforcement of Patriarchal Authority in Early Modern England," in *Order and Disorder
in Early Modern England*, ed. Anthony Fletcher and John Stevenson (Cambridge: Cambridge University Press, 1985), 135–36. Wallace Notestein remarks on the numbers of
accused witches who were teachers (*A History of Witchcraft in England from 1558 to
1718* [1911; reprint, New York: Russell and Russell, 1965], 211–13, 223–24). Many
female activities centered in London: Christopher Hill writes that aristocratic theater was
cynical and contemptuous in its attitude toward women, probably because of rising
middle class households where the wife was the junior partner in the business (*The World
Turned Upside Down: Radical Ideas during the English Revolution* [New York: Viking
Press, 1972], 247–48). There was a scheme to incorporate the midwives of London,
which was turned down by the College of Physicians (J. H. Aveling, *The Chamberlens,
and the Midwifery Forceps: Memorials of the Family and an Essay on the Invention of the
Instrument* [London: J. and A. Churchill, 1882], 34ff.). Women's literacy increased dramatically in London, beginning in 1650 (Peter Burke, "Popular Culture in Seventeenth-
Century London," *London Journal* 3 [1977]: 157). W. K. Jordan notes that while there
was little legal improvement for women in London from 1480 to 1660, the actual rights
of women were increasing in all urban communities; he also notes that there was a rapid
gain from the 1620s through 1650. In London and Bristol, most charitable activities were
handled by women (*Philanthropy in England 1480–1660: A Study of the Changing
Patterns of English Social Aspirations* [New York: Russell Sage Foundation, 1959], 28–
30).

24. Martin Ingram, "Ridings, Rough Music, and Mocking Rhymes in Early Modern
England," in *Popular Culture in Seventeenth-Century England*, ed. Barry Reay (London
and Sydney: Croom Helm, 1985), 166–97. Ingram argues that the skimmington reflected
anxiety about the security of patriarchal norms rather than the totalitarian oppression of
women. See also Susan Dwyer Amussen, *An Ordered Society: Family and Village in
England, 1560–1725* (Oxford and New York: Basil Blackwell, 1988). Amussen points to
families' concern for order as affecting the state. She discusses charivaris organized by
men, mocking women's sexual mistreatment of their husbands. These rituals focused on
sexual misconduct rather than on other forms of aggression because really meek women
would have been less effective in the family economy; sexual modesty thus became a sign
of the good wife in defamation cases (118–22). On women's challenges to patriarchal
authority, see Louis B. Wright, *Middle-Class Culture in Elizabethan England* (Chapel
Hill: University of North Carolina Press, 1935), 490–97. On popular protest, see Reay,

As the bulwarks of social propriety and religious conformity became more and more destabilized in the decades preceding the Civil War period, occult female spirituality acquired an increasingly subversive connotation. Indeed, respectable Englishmen had begun to perceive that, without the entrenched authority to interpret visionary experience, spiritual knowledge might be co-opted, and exploited, by virtually anyone. "All sorts of people dreamed of an utopia and infinite liberty," lamented one Royalist, "especially in matters of religion."[25] For those reacting against the earlier Elizabethan or "Rosicrucian" culture, as historian Frances Yates termed it, feminine spiritual images became less frequently associated with religious harmony or philosophical magic; instead, they were associated with treason and witchcraft.[26] In Ben Jonson's play *The Alchemist*, the Faerie Queene of Spenser's poem has become the Whore of Babylon, representing the false religion of the Elizabethan magus John Dee, who died in extreme poverty and disgrace in 1608.[27] Other writers linked female qualities to those of the obscene papists: decadent, subversive, promiscuous, enemies of the state, all of these associations referring ultimately to real female villains, "Bloody" Mary Tudor and King Charles I's Catholic wife Henrietta Maria. It was during the reign of King James I that the royal power authorized examinations for the discovery of witches' marks on the body, setting a precedent for the trials of the Civil War period. Witchcraft executions, formerly concentrated in London and adjacent counties, now occurred in East Anglia, the Mid-

---

ed., *Popular Culture in Seventeenth-Century England*, 12, and the essay by Buchanan Sharp, "Popular Protest in Seventeenth-Century England," 274, 285, 290.

25. Chestlin, *Persecutio Undecima*, quoted in Hill, *World Turned Upside Down*, 28.

26. Frances A. Yates, *The Rosicrucian Enlightenment* (London and Boston: Routledge and Kegan Paul, 1972). G. L. Kittredge, "English Witchcraft and James I," in *Studies in the History of Religions Presented to Crawford Howell Toy by Pupils, Colleagues, and Friends*, ed. D. Lyon and G. Moore (New York: Macmillan, 1912), 1–65. Kittredge emphasizes the readiness of the English public to accept the more severe punishments for witches instituted at the beginning of the seventeenth century, while Stuart Clark emphasizes the close relation between James's theory of ideal monarchy and his attitudes about witchcraft; he also discusses witchcraft as an inversion of the social order ("Witchcraft and Kingship," in *Studies in the History of Religions*, ed. Lyon and Moore, 156–77). Robert Fludd's work found more favor on the Continent than in England, where he was accused of witchcraft (Allen G. Debus, *The English Paracelsians* [New York: F. Watts, 1966], 178). On the seriousness with which witchcraft was now discussed, see Katherine Mary Briggs, *Pale Hecate's Team: An Examination of the Beliefs on Witchcraft and Magic among Shakespeare's Contemporaries and His Immediate Successors* (London: Routledge and Kegan Paul, 1962), 76.

27. Frances A. Yates, *Shakespeare's Last Plays: A New Approach* (London: Routledge and Kegan Paul, 1975), 116–18, 124–25. See also Yates, *The Rosicrucian Enlightenment*, 161.

lands, and the remote counties of Yorkshire and Lancashire and later in Durham, Wales, and Cheshire.[28]

Not only was the irrational, bestial, and envious nature of woman associated with the enemy from Rome; these female characteristics were also identified with those of the mob, the "giddy" or "promiscuous" body of the people. So the astrologer William Lilly asserted that "Mercury and the moon are significators of the common people" and that "the moon is the general significatrix of women."[29] Women prophets of the 1640s were ridiculed as "tub-preachers," laundresses who turned their washtubs upside down to use as pulpits, in order to incite wifely disobedience and sexual deviance. In a lengthy tome detailing the crimes of sectarian fanatics, the Puritan Thomas Edwards described the heartless Mrs. Attaway, who took advantage of her husband's absence in the army to preach and then left her children of six and seven exposed to the world when she ran away with another man, in the process inspiring another male member of her audience to abandon his own pregnant wife.[30] In A Discovery of Six women preachers, Mary Bilbrowe was said to have interrupted her prayer to converse with a male caller, quieting her gossiping female congregation by serving a roast pig, while Joan Bauford of Feversham taught that women might forsake husbands who crossed their wills, and Susan May of Kent preached that the devil was the father of the pope. "Thus have I declared some of the female academies," wrote the anonymous author, "but where their university is I cannot tell, but I suppose that Bedlam or Bridewell would be two convenient places for them."[31] In yet another so-called exposé of female sectarians, called "The Sisters' Conspiracy," a group of women described themselves as beasts slaking their appetites by indiscriminate sex,

28. Notestein, History of Witchcraft, 51–52, 118–19, 154–55. On the revision of witchcraft legislation during the reign of James I, see Kittredge, "English Witchcraft," 22–26.

29. William Lilly, Astrological Almanac (1680). On the connotation of the word "people," see Christopher Hill, "The Poor and the People in Seventeenth-Century England," in History from Below: Studies in Popular Protest and Popular Ideology in Honour of George Rudé, ed. Frederick Krantz (Montreal: Concordia University Press, 1986), 76: "Upper class writers . . . just did not think of the lowest classes (any more than they thought of women) when speaking of 'the people' whom Parliament represented." On the link between women and political rebellion, see Hill, World Turned Upside Down, 82–83, and Keith Thomas, "Women and the Civil War Sects," Past and Present 13 (1958): 42–62.

30. Thomas Edwards, Gangraena, or a Catalogue and Discovery of Many of the Errours, Heresies, Blasphemies and Pernicious Practices of the Sectaries of This Time, Vented and Acted in England in These Four Last Years (London, 1645), 120–21.

31. A Discoverie of Six Women Preachers . . . (1641).

robbing their families' goods, and cutting their husbands' throats. The sisters' song (to be sung through the nose) went:

> No ordinance shall command us at all,
> For we are above their thrall.
> We care not a straw for reason or law;
> For conscience is all in all. . . .
> We will not be wives and tie up our lives
> To villainous slavery:
> But couple in love and fear;
> When mov'd by the spirit to't;
> For there is no sin to let a saint in,
> When he has the grace to do't. . . .
> We'll cut off the wicked rout,
> And bathe us all in their blood;
> Their houses and land we'll have at command.
> And common upon their goods;
> We'll grind 'em to grist, and live as we list,
> And we will do wonders brave.[32]

In short, *all* enemies of the propertied classes and of the religious establishment, both male and female, were portrayed symbolically as women (most notably the Whore of Babylon), while actual female visionaries were portrayed as tramps, in both the sexual and economic sense.

Critics of the religious establishment and defenders of women's preaching utilized the same feminine symbolism but reversed its meaning. So Doctor John Bastwick ridiculed the pomp of the Anglican prelates by describing a bishop parading down the street, preceded by a servant who pushed back the mob of spectators, crying, "Sirs, I say you common people, you laymen stand back there, give room for my Lord Bang-Whore [i.e., the Bishop of Bangor, having sex with the Whore of Babylon], stand back I say, you women there is a plague of God upon you, what make you here among the clergy? . . . Get you home to spin and learn obedience to the Church."[33] John Rogers, minister of a congregation belonging to the radical Fifth Monarchist sect, linked women's spiritual equality with the rights of other oppressed groups:

The Apostle says it agrees not with the profession to make difference of persons in the Church of Christ, . . . not only in not preferring the rich before

32. *Rump, or an Exact Collection of the Choycest Poems and Songs*, 2 vols. (London, 1662), 2: 196.
33. John Bastwick, *Letany*, 1:7, quoted in Christianson, *Reformers and Babylon*, 160.

the poor, but not the strong before the weak, (nor the men before the women). . . . For where there ought to be no respect of persons, there ought to be no difference betwixt men and women.[34]

Decades later, the Quaker George Keith would argue that education should not be the chief criterion for a preacher, because knowledge of scripture did not reveal whether these men "be truly gracious." On the contrary, the ministry was usually a career choice made by parents for their youngest and dumbest sons, whereas the true servants of God are "mechanic men and tradesmen" and, of course, women. Keith wrote of the biblical woman of Samaria that "her preaching was not any human design . . . it was of the Lord alone . . . whereas their preaching [that of the Anglican clergy] commonly and generally is a human design, and contrivance from first to last, to get money and worldly honor and preferment with much ease and idleness."[35]

PHILOSOPHERS AND FEMALE POWER

Our *Maker* is our *Husband* . . . and all *Forms* . . .
shall melt *away*.

                                    Abiezer Coppe

As magical and visionary practices became more closely associated with fears of impending social breakdown, philosophers of every class and political position strained to accommodate their belief in intuitive spiritual insight with their desire to preserve (or to create) firm structures of knowledge and authority. And since a primary characteristic of both occult spirituality and social disorder was the perceived activity of women, it was on the terrain of gender roles and gender relationships that their thinking most often foundered.

Those thinkers whose concerns were wholly mystical and apolitical continued, with no apparent discomfort, to celebrate both feminine spiritual symbolism and the visionary authority of actual women. John Pordage was an Oxford-educated Anglican minister, physician, astrologer, and mystic who held a prosperous living in Berkshire and enjoyed the patronage of such eminent personages as Elias Ashmole. He was also

34. John Rogers, *Ohel or Beth-shemesh* (London, 1653), reprinted in Joyce L. Irwin, *Womanhood in Radical Protestantism, 1525–1675* (New York and Toronto: Edwin Mellen Press, 1979), 174.
35. George Keith, *The Woman Preacher of Samaria* . . . (London, 1674), 9.

an adherent of the German mystic Jacob Boehme, for whom w[
the Virgin Sophia, was a central figure in guiding the individual'[
regeneration. In Boehme's theosophy, Sophia had been gen̶e̶r̶a̶t̶e̶d̶ ̶b̶y̶
Adam, an androgynous being

> with the *whole Cross in the brainpan*, which signifieth the number three; he
> was both man and woman, yet you are not to understand any woman, but
> a virgin wholly pure and chaste; he had in him the spirit of the tincture of the
> fire and also the spirit of the tincture of the water *viz.* of Venus: . . . he could
> generate *virgin-like* (out of his will, out of his essences, without pain, without
> tearing or dividing his body . . . for he had all three centers in him).[36]

Boehme also paid homage to the Virgin Mary as a vehicle of human
spiritual restoration: "Christ has truly, in the body of the Virgin Mary,
attracted to Him our human essences, and is become our brother."[37]

Pordage adopted Boehme's concept of Adam's original androgyny as
well as the kabbalistic notion that God and humanity were originally
one, "the male representing the deity, the female the pure humanity, or
regenerated part of the soul."[38] Reversing the customary attribution of
reason to men and visionary insight to women, he characterized Sophia
as passive human reason, enlivened by the active, masculine force of
revelation:

> She is a mere passive bright shining virtue, . . . a lustrous shining glance, being
> perfectly passive and moving only according to the motion of the eye of the
> Father. . . . She is free from all desire, will and motion of her own. She desires
> and wills nothing, but as the eternal mind, and will, desires and wills in her.
> [She is] free from all essences whatsoever, being nothing else but the unspotted
> mirror of the glory and excellency of God.[39]

Pordage and his wife Mary, known as "Father Abraham and Deborah," became the center of a group that attracted both Oxford aca-
demicians and tradesmen as well as the Ranter Abiezer Coppe. During
the 1650s, they formed a community that was said to live in continual

36. Jacob Boehme, *The Third Booke of the Author* (1650), quoted in Nigel Smith,
Perfection Proclaimed: Language and Literature in English Radical Religion (Oxford:
Oxford University Press, 1989), 198. For an account of Pordage's group in Bradfield, see
Désirée Hirst, *Hidden Riches: Traditional Symbolism from the Renaissance to Blake*
(New York: Barnes and Noble, 1964), 104–7, 168–70. See also Serge Hutin, *Les disci-
ples anglais de Jacob Boehme* (Paris: Editions Denoèl, 1960).

37. Jacob Boehme, *The Three Principles*, xiii, 41, quoted in Hirst, *Hidden Riches*, 95.

38. John Pordage, *Innocencie Appearing* (1653), 44, quoted in Smith, *Perfection
Proclaimed*, 206–7.

39. John Pordage, *Theologica Mystica, or the Mystic Divinitie of the Aeternal Invisibles* (London, 1683), 67–69.

expectation of heavenly openings, praying and dancing in celebration of their triumph over Satan, all presided over by Mrs. Pordage, attired in white lawn and holding a white wand. The group was apparently both celibate and nonauthoritarian, for Pordage maintained that the biblical verse "I know him, that he will command his children, and his household after him" (Genesis 18:19) did not mean his outward household but his inner will and affections, "for a man . . . cannot command his wife and children."[40] Attacked by his enemies on doctrinal and personal grounds (he was said to have rushed out of church "bellowing like a bull, saying that he was called, and must be gone"), Pordage was put on trial and ejected from his living in 1654, having vainly protested that he was neither a profligate nor a conjuror. After his wife's death he established himself in London, where he became a disciple of another female prophet, Jane Lead.[41]

The Cambridge Platonists were both more explicit and more cautious in analyzing the relation between spiritual reform and social disorder. Firmly wedded to an ideology that linked reason and intellectual elitism, they expressed a strong antipathy toward the use of magic and the naive, misguided enthusiasm of the radical sects. Henry More stressed the soul's inability to perceive accurately through dreams and the imagination: "The *spirit* then that wings the *enthusiast* in such a wonderful manner, is nothing else but that *flatulency* which is in the *melancholy* complexion, and rises out of the *hypochondriacal* humour upon some occasional heat." He also denigrated the spiritual frenzy and physicality of the radical sects:

> And as for *quaking*. . . . That *fear* causes *trembling* there is nothing more obvious . . . when they are to . . . go about some solemn or weighty performance in public, they will quake and tremble like an aspen-leaf; some have been struck silent, others have fallen down to the ground. . . . [So] the fervour of his *spirits* and heat of *imagination* may be wrought up to that pitch that it may amount to a perfect *epilepsy*.[42]

40. Christopher Fowler, *Daemonium Meridianum. Sathan at Noon* . . . (London, 1656), 38.

41. See the account of Pordage's ejection in Jerome Friedman, *Blasphemy, Immorality, and Anarchy: The Ranters and the English Revolution* (Athens, Ohio, and London: Ohio University Press, 1987), 236–50. Friedman defines Pordage as a Ranter rather than a mystic.

42. Henry More, *Enthusiasmus Triumphatus: Or, a True Relation of the Sad and Grievous Torments, Inflicted upon the Bodies of Three Children . . . by Witchcraft*, William Andrews Clark Memorial Library, no. 118 (Los Angeles: University of California Press, 1966), 12. See also Frederic B. Burnham, "The More-Vaughan Controversy: The Revolt against Philosophical Enthusiasm," *Journal of the History of Ideas* 35 (1974): 33–49. More referred to the "low Spirits" (i.e., natural philosophers, Paracelsians) who

The problem was that, like many of the sectarians he despised, More was a mystic as well as a rationalist, committed to a belief in the existence of spiritual forces acting in the material world and to a definition of reason as intuitive, contemplative, and aesthetic as well as logical.[43] He also criticized the elitism of his own intellectual community:

> Neither many words, nor much knowledge, nor the voluminousness of books, which are the disadvantages of our academical education, are anything to this, but it is the perpetual taking up of the Cross, and constant endeavor to shun a man's own will and appetite, that leads directly, to . . . peace and joy. . . . All knowledge to this is but vain fluttering, a feather in a man's cap tossed with the wind.[44]

As a Latitudinarian, More and others also espoused an ideal of toleration in matters of religious belief. Unlike many sectarians, who aimed for literal honesty in all things, Latitudinarians attempted to isolate a few essential principles on which all could agree while defining many other beliefs, including many religious opinions and practices, as nonessential.[45]

---

adopt the practices of artisans under the illusion of gaining knowledge (Charles Webster, *The Great Instauration: Science, Medicine, and Reform, 1626–1660* [London: Gerald Duckworth and Co., 1975], 146–47). He also rejected astrology as detracting from Christ's miracles: "And why might they not pray to [the stars] as *Anne Bodenham* the Witch did to the Planet *Jupiter* for the curing diseases, if they have so much power?" (More, *Enthusiasmus, Triumphatus*, 34).

43. More defined reason as "a Power of Faculties of the Soul; whereby either from her Innate Ideas or Common Notions, or else from the assurance of her own sense, . . . she unravels a further clue of knowledge, enlarging her sphere of Intellectual light, by laying open to herself the close connection and cohesion of the Conceptions she has of things, whereby inferring multifarious Conclusions as well as pleasure of Speculation" (quoted in John H. Stoneburner, "Henry More and Anne Conway," *Guilford Review* 23 (1986): 25. On More's concept of reason as encompassing spiritual intuition, see Marjorie Hope Nicholson, "George Keith and the Cambridge Platonists," *Philosophical Review* 39 (1930): 40–42. See also Barbara Shapiro, *Probability and Certainty in Seventeenth-Century England: A Study of the Relationship between Natural Science, Religion, History, Law, and Literature* (Princeton: Princeton University Press, 1983), 88. On More's affinities with theosophical ideas, see C. A. Staudenbaur, "Platonism, Theosophy, and Immaterialism: Recent Views of the Cambridge Platonists," *Journal of the History of Ideas* 35 (1974): 163–69; Staudenbaur's summary of historiography on More, focusing on whether More was a rationalist or a mystic, is an interesting echo of More's own apparent concern with this issue.

44. Quoted in Aaron Lichtenstein, *Henry More: The Rational Theology of a Cambridge Platonist* (Cambridge, Mass.: Harvard University Press, 1962), 100. See also Marjorie Hope Nicholson, ed., *Conway Letters: The Correspondence of Ann, Viscountess Conway, Henry More, and Their Friends, 1642–1684* (New Haven: Yale University Press, 1930), 76.

45. Shapiro, *Probability and Certainty*, 108. More never took a clear political stand and so retained his position at Cambridge throughout the revolution and Restoration, when he expressed his loyalty to the king (Susan Staves, *Players' Sceptres: Fictions of*

More resolved these quite fundamental contradictions by espousing a firm belief in diabolical witchcraft while denying the spiritual validity of popular prophecy. Writing to his intellectual companion Lady Anne Conway, he maintained that bad souls are capable of migration to other bodies, but good souls are not. Elsewhere he evinced considerable interest in folk stories of occult phenomena, including encounters with spirits and the transmigration of souls, while discounting the words of visionaries as "children's prattle."[46] This perspective, achieved only at the cost of some logical consistency, allowed him to retain his belief that spiritual energy acts in nature while simultaneously denying any positive authority to sectarians who preached without the proper intellectual credentials.

The same contradictions were resolved somewhat differently in the writing of John Smith, author of the most extended work on prophecy by the Cambridge Platonists.[47] Smith maintained that visionary experience is as real as sense perception, that it is perceived by the imagination as well as by the rational faculty, and that it is accessible to the ignorant as well as the learned. "The Scripture was not writ only for sagacious and abstracted minds, or philosophical heads; for then how few are there that should have been taught the true knowledge of God thereby?"[48] He clearly believed that "ecstatical rapture" was basic to the nature of prophecy. The imaginative power, he wrote, "is also the seat of all prophetical vision"; and "we must not mistake the business, as if there were nothing but the most absolute *clearness* and *serenity* of thoughts lodging in the soul of the *prophet* amidst all his *visions*"; and again, "[Prophecy] . . . entered upon the mind *as a fire*, and *like a hammer that breaketh the rock in pieces*."[49] Smith also provided a quite fascinating account of the psychology of the visionary, describing the experience of revelation as spiritual theater, God acting on the imagination of the prophet: "Those things which God . . . revealed . . . were acted over

---

Authority in the Restoration [Lincoln and London: University of Nebraska Press, 1979], 28). See also Rosalie Colie, *Light and Enlightenment: A Study of the Cambridge Platonists and the Dutch Arminians* (Cambridge: Cambridge University Press, 1957), 1–6.

46. On witchcraft and spiritual phenomena, see the letters of More to Lady Anne Conway, reprinted in Nicholson, ed., *Conway Letters*, March 31, 1663; July 14, 1671; October 17, 1671. Ralph Cudworth, Joseph Glanvill, and other Platonists also affirmed the existence of witches (Shapiro, *Probability and Certainty*, 212–13).

47. John Smith, "Of Prophecy," in *Select Discourses* (1660; reprint, Delmar, N.Y.: Scholars' Facsimiles and Reprints, 1979), 167–281.

48. Ibid., 172, 173, 178.

49. Ibid., 191–92, 199, 207.

symbolically, as in a *masque*, in which divers persons are brought in, amongst which the prophet himself bears a part: And therefore he, according to the exigency of this dramatical *apparatus*, must, as the other actors, perform his part."[50]

Yet Smith was fundamentally a conservative scholar, dedicated to the maintenance of a hierarchical order of learning and authority. And so, basing his arguments almost exclusively on quotations from Maimonides and talmudic writers rather than actual biblical prophets or mystical works, he maintained that the greater the harmony between reason and vision, the higher the level of prophecy:

> Now from what hath been said ariseth one main characteristical distinction between the *prophetical* and *pseudo-prophetical* spirit, viz. that the *prophetical* spirit doth never alienate the mind . . . but always maintains a consistency and clearness of reason, strength and solidity of judgment, where it comes; it doth not *ravish* the mind, but *inform* and *enlighten* it.[51]

Thus, it follows that not every individual is suited to be a prophet. Only one who is wise, prudent, and serene, who has subdued his or her animal parts, and who avoids light behavior and frivolous talk can be called a true visionary. Like the greatest of all prophets, Moses, the visionary perceives divine truth not through the concrete images of the imagination but through reason alone.[52]

> It may be considered that God made not use of idiots or fools to reveal his will by, but such whose intellectuals were entire and perfect; and that he imprinted such a clear copy of his truth upon them, as that it became their own sense, being digested fully into their understandings; so as they were able to deliver and represent it to others as truly as any can paint forth his own thoughts.[53]

The type of Mosaic prophecy, being the highest and most rational to be found in the Bible, was also the most fit setting for the inculcation of laws; Moses and the philosopher-king are brothers. Contemporary sec-

50. Ibid., 222.
51. Ibid., 197.
52. Ibid., 195, 245–46, 250–51, 261–65. Henry More agreed, defining reason as "so settled and cautious a Composure of Mind as will suspect every high flown and forward Fancy that endeavours to carry away the assent before deliberate examination" (*Enthusiasmus Triumphatus*, 38). Pure religion is characterized by universal piety, acceptance of the truth of scripture, and "*universal Prudence*, whereby a man neither admits nor acts anything but what is solidly rational at the bottom, and of which he can give a good account. . . . He that finds himself thus affected, may be sure it is the *Spirit of God*, not the powr of *Complexion* or *Nature* that rules in him" (45).
53. Smith, "Of Prophecy," 273.

tarians are false prophets, their minds dominated by melancholy, fancy, and imagination. Needless to say, the female visionary, whether considered historically or theoretically, is virtually absent from Smith's account.[54]

If academic philosophers found themselves unable to sustain a consistent position on the question of the relationship of rational and occult knowledge, or of male and female power, other less august thinkers vacillated even more wildly between the urge to align themselves with radical political movements and the equally powerful urge to dissociate themselves from elements that were condemned as ignorant and disorderly. These were the authors of astrological almanacs, popular yet "scientific" magicians, perched uneasily on the interface between high and low culture. Many of these astrologers, apothecaries, and chemists espoused democratic ideals. They defined occult knowledge as independent from and superior to the knowledge taught in universities, precisely because it was potentially accessible to everyone.[55] Several had specific plans for the general improvement of health, the advancement of horticultural production, and the productivity of human labor. They further asserted that men and women could recapture Adam's direct knowledge of nature, which enabled him to cure all illness. Nicholas Culpepper had a vision that "all the sick people in England presented themselves before me, and told they had Herbs in their gardens that might cure them, but knew not the virtues of them."[56] Culpepper also published a directory for midwives; he in turn was influenced by the popular astrologer William Lilly, who published the prophecies of the fictional Mother Shipton and the sibyls. Some Paracelsians even claimed

---

54. Ibid., 256. The biblical prophetess Huldah is mentioned once, with no commentary.

55. On the link between occult magic and radical politics, see P. M. Rattansi, "Paracelsus and the Puritan Revolution," *Ambix* 2 (1964): 24–32. Rattansi discusses the spread of mystical, antirational Paracelsian and Helmontian doctrines, which denigrated orthodox education, among apothecaries and others. "In a time of crisis . . . that side of the Paracelsian and Helmontian doctrine which exalted the knowledge of illumination above that derived from 'carnal reason' had a particular attraction for reformers and revolutionaries" (26). See also P. M. Rattansi, "The Social Interpretation of Science in the Seventeenth Century," in *Science and Society, 1600–1900*, ed. Peter Mathias (Cambridge: Cambridge University Press, 1972), 6, 12, 21, 31. Michael MacDonald, *Mystical Bedlam: Madness, Anxiety, and Healing in Seventeenth-Century England* (Cambridge: Cambridge University Press, 1981), 230–31; Hill, *World Turned Upside Down*, 24, 70–85. On the astrologers' middle-of-the-road politics, see Bernard Capp, *Astrology and the Popular Press: English Almanacs, 1500–1800* (London and Boston: Faber and Faber, 1979), 68–86, 160–61.

56. Nicholas Culpepper, *Physical Directory* (1666), sig. A2r., quoted in Webster, *The Great Instauration*, 271.

that old women had stronger claims to reliable medical knowledge than physicians.[57]

Regardless of these democratic sentiments, however, many of these same men adopted a tone of amused disdain toward the real female visionary, whom they ridiculed as ignorant, superstitious, and, above all, distinct from themselves. One astrological almanac informed readers that the meaning of a solar eclipse was the continuance of domestic wars "by the subtlety, cunning and plotting of a woman, or women rather; sectaries, sly knaves, witty and well spoken."[58] Astrologers also joked about prophets as though they were throwing stones at a village idiot. "About this time," sneered one writer, "shall a prophecy be found in an old woman's trunk, . . . portending the strange contentions that shall happen at *Billings-gate*, between the fish wives and the oyster women which shall last for many years."[59] In the *Yea and Nay Almanac* satirizing Quakers, the catechism goes: "Q. Why do the women so commonly follow the light? A: Because they are commonly light women."[60] By presenting themselves as intellectuals of a higher species than female visionaries and practitioners of low magic, whom they described as slatterns or even witches, astrologers were disguising the fact that they themselves often had no education beyond grammar school. They were also distracting readers from observing the obvious affinity between their own practices and those of visionaries, thus protecting themselves from charges of sorcery at a time when both witches and magicians were under increased attack by the government.[61] William Lilly, the author of sev-

57. Webster, *The Great Instauration*, 246–48, 256, 259, 262, 268–69, 274–85. Capp, *Astrology and the Popular Press*, 55, 91, 122–23, 131. See also Alan Debus, *The Chemical Philosophy: Paracelsian Science and Medicine in the Sixteenth and Seventeenth Centuries*, 2 vols. (New York: Science History Publications, 1977), 2: 386–406, 509–11; J. R. Jacob, *Robert Boyle and the English Revolution: A Study in Social and Intellectual History* (New York: Burt Franklin, 1977), 161–64; Lotte Mulligan, "'Reason,' 'Right Reason,' and 'Revelation' in Mid-Seventeenth-Century England," in *Occult and Scientific Mentalities in the Renaissance*, ed. Brian Vickers (Cambridge and New York: Cambridge University Press, 1984). The works of the visionary Mary Cary were known in chemical circles (Hill, *World Turned Upside Down*, 260n).

58. William Lilly, *Merlinus Anglicus Junior: The English Merlin Revived . . .* (London, 1644), 6.

59. *Montelion, 1661. Or, the Prophetical Almanack* (London, 1661), September.

60. *A Yea and Nay Almanac* (1678), n.p.

61. On the astrologers' education, see Capp, *Astrology and the Popular Press*, 235–37; on the similarities between so-called high magic and folk beliefs, 211–13. On their sexism, see MacDonald, *Mystical Bedlam*, 37, 288 n. 58. On the change in the climate of opinion concerning high magic, see Yates, *Occult Philosophy*, Chaps. 7, 9, 11, 17. "Fame or respectability offered a degree of protection to the astrologer, whose position . . . was highly ambiguous. While there was no law explicitly against astrology, there were many against witchcraft, sorcery and seditious prophecies, which gave ample scope to hostile magistrates" (54). On astrologers' attitudes to witchcraft, see Capp, *Astrology and the*

eral of the misogynist quips cited in this and the preceding chapter, was actually indicted for sorcery but protected by politicians.

Turning to the leaders of the radical sects, we again find that those thinkers who were avowedly antiformalist or unprogrammatic (the Ranters, the millennarian Fifth Monarchists) were also those who displayed an appreciation of both feminine symbolism and the spiritual power of actual women, while those most concerned with political order—in this case, that of a renovated human community based on strict principles of social justice—were also those whose genuine respect for the rights of all women and men came to be articulated in terms of an exclusively male authority.

The Ranters, whose writing and activity peaked during the late 1640s and early 1650s, were proponents of universal love and salvation and enemies of organized churches, centralized state power, inequalities of property, the sanctity of the Bible, and the doctrines of hell and the devil.[62] Abiezer Coppe, who attended the gatherings of John and Mary Pordage, exulted in a letter to Mrs. Pordage:

> The Lord is risen indeed: I see him, not only risen out of *Joseph's* tomb, *without me*, but *risen* out of the bowels of the *earth within me*, and is *alive in me, formed in me, grows in me:* The *Babe springs in my inmost womb*, leaps for joy *there*, and then I sing . . . to *me a child is borne, a son is given*, who *lives in me* . . . the *saints* are thy *spouse*, our *Maker* is our *husband; We* are no more *twain*, but *one. Halelujah*.[63]

Thus, Coppe affirmed the sensuous, feminine ecstasy of the prophet in full flight, "where I have been, where I have been, where I have been, hug'd, imbrac't, and kist with the kisses of his mouth, whose loves are better then wine."[64] For Coppe, spiritual knowledge and female proph-

---

Popular Press, 128–29, and Rattansi, "Paracelsus and the Puritan Revolution," 29. Barbara Shapiro writes, "In refuting assertions that astrology was itself a form of witchcraft, it was customary to stress the distinctions between them, but not to deny the existence of the witch" (*Probability and Certainty*, 212–13).

62. Christopher Hill, "Abolishing the Ranters," in *A Nation of Change and Novelty: Radical Politics, Religion, and Literature in Seventeenth-Century England* (London and New York: Routledge, 1990), 152–94. "Because they had no organization, the implicit threats contained in their writings never became part of a social and political program" (185). See also A. L. Morton, *The World of the Ranters: Religious Radicalism in the English Revolution* (London: Lawrence and Wishart, 1970) and Friedman, *Blasphemy, Immorality, and Anarchy.*

63. Abiezer Coppe, *Some Sweet Sips, of Some Spirituall Wine* (London, 1649), 45–54.

64. Coppe, *Some Sweet Sips*, quoted in Nigel Smith, ed., *A Collection of Ranter Writings from the Seventeenth Century* (London: Junction Books, 1983), 108.

ecy were both linked to the transcendence of social and intellectual categories. "Dear friend," he wrote, in a letter to a female visionary:

> why doest in thy letter say, (what though we be weaker vessels, women? etc).
> I know that male and female are all one in Christ, and they are all one to me.
> I had as live hear a daughter, as a son prophesy. . . . How sweet art thou, O
> *Word, O God*, to my taste! yea, sweeter than the *honey*, and the *honey comb*,
> my *God, Sweet God*! Awake lute, Awake harp, awake *Deborah*. . . . *Man* is
> the *Woman*, and *thou* art the *Man*, the *Saints* are thy *spouse*, our *Maker* is
> our *Husband*; We are no more *twain*, but *one*. . . . The *elements* . . . shall melt
> *away*, and all *forms*, appearances, *types*, *signs*, *shadows*, *flesh* . . . shall
> *melt away* . . . into *power*, reality, *truth*, *the thing signified*, *substance*,
> *spirit*. . . . Let us not therefore any longer single out any appearance, and
> appropriate it to our selves.[65]

The Ranters' language and reputed activities were so extreme as to lead one historian to speculate that the entire group was nothing but a contemporary metaphor for disorder, which never existed in real life.[66] Perhaps the Ranters' libertinism has been exaggerated (though surely not invented) by historians. For our purpose, however, it is irrelevant whether Coppe's spiritual kisses were metaphorical or actual, for the form of unstructured, bodily (or feminine) knowledge that he espoused was, in its way, as threatening to both traditional and progressive ideals of social order as was physical promiscuity.[67]

At the opposite end of the radical spectrum were the True Levelers, or Diggers, a sect widely considered to have marked the ideological peak of the English Civil War; the *Dictionary of British Radicals* calls their leader, Gerrard Winstanley, "the most remarkable of the radical thinkers of the English Revolution."[68] Certainly, the Diggers were the most

65. Abiezer Coppe, "Epistle V," quoted in Smith, ed., *A Collection of Ranter Writings*, 66. See also Coppe, *Some Sweet Sips*, 46–48, 54–60.

66. J. C. Davis, *Fear, Myth, and History: The Ranters and the Historians* (Cambridge and New York: Cambridge University Press, 1986). For a powerful refutation of this thesis, see Hill, "Abolishing the Ranters," 152–94. David Underdown finds evidence of the group's real existence in Wiltshire and elsewhere and calls them an "isolated handful" who were decimated by 1653 (*Revel, Riot, and Rebellion*, 249–50).

67. Hill writes that the Quakers and other sectarians were accused of turning all things into allegories, but his interpretation is somewhat different from mine; in his view, sectarians brought biblical myths down to earth, to material acts (*World Turned Upside Down*, 115–16). Underdown finds actual sexual promiscuity among Ranters in Wiltshire (*Revel, Riot, and Rebellion*, 249).

68. DBR 3:329. See also Christopher Hill, "The Religion of Gerrard Winstanley," in *Collected Essays of Christopher Hill*, vol. 2, *Religion and Politics in Seventeenth-Century England* (Amherst: University of Massachusetts Press, 1986), 185–252. For an overview of the radical sects, see Frances D. Dow, *Radicalism in the English Revolution, 1640–1660* (Oxford: Basil Blackwell, 1985). She writes that Winstanley's beliefs "mark

eloquent defenders of the laboring classes and the authors of the most
well-developed political program. While the vast majority of Englishmen
viewed "the people" as consisting only of male property holders, the
Diggers advocated absolute equality of servants and masters, male
and female, in a democratic, communistic society. "And by people,"
writes historian Christopher Hill, "Winstanley really did mean all the
people."[69]

Winstanley was an enemy of pride or imagination, which he viewed
as an amalgam of four evil powers: "teaching power" (scholarship, book
learning), "kingly power" (the sword), "the power of Judges" (the will
of the conqueror, masked as justice), and the "buying and selling of the
Earth."[70] Human despair was the result of looking outward, toward
those four powers. Thus, the damned soul seeks restlessly after objects,
whether goods, words, or human chattel, in order to feed his or her own
pride: "Thou lookedst for peace and rest without, and thou art deceived;
thou art afraid to look within, because thy conscience, the light, that is
within thee, . . . condemns thee. . . . Thou lookedst for good to come
from objects without, but behold sorrow."[71] Salvation was an inner
transformation, the awareness of God's indwelling in the soul, which
Winstanley called "the light" or "the seed." Winstanley further argued
that both men and women had the capacity for perfection and that
corrupt earthly power does not know "that their wives, children, servants, subjects are their fellow creatures, and hath an equal privilege to
share with them in the blessing of liberty."[72]

Like the Cambridge Platonists, Winstanley was both a rationalist and
a mystic.[73] Unlike those philosophers, however, he held that the physical

---

the peak of radical, innovative tendencies in the history of political, religious and social
thinking in the 1640s and 1650s" (79).

69. Hill, "The Poor and the People," 89; Hill, *World Turned Upside Down*, Chap. 7.

70. Gerrard Winstanley, *Fire in the Bush: The Spirit Burning Not Consuming, but
Purging Mankinde* (1650), in *The Works of Gerrard Winstanley*, ed. George H. Sabine
(Ithaca, N.Y.: Cornell University Press, 1941), 463–64.

71. Ibid., 460.

72. Gerrard Winstanley, "Truth Lifting Up Its Head above Scandals" (1649), quoted
in T. Wilson Hayes, *Winstanley the Digger: A Literary Analysis of Radical Ideas in the
English Revolution* (Cambridge, Mass.: Harvard University Press, 1979), 115.

73. Winstanley has been discussed as a modern Baconian, a proto-Marxist, a religious mystic, and a synthesis of all three. Arguments on all sides are summarized in Hill,
"The Religion of Gerrard Winstanley," 185–252. See also G. E. Aylmer, "The Religion
of Gerrard Winstanley," in *Radical Religion in the English Revolution*, ed. J. F. McGregor and B. Reay (Oxford: Oxford University Press, 1984), 91–121. Hayes calls Winstanley a radical Christian visionary and emphasizes his creative use of alchemical symbolism,
while J. C. Davis presents him as a proto-Stalinist, emphasizing the importance of soldiers, taskmasters, and executioners in his utopia: "To Winstanley the only freedom that

universe, while filled with spiritual meaning, was not subject to unpredictable intervention by spiritual forces; it could be appreciated and comprehended by reason alone. Reason was a reflection both of divine order and of the essential goodness of human nature; reason was God. "I shall add one word," he wrote,

> as an account wherefore I use the word reason, instead of the word God, in my writings. . . . Reason is . . . the salt that savours all things; it is the fire that burns up dross, and so restores what is corrupted; and preserves what is pure; . . . some may call him King of righteousness and Prince of peace; some may call him Love, and the like: but I . . . call him Reason; because I see him to be that living powerful light that is in righteousness, making righteousness to be righteousness; or justice to be justice; or love to be love: for without this moderator and ruler, they would be madness; nay, the selfwilledness of the flesh; and not that which we call them.[74]

By "reason" Winstanley did not mean the wisdom taught in universities or the ethereal concepts learned in church but the "laborious knowledge" that comes from practical education: husbandry, minerals, the ordering of cattle, the "secrets of nature." "And thus to speak, or thus to read the *Law* of Nature (or God) as he hath written his name in every body," he wrote, "is to speak a pure language . . . giving to every thing its own weight and measure. By this means, in time men shall attain to the practical knowledge of God truly . . . and that knowledge will not deceive a man."[75]

Winstanley's imaginative, gendered use of traditional biblical and alchemical symbolism was complicated and ambiguous. For him, as for other mystical thinkers, the sun represented the masculine light of reason; the moon and Earth, however, represented the dark, fleshly, feminine side of existence: "The moon is the shadow of the sun, in regard they have been led by the powers of the curse in flesh, which is the *feminine* part; not by the power of the righteous Spirit which is Christ,

---

mattered was freedom from economic insecurity" (*Utopia and the Ideal Society: A Study of English Utopian Writing, 1516–1700* [Cambridge and New York: Cambridge University Press, 1981], 199, 202). Nigel Smith argues that Winstanley was not a pantheistic materialist; rather, he saw a continuity between man, nature, and God (*Perfection Proclaimed*, 259–60). George M. Shulman adds a psychoanalytic dimension (*Radicalism and Reverence: The Political Thought of Gerrard Winstanley* [Berkeley, Los Angeles, and London: University of California Press, 1984]).

74. Winstanley, "Truth Lifting Up Its Head," 104–5.

75. Gerrard Winstanley, *The Law of Freedom in a Platform or True Magistracy Restored*, in *Works*, ed. Sabine, 564–65, 577–79. See also "Truth Lifting Up Its Head," 131, and Hill, *World Turned Upside Down*, 115–20, on Winstanley's reliance on the senses and his use of biblical stories as metaphors for practical human truths.

ine power."[76] Winstanley described the Fall in the garden of
..sly:

> ..ason the essential Father, gave this law, that [when] man left off to own
> ..is maker that dwelt within him, and [began] to suck delight from the
> creation, he should then die . . . til the fulness of time came, that he would
> rise up like seed of wheat, from under those dark and heavy clods of fleshy
> earth, and so himself . . . would bruise the serpent's head.[77]

By no means did Winstanley intend to denigrate this "fleshly feminine part." In his view, feminine created flesh is dominated by masculine pride, the childish desire to dominate and possess both material things and people, to suck all of the goodness from Mother Earth like a child who will not share the breast.[78] Human beings must therefore be liberated from pride (which he called the Tree of Knowledge) in order to be reconnected to feminine nature, "our common Mother," which he called the Tree of Life.

> The Tree of Life I say, is universal Love, which our age calls righteous conscience, or pure Reason; or the seed of life that lies under the clods of Earth, which in his time is now rising up to bruise the Serpent's head, and to cast that imaginary murderer out of the creation. . . . And when this tree of Life is fed upon and delighted in, (by the five senses, which is . . . the living soul). Then these five rivers [i.e., senses] are called pure rivers of the waters of life; for the life of truth and peace is in them, and they are the sweet conveyers of the waters, or breathings of life, from one to another through the whole body: and so bringing all into a oneness, to be of one heart and one mind.[79]

Salvation is thus a fusion of masculine and feminine qualities, the triumph of true reason, which has learned to see the world not acquisitively but in a spirit of cooperation and benevolence, no longer seeking to dominate either nature or human beings. When four Diggers were attacked by a pack of men dressed in women's clothing, Winstanley accused the men of dressing as women not only to hide their identity but, in the opinion of one scholar, "to act out their true group identity as men who corrupt and hold the feminine side of human nature in

76. Gerrard Winstanley, "New Law of Righteousness," quoted in Hayes, *Winstanley the Digger*, 114.

77. Winstanley, "Truth Lifting Up Its Head," 133.

78. For an analysis of the masculine power of pride, see Shulman, *Radicalism and Reverence*, 4–5. See also Hayes, *Winstanley the Digger*, 150.

79. Winstanley, *Fire in the Bush*, 453, 454.

bondage, men who must destroy any attempt to show equality with women."[80]

In April 1649 Winstanley and the Diggers attempted to establish a wholly communistic community by digging and planting the common land of St. George's Hill near London; they were dispersed in April 1650. Two years later Winstanley published *The Law of Freedom in a Platform, or, True Magistracy Restored*. The central premise of this, his final and most systematic work, is that misery of every kind is ultimately caused by one thing and one thing only—the exploitation of human beings by one another:

> I speak now in relation between the oppressor and the oppressed; the inward bondages I meddle not with in this place, though I am assured that if it be rightly searched into, the inward bondages of the mind, as covetousness, pride, hypocrisy, envy, sorrow, fears, desperation, and madness, are all occasioned by the outward bondage, that one sort of people lay upon another.[81]

Thus, Winstanley's ultimate response to the human condition was to veer away from the introspection and spirituality of more mystical or biblical thinking, including elements of his own earlier work, and to focus his attention on the transformation of society in this life. Mystical and alchemical knowledge were now intended to increase human mastery of nature, not to transcend material reality, while the function of the minister was to inform the people of current events, the laws of the commonwealth, and (in third and last place) the nature of humanity and the universe. As the Digger song, quoted by Christopher Hill, went, "Glory *here*, Diggers all!"[82]

Winstanley's new law of freedom combined a radical insistence on the needs and rights of the weak with an utterly conservative scenario of the beginnings of patriarchal authority: Adam (not John Pordage's androgynous Adam but the first *father*) was also the first ruler, because his children needed and accepted his authority in order to ensure their own preservation. "By this choice, they make him not only a father, but a master and ruler. And out of this root springs up all magistrates and

---

80. Gerrard Winstanley, *A Declaration of the Bloudie and Unchristian Acting of William Star and John Taylor of Walton* (1649). The quotation is from Hayes's summary of the tract (*Winstanley the Digger*, 153).

81. Winstanley, *The Law of Freedom*, 520.

82. Hayes, *Winstanley the Digger*, 64–65; Winstanley, *The Law of Freedom*, 562. The song is quoted in Hill, *World Turned Upside Down*, 120.

officers."[83] Winstanley railed against the community of women supposedly practiced by other sects not because he wanted to give women
greater independence but because he wanted to preserve the nuclear
family as the cellular basis of society and authority.

> In a private family a father, or master, is an officer. . . . He is to command
> (his children) in their work, . . . he is either to reprove by words, or whip those
> who offend. . . . That so children may not quarrel like beasts, but live . . . like
> rational men, experienced in yielding obedience to the laws and officers of the
> commonwealth.[84]

Boys are to be educated by their fathers, not their mothers, and trained
up in trades; girls will learn reading, sewing, knitting, spinning, and
music.

Seen against the background of much contemporary theory and practice, Winstanley's advocacy of universal human rights was immensely
creative, because he attributed virtues to the poor that the Puritans
applied only to property holders and that the Cambridge Platonists
applied only to high-ranking intellectuals.[85] His program for women was
also partially progressive. Winstanley explicitly condemned rape, and,
rather than define a married woman as a legal nonentity, he gave her a
certain independence; she might choose whom to marry, and, "the wife
or children of such as have lost their freedom, shall not be as slaves till
they have lost *their* freedom, as their parents and husbands have done."[86]
Notwithstanding these important social innovations, we must still observe that Winstanley's social philosophy, while radical in terms of class
relationships, is conservative to the core in terms of gender. In his utopia,
women are not even given authority over the freshness of the meat they
put on the table:

> No master of a family shall suffer more meat to be dressed at a dinner or
> supper, then what will be spent and eaten by his household. . . . If there be
> any spoil constantly made in a family of the food of Man, the overseer shall
> reprove the master for it privately; if that abuse be continued in his family,
> through his neglect of family government, he shall be openly reproved . . .
> before all the people, . . . the third time he shall be made a servant . . . that

83. Winstanley, *The Law of Freedom*, 532.
84. Winstanley, *The Law of Freedom*, 544–45. On Winstanley's patriarchalism, see
also Davis, *Utopia and the Ideal Society*, 197. On Winstanley's repudiation of promiscuity and his denigration of women, see Shulman, *Radicalism and Reverence*, 195–96.
85. Hill, "The Poor and the People," 87.
86. Winstanley, *The Law of Freedom*, 527, 597–99; emphasis added.

he may know what it is to get food, and another shall have the oversight of his house for the time.[87]

Similarly, if a citizen becomes ill, he or she resorts to the herbal medicines of the male surgeon, while if the father of a family becomes incapacitated for any reason, the children are removed to the authority of the overseers of the father's trade; female healers and mothers are simply not there.[88]

Scholars have long disagreed as to whether *The Law of Freedom* represents the culmination of Winstanley's radical vision or the hardened philosophy of a defeated man.[89] Clearly, the mystical elements of Winstanley's earlier writings are absent here. Yet the focus on reason as the chief means of attaining both personal salvation and social justice is thoroughly consistent with the sense of those more visionary tracts. For even though Winstanley's earlier vision of restored humanity included both masculine and feminine elements (reason exercised in a spirit of mutuality and in harmony with nature), the dominant element was always reason, and the struggle for salvation was primarily a male event. "And this shall be your mark," Winstanley wrote to the prophet Eleanor Davies, "that you have lost the breeches, your reason, by the inward boiling vexation of your spirit . . . and that inward power shall chain you up in darkness, til Reason, which you have trampled under foot, come to set you free."[90] Winstanley did say that, once saved, both men and women become true sons of the sun. "All his sons and daughters will then be the second man."[91] He also said that women might preach: "That man or woman that sees the spirit, within themselves . . . is able to make

87. Ibid., 599–600. See also Davis, *Utopia and the Ideal Society*, 197.

88. Winstanley, *The Law of Freedom*, 549, 598. This was in line with seventeenth-century conduct books that guided men in organizing their households rather than advising women on housewifely responsibilities (Jeanette Carter Gadt, "Women and Protestant Culture: The Quaker Dissent from Puritanism," Ph.D. diss., University of California, Los Angeles, 1974, 153).

89. The first view is taken by Christopher Hill in "The Religion of Gerrard Winstanley." The second view is taken by George Shulman, *Radicalism and Reverence*, particularly in his chapter, "The Meaning of Defeat."

90. Gerrard Winstanley, "Letter to Eleanor Davies, Pirton, Hertfordshire, 1650," ed. Paul H. Hardacre, *Huntington Library Quarterly* 22 (1959): 345–49. Winstanley actually became an employee of Eleanor Davies after his attempt to establish a Digger commonwealth had failed. Although he was aware of her fame as a prophet, his relationship with her was apparently limited to an argument over payment of his wages, during which she told him she was the prophet "Melchisedecke" or the Queen of Peace (*The Appearance or Presence of the Son of Man* [1650], 7, quoted in Esther S. Cope, *"Dame Eleanor Davies, Never Soe Mad a Ladie?"* [Ann Arbor: University of Michigan Press, forthcoming], 220).

91. Winstanley, "Truth Lifting Up Its Head," quoted in Hayes, *Winstanley the Digger*, 102, 104, 105.

a sermon, because they can speak by experience of the light . . . within them."[92] But the kind of sensibility and occult knowledge in which women were believed to excel had little or no place in Winstanley's conception of nature, whose secrets were accessible to the observer with both common sense and sympathy with the created world. Needless to say, while hundreds of female visionaries preached and wrote during the Civil War and Interregnum, there were no Digger women prophets. When Winstanley's works were subscribed by others in the movement, the signatories included only male members.[93]

Nor were there any women prophets among the Muggletonians. The members of this quasi-materialist sect agreed with the Diggers in rejecting both the high wisdom of the churches and universities and the intuitive mystical wisdom of the visionary: "The strong imagination of reason being exercised about things that are beyond trades and sciences . . . so it became a familiar spirit because it proceeds from the imagination of reason, . . . the seed of reason being the devil."[94] Muggleton would also castigate the Quakers as mystics and idolators for preaching that spirits can exist without bodies: "This is the heathen philosopher's opinion, they brought into the world that principle of the immortality of the soul."[95]

Not surprisingly, Muggleton had little use for either feminine spiritual symbolism or female authority. He maintained that the world was divided between the saved and the damned because a fallen angel had entered bodily into Eve: "[Women] were created only to let God and the serpent clothe themselves in flesh in a woman's womb to bring forth God's glorious design of the two seeds. But 'the holy angels and all other creatures that are in the presence of God in the creation beyond the stars are all spiritual male creatures.'"[96] The sect did welcome individual women, who were active in raising money and who participated in the

92. Winstanley, "The New Law of Righteousness," quoted in Hayes, *Winstanley the Digger*, 132.
93. Hilda Smith, "Gender Implications of the Execution of Charles I," paper presented at the American Historical Association Annual Convention, December 1991, Chicago, Illinois.
94. Lodowijk Muggleton, *A True Interpretation of the Witch of Endor*, 5th ed. (London: For Joseph Frost, 1856), 1–2.
95. Lodowijk Muggleton, *A Looking-Glass for George Fox the Quaker, and Other Quakers: Wherein They May See Themselves to Be Right Devils* (London, 1667), 64–65; Alexander Delamain to John Ladd, June 5, 1676, Add. MSS. 60183, Muggletonian Archives, British Library, London.
96. John Reeve, *Of the Spiritual Life*, quoted in Christopher Hill, "John Reeve and the Origins of Muggletonianism," in *Prophecy and Millenarianism: Essays in Honour of Marjorie Reeves*, ed. Ann Williams (Burnt Hill, Harlow, Essex: Longman, 1980), 320. See also Davis, *Fear, Myth, and History*, 65.

informal discussions that were the group's chief mode of religious activity, but there was no question of shared authority; indeed, one of the chief canons of the Muggletonians was the absolute primacy of Lodowijk Muggleton and his associate, John Reeve, as associate prophets of a new world.[97] In the recently discovered manuscript collection of seventeenth-century Muggletonian writings in the British Library, there is, to my knowledge, not a single extended work by a woman.[98]

INTERPRETING PROPHECY

The maid looking in the [witch's] glass saw the shape
of many persons, and what they were doing in her
master's house, in particular . . . Mistress *Elizabeth
Rosewell* standing in her mistress's chamber, looking
out of the window with her hands in her sleeves, . . .
and showed others drinking with glasses of beer in
their hands; . . . and the maid relating this to
Elizabeth Rosewell, she replied that Mistress
Bodenham, (meaning the said witch) was either a
witch, or a woman of God.

> Doctor Lamb Revived, or Witchcraft Condemn'd in
> Anne Bodenham, *1653*

Even in these increasingly uncertain political and epistemological conditions, it was still possible for those with power and authority to respect and frequently to co-opt the activities of the individual female visionary. Lady Eleanor Davies's pronouncements were tolerated, even welcomed, by the royal family when she spoke as a harmless but well-bred eccentric and then condemned when she became politically obstreperous in print. Later, when the political climate changed, her prophecy of the king's execution was reprinted and one of her tracts was read before Parliament.[99]

A similar scenario occurred in the case of Anne Bodenham, an elderly teacher and cunning woman living in a village in Wiltshire, who was

---

97. Christopher Hill, Barry Reay, and William Lamont, *The World of the Muggletonians* (London: Temple Smith, 1983). And see the correspondence of Muggleton with his followers, published in Joseph Frost and Isaac Frost, eds., *The Works of John Reeve and Lodowicke Muggleton, the Two Last Prophets of the Only True God, Our Lord Jesus Christ*, 3 vols. (London, 1832).

98. Add. MSS. 60168–60256.

99. Bernard Capp, *The Fifth Monarchy Men: A Study in Seventeenth-Century English Millenarianism* (London: Faber and Faber, 1972), 50.

executed for witchcraft in 1653. Following her arrest, accompanied by shrieks and chain rattling, she asked a witness to accompany her to a private room, called loudly (and in vain) for a glass of beer, and proceeded to tell her own story: She had once been employed as a servant to a client of a popular and notorious astrologer, Dr. Lamb of London. Entertained by his predictions and curious about his magical techniques, she asked him to employ her as his servant and to teach her his trade. For some years thereafter she had applied his methods in her own practice, making predictions of lucky and unlucky days, finding lost objects, advising her aristocratic clientele on lawsuits and romantic liaisons, and dispensing medicines. "She could cure diseases by charms and spells," she bragged, "and had prayers that would do so likewise; and they could cure such diseases as the best doctors could not do; she could discover stolen goods, and show anyone the thief that had them in a glass; and . . . she could raise spirits by reading in her books."[100] She apparently viewed herself as a kind of Faust figure, describing the technique of raising spirits: "If those that have a desire to it, do read in books, and when they come to read further then they can understand, then the Devil will appear to them, and show them what they would know; and they doing what he would have them, they may learn to do what they desired to do, and he would teach them."[101]

Bodenham's career flourished until she became implicated in some rumors of an attempted murder in the household of an aristocratic client, whereupon the family accused her of practicing witchcraft, an accusation designed to divert attention from their own complicity in the affair. The respected, if not quite respectable, cunning woman was now presented to the public with all the theatrical conventions of diabolical witchcraft: a gossiping troublemaker who flirted with papist ideas and could also fly. "She would convey either man or woman forty miles an hour into the air," announced one pamphlet, "she could transform herself into any shape whatsoever, viz.

> A mastiff dog,
> A black lion,
> A white bear,
> A wolf,
> A monkey,
> A horse,
> A bull,
> And a calf.

100. Bower, *Doctor Lamb Revived*, 25–26.
101. Ibid., 32.

She had likewise the marks of an absolute witch, having a teat . . . on her left shoulder, and another likewise was found in her secret place."[102] Bodenham herself seemed perfectly aware of the use to which she was being put. "She had learned much in Dr. Lamb's service," she said,

> and she reading in some of his books, with his help learned her art, by which she . . . had gotten many a penny, and done hundreds of people good, and nobody ever gave her an ill word for all her pains, but always called her Mistress Boddenham, and was never accounted a Witch but by reason of this wicked maid now in prison.[103]

Walking toward the gallows, yelling for beer at every house she passed, she refused to confess any crimes, and when the executioner, according to custom, asked her to forgive him, she shot back, "Forgive thee? A pox on thee, turn me off!"[104] Anne Bodenham was not the only visionary woman to be perceived as a witch or criminal at the moment when her activities began to threaten people in high places or at the moment when attributing extraordinary powers to *her* would distract attention from others who might be vulnerable to prosecution. Jane Hawkins, a peddlar in St. Ives, preached in verse for three days and nights to a huge audience against the Anglican bishops. The local vicar and curate, who had sat at her feet supposedly taking notes, later admitted that they were altering the text, which they planned to publish as popular songs. When their activities were investigated by the magistrates, the vicar publicly confessed his imposture: "He has fully satisfied the people, who [now] cry out against the woman," saying her verses were from the devil. Anna Trapnel spent hours singing in verse to enthusiastic audiences that included members of Parliament, members of the aristocracy, and the future Lord Mayor of London; following her attacks on Cromwell, she was sent to the prison of Bridewell for two months. Susanna Parr testified in writing that the male minister of a Separatist congregation, agitating for support, had insisted she speak publicly in church against her will.[105]

102. *Dr. Lamb's Darling: Or, Strange and Terrible News from Salisbury* (London, 1653), 1–8.
103. Bower, *Doctor Lamb Revived*, 27.
104. Ibid., 36.
105. On Hawkins, see *Calendar of State Papers: Domestic Series of the Reign of Charles I, 1628–1629* (London: Longman, Brown, Green, Longmans, and Roberts, 1859), 530–31, 537. On Trapnel, see P. G. Rogers, *The Fifth Monarchy Men* (London and New York: Oxford University Press, 1966), 4, 7, 138, 147. Susanna Parr, *Susanna's Apology against the Elders* (Oxford, 1659), 103.

Other women sustained their privileged status as prophets because their message bolstered the credibility of those with even higher status. Christian James, a young woman from Cornwall, "died" and came briefly back to life, admonishing all to repent and live in harmony. Her verses were then published by the local magistrates, to be sung to the tune of "In Summertime." The mute Elinor Channel would certainly have died in oblivion or been a victim of petty crime as she wandered aimlessly through the London streets if she had not been discovered by Arise Evans, who, seeing a new visionary "star," published her utterances as a framework for his own Royalist opinions. (Commenting on her own words—"If a man fall into the hands of a creditor . . . if his body pays the debt, his heir shall have the inheritance"—Evans printed in the margin that the king who died was the body that paid the debt, and that heir was his son.) Claiming he had recognized in her an "angel of God," he wrote: "It must be more of God than we are aware of, . . . that by this dumb woman, God will put all vain talkers to silence."[106] The woman was later found standing, again mute, in Fleet Street, until the beadles dragged her to the prison of Bridewell, where she was further abused.

The more respectable Elizabeth Poole instructed an audience of parliamentary soldiers in 1648, in terms that challenged the accepted categories of feminine obedience:

> It is true indeed (I know I appeal by the gift of God upon me) the King is your father and husband, which you were and are to obey in the Lord, and in no other way, for when he forgot his subordination to divine faithhood and headship, thinking he had begotten you a generation to his own pleasure, and taking you a wife for his own lusts, thereby is the yoke taken from your necks.[107]

This was acceptable because it agreed with Cromwell's policy; as Colonel Rich remarked, "I cannot but give you that impression that is upon my spirit in conjunction with that testimony which God hath manifested here by an unexpected Providence. What she hath said being correspondent with what I have made [known] as manifested to me before."[108]

---

106. "A Wonderful Prophecie, Declared by Christian James," broadside (n.d.). Elinor Channel, *A Message from God, by a Dumb Woman,* ed. Arise Evans (London, 1653), 10.
107. Elizabeth Poole, *A Vision: Wherein Is Manifested the Disease and Cure of the Kingdome* (London, 1648), 6.
108. C. H. Firth, ed., *The Clarke Papers: Selections from the Papers of William Clarke* (Westminster: Nichols and Sons, 1894), 2:152. Also see Hill, *World Turned Upside Down,* 224.

Indeed, Poole's appearance before the Council was so opportune that a Royalist report accused Cromwell of lodging her in seclusion at White-hall and rehearsing her for her appearance. When Poole was summoned before Parliament a second time, her advice was much less welcome, and the response of the Council members showed it. After she urged the Council to spare the king's life she was interrogated repeatedly about the authenticity of her visions. She was also expelled from her Baptist con-gregation (whose minister, William Kiffin, was a close friend of Crom-well's) soon after the king was executed.[109]

All of this implies, I think, that female visionaries were a source of profound confusion to their audiences, not the victims of cold-blooded manipulation, for surely Colonel Rich and the members of Parliament were genuinely relieved to learn that God had sanctioned their values and activities through the mouths of his weak vessels. When Eleanor Davies was first tried, the magistrates disagreed about whether she was a lunatic or a criminal, and two of them asked to be spared from condemning her; the leading politician Sir Edward Dering as well as the Anglican cleric Pierre du Moulin believed in her genuine foreknowledge of events.[110] The magistrates in Cornwall, who stormed into the house where the prophet Anna Trapnel was lodging, displayed considerable bluster but not much self-confidence in their ability to discern the real character of the woman they were seeking:

> These justices . . . came to fetch me out of my bed, . . . and some came upstairs, crying, *A witch, a witch*; . . . and a poor honest man rebuking such that said so, he was tumbled down stairs and beaten . . . and they said, *If my friends would not take me up, they would have some should take me up*: one of my friends told them, *that they must fetch their silk gowns to do it then, for the poor would not do it.* . . . They caused my eye-lids to be pulled up, for they said, *I held them fast, because I would deceive the people*: . . . One of the justices pinched me by the nose, and caused the pillow to be pulled from under my head, and kept pulling me, and calling me; . . . (Mr. *Welsted*) stood at the chamber-door talking against me, and said, *She speaks non-sense*: the women said, *Hearken, for you cannot hear, there is such a noise*: then he listened, and said, *Now she hears me speak, she speaks sense*. And this clergy-man durst not come, till the rulers came, for then they say, The witches can have no

---

109. *A Brief Narration of the Mysteries of State Carried on by the Spanish Faction in England* (The Hague, 1651), 69, discussed in Ludlow, "'Arise and Be Doing,'" 231–33.

110. Cope, *"Dame Eleanor Davies,"* 17. Thomas, *Religion and the Decline of Magic*, 137.

power over them: so that one depends upon another, rulers upon clergy, and clergy upon rulers.[111]

The crisis of knowledge and moral authority that dominated the Civil War period was every bit as confusing to ordinary people as it was to the magistrates and intellectuals who interviewed the visionary in Parliament or debated the nature of prophecy in university common rooms. For, once both the monarchy and the monopoly of the Anglican priesthood had been called into question by Puritans and sectarian radicals, there was no longer a dominant standard for distinguishing good from evil. How was ultimate truth to be determined, when both Royalists and Puritans were claiming prophetic sanction for their activities, when Cromwell followed a policy of tolerating almost every sect, and when philosophers could not resolve questions about the very nature of their own enterprise? Certainly the kinds of evidence one looked for in trying to determine the sanctity of a given prophet was as slippery as that admitted in witchcraft trials. When some men threw Mary Tompkins head first down a flight of stairs, they maintained that her survival was proof of her witchcraft; had she been innocent, her neck would have been broken. When a storm threatened to capsize the ship on which Barbara Blaugdone was sailing to Ireland, her prophetic power calmed the seas and convinced the sailors of her own holiness. Earlier, when she was set upon by a pack of dogs, witnesses undoubtedly suspected that the animals had smelled a witch.[112]

Even those magistrates and clerics who might have welcomed the public appearance of a visionary when she confirmed their own official policies were extremely distressed when the phenomenon touched them as private individuals. When parliamentary officer Edward Fairfax's daughter Helen went into a trance, talking with her dead brothers and sisters, he at first made little of it, "In these fits she had perfect symptoms of the disease called 'the mother'; and for a long time we attributed all that she did or said to it." When the girl then claimed to see God in the

111. Anna Trapnel, *Anna Trapnel's Report and Plea, or, a Narrative of Her Journey from London into Cornwal* (London, 1654), 21.

112. George Bishop, *New England Judged* (London, 1661), 2:394. Barbara Blaugdone, *An Account of the Travels, Sufferings and Persecutions of Barbara Blaugdone* (Shoreditch, 1691), 22. Keith Thomas notes that a paradox of the condition of diabolical possession, incidents of which increased during the Interregnum, was that its symptoms could not be differentiated from those of religious ecstasy (*Religion and the Decline of Magic*, 486–87).

shape of a beautiful man, lit up, in shining clothes, he convinced her the
vision was a fake. (The next night she told this to the apparition,
whereupon the beautiful man grew ugly, horns appeared on his head,
and he threatened to slay her.) Yet ultimately, both Fairfax and the
doctors were forced to agree that Helen had been bewitched, and Fairfax
published a tract recounting the agony of a family under spiritual siege
by the devil.[113]

If officers of the state could vacillate about the right interpretation of
visionary behavior, one can easily imagine the agony of indecision experienced by ordinary people trying to decide whether a given individual
was a prophet, a witch, a victim of witchcraft, or merely hysterical,
particularly when that individual was a member of one's own community or family.[114] When Anne Bodenham showed a servant girl a faraway
image in her magic glass, the girl remarked that Bodenham "was either
a witch, or a woman of God." When Margaret Muschamp first saw
visions of angels and trumpets, she so impressed a witness "that he
blessed God for showing such mercy to a child of eleven years old."[115]
Margaret lived for sixteen weeks without solid food, suffering fits and
announcing visions of both angels and the devil, while her mother
summoned all the representatives of secular and spiritual authority: the
minister, in case she turned out to be a true prophet; the physician, in
case her trouble was "only" convulsions; the judge, in case she was the
victim of the crime of witchcraft. The final resolution of the case was
probably as much the result of desperation as deep spiritual conviction.
The mother, aided by clues given in the girl's fits, finally turned on two
different neighbors with an accusation of witchcraft, one of whom
immediately began slandering the other. The published version of the
episode, written by a witness, never reveals whether the prosecution of
the witch actually took place.

The ordeal of Margaret Muschamp was replayed again and again
among people of all classes (Margaret's mother was a lady of privilege).

113. Edward Fairfax, A Discourse of Witchcraft. As It Was Acted in the Family of
Mr. Edward Fairfax of Fuystone in the County of York, in the Year 1621 (Harrogate: R.
Ackrill, 1882), 37. See also Shapiro, Probability and Certainty, 205.
114. On contemporaries' confusion about the differences between prophecy, insanity,
possession by demons, and witchcraft, see MacDonald, Mystical Bedlam, 133–34, 155–
56, 174–75. On the hesitation of magistrates as to whether Eleanor Davies should be
defined as mad, see Cope, "Dame Eleanor Davies," 137. On the numbers of insane people
wandering about the countryside, attracting curiosity and ridicule, see Hill, World Turned
Upside Down, 223, and Briggs, Pale Hecate's Team, 147–48.
115. Mary Moore, Wonderfull News from the North: Or, a True Relation of the Sad
and Grievous Torments, Inflicted upon the Bodies of Three Children . . . by Witchcraft
(London, 1650), 2.

The physician Richard Napier, perplexed about the problem of distinguishing mental afflictions from diabolical ones, collected accounts of
methods of determining bewitchment as well as amulets and formulas
of exorcism.[116] When, decades later, a Quaker girl took to her bed with
visions of the "Tempter," the neighbors were uncertain how to react;
some thought she was really upset because she was in love and wanted
to get married, and it was some time before the girl convinced her mother
that her visions were authentic.[117]

Some prophets themselves were not always certain of the source or
meaning of their own visions. As the family of Helen Fairfax gradually
became convinced that she was bewitched, she fell into trances in which
she both mothered a monster baby and tried to protect an innocent
baby that was herself. Once a woman appeared holding a child in
swaddling clothes and said, "I will have thy life, and this child shall suck
out thy heart's blood." The baby sucked for half an hour, causing great
agony. Then the girl woke up, vomited, and announced that she was
dying, drained of her blood by a demon. In a later trance the devil
appeared. "Then he took out of a poke a thing like a naked child, and
did beat it. She said, 'what a villain art thou so to abuse a pretty child!' "
Then the girl saw that it was not a child but a picture of herself that he
beat. Helen Fairfax's confusion about her own moral identity was reportedly shared by an Anabaptist woman, mother of a newborn infant
and an oracle of her community, who first announced that "Christ did
appear to her gloriously, and perfumed her (and she would ask those
about her, whether they smelt not those perfumes)." When a visitor
returned a short while later, he found that she had become totally
distracted, "and now she cries out of seeing and smelling the Devil in
everything almost."[118] Suicidal Hannah Allen walled herself up in an
attic but was cured when she realized that her attacks of self-loathing
were not signs of insanity but "only" the machinations of the devil.[119]
John Gilpin, hoping to attain the same state of visionary ecstasy that he
had witnessed in the Quakers, attempted to induce quaking in himself.
He first felt great joy when his right hand began to tremble uncontrol-
lably, "apprehending myself as being shaken by the hand . . . imagining

116. MacDonald, *Mystical Bedlam*, 32.
117. Joan Whitrow, *The Work of God in a Dying Maid* (London, 1677), 17.
118. S. F. to a minister in London, October 14, 1645, reprinted in Edwards, *Gangraena*, 88 [sic].
119. Hannah Allen, *Satan His Methods and Malice Baffled* (London, 1683).

it to be figure of my spiritual marriage and union with Christ." In further fits his legs made crosses on the ground, his hand seized a knife and began to cut his own throat, and his mouth swallowed a butterfly, which he declared was a white devil. Gilpin finally succeeded in making himself sick to his stomach but recovered, finally disavowing the Quakers. "I now affirm," he wrote, "that my quaking and trembling was of the devil."[120]

CONCLUSION

> There was a little girl
> And she had a little curl
> Right in the middle of her forehead.
> When she was good
> She was very very good
> And when she was bad
> She was horrid.
>
> *Nursery rhyme*

The modern reader, perusing the pamphlets, broadsides, treatises, plays, and almanacs of the Civil War period, initially comes away with the sense that, in the realm of gender definitions and gender relationships, seventeenth-century men and women lived in a remarkably totalitarian culture. Indeed, what is most striking about the feminine imagery I have described in this and the preceding chapter is its uniformity across class, religious, and political lines. Certainly, the tone of many such writings was one of levity. Just as certainly, many writers expressed scepticism about the supposed feats of devils, imps, and other occult theatrics as well as the powers of the female witch. They also expressed outrage and compassion for those women who were objectified and persecuted as scapegoats for the sins of their betters. "And why on me?" wrote the three male authors of the play, *The Witch of Edmonton*,

> Why should the envious world
> Throw all their scandalous malice upon me?
> 'Cause I am poor, deform'd and ignorant,

---

120. John Gilpin, *The Quakers Shaken: Or, A Fire-Brand Snatch'd out of the Fire* (London, 1653). George Fox accused him of being distracted and a drunkard (*The Great Mistery of the Great Whore Unfolded* [London, 1659], 297–99).

> And like a Bow buckl'd and bent together,
> By some more strong in mischiefs than myself?
> Must I for that be made a common sink,
> For all the filth and rubbish of Man's tongues
> To fall and run into? Some call me Witch;
> And being ignorant of my self, they go
> About to teach me how to be one; urging,
> That my bad tongue (by their bad usage made so)
> Forespeaks their Cattle, doth bewitch their Corn,
> Themselves, their Servants, and their Babes at nurse.
> This they enforce upon me: and in part
> Make me to credit it.[121]

Yet even when contemporary writers overtly criticized traditional feminine symbols and stereotypes, they frequently did so in a way that left basic presuppositions about gender intact. The astrologer Sara Jinner advanced a conspiracy theory of male domination: "It is the policy of men, to keep us from education and schooling, wherein we might give good testimony of our parts by improvement." But her (or his) almanacs were almost exclusively devoted to recipes for fertility potions and advice on resisting the act of venery or expelling stillborn children; they were also full of conventional asides about women's tongues and women's lust.[122] John Wheelwright, a leader of the Massachusetts Bay Colony, criticized John Winthrop's brutality in condemning the monstrous births of Wheelwright's sister-in-law Anne Hutchinson and Mary Dyer, but he also maintained that women should not attempt intellectual "impossibilities," and while he defended Mary Dyer against Winthrop, he thought her "disordered" birth proceeded out of a "disordered" mind.[123] Even radical sectarians supported women's right to worship as equals with men by reinforcing negative female stereotypes. The Fifth Monarchist John Rogers, whose defense of women's preaching is quoted above, argued that women exceeded men in their affection for the truth:

121. William Rowley, Thomas Dekker, and John Ford, *The Witch of Edmonton* (London, 1658), 56.

122. Jinner, *An Almanack and Prognostication*, "To the Reader." Anne Geneva has questioned whether Jinner was not, in fact, a man ("Sarah Jinner: A Woman Astrologer of the Seventeenth Century," paper delivered at North Atlantic Conference of British Studies Conference, Philadelphia, November 1988).

123. John Wheelwright, *Mercurius Americanus* (1645), reprinted in *John Wheelwright His Writings, Including His Fast-Day Sermon, 1637, and His Mercurius Americanus 1645; With a Paper upon the Genuineness of the Indian Deed of 1629*, Burt Franklin Research and Source Work Series no. 131, The Prince Society, vol. 9 (New York: Burt Franklin, n.d.), 197.

Hence it is that Satan so often makes the first trial of women for his turn and service, seeing where they take, their affections are strongest . . . so he found out a Dalilah for Samson, a Jezebel for Ahab, Pharoah's daughter for Solomon, etc. For where they are bad, they are extreme bad; but where they are good, they are exceeding good, . . . so are women more readily wrought upon, and sooner persuaded and formed into the truth than men, who are for the most part like sturdy steel and iron, hard to work upon.[124]

Yet the uniformity of these feminine symbols and stereotypes and the doggedness with which they were repeated masked a social and epistemological crisis, an uncertainty at all levels of society about the interpretation of the occult knowledge represented by that feminine symbolism and by the presence of real visionary women in the public arena. Indeed, contemporaries doubted not only their ability to interpret symbols and stereotypes; they were also uncertain about who owned them, who might justifiably claim the right to speak as a passive vessel of God or an active instrument of divine authority.

There were many who viewed the female visionary as an embodiment of the true wisdom of the heart as well as a positive political emblem. Even more than the male "mechanick preacher," she represented a kind of authority that was inappropriate, even monstrous, by conventional standards, but conforming to a more radical vision of human equality, on earth and in heaven. For many other more conservative men and women, the negative perception of female visionaries was not that they would act like the radical sectarians, who were merely trying to turn the world upside down. The danger was worse. For the volatile inner essence of these women—the blood of childbirth or illicit copulation or infanticide, the milk of women's consuming and destructive mother love, the tears of anger, despair, and their flamboyant piety—had the potential to dissolve the social structure, even culture itself, altogether. This preoccupation with and repulsion over the idea of a body that both absorbed and exuded fluids and could be touched by anybody is not surprising in a culture in which refined body language (table manners, doffing hats, bowing, blowing noses, and spitting discreetly) was becoming increasingly important as a sign of both social respectability and individual autonomy; where, moreover, the body politic that was the basis and touchtone of that respectability and autonomy was being undermined by sectarian fanatics, "creeping into

124. Rogers, *Ohel or Beth-shemesh,* quoted in Irwin, *Women in Radical Protestantism,* 176.

houses . . . [to] lead captive silly women . . . led away with diverse
lusts."[125] In a world that seemed overrun by masterless men, the apparently masterless, untethered female visionary must have been viewed
by many as the ultimate threat.

125. J. C. Davis discusses the collective paranoia about the Ranters as partly a fear of
the inversion of sexual roles (*Fear, Myth, and History,* 105–7). Christopher Hill disagrees
with my interpretation of audience response to women as prophets, arguing that the
magistrates took women's prophecy lightly as long as the women were not organized in
a movement (*World Turned Upside Down,* 200).

CHAPTER THREE

Talking Back: Women as Prophets during the Civil War and Interregnum, 1640–1655

And though I may be counted mad to the world, I shall
speak the words of soberness: and if I am mad, as the
Apostle saith, it is to God; and if I am in my right mind, it
is for the benefit of others.

Elizabeth Avery, Scripture Prophecies Opened, *1647*

INTRODUCTION

Lady Eleanor Davies sits in prison, conversing with an angel who wears scented gloves and lites on her bed. Anna Trapnel, supine and semiconscious for ten months, sings prophecies in verse, apparently oblivious to the onlookers who come and go. Katherine Chidley, standing tall, confronts a minister, berating him in so clamorous a tone that he is glad to hasten away.[1]

Did the female prophet have an authentic religious sensibility? Most observers, from seventeenth-century Puritans to the nineteenth-century puritan Max Weber, have agreed that women are particularly prone to the expression of an ardent, even passionate religiosity. Yet the vast majority of historians observing the women prophets of the 1640s and early 1650s have been inclined to discuss their work from every perspective *except* that of religion. Adopting the feminine stereotypes of seventeenth-century writers but not their spirituality, some have viewed the ecstatic preaching of visionary women as a form of emotional ca-

---

1. Eleanor Davies, *Ezekiel the Prophet*, 5–6, quoted in Esther Cope, *"Dame Eleanor Davies, Never Soe Mad a Ladie?"* (Ann Arbor, University of Michigan Press, forthcoming), 111. Anna Trapnel, *The Cry of a Stone: Or a Relation of Something Spoken in Whitehall, by Anna Trapnel, Being in the Visions of God* (London, 1654), 2, 15. On Katherine Chidley, see Thomas Edwards, *Gangraena: Or a Catalogue and Discovery of Many of the Errours, Heresies, Blasphemies and Pernicious Practices of the Sectaries of This Time . . .* (London, 1645), 79–80.

tharsis and a symptom of women's fundamental psychic instability, a view stated explicitly by Alfred Cohen, who calls his essay on female visionaries "Prophecy and Madness." Other scholars have expressed the same negative perception in more subtle, possibly unconscious ways. Thus, David Lovejoy remarked that Anne Hutchinson did not *think* about religious issues; she "soaked up" antinomianism, while in Christopher Hill's now classic work, *The World Turned Upside Down,* the sympathetic discussion of women in the radical sects occurs only in the chapters on insanity and free love.[2]

Historians of women generally disagree with these perceptions of the causes of women's emotional frustration, but they tend to agree that religious women preached in order to fulfill nonreligious needs, whether emotional, material, or sexual. Confined to an obscure existence, without property, official power, or political status, visionary women supposedly experienced a sense of freedom and self-realization when they spoke in public. "In a world where female freedom was carefully curbed," writes one historian, "to be free to believe was the first step in becoming free to do as one wished."[3]

In short, historians appear to be united in treating women's spirituality as a metaphor for something else; what divides them is the question whether the woman prophet actually had a mind. Most attribute no agency whatsoever to visionary women, no consciousness of their own or the world's problems and of their role in solving them, while others say they had too much. The former have been remarkably credulous in treating contemporary pamphlet literature as objective historical evidence and accepting accusations of women's hysteria and rampant sexuality at absolutely face value, while the latter have simply ignored the cultural discourse that affected visionary women's self-perception and have celebrated the assertive strategies of prophets who did not even claim to be awake during the time they preached. Perhaps these analyses tell us more about their creators' own preoccupations

---

2. Alfred Cohen, "Prophecy and Madness: Women Visionaries during the Puritan Revolution," *Journal of Psychohistory* 11 (1984): 411–30. David S. Lovejoy, *Religious Enthusiasm in the New World: Heresy to Revolution* (Cambridge, Mass. and London: Harvard University Press, 1985), 68. Christopher Hill, *The World Turned Upside Down: Radical Ideas during the English Revolution* (New York: Viking Press, 1972), Chap. 15, "Base Impudent Kisses," and Chap. 3, "The Island of Great Bedlam."

3. Lyle Koehler, *A Search for Power: The "Weaker Sex" in Seventeenth-Century New England* (Urbana, Chicago, and London: University of Illinois Press, 1980), 217. See also Elaine Hobby, *Virtue of Necessity: English Women's Writing, 1649–88* (London: Virago Press, 1988), 27; Dorothy P. Ludlow, "'Arise and Be Doing': English 'Preaching' Women, 1640–1660," Ph.D. diss., Indiana University, 1978, 273.

and experiences than they do about the historical reality of women as prophets.

This chapter will address the issues of women's freedom and religiosity by posing a series of specific and (I hope) productive questions: How did visionary women replicate the discourse on womanhood that formed such an important part of their cultural environment, and how did they seek to shape that discourse to their own ends or, rather, to godly, spiritual ends? Did they constitute a genuine threat to social order? Did the atmosphere of religious freedom, that atmosphere that gave her audience the freedom to attend to lay prophets and preachers, also give the prophet the freedom to speak her own thoughts, or were women as prophets attempting to say something that even the most admiring of their contemporaries could not hear?

TALKING BACK

> . . . Your names
> Of whore and murd'ress, they proceed from you,
> As if a man should spit against the wind,
> The filth returns in's face.
> *Vittoria, in John Webster's* The White Devil

Who were the women prophets of the 1640s and early 1650s, and how did they view themselves?[4] Popular imagination portrayed the female visionary as a human transmitter of divine knowledge, a sort of spiritual battery, humming with the energy of the universe. Prophecy and witchcraft, or prophecy and possession by diabolical powers, were often conflated, not only because the external behavior of both these types was similar but because, in both cases, the woman's body and behavior frequently exhibited tangible signs (catatonia, witches' marks) that betrayed her as a being whose fragile mental and moral powers had been submerged beneath a tidal wave of occult energy.

The visionaries of the Civil War and Interregnum did not share this traditional definition of female prophecy. They saw themselves as seekers embarked on a quest for moral perfection. They frequently experienced a transformation from an obsession with guilt and suicide to an assurance of salvation and of a social mission. Their confessional experiences led them directly into the act of prophecy and to membership in a

4. See Appendix 1.

congregation.[5] Thus, Mary Cary formulated a new, moral definition of prophecy that universalized the experience of communication with the divine:

> Every saint in a sense, may be said to be a prophet . . . for when the Lord hath revealed himself unto the soul and discovered his secrets to it, . . . the soul cannot choose but declare them to others. . . . He that speaketh to edification, exhortation and consolation, though with much weakness, doth as truly prophesy as he that hath greatest abilities.[6]

Anna Trapnel, who had her first vision at the age of nine, was certain that she was damned, was tempted by suicide, and sought for salvation in several Puritan congregations before emerging as a Fifth Monarchist prophet. Trapnel's prophetic work, *A Legacy for Saints*, included a preface by her new congregation that affirmed her high regard for scripture, her respect for the ministry, her beautiful and blameless conversation, and her "sweet, meek, sober, exemplary temper." The preface also noted that Trapnel wished the work to be published posthumously but deferred to their decision.[7]

The female visionary was not only a self-motivated seeker after moral truth; she was also self-educated. Mary Cary, a young woman of London, maintained that her understanding of divine commands did not come from "any immediate revelation—or that she had been told it by an Angel"; it was the fruit of a twelve-year study of scripture, which she had begun in 1636 at the age of fifteen.[8] Mary Pope told her readers, "but it may be some will say, that these . . . of my writings are non-sense? But to such I answer, if they would study the Scriptures as I do, they shall find them very good sense."[9] Elizabeth Warren meditated on the works

---

5. Nigel Smith, *Perfection Proclaimed: Language and Literature in English Radical Religion, 1640–1660* (Oxford: Clarendon Press, 1989), 342–43. Surviving church lists show women outnumbering men (Bernard Capp, *The Fifth Monarchy Men: A Study in Seventeenth-Century English Millenarianism* [London: Faber and Faber, 1972], 82).

6. Anna Trapnel, *Anna Trapnel's Report and Plea, or, a Narrative of Her Journey from London into Cornwall* (London, 1654), 16–17; Mary Cary, *The Resurrection of the Witness: and Englands Fall from (the Mystical Babylon) Rome* (London, 1648), 65–67.

7. Anna Trapnel, *A legacy for Saints, Being Several Experiences of the Dealings of God with Anna Trapnel, in, and after Her Conversion* (London, 1654), Introduction; and see Miriam Garber, "Anna Trapnel and the Protectorate: A Prophet's Challenge to the Government," typescript, University of Michigan, Department of History, 1989, 23–24.

8. Cary, *The Resurrection of the Witness,* "Epistle to the Reader." Christopher Feake, who contributed a preface to her tract *The Little Horn's Doom and Downfall,* called her a "gentlewoman."

9. Mary Pope, *A Treatise of Magistracy* . . . (1647), "To the Reader."

of Plato, Aristotle, Cicero, Plutarch, and Augustine; her texts are laden with mythical images and her margins with Latin quotations.[10] Eleanor Davies was exceptional in that she never displayed much interest in the working of divine moral power in herself or in her own moral or spiritual condition, nor did she ally herself with any of the religious tendencies that arose as a challenge to the Anglican hierarchy, despite the fact that she condemned Archbishop Laud as a rapist and murderer. Yet even Lady Eleanor saw herself less as a sibyl than as a biblical scholar working to decipher and interpret her own divine messages. After one cataclysmic experience in which she was anointed as the handmaid of Daniel, she devoted her life to writing glosses on her own visions, one of which predicted the discovery of a new hemisphere having "magnificent libraries with printed books." She showed particular interest in the numerology and arcane symbolism of Daniel and Ezekiel; indeed, she perceived these prophets as intervening directly in her own personal affairs. The night she received a writ denying her the tithes she was owed on one of her estates, "a bold star facing the moon passed through her body," and she knew that she must speak as Ezekiel.[11]

In short, the mentality of the most eminent female prophets was not, in their view, radically dissimilar to that of male ministers, many of whom also surmounted suicidal impulses, heard voices, and attended to the spiritual import of their own dreams. Indeed, in a different world some of these women might have become ministers.[12] Katherine Chidley and Mary Cary actually insisted that they *were* ministers, not prophets; that is, they spoke out of their "own conviction and learning, not involuntarily as the transmitters of specific angelic messages. Even those visionaries who entered trance states sometimes counseled visitors and family members in a pastoral mode. So Mrs. Joan Drake, following several days and nights of visionary ecstasy, advised her husband on household management, while the adolescent Sarah Wight offered consolation and reasonable counsel to visitors who suffered from depression: "In preaching the Gospel," she told her audience, "light, motion,

---

10. Elizabeth Warren, *Spiritual Thrift. Or, Meditations . . .* (London, 1647). Ludlow, "'Arise and Be Doing,'" 234.

11. Eleanor Audeley, *A Warning to the Dragon and All His Angels* (1625), 90. (Audeley was Eleanor Davies's maiden name.) On the difference between Eleanor Davies and the radical prophets, see Nigel Smith, *Perfection Proclaimed*, 32. On her knowledge of the law and of Latin, see Cope, "*Dame Eleanor Davies*," 12–13, 24.

12. On male ministers' depression and visionary tendencies, see Owen Watkins, *The Puritan Experiment: Studies in Spiritual Autobiography* (New York: Schocken Press, 1972), 93ff.

and power goes out to all: which men resist, and such are destroyed, not
because they could not believe; but because they resist, and will not obey,
and so die."[13]

What *did* distinguish these female visionaries from male clergymen,
besides the obvious disparities in education and background, was their
location of spiritual transformation and creativity in the mother/child
relationship. Anna Trapnel attributed her prophetic gifts to the words of
her mother, "Lord! Double thy spirit upon my child," uttered three times
before her death.[14] Sixteen-year-old Sarah Wight berated herself in her
trances for harsh words and thoughts about her mother, confessing that
*"If any one see and feel what I have seen and felt they would take heed
of murmuring against God and a parent. You never murmured so much
against God, and against my mother, as I have done*; Ah, ah, ah, sighing
and weeping as she spoke."[15] At one moment she contemplated offering
herself to the wild dogs at Moorfield "that her mother might never hear
of her more," and when she lost her sight and hearing, a neighbor bathed
her eyes and held them open so that "she saw and knew her mother."[16]
The Belgian prophet Antonia Bourignon turned to God because her
mother did not love her. Susanna Parr decided to break away from an
Independent congregation after the death of her child:

> When my bowels were yearning towards my child, I called to remembrance
> the Lord's tender bowels toward his children, . . . when I considered the breach
> that the Lord had made in my family, I beheld how terible it was to make a
> breach in his family. . . . Then the work I was engaged in, this sin of separa-
> tion, appeared nakedly unto me to be no other then a wounding of Christ's
> body.[17]

Elizabeth Avery wrote that before her enlightenment she had lost three
children and with them all meaning in life. "[I was left] in a horror, as

13. On Joan Drake, see John Hart, *The Firebrand Taken out of the Fire* . . . (London,
1654). On Sarah Wight, see Henry Jessey, *The Exceeding Riches of Grace Advanced*, 7th
ed. (1658), 95–97, quoted in Barbara Ritter Dailey, "The Visitation of Sarah Wight:
Holy Carnival and the Revolution of the Saints in Civil War London," *Church History* 55
(1986): 450.
14. Trapnel, *The Cry of a Stone*, 3.
15. Jessey, *The Exceeding Riches*, 30, quoted in Smith, *Perfection Proclaimed*, 46.
Dailey, "The Visitation of Sarah Wight," 444; she had lied to her mother about a lost
hood that she told her was at a grandmother's house.
16. Jessey, *The Exceeding Riches*, 25, 30, 39, 130. See also Smith, *Perfection Proclaimed*, 46; Smith implies that Jessey emphasized this aspect of Wight's guilt feelings.
Also see Dailey, "The Visitation of Sarah Wight," 446.
17. Susanna Parr, *Susanna's Apologie against the Elders: Or a Vindication of Susanna Parr* . . . (Oxford, 1659), 14.

if I were in hell, none could comfort me, nothing could satisfy me, no friends, nothing." Katherine Chidley, mother of seven children, made her first public protest in 1626, when she joined with other women in refusing to be churched after childbirth; she and Mary Pope both collaborated with their sons, to whom they dictated their works. Eleanor Davies took a "dumb" prophetic boy into her house shortly before her first vision. She had recently buried her own small child, a handicapped boy named Jack, also mute, who died by drowning. When her daughter Lucy's own son died, Lady Eleanor wrote to her about her dream of a child beheaded for treason and women trying to quiet the bodiless head, which would not stop crying.[18]

One does not need to posit the existence of an innate female nature in order to understand why the prophets' locus of spiritual pain and transformation was the experience of motherhood and daughterhood. One need only remember the social preoccupations of women and conventions of female spirituality that pervaded seventeenth-century culture. Puritan goodwives, Baptist women, and great ladies like Mary, Countess of Warwick, all saw, and were taught to see, moral and spiritual significance in childbirth and in the mother/child relationship.[19]

If women as prophets understood themselves as mothers, daughters, readers, and seekers after truth, one might speculate that, in a culture in which spiritual suffering and communication with the divine were viewed as real, indeed normative experiences, then far from being a marginalized, hysterical fringe group in seventeenth-century society, women like Grace Cary and Anna Trapnel were the ones whose spiritual sicknesses were healed, for the numerous other wives, daughters, and new mothers who succumbed to despair, refused to eat, or dreamed of Jesus as they lay in their beds either died at home (like Joan Drake, who was visited by nine different ministers and numerous physicians and who expired after ten nights of visionary ecstasy) or simply disap-

18. On Avery, see John Rogers, *Ohel or Beth-shemesh: A Tabernacle for the Sun* (London, 1653), 403. On Chidley, see DBR, 1:139. On Davies, see HEH, Hastings Manuscripts HA 2337, quoted in Cope, "*Dame Eleanor Davies*," 41. Davies also wrote a tract about her grandson's death, *Sions Lamentation: Lord Henry Hastings, His Funerals Blessing, by His Grandmother, the Lady Eleanor* (1649). Lady Eleanor had another son, Richard, who died in infancy (Cope, "*Dame Eleanor Davies*," 7).

19. Rogers, *Ohel or Beth-shemesh*; many women in Rogers's sect converted after the death of a child. On the Countess of Warwick, see Sara Heller Mendelson, *The Mental World of Stuart Women: Three Biographies* (Amherst: University of Massachusetts Press, 1987), 81–82.

peared from view, at peace or not at peace, and resumed their domestic responsibilities (like Martha Hatfield, a young girl whose seizures and trances were recorded by her uncle, the vicar of Sheffield, and who later married and bore a child).[20] Prophetic women, however, translated their sense of personal guilt into a vision of external evil, of a society corrupted by sin, and embraced the challenge of expelling that evil from the world. So Grace Cary, a respectable widow from Bristol, after a period of deep internal conflict, had an initial dream that blossomed into a series of visions inviting her to approach the throne of grace, through "glorious shining lights accompanied with vehement rushing winds," finally culminating in a full-blown apparition of "a king's head and face without a body, which looked very pale and wan: it had a crown upon it and the crown was all bloody in a circle about." The message: treason and death, which, after a further period of prayer and fasting, she translated into a public plea for a reconciliation between king and Parliament.[21]

One might also speculate that what distinguished the prophet from the young women and matrons who struggled for their salvation behind closed doors was that they were deprived of the compassionate yet repressive attentions of male family members. For whatever their class background—and women prophets ranged from the impoverished countrywoman Elinor Channel to the aristocrat Eleanor Davies—several who achieved eminence were either single, widowed, or orphaned. Anna Trapnel, the unmarried daughter of a London shipwright, lost her father when she was a child, and when her mother died she lived with two different older women before joining the Fifth Monarchist sect. When a magistrate interrogating her remarked, "I understand you are not married," she replied, "Then having no hindrance, why may not I go

20. Hart, *The Firebrand Taken out of the Fire*. See also George Huntston Williams, "Called by Thy Name, Leave Us Not: The Case of Mrs. Joan Drake, A Formative Episode in the Pastoral Career of Thomas Hooker in England," *Harvard Library Bulletin* 16 (1968): 111–28, 278–300. Martha Hatfield's case was recounted in James Fisher, *The Wise Virgin, or, a Wonderfull Narration of the Hand of God* . . . (London, 1653). For a discussion of Mary, Countess of Warwick's religious diary, see Mendelson, *The Mental World of Stuart Women*, 98–99: Regarding Mary's blaming herself for major catastrophes, such as the burning of London, Mendelson writes, "By playing Jeremiah, Mary felt she was helping to forestall future judgments. . . . Mary's energetic 'wrestling' with God for aims which ranged from personal to international in scope were a similar effort to transform passive impotence into active intervention" (98–99).

21. Theophilus Philaleihes Toxander, *Vox Coeli to England, or England's Fore-warning from Heaven* (London, 1646), 3–11.

where I please, if the Lord so will?"[22] Trapnel also wrote a poem addressed to her unmarried companions:

> Hallelujah, Hallelujah Lord
> For companions I will sing,
> And praises shall be given here,
> Because they have not been
> Carried about not yet enticed,
> From thee by any means,
> And they shall here meet with reproof,
> If on creatures they lean.
> Hallelujah, Hallelujah for
> Companions that do come,
> And are not wedded to anything,
> But to King Solomon.[23]

Sarah Wight, an adolescent living with her mother, a Puritan gentlewoman, also lost her father as a young child, while Eleanor Davies rarely
saw her father during her childhood. Elizabeth Poole apparently disobeyed her father in joining her Baptist congregation in London; he
claimed that the minister William Kiffin had seduced his children and
servants into error, and Elizabeth arranged an abortive meeting between
the two men.[24] Likewise, Elizabeth Avery, daughter of an Anglican
scholar and sister of a theologian specializing in the prophecies of Daniel,
was publicly attacked by her family after she published her own theological work.[25]

Those women who were married frequently had to resist the opposition of their spouses. Elinor Channel was forbidden by her husband to
prophesy, whereupon she became dumb until he relented. Eleanor Davies prophesied against the wishes of *her* two husbands (her second
husband was an insane invalid at the time she published her first work).
She also made it clear that she considered her domestic responsibilities
less significant than her prophetic calling. Describing popular suspicions

22. *The Lady Eleanor Her Appeal. Present This to Mr. Mace the Prophet of the Most High, His Messenger* (1646), quoted in George Ballard, *Memoirs of Several Ladies of Great Britain Who Have Been Celebrated for Their Writings or Skill in the Learned Languages, Arts and Sciences* (1775), ed. Ruth Perry (Detroit: Wayne State University Press, 1985), 258. Trapnel, *Report and Plea*, 26, quoted in Hobby, *Virtue of Necessity*, 33.

23. Anna Trapnel, *Voice of the King of Saints* (1658), quoted in Hobby, *Virtue of Necessity*, 33.

24. On Davies, see Cope, *"Dame Eleanor Davies,"* 8. On Poole, see Ludlow, "'Arise and Be Doing,'" 229ff.

25. Ludlow, "'Arise and Be Doing,'" 260.

that the prophetic boy she took into her house was a witch, she wrote, "immediately upon this, the spirit of prophecy falling likewise upon me, then were all vexed worse than ever, ready to turn the house upside down, . . . when *laying aside household cares all*, and having no conversation with any but the word of God . . . I found out this place." Only two women, Katherine Chidley and Dorothy Hazzard, received their husbands' active support, though Chidley's activities were chiefly in collaboration with her son.[26]

The prophet's spiritual independence may have also been assisted by the fact that she was often economically independent as well. Anna Trapnel defended herself to magistrates as an independent, tax-paying citizen. Katherine Chidley was a businesswoman, supplying the government's troops in Ireland with five thousand pairs of stockings in 1650–51. Elizabeth Poole and Elizabeth Warren lived by their own labor as seamstress and school teacher, respectively. Mary Pope inherited her husband's salting business and paid the costs of her tracts herself. So did Lady Eleanor, whose entire career was punctuated by lawsuits as well as prophecies, as she doggedly defended her rights to her jointure and to the financial benefits attached to the ownership of her estates. At least one of these lawsuits, aimed at the recovery of her estates from her insane second husband, directly challenged strictures on the legal recourses available to women. Thus, the concerned magistrates appended a number of questions to her petition: "Could a wife contradict and void the grant of her husband? Could she plead that he was insane?" Eventually the judges apparently decided to question *her* sanity, whereupon she wrote a letter "without the help or knowledge of any; which I think, that few to this purpose could have done it much better. . . . And that a man of very small understanding could not have done it so well."[27]

Clearly women were dependent on men for patronage once they began to prophesy in public. Indeed, no woman presuming to address a mixed audience on political issues could have survived without male allies, either as editors, apologists, ministers, or, in a very few cases, lovers.

26. On Chidley, see DBR, 1:139–40. On Hazzard, see Claire Cross, " 'He-goats before the Flocks': A Note on the Part Played by Women in the Founding of Some Civil War Churches," in *Popular Belief and Practice*, ed. G. J. Cuming and Derek Baker (Cambridge: Cambridge University Press, 1972), 195–203. Lady Eleanor, *Her Appeal*, 8–9, and Cope, "*Dame Eleanor Davies*," 43.

27. On women's social backgrounds, see Ludlow, " 'Arise and Be Doing,' " 41–42. On Trapnel, see DBR, 3:250. On Chidley, see DBR, 1:140. On Lady Eleanor, HEH, Hastings Manuscripts Correspondence, HA 2344, discussed in Cope, "*Dame Eleanor Davies*."

Excepting Lady Eleanor, every important prophet belonged to a congregation that was supervised by male ministers, and most (again excepting Lady Eleanor) were dependent on male editors who bracketed
their texts by salutations that affirmed their piety and respectability,
inserted supporting biblical citations, and added substantive arguments;
most strikingly is this so in the case of Elinor Channel, whose vague
prophecies were tranformed into a Royalist polemic by her editor, Arise
Evans.[28]

Yet women also exhibited remarkable initiative and persistence in
using or ignoring the patronage system for their own purposes. Grace
Cary consulted some divines from Bristol, who could neither confirm
nor deny the authenticity of the visions she had written down and
attempted to dissuade her from further action. She then decided for
herself that the visions were genuine, traveled to London, and gained
the intercession of the Lord Marquis of Hambleton, who obtained an
audience with the king, to whom she communicated her message of
reconciliation.[29] Mary Pope asked members of Parliament to correct the
flaws in her treatise before she printed it. When they ignored her, she
printed it herself and hired someone to present copies at the doors of
both houses of Parliament. Mary Cary withheld publication of one of
her tracts for seven years, until she felt there was greater general receptivity to prophecies. It was then presented, laden with encomiums from
three male ministers ("in this dress you shall neither see naked breasts,
black patches, nor long trains; but an heart breathing after the coming
of Christ"). It was also dedicated to three prominent gentlewomen, best
among "the many pious, precious, prudent and sage matrons, and holy
women, with which this commonwealth is adorned; as with so many
precious jewels."[30]

Women also appear to have made a distinction between the men to
whom they turned for patronage and the women who provided them
with emotional support. When Anna Trapnel was about to embark on
a dangerous mission to Cornwall, she discussed the project with her
"sisters," ten of whom sat up with her all night to pray for a good
outcome. After her arrest she was visited in Bridewell by a group of

28. On Anna Trapnel, whose theology was examined by the minister John Simpson
during her fast, see Smith, *Perfection Proclaimed*, 51. On Wight, ibid., 45ff.
    29. Toxander, *Vox Coeli*, 6.
    30. Pope, *Treatise of Magistracy*, 130. Mary Cary, *The Little Horn's Doom and
Downfall: Or a Scripture-Prophesie of King James, and King Charles, and of This Present
Parliament, Unfolded* (London, 1651), Preface, A3v. The ladies were Elizabeth Cromwell,
Bridget Ireton, and Margaret Role.

women, one of whom moved into prison with her, staying for seven of the eight weeks of her incarceration. The women preachers described by the Puritan Thomas Edwards were defended by their "sisters" against the taunts of their audience. He also describes Mrs. Attaway and her "sister" beginning their career by preaching together to audiences of women. When Elizabeth Poole's Baptist minister expelled her and circulated a letter condemning her "immoral" behavior, the wife of another minister intercepted it and wrote her own letter of support. Sarah Jones was a friend of the preacher Katherine Chidley and the visionary Sarah Wight. Anna Trapnel also knew Sarah Wight and visited her shortly before the beginning of her own quite similar visions.[31]

Lady Eleanor Davies, the most socially elevated and personally idiosyncratic of all female prophets, cited the work of Grace Cary (circulated in manuscript) in the gloss to an early edition of one of her own tracts. She also met with a group of women in Lichfield to discuss religion before her most bizarre act: pouring hot tar and wheat paste on the hangings of the altar of the cathedral. As a collective gesture of protest, the women went daily to the church, which had recently been embellished by Archbishop Laud, and occupied the seats reserved for the wives of the bishop, dean, and canons. Two of the women invited Lady Eleanor to their homes and later defended her gesture to opponents as an act of conscience. Lady Eleanor's most enduring personal bond was with her daughter Lucy, "your Mother's copartner . . . and sole support under the Almighty." Lucy defended her mother through all of her imprisonments, sent her pies and money, expended effort to preserve her mother's papers, and, judging from the epitaph she composed for Lady Eleanor's grave, was one of the few contemporaries who saw her mother the way she wished to be seen:

> Learned above her sex, meek below her rank. . . . In eminent beauty she possessed a lofty mind, in pleasing affability, singular modesty . . . in most adverse circumstances a serene mind, in a wicked age unshaken piety and uprightness. Not for her did luxury relax her strong soul, or poverty narrow

31. Trapnel, *Report and Plea*, 2, 7. On Elizabeth Poole, see Elizabeth Poole, *An(other) Alarum of War, Given to the Army* (1649), quoted in Hobby, *Virtue of Necessity*, 30, and in Ludlow, "'Arise and Be Doing,'" 228ff.; Poole may have left the congregation for doctrinal reasons. She denied the accusations of immorality. On Jones, see Ludlow, "'Arise and Be Doing,'" 80 n. 103. On Anne Hutchinson's protection of the prophet Jane Hawkins and the women who were loyal to Hutchinson, see Ludlow, "'Arise and Be Doing'" 172, and nn 82, 86, and 89.

it: but each lot with equal countenance and mind, she not only took but ruled.[32]

VISIONS AND WISE COUNSEL

Lucy's estimation of her mother as a tower of moral and spiritual fortitude surely struck many contemporaries as absurd. Yet when we examine the substance of these visionaries' published writings, we find them collectively contradicting a fundamental female stereotype, that of woman as a figure of disorder, an enemy of structured, civilized existence. Indeed, a primary characteristic of many women's visionary pronouncements, whether Royalist or radical, was their tone of moderation and restraint. Sarah Wight, member of a Baptist congregation, counseled visitors from within the moral and scriptural traditions of orthodox Calvinism.[33] Grace Cary followed the king to York to warn him about the evils of Archbishop Laud and Queen Henrietta Maria and pleaded with Parliament to reconcile with the king and tolerate Puritans but not Independents or any radical groups, be they "Prelates, Anabaptists, Antinomians, Adamites, Familists . . . Papists and Arminian Innovators." She also decided not to publish her vision, despite the pleas of friends, but to circulate it in manuscript, thereby keeping God's word out of the hands of "the meaner sort, of vulgar people," whose conversation might discredit it.[34] Elizabeth Poole criticized the king when she appeared before the Council chamber in 1649 but counseled Oliver Cromwell against regicide, asserting that all the "glorious glittering images of state policies, religious ordinances, orders, faiths, lights, knowledges . . . drawn over [with] beautiful pretenses" could not hide the "worldly dark part" in the king's executioners. Ultimately, only fear and self-interest

32. On Eleanor Davies's citation of Grace Cary, see Eleanor Davies, *Given to the Elector, Prince Charls of the Rhyne* (1648). On Davies in Lichfield, SP 16/380/94, London Public Record Office, discussed in Cope, *"Dame Eleanor Davies,"* 50, 116, 118. Cope suggests that the Lady Eleanor's connection to the women may have been exaggerated, since she does not mention them in her own writings. Lady Eleanor's statement is found in *From the Lady Eleanor, Her Blessing to Her Beloved Daughter, the Right Honorable Lucy, Countess of Huntingdon. The Prophet Daniel's Vision* (1644), 38, quoted in Cope, *"Dame Eleanor Davies,"* 159. Lucy's epitaph is printed in *Poems of Sir John Davies* (1876), 2:123.
33. Smith, *Perfection Proclaimed*, 46, 48.
34. Toxander, *Vox Coeli*, 9. Grace Cary, Englands Fore-Warning or: A Relation of True, Strange and Wonderfull Visions, . . . Add, 32. iv and D.d. 14.25. (3), Cambridge University Library, discussed in Margaret J. M. Ezell, *The Patriarch's Wife: Literary Evidence and the History of the Family* (Chapel Hill and London: University of North Carolina Press, 1987), 65.

and a thirst for blood were satisfied. Poole compared the duty of Parliament to that of a loyal wife who bears the pain of her husband's guilt:

> a just woman must deliver up her husband to the just claim of the law, though she might not accuse him to the law, nor yet rejoice over him to see his fall, for all that pass by and behold her, will say this was a strumpet, and not a faithfull wife, that rejoiceth at the fall of her husband; and contrariwise the faithful wife mourneth in secret for him: . . . you owe him all that you have and are, and although he would not be your father and husband, . . . yet know that you are for the Lord's sake to honor his person. For he is the father and husband of your bodies.[35]

Speaking of the document called the Agreement of the People, she also advised the Council not to surrender the power now entrusted to them by giving it to "the people," (i.e. the Levelers): "For it seems to me to be [intended by the agreement] that you shall give the power out of your own hands, whereas God hath intrusted it with you, and will require it of you how it is improved. You are his stewards."[36] Mary Pocock, a disciple of the mystic John Pordage, also published a tract in 1649, the year of the king's execution. In it she described an androgynous Adam, whom she saw as a "shadowing forth" of the ideal political order:

> Here is now the soul in the body, the husband and wife, God and the man. This is the representative, King and parliament, whose happy condition is bound up in the enjoyment of each other, in the union of the manhood, in the power of the Godhead: And this is the glory of the King, in his paradisical kingdom.[37]

Altering Pordage's conception of Sophia, or passive human wisdom, activated by divine masculine revelation, Pocock described the Fall as the sin of the king, or Adam, who loves only himself and self-seeing reason rather than dwelling peacefully with Eve, or divine reason.

Other visionaries were equally restrained in their criticism of the monarchy. Eleanor Davies defied episcopal authority but was apparently an orthodox Anglican in every other respect. Elizabeth Warren counseled men to stay within their stations and women to follow the opinions of their husbands, defended the necessity of traditional learning for the

---

35. Elizabeth Poole, *A Vision: Wherein Is Manifested the Disease and Cure of the Kingdome* (London, 1648), 7, and *An(other) Alarum of War*, 12, paraphrased in Ludlow, "'Arise and Be Doing,'" 210.

36. General Council, January 5, 1648, at Whitehall, reprinted in C. H. Firth, ed., *The Clarke Papers: Selections from the Papers of William Clarke*, 4 vols. (Westminster: Nichols and Sons, 1894), 2:163.

37. Mary Pocock, *The Mystery of the Deity in the Humanity* (1649), 16–17, quoted in Smith, *Perfection Proclaimed*, 211.

ministry, and condemned the Civil War as punishment for the people's greed. Mary Pope reminded Parliament that the brunt of the war had been born by "the middle rank of people, that are the chief upholders of the highest rank, and of the lowest," and urged that the poor be relieved and soldiers be paid on time.[38] For all these women, the natural law that justified the king's survival was presented as more fundamental than the specific misdeeds and oversights of which the king was guilty.

Elizabeth Avery, Mary Cary, Anna Trapnel, and Katherine Chidley *were* radicals: Avery, Cary, and Trapnel supportive of the millennarian Fifth Monarchist sect, which rejected the legality of the Protectorate; Chidley a supporter of the Levelers. Cary was one of the few women prophets who supported the execution of the king: "when the late King was in his height, I declared my confidence, that the Parliament should prevail over him, and at last destroy him."[39] She envisioned a world turned upside down:

> They that seek not [salvation] . . . but that do covet to treasure up most riches for themselves, and to poll, and rob, and cheat the people, to enhance their own estates, and make themselves great in the world, and their children gay and splendid among men . . . these shall become the basest and the vilest among men. . . . There must be such a time, when the saints must be so lifted up out of the dust, as they must be the top and the head of all nations: and whatsoever kingdom and nation will not serve them must perish.[40]

Yet her visionary program was more concerned with poverty and education than with the violent victory of the saints. Her utopia was a world without poverty or famine, in which men and women no longer lived in emnity with nature or each other, and where wild animals were not enemies of men and women but served them.

> "The creatures shall appear in their primitive beauty and goodness wherein they were created, being all in subjection, and useful to man. . . . The wolf shall not destroy the lamb . . . but they shall all feed together."[41]

The pleasures and creature comforts of the world would become innocent, being the fruit of the people's own labor. Clothing would be

---

38. On Chidley, see Katherine Chidley, "Good Counsell, to the Petitioners for Presbyterian Government That They May Declare Their Faith before They Build Their Church," broadside (1645), and *The Justification of the Independent Churches of Christ* (London, 1641), 37–38; on Warren, see DBR, 3:293; on Pope, see Pope, *Treatise of Magistracy*, 123–24.

39. Cary, *The Little Horn's Doom and Downfall*, 46.

40. Mary Cary, *A New and More Exact Mappe or Description of New Jerusalems Glory* . . . (London, 1651), 56–57, 67.

41. Ibid., 293, 298–99.

beautiful but not gaudy. Society would be ordered, for the godly magistrate would still wield the sword, punishing drunkards, whoremasters,
and swearers, yet the full potential of a renovated human nature would
be released. "Let me say," she wrote,

> there is nothing absolutely necessary to the making of a convert, and of a
> convert, a publisher of the gospel, which a soul that is but furnished only with
> understanding and reason is not capable of, if the spirit be poured out upon
> it; whether it be a heathen . . . or one brought up in the profession of
> Christianity: or whether it be learned, or unlearned; or whether it be male,
> or female.[42]

Cary was one of only two writers, male or female, to propose a scheme
of university reform, using colleges as the basis for evangelizing the
world. She was also unique in proposing to extend toleration to papists
and atheists.[43]

Anna Trapnel held similar views of human renovation, education,
and religious toleration: "that [all] might be of one heart and one mind;
and that knowledge might cover the earth, as water the sea; . . . and the
kingdom restored to this old *Israel*, which was the first married wife."
She originally prophesied in favor of the Protectorate, seeing Cromwell
as Gideon "going before Israel, blowing the trumpet of courage and
valor."[44] Later, as a Fifth Monarchist, she became more radical, condemning the Protectorate as illegitimate and unlawful and predicting
that the saints would become earls and potentates. Yet she was also a
pacifist and condemned Thomas Venner's abortive plot to forcibly in-
stall King Jesus on the throne of England.[45] Sarah Wight also pleaded
for harmony among churches and upheld orthodox Puritan doctrines of
justification, while Katherine Chidley wrote extensively on toleration,
although her definition of an acceptable congregation became more
narrow as her own millennarian vision hardened during the course of
the decade.[46] She also defended Separatist congregations as directed by
literate preachers who acknowledge the authority of the magistrates
and assured readers that liberty of conscience would not lead to libertinism.

42. Ibid., 238–39.
43. Mary Rande, *Twelve Proposals* . . . (1653), 4. Capp, *Fifth Monarchy Men*, 189.
Mary Cary took the name Rande at this time.
44. Trapnel, *Report and Plea*, 14; Trapnel, *Cry of a Stone*, 6.
45. Cohen, "Prophecy and Madness," 424. Trapnel, *Cry of a Stone*, 40, discussed in
Capp, *Fifth Monarchy Men*, 144. Venner was a Fifth Monarchist leader.
46. Katherine Chidley, *A New-Yeares-Gift, or a Brief Exhortation to Mr. Thomas
Edwards* (London, 1645).

Above all, and regardless of their political and religious position, women prophets saw the ravaged political edifice of the monarchy less in terms of a conflict among institutions or theological positions than in terms of concrete human suffering, expressed most powerfully by Mary Cary's poignant utopian vision:

> No infant of days shall die; none shall die while they are young; all shall come to a good old age. They shall not be afflicted for the loss of their children; for they shall live till they be an hundred years old. . . . The streets shall be full of boys and girls playing . . . and old men and old women shall live till they come to a good old age, till they walk with a staff in their hand for age.[47]

Cary was unique among members of the sect in her concern for the helpless poor, criticizing those members of Parliament who would consider a poor relief act and then lay it aside for three, six, or twelve months. She suggested a postage fee, to be used for support of those who could not work or had too many children to feed.[48] Katherine Chidley railed against priests who

> will have a share out of him that is born without life! For if a dead child be born into the world, they will be paid for reading a dirge over it before it shall be laid in the earth. . . . Further they will yet have another patrimony for the birth of that child; for before the mother dare go abroad, she must have their "blessing" [i.e., attend the ceremony of churching], that the "sun shall not smite her by day, nor the moon by night;" for which blessing of theirs, they must have an "offering." . . . I am able to prove that they do demand of poor people before they can have a child that is but fourteen or fifteen years of age buried in one of the out-churchyards of the great parishes; which land is the free gift of the dead, for the help of the poor . . . before, I say, they can have such a child buried there, it will cost the poorest parent seven or eight shillings! . . . It is a plain case, therefore, that these men are a greater plague to this land than the natural locusts of Egypt, for they ate up the green things, but these eat up both green and dry.[49]

Chidley argued that ministers should earn their bread by their own manual labor. She further argued that independent sects be tolerated

47. Cary, *A New and More Exact Mappe*, 289–90. See also *Resurrection of the Witness*, 173, and Capp, *Fifth Monarchy Men*, 184: Cary wanted toleration even for papists and atheists; most others disagreed.

48. Rande, *Twelve Proposals*, 4, 6. She was also concerned for the idle poor, advocating workhouses that would dispense small allowances. See Capp, *Fifth Monarchy Men*, 147.

49. Chidley, *The Justification of the Independent Churches of Christ*, 114–15. The phrase "the sun shall not burn thee by day, nor the moon by night" is a part of Psalm 121 that was read during churching. Many opposed it as implying a curse or threat on the new mother (Ludlow, "'Arise and Be Doing,'" 58).

because they maintain all of their own poor "as well as any other man," while Mary Pope inveighed against the materialism of shopkeepers who trade until the last possible moment on Saturday night; she also suggested a program to relieve the poor in individual parishes. The Leveler women's petition of April 1649 was written entirely in Chidley's style:

> Considering, that we have an equal share and interest with men in the commonwealth, and it cannot be laid waste, (as now it is) and not we be the greatest and most helpless sufferers therein; and considering that poverty, misery, and famine, like a mighty torrent, is breaking in upon us, . . . and we are not able to see our children hang upon us, and cry out for bread, and not have wherewithall to feed them, we had rather die than see that day.[50]

In short, however radical their proposals for social and spiritual reform, and however strident the tone of those proposals, women's programs were less destructive of the established social order than those of their male counterparts. Moreover, the tone of their remonstrances against the king was far less hyperbolic and emotional than the contemporary pamphlet literature that presented Charles as a doting husband, a pathetic weakling, and a depraved lover of the Anglican church.[51] The personal claims made by women to be handmaids or spouses of the Holy Spirit were also far less grandiose than those of the male pseudo-messiahs who preached alongside them. Mary Gadbury, who called herself "the bride of the lamb," was completely overshadowed by the Ranter William Franklin, with whom she traveled and preached and who claimed to be a reincarnation of Jesus Christ; she was also a nearly isolated case.[52] Eleanor Davies announced herself proudly

50. Chidley, *The Justification of the Independent Churches of Christ*, 43; Petition of April 24, 4, quoted in Ludlow, "'Arise and Be Doing,'" 121. On Pope, see Ludlow, "'Arise and Be Doing,'" 216–17.

51. Ludlow, "'Arise and Be Doing,'" 209.

52. On Gadbury, see H[umphrey] Ellis, *Pseudochristus: Or, a True and Faithful Relation of the Grand Impostures, Abominable Practises, Horrid Blasphemies, Gross Deceits . . .* (London, 1650). Gadbury and Franklin were arrested for blasphemy in 1650. She was imprisoned and whipped, admitted he had deceived her and said she would have "laid down her life for the truth of what she had declared concerning him." Anne Hall caused a scandal by cohabiting with two male lay preachers who exorcised her demons (T. J., *A Brief Representation and Discovery of the Notorious Falshood and Dissimulation Contained in a Book Styled, The Gospel-Way Confirmed by Miracles* [London, 1649]; Ludlow, "'Arise and Be Doing,'" 150–52); Jerome Friedman, *Blasphemy, Immorality, and Anarchy: The Ranters and the English Revolution* (Athens, Ohio, and London: Ohio University Press, 1987), 161–66. There were other cases of women cohabiting with male prophets and pseudo-messiahs. On Laurence Clarkson and the group "My One Flesh," see J. C. Davis, *Fear, Myth, and History: The Ranters and the Histo-*

as the "handmaiden of the most high God of heaven, this book brought
forth by Her, fifth Daughter of George Lord of Castlehaven."[53] But for
sheer arrogance or self-delusion, even Lady Eleanor could not hold a
candle to Lodowijk Muggleton and John Reeve, who said they were the
two Witnesses of the Spirit in Revelation and cursed to eternity anyone
who opposed them; or John Rogers, "the Shakers' God," who claimed
to be the messiah; or John Moore, who said he was Christ; or Laurence
Clarkson, who tried to prove that he was the only true messenger of
Jesus; or Richard Farnham, another witness in Revelation, who expected
to rise again like Jesus and also claimed he could control the weather;
or Miles Fry, alias Emmanuel Plantagenet, the son of Queen Elizabeth
by God the Father.[54] Many female prophets compared themselves to
famous biblical figures, but these male prophets believed they *were*
famous biblical figures. The introductions to women's tracts, soothing
the reader with an excess of deferential disclaimers, certainly could not
be more different from the "divine fireworks" presented by Abiezer
Coppe: "Read [my tract] through, and laugh not at it; if thou dost I'll
destroy thee, and laugh at thy destruction." Nor did any woman's
behavior compare to that of Coppe, who expressed his spiritual fervor
in an extravagance of indiscriminate kissing.[55]

Clearly, many women had both the spiritual and the intellectual
capacity to contribute to the political discourse that dominated the Civil
War period, and, clearly, their political intention was not to subvert all
traditional morality or destroy every vestige of established authority.
However, regardless of the substantive content of women's visionary
writings and pronouncements and the relative restraint with which they
were presented, their overall effect on most observers was probably to
reinforce traditional preconceptions of the volatile, essentially uncivilized nature of all womanhood. The reason for this was not simply a
preconceived prejudice against women on the part of their audience. It
was also the result of visionary women's own affective and literary style,

rians (Cambridge: Cambridge University Press, 1986), 70–72. On John and Mary Robins, see Friedman, *Blasphemy, Immorality, and Anarchy,* 156–60.

53. Eleanor Davies, *To Parliament* (1641), 11.

54. Keith Thomas, *Religion and the Decline of Magic* (New York: Scribner's, 1971),
133–37. Hill, *World Turned Upside Down,* 160.

55. Hill, *World Turned Upside Down,* 254. Owen Watkins remarks that Trapnel's
writing "shows a remarkable freedom from aggressive self-concern" (*The Puritan Experiment,* 93).

for if respectable women were constrained by convention to behave with humility and modesty, the female visionary was constrained to behave as though she were literally out of her mind.

VISIONARY EXPRESSION AND THE GENDER ORDER

Another question was, "what moved you to silence at
any time when you ceased from speaking? Was it with
you as with other good men, Ministers, . . . who cease
at discretion, either having no more to say, or having
spent their strength of body, or having wearied the
people?" . . . [I answered] "It was as if the Clouds did
open and receive me into them, and I was swallowed
up."

> *Anna Trapnel,* The Cry of a Stone

To the magistrates and congregations who listened to women's accounts of their visionary experiences, the female prophet's right to exercise public authority was not based on the recognition that she possessed qualities of leadership that had previously gone unnoticed. On the contrary, we have seen that beliefs about the traditional and quite familiar qualities of passivity, irrationality, and passion that had justified women's *absence* from the political arena were used to justify their visionary activities as well. "As for . . . Anna Trapnel," wrote a contemporary witness of her trances,

> it is, (to be plain) to me a very strange dispensation, yet I am persuaded she hath communion with God in it. . . . If she did continue in it but for one or two days, I should be apt to think she might do it when she would . . . save for two things. First, she is so stiffened in her God that were she not warm, one would think her dead. Secondly: Because she cannot make a verse when she is her self. But it is strange to me she should continue for eight days.[56]

In one London Baptist church, Anne Harriman threatened to leave the congregation because a male member had said he would not walk with those who gave women liberty to speak in church, and she would not

---

56. Letter of December 21, 1654, quoted by Champlin Burrage in "Anna Trapnel's Prophecies," Rawlinson Manuscripts A. 21. 325, Bodleian Library, Oxford. My thanks to Miriam Garber for allowing me to read her unpublished paper on Anna Trapnel ("Anna Trapnel and the Protectorate").

walk where she had not got this right. The church, untypically, acceded to her demand, stating that "a woman . . . being a prophetess . . . may speak, prophesy, pray, with a veil. Others may not."[57] Even radical sectarians insisted on making a distinction between authority that was spiritual and communal and authority that was political and hierarchical. The Fifth Monarchists, who allowed women to testify, vote, act as spies, and even meet separately from men, insisted on a distinction not only between preaching and prophesying but between prophesying as a leader of the church and as a "mere" vessel of God. Thus, John Rogers argued that women "keep from public preaching, or prophesying, or teaching as officers or ministers do. . . . Now we plead not for this; but for the common ordinary liberty due to them as members of the Church, viz. to speak, object, offer, or vote with the rest."[58] Rogers's admonition to his women congregants, urging them to be both courageous and deferential, painfully conveys the awkwardness of his, and their, position:

> To women, I wish ye be not too forward, and yet not too backward, but hold fast your liberty . . . keep your ground which Christ hath won and got for you; maintain your right, defend your liberty, even to the life, lose it not, but be courageous, and keep it. And yet be cautious too. . . . Your silence may sometimes be the best advocate of your orderly liberty, and the sweetest evidence of your prudence and modesty. . . . And yet ye ought not by your silence to betray your liberty, trouble your consciences, lose your privileges and rights; or see the truth taken away or suffer before your eyes; but I say, be not too hasty nor too high.[59]

Thus, the image of women's essential liminality was given added resonance even by those writers who were most supportive of women's improved opportunities. And for them, as for their less sympathetic contemporaries, a woman who interrupted a parliamentary meeting by babbling or singing, her eyes glazed, would probably seem less of an anomaly than one who tried to appear as a concerned citizen or minister

---

57. Claire Cross, "The Church in England, 1646–1660," in *The Interregnum: The Quest for Settlement, 1640–1660,* ed. G. E. Aylmer (Hamden: Archon Books, 1972), 116–17.

58. Rogers, *Ohel or Beth-shemesh,* quoted in Joyce Irwin, *Women in Radical Protestantism, 1525–1675* (New York and Toronto: Edwin Mellen Press, 1979), 176.

59. Rogers, *Ohel or Beth-shemesh,* 476–77, quoted in Ludlow, "'Arise and Be Doing,'" 23. In another Fifth Monarchist meeting, one Sister Harrison raised the issue of women speaking, causing a fierce dispute, after which ordinary women were given no rights at all, but a prophetess was allowed to speak, prophesy, and pray (Capp, *Fifth Monarchy Men,* 174; Ludlow, "'Arise and Be Doing,'" 20–24).

engaging in public theological debates or rational biblical exegesis. One aristocratic lady learned this to her cost when she tried to address a Separatist congregation in London in 1645. After apologizing for "some bodily indispositions," she began speaking in a low voice on the nature of love. Being urged to speak louder, she became confused and was finally shouted down. "In brief, there was such laughing, confusion and disorder at the meeting, that the minister professed he never saw the like."[60] A woman who disturbed the public peace by singing or mumbling prophecies risked imprisonment or worse, but her audience was far less likely to laugh.

Thus, the prophet's only means of establishing her credibility in a public forum was to present herself as a defender of the natural order in which she was subservient while simultaneously affirming that she had transcended that natural order. She had to convince her audience that she was both less and more than human. So Mary Pope, "finding God over-powering my spirit, and as it were forcing of me on," admonished wives to render unto husbands only what husbands were due and defended her right to speak as a prophet:

> Whatsoever governors we are under, whether magistrates, ministers, husbands, fathers, or masters, we should not obey them . . . farther than is according to God's commission . . . seeing David held it no disparagement, though a king, to take the advice of a woman, (I Sam. 25.33) and seeing that God himself, hath in many great acts honored women as well as men, and above men.[61]

Yet she professed herself to be appalled by the specter of social breakdown that followed upon the claims of a woman's individual conscience:

> Principles of nature, vary not as languages do, and if principles of nature be inviolable, and indispensible, much more is divinity. Opinions ought not to be the rule of things, but the nature of the things it self. . . . In the prophet Jeremiah's time, the women did not bake cakes to the queen of heaven without their husbands (Jer. 44.19). But now in our time there be some teachers that have taught our women to follow their new found out truths, without their husbands: and I think in some families there are as many opinions as

---

60. Edwards, *Gangraena*, 86. On Lady Eleanor's experience before the magistrates, who ridiculed her propensity to compose arcane anagrams, see P. Heylyn, *Cyprianus Anglicus* (London, 1688), Part. 2, 266, quoted in Cope, *"Dame Eleanor Davies,"* 99.
61. Pope, *A Treatise of Magistracy*, 42, 108.

people. . . . When we see such division come to pass, we shall know the end of the world is near.[62]

We find this disjunction between women's portrayal of themselves as supernatural and as human beings—or more abstractly, their rendering of the discourses of religion and politics—permeating the very grammar of their visionary texts. Eleanor Davies's visions were conveyed in fractured feminine images that, to many readers, went well beyond the limits of sane discourse:

> Where belonging to passages of *inns*; the one frequented all hours, and drinking, not more free than the others darksom *grates close*; famished there no few. But requisit *bridges*, and the like, the true *narrow way* (by suffering) that leads *to life*; From him a proper *passage* or mention. Straits of the *virgins-womb* had passed; besides seafaring-persons his followers in that way not unexperienced, afore arrive the *welcome haven*.[63]

In other passages, Lady Eleanor changed the "A" and "O" of the quotation to "Da" and "Do," the abbreviations of her two married surnames, thus making herself the Alpha and Omega, the first and the last. Yet this arrogant woman, who viewed the deaths of her two husbands as vindications of her spiritual calling and who lathered her prophetic texts with accounts of family grievances, also chose the institution of patriarchal marriage as one of her most sustained metaphors for true piety. Interestingly, the moment Lady Eleanor portrayed the voice of a jealous God as that of a husband, she also assumed a syntactically straightforward prose style, expressing herself in quite respectable discursive language:

> Suppose a man after his marriage to a young virgin, should say, my experience is more than yours, I cannot always walk hand in hand with you, neither may I keep you in a cloister that will not be for your health or my profit, neither must you forget your covenant to be subject to my desires not tending to the harm of either of us; . . . many strangers will strive to be your servants; not all for your beauty but some for malice and envy to me: Though your intent be good in all things, yet because I am very jealous of mine honor, entertain none in that manner; . . . in the end they will draw your affection from me; Besides, much resort though she be never so chaste, is dalliance the mark of

62. Ibid., 32, 39.
63. Lady Eleanor, *The Restitution of Prophecy: That Buried Talent to Be Revived* (1651), Introduction, n.p. Cope interprets Lady Eleanor's obscure grammar differently, as a deliberate attempt to confuse the majority of readers ("*Dame Eleanor Davies*," 15, 134).

a known harlot, which sort of woman I would have you differ from. . . . Yes doubtless I am the Lord thy God.[64]

Similarly, Anna Trapnel, who delivered her public prophecies in a trance state, as if inundated by the spirit, combined biblical themes with images of women's fluidity in order to validate her own authority to prophesy. "Then the Lord made His rivers flow," she wrote,

> which soon broke down the banks of an ordinary capacity, and . . . mounted my spirits into a praying and singing frame. . . . The Lord [will] be . . . a place of broad rivers and streams, . . . these are rivers that the waters rise up to the ankles, yea to the knees, and so to the loins, and at length they become a flowing high spring, . . . this is water of Life, it recovers the dying vitals, and fainting spirits, the which none of men's strong liquors of arts and sciences can do, neither can any compounded water of human invention.[65]

This was language and behavior quite unlike her reasoned declaration that she should be respected as an adult, taxpaying citizen. "You call me vagabond," she wrote to the magistrates who attempted to discredit her,

> but how will you make that good? . . . I lived with my mother till she died, . . . then I kept house with the means my mother left me, and payed taxes toward maintaining of the army then in the field; and this I did not grudgingly, but freely and willingly; I sold my plate and rings, and gave the money to the public use; you did not call me vagabond then.[66]

Anna Trapnel was well aware of her audiences' expectation that she would show herself to be either a monster, a whore, or a madwoman:

> My desire is to imitate that approved *Hannah* . . . who was in bitterness of soul, and prayed unto the Lord. . . . And if handmaids in these days pray and weep for their Lord . . . such praying cannot be borne by the inhabitants of this nation; there is such an evil spirit of misconstruing. . . . *England's* rulers and clergy do judge the Lords hand-maid to be mad, and under the administration of evil angels, and a witch, and many other evil terms they raise up to make me odious, and abhorr'd in the hearts of good and bad, that do not know me.[67]

Perhaps Trapnel's ecstatic manner was an authentic attempt to imitate the behavior of the ancient Hannah. It may have also helped her to

64. Audeley, *A Warning to the Dragon and All His Angels*, 94–95. Another factor in her changed style may have been the fact that the more incoherent passage was written after her incarceration in Bedlam, while this tract was composed at the beginning of her career. (Cope, "*Dame Eleanor Davies*," 10, 214.)
65. Trapnel, *Report and Plea*, 20, 57.
66. Ibid., 50.
67. Ibid., Preface, n.p.

endure ridicule. "And . . . there came many to see me," she wrote, "some out of goodwill . . . and others came to gaze, and others to catch at my words, so as to reproach me; but the Lord taught me how to speak before them all."[68] Ironically, her behavior must have also helped reinforce the perception of many in her audience that she was indeed mad.

Given popular preconceptions about the acceptable directions of women's religious and political writing, it should not surprise us that visionary women's strong individual characters and divergent social backgrounds often appear to be submerged beneath the weight of symbolic baggage described in the previous two chapters. The Belgian Catholic Antonia Bourignon and the Fifth Monarchist Mary Cary seem to have been thoroughly opposed both in temperament and in social position. Bourignon, an aristocrat who established her own community of disciples, was dictatorial, ascetic, and elitist, while Cary, a member of a radical sect composed largely of artisans and laborers, was compassionate and democratic. Yet both characterized themselves, and were described by their patrons, as passive and inadequate. Antonia Bourignon defended her right to preach by saying that "they ought to let God speak by a woman, if it be his pleasure, since he spoke in former times to a prophet by a beast." Cary, who presented a systematic program of social reform that dealt with the issues of wage ceilings, a postal service, and a proposed stamp tax, conveyed the same negative message, although in very different tones:

> If any shall hereby receive any light [from my prophecies], . . . let them bless the Lord for it . . . for I am a very weak, and unworthy instrument, and have not done this work by any strength of my own, but have often been made sensible, that I could do no more herein . . . of my self, than a pencil or pen can do, when no hand guides it; being daily made sensible of my own insufficiency to do anything, as of myself.[69]

Does this persistent self-deprecation imply that Antonia Bourignon or Mary Cary were merely parroting the behavior that had been imposed on them by a male-dominated culture? Or does it imply that *men* were the victims of cold-blooded manipulation by *women*, who consciously used traditional language and behavior as a covert strategy of self-expression? Perhaps Katherine Chidley was being disingenuous when she challenged the Puritan Thomas Edwards to a formal debate, saying that,

68. Ibid., 15.
69. Cary, *The Little Horn's Doom and Downfall*, "To the Reader." For a different interpretation of this passage, see Hobby, *Virtue of Necessity*, 30. Cary's economic proposals are in her *Twelve Proposals*.

if defeated, she would submit gracefully: "But if you [ministers] overcome me, your conquest will not be great, for I am a poor woman, and
unmeet to deal with you. . . . This is my charity towards them, though
I know them not by face, and I think I may boldly say that none of them
knows me."[70] In most other cases, however, I am inclined to believe in
the sincerity of women's gestures of self-denial, for while these same
women might have been verbally aggressive and physically brutal in
collective acts of parish protest or in presenting petitions to magistrates,
most were unaccustomed to individual public leadership of any kind.
They may indeed have had to reach a state of near catatonia or hysteria
in order to convince themselves, as well as others, that their inspiration
was genuine.[71] The articulate Mary Cary surely spoke for many women
when she wrote,

> Not but that there are many godly women, many who have indeed received
> the Spirit; but in how small a measure is it? How weak are they? and how
> unable to prophesy? . . . Indeed, they have tasted of the sweetness of the spirit;
> and having tasted, are longing for more, and are ready to receive from those
> few that are in any measure furnished with the gifts of the spirit for proph-
> esying; but they are generally very unable to communicate to others, though
> they would do it many times in their families, among their children and
> servants; and when they would be communicating to others into whose
> company they come, though sometimes some dry sprinklings come from
> them, yet at other times they find themselves dry and barren.[72]

Such a one may have been Mrs. Attaway, who claimed that she had not
taken it upon herself to preach but only to exercise her gifts. After
espousing a doctrine of universal salvation to an audience in Bell-Alley,
she affirmed "that she desired to lay down her crown at the feet of Christ;
and wished that shame and confusion might cover her face for ever if she
had any confidence in her self." Later, standing before a mixed congregation, she responded to a man who advanced an argument for infant
baptism, saying "she was not very fit to argue those questions."[73] When

---

70. Chidley, *The Justification of the Independent Churches of Christ*, 80–81. Chidley made no systematic attempt to counter her adversary Thomas Edwards's attacks on
women, although she was tireless in her arguments in every other respect.

71. On women and parish protest, see Ludlow, "'Arise and Be Doing,'" 48–64.
Women beat Anglican priests, tearing their robes and scratching their faces. Joan Hoby
said she did not "care a pin nor a fart for my Lords Grace of Canterbury" but hoped to
live to see him hanged (Ludlow, "'Arise and Be Doing,'" 49). Women also felt free to
argue with priests on points of theology (53–54). On women in riots, see 263.

72. Cary, *A New and More Exact Mappe*, 237–38.

73. Edwards, *Gangraena*, 119, 120. This account was certainly biased against
women preachers, but it jibes with their own general statements of self-deprecation.

another young woman fell into visionary trances, her mother defended the authenticity of her preaching by saying, "the Judge thought she feigned: but as soon as she was out of her fit, did not know what was past, as all the beholders did see, only an innocent bashful girl, without any confidence at all when she was out of her fits."

Perhaps even more inhibiting than fear of public exposure was the degree to which the thrust of women's spiritual creativity was deflected by social strictures on women as public figures. We have seen that the visionary's spiritual transformation was often triggered by and nourished by her experience as mother or daughter. We have also seen (in chapter 1) that the image of motherhood was one redolent of spiritual and moral authority. But this maternal authority had no relevance whatsoever to the authority of the political thinker or actor. Even Queen Elizabeth, who exploited maternal and virginal imagery to dramatize her fidelity and love for her country, tended to resort to masculine imagery when she presented herself as a head of state, an incarnation of the sacred principle of kingship. "I have the body of a weak and feeble woman," went her famous speech to the forces arrayed against the Spanish Armada, "but I have the heart and stomach of a king, and of a king of England too." She also referred to herself habitually as "prince," using the term "princess" to refer to discredited female monarchs like Mary Queen of Scots. In a message to Parliament in 1601, two years before Elizabeth's death, the speaker noted that "she said her kingly prerogative (for so she termed it) was tender."[74]

Thus, bypassing the true psychological roots of their own visionary impulses, women relied on the image of the good wife, not the mother, in their political writings, an image that connoted not authority but subordination, even when presented in highly positive terms, as in Mary Pocock's mystical tract: "Here is now the soul in the body, the husband and wife, God and the man. This is the representative, king and parliament, whose happy condition is bound up in the enjoyment of each other, in the union of the manhood, in the power of the Godhead: And this is the glory of the king."[75] When women came to justify the au-

74. Leah Sinanoglou Marcus, "Shakespeare's Comic Heroines, Elizabeth I, and the Political Uses of Androgyny," in *Women in the Middle Ages and the Renaissance: Literary and Historical Perspectives*, ed. Mary Beth Rose (Syracuse: Syracuse University Press, 1986), 135–53. Marcus states that Elizabeth's masculine imagery surfaced most frequently in her public pronouncements (137).
75. Pocock, *The Mystery of the Deity in the Humanity*, 16, quoted in Smith, *Perfection Proclaimed*, 211.

thority of their own religious movements vis-à-vis the state, they referred not to the straightforward moral authority of the mother but to
the derivative authority of the wife as steward for the husband who is
unavoidably absent. Thus, Katherine Chidley compared the autonomy
of the Independent congregation to that of a wife who acts as a deputy
husband:

> Yea, the power of the *keys* is as absolutely the *Church's*, which is *Christ's
> wife*, as the power of the keys of the *family* are the mistress's, to whom the
> *husband* giveth full power . . . and I think no reasonable man will affirm (if
> her husband give her sole power in his absence) that she is subordinate to
> any of her servants. Now . . . Christ . . . hath delivered the power to his
> *church*.[76]

Maternal imagery did appear in many women's writings, of course,
but it was generally used in conjunction with abstractions like God or
the church, rarely as a symbol of the prophet's own spiritual experience
or authority. "O the milk that runs through Christ's breasts!" wrote
Anna Trapnel: "Come sucklings take it in."[77] Eleanor Davies also portrayed God and the church as female (though hardly feminine): "the
church of God being then with child, travailing in birth, crying and
pained to be delivered of the man child, roaring like a lion, the whole
forest ringing."[78] When women did use maternal symbols in relation to
their own works, they often emphasized the vulnerability of the baby
and the passivity of the mother. Sarah Jones was positively lyrical when
she described the righteous congregation, "out of whose bellies flow
rivers of waters of life . . . holy brethren such are made partakers of the
divine nature," but the birth of her own text is described thusly: "I
presume to *father* this naked child without scholastic phrases, or school
learning to dress it and garnish it." Elizabeth Warren also worried
about the ill effects of her bad writing: "My dull meditations appearing
unpolished, are produced like abortives in an hour unexpected, and
may seem unreasonable" (an interesting counterpoint to the superla-
tives of her male patron, who praised her "humility of spirit, elegancy
of style, solidity of matter, height of fancy, depth of judgment, clearness
of apprehension, strength of reason, all sweetly met together . . . by the

76. Chidley, *A New-Yeares-Gift*, 13.
77. S.1.42.th., 84, Bodleian Library, Oxford, quoted in Cohen, "Prophecy and
Madness," 425.
78. Audeley, *A Warning to the Dragon*, 3.

phoenix of this age, . . . the envy and glory of her sex"). And thus spoke
Mary Pope:

> Now your unworthy handmaid in Christ, which hath been long in travail, yet
> now in hopes, that the time draweth near of her delivery, doth present to you
> (worthies) these lines. . . . For God hath given me faith to believe, that this
> child shall not be abortive, but shall . . . be born a goodly child. . . . God
> having made me a mother in Israel, I thought it my duty to put my helping
> hand, . . . and finding God over-powering my spirit, and as it were forcing
> of me on, for the improving of those talents he hath given me for His glory,
> and serving of my generation.[79]

Yet if women generally felt unable to apply positive images of cosmic
motherhood to their own spiritual creativity, they also eschewed the
image of the monster mother and her wretched, evil children. There are,
to my knowledge, no passages in women's writings comparable to that
of Abiezer Coppe, denying accusations that he was a Ranter:

> There are many spurious brats, lately born: and because their parents have
> looked upon me as a rich merchant they have took on them the boldness to
> lay them at my door, etc. Some of them (indeed) look somewhat like my
> children. But however, to put all out of doubt, whether they are mine, or no:
> I will not be so full of foolish pity, as to spare them. I will turn them out of
> doors, and starve them to death. And as for those which I know are not mine
> own: I will be so holily cruel, as to dispatch them.[80]

Unlike the male minister, who might refer to himself while preaching
as the breasts of God or the bride ravished by Christ, or the male
sectarian, who might express his own religiosity in sexual metaphors and
actions that were even more explicit, women visionaries did not draw
attention to their own bodies as sources of either passion or nourishment.
In fact, they rarely portrayed their bodies as metaphors at all. Rather,
their passages of damnation and desire are merged with passages of
bodily annihilation.[81] Sarah Wight, who was struck lame, mute, and
blind through guilt over sins committed against her mother, felt her
damnation as a fire that surrounded her: "*I felt myself, soul and body*

---

79. Mrs. Sarah Jones, *This Is the Light's Appearance* (1650), n.p. (emphasis added).
Warren, *Spiritual Thrift*, "To the Christian Reader," n.p. Pope, *A Treatise of Magistracy*,
"The Epistle Dedicatory, To the Christian Reader," C2v. Eleanor Davies also referred to
her pamphlets as "babes" (*The Restitution of Prophecy*, sig. A3r, quoted in Smith, *Perfection Proclaimed*, 63).
80. *Coppes Return* (1651), quoted in Davis, *Fear, Myth, and History*, 56.
81. Nigel Smith emphasizes that women saw their bodies as maps of their spiritual
experiences, but he does not analyze the specific forms of bodily expression women
displayed as distinct from men (*Perfection Proclaimed*, 43, 47–48, 50, 80, 87).

*in fire and brimstone already. If all the fire and brimstone in London,
and all the pitch and tar, should all be in one fire, and I walking in the
midst of that fire; this was my condition.*" She later exhibited her body,
wasted by seventy-five days of partial fasting, as the site of triumphant
combat between the forces of good and evil, announcing to members of
her congregation gathered around the bedside,

> Now I have been four days in the grave, with Lazarus, and now I am risen
> to live with Jesus Christ. . . . Now I have my desire; I desired nothing but a
> crucified Christ and I have him; a crucified Christ, a naked Christ; I have him
> and nothing else. . . . I am so full of the creator that I can take in none of the
> creature. . . . I do eat, but it's meat to eat that the world knows not of. . . .
> His words were found, and I did eat them.[82]

Elizabeth Avery affirmed herself "more enabled to act by the spirit, when
I am most straightened in the flesh."[83] "Vision!" cried Anna Trapnel,
"the body crumbles before it, and becomes weak." Trapnel, who carried
knives to bed and lay in ditches during her obsession with suicide, told
her audience, after fasting for twelve days, "the scent of dead souls
turned out of the grave was still in my nostrils." She also portrayed
herself as an inspired martyr, impaled on the horns of a cosmic bull with
Oliver Cromwell's face.[84]

Women visionaries both before and after the English Revolution,
whose writings were chiefly apolitical or mystical, employed maternal
and sexual imagery with much greater freedom. One example from the
final decade of the century, Ann Bathurst's visionary diary, contains this
account of her praying for the victims of an earthquake in Jamaica:

> And my spirit was at Jamaica lying on my face at prayer. . . . And I lay
> stretched out on the earth, licking the dust and then breathing in the earth as
> brooding over it for a new Creation. . . . I milked milk out of my breasts on
> the earth. . . . Still I see my spirit much on its face, with my breasts touching
> the earth . . . and I feel the witness of fire on my breasts . . . in my left breast,
> brooding, hatching as't were and nourishing a flame to break forth. . . . O'tis
> love's fire that burns and heals and warms! Warm, warm love, warm
> through blood. I am big and warm with expectations what this warm healing

82. Jessey, *The Exceeding Riches*, 27–30, and see Dailey, "The Visitation of Sarah Wight," 447, 448.
83. E[lizabeth] Avery, *Scripture-Prophecies Opened, Which Are to Be Accomplished in These Last Times, Which Do Attend the Second Coming of Christ* (London, 1647), 17.
84. Trapnel, *Cry of a Stone*, 13, 74, analyzed in Smith, *Perfection Proclaimed*, 94.

power will come to. . . . When it breaks open it will be as sun-shine after rain. I flame, and it satisfies most of my desires.[85]

Elsewhere she described herself waiting for night to come and bring with it a vision of God: "[I] hoped at night that I might lie in his arms as I had done the night before . . . there I held Him and would not let Him go, but that He would lie all night as a bundle of myrrh between my breasts, and He was willingly held."[86] Women may well have had such visions during the Puritan revolution, but no one of them ever found the patronage, even within the radical sects, to enable her to publish it. Those few women who believed they had given birth to Jesus expressed themselves verbally or in private letters, and we know they existed only through hostile pamphlet literature or the reports of the magistrates who arrested them.[87] Even Mary Cary, the most radical woman prophet of the 1640s, took care that she was shielded by patrons who introduced her to the public as a virtuous and respectable gentlewoman.

Of course there was no barrier to the visionary's appropriation of *negative* female imagery, particularly maternal imagery, to castigate her enemies, especially the clergy (or "clergy-puff," as Anna Trapnel said), and women used this negative imagery more vividly and with greater energy than they did images of nurturing and fulfillment. Thus, Mary Cary affirmed the equality of women and men in rather pallid prose: "That which is given to the Husband [Jesus], the wife must partake of: for there is nothing that he possesses, which She [the Saints] hath not a right unto."[88] She was much less restrained in describing the feminine decadence of Rome, predicting that the people will hate her "for her filthiness, and cursed lewdness . . . and make her naked . . . [and] they will not only make her naked, but will eat her flesh: will make her destitute, not only of her outward robes of pomp and glory, but will eat

---

85. Diary of Anne Bathurst, 1692, Rawlinson Manuscripts, D. 1262–63/480.
86. Ibid., fol. 45.
87. Mary Gadbury testified that she had given birth to the Spirit (Ellis, *Pseudochristus*, 39–40). Mary Adams claimed that she was pregnant with the Holy Ghost (*An Account of Mary Adams, The Ranters Monster* [London, 1652]). Mrs. Pordage wrote to Abiezer Coppe about a metaphoric birth: "What though we are weaker vessels, women etc. yet . . . we shall mount up with wings as Eagles, . . . when the *Man-Child Jesus* is brought forth *In Us*" (Abiezer Coppe, *Some Sweet Sips, of Some Spirituall Wine* [London, 1649], 40). A Warwickshire woman thought she was the "mother of God and of all things living" (Capp, *Fifth Monarchy Men*, 33). A woman stripped naked in Whitehall to mock a sermon preached there and was chastised in David Brown's *The Naked Woman* (1652). Anne Hall was reported to have cohabited with two male lay preachers and to have expected to give birth to a child who spoke in tongues (T. J., *A Brief Representation*).
88. Cary, *A New and More Exact Mappe*, 54.

her very flesh." Elizabeth Poole envisioned the weak and distressed state of the country as the body of a diseased woman, "full of imperfection, crooked, weak, sickly, imperfect." Eleanor Davies envisioned "the blaspheming blasts of the little Horn, that had eyes like a man, and such a mouth as much to say, *that mouth speaking such great things, a woman's and no man's* . . . Jezebel by name . . . this bloodthirsty mistress of *charms* and spells."[89] She also railed against Parliament, "the nursing mother of *dragons*," against "that strumpet hag *Rome*," and against the Anglican church, "this indulgent witch, the mother of harlots," who may appear beautiful and upright, but whose golden crowns cannot deceive,

> or hair as the hair of women. . . . Think ye those long locks . . . can cover your knotted crowns from the razor, or hide your pined bodies pinched of provender like neighing horses prepared to the battle. . . . The faithful city is become a harlot, having in her hand a cupfull of abominations, witchcraft and blasphemy . . . mixing holy things with filthy excrements. . . . Is this the true mother; is this the woman she is taken for, with eagle's wings? . . . In no wise in her there is no bowels of a mother, though they strive to the end of the world."[90]

Clearly, it was no easy task for women visionaries to navigate between the Scylla of their audiences' praise of them as mindless vessels and the Charybdis of their critics' attacks on them as aggressive or self-serving. The editor of Elizabeth Avery's treatise wrote flatteringly on her behalf, "the power of God doth appear in [this work] in respect of the weakness and contemptibleness of the instrument whom he doth here employ; as formerly it hath been his course in doing great things by weakest means, and so by such foolishness he doth bring to nought the wisdom of the wise." The published reply to the treatise, written by Avery's brother, barely mentioned the substance of her arguments but expressed shock at the fact that she had written a book at all. "You seem to be lifted up," he said, "as if you were a goddess, as if all should bow unto you. . . . Your printing of a Book, beyond the custom of your sex, doth rankly smell, but the exaltation of your self in the way of your opinions, is above all." One can readily empathize with Elizabeth

89. Ibid., 173; on Poole, see *The Clarke Papers*, 151; Eleanor Davies, *Her Blessing to Her Beloved Daughter*, 13–14.
90. Davies, *Her Blessing to Her Beloved Daughter*, 17; *A Warning to the Dragon*, 19–20, 28, 29.

Avery's own rather strained rejoinder: "If I am mad . . . it is to God; and
if I am in my right mind, it is for the benefit of others."[91]

CONCLUSION: WOMEN OUT OF TIME

Methinks I see not only foolish virgins slumbering and
sleeping, but the wise virgins are also in a slumber,
but when the bridegroom's appearance shall be
manifested, shall they still lie in a slumber? I believe
otherwise, that there shall be such an awakening of all
things, the very foundation of all things shall be
shaken by that foundation that shall stand forever.
                                   Anna Trapnel, A Legacy for Saints

Did the female prophet have a mind? Mary Cary, as even her critics
recognized, had a very formidable mind.[92] So, some would argue, did
Eleanor Davies, although she may have lost and regained hers as she
passed in and out of prison and in and out of public favor. Clearly,
visionary women differed in their individual temperaments and intellectual capacities as well as in their prophetic vocations. Mary Cary
viewed herself as a minister and teacher, using language that was at once
ardent and pragmatic; Lady Eleanor was a student of symbolism who
lived at various inns called "Angel" in memory of the angel who visited
her in prison; Anna Trapnel was a mystic for whom the sight of a rock
in a field might trigger a flood of singing on Peter as her rock and
sustainer. Yet even Trapnel found a public voice that was as much the
fruit of her own intelligence and political activism as it was the product
of a disembodied trance state. Not only did women as prophets display
an understanding of the economic and political issues of the time; they
also turned visionary language into a form of political resistance. Thus,
they distanced themselves from negative female stereotypes by applying
those stereotypes to their male enemies; with other women they formed

    91. Avery, *Scripture-Prophecies Opened*, Preface, n.p. *The Copy of a Letter Written
by Mr. Thomas Parker* . . . (London, 1650), 13.
    92. Hugh Peters's preface to Cary's *The Little Horn's Doom and Downfall* stated
that Cary wrote so well and in so scholarly a fashion that "you might easily think she
plowed with anothers Heifer, were not the contrary well known." A published critique
questioned her biblical exegesis but acknowledged her intelligence: "And truly it is a pity
that a woman of her parts should build with so much confidence upon so rotten a
foundation" (*The Account Audited, Or the Date of the Resurrection of the Witnesses,
Pretended to Be Demonstrated by M. Cary a Minister* [London, 1649], 2).

associations that sustained them in the pulpit and in prison; and they exercised pastoral as well as prophetic authority within their congregations, speaking to appreciative men as well as women.

Yet it remains true that, whatever the prophet's individual character and capacity, and however appreciative her audience, her presence in the public arena constrained her as firmly, in some ways more firmly, than the walls of the nunnery did the behavior of the Catholic visionary of the Middle Ages. It also placed her in a profoundly vulnerable position, for the status of visionary or prophet was not a fixed social definition analogous to that of the minister or magistrate; it was one end of a very slippery continuum, the other end of which was the polluted whore or witch. Depending on a host of factors—her own class position, the politics of the moment, the reactions of family members—she was liable to move back and forth along this continuum in the perception of her audience or readership; or, like Anna Trapnel, she might find herself simultaneously abused as a witch and defended as a prophet by the confused mob that jostled for position around her bed.[93] Moreover, the degree of reasonableness or maturity displayed in her writings was often in direct proportion to the degree of hostility she aroused. Katherine Chidley, the most rational and assertive of all preaching women, who organized debates with ministers, led her own Independent congregation, and wrote extensively on political and social issues, was vilified as "a brazen-faced audacious old woman resembled unto Jael." The prophet Elizabeth Poole, who was received as a respectable gentlewoman by members of Parliament, was also described as a "virgin," "girl," and "monstrous witch full of all deceitful craft." The invalid Sarah Wight, the only prominent visionary actually a girl living with her mother and under the constant tutelage of the minister who edited her works, was also the only one not subjected to extremes of adulation and contempt.[94] No wonder Eleanor Davies's daughter Lucy, wanting to honor her mother as a sage after her death, adorned her grave with the tribute, "In a woman's body, a man's spirit."

Indeed, what we have seen in contemplating women as prophets, whether the astute social critic Mary Cary or the flamboyant and abstruse Lady Eleanor, is a collective mentality stretched to the limit, and

93. For a general discussion of the instability of women as subjects in seventeenth-century culture, see Catherine Belsey, *The Subject of Tragedy: Identity and Difference in Renaissance Drama* (New York and London: Methuen, 1985), 150, 153.

94. Edwards, *Gangraena*, 3:170–71, quoted in A. L. Morton, *The World of the Ranters: Religions Radicalism in the English Revolution* (London: Lawrence and Wishart, 1970), 33.

occasionally past the limits of coherent expression, by the contradictions of their public positions as females venturing onto the forbidden planet of male political discourse. Women not only had access to a restricted spiritual vocabulary; they also experienced a conflict between their impulse to preach in the mode of ministers carrying an ethical message and the need to present themselves as sibyls, not teachers. Indeed, no one of these preachers and writers, however personally gifted, could put one foot in front of the other as firmly as did an obscure countrywoman named Dorothy Burch, who composed a purely religious catechism in response to her minister's attacks on her and other members of her church:

> Because my self and others will not honour him in the way he is in . . . now he reviles me and others almost where ever he comes; my self heard him say, that we were poor ignorant simple people, and as concerning God we knew nothing, . . . which much grieved me to hear. . . . The Lord hath promised to teach his people, though not all alike; it came in my mind to see what God had taught me; I set pen to paper, . . . asking my self questions, and answering them.[95]

We have, I hope, attained some insight as to why so many observers have been convinced of the female prophet's emotional and intellectual instability. In terms of conventional definitions of lunacy, the men who insisted that they were incarnations of Jesus or specific messengers out of the Book of Revelation were surely no less demented than the women who claimed to be simple generic handmaids of God.[96] Men, however, were able to fashion a public persona that was at once more coherent and more individualized than women's, one in which the emotions that attended their religious conversions became an integral part of their prophetic discourse. Ironically, they had more access to feminine maternal and sexual symbolism than women did.[97] Indeed, the male mechanic preacher, however aberrant his message or behavior, was part of a cultural tradition reaching back to the long-haired charismatic carpenter's son known as Jesus or even further back, to the unlettered prophets of the Old Testament. Like the *topos* of the medieval hermit or

95. Dorothy Burch, *A Catechism of the Several Heads of Christian Religion* (London, 1646), Preface, n.p.
96. William Franklin had a history of mental illness, wife-beating, and spiritual delusion. He was expelled from his congregation before teaming up with Mary Gadbury (Ellis, *Pseudochristus*, 6–7).
97. For several examples of male maternal visions see Smith, *Perfection Proclaimed*, 58, 60–61, 65, 81.

that of the modern lonesome cowboy, he was entirely recognizable to himself and others in cultural terms, however isolated he might have felt himself to be in personal terms.

For most prophetic women, the final solution to the ambiguities of their position was to project their utopian visions of equality into a spiritual millennium outside normal life. Mary Cary and Eleanor Davies expected the natural order to end in their lifetime; the books of Daniel and Revelation were to be realized in their day. Elizabeth Avery was also concerned with the millennium, particularly the resurrection of the dead. This focus on a world without time, "when the streets shall be filled with boys and girls" and men and women live to a great age, was surely liberating for women. It may have also reflected what some theorists have called "women's time," a sensibility to the cyclical and eternal aspects of existence, as opposed to the linear, organized march of time as it is seen in history.[98] In terms of winning a new position for women within the natural, historical order, it was clearly self-defeating.

A more heartening aspect of visionary women's public identity was their membership in religious congregations, where they were personally known and where their audiences were predisposed to view their visionary insights as credible. Almost every prophet of note preached as a member of an independent church or sect and relied on the physical, moral, and financial support of her spiritual "family." Indeed, the religious ecstasies of prophets like Sarah Wight were profoundly social events, often conducted in rooms crowded with congregational members who supported them in their spiritual "illness" and who, in turn, experienced a kind of vicarious sanctification by their witness of the prophet's own spiritual labor. Women prophets also engaged in more general political activities along with other women, agitating against churching and presenting petitions to Parliament. Eleanor Davies was again the exception, pursuing an aristocratic life-style utterly distant from the ordinary men and women who constituted her audience, though even Lady Eleanor found a circle of women in Lichfield with whom she attended church and discussed religious matters.

In the end, however, the potential of even collective behavior was limited for prophetic women, for all organized congregations, even radical congregations, excluded women from positions of real leader-

98. On linear time viewed as masculine, see Frieda Johles Forman, "Feminizing Time: An Introduction," in Taking Our Time: Feminist Perspectives on Temporality, ed. Frieda Johles Forman and Caoran Sowton (Oxford and New York: Oxford University Press, 1989), 4.

ship. Women spoke at Baptist meetings, but their authority to preach or to lead meetings was contested. No Leveler or Muggletonian tracts were ascribed to women, and despite the women's networks that must have existed in order to mobilize the thousands of signatures seen on petitions to the government, there is no record of women regularly attending the men's meetings. The Fifth Monarchist sect to which Mary Cary and Anna Trapnel belonged respected women as prophets and may even have tolerated separate women's meetings, but the agenda of those meetings was set by men, and much of women's public activity as church members was in support of these male leaders.[99] Mary Pocock, describing herself as a "member of the body" of enlightened people, defended the minister John Pordage when he was accused of heretical doctrine. Anna Trapnel's first vision took place in Whitehall, where she had accompanied the Fifth Monarchist Vavasour Powell when he was accused of sedition. Katherine Chidley's last public act in 1653 was to lead a contingent of women to the doors of Parliament to present a petition, signed by six thousand women, on behalf of the Leveler leader John Lillburne.[100]

By the end of the 1640s, the age of independent female prophecy was over.[101] The atmosphere of free expression and potential equality that had temporarily obscured class barriers during the Interregnum had not been sufficiently powerful to obscure the gender barrier, perhaps because the leaders of even the radical sects were beginning to see a fundamental contradiction in the very notion of a rationally organized society energized by occult spiritual forces. Visionary men like Gerrard Winstanley or John Rogers might have been seen to resolve this contradiction by embodying both unrestrained spiritual energy and practical leadership. Visionary *women*, active in a period of extreme political upheaval and

99. On women in the Levelers, see Ludlow, "'Arise and Be Doing,'" 243ff. On women in the Fifth Monarchy sect, see Capp, *Fifth Monarchy Men*, Biographical Appendix; Anne Laurence, "A Priesthood of She-Believers: Women and Congregations in Mid-Seventeenth Century England," *Women in the Church*, ed. W. J. Sheils and Diana Wood, Studies in Church History (Oxford: Basil Blackwell, 1990), 345–63.

100. On Pocock, see Smith, *Perfection Proclaimed*, 190, 211; on Chidley, see DBR, 1:140.

101. Fewer books by female prophets (excluding Quakers) were published after 1650 (Patricia Crawford, "Women's Published Writings, 1600–1700," in *Women in English Society, 1500–1800*, ed. Mary Prior [London and New York: Methuen, 1985], 211–82). Eleanor Davies died in 1653. Little is known about the later activities of Mary Cary, Katherine Chidley, and Anna Trapnel. Trapnel was in Wales seeking support for the movement in 1656; she was also reported to be considering a trip to the Continent. She published a tract in 1658, *Voice for the King of Saints and Nations*. She may have married at Woodbridge, Suffolk, in 1661 (Capp, *Fifth Monarchy Men*, 266; Garber, "Anna Trapnel and the Protectorate," 8).

intense political consciousness, made the contradiction more explicit. Spiritual women needed a new movement, a larger community whose leaders were explicitly concerned to dissolve *all* barriers to the equality of the saints. In 1654, when the first Quaker prophets appeared in London from out of the north, many must have felt that such a movement had finally been born.

PART TWO

Friends in Eden:
Gender and Spirituality in
Early Quakerism, 1650–1664

CHAPTER FOUR

Ecstasy and Self-Transcendence

"I wish [the Hasidim] weren't so afraid of new ideas."
"You want a great deal, Reuven. The Messiah has not yet
come. Will new ideas enable them to go on singing and
dancing?"
"We can't ignore the truth, abba."
"No. . . . We cannot ignore the truth. At the same time, we
cannot quite sing and dance as they do."

Chaim Potok, The Promise

INTRODUCTION

When old Elizabeth Hooton became the first person in England to preach the doctrines of George Fox the Quaker, her neighbors in the village of Skegby were probably not very much surprised. The wife of a prosperous farmer and mother of five children, she was already active in the local Baptist community, perhaps even a preacher, when she first encountered George Fox, and it was she, not her husband Oliver, who took the lead in converting to Quakerism. Hooton became Fox's disciple, aide, and comrade in the late 1640s. Not only did she preach to newly converted Friends; she opened her own house to meetings, including one in which Fox staggered the community by his miraculous cure of a woman possessed by the devil, who "would make such a noise in roaring, and sometimes lying along upon her belly upon the ground with her spirit and roaring and voice, that it would send all Friends in a heat and sweat."[1]

Thrown into prison as a disturber of the peace in Derby (1651), in York (1652), and in Lincoln (1654), Hooton became an aggressive agitator against the corruption of clergy and magistrates. "You make yourselves ridiculous to all people who have sense and reason," she wrote to Oliver Cromwell. "Your judges judge for reward, and at this York many which committed murder escaped through friends and money, and poor people for lesser facts are put to death. . . . They lie [in prison] worse

---

1. George Fox, *The Journal of George Fox,* ed. John L. Nickalls (London: Religious Society of Friends, 1975), 42.

than dogs for want of straw."[2] Years later, preaching in Barbados, she addressed the magistrates of the island about the rights of the black slaves of wealthy plantation owners who were accused of robbery. "Now it is the duty of every man to take care and see their family have sufficient food and anything else they stand in need of . . . that they may be kept from stealing and doing any thing that is evil."[3]

She seemed to be without terror of any worldly authority. When her husband died, making her proprietor of the family house, lands, and livestock, she embarked on a missionary voyage to America in the company of another old woman, Joan Brooksop. There she offended magistrates in Massachusetts and Rhode Island by returning to preach again and again and again, after being stripped, whipped from town to town while tied to the back of a cart, and abandoned in the forests. Once, having accompanied a pregnant friend several miles through the forests outside Boston, she made her own way back through the woods by following a track that had been made in the snow by a pack of wolves. In 1662, again in England, she harangued King Charles II in Whitehall in a state of such ecstasy and audacity that she was said by some to be a witch:

> I waited upon the king which way soever he went, . . . but the people murmured because I did not kneel, but I went along by the King and spoke as I went. . . . The power of the Lord was risen in me . . . and some wicked ones said that it was of the devil and some present made answer and said they wish they had that spirit, and then they were my disciples. . . . And it came upon me to get a coat of sackcloth, and it was plain to me how I should have it, so we made that coat, and the next morning I were moved to go amongst them again at Whitehall in sackcloth and ashes, and the people was much stricken, both great men and women was stricken into silence. . . . The Lord . . . made me an instrument to make way. . . . So is the Lord now filling up his viols of wrath to pour on the throne of the beast.[4]

Yet this radical visionary and social critic was cursed by that other notorious radical, Lodowijk Muggleton, and praised by King Charles II, receiving a certificate of her loyalty and usefulness to the crown. And in fact, Hooton did defend the king's authority in the New England col-

2. Elizabeth Hooton to Oliver Cromwell, 1653, Portfolio Manuscripts 3/3, 10, Library of the Society of Friends, London, quoted in Emily Manners, *Elizabeth Hooton: First Quaker Woman Preacher (1600–1672)* (London: Headley Brothers, 1914), 10.
3. "To the Rulers and magistrates of this island that ought to rule for God," Portfolio Manuscripts 3/25, quoted in Manners, *Elizabeth Hooton*, 71.
4. Portfolio Manuscripts 3/43, quoted in Manners, *Elizabeth Hooton*, 49. Letter of Elizabeth Hooton to Friends, London, October 17, 1662, Portfolio Manuscripts 3/34, reprinted in Manners, *Elizabeth Hooton*, 36–37.

onies; she also maintained that she was a loyal subject who broke no laws and submitted to physical punishment without resistance. "I was whipped before it was light," she remembered:

> Then fetched he down Sarah Coleman who was, I thought, older than myself and then my daughter and whipped us each 10 stripes a piece with a 3 corded whip, and said to my daughter are you not glad now it's your turn she said I am content, so they put her hands in a very strait place which pressed her arms very much.[5]

An established leader of her own local meeting, Hooton displayed great deference toward her "mother in Israel," Quaker leader Margaret Fell. "What a rebellious daughter-in-law art thou," she wrote to a relative who was attempting to alienate Fell's estate; "Was there ever such a wicked thing done in England or in any age before, that thou should reuinate thy husband's mother."[6] Hooton also traveled and suffered with other female missionaries, most notably her own daughter Elizabeth. Yet she was also a woman who made exuberant use of the traditional stock of vicious antifemale metaphors. In her "Lamentation for Boston and Cambridge her Sister," she wrote:

> by your unrighteous decrees hatched at Cambridge and made at Boston you are the two breasts of New England where all cruelty is nursed up, and feeds both priests and professors, and by these two breasts they are blood suckers persecuters and murderers. . . . [God] will rend and tear and deliver His little ones out of your hands, and shake terribly, and put out your two eyes.[7]

She was an ascetic who wrote to friends of the need to suffer continually: "O dear friends," she confided in a private letter, "when the Lord hath set you free and brought you into joy, then you think you have overcome all, but . . . the serpent there gets hold, and brings into death and darkness so that there is a continual warfare, for there is nothing obtained but through death."[8] Yet she was also protective of her own property: her house, lands, and cattle. In several letters to the king, she requested that

5. Portfolio Manuscripts 3/27, 2d portion, quoted in Manners, *Elizabeth Hooton*, 42–43. See also page 50.

6. Elizabeth Hooton to Hannah Fell, quoted in Isabel Ross, *Margaret Fell: Mother of Quakerism* (London: Longmans, Green, and Co., 1949), 226.

7. "Lamentation for Bosston and Camberig Her Sister," Portfolio Manuscripts 3/36, quoted in Manners, *Elizabeth Hooton*, 51. Elizabeth was married in 1669.

8. Elizabeth Hooton to Captain Amor Stoddard and his wife, n.d., Portfolio Manuscripts 3/35a.

he restore her property to her, "that I may have a horse to ride on in my old age."[9]

> Samuel Hooton [was] taken . . . and fined 5 pounds for which they took from me his mother being a widow 3 Mares with their furniture out of a cart laden with corn in harvest time, . . . Matthew Babington . . . took him from the plow . . . so they kept him in prison both in seed time and in harvest. And all this loss and damage fell upon me a widow besides the spoiling of my other cattle which I was forced to make use of (for want of my team) because I could not otherwise sow my seed. . . . If I be thus abused which am a widow . . . how should I pay my rents and taxes.[10]

Visiting Barbados and Jamaica in 1672, her third missionary voyage across the Atlantic, Hooton exhorted the Quaker settlers to sustain their faith. One of those Friends, James Lancaster, remembered that the next day,

> they had . . . taken her out of her bed into a chair, she was much swelled, and [I] said let her have air and they opened the windows and opened her bodice and then her breath came and she looked up and see me but could not speak, [I] said let us put her into her bed lest she get cold and we did and she looked upon me and I her, my life rose towards her and also her life answered mine again with great joy betwixt us and she said it is well James thou art come and fastened her arms about me . . . and embraced me with a kiss and laid her self down and turned her self on her side and so her breath went weaker and weaker till it was gone from her and so passed away as though she had been asleep and none knew of her departure but as her breath was gone.[11]

The contemporaries of Elizabeth Hooton would have agreed that there was no truer Quaker than that old woman, though her daughter, Elizabeth, and her antagonists, the magistrates and ministers of Boston, would surely have had different images of Quakerism in mind when they said the words. Most audiences were impressed, above all, by the collective energy and audacity of Quaker women prophets, so unlike the softer, catatonic ecstasies of visionaries like Anna Trapnel and Sarah Wight. The first Quaker missionaries to appear in London were two

    9. Portfolio Manuscripts 3/73, reprinted in Manners, *Elizabeth Hooton*, 60. Her arrest in Massachusetts followed her attempt to purchase a house and burial ground for the use of Quakers. The house and land were rented by her in the early 1660s; she still retained the farm at Skegby (Manners, *Elizabeth Hooton*, 35, 54).
    10. "The unjust Usage of Eliz. Hooton by some Magistrates in Leicestershire, 17/ 2nd mo/63," Portfolio Manuscripts 3/41.
    11. "A testemony of elesebeth hoton before she dyde by Ja: Lancaster," 1672, Library of the Society of Friends, London, MS. vol. 366 (SR 101).

women, Isabel Buttery and a friend, who arrived from the north in 1654 carrying books and papers to distribute. The first Quaker in Norfolk was a woman, Anne Blaykling, who won the first important local convert and was also the first arrested. Among the first missionaries in Ireland was a woman, Elizabeth Fletcher, sixteen years old, who arrived in 1655 and who had also been the first Quaker to evangelize Oxford. A woman was among the three first pioneers to evangelize Holland in 1655 and 1656. The first missionaries to America were Elizabeth Harris, Mary Fisher, and Ann Austin, who arrived in Maryland and Boston at that same time. One of the first missionaries to Turkey was a woman, the same Mary Fisher, who walked alone five hundred miles to visit the Sultan, knowing "it would be given her in that hour, what she should speak." The youngest and oldest Quakers to preach in public during the 1650s were female: Mary Fell of Swarthmore sent a message to the local Anglican priest, "Lampitt, the plagues of god shall fall upon thee and the seven viols shall be poured upon thee and the millstone shall fall upon thee and crush thee as dust under the Lord's feet how can thou escape the damnation of hell." Mary Fell was eight. Elizabeth Hooton admonished the king in the words of a reproving parent: "How often have I come to thee in my old age, both for thy reformation and safety, for the good of thy soul, and for justice and equity." She was about seventy.[12]

While many in their audiences recoiled at the personal audacity of

12. On London, see Alexander Delamain and John Bridges to Thomas Willan, April 1654, reprinted in Abram Rawlinson Barclay, ed., *Letters, etc. of Early Friends* (London, 1841), 8–9, and William Crouch, *Posthuma Christiana* (London, 1712), in EQW, 85–86, in which Ann Downer is cited as the first Londoner with a public testimony. On Norfolk, see Richard Vann, *The Social Development of English Quakerism, 1655–1755* (Cambridge, Mass.: Harvard University Press, 1969), 10. On Ireland, see Mabel R. Brailsford, *Quaker Women, 1650–1690* (London: Duckworth and Co., 1915), 179. On Holland, see Brailsford, *Quaker Women,* 219. On America, see Kenneth L. Carroll, "Elizabeth Harris, the Founder of American Quakerism," QH 57 (1968): 96–98; on Fisher and Austin, see BQ, 402. On women missionaries, see Rufus M. Jones, *The Quakers in the American Colonies* (London: Macmillan and Co., 1911), 26ff. Twelve of the twenty-two missionaries to Massachusetts before 1660 were women (Hugh Barbour, "Quaker Prophetesses and Mothers in Israel," in *Seeking the Light: Essays in Quaker History in Honor of Edwin B. Bronner,* ed. J. William Frost and John M. Moore [Wallingford and Haverford, Pa.: Pendle Hill Publications and Friends Historical Association, 1986], 44). Mary Fisher, Dorothy Waugh, and some male Quakers were the first in Buckinghamshire (Vann, *The Social Development of English Quakerism,* 10). On Mary Fell, see Fox, *Journal* (1656), quoted in Lucy V. Hodgkin, *A Quaker Saint of Cornwall: Loveday Hambly and Her Guests* (London: Longmans, Green, and Co.: 1927), 101–2. On Hooton, *see* Portfolio Manuscripts 3/57, quoted in Brailsford, *Quaker Women,* 36.

On Quaker children prophesying in America, see Lyle Koehler, *A Search for Power: The "Weaker Sex" in Seventeenth-Century New England* (Urbana, Chicago, and London: University of Illinois Press, 1980), 303, and James Bowden, *The History of the Society of Friends in America,* 2 vols. (London: Charles Gilpin, 1850), 1: 168–69.

Quaker woman prophets, others observed a quality of personal integrity and an extraordinary capacity for physical and emotional restraint. "[I] am a witness of the new covenant," announced Rebeckah Travers to the inhabitants of one London parish, "setting before you all this day, life and death . . . that you may . . . love and follow that which condemns all injustice, deceit, vain, wanton and unprofitable words and actions, and leads to justice, righteousness and soberness."[13] The mob that pushed Travers down in the street would never have characterized her sermon as one of sober counsel or passive resistance, but other witnesses saw the Quakers as excelling in precisely that; for Friends (as Quakers called themselves) sought verbal confrontations with clergy and magistrates and submitted to the inevitable persecution in order to dramatize the contrast between their own apostolic innocence and the magistrates' unenlightened souls, and they did this even before pacifism had become the official policy of the movement after 1660.[14] "*Now the image of Christ is . . . meek and a dove-like image,*" wrote Katherine Evans from her prison in Malta, "*an innocent and a lamb-like image, a righteous and a glorious image.*"[15] When the Inquisitors threatened to chain Sarah Cheevers for preaching against images, "she bowed her head, and said to him, *Not only my feet, but my hands and my neck, also, for the testimony of Jesus.*"[16] Quaker women surely suffered more theatrically, if not more harshly, than men, if only because the sight of a woman being whipped, clutching her baby to her naked chest, had a different social and sexual resonance than the sight of a man in the same cruel position.[17]

Righteous and sober Quakers were, in fact, more obedient citizens than the members of some other radical sects. Unlike the Diggers, no Quaker advocated the seizure of any property, and all would celebrate the restoration of the monarchy in 1660.[18] Like most other female

13. Rebeckah Travers, *Of That Eternal Breath Begotten and Brought Forth . . .* (n.d.), 8.

14. For an early example of this behavior, see *The Saints Testimony Finishing through Sufferings . . .* (London, 1655).

15. K[atherine] Evans and S[arah] Cheevers, *A Short Relation of Some of the Cruel Sufferings (for the Truths Sake) of Katherine Evans and Sarah Chevers . . .* (London, 1662), 81.

16. Ibid., 29.

17. In 1658 Horred Gardner was whipped in New England while holding her baby (Bowden, *The History of the Society of Friends in America*, 1:142). Lydia Wardell walked half naked to the Newbury, Massachusetts, meeting house to testify against the whipping of women (Arthur J. Worrall, *Quakers in the Colonial Northeast* [Hanover, N.H.: University Press of New England, 1980], 29).

18. J. S. Morrill and J. D. Walter, "Order and Disorder in the English Revolution," in *Order and Disorder in Early Modern England*, ed. Anthony Fletcher and John Stevenson (Cambridge: Cambridge University Press, 1985), 162. For a different view of the

visionaries, women (and men) Friends were also restrained in their sexual behavior. Historians have understandably dwelt on the salacious pamphlet literature that labeled both Quakers and Ranters as antinomian and described women and men cavorting through the countryside during the upheavals of the Civil War and Interregnum, claiming to be Adam and Eve or the Messiah and his adoring disciples.[19] The fact is, however, that of the hundreds of Quaker prophets and visionary writers active during the 1650s, only one man was formally accused of sexual misconduct; indeed, we shall see that a more pressing problem in the early movement was the insistence of some extremists in New England on abstaining from sex with their husbands.

Whatever their degree of sympathy for the tenets and practices of early Quakerism, audiences were in no doubt that Quaker women had departed from the conventions of acceptable feminine behavior far more radically than was the case for the visionaries who spoke and wrote before them or alongside them. Those other women—women like Anna Trapnel and Sarah Wight or the anonymous maidens who returned from the dead to advise the living—engaged in political and ethical discourse both in person and in print, but they were recognizable and acceptable as women nonetheless: feminine in their apparent susceptibility to emotional outbursts, in their use of images of motherhood and whoredom to convey their spiritual insights, and above all in their physical passivity and in the trances that allowed their audiences to observe them not as spiritual actors but as sibyls, semihuman transmitters of divine wisdom.

Elizabeth Hooton also used gendered images of virgins, mothers, and whores to praise the righteous and castigate the unjust, but there her resemblance to most other, non-Quaker visionary women ended. For the Quaker prophet did not appear to act out of the popular tradition of pagan divination; on the contrary, the Quaker prophet appeared as an active messenger out of the pages of the Old Testament. Her duty was to initiate direct encounters, to teach hard truths, to condemn moral decadence and social injustice, and, above all, to warn the sinner "that God may be justified in his judgements."

In assuming the personae of biblical prophets, Quaker women seemed to be denying the reality of all outward cultural constraints. They denied

---

Quakers' militancy during the 1650s, see Barry Reay, *The Quakers and the English Revolution* (London: Temple Smith, 1985), 32–45.

19. For example, see the treatment of Quakers by David S. Lovejoy in *Religious Enthusiasm in the New World: Heresy to Revolution* (Cambridge, Mass.: Harvard University Press, 1985), 111–34.

class and status differences by refusing to use the verbal or body language of deference; they denied gender differences by insisting that they preached as disembodied spirits "in the light," not as women. Indeed, if Quaker women prophets could be said to resemble any cultural archetype, it was that of the aggressive, male Old Testament hero.

WOMEN'S EMOTIONS

What were the deeper reasons for Elizabeth Hooton's unorthodox, unfeminine behavior? Most traditional historians of Quakerism, while invariably courteous toward Margaret Fell, the revered mother of the movement, have emphasized the hysterical, self-serving, and ultimately trivial character of early Quaker women. So in William Braithwaite's classic study of the beginnings of Quakerism, no women's writings are mentioned except those of Fell, but every case of "light behavior" by a woman is described in detail. Other historians have attempted to vindicate that emotional character as a covert strategy of self-realization. Mabel Brailsford tells the story of the Dutch Quaker Judith Zinspinning, whose father was often heard to regret that she had not been born a boy, to "become an eminent instrument in the Church." While married, her "buried talent and stifled ambition revenged themselves in moods of discontent and morbid introspection." As soon as her husband died, she sent her only son to live with an uncle and began a career as a famous, and presumably more fulfilled, polemicist and preacher. Dorothy Ludlow views women's missionary activities as evidence of a craving for adventure and excitement. Bonnelyn Kunze presents a revisionist account of the life of Margaret Fell, one that emphasizes her arrogance and manipulative behavior as well as her undoubted piety.[20]

These approaches to the subject of Quaker women's spirituality are emphatically opposed in their conclusions, but, like interpretations of earlier, non-Quaker visionaries, they rest on two identical assumptions about the meaning of female behavior. The first is that women's religiosity should be understood primarily as evidence of a desire for self-expression; the second is that the place to look for the true character of this self-expression is in overt demonstrations of aggression and emotion. I would like to take issue with both of these assumptions and to argue

20. BQ, 105, 244ff., 345, 346, 349, 364, 372, 388–89, 391, 409. Brailsford, *Quaker Women*, 223–25; Bonnelyn Young Kunze, "The Family, Social, and Religious Life of Margaret Fell," Ph.D. diss., University of Rochester, 1986.

that the Quakers' most passionate, apparently willful behavior was not an articulation of their deepest personal desires; nor was their public assertiveness, whether interpreted as uncontrolled hysteria or as a gesture of defiance—oppressed women trying to act like men—actually a form of self-expression.

The Quakers' attitude toward the self differed radically from the one that dominates our own, late twentieth-century Western culture, informed by fairly rigid standards of self-control and self-integration. Modern Freudian and post-Freudian theory, progressive children's literature, popular how-to-do-it books on love, hobbies, or making money, all these artifacts of our society teach us, with varying degrees of subtlety, that a mature, self-aware personality or ego is the foundation that supports the entire edifice of one's emotional, sexual, and spiritual being. We view the ego or conscious self as a sort of command center, mediating between conscience (or superego), the internalized voice of the larger culture, and instinct (or id), the hidden, volatile inner core of the self. Without a strong, independent ego and a firmly orchestrated personality (in modern slang, "having it all together"), one becomes, at best, a mediocrity in a society that values independence and achievement and, at worst, a professional failure, a social and moral cripple, a hopeless neurotic, even insane.

Within this psychological framework, emotional behavior does appear as a loosening of outward habits of control, the individual's deep, hidden essence spilling out. If we come upon a man or woman in a crowded city street, shouting or weeping loudly, clothes disheveled, we assume that we are witnessing an act of greater personal intimacy than that of a man or woman in a neat business suit, writing a check or delivering a paper at a conference. We might also assume that such behavior is a by-passing of the superego, the self erupting through the constraints of the culture, either through indifference to one's surroundings and to potential embarrassment (a father wailing over the body of his dead child after an earthquake) or in conscious defiance of conventional standards of behavior (an audience at a rock concert).

The Quakers' conception of the self turns our modern archaeology of the personality virtually upside down. Quakers viewed all human drives or appetites as superficial and transitory, as things that pass away with the death of the individual, and they included in this the drive to satisfy the cravings of the intellect as well as those of the stomach and the genitals. They further believed that the deepest, most hidden, most authentic aspect of the self was something akin to conscience, our superego. Conscience was a shard of universal truth, God's voice embedded in the self, which they called "the light" or "the seed." "Every one of you to whom I speak," wrote Edward Burrough to the inhabitants of Underbarrow, "hath this light, which shows you sin, your lying, swearing, pride, and wicked ways, covetous and wantonness to be sin. . . . This is the light which your Pharissee denies to have lighted every one, and this light shall for ever witness me to be true."[21]

In the act of preaching, this light or voice of conscience was catapulted from the depths of the soul, through layers of temperament, appetite, and habit, finally bursting through the individual's outer husk—her social status, her physical shape, her gender—to unite with the voices of other Friends in prayer or to enlighten strangers in the public arena. Unlike some other visionaries, the Quaker prophet was not in a trance when she preached (her whole being on hold, so to speak), for the voice of God was also the voice of her own conscience or integrity, the light within, or rather beneath, her deepest self, which put her in harmony with universal moral truth. "The more we taste of this heavenly banquet," wrote Sarah Cheevers,

> the much the more are we broken down into self denial, sealed down forever in the true poverty, and upright integrity of heart and soul, mind and conscience, wholly ransomed by the living word of life, to serve the living God. . . . [Then] we cannot hold our peace; the God . . . of glory doth open our mouth, and we speak to his praise, and utter his voice, and sound forth his word of life, and causeth the earth to tremble . . . my heart, soul and spirit that is wholly joined to the Lord, stream forth to you. . . . [I] am a partaker of . . . living virtue.[22]

Jane Withers also affirmed the fundamental difference between the catatonic ecstasy of the traditional visionary and the suspended ego of the Quaker prophet:

> The power of God seized upon me, but . . . I did not obey at the first movings; but the power of the Lord so seized on me again, that I was bound about my body above the middle as if . . . with chains. . . . And in the afternoon, I was forced to go [into the church], and as I went in at the door, I should have said, "the plagues of God must be poured upon thee;" but I did not speak the words then; and then the power of the Lord came upon me; but if that priest Moore

21. Edward Burrough, *A Warning from the Lord to the Inhabitants of Underbarrow, and So to All the Inhabitants of England* (London, 1654), 20.
22. "Sarah Chevers Epistle to Friends to read at Bull and Mouth," Portfolio Manuscripts 31/60.

says, I was in a trance, it is a lie, for I was as sensible all the while as ever I was.[23]

Quaker women also sincerely argued, in terms that were only apparently contradictory, that they were not being assertive when they preached; on the contrary, they were actually preaching against their own wills and minds. Margaret Killam recalled (writing in the usual passive voice), "I was moved to go to the steeplehouse. . . . [They] said that that I was subtle, but it was false, for I was kept in innocency, and found nothing rising in me til [the minister] was down . . . I was made in much meekness to declare the truth."[24] Thus, Quaker prophecy both was and was not an expression of the prophet's individual character; it was emphatically not a spontaneous outpouring of mood or individual imagination.

QUAKER LANGUAGE

"Literature," writes Terry Eagleton,

> transforms and intensifies ordinary language, deviates systematically from everyday speech. If you approach me at a bus stop and murmur, "Thou still unravished bride of quietness," then I am instantly aware that I am in the presence of the literary. . . . Your language draws attention to itself, flaunts its material being, as statements like "Don't you know the drivers are on strike?" do not.[25]

When Quaker prophets approached their audiences at crossroads, churches, and marketplaces, they invariably spoke not in conversational English but in literature; in language that was noticeably formalized and uniform.[26] Like many other contemporary visionaries, they assumed the existence of a shared mnemonic culture, a range of symbols and stories derived from the Old and New Testaments whose meanings would be universally understood and whose power, they hoped, would be universally acknowledged. When Katherine Evans declared that "whatsoever I have written, it's not because it is recorded in the Scripture, . . . but in obedience to the Lord I have written the things which I did hear,

23. Jane Wither's testimony, in James Nayler, *A Discovery of the Man of Sin* (London, 1656), 45, quoted in QPE, 117–18.
24. Margaret Killam to G[eorge] F[ox], about 1653, SM, 1/2 (II, 667).
25. Terry Eagleton, *Literary Theory: An Introduction* (Minneapolis: University of Minnesota Press, 1983), 2.
26. For an extended study of Quaker language, see Richard Bauman, *Let Your Words Be Few: Symbolism of Speaking and Silence among Seventeenth-Century Quakers*, Cambridge Studies in Oral and Literate Culture (Cambridge and New York: Cambridge University Press, 1983).

see, tasted and handled of the good word of God," she did not mean that
her own revelations were entirely independent of the Bible but that her
own direct experience of God was identical to that of biblical figures.
(Indeed, the phrase "hear, see, tasted and handled" was itself a biblical
paraphrase.)[27] Thus, the Quakers' attacks on clergy and magistrates
were of an entirely different order from the uninhibited insults (themselves, perhaps, another kind of literature) commonly hurled at unpopular officials: "I am a better man than thou art knave parson a turd in
thy teeth"; "he take away my license he kiss mine arse . . . he is a rogue
and a shitten jackanapes and I care not a turd for him go you and tell
him."[28]

The Quakers' symbolic actions were also more conventionally biblical
than those of other prophets. Some Friends appeared in sackcloth and
ashes and a few preached partially naked, but none approached the
symbolic exoticism of Lady Eleanor Davies, who smeared church hangings with hot tar and wheat paste, or the famous contemporary Jewish
mystic Sabbatai Sevi, who announced his own messianic birth under the
sign Pisces by buying a large fish, dressing it up like a baby, and displaying
it nestled in a cradle.[29] Nor did Friends display the lack of inhibition of
many of their more ordinary female neighbors, who expressed anger at
the Anglican clergy by throwing stones at priests, threatening them with
scissors, or tearing down church images.[30]

In 1660 Esther Biddle wrote to the people of London, in words close
to those of Jeremiah: "O my soul mourneth for thee, and my bowels is
troubled, and my heart is pained within me, to see thy desolation, my
eyes runneth down as a Fountain for the misery that is overtaking
thee."[31] Of course the language and behavior of Esther Biddle, Kath-

27. Evans and Cheevers, *A Short Relation*, 12–13. The issue of Friends' biblicism is
a thorny one in Quaker historiography. See Douglas Gwyn, *Apocalypse of the Word: The
Life and Message of George Fox (1624–1691)* (Richmond, Ind.: Friends United Press,
1986).

28. Susan Dwyer Amussen, *An Ordered Society: Family and Village in England,
1560–1725* (Oxford and New York: Basil Blackwell, 1988), 147, 151.

29. Gershom Scholem, *Sabbatai Sevi: The Mystical Messiah, 1626–1676*, Bollingen
Series 93 (Princeton: Princeton University Press, 1973), 161. Sabbatai Sevi's feats were
known in England and compared to the messianic raptures of the Quakers, particularly
the deeds of James Nayler (see below, chap. 5). In 1666 it was rumored that a ship had
set out from Bristol, a center of Quakerism, to investigate reports of Sabbatai Sevi's
messianic acts (Scholem, *Sabbatai Sevi*, 420, 547–58).

30. Dorothy P. Ludlow, "'Arise and Be Doing': English 'Preaching' Women, 1640–
1660," Ph.D. diss., Indiana University, 1978, 49–50.

31. Esther Biddle, *A Warning from the Lord God of Life and Power, unto Thee O
City of London* (London, 1660), 1.

erine Evans, Margaret Killam, and Elizabeth Hooton were emotional, and the intensity of their public voices, which hostile contemporaries described as shouting or screaming, may well have held a residue of personal frustration or exultation; more importantly, it was an expression of the prophet's ritually expressed anguish over the nation, mediated through the conventional language and behavior of biblical figures.[32] Indeed, rather than serve as a vehicle of self-expression, the prophet's strident voice and gestures probably worked to blot out whatever emotions of terror, timidity, or arrogance she might have felt in the moments that preceded her public act. It is in this context, rather than that of egoistic self-expression or neurotic masochism, that we find the most appropriate starting point from which to view the energy and persistence of Elizabeth Hooton's challenge to the magistrates of New England and the seeming compulsion with which she kept baring her back to the whip.

And yet, having discussed what we might call the Quakers' reversed psychology, and having observed an affinity between Quaker styles of expression and those of biblical figures, one comes back to the question of personal motivation: Why imitate *these* biblical figures and not others? Why make *these* symbolic gestures and not others? Why do *these* women convert, write, and preach and not others? The mentality and motivation of Susanna Ferris, who once paused from milking her cow in order to admonish a passing priest, was surely different from that of Margaret Fell, who pursued a forty-year career as a minister, writer, and organizer. And the mentality of an educated thinker like Fell, whose elegant treatises and polemics were translated and exported to the Continent, must have been equally different from that of Elizabeth Hooton, author of the following crude fragment, addressed to the Anglican priests: "Wo unto you, for you shut up ye kingdom of heaven a ganst man and will neither go in your selves nor sufer them yt would go to inter in a way with your lukewarmnes and formmality . . . wen your eyes ar open you will know me to be your frind." Quaker farmers and servants, women like Elizabeth Hooton and Jane Holmes, preached chiefly against material and moral corruption, inspiring the inhabitants of one town to hurl their finery on a bonfire, while the gentlewoman Margaret Fell

---

32. On the meaning of signs—tearing clothes, going naked, breaking pottery, and so on—see Kenneth L. Carroll, "Early Quakers and 'Going Naked as a Sign,'" QH 67, no. 2 (Autumn 1978): 69–87.

composed doctrinal essays and ordered ribbons and petticoats from London.[33]

One also comes back to the question of the meaning of gender. A primary tenet of early Quakerism was that the hierarchical character of gender relationships, indeed of all social relationships, was a product of human sinfulness, an outcome of the original Fall from grace. That Fall had shattered humanity into fragments, and the placement of those fragments, far from reflecting the moral and aesthetic unity of a universal Chain of Being, were uniquely human and imperfect forms of expression and oppression, invisible prisons whose walls could be demolished only by the painful annihilation of the outward self. Yet Quakers lived in a society where the language of social roles and moral values was completely gendered; where, as in biblical tradition, every transgression was expressed in metaphors of wifely infidelity and every soul in anguish as a woman in labor; where, in political discourse, the most antisocial crime was perceived as female witchcraft and the pinnacle of social harmony as the king or familial patriarch. In such an atmosphere, speaking and writing in a culture where one hoped to be able to communicate and proselytize, it would have been impossible to convey the meaning of the Quaker's rebirth "in the light" or the warnings of an angry God and avoid using the language of masculine and feminine. Indeed, the Quakers' concentration on the life of the soul necessarily implied that their mode of worship would be conceived in gendered terms, for the soul, whether housed in the body of a man or a woman, was invariably defined as feminine in its relationship to God.

The importance of gender and social context in shaping the expression of Friends' spirituality was as much their own concern as it must be the historian's. The earliest Quakers did insist that each of their impulses and actions was animated by a purely spiritual power that overrode their own individual reasoning or inclination, their outward social constraints, indeed, their whole previous experience. George Fox remembered that in 1652, when he preached before some hostile ministers in Lancashire, "one of them burst out into a passion and said he could speak his experiences as well as I; but I told him experience was one thing, but to go with a message and a word from the Lord as the prophets and the apostles had and did, and as I had done to them, this was another

33. On Ferris, GBS, vol. 2 (Wiltshire, 1658), 4; Elizabeth Hooton, "To the priests" (1654), Portfolio Manuscripts 3/12; on burning finery, see Thomas Aldam to George Fox from York, 1652, SM, 1/373 (I, 13); on Margaret Fell's ribbons, see Kunze, "The Family, Social, and Religious Life of Margaret Fell," 145.

thing."[34] Yet Fox also insisted on the relevance of personal experience in determining the proper direction of the prophet's expression and activity. Indeed, experience was not merely relevant; it was essential to the concept of unity that was the Friends' chief means of validating their calls or "leadings" to travel or prophesy. In an epistle to Friends written in 1653, Fox wrote:

> To you all, . . . which be babes of God wait for living food from the living God . . . that orderly and in order you may all be guided and walk, servants in your places, young men and women and rulers of families; that everyone in your places may adorn the truth, everyone in the measure of it. . . . And that no strife nor bitterness nor self-will amongst you may appear, but with the Light may be condemned, in which is the unity. And that every one in particular may see the order and ruling of their own family; that in righteousness and wisdom it may be governed . . . that stewards of his grace ye may come to be, to dispense it to everyone as they have need . . . and none amongst you boast yourselves above your measure.[35]

Thus, the prophets' exalted words and acts, while carrying them momentarily far outside themselves, were also to be shaped and constrained by their own experiences as members of a specific family, social station, and geographic space.

The remainder of this and the following three chapters is an analysis of the meaning of gender to early Quaker women and men in terms of the Quakers' own religious expectations, both in this world and out of it. How did a people whose aim was to transcend the limitations of their outward circumstances, including differences of gender, come to terms with the gendered discourse of the larger culture, and how did they attempt to shape that discourse to their own ends, or rather to godly, spiritual ends? Why did the female leaders of a sexually egalitarian movement speak with the voice of male biblical figures and not those of Deborah or Esther or Miriam? Conversely, what elements of a traditionally feminine identity influenced the language and behavior of contemporary Quaker men? I also explore the language and behavior of Quaker visionaries as workers, wives, friends, and parents, in groups and as individuals, looking for clues to personal motivation and attitude. What were the sources of Elizabeth Hooton's conviction that she must leave her own prosperous farm in order to expose herself and her daughter, and other old women, to the hazards of the American wilderness,

34. Fox, *Journal*, 123.
35. Ibid., 173.

inhabited by savage, ungodly Puritans? Was it the same conviction as
that of male Quakers who made similar sacrifices and faced similar
dangers? What was the mentality that allowed Quaker women to be both
tender and abrasive, mothers in Israel and scourges to humble the unrighteous? Can we discern, alongside or beneath their avowed ideals of
self-denial and community solidarity, other more personal agendas? And
if so, how did Quaker women attempt to fulfill those agendas within the
context of the dominant Quaker values they espoused?

THE CARNAL MIND

I am vile and abhor my self in dust and ashes. . . . I
am not worthy to be called thy child.
                    Ann Burden to George Fox, 1662

Glad to just be, glad to just be, glad to just be me!
          Marlo Thomas, "Free to Be You and Me,"
                    song for children, 1974

From the perspective of Enlightenment philosophy, and from the post-
Enlightenment perspective of many modern historians, the key, often
pejorative word for the troubles of the mid-seventeenth century is "enthusiasm": impulsive, emotional behavior involving a loss of reason and
self-control. For seventeenth-century Quakers, "enthusiasm" and "exaltation" were also dirty words, but not because they implied a *loss* of
selfhood; on the contrary, they conveyed a sense of self-generated, self-
centered, willful energy.[36] In both the flamboyant behavior of contemporary groups like the Ranters and the more sedate, intellectual preaching of the Anglican and Puritan clergy, Quakers saw the self run rampant.
For these Quakers, both will and mind were, quite simply, the enemies
of the soul, and the first object of Quaker meditation, prayer, good deeds,
or visions was to suffocate impulses toward personal expression and
achieve the annihilation of the thinking self. "Judge all thoughts and
believe," William Dewsbury counseled, "for blessed are they that believe
and see not." "See your thoughts, and deny them," declared Priscilla
Cotton; "deny thy own will, thy own thoughts, and thy own self." "I am

---

36. A more positive interpretation of the term "enthusiasm" in relation to seventeenth-century Quakerism is found in Geoffrey F. Nuttall, *Studies in Christian Enthusiasm: Illustrated from Early Quakerism* (Wallingford, Pa.: Pendle Hill, 1948).

vile," wrote Ann Burden to George Fox, "and abhor my self in dust and ashes. . . . I am willing to give up all to him freely for ever. . . . [Signed], I am not worthy to be called thy child Anna Burden."[37]

In order to appreciate this relentless self-negation in terms the early Quakers would have understood, we must begin by admitting that our own life goals of happiness, self-respect, and individual self-expression would have seemed to them to be both deluded and trivial. Quakers aimed for nothing less than the experience of a divine presence, or indwelling, in their own bodies. They also wanted friendship and spiritual empathy with the entire community of Quakers. Ultimately, they even wanted to transcend death: "There is a pure, and heavenly cry in me," wrote Thomas Lawson, "to dwell out of time, in that which was before all time, out of willing and running, and when I am kept stilly, and quietly in it, I find joy and peace."[38] As Mary Howgill put it to Oliver Cromwell: "We are all soldiers against all sin and deceit, and have overcome death, hell, and the grave."[39]

Such exalted feats of self-transformation were not achieved through the mere intellectual comprehension of a particular set of doctrines. Not only was intellectual activity a dangerous pastime that encouraged the sin of pride and the idolatry of the Anglican priests; it was also simply irrelevant to the existential experience Quakers sought. One male Quaker who felt the call to speak at a meeting and was afraid forced himself to think about the subject and immediately the spirit left him. "I saw I could do nothing, having quenched the spirit, and I was under trouble and exercise for my disobedience."[40] When the intellectual Judith Zinspinning arrived from Holland to preach in England, she intended to use a translator, but the Quakers asked her to preach in Dutch even though they could not understand a word she said. They knew well that the prophet's deeper message was nonsense; literally non-sense.[41]

The Quakers' insistence on distinguishing between reason and spirit was partly rooted in their belief (described in greater detail in chapter 1) that the activities of the mind and heart resembled bodily drives. In their psychology, as in that of their contemporaries, attitudes and emotions did not sit securely buttressed by fixed attributes of personality, as today

37. Ann Burden to G[eorge] F[ox], SM, 3/102 (III, 183).
38. Thomas Lawson to M[argaret] F[ell], 1653, SM, 1/245; II, 709.
39. Mary Howgill, *A Remarkable Letter of Mary Howgill to Oliver Cromwell . . .* (London, 1657), 1.
40. Christopher Story, *Life*, quoted in Luella M. Wright, *The Literary Life of the Early Friends, 1650–1725* (New York: Columbia University Press, 1932), 228.
41. Brailsford, *Quaker Women*, 237.

one might say, "I am, was, and will be an intellectual, a heterosexual, a shy person, and a lover of ice cream." Rather, attitudes and emotions were portrayed as physical forces or actual fluids that permeated and exited the body, like a dye that could be washed out.

In negative terms, this fluidity of the ego and of the emotions implied that activities of the mind were linked to the will, to sexuality, and to the lust for power. Faust legends, in which egotistical and impious students, magicians, and others sold their souls to the devil in exchange for knowledge, abounded in the seventeenth century. Anyone unacquainted with Faust or with the biblical language conflating knowledge and sexuality ("Abraham knew Sarah") had only to listen to a sermon on Eve and the apple to know that the pursuit of knowledge was a carnal and prideful act. "But if you look into the earthly mind," wrote James Nayler,

> there the worldly spirit meets you with his counsel, and . . . you take counsel in the night, from which the counsel of God is hid . . . and instead of that you will be presented with the pleasure, and glory of this world, which stands in visible things, and is pleasing to the visible eye and senses . . . and this you cannot avoid if you . . . counsel with your own reasonings . . . which cumbers the mind, checks the seed, and kills the holy child, and covers the pearl with earthly affections and lusts . . . and so puts the just to death in the womb . . . which being begot, and not brought forth, it withers, and become as dry bones in the womb.[42]

In many Quakers' actual conversion experiences, it was words—the seducers of the mind—not the flesh, that proved to be the real whore, because the enjoyment of one's own wisdom and eloquence fed the carnal appetite for self-esteem long after the other appetites of the body had been subdued. "I ran forth in my wisdom comprehending the mysteries of God," wrote Edward Burrough,

> and I grew up into notion, to talk of high things . . . and then was I above many of the priests and professors . . . and so I became one of them in their discoursings, and was looked upon by them to know much . . . and my delight was much in discoursing, where I played the harlot . . . here I was run from my husband after other lovers . . . then it pleased the Lord to send . . . Geo[rge] Fox; he spoke the language which I knew not, notwithstanding all my high talking, for it was higher, and yet lower: . . . and then I saw myself to be a

    42. James Nayler, *How Sin Is Strengthened, and How It Is Overcome* (London, 1657), 7, 8.

child of wrath, . . . and that harlots had been my companions, and was no more worthy to be called a son.[43]

As an old woman, Margaret Fell remembered sitting in the parish church near her estate at Swarthmore, listening to George Fox rebuke those who understood the scriptures only with their minds: "This opened me so, that it cut me to the heart; and then I saw clearly that we were all wrong. So I sat down in my pew again, and cried bitterly; and I cried in my spirit to the Lord, 'We are all thieves; we are all thieves; we have taken the Scriptures in words, and know nothing of them in ourselves.'"[44]

NORTH AND SOUTH

The Quakers' deep mistrust of "high things," their conviction of the irrelevance of all intellectual and social attainments, was far more profound than it had been for the visionaries of the 1640s, and it testifies to Friends' frustration, even horror, at the spiritual chaos and the injustices against king and people that had dominated the Civil War period. More important, it characterizes a movement of outsiders, one led by men and women of the northern and midlands counties, denizens of a culture that was austere, remote, and narrowly biblical, purer, in their eyes, than that of the cacophonous, sensuous cities of the south. So two early missionaries wrote home to Margaret Fell in Lancashire in 1654: "They have not so much heard of a cross, but lust and pride and all manner of filthiness. . . . O, the rich and boundless love of God unto us, the people of the north, who hath separated us from the pollutions of it, and hath gathered us together into the unity of the spirit."[45]

For these purists, disengagement from the carnal world was remembered as a sharply painful but relatively straightforward internal event. When Elizabeth Hooton sought vainly among the Baptists for a true spiritual encounter, she expressed her dissatisfaction not in terms of personal confusion but as a chastisement against the weakness of others; so her son Oliver wrote many years later: "And my mother joined with

43. Burrough, *A Warning from the Lord*, 32, 33, 34.
44. Margaret Fell, *Leeds Journal*, 1:lxii, quoted in Ross, *Margaret Fell*, 11.
45. Francis Howgill and John Camm to Margaret Fell, March 27, 1654, EQW, 384–85. On the atmosphere of the northern counties, see QPE, 43–44, 72–84. Almost all northern women whose backgrounds are known were either wives or servants in farming families. Ann Audland was married to a shopkeeper. She, Dorothy Benson, Margaret Killam, Elizabeth Fletcher, and Margaret Fell belonged to prominent or well-to-do families. Grace Barwick and Rebecca Ward had husbands in the military. Jane and Dorothy Waugh, Ann Cleaton, and Mary Fisher were servants. Elizabeth Leavens, Elizabeth Cowart, and Alice Birkett were referred to as poor. (DQB; Appendix 2).

the Baptists but after some time finding them that they were not upright hearted to the Lord but did his work negligently and she having testified against their deceit left them who in those parts soon after were scattered and gone."[46] The young Elizabeth Farmer, daughter of strict Puritans from a village near Shrewsbury, wallowed in the sin of pride as she received the praises of the local nobleman whom she served at her father's table. In 1653, having read of the trial of George Fox and James Nayler and believing they were holy men, she went by herself to visit Fox in prison. "The first meeting I was at . . . then did I stand boldly for the truth, and took up my cross and did bear my testimony for the truth." Again serving at table, she refused to bow to the assembled notables, amusing a guest, Lord Newport, who offered her a bribe of twenty pounds if she would make him a curtsy. "I answered: 'If I might have all Eyton Hall to do it, yet I durst not do it, for all honor belongeth to God.'"[47]

For women from the more complex, urbanized culture of the southern counties, disengagement from worldly habits proved to be a far more tortuous and protracted process. Unlike the vast majority of northern women, who were servants, daughters, or mistresses of farming families, these southern Friends were married to tradesmen, artisans, or publishers. Judging from the language and biblical citations in many of their works, they were also relatively well educated, with access to a wide range of religious writing, including the literature of Continental mysticism.[48] Other women were exposed to the preaching

46. "Oliver Huttons Certificate Concerning G: ff:" (1686/7), Portfolio Manuscripts 10/42, quoted in Manners, *Elizabeth Hooton*, 4.
47. "An Account of the Birth, Education and Sufferings for the Truth's Sake of that Faithful Friend Elizabeth [Farmer] Andrews," reprinted in JFHS 26 (1929): 4, 5.
48. Almost every woman from an artisan, trading, or publishing family was from the south. They included Elizabeth Farmer Andrews, Esther Biddle, Mary Clark, Anne Curtis, Tacy Davies, Mary Dyer, Ann Hersent, Temperance Hignell, Frances Raunce, Rebeckah Travers, Hannah Stranger, Martha Simmonds, and Elizabeth Stirredge. Ann Downer's father was a clergyman. Dorothea Scott Gotherson, Mary Penington, Mary Akehurst, Sarah Blackborow, Ann Burden, Margaret Newby, Ann Curtis, Mary Dyer, Ellen Embree, and Katherine Evans were from prominent or prosperous families. Barbara Blaugdone was a teacher with aristocratic friends. Ann Upcott's brother was a constable; Lucretia Cooke was married to a cornet in Cromwell's cavalry. Servants from the south were Ann Austin, Elizabeth Cox, and Mary Powel. Jeane Bettris was listed as "poor." (DQB; Appendices 2 and 3).
    The question of women's education is a vexing one. Many surviving letters are not in the writer's own hand but were copied soon afterward. While every woman discussed here was a reader of the Bible and other works, not all could write. Margery Clipsham, wife of a prosperous London merchant and the coauthor of a tract published in 1685, affixed a mark rather than a signature to a document that she and her husband presented to the six weeks meeting ("To all people to whom this present writing shall come" [September 20, 1687], Portfolio Manuscripts 41/77).

of non-Quaker female visionaries. Rebeckah Travers, wife of a well-to-do London tobacconist, frequented the same society that attended the bedsides of the visionaries Anna Trapnel and Sarah Wight. Dorothea Scott Gotherson, a wealthy gentlewoman, was related to the American prophet Anne Hutchinson, while Mary Dyer had been Hutchinson's friend and ally over a decade before her conversion to Quakerism.[49]

Many of these literate women were not merely witnesses of the upheavals of the Civil War; they had been active seekers among the profusion of sects and independent churches that proliferated during the 1640s. Katherine Evans told her inquisitors at Malta that she had first been a Lutheran, then a Baptist, then an Independent, and finally a Puritan.[50] Martha Simmonds spent the years of her childhood and adolescence in a fruitless search for a people who would be both a touchstone of moral integrity and a sounding board for her own anxieties:

> For seven years together I wandered up and down the streets inquiring of those that had the Image of honesty in their countenance, where I might find an honest minister, for I saw my soul in death . . . and finding none sensible of my condition, I kept it in, and kept all close within me. . . . I found breathing in me groaning for deliverance, crying out, oh when shall I see the day of thy appearance.[51]

Esther Biddle, wife of a prosperous shoemaker, was so wracked by her own and the world's condition that she became deaf until her convincement by Friends:

> I spent many years in *Oxford*, where the carriages of the scholars, did trouble me in that day, they were so wild; . . . then the Lord drew me to

49. G. D. Scull, *Dorothea Scott, Otherwise Gotherson and Hogben, of Egerton House, Kent, 1611–1680* (Oxford: Parker and Co., 1883), 33–35. On Mary Dyer, see Bowden, *The History of the Society of Friends in America*, 1:193, 197–203. Travers socialized with the leading London Quaker minister, James Nayler, who consorted with the same society that frequented the bedsides of the prophets Anna Trapnel and Sarah Wight (Geoffrey F. Nuttall, "James Nayler: A Fresh Approach," JFHS Supp. 26 [1954]: 10–11). Eleanor Davies, Elinor Channel, Mary Pordage, and Mary Cary all lived in or near London, and all prophesied to the same London audiences; Trapnel actually preached to mixed audiences of Fifth Monarchists and Quakers (Bernard Capp, *The Fifth Monarchy Men: A Study in Seventeenth-Century English Millenarianism* [London: Faber and Faber, 1972], 153).

50. Stephen C. Morland, ed., *The Somersetshire Quarterly Meetings of the Society of Friends, 1668–1699* (Old Woking, Surrey: Somerset Record Society, 1978), 6.

51. Martha Simmonds, *A Lamentation for the Lost Sheep of the House of Israel* (London, 1655), 5–6.

> [London], . . . where I applied my heart both evening and morning, and at
> noon day, unto reading and hearing the *common-prayer*; when there was
> but one place of worship left in this city, I went to it, and when their books
> were burned, I stood for them . . . and when the King's head was taken off,
> my heart and soul was burdened, that I was even weary of my life. . . . Then
> did the Lord take away my hearing for a year.[52]

For these articulate and introspective women, the trauma that preceded their conversion to Quakerism was the realization that they themselves were implicated in the corruption that surrounded them by their
own social vanity and intellectual ambition. So wrote Elizabeth Stirredge, who had read and meditated on religious matters since childhood:

> I lent out an ear unto the enemy of my soul, and let my mind go forth after
> fine clothes; but when it was drawn out, it went without limit; and when I
> bedecked myself as fine and as choice as I could, it would hardly give me
> content; for when I had one new thing, when I saw another, or the third, I
> was as desirous as for the former, so ever unsatisfied. Oh! The lying enemy,
> who promised me rest and peace, but could not give it me.[53]

When Stirredge first heard the preaching of the northern Quakers John
Audland and John Camm in 1654, she was twenty years old. "It struck
a dread over my heart, hearing of their plainness. I began to think, 'How
shall I demean myself to go to hear them.'" The following year, Stirredge
approached William Dewsbury after a meeting, hoping he would see
through to her hard heart; his message was, "Dear lamb, judge all
thoughts and believe, for blessed are they that believe and see not." "He
was one who had good tidings for me," she said.[54] Attending a debate
between the Quaker James Nayler and some Baptists in London, Rebeckah Travers was appalled at the inferior performance of the more educated Baptists: "She could feel [Nayler's] words smote them, that one
or two of them confessed they were sick and could hold it no longer, and
the third . . . shamed himself in bringing scriptures that turned against
him, and she was confounded and ashamed that a Quaker should exceed
the learned Baptists." Travers again encountered Nayler at a London
gathering, where she tried to engage him on her own ground by ques-

---

52. Esther Biddle, *The Trumpet of the Lord God Sounded forth unto These Three
Nations* (London, 1662), 14–15.
53. Elizabeth Stirredge, *Strength in Weakness Manifest* . . . 3d ed. (London, 1772),
12.
54. Ibid., 28.

tioning him about the fine points of Quaker theology. Nayler took her hand across the table and answered, "Feed not on knowledge. It is as dangerous to you, as ever it was to Eve. It is good to look upon but not to feed on, for he who feeds on knowledge dies to the innocent life." Travers ultimately embraced the Quaker doctrine of the mortification of the intellect, a sacrifice that opened for her an entirely new mode of visionary discernment. "When you read Scripture," she wrote to former friends,

> is the veil yet rent off your faces? Friends and neighbours, and relations, if it were, you would see him whom you have pierced, who are yet eating and drinking your own damnation . . . though I have been a reader of the Scriptures . . . from a child of six years old . . . yet when . . . I was turned from darkness to light, I saw things unutterable. . . . O man and woman . . . [thou] art become as a brute beast that perishes, and knowest nothing but what thou knowest naturally.[55]

Thus, southern women portrayed their own experience of conversion not as a passage from which they emerged as liberated individuals, ready for assertive action on behalf of themselves and their sex, but rather as a passage in the opposite direction, one that stripped them of individual pretensions and relieved them of the burden of endless spiritual speculation, of weighing the virtues of myriad sects and prophets, and of engaging in fruitless competition to display social status by means of their wealth or their wardrobe. Once convinced, they expressed their fulfillment, quite precisely, as that of disengagement and sacrifice as well as union with the group, yet they continued to dwell upon their previous personal struggles as they made themselves objects of instruction for the unregenerate. So the gentlewoman Mary Penington remembered, many decades after her convincement:

> I never had peace or quiet from a sore exercise in my mind for many months . . . not . . . ever disputing . . . against the doctrine [of Friends], but I was exercised against taking up the cross to the language and fashions, customs, titles, honors and esteem in the world, and the place and rank I stood outwardly in. . . . But . . . as I gave up out of reasoning or consulting how to provide for the flesh, I received strength and so went to the meetings of those people. . . . I longed to be one of their number . . . [and] judged it to be worth

---

55. BQ, 242; Rebeckah Travers, *For Those That Meet to Worship at the Steeple-House, Called John Evangelist in London* (London, 1659), 17–44.

the cost and pains, if I came to witness such a change as I saw in them, and such power over their corruptions.[56]

ECSTASY AND COMMUNITY

It pleased the Lord to raise up the ancient horn of
salvation among us, who were reckoned in the north
part of *England*, even as the outcasts of *Israel*, and as
men destitute of the great knowledge which some
seemed to enjoy . . . and as we waited upon him in
pure silence, our minds out of all things, . . . when
there was no language, tongue nor speech from any
creature; . . . the kingdom of heaven did gather us,
and catch us all as in a net, and . . . we did come to
know a place to stand in, and what to wait in, and
the Lord did appear daily to us, to our astonishment,
amazement, and great admiration, insomuch that
we often said one unto another with great joy of
heart, *What, is the Kingdom of God come to be with
men? . . . And what, shall we that were reckoned as
the outcasts of Israel, have this honor of glory
communicated amongst us.*[57]

> *Francis Howgill's testimony to*
> *Edward Burrough, 1662*

As Quakers gathered in silent meetings, waiting, as had earlier seekers, for the signs of a divine visitation, they perceived a space in both mind and body that was suffused, both from within and without, by divine light, that same light, or seed, that had lain buried under layers of personality and habit and was now dissolving not only the trappings of social adulthood but the boundaries that separated individuals from one another. This dissolution of the individual personality, a dissolution that Friends perceived as a sensation of melting, was expressed through the loosening of all bodily inhibition in tears, groans, and shaking. So Esther Biddle, deaf before her convincement, saw the word of God not as an abstraction but as a living force, "which proceedeth out of thy bowels,

56. Mary Penington, *A Brief Account of My Exercises from My Childhood* (Philadelphia, 1848), 12–13.
57. F[rancis] H[owgill], *A Testimony concerning the Life, Death, Trials, Travels and Labours of Edward Burroughs* . . . (London, 1662), 5.

which is the word of god, which raised our souls . . . and quickened our mortal bodies."[58]

Thus, Quakers were at once ascetics, rejecting both carnal reason and carnal sensuality, and celebrators of bodily sensation as a vehicle for experiencing and expressing the soul's new capacity to discern truth—a kind of x-ray vision that enabled them to see through the meaningless categories and colors of external reality to the real essence of people and of nature.

> Life gives [the soul] a feeling, a sight, a tasting, a hearing, a smelling, of the heavenly things, by which senses it is able to discern and distinguish them from the earthly things. And from this measure of life . . . the senses grow stronger; it sees more, feels more, tastes more, hears more, smells more. Now when the senses are grown up to strength, then come settlement and stability, assurance and satisfaction. . . . Where the senses are grown strong . . . the soul is enlarged.[59]

Hence the Quakers' practices of quaking, staring, and weeping, all of which expressed both the intensity of their spiritual and bodily experiences and the irrelevance of their own intelligence or common sense in attaining those experiences. Hence also the Quakers' use of both lyrical and grotesque bodily imagery in their visionary language: "Exceeding . . . beautiful . . . do I feel thee in me, as ointment poured out, thy smell is sweet and lovely"; "My bowels do yearn toward thee"; "thy eyes pierce through me . . . my heart is often melted within me"; "Oh *drink, drink* . . . of the *streams* of my *heavenly Father's love*"; "I even feed with thee and lie down with thee in the life forevermore"; "I could weep tears of blood"; "I will roar as a lion bereaved of her young, I will tear through the darkness"; "[You have] paleness of face, with thy hands on thy loins, as a woman in travail, crying to be delivered from the body of sin"; "thou . . . art as a stinking dunghill in the sight of God"; "*you have*

58. Esther Biddle to Francis Howgill, Bridewell, London, October 17, 1664, in Norman Penney, ed. *Extracts from State Papers Relating to Friends, 1654 to 1672* (London: Headley Bros., 1913), 222.
59. Isaac Penington, "To Friends of Both the Chalfonts," quoted in R. Melvin Keiser, "From Dark Christian to Fullness of Life: Isaac Penington's Journey from Puritanism to Quakerism," *Guilford Review* 23 (1986): 56. On the Quakers' belief in "spiritual senses" as opposed to objective knowledge involving a split between subject and object, see Melvin P. Endy, Jr., *William Penn and Early Quakerism* (Princeton: Princeton University Press, 1973), 158–59. Endy suggests that Fox may have believed that the worshiper experienced an actual change in his body as he "ate" the spiritual body of Christ (187–88). My analysis differs from that of Professor Greven, who emphasizes the physical self-loathing of "evangelicals" and their "alienation from their own bodies" (*The Protestant Temperament: Patterns of Child-Rearing, Religious Experience, and the Self in Early America* [New York: Alfred A. Knopf, 1980], 65–73).

forsaken the Lord, the fountain of living waters, and are greedily swallowing the polluted waters, that come through the stinking channel of your hireling-masters, unclean spirits."[60]

The Quakers' peculiar style of worshipful expression—their quaking—was also a social statement, a commentary on the body language of their contemporaries. For Quakers lived in a world in which many of the physical gestures of affection, association, deference, and punishment (kissing, eating, bowing, whipping, and the range of emotions that accompanied them) were often more closely associated with public ritual and convention than with authentic feeling or impulse. The early Quakers repudiated all such gestures of deference and oppression, and their displays of tears, symbolic dress and undress, partial paralysis, and involuntary quaking were clear statements that they had divorced themselves from all corrupt habits of social ritual, self-glorification, or control. Thus, one Friend judged bowing and curtsying as false feeling, arguing that real honor was expressed in "certain natural, lively actions, that are inseparable from it, and so consequently true and infallible, according as the indwelling honor leads, moves, guides, directs, and puts forth itself, either by giving the hand, falling on the neck, embracing, kissing."[61] Indeed, behavior that expressed social deference was not only inauthentic, it was also anachronistic, for Friends believed that they had already entered into the last times and that Christ had been spiritually resurrected on earth, within their own souls. Thus, their quaking was a sign that the earthquake prophesied in Revelation had actually come to pass, a prelude to the opening of the seventh seal, when the truth of the scriptures would be opened to human understanding.[62] "But the time cometh," wrote Dorothy White, "that a day of quaking shall pass over

60. Barbara Blaugdone to M[argaret] F[ell], n.d., SM 1/155 (I, 209). Mary Page to William Dewsbury, Wellingborough, September 26, 1657, Temp. Manuscripts 61/6. Margaret Kilham to G[eorge] F[ox] about 1653, SM (II, 667). Joan Brooksop, *An Invitation of Love unto the Seed of God* (London, 1662), 11. Ann Audland to M[argaret] F[ell], February 8, 1655, William Caton Manuscripts 3/140, III, S.81, folls. 431–432. Martha Simmonds, Hannah Stranger, James Nayler, William Tomlinson, *O England: Thy Time Is Come*, (n.d.), 1. Dorothy White, *A Trumpet of the Lord of Hosts* (1662), 3–4. Judith Eedes, *A Warning to All the Inhabitants of the Earth . . .* (1659), 4. Mary Howgill, *A Remarkable Letter of Mary Howgill to Oliver Cromwell, Called Protector . . .* (London, 1657), 1. Mary Trask and Margaret Smith to Governor Endicott, December 21, 1660, reprinted in Besse, 2:212.

61. Benjamin Furly, *The World's Honor Detected* (London, 1662), quoted in Barry Levy, *Quakers and the American Family: British Settlement in the Delaware Valley* (New York and Oxford: Oxford University Press, 1988), 60.

62. Gwyn, *Apocalypse of the Word*, 187. T. L. Underwood, "Early Quaker Eschatology," in *Puritans, the Millennium, and the Future of Israel: Puritan Eschatology, 1600 to 1660*, ed. Peter Toon (Cambridge and London: James Clarke, 1970), 91–104.

all that have not yet known quaking, the earth shall be terribly shaken, and not the earth only, but the heavens also."[63]

Perhaps the Quakers' physical quaking was also resonant of the uninhibited, involuntary motions of infancy, for Friends portrayed the experience of salvation as the bliss of babyhood, the soul eating or sucking God's word, or the soul as a seed, nestled and burgeoning under God's maternal wing, "where his children all sit together (under his banner of love) and feed together, and drink together, and are satisfied."[64] God's offer of salvation to all was made "with as great cheerfulness and willingness, as a hen gatherest her chickens. Such as is the love and care of the hen towards her brood, such is the care of Christ to gather lost men and women."[65] God's word itself was portrayed as milk, and the bliss of salvation was to be cradled in arms of divine love, safe from the unreal individuation and loneliness of the carnal world. "The image of God is renewed in you, and ye come to grow up in it. . . . And the Babe's food is known, the children's bread, which comes from the living God, and nourishes up to eternal life; which babes and children receive their wisdom from above, from the pure living God, and not from the earthly one."[66] Like the newborn baby who instinctively knows how to suck, so the individual has an innate ability to turn toward God.

The symbolic and emotional focus of this experience of blissful infancy were the parental figures of Margaret Fell and George Fox, whose relationship to Quakers was portrayed in terms of a fluidity that was both erotic and maternal, with images of mutual penetration, holding, and feeding, all derived from biblical language. "My life flows into thee," wrote Richard Hubberthorne to George Fox. "The world knows thee not but I know thee and feel thee. . . . Thy eye pearceth through me and is as the Arrows of god within me. . . . I am broken into unfeigned tears."[67] Sitting in prison, Ann Audland wrote to Margaret Fell in tones of the deepest personal and spiritual intimacy: "My dear and precious sister in whom my life is bound up, after thee my life breatheth, oh that

63. Dorothy White, *This to Be Delivered to the Counsellors That Are Sitting in Counsel* (London, 1659), 8.

64. H[enry] Fell to M[argaret] F[ell], June 11, 1660, Thetford Prison, Norfolk, SM 1/73 (II, 135).

65. *An Apology for the True Christian Divinity Being an Explanation and Vindication of the Principles and Doctrine of the People Called Quakers* (Philadelphia, 1908), 155, quoted in Jeanette Carter Gadt, "Women and Protestant Culture: The Quaker Dissent from Puritanism," Ph.D. diss., University of California, Los Angeles, 1974, 208.

66. Fox, *Journal*, 2:326.

67. Richard Hubberthorne to G[eorge] F[ox], November 13, 1654, Norwich Castle prison, SM 4/235 (II, 567).

I could hear from thee. . . . I even long to open my heart into thy bosom, my dear and near and eternal mother, by thee I am nourished. . . . I even feed with thee and lie down with thee in the life for evermore." Again she wrote, "thou art my natural mother, by thee I have been nourished and refreshed. . . . My heart is open into thy bosom."[68] "Oh my dear sister my mother my well beloved one my life my Joy," cried Ann's husband, John Audland, to Margaret Fell: "I read thee daily thou art bound up in me sealed closed and enjoyed for evermore: thy garments are sweet thy countenance is beautiful and glorious; breathe to me more and more and I shall feel thee I am open to thee my most dear sister glorious is thy dwelling place."[69] For William Caton, Margaret Fell seemed to embody the emotional and spiritual function, if not the divine status, of Mary and the saints:

> Oh evermore give me of thy living food with which thou feeds them who are born again of the immortal seed, I know the everlasting treasury out of which thou administers is always full, and bread is never wanting in thy father's house who hath highly favored thee, and made thee a joint heir. . . . [You] often appear before the throne of grace making vehement supplication, sometimes with sighs and groans which cannot be expressed, and sometimes with a pleasant melodious voice, pleading the cause of the innocent, and crying for vengeance upon the head of the oppressor. . . . I feel thee taking part with me whether it be in suffering or rejoicing. . . . my life is raised and quickened when I feel thee, who remains nigh unto me, glory, glory for evermore.[70]

The earliest Quakers did more than replicate the traditional Christian symbolism of the worshiper as a child or the community as the bride of Christ; they also conflated masculine and feminine symbols. Thus, in one of his treatises addressed to Friends, George Fox depicted the church as a father who gives milk:

> All changeable things that are in the world . . . are as the moon for the moon changes but the sun doth not change. . . . The true Church which Christ is the head of which is in god the father . . . this church is clothed with the son Christ Jesus her head who doth not change and hath all changeable things

68. Ann Audland to Margaret Fell, Banbury, February 8, 1655, William Caton Manuscripts 3/140, III, S.81, fols. 431–32, Library of the Society of Friends, London.
69. John Audland to M[argaret] F[ell], Swanington, January 3, 1656, SM, 1/7 (I, 99).
70. William Caton to M[argaret] F[ell], July 23, 1656, Launceton, SM, 1/313 (I, 363).

under her feet and there are the living members born again . . . and feed upon the immortal milk.[71]

Of course, Puritans also portrayed God as both mother and father, as did Catholic mystics of the High Middle Ages, but Quakers went farther, extending the symbolic depiction of a divinity with masculine and feminine qualities to a belief in the unity and perfectability, some said divinity, of actual men and women.[72] This doctrine of perfection, the sense that someone "in the light" had transcended all carnal aspects of his or her individual being, caused some Friends to express themselves in terms that approached the heresy of antinomianism: "Them who drink of [the blood of the Lamb]," wrote Mary Howgill, "it taketh away all guilt of sin, and there is no sin remaining where guilt is taken away; the Son of God hath redeemed us from all evil, and there is no evil in them who are in the Son . . . so we witness the Scripture fulfilled in us."[73]

The Quakers' doctrine of perfection and their use of feminine spiritual symbolism obviously had a positive impact on women's confidence as interpreters of the divine will and as actors in the divine cause; Elizabeth Hooton's story is only one instance of the importance of women's contributions to the movement, both within and outside the religious community. From the Quakers' own perspective, however, the importance of the doctrine of perfection was not only, or even primarily, in granting authority to individual women but in what we might call its liquifying aspect, its potential for decomposing the individual, gendered personality and encouraging women and men to speak and act with the traditional attributes of both sexes. Thus, George Fox was portrayed as being "so meek, contented, modest, easy, steady, tender, it was a pleasure to be in his company. . . . [He] experienced no authority but over evil, and that . . . with love, compassion, and long suffering. A most merciful man, as ready to forgive as unapt to take or give an offence."[74] Fox himself addressed Quakers both as "dear babes of God" and as "my babes." Margaret Fell, on the other hand, was ad-

71. George Fox, "Concerning the Church of Christ being Cloathed with the Sun & having the Moone under her Feet, etc.," read in monthly and quarterly meetings January 1667, Portfolio Manuscripts 10/58–59.
72. On Puritans, see David Leverenz, *The Language of Puritan Feeling: An Exploration in Literature, Psychology, and Social History* (New Brunswick, N.J.: Rutgers University Press, 1980), 1ff. On medieval mystics, see Caroline Walker Bynum, *Jesus as Mother: Studies in the Spirituality of the High Middle Ages* (Berkeley: University of California Press, 1982), 170–262.
73. Howgill, *A Remarkable Letter of Mary Howgill to Oliver Cromwell*, 5.
74. Fox, *Journal*, 1:xxxix, quoted in Gadt, "Women and Protestant Culture," 185.

dressed not only as bride, mother, and sister but as hero and friend: "Arise thou daughter of Zion," wrote Thomas Aldam. "Thresh o thresh upon the mountains; stand up for the everlasting truth. The sword is put into thy hand; go forth in the strength of the Lord as he calls, sit not still when the Lord bids go. . . . Thy appearance in life, in that which is eternal, is to judge."[75]

Quaker private correspondence often conveys the sense that the early Friends' emotional and spiritual lives were conducted in a sort of gravity-free zone, in which personal relationships attained a fluidity impossible to achieve "in the flesh." So Thomas Holme wrote to Margaret Fell that he had married Elizabeth Leavens "contrary to my will before diverse friends" (that is, *in* the will of God).[76] John Killam wrote to Fell in terms that would have been inadmissible in any earthly context:

> My love . . . flows forth unto thee, my dearest Love of loves, thy love towards me is answered with the same love which flows from me to thee again, which love runs out freely unto thee. . . . in the bowels of love I do thee greet, where we have unity together, and lie down in the arms of love embracing each the other, in that where we cannot be separated.

Killam went on to give news of his wife, the prophet Margaret Killam, who was traveling and preaching elsewhere, and concluded his letter, "Captain Siddall's wife is my near and dear company in the bonds of love she above all the rest . . . she is my yoke fellow, in the true fellowship of love."[77] Francis Howgill poured himself out to George Fox: "I am melted I am melted with thy love it is not lawful to utter, pray for me thy dear son begotten to an inheritance incorruptable. . . . Farewell for evermore my beloved one, [addressed] To him who is invisible out of time."[78] Elizabeth Morgan wrote to Margaret Fell with the same ardor: "Fair art thou as the noon, clear as the sun, terrible as an army with banners . . . thy presence to me is life, joy and peace is on thy right hand and on thy left pleasure forever more thy love is better than wine yea more precious to me than life."[79] Henry Fell addressed George Fox

75. Thomas Aldam to G[eorge] F[ox], n.d. SM 3/39 (I, 25).
76. Tho[mas] Holme to M[argaret] F[ell], about 1654, SM 1/195 (II, 346).
77. John Killam to Margaret Fell, York Castle, June 9, 1655, SM 4/88 (II, 675).
78. Francis Howgill to G[eorge] F[ox], 1655, A. R. Barclay Collection, reprinted in JFHS 48 (1956): 93.
79. Eliz[abeth] Morgan to M[argaret] F[ell] from prison in Cambridge, sent from Chester, November 9, 1654, SM, 1/192 (II, 339). The letter was also signed by Richard Hubberthorne and James Parnell.

as "all glorious within and beautiful: and the savour of thy sweet ointment which thou pourest forth abundantly doth cause the virgins to
love thee. . . . How greatly doth my soul love thee, and long after
thee. . . . Words fail me to express the breathings and thirsting that is in
me after thy life." He signed his letter, "thy babe in my measure of the
eternal truth."[80] Quakers not only bathed in a sea of polymorphous
spiritual nurture and eroticism; they occasionally wrote as if they had
succeeded in floating above gender altogether. Thus, "one Williamson's
wife . . . said in the hearing of divers [people] . . . that she was the eternal
Son of God; And when the men that heard her, told her that she was a
woman, and therefore could not be the Son of God: She said, no, you
are women, but I am a man."[81] John Perrot signed a letter to Quakers,
"I am your sister in our spouse, John."[82]

If the sceptical outsider found the Quakers' verbal and body language
tinged with antinomianism, Quakers themselves felt assured of their
essential righteousness because their most ecstatic outbursts took place
within the shelter and authority of their own community, one composed
in great part of families and their servants and neighbors. Quakerism
began, in fact, as a family and neighborhood movement, one that drew
on the ethics and emotions associated with kinship and friendship but
divested them of the aspects of patriarchy and clientage, which were
commonly attached to those relationships. "No man can speak the
language of the spirit in flattering titles," wrote James Nayler, "neither
doth the spirit frame any such speech."[83] Quakers saw the community
as a practical basis of organization, a source of emotional sustenance,
and a kind of spiritual template—a pattern of sanctified, egalitarian
social behavior that would serve as a model for outsiders. "There is a
summer religion," said George Fox,

> that is up and flourisheth while the sun shineth. . . . But this is not the nature
> of the sheep of Christ. . . . The sheep will get atop of the highest hill, and

80. Henry Fell to George Fox, 1655, SM 4/182 (II, 87).
81. Francis Higginson, *A Brief Relation of the Irreligion of the Northern Quakers*
(London, 1653), 3–4. When the minister of a country church quoted St. Paul's injunction
against women preaching to the prophet Dewens Morry, "she denied that it was the voice
of a woman who spoke, but said that it was the voice of the spirit of God" (QPE,
132–33).
82. John Perrot to Quakers from Lyons, about 1661, quoted in SPQ, 231–32.
83. James Nayler, *An Answer to Twenty-Eight Queries Sent out by Francis Harris
to Those People He Calls Quakers* (London, 1655), 8.

mountain, and set their backs and tails against the storm and tempests, and
bleat for one another; and when the dogs are abroad among the sheep, they
will run together . . . and so Christ's sheep beareth fruit in the winter
storms.[84]

"Let thy prayers be for me," wrote Ann Audland to Margaret Fell, "for
except I abide in the root I cannot bring forth fruit."[85]

There was no lack of biblical models for the Quakers' sense of community. Friends were the elect nation,

brought forth by the same Womb, and have sucked the same breasts. . . . By
faith with *Abraham* are ye come out of your native country from among your
kindred . . . and with *Moses* have you forsaken the glory of *Pharoah's*
house. . . . Look not back at the glory of Sodom, nor at the riches of Egypt,
but follow [God].[86]

The Quaker community was also modeled on the tradition of apostolic
friendship and mutual sacrifice. When George Whitehead languished in
prison, Margaret Sutton offered her own body as a replacement for his:
"herein I do own the Scriptures, and witness them, and the fulfilling of
them in me by Christ Jesus, who suffered and laid down his life for his
flock, and greater love hath no man than this to lay down his Life for
his friend."[87]

The Quaker meeting was a moral and spiritual reference point, a way
of validating the objective authenticity of one's own experience of God.
Thus, Friends expected that their behavior toward each other, being in
the light, would also be both conscientious and loving, both judgmental
and nonviolent. Richard Farnsworth counseled Friends to

meet often together . . . and stir up that which is pure one in another. Live
not in words but mind the power of words . . . words that cometh from
the life will go to the life and raise up that which is pure, and so you will
have unity with that which is pure in one another. . . . It will cross and
crucify that which would consult with wisdom and reason, and so you will
be brought into a discerning and a perfect savor . . . both in your selves and

84. G[eorge] F[ox] to Friends, Book of Epistles of George Fox, Richardson Manuscripts, 975c, Haverford College Library Quaker Collection.
85. Ann Audland to Margaret Fell, Banbury, March 30, 1655, William Caton
Manuscripts III, 3/144, S.81/440–41.
86. Burrough, *A Warning from the Lord*, 27–29.
87. Margaret Sutton to the Judge of Assize at Bury, August 20, 1656, printed in
Besse, 2:662.

also in one another, to savor every ones words from what center they do arise.[88]

We can appreciate the totality of the individual's identification with the group (or, more accurately, the individual's perception of the group as a prism that would refract his or her own emotions) by observing the struggles of one William Caton, a young and very dedicated Quaker who experienced a "leading" toward the act of marriage. Caton, a former member of Margaret Fell's extended household at Swarthmore, became a missionary in Holland in the early 1650s, where he conceived an affection for a member of an important Dutch Quaker family, Annekin Diericx. "And now," he wrote to Margaret Fell and George Fox,

> it is upon me to impart a matter . . . unto you, hoping and expecting your council and advice . . . even as a child would expect advice from his parents in a thing which was beyond his capacity. . . . [I felt a] mighty clear opening of my proffering of my self to take [Annekin's] part in marriage. . . . This thing settled in me, and grew clearer and clearer, neither could I expel it as heretofore I could have done [a] flashing thought which have come as lightenings in some cases, . . . for the longer it continued the more assurance I came to have in my self, of the thing being of the Lord. . . . And in the mean time it came to be shown unto me, how I should proceed in the thing: As first of all . . . I was to propound it to some dear friends to hear and receive their advice . . . and so much subjection I found then in my spirit that if they . . . had been against the thing, and had not seen it in part to have been of the Lord, and that they also had no unity with the thing that then I could (I believe) have let the thing have fallen and have rested satisfied in myself about it; for after I had given up to the will of the Lord in the thing I had little trouble in my spirit about it, but felt rather much peace and contentedness. . . . But further . . . I saw that if the friends to whom I was to propound the thing had . . . unity with it, then I was to proceed so far as to ask her a question. . . .
>
> Now after that I had cleared my self of the thing by propounding it to her (which I can truly say I did in the cross) I was afterwards as free and as clear . . . as if the thing had never been.[89]

The importance that Friends placed on their collective identity within the meeting must partially account for the formulaic and "literary"

88. Rich[ard] Farnsworth to M[argaret] F[ell], Balby, 1652, SM, 3/45 (II, 19–20).
89. William Caton to G[eorge] F[ox] or Margaret Fell, Amsterdam, June 6, 1662, SM, 1/329 (I, 481–85).

quality of their hundreds of personal letters. Quakers of the second and third generation have left us journals, poems, even full-blown autobiographies; but for all that the earliest Friends wrote and published, and for all the fervent lyricism of their salutations to Margaret Fell and George Fox, they had remarkably little to say about their own emotions, other than that of love, once they had become regenerated; the passages quoted above, describing southern women's despair *before* their convincement, were embedded in their published tracts and epistles, intended as exempla for the unconverted. Occasionally, Friends did admit the persistence of weakened resolve, of lustful thoughts, or confusion about the interpretation of the inner voice; but in general (and in strong contrast to contemporary Puritan literature), introspection or conscious self-castigation virtually disappeared from private writings once the initial upheaval and convincement was resolved. Indeed, Quakers never displayed the obsessive preoccupation with personal depravity that some Puritans did, once their convincement had been accomplished. No Quaker, man or woman, wrote like Edward Taylor, who described himself as "a dirt ball, a muddy sewer, a tumbrel of dung, a dung-hill, a dot of dung, a varnished pot of putrid excrements, drops in a closestool pan, guts, garbage and rottenness."[90] And no Quaker ascetic approached the self-loathing of the Fifth Monarchist John Rogers, who, when in a state of severe poverty, felt that he should even eat himself.[91]

The relative absence of personal introspection in Friends' correspondence may have also resulted from the fact that their letters were not truly personal in the modern sense. Hundreds would be recopied as inspirational messages of self-transcendence and loyalty to the group (sometimes edited by George Fox to tone down the most adulatory passages), while many were explicitly framed as epistles, to be circulated and read aloud at meetings. Letters were also the primary means of organizing the movement, and the communication of ministers' itineraries or Friends' suffering in prison was clearly of more immediate importance than the luxury of personal intimacy. Thus, John Camm reported that a Friend had recently arrived with a letter to another minister from the man's wife:

90. Edward Taylor, quoted in Koehler, *Search for Power*, 18. Isaac Penington's early writings, done when he was a Puritan, do resemble these works to some degree; his later writings, following his conversion to Quakerism, do not (Keiser, "From Dark Christian to Fullness of Life," 44–63).
91. John Rogers, *Ohel or Beth-shemesh: A Tabernacle for the Sun* (London, 1653), 434, quoted in Nigel Smith, *Perfection Proclaimed: Language and Literature in English Radical Religion, 1640–1660* (Oxford: Clarendon Press, 1989), 37.

"I opened it to see if there were anything of haste in it, but there is but little, but love from his wife."[92]

I suspect, moreover, that the Quakers' emphasis on the unity of Friends not only validated and reinforced the individual's own conviction of being "in the light"; it must have also influenced the believer to suppress feelings that would not immediately resonate with the group as a whole. The Quakers' reluctance to scrutinize their own negative emotions may have also been due to their acute sensitivity, even defensiveness, about the potential for emotional chaos in their practices of physical quaking and ecstatic prayer.[93] In any case, none of these suppositions should lead us to dismiss the Quakers' private letters as emotionally inauthentic. Indeed, Friends' inner assurance that their passionate feelings *were* authentic, that they emanated from God and not the devil or mere ego, was based largely on the resemblance of their own sponta-

92. John Camm to Margaret Fell, 4th mo. 1656, William Caton Manuscripts III, 3/159, S. 81/478–79. William Caton copied Friends' personal letters in order to glorify Margaret Fell and highlight the travels and suffering of Friends (William Caton Manuscripts S. 81, 3/1). One letter of Mary Howgill to George Fox was edited by Fox to tone down the language; Fox crossed out phrases like "George my dear life" and substituted "my dear friend" (Mary Howgill to George Fox, Lancaster, 1656, A. R. Barclay Manuscripts, vol. 323, no. 41, Library of the Society of Friends, London; see also BQ, 105 n. 1).

93. See chapter 2, pp. 82–83, on John Gilpin's mental distress. James Nayler, who himself experienced something like a nervous breakdown and was one of the few Friends to write about his distress, informed Margaret Fell about a young male Quaker who, being persecuted by his father, an Anglican priest, heard a voice telling him to set himself on fire; the man thrust his hand into a kettle of boiling liquid, but he recovered (Nayler to Margaret Fell, 1653, SM 3/192 [II, 869], passage crossed out). Several ex-Quakers published works recounting their experiences of mental imbalance, which they blamed on Friends. John Toldervy became convinced that a fly that flew into his face was a messenger from God, and he claimed he was subsequently "guided by Flies in many things; being very certain, that they were moved by God in them, to make known what was his will to me." Once he held his leg over a flame where a fly hovered for twenty minutes, burning himself severely. He preached that God wanted Quakers to stack the sticks, stones, leaves, and bricks in their gardens separately, and when he saw two white stones in his path, he threw away the larger one, which represented Esau, and kept the smaller, which "did not only signify Jacob, but the white Stone spoken of in the *Revelations*, which was sent as a token from Christ in Heaven to me; and so long as I kept that stone I had unity with God; but if lost, I should be disunited" (John Toldervy, *The Foot out of the Snare Being a Brief Declaration of His Entrance into That Sect Called Quakers* [1656], 3, 32–42, quoted in Vann, *The Social Development of English Quakerism*, 29–30). Jane Turner had a similar though more restrained experience. Sitting silently in meetings, she thought she had the power, and once she thought she had communion with God, "but I do believe it was no such thing, but a mere Spirit of delusion . . . for after a little time I began to lose my peace, and was very much troubled, having little or no communion with God, nor scarce any thing to speak to or for God." She was told to be patient but finally began questioning God's existence; ultimately she reread scripture and was restored to peace (Jane Turner, *Choice Experiences of the Kind Dealings of God before, in, and after Conversion* [London, 1653], 116–18).

neous language to that of other regenerate Friends and to that of the traditional sacred language of the Bible.

THE SOUL AS FEMININE

Wisdom is my mother and Counsel are her breasts. I am a child and desire ever to be found a sucker of the substance thereof.

John Perrot

Why should Quakers have taken such deep satisfaction in the portrayal of their own regenerate selves as infantilized or feminine, and why were metaphors of wifely ardor and passive, blissful feeding on the word embraced by men more often, and with greater fervor, than by women? Men outnumbered women in the movement, and men were more fully literate. Men (and women) were also inevitably aware of the long Christian tradition that placed both the male and female worshiper in the position of a child or bride in relationship to God. Yet the male Friend's adoption of feminine images was far more than lip service to an old tradition or an ornamental salutation in a scrawled private letter. Clearly, men felt a particularly acute sense of release in identifying with the infantile and feminine qualities of passivity, emotionalism, and loss of bodily inhibition, for in doing so they proclaimed their victory over the recalcitrant, masculine attributes of rationality, aggressiveness, and arrogance, which had formed the hard carapace of the old self. At this historical moment, when the values of the patriarchal family and state were promulgated and defended at all levels of culture, Quaker men experienced a powerful emotional catharsis as they abandoned themselves within the collective authority and succor of their new community. So the seventeen-year-old Charles Marshall, seeing a leading Quaker rise to speak at a meeting, felt himself begin to shake, "and all my limbs smote together and I was like a drunken man because of the Lord and because of the word of His holiness, and I was made to cry like a woman in travail."[94]

Women shared wholeheartedly in the Quaker theology of perfection and in the Quakers' rejection of an aggressive and rational egoism. For a woman to affirm her own spiritual babyhood, however, implied a less dramatic reversal of status and a less radical emotional shift than it did

94. Charles Marshall's testimony in *The Memory of the Righteous Revived* (1689), quoted in BQ, 167.

for a man, not least because all babies and young children were commonly dressed as girls.[95] It also offered a narrower opening for the uninhibited expression of emotion, for women cannot have been oblivious to their greater vulnerability to criticism as creatures prone to hysteria and inconstancy. Indeed, historians of Quakerism never fail to quote Margaret Fell's one effusive letter to George Fox and Fox's good influence in steadying her shaky feminine temperament, but they rarely quote the dozens of equally effusive letters by men.[96] As a gesture intended to redress that imbalance, we note that Elizabeth Hooton wrote repeatedly of her love of God and loyalty to Friends, but for sheer feminine abandon (expressed, as always, in biblical imagery) she never wrote a word to compare with this passage by her son Samuel:

> The strength of my god apeared in me so was I made perfect, through weakness. . . . With his love he doth embrace me . . . he fills me with sweet smelling savours, perfumed with heavenly odors . . . he waters me with the heavenly dews . . . he hath fashioned me according to his will, a vessel fit to put in what he will; I am not mine own but the lords; I am my beloved's and my beloved is mine.[97]

Images of femininity and infancy had a further significance for regenerate Friends, for womanhood stood to contemporaries as an emblem of timelessness, of an eternal and repetitive reality quite outside the ordered march of history. George Fox once had a vision of his own spiritual destiny:

> I was walking in the fields and many friends was with me, and I bid them dig in the earth: and they did and I went down: and there was a mighty vault top full of people kept under the earth, rocks, and stones: and so I bid them break open the earth and let all the people out: and they did, and all the people came forth to liberty and it was a mighty place. . . . And I went on again, and bid them dig again, and friends said unto me: George, thou finds out all things.

95. On the male fear of becoming feminine, see Marianne Novy, "Shakespeare and Emotional Distance in the Elizabethan Family," *Theatre Journal* 30 (1981): 316–26. Novy describes a personality ideal that kept tears and grief under control but not anger. Coppelia Kahn, writing on *King Lear*, speaks of a "maternal subtext," a discourse that underlay the dominant, patriarchal, and misogynist one and that expressed a yearning—particularly acute during this period of heightened patriarchal values—for a relaxation into the solace of remembered images of nurturing motherhood (Coppelia Kahn, "The Absent Mother in *King Lear*," in *Rewriting the Renaissance: The Discourses of Sexual Difference in Early Modern Europe*, ed. Margaret W. Ferguson, Maureen Quilligan, and Nancy J. Vickers (Chicago and London: University of Chicago Press, 1986).

96. See, for example, BQ, 105–6.

97. Samuel Hooton, "Something concerning my travell, & of the dealings of the lord with me since the lord brought me from my dwelling" (n.d.), Portfolio Manuscripts 3/80. This may have been the Samuel Hooton who became insane in 1694. (Manners, *Elizabeth Hooton*, 82).

And so there they digged, and I went down, and went along the vault, and there sat a woman in white looking at time how it passed away.[98]

Yet in another sense, history was also at the very center of this millennarian movement, for Quakerism's liminal aspect, its ecstatic blurring of the boundaries between individuals, classes, and genders, was merely a prelude and an ongoing background to Friends' assumption of a prominent role at the climax of human history, as public prophets of the apocalypse; a role, we shall see, that they imbued with the attributes of a firmly masculine persona.

98. Fox, *Journal*, 2:175, quoted in Brailsford, *Quaker Women*, 337.

CHAPTER FIVE

Prophecy

I am moved to declare unto thee how it hath been with me
since I saw thy face in the flesh. Upon the seventh day, . . .
being come about five miles, I sat me down to rest, and
sitting upon the ground a while, I [was as?] if I had been
taken out of the body, . . . and upon the fourth day after, I
dreamed that I was carried into a pleasant garden . . . and
as I came from the garden there stood in the way many . . .
and they was very vicious, but . . . I was made to come
boldly through the midst of them, declaring and spreading
forth my hands at them, and they was all put to silence. . . .
Upon the third day of the week after, there was at the next
house to ours a company of proud men and some of them
they call gentlemen which did highly dishonor the Lord . . .
and in obedience to the Lord I was said to rise out of bed in
the night and writ unto them, and in obeying I had sweet
peace.
                              Susanna Arnold to George Fox, 1657

Dear George thou mayst think, but little do friends know or
consider what I go through to bring up seven small children
and to answer uprightly on all occasions.
                              Mary Forster to George Fox, 1663

INTRODUCTION

As Friends held themselves to a condition of perfection in prayer, work,
friendship, even sleep, they experienced visions, dreams, and auditory
commands that intruded upon both the habits of everyday life and the
harmony of the meeting, moving them to engage in bold prophetic acts.
The substance of these visions and commands was, in many cases, similar
to that of other contemporary prophets; so Anna Trapnel's vision of wild
animals, and of a bull with Oliver Cromwell's face, was echoed in Mary

Howgill's sudden sight of a wood full of beasts, "which had many horns and sharp, and great jaws, and great paws also. . . . The Lord had showed me these things in the vision of the cloud, and that it should spread over the nation . . . and that the bloody men therein should fall upon many with cruelty."[1]

What distinguished Quaker women prophets from other female visionaries was less the content of their challenges to political and ecclesiastical authority than their mode of self-presentation. In a world of cascading wigs, extreme décolletage, high-heeled shoes, and massively applied cosmetics, Quaker women preached in public with loose or covered hair and wearing clothing stripped of buttons, lace, or any sort of trimming. Standing alone or accompanied by other Friends, they chastised neighbors, judges, clergymen, and monarchs, face to face, in churches, graveyards, private houses, and before the doors of Parliament. As worshipers they had melted, wept, and quaked in an atmosphere of ecstatic, sympathetic bonding. In public they shouted, insulted, and provoked, seeking to trigger in their audiences a process of self-scrutiny and inward repentance, proving the authenticity of their message by their own upright bearing as they were punched, bludgeoned, and whipped by enraged ministers and magistrates.

"Come down thou well favored harlot, thou deceivest this people," cried a spinster of Overkellett, Lancashire, to the rector of Aldingham. "Come down thou greedy dog, woe unto thee," called Ann Cleaton, a servant in the household of Margaret Fell, to the same clergyman. Mary Tompkins, ordered by a Boston magistrate to remove her hat, threw it on the ground, clapped her foot on it, and said, "See I have your honor under my feet." Mary Boreman, being taken from a meeting in London, was asked by the alderman what her name was. "You may, instead of my name," she replied, "write thus, 'Afflict not the widow and the fatherless,' and then when you look over the roll you may see your duty." Dorothy White battered the congregation of a church in her home town of Weymouth:

> The *Lord* . . . moved me to go into your steeple house, . . . foreseeing the great misery and desolation that is coming upon you. . . . But before I could deliver what the *Lord* sent me to deliver, they set hands on me, and put me forth. . . . But when I came up again, the *Lord* led me in again, and many strived against me, and put me out again before I had done delivering the message of the

---

1. M[ary] H[owgill], *The Vision of the Lord of Hosts* . . . (1662), 3, 4. There were two Mary Howgills who prophesied, this one a sister of the prophet Francis Howgill, the other a spinster of Overkellet, Lancashire.

Lord; Again the word of the *Lord* came unto me, *Go and say the Lord of hosts hath sent thee to bear witness against the idol shepherds*; But many strived against me, but wo from the *Lord God* unto them that strive to hinder the messenger of the Lord: Again the word of the *Lord* came unto me: *Go cry against the foolish prophets that preacheth lies in my name* . . . which word is like a fire, and like a hammer. . . . But two fierce spirited men . . . came and haled me forth, and said it was the Devil's work, and that I looked like the Devil.[2]

Elizabeth Peacock walked into a London church, admonished the congregation to have contrite spirits, and was sentenced to hard labor for two months. She then returned to the same church, preached against hypocritical worship, and was jailed for four weeks. She then reappeared in another church, where she told the congregation that the kingdom of God was within them, and was removed from the building and released near her house. The following day she walked out of a Quaker meeting and into the chapel at Whitehall, where she announced that it was impossible to please God without faith; she was put in jail for six more weeks.[3] After Deborah Harding was arrested for attempting to preach in a church in Gloucestershire, the magistrate offered to release her if she paid a fine (she refused); then if she promised to be good (she refused); then if she promised to leave by a back door (she still refused); he reluctantly sent her to jail.[4]

Women transformed themselves into visual signs of the corruption of church and state. Elizabeth Adams left her farm in Kent and traveled to London, where she stood in front of the houses of Parliament for two days with a vessel on her head; she then overturned it, "as many things were turned, and aturning," sat down on it, and finally smashed it. The following year she bought two torches, lit them, and rode silently through the streets of Canterbury on horseback. When questioned by the magistrate she announced, "Friend, I seek . . . an honest man that truly fears the living God, and will stand up to vindicate the Truth." When he threatened her with hanging, she replied laconically that, "He was not the man she looked for."[5] Elizabeth Simcock stood in a church in Cheshire holding a lantern, a candle, and a sheet of white paper. She

2. BQ, 199. George Bishop, *New England Judged, Not by Man's, but by the Spirit of the Lord* (London, 1661), 460. Besse 1:398. Dorothy White, *A Diligent Search amongst Rulers, Priests, Professors, and People* . . . (1659), 7.
3. Sarah Fell, *Household Account Book of Sarah Fell of Swarthmoor Hall* (Cambridge: Cambridge University Press, 1920), 541n. Besse, 1:398. GBS, 2:1–2 (1659).
4. Besse, 1:209.
5. GBS 1:547 (1661).

burned the paper, broke the lantern, and cried out, "Even as you see this paper consumed with the fire so shall the wicked be consumed before the Lord, for he is a consuming fire."[6] Katherine Evans and Sarah Cheevers, being taken to a Catholic communion service in Malta, stood quaking for nearly an hour, "and being so overcome with their abominations, we went along the street reeling to and fro, and staggering like drunken men, so that we were a wound to all that saw us."[7] Sarah Goldsmith sewed a full-length coat of sackcloth, which she put on with no other clothing save shoes, her hair hanging loose and smeared with ashes; on seven different days she walked through the streets and stood silently in front of the high cross before the marketplace as a sign against the pride of the city of Bristol.[8]

For more than a hundred of these girls and women, the confrontation with authority in one's own church or marketplace was the first stage in a career of itinerant prophecy in England, Ireland, Scotland, Wales, America, and the European continent.[9] Mary Fisher first heard Quakers preach in 1652, when she was thirty years old, an unmarried servant living in the household of Richard and Elizabeth Tomlinson of Selby, Yorkshire. Convinced along with the master and mistress (who immediately rushed out into the street, "carried almost off her feet" in order to prophesy), Fisher entered a church to admonish the minister and was thrown into the prison of the castle of York. There she met Elizabeth Hooton, serving her second prison term as a Quaker prophet, and Jane Holmes, who had been ducked as a scold for preaching in the streets of Malton, inspiring the shopkeepers to hurl their silks and ribbons on a bonfire; together they signed a tract by another prisoner, Thomas Aldam, which condemned the imposition of tithes.[10] It may also have been during this prison term that Fisher wrote to the judge, protesting his sentence of death against three horse thieves: "Thou doth . . . contrary to that in thy conscience which tells thee thee should not put any to death for the creature. . . . Lay it to heart and let the oppressed go free. . . . Written by one who desires the good of all people Mary Fisher prisoner . . . who cryeth for justice and true judgement

6. GBS 1:139 (1661).

7. Katherine Evans and Sarah Cheevers, A True Account . . . (London, 1663), 144–45.

8. GBS 1:139 (Cheshire, 1661).

9. See Appendices 2 and 3. There are varying estimates of the number of missionaries to America; I find twenty-two women before 1664.

10. Tho[mas] Aldam to G[eorge] F[ox], York, 1652, SM 1/373 (I, 13); 3/36 (I, 19). On the Tomlinsons' conversion, see EQW 58–59.

without partiality."[11] When she was released over a year later, Fisher traveled south with another Friend, Elizabeth Williams, twenty years her senior. In Cambridge the two stood at the Sidney-Sussex college gate and admonished the students, becoming the first Quakers in England to be stripped to the waist and whipped, "and all the while they were in their punishment," writes the Quaker chronicler, "they sang and rejoiced, saying, *The Lord be blessed, the Lord be praised, who hath thus honored us . . . to suffer for his name's sake."*[12] Imprisoned again in York, where she had no money to share a room with other Friends, and in Buckinghamshire, in 1655, Fisher then took ship for Barbados and New England with Ann Austin, a London matron with five children. In Boston their books were burned, their bodies were searched for witches' marks, and they were kept in confinement with no one permitted to visit or assist them. Forced to leave the colony, the women were shipped back to Barbados, where Fisher preached for some months and received financial assistance for the journey home. ("Mary Fisher is a precious heart," wrote a Friend to Margaret Fell, "and hath been very serviceable here.")[13] Once in England, she addressed an epistle of encouragement to the Friends who had received her ministry in Barbados:

> Dear hearts go on in the power and might of our God, that you may conquer the whole earth, and rule over the inhabitants thereof, go on, look not back, press forwards. . . . My dear babes, love not your lives unto the death . . . give up freely, soul and body as a living sacrifice. . . . Truly our righteousness is of God, all other righteousness is as a menstruous cloth, and an unclean garment, which is a shame to be worn.[14]

In 1657, laden with books, Fisher embarked on a mission to Turkey with the Irish Quaker John Perrot and two other women. In Leghorn they preached for two weeks to Jews, Roman Catholics, and English residents. Traveling on to Smyrna, the party became separated, and Fisher ultimately reached Adrianople alone, where she was granted an audience with Sultan Mohammed IV, complete with state ceremony. Face to face with the tyrant, she announced that he was the one man in Europe most

11. Mary Fisher to the Judge in York, n.d., A. R. Barclay Manuscripts, vol. 324, no. 173, Library of the Society of Friends, London. Two were brought back from the gallows.
12. Besse 1:85.
13. T[homas] A[ldam] to M[argaret] F[ell], 1653, SM 3/42 (I, 37). Henry Fell to Margaret Fell, Barbados, November 3, 1656, SM 1/66 (II, 101).
14. Mary Fisher to Friends in Barbados, London April 9, 1657, Portfolio Manuscripts 33/112, 113, Library of the Society of Friends, London.

in need of her message. She was honorably received and dismissed; "yet have I borne my testimony," she wrote to three Yorkshire friends and their wives,

> before the king unto whom I was sent, and he was very noble unto me. . . .
> He received the words of truth without contradiction, they do dread the name
> of God many of them. . . . The English [in Italy and Turkey] are more bad
> most of them yet there hath a good word gone through them, and some have
> received it but they are few.[15]

In 1659 Mary Fisher was back in England, signing a petition with seven thousand women against the imposition of tithes. In 1662 she married William Bayly, a Dorset shipmaster, former Baptist preacher and leading Quaker with whom she had three children; he died in 1675. Three years later she married John Cross of London and settled in America. In 1697 she was a widowed landlady in Charleston, South Carolina, where she nursed a traveling Quaker back to health. Her children and grandchildren remained Friends, and one granddaughter, Sophia Hume, became a noted preacher and author; some also received bequests in her will, an estate that included some modest property and one black slave.[16]

    Visions and calls to prophesy were experienced by every sort of person in all parts of England where Quakerism spread. Indeed, every word spoken at a Quaker meeting was, in a sense, prophetic, because it was perceived as a direct communication of God's own voice. Thus, the actual number of female prophets or visionaries was far greater than the 243 girls and women whose actions or writings came to the attention of the authorities, the reading public, or the leaders of the movement and hence to the notice of the historian.[17]

    15. Mary Fisher to Tho[mas] Killam, Tho[mas] Aldam, and John Killam "with your dear wives," London, March 13, 1658, William Caton Manuscripts vol. 320, I/165, Library of the Society of Friends, London.
    16. DBR; Isabel Ross, *Margaret Fell: Mother of Quakerism* (London: Longmans, Green, and Co., 1949), 78; BQ, 421–24.
    17. See Appendices 2 and 3. With the exception of more eminent writers and prophets, the main source of women's public activities is the *Great Book of Sufferings* (Manuscripts in the Library of the Society of Friends, London), from which Besse's printed work is culled. This makes numerical accuracy impossible. On the one hand, some women may have preached in public but escaped arrest, while on the other hand, magistrates may have cited women as prophets who were actually silent. In Worcestershire, the sheriff arrived at a meeting and asked which one was the preacher. "A rude boy standing by pointed to a woman, and said, 'She was;' which was not true, the meeting being altogether silent. Nevertheless, those fellows went and swore before the Mayor, not only that 'there was a conventicle,' but that 'the woman preached at it'" (Besse, 2:77).

The call to prophesy was answered differently by different Friends. Some cleared their consciences by a single phrase or act, writing their warnings on scraps of paper that they pressed into the hands of the powerful. So Mary Howgill concluded her brief tract to Oliver Cromwell, "This in one of its first copies was delivered to *Oliver Cromwell's* own hands by the author her self, at or about the eighth day of the fourth month 1656, about ten a clock at night, with whom thereupon she had much discourse."[18] Other women, perhaps even more audacious, presumed to chastise their own kin and neighbors. "[I] am a witness of the new covenant," Rebeckah Travers wrote to the parishioners of Ashted, "knowing the pouring forth of spirit upon sons and upon daughters, and in it prophesy of the things which shall shortly come to pass . . . setting before you all this day, life and death."[19] Friends in prison, in anticipation of or recovery from whippings, beatings, and fines, put their signatures to collective protests, demanding more air, more straw, more justice. Still others composed lengthy epistles that were crafted from an initial visionary experience or spontaneous sermon, as in the poetry of Rebeckah Travers and Dorothy White or the theological reflections of Sarah Blackborow.[20] The resulting pamphlets and broadsides were then bound and distributed by booksellers and on streetcorners and marketplaces by the prophets themselves, who carried trunkloads of books with which to till the spiritual wastelands of Boston, Barbados, and Turkey.

The specific audiences for women's public writings were also different. Their social critiques and pleas for repentance were addressed to individuals (the rector of Aldingham, the gentleman John Lowther, the Protector Oliver Cromwell) and to larger groups (the houses of Parliament, the corrupt cities of London and Oxford, the whole people of the world). Or they were epistles addressed to other Friends, in meetings they themselves had established; so Mary Fisher acted as a pastor, not a social critic, as she encouraged the flock in places where she had already preached.

18. Mary Howgill, *A Remarkable Letter of Mary Howgill to Oliver Cromwell* . . . (London, 1657), 4.

19. Rebeckah Travers, *Of That Eternal Breath Begotten and Brought Forth* . . . (n.d.), Manuscripts Box 71, 8, Library of the Society of Friends, London (hereafter referred to as Friends Manuscripts).

20. Quaker women wrote 220 tracts of the 3,853 published before 1700. Eighty-two of the 650 authors were women (Hugh Barbour, "Quaker Prophetesses and Mothers in Israel," in *Seeking the Light: Essays in Quaker History in Honor of Edwin B. Bronner*, ed. J. William Frost and John M. Moore [Wallingford and Haverford, Pa.: Pendle Hill Publications and Friends Historical Association, 1986], 46). On the relation between prophetic messages, sermons and tracts, see EQW, 49–55.

What overall patterns can be discerned within this complicated array of activities, and how were acts of prophecy inwardly experienced? Did the prophet wearing sackcloth cower in front of the high cross, or did she gloat? Was the dreamer always confident of her ability to distinguish between inspiration and illusion? Did the aggressive speaker ever claim a personal authority "above her measure"? Were the acts of writing, speaking, and suffering understood in just the same way by both the fathers and mothers of the movement? We begin at the level of broadest generalization, with the Quakers' language and theology of prophecy and its significance for women as a group in relation to their male coreligionists.

FEMALE IDENTITY AND MASCULINE IMAGERY

Amos was a Herdsman, and a gatherer of Sycamore
fruit, . . . and the Lord said unto him, *Go
prophesy.* . . . And I do witness the same call, who
was a husbandman, and had a vineyard, and gathered
fruit.

> *Richard Hubberthorne, "A true testimony"*

Moses . . . refused to be called the son of Pharoah's
Daughter, but rather chose to suffer affliction with
the people of God than to enjoy the pleasures of sin
for a season, and so had I.

> *Elizabeth Farmer to Lord Newport*

On what grounds did Elizabeth Farmer claim the right to address her social superior in the person of Moses? Like the proponents of other egalitarian religious movements, Quakers defended women's public speech by citing the ancient Christian tradition of paradox, which held that the last—the poor, the ignorant, the diseased and despised—shall ultimately be first. So Daniel Baker affirmed the authority of the prophet Katherine Evans, calling her "the foolish vessel, . . . base, contemptible, and despised in the eyes of lofty men that must be laid low." Mary Dyer admonished the magistrates of Boston to remember the request of Queen Esther: "You will not then repent that you were kept from shedding of blood, though it was by a woman."[21] Priscilla Cotton told the magis-

---

21. Besse, 2:202, quoted in James Bowden, *The History of the Society of Friends in America*, 2 vols. (London: Charles Gilpin, 1850), 1:180.

trates in London that early Christian women had prophesied, and when the judge said it was a great while ago, "she told him, it was when the Church was in her beauty and glory but since darkness hath covered the Earth."[22]

These were traditional and historical arguments, but they were not doctrinal ones. The Quakers' main *substantive* argument for female preaching was not the glorification of weak and pious femininity but the assertion that a woman preaching in public had actually transcended her womanhood. "What I have seen and known, heard and felt," wrote Sarah Blackborow, "that declare I unto you, and my witness is true; if I bore witness of my self, it were not true; but my witness stands in him."[23]

Self-annihilation was, of course, a prerequisite for the preaching of both sexes. "I am as a white paper Book," wrote Richard Farnsworth, "without any line or sentence but as it is revealed and written by the spirit the revealer of secrets."[24] Far more often than not, however, both men and women depicted this self-annihilation as killing the woman within the self. As Farnsworth elaborated, "where [the Spirit of God] is manifested, either in male or female . . . then it is the man Christ that speaks in them."[25] "Oh! come out of words," wrote Edward Burrough,

> into the Word, which is nigh in the heart, in the mouth. . . . Let . . . [the Word] dwell richly in you, which will cut down, and wholly root out the whorish wo-man within your selves, which is not permitted to speak in the church, the which steals the prophets, Christ's, and his apostles words; O that's the clamberer, the thief, and the robber . . . from which the wo-man, the unprofitable talker, the vain babbler, boasts in the line of another man. . . . O *male* and *female*-man, wherefore keep thine *to within* in *thy head*, and *the head* of every man is *Christ Jesus*.[26]

Both the "male and female-man" must die in order for the "man Christ" to speak, but the "female-man" is clearly the most essential casualty.

22. GBS, 2:64 (London, 1662).
23. Sarah Blackborow, *A Visit to the Spirit in Prison* . . . (London, 1658), 7.
24. Richard Farnsworth to George Fox and Margaret Fell, November 12, 1654, SM, 3/51 (II, 64).
25. Richard Farnsworth, *A Woman Forbidden to Speak in the Church* . . . (London, 1654), 5.
26. Edward Burrough, *An Alarm to All Flesh* . . . (London, 1660), 7–8. See also the argument by Richard Farnsworth in his tract, *A Woman Forbidden to Speak in the Church*, 3–4: "The woman or wisdom of the flesh is forbidden to speak in the church, that is, of the things of God, for that which is flesh is flesh . . . it is the man child *Christ Jesus*, . . . that is to declare the Father's will, and that is permitted to speak." For another similar argument, see Patrick Livingstone, *Truth Owned and Deceit Denyed and Witnessed Against* . . . (London, 1667), 46.

Quakers further argued that, when a woman was in the light, she was God's bride, "at home" and in her proper place in the sense of being obedient to God, entirely passive and speaking only in his voice, even though her carnal self appeared to be screaming at a magistrate in front of the town hall. "And so," wrote George Fox, "by the leading of the spirit you come to Christ, another husband, of whom you are to learn as people were to learn of the Law; and such as are led by the spirit are the sons of God."[27] Thus, the liberation that allowed Quaker women to assume authority as political prophets had little to do with their conception of the rights of women (although most male Quakers did welcome the prophecies of women Friends); on the contrary, the Quaker female prophet was more aggressive than the visionaries of the 1640s because her disengagement from her own social identity or "outward being" was more radical.

Not surprisingly, both male and female prophets employed a repertoire of symbols that were weighted with images of masculine authority. Those same women who portrayed themselves privately as sucking infants or as the bride in the Song of Songs rarely presented themselves in public as the courageous Queen Esther, the heroic Jael, the praise-singer Miriam, or the militant judge Deborah; instead, they spoke as virtual incarnations of angry male biblical prophets. The tone and imagery of Ann Audland's private letter to Margaret Fell, her spiritual mother, was completely in tune with contemporary stereotypes of worshipful femininity:

> Oh my dear heart my love and life is with thee . . . blessed art thou amongst all women . . . for with thee there is a fresh spring which flows freely to the lambs and plants of god. . . . My tongue cannot utter the joy that I have concerning thee . . . my dear and near and eternal mother, by thee I am nourished.[28]

Audland's public language, spoken aloud to a group of magistrates and published in a long account of her trial, conformed just as fully to the stereotype of the harsh, judgmental patriarch:

> Ye stiff-necked and uncircumcised in heart and ears . . . truly you will be found as stubble before the fire, and as dust before the wind, *the whirlwind from the Lord God is gone forth, which will scatter the wicked, and the fire is kindled which will consume you.* . . . *Do you think the trumpet is sounded,*

27. George Fox, *Concerning Sons and Daughters, and Prophetesses Speaking and Prophesying* . . . (London, n.d.), 2.
28. Ann Audland to M[argaret] F[ell], 1655, SM 1/13 (I, 87).

*and the alarum given for nothing, or will you gather together your selves
against me, and set the briars and thorns in battle?*[29]

Mary Howgill also drew on a specific cultural archetype when she wrote
privately to Margaret Fell,

> Dear mother in the everlasting fountain of life I dearly salute thee and my love
> runs forth to thee daily in the unity of life which the lord hath called us unto
> into a newness of life when my soul is nourished and refreshed daily by that
> which is eternal. . . . I am out of all visible things . . . and so I rest thy dear
> sister in that which never changes.[30]

And she drew on another cultural archetype when, during the same
period, she addressed a letter to the people of England:

> You who have nursed your selves up in that great abomination, which is
> fornication, you are found in idolatry, and the mother of that Idolatry is a
> whore . . . your gay and glorious clothing, it's of your selves, and of the
> whorish woman, which hath the cup of abomination in her hand, and you
> are found in an ill smell, stinking in the nostrils of God . . . a day of terror
> will overtake you; a day of sorrow, and all your gallant flesh shall come down,
> and you shall be laid waste.[31]

The degree to which Quaker women disengaged their individual
gendered selves from their personae as prophets can be seen by the use
they made of feminine images in defense of women's spiritual authority.
Some women did cite biblical figures like Hannah or Deborah as justi-
fications for women's public acts; far more often, however, "womanhood" was used metaphorically to identify those who could *not*
preach. Dorothy White maintained that

> all, before they come into [preaching], must come unto silence, and so learn
> of Christ, the husband, the head of the woman, which is to keep silence: in
> the Church all flesh ought to be silenc'd, but he or she that is born of God,
> who are members of the same body . . . as this prophet speaketh, here the man
> speaketh, which is Christ in all.[32]

Priscilla Cotton argued that without God all men are reduced to being
women:

> Man in his best estate is altogether vanity, weakness, a lie. . . . Now the woman
> or weakness, that is man, which is his best estate or greatest wisdom is

29. Ann Audland, *A Warning from the Spirit of the Lord (in His Handmaid) Ann Audland,* . . . in *The Saints Testimony Finishing through Sufferings* (London, 1655), 11.
30. Mary Howgill to Margaret Fell, n.d., SM 1/378 (II, 493).
31. Howgill, *A Remarkable Letter,* 4, 5.
32. Dorothy White, *A Call from God out of Egypt, by His Son Christ the Light of Life* (London, 1662), 6.

altogether vanity, that must be covered with the covering of the Spirit . . . that
its nakedness may not appear. . . . Here mayst thou see . . . that the woman
or weakness whether male or female, is forbidden to speak in the Church; . . .
*Indeed you yourselves are the women, that are forbidden to speak in the
church, that are become women.*[33]

Katherine Evans agreed that while individual women might indeed
preach, the *real* women were those unsanctified Jezebels, male and
female, who were to keep silent in the church:

They say Paul would not permit of a woman to speak in the church; it is true
. . . no more do not the Quakers; neither do they permit a woman to speak
in the church, nor a man that is born of a woman; but he that is born of God,
whether in male or in female, let him speak freely. . . . But Paul nor John
neither would not permit that Jezebel, that painted harlot, should speak in the
church, who hath painted herself with the saints words.[34]

Rather than attempting to refute conventional symbols and stereotypes
of womanhood, Quakers tried to deflect misogynist sentiments away
from themselves and toward any individual, man or woman, who flouted
truth. So Margaret Lynam accused the Anglican ministers of being "silly
women—ignorant and unstable." Margaret Fell, who would later compose the first published work in defense of women's preaching, assailed
an Anglican priest: "The whore of Babylon is the mother of harlots, And
thou Shaw art one of her children . . . and thou drinks deep of her
abomination and filthiness and fornication."[35] Elizabeth Hooton, the
first Quaker woman preacher and a venerated "mother in Israel" within
the movement, admonished King Charles II, "Oh that thou would not
give thy kingdom to your papists nor thy strength to women."[36]

As we shall see, several women writers, usually those from the southern counties, did sometimes employ feminine images, but these usually
referred to abstract qualities or institutions, not their own authority as
visionaries. Thus, we read of Zion as a bride, the congregation as a wife,
London as a sick woman, Jerusalem or the purified soul as the espoused
virgin, the struggling sinner as a woman in childbirth. Like the non-

33. Mrs. Priscilla Cotton and Mary Cole, *To the Priests and People of England, We
Discharge Our Consciences, and Give Them Warning* (London 1655), 7–8.
34. K[atherine] Evans and S[arah] Cheevers, *A Short Relation of Some of the Cruel
Sufferings (for the Truths Sake) of Katherine Evans and Sarah Chevers . . .* (London,
1662), 35–36.
35. Margaret Fell to Thomas Shaw, Priest, Answer to Queries, 1654, Spence Manuscripts III, no. 138, Library of the Society of Friends, London.
36. "El. Hooton to some Spirits who were gone out from ye truth," August 13,
1667, Portfolio Manuscripts 3/33, quoted in Emily Manners, *Elizabeth Hooton: First
Quaker Woman Preacher (1600–1672)* (London: Headley Brothers, 1914), 57.

Quaker prophets described in chapter 3, these southern women gave
more energy, and far greater specificity, to their descriptions of womanhood as a figure of betrayal and corruption. "O a woe," cried Rebeckah Travers, organizer of the first women's meetings in London, "a woe
unto all that discerns not the signs of his coming . . . and the adulterous
eye cannot see him, which hath run a lusting after many lovers, yet pays
her vows, offers her offerings, and wipes her mouth, and saith she hath
done no evil, but her steps lead to hell."[37]

From the Quakers' own perspective, their altering of the popular
meaning of womanhood, holding to it as a negative abstraction while
rejecting its descriptive value for individual, sanctified women, must have
seemed a very effective argument—indeed, the only possible argument,
both theologically and strategically—that could justify the public authority of female prophets in a patriarchal world. This seems the only
way to view Richard Hubberthorne's tract in defense of the prophets
Elizabeth Leavens and Elizabeth Fletcher, a tract with the subtitle "Also
the lewdness of those two great mothers discovered, who have brought
forth so many children, and never had husband." The "mothers" were
the two male justices who had persecuted the ministers, while the real
women were referred to only as "two servants of the Lord."[38] It must
also be said that Quakers shared prevalent assumptions about the subjection of women in marriage and their unsuitability for positions of
political authority—that is, authority in the world, in the body. As
George Keith explained it some years later in a tract defending women's
preaching:

> It is permitted unto men, at times, to speak in the church. . . . An unlearned
> man may be permitted to ask a question in the church, which is not permitted
> unto a woman, nor is it needful, for She may ask her husband at home. But
> if the spirit of the Lord command or move a godly and spiritually learned
> woman to speak, in that case she is the Lord's more than her husband's, and
> she is to speak, yea, though the husband should forbid her.[39]

Whatever the intentions of these writers, the effect of Friends' theology
must have been to impose on women a greater distance between their
sense of themselves as individuals and as prophets and to force them to
demonstrate, over and over again, their essential absence from a scene

---

37. Rebeckah Travers, *For Those That Meet to Worship* (London, 1659), 13.
38. Richard Hubberthorne, "A True Testimony of the Zeal of Oxford-Professors,"
in *A Collection of the Several Books and Writings of That Faithful Servant of God
Richard Hubberthorne* . . . (London, 1663), 41, 42.
39. George Keith, *The Woman Preacher of Samaria* . . . (London, 1674), 11.

that they outwardly appeared to dominate. So Margaret Fell addressed
a local magistrate,

> thou said that I was puffed up with malice and pride and that the people saw
> it so, and that I did not see my self so, thy sight and the peoples is all one,
> you could but see me . . . with a carnal eye, which is the eye that offends the
> Lord, and must be put out before ever thou can see me or what condition I
> was in . . . thou art the woman that goes abroad and dost not abide in thy
> own house.[40]

In short, the self-transcendence of Quaker men was different from the
self-alienation of Quaker women. The public authority of Richard Hubberthorne was at least analogous to, if not derived from, his own gendered individuality: "*Amos was a herdsman, and a gatherer of sycamore
fruit*, . . . *and the Lord said unto him, Go prophesy unto my people
Israel.* . . . And I do witness the same call, who was a husbandman, and
had a vineyard, and gathered fruit, till the Word of the Lord came and
called me from it."[41] The authority of Elizabeth Farmer to speak as
Moses was grounded in her radical disengagement from self.

PROPHETS AS MOTHERS

If the theology of Quakerism dictated that women might prophesy only
insofar as they transcended their identity as women, it also dictated that
women who converted into Quakerism did not convert out of motherhood and family life. The vast majority of female prophets active in the
early years of the movement preached in the vicinity of their homes, or
they left on missionary journeys of a few weeks or a few months at most.
Most, though not all, of the women who traveled overseas as missionaries *did* leave their children entirely in the care of others for more
extended periods; yet even for these women, there was no question of
abandoning one's long-term domestic responsibilities if one chose to
become a Friend.[42] Indeed, Quaker polemics insisted on presenting
women not only as prophets and martyrs but as mothers, thereby high-

40. Margaret Fell to Justice Sawrey, 1653, Spence Manuscripts 3/146.
41. Hubberthorne, "A True Testimony of Obedience to the Heavenly Call," in
Hubberthorne, *A Collection*, 4.
42. Older children sometimes accompanied their parents on missionary journeys.
Elizabeth Hooton, a widow, made her second trip to America with her daughter Elisabeth. Margaret Fell traveled with *her* older daughters, although she also left some of her
six children for long periods (Bonnelyn Young Kunze, "The Family, Social, and Religious
Life of Margaret Fell," Ph.D. diss., University of Rochester, 1986, 43, 45, 61).

lighting both the brutality of the magistrates and their own normality and virtue. So Margaret Fell complained to Oliver Cromwell:

> And Gervase Benson wife being moved of the Lord to go to the great stee-plehouse, called the minster in York, being great with child, going to speak against the deceit of the priest, . . . was abused by the rude multitude, and thrown down under their feet, the magistrate looking on . . . and hath been imprisoned th[ere] a quarter of a year, and was delivered of the child in the prison, contrary to all humanity or any appearance of God in the least measure. Thieves and murderers might have had as much favor as she had there, her husband was a Colonel in the army . . . and is a friend to the commonwealth, but is brought into truth.[43]

Richard Davies remembered that when the bailiffs of Welch-Pool came into the meeting and took down the names of those present:

> When they had done, my wife called to justice Corbet, and told him, they had not taken the names of all that were at the meeting; he asked her, who was untaken? And she put her child towards him, about a quarter [three months] old. He said, that was under age. She answered him and said, We are all as innocent from plotting and contriving, or thinking any harm to any man, as this little child: which smote much this Thomas Corbet, and several others that were present. . . . Corbet [later said], . . . "I wish I were a Quaker in my life and conversation."[44]

For Mrs. Benson and Mrs. Davies, and for numerous other women Friends, family life included the raising of very young children. The visionaries of the 1650s did not resemble those medieval adolescent mystics whose visionary activities had the indirect result of helping them to avoid marriage, nor did they resemble other contemporary prophets, who were generally single; nor, indeed, did they resemble Quaker female ministers of the eighteenth century, who were generally described as either young maidens or "seasoned" widows and matrons.[45] Early Quaker prophets were a demographically diverse group, with a dispro-portionately large number of single women, but most were married or widowed, in their twenties and thirties, and therefore the heads of growing families.[46] So in Cumberland, Katherine Fell asked a question

43. M[argaret] F[ell] to Oliver Cromwell, 1657, Spence Manuscripts III, nos. 94–95.
44. Richard Davies, *An Account of the Convincement, Exercises, Services and Travels of That Ancient Servant of the Lord, Richard Davies* . . . (London, 1710), 124, 131.
45. See below, chapter 10.
46. See Appendix 2. Of the women cited as active prophets and missionaries for whom there is specific information, forty-eight were married or widowed, twenty were single and twenty-six were unknown. Hugh Barbour states that while many women had young children, they had fewer than the population at large ("Quaker Prophetesses," 50).

of a priest and was thrown into jail for nineteen weeks, "a young child sucking her breasts." In Staffordshire, Alice Bowman also went to jail carrying a nursing child who died there. After preaching against the "false hireling priests," Jane Waugh walked into Ilchester prison with a nursing child, having left her four other young children at home. In Essex, the pregnant Ann Child was beaten after speaking in a church. Elizabeth Leavens Holme, who had given her first baby to the care of Friends in order to travel and preach, later spoke to the judge in Westmoreland accompanied by her two small children; so did Margaret Fell, who stated at her trial, "I am clear and innocent of the wronging any man upon the Earth, as my little child that stands by me here." For opening her London shop on a Sunday, Elizabeth Baker was arrested and taken from one nursing baby and another small child who was "left to the wide world."[47]

It is not difficult to imagine the material and emotional suffering implied in these bare facts; or perhaps it is, given some historians' insistence on the absence of maternal feeling in periods of great maternal hardship.[48] Nevertheless, Quaker mothers did ache, both for their children and for themselves as seekers and leaders who were moved to leave their families in order to preach or to join other Friends. So Dorothy Howgill, writing to George Fox in the first flush of her conversion, struggled to accommodate her spiritual epiphany to the ongoing rhythm of her domestic responsibilities:

> Thou told me [a pure light] was arising in me when thou was here yet I could not believe because I felt no such thing . . . but now I know thou hast the anointing of the holy one and thou knows all things. . . . Oh, oh, praises, praises unto that God which brought ye hither and caused thee to come under my roof. . . . I cannot tell thee how dearly my love runs out to thee nor how fain I would see thy face, if the lord so order it that thou come to . . . Lancashire or to Sedbergh get me word if I can come to thee of a day for my little one cannot be without the breast of the night.[49]

47. GBS, 1:169 (1653); 2:4 (1664); 2:142 (1671); 1:407 (1657); 4(Part 2): 427 (1664). Besse, 2:379: "Abstract of the Trial of Margaret Fell, at the Assizes Holden at Lancaster, the 29th Day of the 6th Month, 1664." GBS, 2:2 (1662).

48. Lloyd de Mause, ed., *The History of Childhood* (New York: Harper and Row, 1974), Chaps. 1–7. Lawrence Stone, *The Family, Sex, and Marriage in England 1500–1800* (London: Weidenfield and Nicolson, 1977), 161–78. Elisabeth Badinter, *Mother-love: Myth and Reality* (New York: Macmillan, 1981), 1–114. An antidote to this view is the work of Patricia Crawford (see Bibliography). The Quaker historian Richard T. Vann observes that Quakers produced no child-rearing literature during the early years of the movement, deducing that the issue of nurture in the family was not of great concern to them (*The Social Development of English Quakerism, 1655–1755* [Cambridge, Mass.: Harvard University Press, 1969], 167–68).

49. Dorothy Howgill to George Fox, 1652, A. R. Barclay Manuscripts vol. 323, no. 32.

Mary Page would have understood her predicament. "Something there is stirring in me as to come unto thee," she wrote to William Dewsbury, "and the cross is much and hard concerning my husband, and my children hath been visited with sickness and doth recover but are not yet all recovered and I am often called from them and I do not see it clearly concerning my coming. I would have thee send unto me what thou seest more of it alway."[50] So would Mary Forster, who worried about earning enough money to feed her children while maintaining her moral integrity as a Friend. "[Let me be] kept out of the many temptations that attend my condition," she wrote to George Fox,

> in my worldly employment to provide food and raiment for my great family, dear George thou mayst think, but little do friends know or consider what I go through to bring up seven small children and to answer uprightly on all occasions, yet I complain not . . . their father . . . was made willing with me to give up our subsistance in faithfulness to god . . . for I have had very little trade this good while . . . yet all is well with me and mine, and I desire thou shouldst know we lack no good thing at present, and my great desire is that my children may grow up in the . . . faith and favor of the Lord.[51]

Elizabeth Stirredge prophesied as though she were willing and able to take on the whole, corrupt world single-handedly: "This is unto thee, oh King! Hear what the Lord hath committed unto my charge concerning thee: As thou hast been the cause of making many desolate; and as many as have been the cause of . . . the shedding of the blood of my dear children . . . hear and fear the Lord God of heaven and earth." King Charles II, to whom she handed the message in person, would have been surprised to learn that his chastiser was also a parent, one who felt intense ambivalence about leaving her children to preach. "I could not believe," she wrote in her journal,

> that ever the Lord would require such a service of me, that was so weak and contemptible, so unfit and unlikely, my understanding but shallow, and my capacity but mean, . . . to leave my habitation and tender children, that were tender and young, to go to King Charles, which was an hundred miles from my habitation, and with such a plain testimony as the Lord did require of me; which made me go bowed down many months under the exercise of it; and oftentimes strove against it . . . when I was going from my tender children, and knew not but my life might have been required for my testimony, it was

50. Mary Page to William Dewsbury, September 26, 1657, Temp. Manuscripts 61/6, Library of the Society of Friends, London.
51. Mary Forster to G[eorge] F[ox], February 15, 1663, SM IV, 167–68.

so plain; and when I looked upon my children, my bowels yearned toward them.[52]

Letters from some male Friends convey their awareness of women's (and, to a lesser extent, their own) struggles to fulfill both parental and spiritual obligations. So Thomas Aldam affirmed that the poor and foolish must forsake their families in order to confront the wise and prudent and then advised Margaret Fell to get her daughters home from York because they were under a bad influence.[53] Joseph Nicholson also wrote to Fell, telling her that his wife, sitting in a Boston prison, was in labor, and that some Quaker extremists refused to associate with them because they were clearly not celibate.[54] The following year, writing from Dover, he discussed his and his wife's plans in a long, depressed letter to Fell. He himself was going back to Virginia,

> but which way Jane will go . . . as to that I can not much say how it will be with her, maybe thou or G[eorge] F[ox] may see more of it, thou mayest see what I have writ to her at this time which comes with this letter . . . if there lie any thing upon Jane to go into the country she may use her liberty but if she be not clear of that place . . . it seems to me for her to leave the child if she could be sent into the north to the rest of our children. . . . My trouble hath been great many times since I went from this nation . . . but I hope in the lord the tempest as inward is much overcome but I am much short of what hath been or may be required of me.[55]

Elizabeth Leavens and Thomas Holme also struggled to integrate their desire for family attachment with their vocation as intinerant prophets. Preaching and singing together as they traveled through England and Ireland, they also married. "While I was with George [Fox]," Holme wrote to Margaret Fell, "[my wife] was delivered from her child, and was moved . . . in a cross to her will to give up her child to the friend which so long before had desired her, so a way it's like will be made that she may continue in the ministry which the desire of our souls is. . . . It's eight days since she was delivered."[56] This was not an unheard of strategy in that time; indeed, Joseph Nicholson suggested his wife Jane follow a

52. Elizabeth Stirredge, *Strength in Weakness Manifest* . . . 3d. ed. (London, 1772), 35–40. This was in 1670.
53. Thomas Aldam to G[eorge] F[ox], York, 1652, SM 1/373 (I, 16).
54. Joseph Nicholson to M[argaret] F[ell], Boston prison, SM, 4/107 (II, 923). A small group of Quakers, mainly in America, advocated total celibacy (BQ, 236; EQW, 520, 536).
55. Joseph Nicholson to M[argaret] F[ell], Dover Castle April 20, 1661, SM 4/106 (II, 939–40).
56. Thomas Holme to M[argaret] F[ell], quoted in Mabel R. Brailsford, *Quaker Women, 1650–1690* (London: Duckworth and Co., 1915), 153.

similar course with their own new baby. However, to the Holmes' undoubted surprise and chagrin, they were severely reprimanded by Margaret Fell, who chastised them for imposing on the hospitality of other Friends. The contrite parents then traveled in different directions to preach, Elizabeth engaging in manual labor in Cardiff to make her living. "And concerning our going together that shall be mended," wrote Holme,

> and what ever I have done amiss in that or other things I shall condemn. . . . If thou hadst known my burden thou would have dealt tenderly with me, but I am smitten of every hand. . . . Let things be weighed in just balance and do not judge us from reports . . . if our going together be the ground of what is against us, the ground shall be removed, . . . for we had both of us determined long before thy letter came to keep asunder . . . seeing the thing I am willing to part with all, and to give up all to the death of the cross.[57]

Years later, Elizabeth Leavens Holme came to visit her husband in prison, accompanied by two or three small children.

PROPHECY AND SELF-EXPRESSION

The different implications of Quaker theology for women and men, as well as their different material conditions, may help to explain why women's public language and behavior were, overall, considerably less idiosyncratic and pretentious than those of men. No woman described her experience as a prophet as Richard Sale did in a letter to George Fox: "My countenance was as fierce as a lion which was dreadful unto the wicked, and when the lion roared through the streets, the beasts of the field began to tremble and many faces gathered paleness before me . . . for my mouth was opened in much power."[58] Women did not pile image upon image with the energy of Edward Burrough:

> Howl, howl, shriek, yell and roar, ye lustful, cursing, swearing, drunken, lewd, superstitious, devilish, sensual, *earthly inhabitants* of the whole Earth; Bow, bow ye most surly trees, and lofty oaks, ye tall cedars, and low shrubs, *cry out aloud*; hear, hear ye proud waves, and boistrous seas, also listen ye uncircumcised, stiff-necked, and mad-raging *bubbles*, who even hate to be reformed.[59]

Women did not skirt the boundaries of coherent discourse as closely as did George Fox, writing on the powers of the earth: "Oh hypocrisy it

57. Thomas Holme to M[argaret] F[ell], Newport, April 30, 1656, SM 1/203 (II, 361–62).
58. Richard Sale to George Fox, October 28, 1655, SM 4/211 (III, 289).
59. Burrough, *An Alarm to All Flesh*, 1.

makes me sick to think of them. . . . There is an ugly a slobbering hound an ugly hound an ugly slobbering hound but the Lord forgive them—destruction—destruction."[60] And no woman wrote with the exuberant hyperbole of John Perrot, who called one tract "A wren in the burning bush, waving the wings of contraction to the congregated clean fowls of the heavens, Holy Host in the ark of God, Salutation."

As we shall see, a few women prophets were accused of unruly behavior by Quaker leaders during the movement's first fifteen years. Martha Simmonds was judged to have made an idol of Quaker leader James Nayler. Susanna Pearson attempted to resurrect a drowned man at Worcester.[61] Jane Holmes "did hold forth that all was destroyed in her . . . [and] she did kick against exhortation." So did Mildred Crouch, when she reputedly said that she was above the apostles.[62] The aspect of these delinquent women may have been grandiose or hysterical, but it was also less bizarre than that of Thomas Ibbott, who ran through the streets of London with his clothes loose, in the posture of one fleeing from a fire, or Thomas Holme, who lay on the floor of his prison singing for two nights running, or Solomon Eccles, who climbed into a pulpit and sat sewing before the congregation and who appeared in the doorway of a church with a pan of coals on his head, or Richard Sale, who threw weeds and flowers on his own head, or Francis Howgill, who attempted to cure a crippled child by touch, or James Nayler, who rode into the city of Bristol on an ass in imitation of Jesus' entry into Jerusalem, or James Milner, who claimed that he was Adam and his wife Eve, that George Fox was John the Baptist, and that a four-cornered sheet holding a sheep was shortly to descend from heaven.[63] Quaker men also appeared naked in public far more often than Quaker women.[64] Of course this symbolic

60. George Fox, *Journal of George Fox*, 2 vols. (Cambridge: Cambridge University Press, 1911), 2:172, quoted in QPE, 137.
61. Thomas Willan to Margaret Fell, February 1657, quoted in EQL, 368.
62. On Holmes, DBR 2:108. On Crouch, EQL, no. 429.
63. On Thomas Ibbott, see Brailsford, *Quaker Women*, 301–2. The women Friends who saw him were sceptical of his warning of fire, "fearing that he was under some Discomposure of Mind," but Ibbott was right; the London fire broke out two days later. On Holme, see his letter to Margaret Fell from Chester Prison ca. 1653, SM, 1/190 (11, 329); on Sale, see his letter to George Fox, October 28, 1655, SM 4/211 (III, 289). Solomon Eccles, *In the Year 1659 . . . the Presence of the Lord God Was Felt Within Me* (1659), 1–7. On Burrough and Howgill's unsuccessful attempt to cure a sick boy, see Fox's *Book of Miracles*, 12, from A. R. Barclay Manuscripts, vol. 323, no. 21, and crossed out. On Milner, see Kenneth L. Carroll, "A Look at James Milner and His 'False Prophecy,'" QH 74 (1985): 22, and BQ, 147. See also Barbour, "Quaker Prophetesses," 47. Women made predictive prophecies less often than men.
64. Kenneth L. Carroll, "Early Quakers and 'Going Naked as a Sign,'" QH 67, no. 2 (Autumn 1978): 69–78. Hugh Barbour notes that "No women Friends felt [the burden

behavior was derived from biblical exemplars, as was that of women, but the exemplars were chosen differently, and from a broader range. Quaker women did not see themselves as lions, and they did not climb into pulpits.

Like the non-Quaker prophets described in chapter 3, Quaker women labored in an environment that constrained them as females in direct proportion to the degree of public authority they sought to claim. They also labored as wives and parents, shouldering the ordinary responsibility of motherhood while they simultaneously attempted to transcend their material and emotional concerns as they were moved to preach. Not surprisingly, while women undoubtedly experienced their visionary moments as moments of personal catharsis, they acknowledged the experience purely as a catharsis of sacrifice (though, as we shall see, the sacrifice was not always performed with the same confidence or sense of calm inevitability). Jane Waugh began her career as an ignorant servant who had to ask Friends to write her letters for her. She died as one of the "valiant sixty" and as wife to another respected Quaker; she was a woman described by Friends as a hero of the movement. Clearly, she had grown and benefited by her conversion to Quakerism, yet she often confided to her husband that she would prefer to have died rather than endure what she had undergone as a prophet.[65] Rebeckah Travers was an even more prominent Friend. "I who know how precious your souls are," she wrote, "with thousands more, have been made willing . . . to go forth with our lives in our hands, denying all that has been dear to us, that you might be brought from under the power of the Prince of darkness."[66] To the extent that we *can* characterize Quaker public prophecy as a direct extension of the individual's sense of personal identity and expressiveness, it was an element in the activity of men rather than in that of women.

This familiar pattern of female self-denial may be dismaying to the modern observer. Yet when we remember that self-transcendence, not self-expression, was the ultimate goal of Quaker worship, we realize that women as prophets may have achieved that goal more completely, and with a greater sense of inward contentedness, than their male coreli-

---

to go naked as a sign] as regularly as did William Simpson, Richard Robinson, Samuel Cater, . . . and Solomon Eccles; two Massachusetts women Friends along with three Englishwomen did so once" ("Quaker Prophetesses," 47).

65. *A Testimony concerning the Life and Death of Jane Whitehead, That Faithful Servant and Handmaid of the Lord* . . . (1676).

66. Travers, *For Those That Meet to Worship*, 23.

gionists. For while men's finest moments of self-transcendence occurred in private or in the meeting, as their tears and quaking signaled their repudiation of the traditionally masculine traits of rationality, competitiveness, and aggression, it was in the act of prophecy that women proclaimed their utter separation from the traditionally female qualities of vanity, selfishness, duplicity, and lust, which, in the image of the Whore of Babylon, they then attributed to corrupt rulers and institutions. In this sense, their acts of public prophecy and visionary writing must stand, for the reader of their texts, as *their* own finest moment.

NORTH AND SOUTH

[Come] where the feast of fat things is prepared, . . .
where the streams of the pure fountain freely flow in
the still habitation, . . . feel the breast of everlasting
consolation, draw, drink abundantly . . . where the
turtle-doves do fly from the throne of his glory, whose
majesty and brightness hath ravished my heart.
                    Dorothy White, Weymouth, Dorset

God hath so ordered that the taking away of my
cattle hath been very serviceable, for by that means
have I had great privilege to speak to the faces of the
great men.
                    Elizabeth Hooton, Syston, Leicestershire

Quakerism began as a movement of country people from the midlands and northern counties, and it was a crusade for social justice as well as a quest for personal salvation. Margaret Killam, sister of a farmer from Yorkshire, spoke to the rich men of England:

> Howl ye rich men, for the misery which is coming upon you, for the rust of your silver and gold shall eat you through as a canker. . . . Howl ye proud priests, for the misery that is coming upon you, for ye shall run to and fro, as drunken men, and none shall be to pity you. Woe to you that have fed yourselves with the fat, and clothed your selves with the wool, and the people perish for want of knowledge; . . . because ye have departed out of my counsel, I will spread dung on your faces, yea I have cast dung on your faces already.[67]

67. Margaret Killam and Barbara Patison, *A Warning from the Lord to the Teachers and People of Plimouth* . . . (London, 1656), 2. This passage is by Killam.

Margaret Braidley of Westmoreland addressed a letter to the gentleman John Lowther:

> Woe unto thee that layest house to house, and land to land, till there be no room for the poor to dwell; the earth is the Lord's . . . thou art one of those that devours widows' houses . . . the Lord God will trample upon thee in the wine-press of his indignation; . . . the coming of our Lord Jesus Christ will be dreadful to thee, for oppressing the poor.[68]

Grace Barwick of Yorkshire traveled one hundred fifty miles to address the officers in the parliamentary army:

> There is a great darkness over you . . . and I feel a renting and tearing. . . . Is it not high time to remove the oppression of *tithes*. . . . There is a weight of blood cruelty and injustice lying under this great mountain, and it is time to be cast down . . . and the people eased from it: . . . and the people loves liberty, and however that shall come to them, it will be thankfully received, whether by a law or contrary to a law. . . . It is not the changings of government into new titles and names, but it is truth and perfect freedom that the best of men delights in, and it is that, that will satisfy the hungering people.[69]

The aggressive language of Old Testament prophets and their masculine, heavily rural imagery were characteristic of all Quaker public speaking and writing. The quotations in the preceding section of this chapter are taken from the writings of women in all parts of England where Quakerism flourished. However, in visionary writings by women from the cities of the south, the blood and thunder of their political prophecy was often tempered by a gentler, more mystical and meditative tone and a greater emotional range and self-absorption, sometimes expressed in positive feminine images. "Oh! love truth and its testimony," wrote Sarah Blackborow, a London matron,

> that into my mother's house you all may come, and into the chamber of her that conceived me, where you may embrace, and be embraced. . . . Love is his name, love is his nature, love is his life. . . . See the seed of the Woman, and the seed of the Serpent . . . and . . . see birth each of these bring forth; the wombs they are conceived in, which it is that bears, and which it is that is barren.[70]

68. Margaret Braidley, *Certain Papers Which Is the Word of the Lord* (n.d.), 10, 11, 13.
69. Grace Barwick, *To All Present Rulers, Whether Parliament, or Whomsoever of England* (London, 1659), 2, 3, 4.
70. Blackborow, *A Visit to the Spirit in Prison*, 10–11, 12. Compare these statements with the observation by Barbour and Roberts that "Friends had almost nothing to say about love in their message to the world, for fear of any word that would cater to man's self-esteem" (EQW, 52).

Esther Biddle, wife of a prosperous artisan, had a more feminine, sensuous vision of the world and of her own city of London than any
northern prophet had of York or Lancaster:

> Oh thou city! saith the Lord, who formed thee in the womb, and gave thee
> life and breath . . . have not I made the earth to bring forth her corn, and oil,
> and wine for thee?. . . Have not I caused to distill upon thy flowers and vines
> that they might give a fragrant smell unto thee? . . . Have not thine eyes beheld
> the glorious colors of the flowers and workmanship of my hands. . . . Oh
> *London!* . . . thou art full of running sores. . . . Have not I opened a well of
> pure water to bathe and made thee white?[71]

Katherine Evans, imprisoned by the Inquisition in Malta for three years,
had a vision in which she rescued a child who was herself:

> It had no clothes on but a little fine linen about the upper parts. . . . The fire
> did flame on every side of it, yet the child did play and was merry: I would
> have took it up, for fear it should have been burnt . . . and then [Christ] bade
> me take up the child, and it had no harm. . . . And then I did awake, and I
> called to my friend *Sarah*, and bid her she should not fear . . . and as we do
> believe, who can harm us.[72]

She also had a sight, rare among Quaker women, of the woman clothed
with the sun:

> And I saw a great wonder in heaven, the Woman clothed with the Sun, and
> had the moon under her feet, and a crown of twelve stars upon her head, and
> she travailed in pain ready to be delivered of a man-child; . . . and there was
> given to the woman two wings of a great eagle to carry her into the desert,
> where she should be nourished for a time.[73]

Yet another southern writer, Dorothy White (whose behavior as a
prophet is quoted on pages 166–67) used the Song of Songs, rather than
the invectives of the prophets, in her epistle to Friends; she also used that
imagery in a fashion that was less punitive, more lyrical, and more
self-consciously artistic than the language of female prophets from the
north. The "I" of her prose is not God's voice (as in Margaret Killam's
"I have cast dung in your faces already"); it is openly her own voice.

---

71. Esther Biddle, *The Trumpet of the Lord Sounded Forth unto these Three Nations* (London, 1662), 4.
72. Evans and Cheevers, *A True Account*, 264.
73. Ibid., 21, 23, 33, 35, 37.

"And the Lord God hath spoken," she wrote, "and therefore I will speak":

> The *dissolving power* of the Lord God, is dissolving *hell* and *death*; . . . and this is the birth which is brought forth through the *travail*, through *death*, . . . for the *bridegroom* is come, the *virgins* have *met* him, and the *damosels* dance at the glory of his *brightness*, . . . for the *ravishing* glory of God did over-shadow me. . . . And in the deep his voice is very sweet, unto the hungry is bread, both life and meat . . . and unto my beloved, unto thee, I sweetly sing, as the turtle in the time of spring; who for joy that she hath found her mate, what from thy love shall me separate? My soul doth swim within the sea of love, as doth the fishes in the water move.[74]

Like the London Fifth Monarchist Anna Trapnel but unlike northern Quaker women, Dorothy White attempted to express herself in rhyme, as did Rebeckah Travers, Dorothea Gotherson, and Katherine Evans as well as several Quaker men.

Certainly, the emotion expressed by Dorothy White and other southern women was no more ardent than that found in the prophecies and private letters of Ann Audland or Margaret Killam. Yet it was a qualitatively different emotion, for even the private letters of northern women primarily conveyed a sense of self-transcendence and fusion with the group, while southern women frequently placed their own individual struggles at the center of their published spiritual narratives. Even in expressing their principle of nonviolence, southern women wrote in a tone that overall was far less harsh and one-dimensional. Here is Ann Audland, of the northern county of Westmoreland, chiding Englishmen for their violent behavior: "O blush, and be ashamed of that which you call your Church, who are so suddenly in a tumult! Was there ever such a thing heard of amongst the saints, that they would be in a tumult, when one came in peaceably among them, not offering wrong to any?"[75] And here is a similar peace testimony by Dorothea Gotherson, a gentlewoman of Kent:

> Oh friends, that you could enter into the closet where the jewels are made up, and shut the doors about you. . . . [God] will reward you . . . when you can desire God to forgive you no further than . . . you forgive others; and when you can pray for such as hate you, and despitefully use you, even your

74. Dorothy White, *An Epistle of Love, and of Consolation unto Israel* (London, 1661), 2, 3, 4, 5, 6, 8–9.

75. Ann Audland, *A True Declaration of the Suffering of the Innocent*, in *The Saints Testimony Finishing through Sufferings* (London, 1655), 30.

enemies. . . . What and if thy brother be led by a fallible spirit? so art thou; and nothing shall overcome but a spirit of meekness.[76]

To be fair, this, and several other quotations of southern women belong to different genres; Ann Audland is addressing her persecutors directly, while Dorothea Gotherson and Dorothy White wrote general epistles whose thrust is more conciliatory than adversarial. Still, the epistle was a form adopted more frequently by southern writers than by visionaries from the north, and it is a form that lends itself more readily to the author's own craft and personality than the political prophecy.

Credible interpretations of these sharp differences in the spiritual styles of women writers seem eminently ready to hand. One easily frames the stern, evangelical preaching of northern women in the stark, complementary colors of rural simplicity and traditional biblical piety while setting the subtler preaching of southern women against the more richly textured background of the written and oral culture of the city. The differences between the writings of north and south are clearly reflective of a difference in education as well as that between town and country. The prophet Martha Simmonds, for instance, was the wife of one of the two most eminent Quaker publishers, Thomas Simmonds, and sister of the other one, Giles Calvert; historian Hugh Barbour suggests that it may have been her initiative that caused her husband to begin issuing Continental mystical literature in England.[77] Of the women who wrote five or more tracts, only the cultivated gentlewoman Margaret Fell came from the north (the others were Esther Biddle, Sarah Blackborow, and Rebeckah Travers, all of London, and Dorothy White, of Weymouth).

So much is obvious. Yet the real impact of these cultural differences on the mentality of visionary women is not at all self-evident. We might speculate that southern women, whose day-to-day experience was certainly more cosmopolitan and arguably less severe than that of most northerners, had a more positive sense of themselves as autonomous individuals. Certainly, the career of a Friend like Rebeckah Travers, the widow of a prosperous London tobacconist, seems to argue for an

76. Dorothea Gotherson, *To All That Are Unregenerated: A Call to Repentance* (London, 1661), reprinted in G. D. Scull, *Dorothea Scott, Otherwise Gotherson and Hogben, of Egerton House, Kent, 1611–1680* (Oxford: Parker and Co., 1883).
77. Barbour, "Quaker Prophetesses," 50. Thomas Simmonds also owned a bookstore from which he sold Friends' works. He published most of the works written by Friends from 1656 to 1660, although he was not a Quaker himself (*The Friend* [Philadelphia, 1843] vol. 16, 374).

interpretation in which southern, urban women are seen to be more self-aware, more socially evolved, and more cognizant of their interests as women—more modern, in short—than were northerners like Elizabeth Hooton or Mary Fisher. Travers, who "discovered" the Quakers while dining in eminent company with one of its chief male leaders, published several spiritual tracts, was instrumental in setting up the first women's meetings in the country, and presumably helped to run her husband's business on the side.

This rendition of Quaker women's mentality may be appealing to the observer seeking the origins of modern feminism. Yet it tells, at most, only a partial truth, for if southern prophets did indeed feel inspired to affirm their personal identities by using feminine spiritual imagery, they also felt impelled to deny those very identities as they sought to achieve a condition of self-transcendence, of "power over their corruptions," as the southerner Mary Penington wrote. And just as these efforts to achieve self-transcendence were undermined by the siren call of social and intellectual vanity (described in chapter 4), so their calls to prophesy involved a more radical distancing from familiar habits and privileges than was the case for most northerners: "your women in their sedans, running up and down with your meat from the cooks' shops, and drawing of your coaches up and down about the streets, that people can sometimes hardly pass up and down for them."[78]

Perhaps sensing the self-affirming aspect of their writing and behavior, southern women labored painfully to sustain a condition of moral purity, inserting themselves into their texts while simultaneously insisting on their complete disengagement from self. Thus, Dewens Morry told her readers that she had fasted for five days in order to prepare herself to compose a visionary tract. Sarah Cheevers and Katherine Evans, imprisoned in Malta, proudly informed readers that they had shocked even their Inquisitors by the extent of their fasting: "Then [the Inquisitors] did run to and fro like mad men, and the friars did come and say . . . we might have any thing we would eat; and they did say, it was not possible that ever creatures could live with so little meat for so long a time together. . . . It was a glorious fast indeed, the Lord did appear wonderfully in it."[79] Barbara Blaugdone, a schoolteacher of Bristol, wrote an autobiography

---

78. Anne Gould et al., *An Epistle to All the Christian Magistrates and Powers in the Whole Christendom* (London, 1659), 11.
79. Morey, 5; Sarah Cheevers to her husband and children, in Evans and Cheevers, *A True Account*, 113; Evans and Cheevers, *A True Account*, 151. On Evans's theology of perfection, see her *A Brief Discovery of God's Eternal Truth* . . . (London, 1663).

in which she emphasized both her connections with eminent local gentry and her own extreme asceticism. Blaugdone fasted repeatedly as a means of self-transcendence:

> I . . . willingly took up the cross . . . in plainness of speech and in my habit: and the people were so offended with it, when I went into their public places and steeple-houses to speak, that they took away their children from me, so that I lost almost all my employment . . . and great was my sufferings in that day. . . . And then the Lord caused me to abstain from all flesh, wine and beer . . . and I drank only water for the space of a whole year. . . . And then I was made to go and to call the people forth. . . . I fasted six days and six nights, and neither eat bread nor drank water. . . . Then I came to a feeding upon the Word . . . and I went to the Earl of Bath's, where I had formerly spent much time in vanity, to call unto them to come out of their vanity.[80]

One can only speculate on the impression she made as she preached outside Bristol, having slept in an abandoned pig trough the night before.

Northern women expended far less visible effort in distancing themselves from the decadent habits of their own culture. Whether poor farmers and servants like Mary Fisher or comfortable citizens like Fisher's master and mistress, Richard and Elizabeth Tomlinson, their feet appeared to be squarely planted on the high ground of moral superiority and moral outrage: the deprived Israelites assaulting the citadels of learning and corruption. Indeed, compared to the extreme asceticism of Barbara Blaugdone, Mary Fisher's counsel of frugality seems rather tame: "Never desire to have more in your disposing then you have present need of . . . for if we were provided for many days the thing would come to an end . . . and plenty would cause the thing to be loathed."[81] So, oddly enough, do the writings of Elizabeth Hooton and Ann Audland, who recounted their sufferings purely in order to expose the corrupt hearts of the magistrates who afflicted them. "A malignant woman keeps the jail," wrote Hooton from her prison in Lincolnshire.

> Oppression in meat and in drink . . . and in that which they call garnishes, and in many other things, and I my self am much abused . . . so that I cannot walk quietly abroad but be abused with those that belong unto her. . . . And so in drinking and profaneness and wantonness, men and women together

---

80. Barbara Blaugdone, *An Account of the Travels, Sufferings and Persecutions of Barbara Blaugdone* . . . (Shoreditch, 1691), 6, 9, 10, 11, 12.
    81. Mary Fisher to Tho[mas] Killam, Tho[mas] Aldam and John Killam "with your dear wives," London, March 13, 1658, William Caton Manuscripts vol. 320, I/165.

many times part of the night, which grieves the spirit of god in me night and day. This is required of thee o man, to reform this place.[82]

Interestingly, the most notable case of self-imposed fasting among northern women occurred in the gentry family of Margaret Fell, when all the girls of the household, including servants, joined in a display of collective self-denial lasting several days.[83]

Not only did southern women take greater pains to distance themselves from their own corrupt habits; they were also more concerned to validate their own leadings to prophesy in terms of the group as a whole. So Elizabeth Adams, having mounted a horse and ridden through Canterbury with a burning torch in her hand, wrote to George Fox, "I hope thou need not be ashamed of me, but if I have misbehaved my self in any thing as concerning the truth, if thou have a word from the lord, dear friend, deal plainly with me."[84] Elizabeth Cox, a former servant of Canterbury, wrote to Fox from Amsterdam, where she had settled as a missionary:

> It hath been upon me to visit friends in . . . [Germany]. At first when the thing came before me, my heart was filled with sorrow, and I begun to question what I should do there, and to look how hard a thing it was to go, and so many other thoughts came into my mind . . . and so I endeavored to shut it out, and to be still in the thing . . . and so after that W. Ames came here, and I understanding that he had drawings to visit those friends, then I also waited to see if his going might clear me, but since his departure the thing hath lain more heavy upon me than before, and I see nothing at present that will clear me except I go, nevertheless I had great freedom to lay the thing a little before thee, that if it were so, that I might be cleared of it, and not go, I should be glad.[85]

Elizabeth Harris, organizer of the first Quaker meeting in Maryland and a highly respected minister, sometimes appeared in London churches wearing sackcloth and ashes. She was distressed when her behavior was criticized by Friends, and she spoke of it repeatedly, "with many tears"; she felt she could not follow her own inspired leading to undertake a missionary journey to Manchester before George Fox had advised her

82. "E. H. Prisoner in Lincolne Castle, pleads to him in Authority to reform the abuses of ye Gaol," ca. 1654, reprinted in Manners, *Elizabeth Hooton*, 14–15.
83. Ross, *Margaret Fell*, 82. Several Quaker men also fasted for as long or longer periods.
84. Eliz[abeth] Addames to George Fox, Whitfield, May 26, 1657, SM, 3/118 (IV, 5).
85. William Caton and Elizabeth Cokes to G[eorge] F[ox], Amsterdam, March 8, 1661, SM (I, 414–16).

what to do.[86] Barbara Blaugdone, whose aggressive preaching caused
one observer to set dogs on her and another to set upon her with a cleaver,
also wrote to Fox, asking for the proper response to her prophetic call:

> George, I had these words rose in me: "Wo be to that nation whose teachers
> are fools and princes are children, that hew unto themselves broken cisterns
> that will hold no water; therefore everyone to your tents. . . ." This rose in
> me the first day the parliament sat; but I was then in prison, and I knew not
> whether that might be shown to me which was done by another to them in
> the steeple-house. If it hath not been done, and thou see the work be mine,
> I desire a line from thee the second or first post. . . . If I hear not from thee,
> I shall abide here till the understanding of those I writ to thee of be opened,
> that should go with me to Jerusalem; they have all been very sick.[87]

Northern women's letters, in contrast, betray little or no confusion about
the validity of their private leadings in relation to those of the group.
"Dearly beloved George," went this wholly typical passage by Mary
Howgill, "my dear life . . . my strength grows, and discerning grows and
the mysteries of the kingdom come to be opened. . . . Pray for me . . .
that I may be kept out of all visible things in my measure, and led up to
God."[88]

Thus, southern women Friends struggled harder (or at least more
overtly) to achieve a state of mind that northern women appeared to take
for granted. They traveled farther to reach a condition of perfection "in
the light," and, having reached it, they were more concerned about their
position within the larger community of Friends. Their heightened self-
consciousness is partly explicable in terms of their own effort to grapple

86. John Stubbs to George Fox, London, 1660, Crosfield Manuscripts, quoted in
Rufus M. Jones, *The Quakers in the American Colonies* (London: MacMillan and Co.,
1911), 266n. This was a period when Friends' concern for public opinion was becoming
more acute and the practice of preaching naked or wearing sackcloth was in decline.

87. Barbara Blaugdone to George Fox, October 1656, SM 3/194 (I, 211), quoted in
EQW, 479–80. Sarah Hollyman, being moved to go to Barbados, wrote to ask George
Fox's advice (1656, SM 4/173 [IV, 213]). Dorothy White sent her paper to George Fox
or Francis Howgill for directions (BQ, 304). An exception was Esther Biddle, who told
George Fox in 1659 that she had a prophecy concerning King Charles II three years before
he was restored. Fox warned her not to deliver it, lest it be considered treason, but she
insisted on going to Charles and telling him to return to England (George Fox, *The
Journal of George Fox*, ed. John L. Nickalls [London: Religious Society of Friends, 1975],
p 355.

88. Mary Howgill to George Fox, 1656, FPT, 201n. Fox crossed out "Life" and
inserted "Friend." Other northern women who wrote letters to Margaret Fell or George
Fox were Susanna Arnold, Joan Brooksop, Elizabeth Cowart, Mary Fell, Margaret Fell,
Jr., Ann Audland, and Margaret Killam; none of them expresses the confusion found in
letters by southern women.

with the issues and temptations of their wider intellectual and material culture. It may also be taken as evidence that they felt their smaller community of Friends to be less solid. In London, where missionaries from the north arrived in 1654, so many meetings had been established that Friends did not know how to recognize each other, and individuals who questioned the authority of one eminent missionary could easily appeal to the authority of another.[89]

I would speculate that southern visionaries were also reacting to an environment that was especially uncongenial to the public activities of women. Southern prophets might well have received a broader cultural education (including that offered by the preaching of other female visionaries), but they might also have been inhibited by what some Friends (and some historians) have taken to be a general hostility to women in these urban areas. Thus, William Caton reported that people there did not always want to hear women preachers. Ministers are desired for those parts, he said, "by many who accepts rather of ministresses then none, although to some they are all one, both male and female . . . but thou knows as well as I, it is not so with every one." Another Friend wrote to George Fox from Plymouth that the people of Devonshire and Cornwall "do not care to hear any women Friends." Still another northern minister wrote that London was such an explosive environment that women should be discouraged from coming there to evangelize:

At London we found very many who have a true principle of honesty in them, but they are . . . so high flown in wisdom and notions, that it is hard to reach them . . . and if they be judged then presently they rage . . . they have had the truth in notions and all cry out: what do these men say more than others have said . . . and there are so many rude savage apprentices and young people and ranters that nothing but the power of the Lord can chain them. Women are a stumbling block for the present amongst them.[90]

89. See below, chap. 6, for examples of aid dispensed to northern prophets.
90. William Caton to Margaret Fell, October 1658, William Caton Manuscripts, 3/29, 478–79. Anthony Pearson to George Fox, A Collection of Letters, Dreams, Visions, and Other Remarkable Occurrences of Some of the People called Quakers, fol. 5, Library of the Society of Friends, London. A London apprentice was taken to task by his master for going to a meeting led by two women preachers (Emilia Fogelklou, *James Nayler, the Rebel Saint 1618–1660: An Attempt to Reconstruct the Chequered Life History of a Singular Personality from the Age of the Commonwealth*, trans. Lajla Yapp [London: E. Benn, 1931], 140). On gender relations in general, see David Underdown, "The Taming of the Scold: The Enforcement of Patriarchal Authority in Early Modern England," in *Order and Disorder in Early Modern England*, ed. Anthony Fletcher and John Stevenson (Cambridge: Cambridge University Press, 1985), 116–36. Barry Levy writes, "Southern Puritan reform assumed human relations impossible to replicate in northwestern England's economy and society: . . . strong, patriarchal nuclear households in which fathers played domestically the ministerial role" (*Quakers and the American Family: British*

The evidence is far from complete or conclusive, but it is worth noting that surviving documents that describe the prophet converting against her family's wishes, or being "out of unity" with her relations, are largely from the south. Ann Downer was permanently disowned by her father, the vicar of Charlbury, after her conversion. Rebeckah Travers referred to some "near relations" who mocked her when she preached in the streets of London, while Barbara Blaugdone had the same experience among her relations in Cork (Ireland), where "many of her former friends grew afraid of her, speaking in so solemn and awful a manner as made them tremble. Others called her a witch, and kept out of her way, till their servants turned her out of doors." When Ann Upcott was seen mending her waistcoat to go out on a Sunday, ignoring the sabbath, her brother, a constable, had her arrested and put in the stocks, asking his friend if he was coming to Ann's wedding, for "she is to be married to the stocks." Another brother announced that he would fetch all the boys in the town to dance before her and ordered her maid to provide beer, pipes, and tobacco. Then the father arrived and joined the jeering crowd, whereupon the whole family went back into their house, where they enjoyed the spectacle from a window. Dorothea Gotherson was reported to be on bad terms with her husband, who abandoned her in 1660. Mary Akehurst was beaten by her husband and bound with chains for a month after her first appearance as a prophet.[91] Sarah Cheevers, writing to her husband and children from her prison in Malta, adopted the tone of a missionary instructing the unconverted:

> I am a witness of . . . the messengers of Christ, who [are] . . . directing you where you may find your saviour to purge and cleanse you from your sins, and to reconcile you to his Father. . . . I breathe to thee . . . that your minds may be joined to the light, . . . that I may enjoy you in that which is eternal, and have community with you in the spirit.

Mary Dyer's husband William was also not a Friend, and his letter to the magistrates of Boston regarding his wife was uncomprehending and desperate. "'Tis true, I have not seen her above this half year, and cannot tell how, in the frame of her spirit, she was moved to run so great a hazard

---

Settlement in the Delaware Valley [New York and Oxford: Oxford University Press, 1988], 11).
    91. On Downers, see DQB; on Travers, see her To Those That Meet to Worship, . . . 3; on Blaugdone, see An Account, 27, and Besse, 2:458, 459; on Upcott, see GBS, 1:146 (1658); on Gotherson, see LEF, no 506; on Akehurst, see GBS, 2:5 (1659).

to herself . . . by her inconsiderate madness; Oh! do not deprive me of her, but I pray give her me once again. . . . Pity me!"[92]

MARTHA SIMMONDS AND JAMES NAYLER

All of the elements of southern women's culture described above—the importance of self-annihilation and mystical religiosity, the absence of a unified community, the existence of relatively strained gender relations—contributed to the crisis caused by James Nayler, Martha Simmonds, and their followers in 1656. James Nayler, a Yorkshire farmer and former quartermaster in the parliamentary army, arrived in London in 1655 and quickly became one of the leading "publishers of Truth." Martha Simmonds was a respected London prophet, close to the center of Quaker activity in the city, who began her activities in 1654.[93] Two years later, when Baptists and Fifth Monarchy prophets were proclaiming the thousand-year reign of Christ, she and several other women began disputing with two eminent male ministers in public meetings. One of the men, Francis Howgill, judged Simmonds to have spoken "in her will." The other, Edward Burrough, wrote to her:

> This is the truth from the Lord God concerning thee Martha Simmonds . . . you are out of the truth, out of the way, out of the power, out of the wisdom and out of the life of God. . . . It is not the spirit of God, but the voice of the stranger which you follow; and are become goats, rough and hairy . . . though . . . some of you have prophesied in the name of Christ yet now you are workers of iniquity.[94]

Simmonds turned to James Nayler for support, but he hesitated to take action against either her or her accusers, telling her "she sought to have

92. Evans and Cheevers, *A True Account*, 112–13. William Dyer to Governor Endicott, 1660, quoted in Bowden, *The History of the Society of Friends in America*, 1:199–200. Two northern women who did suffer from their relations were Jane Waugh and Elizabeth Wheatley, the latter being turned out of the house by her mother when she converted; Waugh was later reinstated by her family (Townsend, "A Testimony to Jane Whitehead," 12; on Wheatley, see DQB, "Wheatley").

The northerner Elizabeth Hooton was opposed by her husband, "in so much that they had like to have parted," but succeeded in turning him to Quakerism; her son Samuel opposed her first visit to America but later defended her and preached in America himself (George Fox's testimony to Elizabeth Hutton, November 17, 1690, Portfolio Manuscripts 16/74; Portfolio Manuscripts 3/80). Margaret Fell's husband never became a Friend but actively supported the movement.

93. For a lucid account of the episode, see Kenneth L. Carroll, "Martha Simmonds, a Quaker Enigma," JFHS 53 (1972): 31–52.

94. Markey Manuscripts, Fol. 120 (also listed as 104), Library of the Society of Friends, London.

the dominion and charged her to go home and follow her calling."[95] She then reappeared at a meeting, "and when we had waited in silence a while," reported Richard Hubberthorne:

> she stood up and spoke, judging all Friends that they were not come to the cross, nor that there was not one to take her part, and would have drawn them from the meetings . . . with her . . . and then she fell on singing, with an unclean spirit. And the substance of that which she said in her singing was, "Innocency, innocency, many times over, for the space of one hour or more, but in the power of the Lord I was moved to speak . . . with many tears . . . and when she saw the power of god arising against her . . . she . . . cried . . . that we were all the beast, and I [was] the head of the beast.[96]

Martha Simmonds again approached Nayler and berated him loudly for his indecision. "Hereupon Martha fell into a passion, in a kind of moaning or weeping, and, bitterly crying out with a mournful, shrill voice, said, 'I looked for judgment, but behold a cry,' and with that cried aloud, in a passionate lamenting manner." Nayler was struck dumb; "it smote him down into so much sorrow and sadness, that . . . fears and doubting then entered him, that he came to be clouded in his understanding, bewildered, and at a Loss in his judgment."[97] Nayler collapsed and lay at Simmonds' house for three days and nights, in a state of depression close to catatonia. He was then sent by anxious Friends on a therapeutic mission to Bristol, where Simmonds followed, at one point kneeling at his feet; the two were forcibly separated by Friends. Shortly afterward Nayler was seized and imprisoned at Exeter, and Simmonds obtained an order for his release from Oliver Cromwell, whose sister she had nursed in London. She also traveled to Launceston, where George Fox was in prison, and demanded that Fox submit to Nayler's higher authority. (Fox later wrote to Nayler, "Martha Simmonds which is called your mother she bid me bow down, and said . . . that my heart was rotten, and she said, she denied that which was head in me, . . . and she came singing in my face.")[98]

Once released from prison in October 1656, Nayler, Simmonds, and a group of disciples staged a procession through the gates of the city of Bristol in imitation of Jesus' entry into Jerusalem, Nayler riding on an ass and the others accompanying him, waving branches and crying

95. Richard Hubberthorne to Margaret Fell, London, August 26, 1656, William Caton Manuscripts III, 3/116, 364–68.
96. Ibid.
97. James Nayler, *Works*, ix, quoted in Carroll, "Martha Simmonds," 41.
98. George Fox to James Nayler, 1656, SM, 3/193 (II, 233).

"holy, holy, holy, Lord God of Sabaoth," the women spreading garments before him. They were arrested almost immediately, and letters written by his male and female followers addressing him as Christ or the messiah were found in his pockets, one young woman claiming that Nayler had raised her from the dead in prison, crying "Dorcas, arise."[99] Following an extended and impassioned parliamentary debate and trial, Nayler was publicly whipped, was branded on the forehead with a "B" (for blasphemy), and had a hole bored through his tongue.

In the chaotic aftermath of these events, one of the women disrupted a meeting by crying out against the male ministers, "You have lost the power; you have lost the power," while another, Mildred Crouch, reportedly announced that she was above the apostles. After having a vision that her Quaker antagonist Richard Hubberthorne would be struck dumb, she disrupted a large meeting by staging a filibuster. As Hubberthorne told it,

> we had a meeting . . . & Mildred was there in all impudence & I having spoken something in the living power of the lord to the people she was tormented & she resolved so to speak as that I should not speak any more to them & . . . told the people that they should not hear a word from me . . . for she intended to speak as long as they stayed . . . we stayed almost until midnight . . . until all her natural parts was spent, and her senses distracted, that she was even really mad; and truth reigned in pure dominion . . . yet she said that the next meeting she would come in more power & we should not speak a word.[100]

Simmonds herself improvised a ritual that suspiciously resembled a communion service, a direct violation of Quaker practice.

> [She] took a bible and read a psalm and they sung it after her, as they do in the steeplehouses. . . . [Then she] took a chapter in Ezekiel which speak to the rebellious children and she said that the Lord had sent that chapter to be read unto us. . . . The people . . . met again . . . after we were gone and they

99. Hannah Stranger and her husband John wrote to Nayler, "Oh thou fairest of ten thousand, thou only begotten son of God, how my heart panteth after thee." Jane Woodcock, Ruth Hill, and Richard Fairman wrote similar letters (Ralph Farmer, *Sathan Enthron'd in His Chair of Pestilence, or Quakerism in Its Exaltation* . . . (London, 1657), 4, 5, 7–8. Farmer was a Presbyterian minister in Bristol and an avid and hostile witness of Friends' activities in that city. On Dorcas Erbury, see BQ, 247. The Friends put in prison were Nayler, Dorcas Erbury, Martha Simmonds, Hannah and John Stranger, Samuel Cater, Robert Crab, and Timothy Wedlock (BQ, 252–53).

100. Richard Hubberthorne to George Fox, London, March 20, 1656, SM, 4/12 (II, 393). Mildred did not appear at the next meeting, "for she hath so destroyed her natural parts that she is so hoarse that she cannot speak at present: and it is like god's judgment will come upon her suddenly."

broke bread and drunk drink and gave [it] to the rude multitude that would take any, and so fulfilled an imagination of their heart. [101]

Like many of Martha Simmonds' contemporaries, historians of Quakerism have been generally so bemused by her apparently hysterical and self-serving behavior that they have rarely considered whether Nayler's followers might have felt an authentic spiritual affinity with his doctrines. The first point to be made about the Nayler episode, therefore, is that the women and men who followed him did so, at least in part, because they believed in what he said. Unlike Edward Burrough, who had first censured Martha Simmonds, Nayler placed particular emphasis on both the uselessness of intellectual achievements and the capacity of all men and women to be totally inhabited by Christ, teachings that several contemporaries, and at least one historian, have described as behmenist or familist.[102] Such principles must have been especially meaningful to women and men who perceived their own convincement as, above all, a renunciation of all personal pretensions. Indeed, those most loyal to Nayler, even after his disgrace and condemnation by George Fox, were not only flamboyant women like Martha Simmonds but pillars of the local community: women like Rebeckah Travers, whom Nayler had inspired to renounce her own intellectual pretensions and who later washed the blood from the wounds on his back, and the highly educated Sarah Blackborow, organizer of the first London women's meeting, who arranged for the publication of a tract by Nayler after the crisis. "This came to my hand," she wrote in her preface, "and having its witness in me, finding the same spirit sealing to it, a necessity was laid upon me to put it in print, that so it might do it service, and have unity with its own." Nayler himself wrote:

> Thou wilt feel the fruit of that Holy One springing in thee, moving to be brought forth in thee towards God and man. . . . If you take heed to your own ways, and make nothing in your minds, you must not create that which must stand before God, for he will be served with his own begettings in you. . . .

101. Richard Hubberthorne to Margaret Fell, London, February 10, 1657, William Caton Manuscripts 3/118, 372–76. Other southern women in trouble: Katherine Crooke was reported to have been "hasty and rash" by saying in a public debate that she would have known God even without Scripture (Edward Bourne to G[eorge] F[ox], Hereford Prison, June–July 1664, SM 4/52 [I, 237]); Esther Corker talked too much at meeting (Leonard Fell to Esther Corker, n.d., SM, 1/115 [I, 169]); Mary Powel was criticized by John Perrot in a letter to Fox (Robert Rich, *Hidden Things Brought to Light* . . . [1678], 13).
102. Geoffrey F. Nuttall, "James Nayler: A Fresh Approach," JFHS, Supp. 26 (1954): 2–20.

As you come into the patient stillness, you must feel the begettings of the
Father moving in you to be brought forth . . . setting aside all subtlety, and
that which is hasty, and whatever is your own.[103]

It is not surprising that such words would resonate in the mind of a
woman whose own spiritual language (quoted above, page 187) was also
replete with images of intellectual renunciation, rebirth, and reconciliation.

The second point to be made about the Nayler episode is that Simmonds and her cohort were exhibiting an extreme form of the behavior
pattern we have already discerned among southern women as a group.
For fourteen years, since the age of seven, Simmonds had engaged in a
protracted and traumatic search among the profusion of religious sects,
finally appearing on the streets of Colchester as a Quaker, barefoot and
in sackcloth. "God! How I have been tossed in this dark world!" she
wrote:

Surely thou hadst a purpose to make use of me in thy will and time; for the
devil hath set very sore against me; for before ever I saw the light of the sun,
or received a natural birth in this visible world, I was rejected of men, for my
parents denied me a birth; and as concerning self, it had been good I had not
been born; for I have not had pleasure in this world, but have stood as one
alone, and since I knew the way to thee, I have exceedingly hasted out of it.[104]

Her husband, who published Quaker writings but was not a Quaker
himself, was strongly critical of her spiritual excesses.[105] Certainly, her
behavior in 1656 showed a confusion both about the ultimate source of
authority or validation of her own individual experience (expressed in
her hero worship of Nayler and condemnation of George Fox) and about
her own authority to preach (expressed in the attempt to dominate
meetings and her repentance soon after her disgrace).

Another renegade prophet, Ann Gargill, displayed the same conflicted
desire for a strong authority both outside herself and within herself.

103. James Nayler, *How Sin Is Strengthened, and How It Is Overcome* (London,
1657), Preface. Mary Booth also wrote prefaces to Nayler's work *Milk for Babes: And
Meat for Strong-Men* (London, 1661); her sister Rebeckah Travers also wrote a preface
to his *A Message from the Spirit of Truth, unto the Holy Seed* (London, 1658). I know of
no other works by men containing prefaces by women Friends. Kenneth L. Carroll does
point out the affinity between Simmonds' belief in the indwelling of the spirit and Nayler's
own doctrine ("Martha Simmonds," 37).
104. Martha Simmonds, Hannah Stranger, James Nayler, William Tomlinson, *O
England; Thy Time Is Come* (London, n.d.), 9–10.
105. Carroll, "Martha Simmonds," 46. Thomas Simmonds wrote, "Dear heart my
love is to thee, . . . but this I could not but write, to warn you that you stand single to the
Lord, and not believe every spirit. Your work is soon come to an end."

Gargill had already journeyed alone to Lisbon in order to confront King
John IV but was detained by the Inquisition and banned from Portugal.
In 1657 she was disowned by London Friends for "Ranterish," or unruly,
behavior, reportedly throwing herself between George Fox's feet and
calling him "the son of the living God." Before her departure from
London she wrote to Fox, "I am weary and burdened until I come where
thou feedest thy flocks . . . where none is equal with thee, but he who
is the shepherd. . . . Above all men art thou called blessed of him . . .
nations and kingdoms shall be under the shadow of thy wings." A few
months later she traveled to Holland, where she organized an independent faction within the community that was attempting to evangelize
Amsterdam, attacked the male ministers physically and in public, and
was turned out of the Quaker house where she lodged. Two years later
she was still in Amsterdam, challenging the authority of resident
Friends.[106]

Compare the behavior of Simmonds and Gargill to the more straightforward arrogance of Samuel Hooton, who, unlike his mother Elizabeth,
actually claimed the capacity to work miracles. Hooton wrote of curing
two dying women in New England:

> I was led into the wilderness . . . the Lord wrought great things of me there. . . .
> And this woman was after [her cure] a fine and tender hearted woman, who
> much loved me. . . . I was three times there, and the people much loved me.
> I was made to pass through all New England . . . to warn them and lay weight
> on them . . . and the lord gave me . . . authority and power over all their
> heads. . . . I came to a court at Cambridge . . . and many of the younger sort
> of people had a great love to me. . . . So I passed to Boston . . . and truly the
> lord's power went along with me, and gave me both valour and courage and
> made me as bold as a lion, and my forehead hard against their foreheads.[107]

Or compare Simmonds and Gargill with Quaker women from the north,
several of whom also displayed ambitions toward personal authority but
who did so in a much less contorted fashion. Thus, Ann Blaykling was
judged to be "out of unity" with Friends because she gathered a party
that agreed to work on Sundays and not pay taxes but to pay tithes. Isabel
Buttery was criticized for misjudgment when she came to London and

---

106. Ann Gargill to George Fox, Plymouth, 1656, quoted in William Hull, *The Rise
of Quakerism in Amsterdam, 1655–1665*, Swarthmore College Monographs on Quaker
History, no. 4 (Philadelphia: Patterson and White, 1938), 276–77. William Caton to
Margaret Fell, Amsterdam, May 20, 1657, quoted in Hull, *The Rise of Quakerism*, 273.

107. Samuel Hooton, "Something concerning my travell, and of the dealings of the
lord with me since the lord brought me from my dwelling," n.d., Portfolio Manuscripts
3/80.

proceeded to borrow a large sum of money, which she used to print and distribute books, selling them up and down the streets. Agnes Wilkinson acted "in filthiness." Mary Howgill refused to leave the area where she preached as a missionary, even though she had caused confusion among Friends for six months. Elizabeth Morgan "bred dissension" among Bristol Friends. Isabel Garnet and Thomas Wilson organized a Separatist movement in Westmoreland. A group of Friends sitting in prison in York were split into two factions, one led by Jane Holmes, and when Holmes was accused of "exalted" behavior (organizing her own faction), she replied that the man was a liar:

> and said it was the whore that spoke in him; . . . she did kick against exhortation, and [Richard Farnsworth] was made before us all to examine her to give an account of her faith . . . where in she did make it appear that it was the devil which spoke in him or the whore. But she said she was not commanded of the Lord to give an account to him, but fell into passion and loudness and said we was all in deceit. . . . She did hold forth that all was destroyed in her.[108]

If the Nayler episode exposed the confusion and extremism characteristic of some southern women, it also exposed the degree to which Quakers shared the prejudices of their contemporaries regarding the fallibility of the female temperament. For while it is certainly possible that Martha Simmonds and her cohort *were* hysterical, self-centered, and entirely deserving of censure, it is equally possible that Simmonds was a victim of the Quaker double standard regarding women's public lan-

108. On Blaykling, see BQ, 345–46; on Buttery, see Francis Howgill and Anthony Pearson to Margaret Fell, London, July 10, 1654, William Caton Manuscripts III, 3/74, 184; she also gave some of the money away as charity. On Wilkinson, see Thomas Aldam to Margaret Fell, October 30, 1654, SM, 4/89 (I, 53). On Howgill, see Richard Hubberthorne to George Fox from London, March 20, 1656, SM 4/12 (II, 593). See also the letter of Thomas Robertson to Margaret Fell, n.d., SM 4/206 (III, 217). Howgill did write an adulatory letter to Fox, calling him "Dear life"; he crossed out "life" and put "friend" (FPT, 201n). On Morgan, see BQ, 388 and n 10. On Garnet, see John Camm to Margaret Fell, Camsgill, Preston Patrick, June 1655, SM 4/119 (I, 339), and Craig W. Horle, "John Camm: Profile of a Quaker Minister during the Interregnum," QH 71, no. 1, p. 10. On Jane Holmes, see Thomas Aldam to Friends, 1653, SM 3/40 (I, 29). On Wilkinson, see Thomas Aldam to Margaret Fell, York Castle prison, October 30, 1654, SM 4/89 (I, 53). Elizabeth Williams and Thomas Castley were ruled out of order when preaching (Edward Burrough to George Fox, July 5, 1654, A. R. Barclay Manuscripts, vol. 324, no. 161, transcpt. 104). Agnes Ayrey was the only woman explicitly condemned for fornication (QPE, 121).

We do not know, of course, what terms like "out of order" actually meant or whether they meant different things for men and for women; John Camm, who judged Isabel Garnet and Thomas Wilson, also maintained that Quakers "were pretty subjected under me before [Wilson] came" (John Camm to Margaret Fell, Cammsgill, June 4, 1655, SM 4/119 [I, 339]).

guage. As William Sewel, the son of another Quaker woman minister, analyzed her behavior:

> These women's practice we may suppose to be somewhat like that which gave occasion to the apostle Paul to say "Let your women keep silence in the churches. . . ." This prohibition of speaking, must be voluntary discourse, by the way of reasoning or disputing, and not when they had an immediate impulse, or concern to prophesy; for the apostle in the same epistle, has . . . made express mention of women's praying and prophecying, together with the men.[109]

As a woman, Martha Simmonds could not debate or argue with male Quaker leaders in a public meeting, for she had only one claim to public authority, and that was as an instrument of God. Whether she criticized the male ministers hysterically or rationally, her very attempt to dispute with them in public would probably have resulted in accusations of self-seeking and, ultimately, in personal disgrace. She herself insisted that *all* of her public speech was inspired by "the power" and that the male ministers were motivated by an all-too-human envy of her success:

> I was moved to *declare to the world*, and often they would judge me exceedingly, that I was too forward to run before I was sent, . . . but I was moved by *the power*, I could not stay tho they sometimes denied me, yet I was forced to go, and *my word did prosper*, . . . and then I was *moved of the Lord* to go to *James Nayler*, and tell him I wanted justice, and he being harsh to me, at length these words came to me to speak to him, which I did, and struck him down; . . . which pierced and *struck him down* from that day; and he lay from that day in exceeding sorrow for about three days, and all the while *the power arose in me*, which I did not expect. . . . But after 3 days he came to me, and confessed *I had been clear in service to the Lord*, and that he had wronged me, . . . I was as innocent as a child.[110]

We can never know, of course, what the unconscious motives or ambitions of either Simmonds or the male ministers really were. I suspect that Quaker leaders in general were quite willing to applaud women's reasoning or disputing as a God-inspired act when it was directed at non-Quakers (as, for example, in the public trials of Ann Audland and Margaret Fell) but inclined to condemn similar behavior as prideful and self-motivated when it was directed against themselves.[111] Certainly, it

109. William Sewel, *The History of the Rise, Increase, and Progress, of the Christian People Called Quakers*, 2 vols. (1722; reprint, Philadelphia, 1823), 1:255.
110. Farmer, *Sathan Enthron'd*, 10–11.
111. See, for example, the account of Elizabeth Holme in "An epistle from Dublin (May 14, 1655) to be read at meetings in Cheshire, Wales and Lancashire": "here is many which comes to us one multitude after another which we do reason and dispute withall,

made good political sense to blame the women rather than Nayler, who was, after all, the central sinner and the focus of the parliamentary trial and debate. For, as the members of Parliament well understood, their discrediting of Nayler, one of the chief leaders of the movement, was a discrediting of all radical religious sects. From the *Quakers'* perspective, shifting the blame to women invalidated neither the movement as a whole nor its theology. It only proved what many had suspected all along: the unsuitability of the female for positions of public authority. Indeed, the scandal ultimately resulted in a more suspicious attitude toward female prophets on the part of the Quaker leadership. No one suggested that, because of Nayler's outrageous behavior or that of his disciple Robert Rich (who placed a paper over him at the pillory saying "This is the King of the Jews" and who afterward licked the burn on Nayler's forehead), it would be dangerous to allow men to preach.[112]

Yet the Quakers' compassion for Nayler and their eagerness to condemn Martha Simmonds surely had even deeper roots. Quakers had always ridiculed contemporaries' fears of them as ludicrous superstition. Soon after Elizabeth Morgan preached in Bristol, they disdainfully reported rumors that Friends had bewitched two men by putting black strength about their arms, preventing them from moving. The Bristol writer George Bishop also reported that when Mary Tomkins farted while on a mission to America, a male witness said she had a devil in her.[113] Yet Bishop himself feared that he had been bewitched by Elizabeth Morgan in 1655.[114] Certainly, the leaders' extreme reactions to Simmonds and Ann Gargill show how quickly their own adoration of women as vessels of God could reverse itself into virtual terror of women's diabolical energy. After Gargill had disrupted a Quaker meeting in Amsterdam, William Caton wrote home to his spiritual mother, Margaret Fell, about the machinations of the spiritual whore:

> A. Gargill a woman of an exalted spirit of whom thou hast heard her envy and malice against friends is very great; if the living power of god did not preserve me she would triumph over me and make me as the ashes under her feet, but the Lord hath hitherto preserved me . . . over that unclean spirit over which friends also are coming to reign. . . . I cannot say that my garments are

---

and they are much confounded by us" (Markey Manuscripts, fols. 50–51, also listed as 36–37).

112. BQ, 248, 266. On the perception of Nayler's group as dangerous, see Gertrude Huehns, *Antinomianism in English History: With Special Reference to the Period 1640–1660* (London: Cresset Press, 1951), 139–41.

113. FPT, 110; Bishop, *New England Judged*, 400.

114. BQ, 388 and n.

either spotted or stained by this muck and filth, nay though I walk through it, it doth not so much as defile my feet.[115]

Some months later, Caton wrote again to Fell:

> They that entertained Ann Gargill (that wicked woman that . . . set herself impudently against the truth) have lately turned her out of their house . . . so that her skirts being discovered as they are, she is become loathsome and odious even to all that knows her malignity. . . . She hath made a young man almost weary of his life, who can by no means get quit of her.[116]

Similarly, the Quaker leadership treated Simmonds and her female companions (ignoring the men who had accompanied them) not as nuisances or criminals but as threats to their very lives. "The agents of J[ames] N[ayler] have come creeping on their bellies to be owned yea: Martha their miserable mother, this day hath been [at] us, & all her witchery & filthy enchantments is set at naught . . . and fleshly liberty was their overthrow."[117] In Nayler's own mind, his role had been that of a tragic Faust or Icarus figure, whose pride had led him to impersonate God, while Martha Simmonds and the other female "evil spirits" were cast as the villains who seduced the gullible hero by witchcraft:

> And all those ranting wild spirits which then gathered about me in the time of darkness and all their wild actions and wicked words . . . which darkness came over me through want of watchfulness and obedience to the pure eye of God . . . so the adversary got advantage, who ceases not to seek and devour, and being taken captive from that true light, [I] walked in the night . . . as a wandering bird fit for the prey. And if the Lord . . . had not rescued me, I had perished.[118]

115. William Caton to Margaret Fell, Amsterdam, May 20, 1657, William Caton Manuscripts III 3/15, 34.

116. William Caton to Margaret Fell, Leyden, March 15, 1658, William Caton Manuscripts III, 3/172 fols. 507–8.

117. John Perrot, Humphrey Norton, and William Shaw to William and Margaret Blanch, Ireland, April 1657, quoted in Carroll, "Martha Simmonds," 50. William Dewsbury wrote against Simmonds' "sorcery" (Markey Manuscripts, fols. 120–22, quoted in Carroll, "Martha Simmonds," 41). It may not have been only Quaker leaders who saw the women this way. Christopher Hill speculates that Milton's characterization of Delilah was partly inspired by his knowledge of the role of Martha Simmonds in Nayler's downfall. "Martha Simmonds was the Eve who led Nayler astray, the Dalila (Nayler had long hair) who took political decisions upon himself" (*Milton and the English Revolution* [London: Faber and Faber, 1977], 136, 443). In contrast to these reactions to women, Braithwaite writes that "Friends disapproved of the outward things which had been acted to Nayler, but were tender towards him, and anxious that the matter should make no rent in the Church" (BQ, 257).

118. James Nayler, *A Collection of Sundry Books, Epistles and Papers Written by James Nayler* . . . (London, 1716), liii–liv, paper beginning "Glory to God Almighty."

When Mary Fisher, the serving maid of Yorkshire, instructed the sultan of Turkey with the word of the Almighty, when the adolescent Elizabeth Farmer refused the patronage of an aristocrat with the authority of Moses, they clearly saw the tradition of male biblical prophecy as an authentic expression of their own public personae. Yet if, in those exalted moments, their spiritual identity as prophets was more real to them than their social identities as daughters and servants, it was also more ephemeral. Indeed, many of the texts we have surveyed convey the sense that the soul of the female prophet was viewed by Friends in the way a modern person would view a character in a fairy tale: touched by the magic wand of divine light, lifted out of her body, and dressed in the glorious garments of biblical heroes to speak in churches and palaces. So Edward Burrough wrote to Margaret Fell from Dublin, "Little Elizabeth Fletcher is at present here. . . . Truly I suffer for her, she being as it were alone, having no other woman with her in this [ruinous?] nation, where it is very bad traveling,—every way a foot, and also dangerous; but we are much above all that."[119] However, should the prophet ever lose her integrity in their eyes, all the stereotypes of her gender and social position would instantly reappear and envelop her as if by magic, and she would find herself back by the hearth, dressed in the rags of her own shabby individuality. So at least one young woman might have felt when, in 1656, Edward Burrough sent her to George Fox with a note, "This little short maid that comes to thee, she has been this long while abroad, and in her there *is little or no service* as in the ministry. It were well to be laid on her to be a *servant* somewhere. *That* is more her place. . . . Friends where she has been have been burdened by her."[120] The tale of Martha Simmonds had an even more sinister dénouement, for this heroine did not collapse by the hearth at a snap of the magician's fingers. Instead, she transformed herself into an even more powerful supernatural figure,

119. Edward Burrough to Margaret Fell, Dublin 1655, reprinted in Abram Rawlinson Barclay, ed., *Letters, etc. of Early Friends* (London, 1841), 263. Elizabeth Fletcher was about sixteen years old.

120. Edward Burrough to George Fox, 1656, quoted in Robert Barclay, *The Inner Life of the Religious Societies of the Commonwealth* (London, Hodder and Stoughton, 1876), 345. William Dewsbury rebuked another woman, Elizabeth Coates, ordering her "to return to her place in the outward and wait" (n.d., SM 3/21 [I, 678]). The same happened with Sarah Knowles (John Audland to Edward Burrough, Olveston, April 26, 1656, A. R. Barclay Manuscripts, vol. 323, no. 116, reprinted in JFHS 48, no. 2 [Autumn 1956]: 92). On women rebuking men, see chapter 6. Thomas Morford wrote to Margaret Fell, "A friend came where I was . . . and she charged me to be a deceiver, . . . giving me very cruel language. . . . I was in great fear lest I should be a preacher to others and myself be a castaway" (quoted in Brailsford, *Quaker Women*, 191). Morford eventually gave up preaching.

one that contemporaries recognized from their own fervid imaginations: an evil, screaming witch.

THE PROPHET AND THE COMMUNITY

Several Quaker women who had experienced difficulty with authority, either their own authority to preach and interpret visions or the authority of the Quaker leadership to direct their activities, eventually left England, sometimes as missionaries, sometimes as emigrants. Barbara Blaugdone traveled to Ireland; Elizabeth Cox and Ann Gargill went to Holland; Elizabeth Harris traveled to America, Venice, and Jamaica; Jane Stokes went to Italy and America; Martha Simmonds traveled to Maryland. Perhaps, as historian Hugh Barbour suggests, these and other women were seeking personal independence by abandoning unhappy marriages or lives that were otherwise unrewarding.[121] Or perhaps they were seeking opportunities for a wider *spiritual* arena, away from the scrutiny of their neighbors or the Quaker leadership. Or perhaps they found it impossible to sustain both preaching and domestic life in the relative absence of family and community support. A woman might have felt impelled to leave her family for an extended period not because she was excited by a vision of greater opportunity elsewhere but because she simply found herself unable to stand in front of the high cross, dressed in sackcloth and ashes, and succeed in emptying her mind of thoughts about the sick child or the work to be done at home.

What is incontrovertible in this story of early Quaker prophets is that, both in terms of Friends' own explicit testimony and the objective numerical facts, it was their collective identity that mattered most. When we learn of Mary Fisher, an illiterate serving maid, instructing Moslems, Puritans, and pagans on the other side of the world, it is difficult to "read" her experience as anything other than a quest for personal freedom and autonomy. Yet the tiny events that punctuated those bold deeds—the letters to Friends long absent, the money given for a sea voyage, her companions' expressions of respect—explain to us what really made those deeds possible and gave them wider meaning in her own time: the collective escape from the flux and ultimate despair of a purely personal life. "They who are of God," she wrote, "that doth discern the ground, the rise, the being, of that which is out of times,

---

121. For example, Mary Clark left her husband and children in London to preach in New England; she also was said to advocate the separation of married couples (BQ, 236).

comprehending time . . . who feeds on the living bread . . . salute one another with a holy kiss."[122] When Katherine Evans and Sarah Cheevers sat in isolated confinement in Malta, hallucinating from lack of food or any other comfort,

> as owls in deserts, and as people forsaken in solitary places; then did we enjoy the presence of the Lord, . . . and we did see you our dear friends, . . . and did behold your order, and steadfastness of your faith and love to all saints, and were refreshed in all the faithful hearted, and felt the issues of love and life which did stream from the hearts of those that were wholly joined to the fountain, and were made sensible of the benefit of your prayers.[123]

Quakers shared a profound sense that the community of Friends formed one single living organism. Records of arrests frequently mention Friends who were jailed even though they did not speak, because they had accompanied a woman to the church or marketplace and stood beside her as ballast during those moments when she prophesied "out of the body."[124] Women traveling companions, many coming from the same villages and towns, often remained together for years, sustained by mutual encouragement as they waited for letters from Friends to reach them.[125] Indeed, those who were most effective as prophets and writers were also those who felt their connection to the body of Friends to be unassailable and who were ready to defer to those connections; those who broke down or broke away were also those who were most individualistic, and the proof of their rejection by God was the hell of their isolation. As James Nayler and his followers straggled out of Bristol after their first visit, during which he had to be forcibly separated from Martha Simmonds, they somehow became separated from each other. Two Friends reported to Edward Burrough:

> We write by the last post of those people passing out of the town . . . some friends followed: and the other in hasting lost one an other: so they were parted in three, the two men was together and the other each alone: . . . and so yesterday [Nayler] went . . . west[wards] and . . . [John] Stranger said he would come for London. Hannah [Stranger] came to us . . . [on Thursday] and had lost all the rest: . . . but Martha [Simmonds] we have not heard on since: a mighty thing was in it that they should be so parted: even by nothing,

122. Mary Fisher, Portfolio Manuscripts 33/34.
123. Evans and Cheevers, *A True Account*, 62.
124. GBS 1:153, 580.
125. Francis Howgill and John Audland to Edward Burrough, Bristol, August 2, 1656, A. R. Barclay Manuscripts vol. 323, no. 114, reprinted in JFHS 48, no. 2 (Autumn 1956): 90.

as to the outward. . . . We went with [Nayler] yesterday about fifteen miles
he said little to us but he did one while weep exceedingly.[126]

Ultimately, Friends' conviction that salvation and peace of mind were
conditional on the unity of the group prevailed over both the unac-
knowledged misogyny of some Quaker men and the equally unacknowl-
edged ambition of individual Quaker women. Thus, Ann Blaykling, who
defected from Friends in 1657 in order to gather her own meeting,
returned to the fold and later married a Quaker. Mary Howgill, who had
also been an obstinate nay-sayer and usurper of authority, continued to
serve the movement. James Milner, who had once claimed to be Adam
and Abraham, submitted a testimony of denial to Friends. A group of
Friends in Kent who burned their Bibles in 1657 repudiated their act in
order to restore unity. Agnes Wilkinson condemned herself, "kneeling
upon her knees." Elizabeth Morgan condemned her behavior to Bristol
Friends and returned home to Cheshire, where she was "pretty low and
goes not forth much"; the following year she resumed her missionary
activities, preaching in Ireland with another woman Friend.[127] Most
extraordinary of all, every important participant in the Nayler episode
was eventually reconciled to Friends. Martha Simmonds died on a ship
bound for Maryland nine years after the Nayler crisis, having long since
been reunited with the Quaker community. Hannah Stranger was chosen
by Fox to petition King Charles II for Margaret Fell's release from prison
some years later. Nayler himself was supremely anxious to make his
peace with Friends. "I have taken this time," he wrote in 1658, two years
before his death,

in the tender bowels of love, (as one wounded therewith), to warn you hereof:
Beseeching you all . . . that you all search low for the bowels of him who loved
you, . . . when you were his enemies, . . . especially towards one another, who
have been called by one spirit into one truth; that so the holy spirit be no more
grieved. . . . And the lord god of love give us all to see, that whatever our gifts

126. On Blaykling, see DBR, 1:74. On contrite Friends who burned their Bibles in
Kent, see Richard Hubberthorne to George Fox, 1657, SM 4/14 (II, 607). On Milner, see
Carroll, "A Look at James Milner," 25. On Wilkinson, see Thomas Aldam to Margaret
Fell, York Castle prison, 1654, SM 4/89 (I, 53). On Morgan, see BQ, 388n.
127. James Naylor, "To all the Dearly Beloved People of God, Mercy and Peace," in
Nayler, Works, xxix, xxx. Fogelklou, James Nayler, 146. Hannah Salter and Elizabeth
Hooton to Margaret Fell Fox, 1670, SM 1/152 (IV, 333–34). (Hannah Salter was for-
merly married to John Stranger.) Even Richard Hubberthorne wrote to Margaret Fell in
1659 that there was "something of god stirring [Simmonds] to reconciliation" (William
Caton Manuscripts III 3/123, 391). An exception was "Mildred," whom Fox said ran out
and gathered a company of Ranters and never came into truth again (Journal of George
Fox [1911], 2:314).

or powers be, yet if we have not the life and power of love, it avails not with God. . . . it was never in my heart to cause you to mourn.[128]

Clearly, Friends' desire for unity cannot be understood as that of total surrender to a charismatic leader, though Quakers had leaders in abundance (some thought overabundance); rather, it was a desire to belong to a family that was both spiritual and material, universal and concrete. Women who prophesied once or twice came from all parts of England where Quakerism spread, while those who sustained a career of writing and preaching came from a few, clearly defined neighborhoods; in the north, the areas of Kendall in Westmoreland, Lancaster in Lancashire, Selby and Sedbergh in Yorkshire; in the south, London (where several stable meetings were eventually established), Bristol, and Wellingborough in Northamptonshire. Those isolated, largely rural Friends who felt moved to speak in Hampshire, Kent, Cornwall, or Worcestershire did not continue as public Friends, although many remained loyal to the movement, being fined for tithes or attendance at meetings for many years thereafter. "We meet together as children of one birth," wrote Anne Gilman to Friends, "and are refreshed in one banqueting-house of his loving-kindness: and here is no vain jangling, but all agree together, and can lie down in the counsel of the Lord; and as we are kept to this, there is no place for the Enemy to enter."[129]

128. See Appendices 2 and 3. The largest single group came from the Kendall area.
129. Anne Gilman, *An Epistle to Friends* (London, 1662), 5.

CHAPTER SIX

Ecstasy and Everyday Life

INTRODUCTION

Here is a passage from a letter by Susanna Arnold, written to George Fox and partially quoted at the beginning of chapter 5, in which she describes her prophetic call:

> There was at the next house to ours a company of proud men . . . which did highly dishonor the Lord in drinking and vain pastime which I was much burdened withall, but at that present I had nothing given from the Lord and so I was willing to be silent; . . . and upon the seventh day after, it came in great power: "hitherto I have wrought, and work thou"; and it continued with me all the day. . . . And so I rest waiting upon the Lord . . . that I may be kept faithful and obedient unto the Lord Jesus Christ.[1]

What was the character of Susanna Arnold's life during the seven days she rested, waiting for God to tell her how to deal with those proud men?

Despite their infantile and apocalyptic imagery and the antisocial appearance of their quaking and prophesying, the Quakers' ultimate ambition was not to live in a spiritual utopia free from worldly concerns; it was to imbue worldly concerns with the intensity and moral stature of an exalted spiritual life. In this respect, Quaker women prophets

---

1. Susanna Arnold to George Fox, SM 4/37 (IV, 9), and see Hugh Barbour, "Quaker Prophetesses and Mothers in Israel," in *Seeking the Light: Essays in Quaker History in Honor of Edwin B. Bronner*, ed. J. William Frost and John M. Moore (Wallingford and Haverford, Pa.: Pendle Hill Publications and Friends Historical Association, 1986), 48.

cannot be compared to the virtuous widows and celibate wives of the early Christian movement, nor to the virgins who stood unveiled in the church as a sign of their separateness and high vocation. Nor did they have an affinity with pious medieval nuns, nor with those adolescent mystics living at home, full-time adepts at self-mortification and visionary ecstasy. Nor, finally, did Quaker prophets resemble the Beguines or any other female lay order of the late Middle Ages whose members lived in the world but practiced celibacy and identified with a single-sex community.[2]

In contrast to all of these earlier groups, Quaker prophets were explicitly instructed to serve God in ordinary ways, as wholly ordinary people, and this was doubly true after the scandal caused by James Nayler had undermined Friends' conviction of their ability to correctly interpret their own prophetic "leadings." In an address to Quaker ministers, written and delivered in 1657, George Fox counseled Friends not to travel and prophesy as a way of life but, once their message had been delivered, to go home, stay home, and lead a sanctified life "in the flesh":

> Now there is a great danger too in traveling abroad in the world, except a man be moved of the Lord, by the power of the Lord, for then he keeping in the power is kept in his journey and in his work. . . . One may have openings when they are abroad to minister to others, but *as for their own particular growth,* [*it*] *is to dwell in the life which doth open.* So if any one have a moving to any place and have spoken what they were moved of the Lord, return to their habitation once again, and live in the pure life of God and fear of the Lord. And so will ye in the life and the sober and seasoned spirit be kept.[3]

Thus, Elizabeth Hooton was "moved of the Lord" to attempt to purchase property in Boston, just as she was moved of the Lord to deliver her visionary prophecies; the apocalypse and new age to come would be heralded in this world by visionary preaching—and by giving fair weight in the marketplace.[4]

---

2. On early Christian women, see Peter Brown, *The Body and Society: Men, Women, and Sexual Renunciation in Early Christianity* (New York: Columbia University Press, 1988) 150. On medieval women, see Caroline Walker Bynum, *Jesus as Mother: Studies in the Spirituality of the High Middle Ages* (Berkeley: University of California Press, 1982), Chaps. 4 and 5.

3. "George Fox's Address to Friends in the Ministry," given at John Crook's house, March 31, 1657, reprinted in EQW, 490 (emphasis added).

4. On Hooton, see "M[argaret] F[ell] to the King and his Counsell," Spence Manuscripts III, no. 116, Library of the Society of Friends, London. See also George Fox's letter

The fact that prophetic preaching was a transient experience and not a permanent office or lifestyle meant that all Quakers, men and women, had to integrate moments of being "in the power" with other aspects of their social and personal existence "in the body." In order to be a good Quaker, one had to live on more than one level, as John Camm and John Audland did when they wrote to Friends:

> You are clothed with beauty and you grow in a pleasant place [and] the hand of the Lord is with you. . . . Tell [widow Alcoke] that the Bristol woman did deliver her letter, and the woman saith she will pay her when she is able. She confesseth she owe her about ten pounds. . . . Send our letter away to the north by the first post. Remember me to the woman which heard the voice, that she must leave her country. I heard she was at the meeting which I was glad of.[5]

Now it may have been a simple enough matter to synthesize ecstatic and domestic modes of expression in a private letter or in a single gesture (as when the sheriff of Nottingham, obeying a sudden impulse to preach in the streets, rushed out of the house in his slippers).[6] Indeed, the very idea of changing one's social and spiritual identities, living as a shopkeeper and parent one moment and a prophet the next, may have been a relatively comfortable one for contemporaries accustomed to the formalized ardor of the church preacher or the periodic social reversals of carnival and charivari. Quakers, however, experienced these shifts of identity not according to the ritual of religious celebration or communal consent but spontaneously, as the spirit moved them. How, then, in actual daily life, were they to sustain the integration of ecstatic prayer with keeping a budget, itinerant preaching with caring for children and the necessities of business, the transcendence of all carnal needs with the needs and obligations of marriage?

---

on economic ethics, "The Line of Righteousness and Justice Stretched forth over All Merchants, etc." (London, 1661), reprinted in EQW, 433–37, and the passage in Fox's journal quoted in BQ, 152. Friends introduced fixed prices because they regarded haggling over prices a form of lying. Other religious groups, those of the "middling sort," regarded honesty in business as an important way of honoring God (Christopher Hill, *A Tinker and a Poor Man: John Bunyan and His Church, 1628–1688* [New York: Alfred A. Knopf, 1989], 23–24).

5. John Audland and John Camm to E[dward] B[urrough] and F[rancis] Howgill, September 9, 1654, A. R. Barclay Manuscripts vol. 324, no. 158, transcpt. 89–90, Library of the Society of Friends, London.

6. On the sheriff of Nottingham, see George Fox, *The Journal of George Fox*, ed. John L. Nickalls (London: Religious Society of Friends, 1975), 41.

MOTHER IN ISRAEL

Salute me to the church in thy house.

    Thomas Holme to Margaret Fell

Given the practical and emotional difficulties of early Quaker life, both in and out of the body, one is struck by the extent to which leading Quaker women succeeded in combining ecstatic prayer and public evangelizing with the more conventional activities of child-rearing, charity work, caring for Quakers in prison, petitioning Parliament, and negotiating with magistrates. Elizabeth Hooton was active buying and selling property, distributing charity, and advocating prison reform during the same period when she was admonishing the English king and the magistrates of Boston and (aged at least sixty) was stripped to the waist, tied to a cart, and whipped out of town and into the wilderness at least three different times because she kept coming back to preach. Elizabeth Farmer Andrews discoursed on Quaker doctrine with the customers who came into her shop. Anne Burden traveled to America to prophesy and to collect her late husband's debts. Ann Downer, later a pillar of the London women's meeting, walked two hundred miles to visit George Fox in prison, where she acted as his secretary, prepared his meat, handled the prisoners' money, and prophesied in the neighborhood. Sarah Cheevers and Katherine Evans sat in a Maltese prison for three years, writing verse, having ecstatic visions, and addressing impassioned appeals to the Inquisitors. When a Quaker was finally able to visit them, he found them sitting calmly in their cell, knitting. This integration of visionary ecstasy with more ordinary behavior was often sustained on an almost daily basis. Some prophets made missionary journeys lasting months before returning home to their families, but in many other cases they preached in the streets or at meetings for worship and then came home, nursed their babies, and served supper. "I delivered [my testimony] into [the king's] hands," wrote Elizabeth Stirredge in her journal. "And I can truly say, that the dread of the most high God was so upon me, that it made me tremble, and great agony was over my spirit; insomuch that paleness came in his face. . . . So the Lord blessed my going forth . . . and preserved my family well, and my coming home was with joy and peace in my bosom."[7]

    7. On Hooton, see Manners, *Hooton;* "Life of Elizabeth Andrews," reprinted in JFHS 26 (1929):7. On Burden, see James Bowden, *The History of the Society of Friends in America,* 2 vols. (London: Charles Gilpin, 1850), 1:52–53. On Ann Downer, see G[eorge] F[ox], "Concerning the Life and Death of . . . Ann Whitehead," Manuscript

The name for this archetypal female Quaker was the "mother in Israel." It was in the persona of Margaret Fell, and in that of Elizabeth Hooton, Mary Penington, Ann Downer, Rebeckah Travers, Margaret Newby, and many others, that the Quakers' ability to integrate life in and out of the body was most fully expressed, and it was these women who made the transition between ecstasy and sanctified daily life at least a partial reality for other Friends, male and female. As Joseph Nicholson struggled to reconcile the dissonant modes of his existence as father, husband, and minister (described in chapter 5), he turned to Margaret Fell as a practical and symbolic parent, both to the movement and to him personally:

> I was not free to write so much to [my wife] about the child but I have
> somewhat hinted at it in her letter which she will let thee see. . . . I was free
> to let thee know what I think in it. . . . God almighty be with thee and thine
> who hath been and art famous above the rest of families upon earth because
> of the abundances of his ointment poured forth upon thee, . . . the lord God
> order thee for thou hast ordered many aright.[8]

During the Nicholsons' absence in New England, Margaret Fell sent money, and her daughter Sarah managed their land.[9]

For all itinerant Quakers, particularly those who lost their families upon their conversion or who were separated from neighbors and relatives, the Fell family, and later the family constituted by the marriage of Margaret Fell and George Fox, had immense symbolic and material importance. Margaret Fell preached at meetings. She wrote treatises, polemics, formal epistles, and private letters, including four tracts addressed to the Jews in Holland, one of which was translated into Hebrew and probably read by Spinoza. She organized the itineraries of missionaries. She acted as a clearinghouse for Quaker correspondence between two continents and advised Quakers on the publication of their writings. She also made sure that traveling Quakers had the most intimate necessities of daily life. So Thomas Holme received breeches and shoes;

vol. 366, Library of the Society of Friends, London (hereafter referred to as Friends Manuscript). On Evans and Cheevers, see Henry Fell to Gerrard Roberts, June 18, 1661, SM, 4/184 (II, 147). Elizabeth Stirredge, *Strength in Weakness Manifest* . . . 3d ed. (London, 1772), 39–40.

8. Joseph Nicholson to Margaret Fell, Dover Castle, April 20, 1661, SM 4/106 (II, 939–40). In 1666, Nicholson wrote that the child had died.

9. Isabel Ross, *Margaret Fell: Mother of Quakerism* (London: Longmans, Green, and Co., 1949), 274.

Edward Burrough (who had been disinherited by his own family) required traveling cutlery; Francis Howgill's cloak was sent after him at a cost of a shilling; Elizabeth Leavens received clothing and Elizabeth Fletcher a hat; Alice Birkett, Jane Waugh, and Elizabeth Cowart were given money, while Jane Waugh also received shoes and Elizabeth Cowart a waistcoat and petticoat; Thomas Lawson received funds to buy a Hebrew lexicon and a Greek dictionary.[10] Friends in prison were also supplied with books, while some families received supplies in the absence of a breadwinner.

Margaret Fell also absorbed the rare complaints and uncertainties suffered by even the true believer. She was told about Mary Pease's bruised arm and Joseph Nicholson's fever and John Camm's aching back, and she learned, and presumably forgave the fact, that John Rous had been tempted to lie to the magistrates of New England about his religious beliefs in order to avoid the torture of losing an ear. For the scholar and missionary John Stubbs, whose children were cared for by Fell during his travels, she was the confidante of his most secret doubts:

> The truth is I have none now in England that I know of that I have so much freedom to impart my secret intent as thou and [my wife], neither do I judge any so fit . . . as thyself to determine upon my present condition, for all hath not the spirit of knowledge and wisdom and discerning, or rather not the spirit of pity, compassion and love to mourn with those that mourn, and to have a fellow-feeling of another's misery, and so cannot mourn with them. . . . It hath been revealed unto me, that the Lord had made thee . . . an interpreter one of a thousand.[11]

For John Camm, sick and dying at his home in Preston Patrick, a letter from Fell was "full of marrow and fatness . . . it was like balm unto my head."[12] For the prisoners in the jail at Appleby, her letter of encouragement must have been equally treasured: "You have peace, you have Joy, you have boldness, and you stand over all the world. . . . I do see the secret work of God going on in people's minds; . . . the earthly mind

10. Ibid., 64–65. On coordinating missions, see Edward Burrough to Margaret Fell, Dublin, September 1655, in EQW, 476–78. Elfrida Vipont, *George Fox and the Valiant Sixty* (London: Hamish Hamilton, 1975), 74.

11. John Stubbs to Margaret Fell, October 19, 1657, SM 1/92 (III, 465), quoted in Ross, *Margaret Fell*, 61–62. Stubbs helped Fell arrange for the translation into Hebrew of her books for the Jews.

12. William Caton Manuscripts III, 482, Library of the Society of Friends, London, quoted in Ross, *Margaret Fell*, 58.

is in the earth, and so it faints, but I know there is that in you which is eternal."[13]

Not only did the mother in Israel assist others in the transition from daily life to preaching; she also maintained the family as a locus of worship, moral education, and spiritual shelter. In many cases it was she who initiated the conversion of other family members and servants; so Margaret Fell's children and servants followed her lead in accepting the testimony of George Fox when he visited her estate, her husband acting as a sympathetic patron.[14] For Anthony Pearson, an eminent local magistrate, the sight of Margaret Fell's family was the inspiration for his own conversion:

> O how gracious was the Lord to me in carrying me to Judge Fell's to see the wonder of his power and wisdom, a family walking in the fear of the Lord, conversing daily with him, crucified to the world, and living only to God. I was so confounded . . . my mouth was stopped, my conscience convinced, and the secrets of my heart made manifest.[15]

Women also held meetings in their own houses (often for family members, sometimes for groups of a hundred), acting as both hostess and minister, often at the risk of imprisonment and loss of property. In London, several prosperous widows were paid to hold regular meetings in their homes. Rebeckah Travers later became the only woman to attend the Six Weeks Meeting in London, which was regularly held at her house.[16] London women also took the initiative in organizing an independent women's meeting, perhaps the first of its kind, which collected

13. Margaret Fell to Francis Howgill and others, when they were prisoners at Appleby, 1653, in Margaret Fell, *A Brief Collection of Remarkable Passages and Occurrences Relating to . . . Margaret Fell* (London, 1710), 51–52.
14. Spence Manuscripts III, nos. 135, 124, quoted in Ross, *Margaret Fell,* 35. On women as initiating conversions of families in America, see Jonathan M. Chu, *Neighbors, Friends, or Madmen: The Puritan Adjustment to Quakerism in Seventeenth-Century Massachusetts Bay* (Westport, Conn., and London: Greenwood Press, 1985), 155.
15. Anthony Pearson to a Friend, Ramshaw, May 9, 1653, SM 1/87 (III, 115), and 3/33 (III, 109), quoted in Ross, *Margaret Fell,* 20–21. And see the letter of Margaret Drinkwell, a London Friend, to Fell, June 12, 1664, SM 1/160 (I, 788). William Caton described meetings at Swarthmore with Friends from five or six counties (*Life of William Caton,* 7–10, quoted in Ross, *Margaret Fell,* 19). Barry Levy stresses the importance of the Fell family in the development of George Fox's theology of domesticity, writing that Swarthmore Hall was "decisive" in determining the family orientation of Quakerism. By converting Margaret Fell, Fox "gained not simply a safe-house protected by gentry patronage but also a compelling demonstration of how the Light could regenerate middling northwestern family life. By following, learning from, and using this experience, Fox grew to lead the Quaker movement" (*Quakers and the American Family: British Settlement in the Delaware Valley* [New York and Oxford: Oxford University Press, 1988], 66, 68–69).
16. Six Weeks Meeting Minutes, Library of the Society of Friends, London.

and dispensed funds for the relief of Friends in prison, an institution that would later evolve into a full-blown system of women's meetings.[17]

STATUS AND SERVICE

Like Elizabeth Hooton, many of the women extolled as mothers in Israel were simultaneously active as prophets, writers, or missionaries. Yet when we consider these leaders collectively, we find that the most prominent female organizers of the movement tended to be those with some money, property, or education, while the group of long-term prophets and missionaries included several former servants but not a single member of the higher gentry.[18] This tendency of some more socially prominent women to limit or entirely eschew itinerant prophecy was certainly not the result of cowardice. On the contrary, women who offered their homes as meeting houses had more to lose, in a material sense, than servants who prophesied to outsiders. Margaret Fell, for one, remained in prison for several years and endured the temporary loss of her entire estate. Rather, it must have seemed to these middle and upper class women that by acting as mothers in Israel they were also serving, and suffering, "in their measure."

The social position of Margaret Fell and other eminent women was clearly important for pragmatic reasons. A movement without a church needed large, safe houses in which to hold meetings and allow members to recuperate from physical harassment. It also needed funds for impoverished Friends and members with the organizational and diplomatic skills to administer those funds effectively and to negotiate with magistrates for the care and release of prisoners. Not surprisingly, mothers in Israel tended to be women whose personal capacities answered those needs, women whose positions had always accustomed them to deference and who also had the skills to manage both servants and magistrates. Margaret Fell wrote four times to Oliver Cromwell, to the council

17. The meeting was organized under Fox's auspices in 1658 or 1659. *George Fox's "Book of Miracles*," ed. Henry J. Cadbury (Cambridge: Cambridge University Press, 1948), 46–47.

18. Margaret Fell cites one instance of her preaching to non-Quakers, when she went to her local church and the minister tried to pull her toward her own pew. She said "hold thy hands off me, and . . . spoke to the priest, . . . and she charged him to do justice, and not to wrong nor oppress the poor people, whereupon he was vexed, and writ a letter to her . . . and charged her to prove what Injustice he had done . . . and within a few years after was drowned in a water upon the Road [i.e., a puddle]" (P.S. attached to letter of Margaret Fell to Justice Sawrey, 1653, Spence Manuscripts III, no. 146). She is also mentioned as a missionary to Warwickshire (FPT, 239).

and officers of the army, and every member of Parliament. Her address to King Charles II, the first formal peace testimony to be issued by any Quaker, was endorsed by thirteen leading male Friends, including George Fox. "We are a people," she wrote,

> that follow after those things that make for peace, love, and unity, . . . and do deny and bear our testimony against all strife, and wars, and contentions . . . and our *weapons* are *not carnal*, but *spiritual*. . . . And so we desire, and also expect to have the liberty of our consciences and just rights and outward liberties, as other people of the nation. . . . Treason, treachery, and false dealing we do utterly deny; false dealing, surmising, or plotting against any creature upon the face of Earth, and speak the truth in plainness, and singleness of heart . . . and this many thousands will seal with their Blood, *who are ready not only to believe, but to Suffer.*[19]

Sarah Fell, one of Margaret Fell's six daughters, kept the Swarthmore account books and acted as a local banker, extending short-term loans to many of her neighbors. She and her sisters also used their knowledge of herbs, both medicinal and culinary, to benefit neighboring Friends. Lady Margaret Hamilton organized the distribution of books and collections of sufferings in Scotland. Loveday Hambly's rural estate was the central refuge and gathering place for Friends in Cornwall. Anne Curtis, wife of a justice of the peace and daughter of a sheriff of Bristol who was hanged as a Royalist, was an important negotiator for the release of imprisoned Friends at the court of Charles II. Likewise, Elizabeth Trelawney successfully applied to her own brother, a colonel, for the release of Friends from prison. Sarah Blackborow, an educated matron, was the originator of a system to collect and distribute aid to prisoners in London jails. Indeed, the Quakers' reputation for financial integrity and honesty in business was partly due to the influence of these prominent women, particularly Margaret Fell, who led in establishing and administering a fund collected at Kendall "for the service of truth," beginning already in 1654, before the distribution of funds was regularized by George Fox in women's meetings.[20]

19. Margaret Fell, "A Declaration and an Information from Us the People of God Called Quakers, to the Present Governors, the King and Both Houses of Parliament, and All Whom It May Concern," June 1660, in Margaret Fell, *A Brief Collection*, 202–10. See also Ross, *Margaret Fell*, 128–29.

20. FPT, 242, 250–51, and Ross, *Margaret Fell*, 60–61. On Sarah Fell, see Bonnelyn Young Kunze, "The Family, Social, and Religious Life of Margaret Fell," Ph.D. diss., University of Rochester, 1986, 141–43, and Ross, *Margaret Fell*, 13, 39, 259, 265. (Sarah Fell was bailiff on the estate from the age of twenty-two [1664] until her marriage in 1681. She was also the only woman in the district to manage an iron-smelting forge (Kunze, "The Family, Social, and Religious Life of Margaret Fell," 119–20, 268). On

Indeed, some Quaker mothers in Israel may have been more powerful within their families and neighborhoods, even before the rise of Quakerism, than women in the general population. Elizabeth Hooton was a leader in her Baptist community, and it was she, not her husband, who took the initiative in converting to Quakerism; later, as a widow, she controlled her property and traveled as a missionary against the advice of her adult son. Mary Penington was an independent-minded Puritan gentlewoman who, as a young widow, refused to baptize her child, against the advice of the ministers sent to persuade her. She was also schooled by her guardian as an oculist and manufacturer of patent medicines. The widowed gentlewoman Loveday Hambly was known for her wide hospitality before George Fox ever saw Cornwall; she had also been named sole executrix of her husband's estate. Hambly's relative, Elizabeth Trelawney, was mistress and overseer of her widowed father's house, where she brought up twelve younger brothers and sisters. Margaret Fell's position on her estate of Swarthmore was also less subservient than that of many other gentlewomen of the period. One biographer describes her moving to publish a Quaker tract quickly, before her husband should find out and oppose the project. The biographer also contrasts the experience of Fell with that of another gentry family, that of Ralph Verney, where the wife and children were beholden to the steward, who exercised authority in the father's absences. Indeed, Margaret Fell, and later her children, had sole responsibility for their estate in the absence of Judge Fell; each sister had her own expense account, and Susanna, for one, was able to lend large sums of money.[21]

Lady Margaret Hamilton, see her letter to George Fox, June 20, 1659, SM 4/217 (IV, 217). On Curtis, see Lucy V. Hodgkin, *A Quaker Saint of Cornwall: Loveday Hambly and Her Guests* (London: Longmans, Green, and Co., 1927), 16; on Elizabeth Trelawney, see Hodgkin, *A Quaker Saint*, 99.

21. Hooton and her husband almost separated when she became a Quaker, but he was later convinced ("Testimony to Elizabeth Hooton by George Fox, Nov. 17, 1690," Portfolio Manuscripts 16/74, Library of the Society of Friends, London). On Mary Penington, then Mary Proud, see Linda Ford, "William Penn's Views on Women: Subjects of Friendship," QH 72, no. 2 (Fall 1983):86. Penington's teacher was her guardian and mother-in-law, Mrs. Springett, also an eminent oculist (Lucy V. Hodgkin, *Gulielma: Wife of William Penn* [London, New York, and Toronto: Longmans, Green, and Co., 1947], 20, 24–25). On Hambly, see Hodgkin, *A Quaker Saint*, 19, 24–25; Hambly belonged to an important Cornish gentry family, was married at thirty-five, and widowed in 1651, at forty-seven. On Trelawney, see Hodgkin, *A Quaker Saint*, 95. Kunze, "The Family, Social, and Religious Life of Margaret Fell," 37, 50–51, 58. See also the discussion of Fell in Carole Shammas, "The World Women Knew: Women Workers in the North of England during the Late Seventeenth Century," in *The World of William Penn*, ed. Richard S. Dunn and Mary Maples Dunn (Philadelphia: University of Pennsylvania Press, 1986), 99–115. Shammas writes, "'Typical' would be a poor word to use in describing the

The respectable social position of Quaker mothers in Israel was also of great symbolic importance to the movement. Above all, Margaret Fell's status as the head of a well-to-do gentry family enhanced her authority as a moral arbiter and as a focus of deference, even adoration, for her larger spiritual family. So Mary Pease, a servant in the Fell household, saluted her earthly and spiritual mistress, "(I am) thy daughter and I hope shall be found obedient to that which shall be required of me." Thomas Holme, a weaver turned minister, wrote to Fell after being judged by her: "forgive me I pray thee I fear to offend thee the lord knows . . . thy brother in the unchangeable love of god according to measure."[22] In this respect, Margaret Fell's role paralleled the later career of William Penn, whose social stature enhanced his capacity to serve as a source of moral and practical authority within the movement and improved Friends' credibility with outsiders.[23] Certainly, the importance of these Quaker gentlewomen was not lost on the male leaders of the movement. The adulatory phrases addressed to Fell as a spiritual wife and mother have already been quoted at length in chapter 4. The reader of George Fox's journal finds him also extolling Fell (whom he later married) as well as the gentlewomen Elizabeth Trelawney and Loveday Hambly, neither of them prophets but both of them benefactors of the movement; yet there is no extended mention of the prophets Ann Blaykling, Margaret Killam, or Ann Audland, all of whom came from an area Fox knew well.[24]

Individual Quaker men were, of course, equally successful as organizers and sustainers of the movement, just as individual women were successful as theological writers and ministers. Yet many male Friends appear to have been as much preoccupied with issues of separation as with integration. Male Quakers were often the only members of their

family unless one was also prepared to argue that matriarchy was the dominant form of household organization . . . in . . . Lancashire" (101). For a more positive account of gentlewomen's autonomy on their estates, see Margaret J. M. Ezell, *The Patriarch's Wife: Literary Evidence and the History of the Family* (Chapel Hill, N.C.: University of North Carolina Press, 1987), 142–43.

22. Mary Pease to Margaret Fell, n.d., SM, 4/72 (III, 131). Thomas Holme to Margaret Fell, April 16, 1657, SM 1/196 (II, 373).

23. Kunze, "The Family, Social, and Religious Life of Margaret Fell," Chapter 5, "Margaret Fell and William Penn: A Seventeenth-Century Friendship."

24. Elizabeth Trelawney (1617–ca.1662) was a gentlewoman Friend in Cornwall, married to Thomas Lower (Hodgkin, *A Quaker Saint*, 93–100). Fox cites a meeting at Audland's house (Fox, *Journal*, 453). The Cambridge journal cites her being in jail in 1655 (*The Journal of George Fox*, 2 vols. [Cambridge: Cambridge University Press, 1911], 2:236). Ann Blaykling's defection is mentioned in the Cambridge journal (2:314, 1657).

families to join the movement. Many were younger brothers without family advantages, and they adopted Quaker plain manners in opposition to the status hierarchy within their own households.[25] Several were disinherited as a result of their conversion, and this fact was highly dramatized in their writings, in which honor and pride were contrasted with salvation as a reversal of status. So Francis Howgill's testimony to his dead friend, Edward Burrough, emphasized the trauma of Burrough's conversion, after which he was cast out into the street by hardhearted parents, and his subsequent ecstatic fusion with the group: "His nearest relations, even his own parents cast him off as an alien, and turned him out from their house, as not to have any part or portion therein as a son, nay, not so much as a hired servant, which this young man bore very patiently."[26] Ambrose Rigge, remembering his own conversion, wrote in his journal:

> So then I became as a stranger to my near relations; for my father and mother forsook me; my friends and acquaintances stood afar off wondering at me, and I was a hissing to many; and I was sorely beaten by those who formerly would have hugged me, because I now feared the Lord . . . yea, and at the last I was cast out of all which might administer comfort to my outward man; so that for some time I had not whereon to lay my head.[27]

When the young Thomas Ellwood refused to remove his hat in the presence of his father, in conformity with Quaker practice, the father beat him and threatened to ram it down his throat. Ellwood reflected:

> I considered thereupon the extent of paternal power; which I found was not wholly arbitrary and unlimited, but had bounds set to it; that as in civil

25. Richard T. Vann, *The Social Development of English Quakerism, 1655–1755* (Cambridge, Mass.: Harvard University Press, 1969), 85, 174–75.

26. F[rancis] H[owgill], *A Testimony concerning the Life, Death, Trials, Travels and Labours of Edward Burrough* . . . (London, 1662), 7. See also Edward Burrough, *A Warning from the Lord to the Inhabitants of Underbarrow, and So to All the Inhabitants of England* (London, 1654), 3–5. Burrough was disowned and did not visit his family after the death of a parent (BQ, 72–73). On Richard Hubberthorne, see his "A True Testimony," in *A Collection of the Several Books and Writings of That Faithful Servant of God Richard Hubberthorne* . . . (London, 1663), 2. On Isaac Penington, see Vann, *The Social Development of English Quakerism*, 174–75. On Richard Davies, see his *An Account of the Convincement, Exercises, Services and Travels of That Ancient Servant of the Lord, Richard Davies* . . . (London, 1710), 7. On Thomas Rawlinson, see his Epistle to Margaret Fox and Friends, ca. 1673, quoted in Kunze, "The Family, Social, and Religious Life of Margaret Fell," 322. On William Penn, see Melvin P. Endy, Jr., *William Penn and Early Quakerism* (Princeton: Princeton University Press, 1973), 106–7. George Fox hardly saw his family after he became a minister. Fox's letter to his parents, written probably in 1652, is quoted in EQL, 486; the editors note Fox's "need to establish the authority of his own inner voice over against his father's judgment."

27. "A True Relation of Ambrose Rigge, by way of Journal," Box D(24), fol. 53, Library of the Society of Friends, London.

matters, it was restrained to things lawful; so in spiritual and religious cases, it had not a compulsory power over conscience; which ought to be subject to the heavenly Father.[28]

Once convinced, male Friends tended to present themselves not as "fathers in Israel" but as zealots wholly dedicated to the vocation of itinerant preaching. James Nayler wrote that his spiritual impulse impelled him simply to walk away from his village, leaving his wife and children permanently, without his knowing why and without a word to anyone. "[People were] clearly convinced," he later wrote, "and stayed in silence a great while after the meeting . . . and many desires was that I would come to their houses, but I am made to go on in the work, and I am made free to wander any way the lord shall move me so that I may do his will, for there is my peace."[29] Edward Burrough was thus described by his best friend: "He made the work of the Lord [i.e., preaching] his whole business, without taking so much liberty unto himself or about any outward occasion in this world, as to spend one week to himself . . . these ten years."[30] The emotional bonding of male traveling companions, or "yokefellows," was described with an intensity as great as, if not greater than, that found in their letters to their own wives.[31] "Dearly beloved brother," wrote William Robinson to Christopher Holder, then in prison in Boston, "Oh! my dear beloved, my soul doth greatly love thee. Oh! I cannot express it . . . feel me with thee where neither length of time nor distance of place can separate us. . . . Dear heart, the remembrance of thee doth ravish my soul. Oh! the Lord God knows how greatly I long to see thy face."[32] In later years, Thomas Camm described the marriage of John and Ann Audland as being "a great comfort and blessing each to other, while they both lived together"; the friendship of John Audland and Thomas' father, John Camm, was described thusly:

> their hearts being firmly knit together, as *David* and *Jonathan*, by the bond of unspeakable love, their very lives being endearingly bound up in each other. . . . Many comfortable days and times have I [Thomas] enjoyed with

28. Thomas Ellwood, *The History of the Life of Thomas Ellwood: Written by Himself*, in vol. 6 of the Friends Library (Philadelphia, 1843), 359.
29. James Nayler to George Fox, 1652, SM 3/60 (II, 843). John Perrot was separated from his wife and children for nine years (Kenneth L. Carroll, "John Perrot, Early Quaker Schismatic," JFHS, Supp. 33 [1971]:81).
30. H[owgill], *A Testimony*, 9.
31. I am not aware of any testimonials to women traveling companions or "yokefellows."
32. William Robinson to Christopher Holder, ca. 1659, reprinted in EQW, 128–29.

him . . . our hearts being perfectly united and knit together, in that love that's everlasting, passing the love of women.[33]

Certainly, these men were not indifferent to their families' needs and demands; Nayler supported his family financially and undoubtedly welcomed his wife's visits to him in prison. Gervase Benson was relieved that a female minister had arrived to attend his wife, who lay in prison on the verge of going into labor, enabling him to leave the town in order to join George Fox, but two years later, Benson decided *not* to travel and preach because his wife was ill. Thomas Holme, who had preached separately from his wife at the behest of Margaret Fell, wrote to George Fox some years later,

> this may let thee know why I come not as I intended, my wife hath been very sick, more then ten days, . . . so that at present I am stopped, she is troubled with the rising of the mother in one side, and the spleen in the other . . . so her body is all out of order, her love is dear to thee and she doth salute thee dearly.[34]

Just as certainly, women sometimes devoted their whole energy to itinerant prophecy and insisted on *their* freedom to wander as they were moved. Thus, Joan Brooksop affirmed, "I . . . am preserved through all straits by sea and by land . . . who have forsaken all my relations, husband, and children, and whatsoever was near and dear unto me, yea and my own life too."[35] The point is rather that men portrayed the social reversal, the casting-off from family, the actual physical removal, as more prominent in the drama of their conversion and preaching experience than women did.[36]

Fortunately for these zealous male Friends, Quaker women were there to mediate between the world of flesh and that of the spirit. The romantic heroism of the male seeker and prophet was sustained by the somewhat less romantic heroism of the benign, reassuringly stationary (but no less dedicated) mother in Israel. "And George Fox being gone out of the country," Margaret Fell remembered, "Friends brought things to me,

33. Thomas Camm and Charles Marshall, eds., *The Memory of the Righteous Revived* . . . (London, 1689), n.p.

34. Thomas Holme to George Fox, Kendall, March 1663, SM, 4/251 (II, 385).

35. Joan Brooksop, *An Invitation of Love unto the Seed of God, throughout the World* . . . (London, 1662), 8, 12.

36. For a parallel phenomenon in the writings of medieval Catholics, see Carolyn Walker Bynum, "Women's Stories, Women's Symbols: A Critique of Victor Turner's Theory of Liminality," in Robert L. Moore and Frank E. Reynolds, eds., *Anthropology and the Study of Religion* (Chicago: University of Chicago Press, 1984), 105–25. See also Hill, *A Tinker and a Poor Man*, 226–27, on John Bunyan's pilgrim.

and I answered them. And I was but young in the truth, yet I had a perfect and a pure testimony of God in my heart. . . . And I believe I could at that day have laid down my life for it. And I was very zealous in it."[37] Isaac and Mary Penington were both visionaries, but Isaac, characteristically, did not want to encumber his ministry by buying or furnishing a house. His wife resolved the problem by selling her own estate in order to buy and refurbish another house:

> My husband was averse to building, but . . . he considering the estate was mine and that he had lost all his and brought that suffering upon me, was willing I should do what I would, and added he took delight, I should be answered in this thing.[38]

MARRIAGE

"He, considering that the estate was mine . . . was willing I should do what I would." The authority of the mother in Israel was grounded not only on the biblical archetypes of Sarah and Rebecca and the good wife in Proverbs. It derived from the Quakers' vision of marriage as a union of spiritual equals, men and women restored to the state of Adam and Eve before the Fall—that is, before human disobedience created the need for relationships of subservience and oppression. In Friends' marriage ceremonies, there was no "giving away" of the bride by her male relations; instead, the two parties spoke their own vows as they were moved.[39] In Margaret Fell's prayer at her marriage to George Fox in 1669, she compared herself to the new Jerusalem, the perfected city, married to the Lamb: "Jerusalem is come down from heaven, . . . the bride, the Lamb's wife, whose light is as of jasper stone, . . . whose firstborn of the womb of eternity is coming out of the wilderness to be comforted and nourished, to be nursed and clothed with the eternal free spirit of the living God."[40] Not only were husband and wife to be *spiritual* equals (as they were in conventional Puritan marriages); the independent obligation of women as mothers was also respected. When Fox married Margaret Fell he surprised contemporaries by signing a contract that waived his legal claim to her property, thereby protecting

37. Spence Manuscripts III, nos. 135, 124, quoted in Ross, *Margaret Fell,* 36.
38. Mary Penington, *A Brief Account of My Exercises from My Childhood* (Philadelphia, 1848), 18. A similar distribution of effort occurred in the family of Thomas Salthouse and Anne Upcott; she ran a linendraper's shop while he preached as a missionary in the southwest counties (Hodgkin, *A Quaker Saint,* 87–88).
39. Caroline Whitbeck, "Friends Historical Testimony on the Marriage Relationship," *Friends Journal: Quaker Thought and Life Today* 35, no. 6 (June 1989):13–14.
40. Portfolio Manuscripts 10/53, quoted in Whitbeck, "Friends Historical Testimony," 15.

her own children from a previous marriage. He also insisted that all couples contemplating marriage make provision for the children of earlier unions.

George Fox was forty-five years old when he married Margaret Fell; she was fifty-five. Most Quaker historians have insisted that the union was a wholly spiritual and symbolic one, citing Fox's answer to the question whether marriage was only for the procreation of children: "I judged such things as below me," he said.[41] Yet Fox lent no particular weight to the concept of celibacy, either as symbol or as a moral precondition of sanctity. Indeed, in an epistle defending the right of women to prophesy, he wrote of marriage,

> men [should] love their wives as their own bodies, he that loveth his wife loveth himself; for no man ever hateth his own flesh, but nourished it, and cherished it, even as the Lord the Church; for we are members of his body of his flesh and of his bones; for this cause shall a man leave his father and mother and be joined to his wife and they twain shall be one flesh.[42]

Whatever the dimensions of Fox's own marital relationship (and the implication of another of his epistles is that it was *not* celibate), the sense of all of Fox's writing is that life is to be lived, and lived spiritually—that is, authentically, not fastidiously.[43] It was good to kiss a father or a friend or a husband in a spirit of love; it was bad to bow to him in a spirit of hypocrisy or subservience to a false authority. William Caton's description of his first weeks of marriage perfectly expresses this ideal of exalted physicality. "I continued several weeks with my dear wife, and the Lord was pleased very much to comfort and refresh us together with his infinite loving kindness which abounded to us, and with his heavenly blessing which he caused to descend upon us: for which our souls have cause for ever to praise and magnify his name."[44]

Ironically, celibacy did become an issue for early Friends when a few individuals, misinterpreting Fox's intent, insisted on abstaining from sexual relations with their spouses.[45] It was also an issue because of Fox's

41. Jeanette Carter Gadt, "Women and Protestant Culture: The Quaker Dissent from Puritanism," Ph.D. diss., University of California, Los Angeles, 1974, 108–9.

42. G[eorge] F[ox], *Concerning Sons and Daughters, and Prophetesses Speaking and Prophesying, in the Law and in the Gospel* (London, n.d.), 4.

43. Whitbeck refers to an epistle of Fox's that defends the sanctity of his "marriage bed" ("Friends Historical Testimony," 15). A letter from Elizabeth Bowman to William Penn implies that Margaret Fell Fox believed she was pregnant at one time (July 16, 1670, PWP 1:158, 159 n. 6).

44. Caton, *Life*, 27, quoted in Levy, *Quakers and the American Family*, 72.

45. BQ, 1:236, EQW, 520, 536. Two advocates of marital celibacy were the prophets Dorothy Waugh and Mary Clark. Joseph Nicholson wrote to Fell from Boston that

and Margaret Fell's insistence that spouses leave each other free to do God's work (although, judging from confessions of lustful thoughts in private letters, it appears to have been a more pressing issue for men than for women). Moreover, the exigencies of itinerant prophecy made periodic celibacy an *ad hoc* necessity because of Friends' concern to avoid giving cause for slander by sceptical outsiders. Most missionaries therefore traveled in single-sex pairs.

Just as the model for the mother in Israel was the northern family of Margaret Fell and her children, so the models for the companionate married couple were the households in the northern counties where Fox made his first important converts. Not surprisingly, families in which husbands and wives were both active as prophets also clustered in the northern counties.[46] Their surviving letters provide very few concrete details about individual family relationships, yet they are eloquent in conveying a sense of mutual purpose and a respect for each other's independent activities in the Lamb's war. Here is Ann Audland writing to her husband John:

> John Audland joy it is to me to hear from thee in the unity where our unity stands for ever . . . let nothing enter that would break thy spirit. . . . I am preserved, thy little one is well, dear heart neglect no opportunity to write unto me for it is much refreshment to hear from you in the Life, Dear heart I am with thee in that which was, before the world was. Cease not to pray for me, that I may be kept out of pollutions, of the world, clear and single.[47]

John Audland, writing to Margaret Fell, affirmed both his own importance to his wife's well-being and her spiritual independence:

> I was at Banbury with my dear wife and there I left her, she is well every way in great service, I was a great strength to her in that place, and I had movings to stay with her about fifteen days . . . how long she stays there I know not, Jo[hn] Camm's wife hath been here with John all the time of his sickness, great

---

one man refused to lie with his wife and two women refused to lie with their husbands (Joseph Nicholson to Margaret Fell, 1660, SM 4/107, 108 [II, 919, 927]).

46. Several southern women were married to Friends or sympathizers of Friends, but few of the husbands were listed as in any way important in the movement. Katherine Evans *was* married to a Quaker minister; her letter to him is similar to those by northern women quoted below (K[atherine] Evans and S[arah] Cheevers, *A True Account . . .* [London, 1663], 109–10).

47. Ann Audland to John Audland, n.d., Markey Manuscripts, fols. 30–31 (also listed as 16–17), Library of the Society of Friends, London.

was the Love of god in preserving her and bringing her to him . . . she is very precious.[48]

Audland and his close friend John Camm had evangelized the town of Banbury, Oxfordshire, in 1654. The following year their wives arrived and carried on the work. Camm wrote to Margaret Fell:

> Dear heart my wife hath been at Banbury the last week to see friends there . . . truly her coming to me was exceeding serviceable and great refreshment unto me, She came in my saddest time of affliction, she is A faithful yokefellow unto me, prayers to the Lord for her: she was at a steeplehouse here and was exceedingly beaten; Walter Clement wife was with her and she suffered for my sake.[49]

John Audland died in 1664, tended by his wife and daughter. "He was greatly afflicted in the sense of my Sorrow," Ann remembered, "lamenting my desolate condition, to be left so big with child, as that I within a few days after his death delivered." Two years later she married John Camm's son.[50]

Northern Friends' private writings clearly indicate that women prophets had challenged contemporary notions of the conventional wifely role. Indeed, a very few letters reveal strains in family relationships, strains that were attributed to the behavior of the women. Gervase Benson, writing to Margaret Fell, was pleased that his wife Dorothy, also a prophet, had recovered from a persistent cough and, though still weak, "was very free that I should come over to Lancaster." He continued, "as for my wife she is come more of late into moderation in words. And surely the forwardness of some that came to her, in judging her who them did comprehend and their judgment did hurt and no good at all: but rather gave the deceipt advantage."[51] Later he wrote, "My wife is in a pretty sober silent and stayed condition waiting for the time of refreshing from the lord . . . into whose hands I us commit who am thy brother in the unchangeable."[52] When Dorothy Benson died, sometime before

---

48. John Audland to Margaret Fell, Bristol, February 10, 1654, William Caton Manuscripts III, 3/141, 434.

49. John and Mabel Camm to Margaret Fell, possibly March 5, 1654, William Caton Manuscripts III S.81, 3/162, fol. 483. See also Craig W. Horle, "John Camm: Profile of a Quaker Minister during the Interregnum," QH 71 (1982): 9.

50. Camm and Marshall, eds., *The Memory of the Righteous Revived*, "The Testimony of Ann Camm concerning John Audland Her Late Husband Deceased" (1681), n.p.

51. Gervase Benson to Margaret Fell, n.d., SM 4/230 (I, 179).

52. Gervase Benson to Margaret Fell, n.d., SM 4/231 (I, 181).

1660, he married another Westmoreland prophet, Mabel Camm, John Camm's widow.

Another northern Friend, Francis Howgill, confided a similar feeling of relief to George Fox; "My wife was here as she came from Newcastle and stayed with me, she is much down and loving and tender towards me now, for which I give the Lord thanks."[53] Joan Killam worried about the emotional stability of her husband Thomas, who, in his grave depression, was unable to eat:

> The earth reeleth to and fro, and is often moved out of its place. My husband . . . often cryeth out his sin is gone over his head and his iniquity is too heavy for him to bear. . . . Sometimes he saith he hath a little refreshment, but it tarryeth not . . . and his grief is great for the people of God least they should be offended by him. My sister Margaret [the prophet Margaret Killam] hath added much to his affliction.[54]

Preaching as a missionary in Wiltshire, the yeoman Miles Halhead instructed his wife as a minister would a new convert: "I am moved . . . to show thee the way that leads to peace. . . . Therefore in dear love I exhort thee to walk in obedience to thy measure." She, however, was recalcitrant. "I would to God I had married a drunkard," she complained, "I might have found him in the alehouse." Later he told her their son's death was God's punishment for her rebellious spirit in criticizing his prophetic vocation.[55] The wife of another prophet, Samuel Fisher,

> was under strong temptations and a wicked spirit of jealousy which ruled her . . . which brought wicked lying thoughts into her mind which she believed and with it her mind set against her husband and others, and she would not suffer him to come near her . . . there is a vain light mind in her full of vain imaginations and jealousies and she doth feed and nourish them with slothfulness lying in bed for the most part every day: and when she feels any guilt and judgment coming upon her then she keeps it off as much as she can by lightness: but he is in a pretty condition.[56]

Fisher was apparently forebearing, but not secretive, about his wife's laziness and jealousy; other Friends intervened, and two years later

---

53. Francis Howgill to George Fox, Appleby, 1664, A. R. Barclay Manuscripts no. 104, reprinted in JFHS 46, no. 2 (Autumn 1954): 90.

54. Joan Killam to George Fox, Balby, October 15, 1658, A. R. Barclay Manuscripts vol. 323, no. 124, reprinted in JFHS 48, no. 3 (Spring 1957): 130.

55. Miles Halhead to Anne Halhead, September 3, 1655, reprinted in Hodgkin, *A Quaker Saint*, 69. EQW, 595. He was a yeoman from Westmoreland who traveled to Wiltshire in 1655 and Devon in 1656.

56. Richard Hubberthorne to George Fox, 1657, SM 4/14 (II, 607).

Fisher, an eminent Quaker controvertialist, was on a mission to Venice and Rome.[57]

Yet the primary emotional thrust of these early letters was less the assertion of personal autonomy on either side than the desire to conflate physical and spiritual independence with family and community fidelity. A few letters, generally those written in prison, succeed in conveying something deeper: the expression of personal emotion transfigured, but not effaced, by piety. Thus, Ann Audland addressed her husband John:

> Dear brother, dearer to me than ever . . . all my soul desireth, is to hear from thee in the life . . . there I am with thee out of all time, out of all words, in the pure power of the Lord. . . . I am full . . . of love towards thee, never such love as this . . . my love to thee is purer than gold seven times purified in the fire. . . . A joyful word it was to me to hear that thou wast moved to go for *Bristol*: Oh! my own heart, my own life in that which now stands, act and obey.[58]

With greater reticence but no less feeling, the farmer Hugh Tickell, in jail in Carlisle, wrote to his wife Dorothy:

> I have not received any Lines from thy hand since we were together, let me hear as often as thou can in thy freedom, I think thou would receive five pounds all but five shillings from Thomas Watson, I will let thee know when I have use for it. Let me know how thou gets on with thy work and when thou be going to mow and what is in thy mind. Let me feel thee.[59]

And John Killam, in jail in York castle, received a letter from his wife Margaret (the same who had apparently abused Thomas Killam): "We are seen and read in one another's hearts, nearer then if we was embracing one another in our arms; I am well . . . and my mother, and my sister, and our children." Margaret also informed him that she had felt movings to visit a female friend, Ann Blaykling, then in prison at Cambridge, where she preached and was stoned in the streets. Killam traveled with a maidservant of John Camm's, and she must have drawn on the support of relatives or neighboring Quakers to care for her children

57. See William Dewsbury's letter to Margaret Fell on the same subject. Quakers wanted to remove Fisher's wife to another place and liberate Fisher to follow his "leading" to travel to convert the Jews, but until she herself accepted the removal as God's will, he would have to be patient and remain at home (William Caton Manuscripts III, 3/168, 492–93; BQ, 426–27).

58. Ann Audland to John Audland, 1654, reprinted in Camm and Marshall, eds., *The Memory of the Righteous Revived*, 92, 94.

59. Hugh Tickell to Dorothy Tickell, Carlisle Prison, July 8, 1665, Gibson Manuscripts II, 335/119, Library of the Society of Friends, London. Tickell's first wife was drowned traveling to evangelize Holland in about 1663 (DQB).

during her absence; she presumably also trusted that her husband would accept the spiritual imperative of visiting Ann Blaykling in prison rather than himself.[60]

WOMEN'S SELF-EXPRESSION

No Quaker woman ever described her activities in terms of a desire for self-expression, least of all the selfless, nurturing mother in Israel. Yet it was in her role as mother in Israel that the Quaker woman came closest to expressing her own, self-generated moral authority and personal talent. For just as Quaker models allowed men to view their prophetic activity as a direct reflection of an Old Testament archetype, so the image of the mother in Israel allowed women to view both their domestic activities and their moral authority among Quakers as emanating from an equally powerful biblical archetype. So Mary Penington described her delight in supervising the reconstruction of her house as a center of Quaker activity:

> My rents came in towards the building, as also the selling of old houses and bark and several other things. I had pleasure instead of pain in laying out my money. Indeed my mind was so daily to the Lord in this affair, and so continually provided with money that I often . . . said, that if I had lived in the time when building of houses for the service of the Lord was accepted and blessed, I could not have had a sweeter, stiller or pleasanter time.[61]

Margaret Fell's visionary prose and her motherly advice flowed into each other with relaxed spontaneity as she wrote to her daughters:

> My dear lambs and babes of God . . . in the bowels of endless love be ye refreshed and nourished for ever, and there do you drink freely and eat abundantly and be satisfied. . . . The last week we received a letter which made mention of Bridget not being well. I would have her to drink at least twenty

60. Margaret Killam to John Killam, Balby, January 5, 1654, Watson Manuscripts 41/130–31, Library of the Society of Friends, London. John Killam's sister Joan also wrote to her brother about the difficult delivery of her baby daughter and described meetings attended by her brother and sister-in-law, both preachers, and other members of her family (Joan Killam from Balby, April 13, Portfolio Manuscripts 36/125). In another letter, she mentioned a male Friend, one Wilkinson, recently married, who arrived with his wife and was traveling south; she also mentioned Gervase Benson, who had gone toward London with his wife and young child (Joan Killam to "Brothers," Balby, November 15, Portfolio Manuscripts 36/123). Ann Audland wrote to Francis Howgill and Edward Burrough from Banbury on April 6, 1655: "If you hear any thing out of the North, let me hear how the child at Kendall doth" (A. S. Barclay Manuscripts, no. 175, 147, transcript). Audland lived in Preston Patrick, near Kendall; presumably her child was cared for there.
61. Penington, A Brief Account, 19.

days of her janesse drink and I would have her take a quantity of alice three mornings together, and keep warm. . . . The arm of the almighty reach over you and His blessing rest upon you for ever. . . . [P. S.] Bridget my dear love, keep in the patience and be subject to the will of the Lord. My dear love to little Rachel and all the rest.[62]

(In the winter of 1662–63 Margaret Fell traveled across England to be with Bridget during her confinement. She and her baby Isaac both died.)

The mother in Israel also felt perfectly free to offer moral and personal advice to men as well as women. So Margaret Lynam counseled a Friend:

> I feel the cause why there has been such trouble attending thee, there has not been a weighty coming down into a true consideration of thy ways. Thou must come to be more weighty. . . . When things appear of different kinds, weigh and prove them, that thou mayest in judgment be upon certain and sure ground. . . . Both in spiritual and temporal concernments thou art to be very cool, still and stayed in thy mind.[63]

In a more mundane context, Ann Audland and Joan Yealle criticized Benjamin Maynard "about his foolishness in showing his shoes and telling them of his want of a shirt when as he had too shirts and neither of us have more . . . and yet he spake to Joan Yealle to let him have three shillings and six pence."[64] Grace Barwick wrote to George Fox, asking him to admonish a male Quaker who had been too noisy in meetings: "who is he in his comprehensions that thou may charge him to keep silence in the church of God."[65] Margaret Fell, Jr., warned her mother, "Humble Thatcher is in Wapping in a distracted condition and truth will suffer by his carriage."[66] Margaret Fell chided a male Quaker for attending meetings only when he felt moved to do so.[67] She also received delinquent Friends who were sent to her for guidance. In 1654, Agnes Wilkinson arrived at Swarthmore with a message from Thomas Aldam

62. Margaret Fell to her children, Spence Manuscripts III, no. 70, reprinted in Ross, *Margaret Fell*, 133, 149–50. "Janesse drink" was an herbal medicine made from barbary. "Alice" is one of the alyssum plants.

63. Margaret Lynam to T. W. at Woodburne, in Margaret Lynam, *Extracts from Letters by Margaret Lynam Written about the Year 1660* (Gloucester, n.d.), 6–7.

64. Edward Pyott to George Bishop, Launceton Prison, May 20, 1656, 91, Craig W. Horle, "A Listing of the Original Records of Sufferings," Numbers 1–500 (vols. 1–4), Library of the Society of Friends, London.

65. Grace Barwick to George Fox, Yorkshire, 1655, SM, 4/174 (IV, 35).

66. M[argaret] F[ell] Jr., to M[argaret] F[ell], Wapping, January 3, 1660, Spence Manuscripts III, no. 64. Other Friends informed Fell of misbehavior by Quakers and asked to intervene; see, for example, Richard Hubberthorne to Fell, SM I, 341.

67. Margaret Fell to John Hall, April 16, 1657, Spence Manuscripts III, no. 52. On Margaret Fell's visit to London in 1660, to address King Charles II and the Duke of York on behalf of imprisoned Quakers, see Kunze, "The Family, Social, and Religious Life of Margaret Fell," 44.

about an unknown offence: "Agnes . . . hath been made to own her condemnation divers times; But dear heart, it is not yet right. . . . See that she be set and kept to Labor, that flesh may be brought down . . . and the life raised up to reign over the will, which now doth her filthiness condemn."[68] Fell also wrote to two Friends who had apparently accused her of laughing at them "behind my back openly in your meeting." Her reply reveals her vindictive (and prophetic) manner toward those coreligionists who failed to acknowledge her preeminence:

> Isabel Gardner and Peter, that day that you came to me with that lying false message . . . after you were gone I walked into the garden, and it was revealed unto me from the lord god, that it was the betraying spirit that brought you. . . . You said that I laughed at you, truly the Lord God is my witness . . . how I have borne with you, and with the deceit that I saw in you both. . . . I have stretched out my hand, and you have not regarded, but you have set at nought all my counsel, and would none of my reproof. I also will laugh at your destruction and will mark when your fear cometh and when your desolation and calamity cometh and anguish and distress cometh upon you as a whirlwind, in the day of your calamity then shall you remember me.[69]

In all their activities, Quaker women continued and amplified a number of customary female roles, for the figure of the matriarch as a nurturer, provider, and overseer of family and dependents, as well as a political activist and dispenser of public charity, was a traditional one for seventeenth-century women. Widows, ministers' wives, and women as deputy husbands all engaged in similar kinds of activities, but in early Quakerism such behavior was not an *ad hoc* measure—taking over in the absence of male authority—but a positive precept of the movement.[70] Quaker women's roles as hostesses, patrons, and general stabilizers of the movement are also reminiscent of those of aristocratic Calvinist women and of the Puritan goodwife—exercising spiritual authority over their children and servants (and occasionally their husbands) through

68. Thomas Aldam to Margaret Fell, York Castle, October 30, 1654, SM 4/89, reprinted in EQW, 471–73. See also Barbour, "Quaker Prophetesses," 49. An unruly orphan named Mary Benson was taken into the Fell household as a servant (Kunze, "The Family, Social, and Religious Life of Margaret Fell," 84).

69. Margaret Fell to Isabell Gardner and Peter Moses, 1653, Spence Manuscripts III, no. 32. Gardner and Moses were accused of witnessing against Fell in meetings and lying to her (Kunze, "The Family, Social, and Religious Life of Margaret Fell," 295–96).

70. Historian Hugh Barbour has pointed out that, whereas all women helped husbands and lovers in jail, bringing food and paying jailer's fees, Quaker women systematically assisted male and female prisoners with tools as well as food and bedding, "whose suffering was part of their common campaign, 'the Lamb's war'" (Barbour, "Quaker Prophetesses," 51).

exemplary behavior and counsel.[71] Yet none of these women or the churches that sheltered them gave as much spiritual weight to the activities of ordinary, domestic life as Quakers did or as much spiritual authority to those who accomplished them.

As providers of charity to imprisoned Friends and as real mothers and nurses, these Quaker mothers in Israel imbued even their public writings with the humanity of the homeliest domestic gestures. Sarah Blackborow was an eminent prophet and the author of several theological tracts. In her published account of the death of Richard Hubberthorne, she addressed the reader:

> Dear Friends, Richard Hubberthorne . . . was a vessel filled with a mighty weighty spirit. . . . The seventh day in the morning, he asked for me, and . . . after a while sitting by him, he put his arm about me, and said Do not seek to hold me, for it is too strait for me; and out of this straitness I must go, for I am wound into largeness, and am to be lifted up on high, far above all. . . . This I was free to give forth, because in the time of his sickness, sometimes I kept friends from him, desiring that he might have slept, and hoping that therein he might have been refreshed.[72]

71. See the discussion of Puritan marriage in Mary Beth Rose, *The Expense of Spirit: Love and Sexuality in English Renaissance Drama* (Ithaca, N.Y., and London: Cornell University Press, 1988), 119–31. On the spiritual leadership of one Puritan gentlewoman, see Peter Lake, "Feminine Piety and Personal Potency: The Emancipation of Mrs. Jane Ratcliffe," *The Seventeenth Century* 2 (1987): 157–58.

72. Hubberthorne, *A Collection of the Several Books and Writings*, Preface.

CHAPTER SEVEN

How Were Quakers Radical?

Discourses are not once and for all subservient to power or
raised up against it, any more than silences are. We must
make allowance for the complex and unstable process
whereby discourse can be both an instrument and an effect
of power, but also a hindrance, a stumbling-block, a point
of resistance and a starting point for an opposing strategy.

Michel Foucault, The History of Sexuality

Quaker visionaries claimed to have transcended their identities; the
modern observer might say that Quakers felt free to assume many
identities. In divesting themselves of their specific individual virtues and
attributes, they experienced that sense of personal nullification and
infantilization that Freud viewed as the ultimate desire of the religious
seeker: the recapturing of the nursing infant's sense of completion in
merging with the source of its own being. So George Fox and others
referred to the light within as "blood" or "milk" or a "spring of water"
that both cleanses and gives new life. Indeed, the Quakers' perception
of their maternal God was so immediate that they felt divine love pro-
ceeding from God's womb or bowels, while Friends themselves had
become so devoid of adult inhibition that, as one witness (perhaps
exaggeratedly) observed, they sometimes defecated while quaking.

> [They] lie groveling on the earth, and struggling as it were for life, and
> sometimes more quietly as though they were departing . . . their lips quiver,
> their flesh and joints tremble, their bellies swell as though blown up with wind,
> they foam at the mouth, and sometimes purge as if they had taken physic.[1]

The Quakers' language, and hence the shape and meaning they gave
to their experience, was significantly altered as a result of this suspension
of the self. Quakers portrayed themselves not merely as individual,

---

1. Francis Higginson, *A Brief Relation of the Irreligion of the Northern Quakers*
(London, 1653), quoted in EQW, 73. Higginson was a Puritan pastor in Lancashire and,
according to the editors, "the best at reproducing early Quaker writing and preaching"
(64).

biological men or women but as souls with the potential for both masculine and feminine expression. When they described the ordeal of self-mortification and the loosening of social (that is, adult) modes of behavior and constraint, they resorted to phrases saturated with biblical images of brides, whores, and nurturing mothers. So William Caton wrote to Friends,

> although for the present you be in pain and sorrow like a woman in travail, groaning to be delivered from the bondage of corruption . . . do not fret yourselves . . . come hither all you that thirsteth, come ye to the waters, and he that hath no money come ye buy and eat, yea come, buy wine and milk without money and without price, yea eat O friends, eat abundantly and be satisfied.[2]

The Quakers' mode of expression was also "feminine" in ways that were less explicit. Mary Penington remembered that at the first meeting held at her house, "the Lord enabled me to worship Him in that which was undoubtedly his own, and give up my whole strength, yea, to swim in the life which overcame me that day."[3] When we remember the conventional association of women with emotional and physical fluidity and nurture (analyzed in chapter 1), we realize that images of fluidity in the Quakers' private writings were also feminine images. To be feminine, in short, was to be both lower and higher than before. It was also to be in a position of equality with every other Friend. As brides of Christ and as his infants, all were reduced to a common level of loving subservience before God; conversely, all were raised above their own, individual humanity by resting in the light.

At other moments, Friends adopted a different feminine identity, that of the mother in Israel, whose competence and virtue made her a dispenser of that very sustenance that, in her mode of silent worshiper, she waited to imbibe from others. At still other moments, when Quakers turned outward toward a public audience, acting as adults to chastise and teach, they adopted a masculine posture and language. Just as men sometimes dressed as women to express the triumph of disorder in riots

2. William Caton to Friends, Amsterdam, May 15, 1657, SM 4/259 (I, 374, 380), quoted in Howard H. Brinton, *Friends for 300 Years: The History and Beliefs of the Society of Friends since George Fox Started the Quaker Movement* (Wallingford, Pa.: Pendle Hill Publications and Philadelphia Yearly Meeting of the Religion Society of Friends, 1983), 42–43.

3. Mary Penington, *Experiences in the Life of Mary Penington (Written by Herself)*, ed. Norman Penney (Philadelphia and London: The Biddle Press and Headley Bros., 1911), 45.

or charivaris, so Quaker women behaved like men when they appeared in marketplaces, churches, and graveyards to address the unregenerate.[4] Not surprisingly, Quakers often dwelt on images of the motherly, compassionate Christ in their private letters and theological writings and on images of the patriarchal, Old Testament Jehovah in their public speeches.

The Quakers' attempt to balance these diverse modes of expression gave Quaker women a complex identity as worshipers, as prophets, and as mothers in Israel. It also gave them an immensely complicated, even contradictory set of relationships to the feminine symbolism that informed their visionary language. As mothers in Israel, Quaker women were defined as gendered, social beings, embedded not only in their own spiritual community but in biological families and physical neighborhoods. Like the orthodox Jewish matron presiding over her Sabbath table, their religious expressiveness emanated from a female identity that was both personalized and traditional. As public prophets, however, Quaker women were utterly distanced from traditional forms of female self-definition. The same situation, in reverse, applied to Quaker men. *Their* personae as prophets comprised elements of their "real" identities as farmers or chastising fathers, while in private or at Quaker meetings they surely experienced a contrast between conventional norms of masculine behavior and the highly fluid and physical style of Quaker worship. Thus, the individual's different vocations must have been perceived as authentic or fulfilling in very different ways, for Quaker religious symbolism both referred the believer back to his or her concrete identity and pointed him or her away from it.[5]

The Quakers' mode of expression was both a replication of a traditional cultural discourse and a creative use of that same discourse. By viewing attributes of gender as superficial, as detached from the inner life of the spirit, Friends were able to use traditional symbols of male authority as instruments to chastise bad men, while symbols of female corruption issued from the mouths of pious women as weapons to provoke the unregenerate. Similarly, biblical images of *family* were used to dissolve and reconstitute new, spiritualized family relationships, en-

4. On cross-dressing, see Natalie Z. Davis, "Women on Top," in *Society and Culture in Early Modern France* (Stanford: Stanford University Press, 1975), 124–52; Rudolf M. Dekker and Lotte C. van de Pol, *The Tradition of Female Transvestism in Early Modern Europe* (New York: St. Martin's Press, 1989).

5. For an interesting theoretical discussion of religious symbols in this context, see Carolyn Walker Bynum, Stevan Harrell, and Paula Richman, eds., *Gender and Religion: On the Complexity of Symbols* (Boston: Beacon Press, 1986), 1–23.

ergized by mutual support and religious zeal, at a time when the hierarchical, patriarchal family was as deeply entrenched in English society as it had been a century earlier. Images of biblical *friendship* like that between David and Jonathan were used to establish egalitarian friendship as the highest form of human interaction at a time when there was a general weakening of the ideal of mutual responsibilities among friends. Images of *childhood* were used by Friends to convey their rejection of conventional forms of authority at a time when childhood was a socially despised state and childish behavior held in contempt. And the imitation of the aggressive *behavior* of biblical prophets was used to challenge habits of social deference at a time when rules of etiquette were becoming more rigidified as part of the language of power and status among social groups.[6]

Yet the most creative aspect of early Quaker life was not the communal meeting or plain language or Friends' spiritualized friendship and marriage. It was the integration of the fluid elements of an ecstatic movement with social identities that were stable and also surprisingly traditional. Quakers anchored themselves to the specific social position into which they were born and raised while allowing themselves to be possessed by forces that rendered that position temporarily null and void. By so doing, they did not demean the importance of that outward identity; on the contrary, social station and family responsibility were, along with the rhythm of the weekly meeting, the fixed points of reference that controlled the centrifugal force of the individual's spiritual energy and made it possible for the movement as a whole to survive and grow.

The traditional wife and mother, dignified by the title of "mother in Israel," was a linchpin of this creative effort. This is a strange assertion, to be sure. One might more easily argue (as some historians *have* argued) that Quakers were most original when they were most militant and that their emphasis on traditional values ultimately meant the loss of their creative edge. Yet Friends' real originality lay in their attempt to contain both the liminality of a charismatic mass movement and the solidity of

6. On contemporary notions of friendship, see Benjamin Nelson, *The Idea of Usury, From Tribal Brotherhood to Universal Otherhood*, 2d ed. (Chicago: University of Chicago Press, 1969), 141–66, and Miriam Slater, *Family Life in the Seventeenth Century: The Verneys of Claydon House* (London: Routledge and Kegan Paul, 1984), 34–35; on family, see Lawrence Stone, *Family, Sex and Marriage in England 1500–1800* (London: Weidenfield and Nicolson, 1977), Chap. 5, "The Reinforcement of Patriarchy." On childhood, see Leah Sinanoglou Marcus, *Childhood and Cultural Despair: A Theme and Variations in Seventeenth-Century Literature* (Pittsburgh: University of Pittsburgh Press, 1978), 7, 31, 51.

a permanent, disciplined community within a single historical moment. To this end, they propounded an image of womanly virtue that went far beyond the persona of the goodwife or the traditional ecstatic visionary, and this at a time when the issue of gender roles and gender relationships was most problematic. Nor was the relationship of these women to eminent male Quakers comparable to that of, say, Muggletonian women with their male messianic and paternalist leader or of Baptist and Puritan women with the ministers who recorded and categorized their experiences of convincement.[7] Thus do the facts belie the stereotypes. Our image of the hysterical female visionary has more to do with expectations of female behavior than it does with objective reality. Far from being excessively undisciplined, formless, or hysterical, the behavior of most early Quaker women was instrumental in holding the movement together.

All of this is not to claim that women owned the movement. On the contrary, Quakers, more than any other contemporary group, were clearly inspired, mobilized, and sustained by the ideas and personality of a single great man. But as George Fox affirmed from the very beginning of his career, the achievement of full human perfectability and sustained moral endeavor could occur only by attending to private as well as public virtues and to the traditional activities of mothers, negotiators, and heads of households as well as prophets and theologians.

QUAKERS AND DIGGERS

What fundamental worldview underlay Fox's vision of the interpenetration of public and private spheres of existence? Why was Fox so receptive to the authority of women and to images of parenthood and family life? Certainly, he felt the influence of the northern, family-based culture of his earliest converts, for the extended families of Margaret Fell, Ann Audland, Dorothy Benson, Elizabeth Tomlinson, Mary Howgill,

7. The Baptists John Rogers and Henry Walker had great influence over their communities (Nigel Smith, *Perfection Proclaimed: Language and Literature in English Radical Religion* [Oxford: Claredon Press, 1989]). On the Muggletonians, see, as one example among many, the letter of Lodowijk Muggleton to Mrs. Elizabeth Dickinson of Cambridge, August 28, 1658: "John Reeve and myself, the chosen Witnesses of the Spirit, we having the commission and burden of the Lord upon us, We are made the object of your faith, . . . so that you shall be perfectly whole as to the relation to the fears of eternal death . . . and your faith being in me, as the object in relation to the commission of the Spirit . . . and . . . you may be sure, I do declare you one of the blessed of the Lord to all eternity" (A. Delamaine and T. Terry, eds., *A Volume of Spiritual Epistles . . . by John Reeve and Lodowijk Muggleton* [1755], 14–15).

Margaret Killam, and others became the spiritual and organizational core of the new movement.[8]

The primacy that Fox gave to family relationships and to images of parental authority was also linked to his fundamental indifference to public, political relationships or organized political programs. Certainly, Fox was, along with Margaret Fell, the great organizer of early Quakerism; as such, he was distrustful of the mystical tendencies of Quakers like James Nayler as well as the arcane symbolism of alchemy and the cabbala.[9] He was also at pains to distinguish Friends from anarchic or incendiary groups like Fifth Monarchists or Ranters. Indeed, Friends consistently affirmed their loyalty to the state; many served in the army, while others were local magistrates who excelled at using the law as a negotiating tool with those in power.

Notwithstanding these disclaimers, Fox in the 1650s was a staunch antiformalist. He and other leading Friends insisted on their radical disengagement from all social structures, whether of language, of personal interaction, or of politics. They rejected baptism, formal marriage ceremonies, oaths of allegience to the state, even the language of the calendar. Quakers were not undisciplined or anarchic. They were always conscious of the need to reconcile spontaneous preaching and freedom

8. On the radical nature of George Fox's concept of the family, see Barry Levy, *Quakers and the American Family: British Settlement in the Delaware Valley* (New York and Oxford: Oxford University Press, 1988), 71. Levy emphasizes that northwest Quakers did not have the extra-household resources, like the congregation, through which to instill moral teachings. Fox therefore focused on household and kinship relations. "The idea that households and family relations should bear such massive moral weight was of course as revolutionary as the extreme spiritualization Fox advocated."

9. Quakers differed in their attitudes toward mysticism. On the affinities between Quakers and intellectual mystics, see Owen Watkins, *The Puritan Experiment: Studies in Spiritual Autobiography* (New York: Schocken Press, 1972), 218; Watkins believes that Winstanley was also a mystic and discusses possible connections between the Diggers and Quakers (219). See also Geoffrey F. Nuttall, "James Nayler: A Fresh Approach," JFHS, Supp. 26 (Spring 1954): 1–20; Serge Hutin, *Les disciples anglais de Jacob Boehme* (Paris: Éditions Denoèl, 1960), 42–114; Désirée Hirst, *Hidden Riches: Traditional Symbolism from the Renaissance to Blake* (New York: Barnes and Noble, 1964), 102–7; Marjorie Hope Nicholson, "George Keith and the Cambridge Platonists," *Philosophical Review* 39 (1930): 36–55; Nils Thune, *The Behemists and the Philadelphians: A Contribution to the Study of English Mysticism in the Seventeenth and Eighteenth Centuries* (Uppsala: Almquist & Wiksells Boktryckeri, 1948); Christopher Hill, *The World Turned Upside Down: Radical Ideas during the English Revolution* (New York: Viking Press, 1972), 233.

Despite their affinities, Quakers and mystical philosophers were generally wary of each other; George Fox mistrusted the elitism and obscurantism of the chemist-turned-Quaker Francis Mercury van Helmont, while Henry More was appalled by what he saw as the intellectual sloppiness and insurrectionary character of the Quakers (Alison Coudert, "A Quaker-Kabbalist Controversy: George Fox's Reaction to Francis Mercury van Helmont," *Journal of the Warburg and Courtauld Institutes* [1976]: 171–89). For arguments that the Quakers were not mystics, see EQW, 21, 25.

of movement with discipline and orderly communication, but they did this largely by persuasion and collective discussion rather than by formalized legislation. In terms of formal theology, the cornerstone of the Quaker community was that, once in the light, men and women were out of the law and out of politics. Adam and Eve were believed to have been created

> of one mind and soul and spirit, as well as one flesh, not usurping authority over each other . . . and the woman was not commanded to be in subjection to her husband till she was gone from the power . . . the power and image and spirit of God is of the same authority in the female as in the male. . . . And whereas it is objected against women that their husbands and parents have power to disannull and make void all their vows or resolutions, this was under the law and under the curse, but who comes to Christ Jesus the end of the law . . . no man hath power . . . to disannull it or make it void.[10]

George Fox counseled Friends against going to war on the grounds that fighting, "destroying mens lives like dogs and beasts and swine, goring, rending, and biting one another . . . and wrestling with flesh and blood, . . . all this is in Adam in the fall for all that pretends to fight for Christ, they are deceived, for his kingdom is not of this world."[11]

We have seen (in chapter 2) that the operative energy in Gerrard Winstanley's utopian vision was the power of the light of reason to organize a just society. For George Fox, the operative energy was a light manifested as both compassion and intuitive insight. Quakers in the light perceived themselves as having transcended not merely the boundaries of their own individuality but the entire visible social order. They were competent and trustworthy in their business dealings and critical of social corruption, not because they were implementing a social or economic theory or model but because they were attempting to demonstrate high standards of affection and integrity, standards that the members of

10. "Concerning the Authority and Dominion in the Church and in the Outward Creation, whether it be in the male or female, or in Christ Jesus the power of God only both in the male and female," Portfolio Manuscripts 1/140.

11. "G. ffs paper to ffriends to keepe out of warrs and fightings," SM (VII, 47), quoted in T. Canby Jones, *George Fox's Attitude toward War* (Richmond, Ind.: Friends United Press, 1972), Appendix A, 75. See also Luella M. Wright, *The Literary Life of the Early Friends, 1650–1725* (New York: Columbia University Press, 1932), 32. Actually, the Quakers' politics were so pragmatic and fluid, especially during the 1650s, that historians are still arguing about whether they were supporters of the Cromwellian army or pacifists, political or apolitical. On the Quakers as a militant sect, see Barry Reay, *The Quakers and the English Revolution* (London: Temple Smith, 1985). Most scholars seem to agree that before 1660 Quakers were of different opinions about the use of violence; after that date, they espoused a policy of nonviolence.

an ideal family might display toward one another, acting in the spirit of divine parental love. Thus, a true prophet was defined as one who preached freely, without intellectual preparation, self-glorification or material gain.

Fox and Winstanley's different attitudes toward the social order were linked to their equally different epistemologies, including the role of the body in acquiring and expressing knowledge. Winstanley believed that the mind understood nature and organized society by means of the clear information transmitted by sense perception:

> The first particular (in mankind) is the living soul, or that estate of simple plain heartedness, which hath the life of the five senses only, and by that life preserves that single body. . . . But the life of the spirit, in sound reason lives not yet in the senses; for pure reason lives like a corn or wheat, under the clods of earth, or beast, and is not yet risen up to rule as king.[12]

In other words, in order for the senses to perceive truly—that is, un-clouded by egoism or imagination—they must be infused by the organizing power of pure reason.

Quakers also believed that salvation gave women and men a true understanding of the natural world through the senses, but for them the inspiration or organizing power that guaranteed true perception was not reason but intuitive revelation. "The Lord hath given me a spirit of discerning," wrote Fox,

> by which I many times saw the states and conditions of people, and would try their spirits. . . . I came among a people that relied much on dreams, . . . and I told them, except they could distinguish between dream and dream, they would mash or confound all together; for there were three sorts of dreams; for multitude of business sometimes caused dreams; and there were whisperings of Satan in man in the night-season; and there were speakings of God to man in dreams.[13]

Fox actually considered becoming a physician after his initial revelatory experience, and throughout his career he continued to practice both physical and mental healing. Yet Fox's mode of treatment involved the spiritual laying on of hands as well as a judicious use of herbs and clysters. His skills were mystical as well as practical, more akin to those

12. Gerrard Winstanley, *Fire in the Bush: The Spirit Burning Not Consuming, but Purging Mankinde* (1650), reprinted in *The Works of Gerrard Winstanley*, ed. George H. Sabine (Ithaca, N.Y.: Cornell University Press, 1941), 478.
13. George Fox, *The Journal of George Fox*, ed. John L. Nichalls (London: Religious Society of Friends, 1975), 9, 155–56.

of a modern faith healer or psychiatrist than those of a conventional doctor. "I bid the lass wash his face," Fox wrote of one patient,

> and I bid her take him and wash him again for she had not washed him clean, then I was moved of the Lord God to lay my hands upon him and speak to him. . . . And sometime after, I called at the house, and I met his mother but did not light. "Oh, stay," says she, "and have a meeting at our house for all the country is convinced by the great miracle that was done by thee upon my son."[14]

Gerrard Winstanley reconciled his belief in the primacy of reason with his preconceptions about feminine and masculine capacities by viewing women as equal but passive citizens of a community rationally structured down to the smallest aspects of domestic life. Quakers could envision a wider role for women because they propounded a view of knowledge in which moral integrity, bodily sensation, emotion, and spirituality were conflated, "where righteousness and peace kisseth each other."[15] They also adhered to a communal structure so minimal that the flow of spiritual authority was relatively unrestricted; shopkeepers, artisans, and gentry, both male and female, might become weighty Friends.

Certainly no one in any of these groups sought to overturn traditional stereotypes of the nature of womanhood. It was rather that those who thought most creatively about women's participation in religious and social life had a social vision and a view of knowledge that harmonized with traditional views of women as more intuitive, more spiritual, and—if you will—more unstructured than men. George Fox, who believed that salvation gave men and women automatic and direct knowledge of the workings of nature, enabling them to speak with God's voice, could envision women as healers, moral teachers, and prophets. Gerrard Winstanley, who wanted to understand nature through common sense and practical education, envisioned an elaborate postal system, whereby new information would be carried from one community to another. It was inconceivable, given contemporary

---

14. Fox, *Journal*, 172. See also *George Fox's "Book of MIracles,"* ed. Henry J. Cadbury (New York: Octagon Books, 1973), Introduction, 12, 52, for a failed attempt at a cure by Francis Howgill and Fox's criticism of conventional medicine. Fox later claimed to have cured over seventy hopeless patients. He carried a clyster pipe with him and bequeathed medical instruments to his family and friends. The most prominent second-generation Quakers in Philadelphia were all physicians and surgeons, "vernacular healers, not formally trained physicians" (Levy, *Quakers and the American Family*, 57).

15. Epistle of James Nayler, 1653, SM, 3/72 (II, 861). Gerrard Winstanley may have been a Quaker in later life; he also renounced his political and social programs (George M. Shulman, *Radicalism and Reverence: The Political Thought of Gerrard Winstanley* [Berkeley and Los Angeles: University of California Press, 1984]).

values, that he could have imagined women as postmasters. (The irony, of course, is that the Quakers actually did have an informal but effective international postal system, and it was organized and directed by a woman, Margaret Fell, who used her home at Swarthmore as a clearinghouse for letters and who was the chief correspondent of almost every leading male and female Quaker.)

Contemporary values also implied that women's spiritual power was never unequivocally benign. The spiritism of the Quakers not only allowed for the prominence of women in the spiritual and practical life of the community; it also implied that women might as easily be witches. Martha Simmonds, formerly a respected Quaker minister, was accused of witchcraft by her own people after she and James Nayler staged an imitation of Jesus' entry into Jerusalem. In the miraculous episodes that George Fox recounted in his journal, the witches and possessed people he discovered were almost invariably female.[16] In this regard it makes little sense to argue that some religious groups "liked" women more than others, for all of them imbued women with a spiritual potential that was always fluid and often sinister.

We may thus understand not only why Quakers were sympathetic to women and to feminine behavior in both women and men but why the persona of the mother in Israel was absolutely fundamental to the ethos of the movement. Because the mother in Israel was female, all of her activities could be regarded as private and apolitical, done from motives of love and charity rather than from the desire for power or formal authority. As a *virtuous* woman, she also symbolized stability; not the lifeless stability of entrenched social hierarchies, but the security of an unchanging, endlessly renewed strength and nurturance. By exalting women as spiritual mothers rather than as administrators or deputy husbands, Friends not only avoided the problem of defining the nature of women's formal public role; they also defined even the organizational activities that stabilized the movement as being outside the law. As a mother in Israel, a leader in the family of Friends, a woman preached, wrote, and counseled as a strictly private person, for while the family might be viewed as a microcosm of the state or a nursery of political education, it was not a public political institution. Quakers thereby benefited from women's commodious houses, their administrative skills, their extensive charitable activities, and their ability to negotiate with those in power while continuing to portray themselves as having risen

16. Fox, *Journal*, 18, 42, 43.

above, or, more accurately, sunk below all formalities, all rituals of social deference and social control.

The propensity of male Quakers to view their own spiritual sojourn as a heroic quest while relying on the mother in Israel to carry on the business of daily life may strike some readers as disingenuous. Still, the figure of the mother in Israel betokened a genuine radical spirit, though of a very different kind from that practiced in other contemporary sects. The mother in Israel was not a New Woman but a traditional woman with vastly augmented spiritual status as well as new latitude for intellectual and administrative authority. No other movement had attempted with so much fervor to project domestic values into the public sphere; nowhere had women been given such great spiritual authority without being told to lead a celibate or retired life. For Quakers recognized women as both prophets and heads of families, allowing them to live "in the body" without regarding the bodily aspect of their existence as necessarily polluting. In this respect it was Quakers, not Diggers, who were the most radical proponents of the essential worthiness of all human beings in all their aspects.

The Quakers claimed that they had attained the perfection of Eden. In a sense they *were* in Eden, for the open atmosphere of the Interregnum gave them space to attempt new modes of worship and behavior, before their apocalyptic hopes were disappointed and before increased persecution and their own spiritual excesses forced them to recast their public posture in a more conventional mode. What the Quakers experienced in those early years was not a liminal movement of hysterics or lotus eaters. It was a quite conscious and frequently successful struggle to integrate disparate modes of being—times of being "in the power" (traveling, writing, prophesying, and ecstatic suffering) with other, much longer periods of mundane existence. This most characteristic element of early Quakerism could not have evolved as it did, nor could it have been sustained in the concrete lives of early Friends, without their belief in both the fluidity of the personality and the solidity of the group, a faith demonstrated by the readiness of Quaker men to exhibit traditionally feminine and childlike behavior and by the capacity of Quaker women to take on the activist and leadership dimensions of prophecy and public evangelizing. We have seen that in their weakest moments the Quakers' struggles to achieve this exalted condition were clumsy and painful. Yet in their finest moments, Quaker men and women were able to balance states of spiritual ecstasy and self-annihilation with a concern for personal integrity and the practical and emotional elements of everyday life. This fusion of spiritual intensity, moral integrity, and attentiveness to the human needs of Friends was expressed with great power in a single sentence by the prophet Margaret Newby, a stout, comfortable, well-to-do widow with several children, who preached and was martyred in 1657: "A friend did hold me in her arms, the power of the Lord was so strong in me, and I cleared my conscience, and I was moved to sing."[17]

THE PROPHET AND HER AUDIENCE

The king was pregnant.
Ursula LeGuin, The Left Hand of Darkness

The Quakers' portrayal of themselves as both ecstatic visionaries and upholders of family morality and personal integrity attracted thousands of converts, who described them not only as prophets speaking wonders but as good men and women, possessing a still spirit, showing dignity in suffering, standing loyally together, honest, and incorruptible. "I desired in my heart a man of love," wrote one such convert,

> or a people in whom one might put confidence, . . . and as God did raise me, so in the end he did answer it to me outwardly, by sending one of his dear servants . . . whose name was Elizabeth Harris, who soon answered that which was breathing after God in me, by which means I came with many more, to be informed in the way and truth of God, having a seal in my heart and soul of the truth of her message, which I had long waited for.[18]

Indeed, the Quaker movement attracted more adherents than any other seventeenth-century sect, about sixty thousand in its first decade.[19]

17. Margaret Newby and Elizabeth Cowart to Margaret Fell, Tewksbury, November 25, 1655, SM, 1/359 (I, 650).
18. Charles Bayly, *A True and Faithful Warning unto the People and Inhabitants of Bristol* (London, 1663), 11.
19. See, for example, Lady Anne Conway's letter to Henry More, in which she describes the Quakers as a quiet people who have compassion for suffering (Ann Conway to Henry More, February 4, 1676, in Marjorie Hope Nicholson, ed., *Conway Letters: The Correspondence of Anne, Viscountess Conway, Henry More, and Their Friends, 1642–1684* [New Haven: Yale University Press, 1930], 421). Jonathan Chu writes that New England converts were attracted to the Quakers' good conversation and to their moral and familial virtues rather than to their exoticism (*Neighbors, Friends, or Madmen: The Puritan Adjustment to Quakerism in Seventeenth-Century Massachusetts Bay* [Westport, Conn., and London: Greenwood Press, 1985], 154ff.).

Yet Quaker prophets also provoked more violent hostility than those of any other group. In Sussex, Margery Caustock was punched in the stomach and her daughter stoned for going to a Quaker meeting. In Wales, Elizabeth Holme was chained to the wall of the prison to prevent her from speaking to the people as they passed, forcing her to drink by sucking through a cane stuck through a hole in the door. In New England, Anne Coleman almost died when the knots of a whip split open one of her nipples, and when Deborah Wilson and her mother were whipped too lightly, the magistrate arranged for a more rigorous constable to be installed at the next town election. In Ireland, a butcher threatened to cut open Barbara Blaugdone's head with a cleaver. In Northamptonshire, when Anne Cox said she dared not swear for her soul's sake, the justice answered that a woman had no soul and sent her to jail. In Nottinghamshire, Elizabeth Hooton's preaching stuck in the mind of the sectarian Lodowijk Muggleton, who wrote to her:

> It is supposed that you are the mother . . . to that Samuel Hooton of Nottingham, who was damned to eternity by me in the year 1662. It is no great marvel unto me that he proved such a desperate devil, seeing his mother was such an old she-serpent that brought him forth into this world. . . . She hath shot forth her poisonous arrows at me in blasphemy, curses, and words, thinking herself stronger than her brethren. . . . Therefore . . . I do pronounce Elizabeth Hooton, Quaker . . . cursed and damned, both in soul and body, from the presence of God, elect men and angels, to eternity.[20]

Not surprisingly, considering the relative youth of many prophets, sadism toward Quaker women was laced with sexual innuendo and with the public frivolity associated with the skimmington and charivari. In York, Jane Holmes was ducked as a scold, and when Dorothy Waugh tried to preach in the streets of Carlisle, "they did put a bridle on her head with a stone weight and much iron in her mouth like an egg." In Evesham, Margaret Newby and a friend were put in the stocks, their legs spread apart, and when they asked for a block to sit on, the mayor had

---

20. On Margery Caustock, see Besse 1:709, 710, 711. On Elizabeth Holme, see Besse, 1:737. On Ann Coleman, see Besse 2:233. On Deborah Wilson, see Arthur J. Worrall, *Quakers in the Colonial Northeast* (Hanover, N.H.:University Press of New England, 1980), 29. On Barbara Blaugdone, see Besse, 2:459. On Hooton, see Emily Manners, *Elizabeth Hooton: First Quaker Woman Preacher (1600–1672)* (London Headley Brothers, 1914). For a general discussion of treatment of Quakers, see Craig W. Horle, *The Quakers and the English Legal System, 1660–1688* (Philadelphia: University of Pennsylvania Press, 1988), 101–61.

the block thrust between their legs "and said they should not have them between their legs they would have, and other uncivil words."[21] A popular satire ridiculed the Quakers' use of the word "seed," referring to God's presence in the worshiper: "when the Quakers have a mind to the act of generation, they do . . . use the compliment that *Mary* and *Martha* used at *Bristol* to *James Nayler*, in these words, viz. *Hast thou*, James, *any seed*? He answered, *Mine is pure*. Wot you not what followed?"

Historians are generally agreed that these negative reactions to Quaker prophets stemmed from the public's increasing fear of disorder. For Puritans in New England, itinerant Quakers were linked with Indians as symbols of the untamed wilderness, while for some English commentators they were linked with Catholics as purveyors of an insidious idolatry. Both papists and Quakers, it was alleged, gave salvation away too cheap, for without the moral scaffolding provided by biblical authority, the doctrine of predestination, and conservative habits of social restraint, the body of the nation would soon be infiltrated and destroyed by her enemies from Rome:

> Our New *Quaking female prophetesses*, . . . who . . . in imitation of the new order of Jesuitesses, . . . out of a pretended zeal of propagating the Gospel . . . presumed to wander abroad, and preach publicly in England and elsewhere to women and others, . . . beyond the modesty of their sex for sundry years, . . . [now] presume to speak publicly to the people in some of *their congregations. . . . Let your women keep silence in your Churches. . . . FOR IT IS NOT PERMITTED UNTO THEM TO SPEAK.*[22]

Quakers were also linked repeatedly with witches. Thomas Smith asserted that several Quaker men and women had confessed to devil worship and copulation with Satan and maintained that most of those attending the witches' meeting were Quakers and Anabaptists.[23] Another pamphlet recounted the visit of Quakers to a town where those who refused to listen went into fits, roared, barked, and tried to commit suicide.[24] George Fox was also accused of being able to bewitch people

21. On Waugh, see FPT 69. On Newby, see GBS, 2:9 (Worcestershire, 1656).

22. William Prynne, *The Quakers Unmasked, and Clearly Detected to Be But the Spawn of Romish Frogs*, . . . 2d ed. (London, 1655), 18.

23. Thomas Smith, *A Gagg for the Quakers, Speaking by the Inspiration of the Papists* (London, 1659), Preface, n.p. Also see Higginson, *A Brief Relation*, 16–19. I know of no incidents of comparable brutality in the treatment of non-Quaker female visionaries.

24. *Quakers Are Inchanters, and Dangerous Seducers. Appearing in Their Enchantment of One Mary White* (London, 1655), 6–7.

by holding their hands or touching them on the forehead.[25] Contemporaries also did not fail to notice that the most militant Quaker prophets came from the northern counties, where the most notorious witchcraft episode of the period had originated; indeed, the exact spot where George Fox had his first great vision, Pendle Hill in Lancashire, was also the home of the famous Pendle Hill witches.[26]

In Thomas Heywood's extremely popular play, *The Late Lancashire Witches*, an account of the episode at Pendle Hill, the result of the witches' activities was a complete upsetting of the social structure: wives ruled husbands, children ruled parents, and servants ruled mistresses. The skimmington, a "real-life" ritual expressing sexual hostility, was an important feature of the play.[27] Quaker prophets were likewise prosecuted not for heresy or magical practices but for destroying the right ordering of society; for vagrancy or disturbing the peace.[28] So Thomas Dowslay testified against the Yorkshire prophet Jane Holmes (who was said to carry a mysterious bottle, whose contents would cause trances, and who advised one man to walk on water),

> that his wife did usually resort to Roger Hebden's house and did not come home any night until 12 o'clock, and some nights not at all; also that his son Thomas had denied true obedience unto him. He alleged that the said Jane was the only instrument of drawing his wife and son from him, and the cause of tumults and assemblies at unseasonable times of the night.[29]

Like the witch, the Quaker prophet's behavior was assertive in unfeminine ways; it was also feminine in unpopular ways, for the Quaker preaching woman was the ultimate scold.[30]

25. Reay, *Quakers and the English Revolution*, 69–70. Wallace Notestein, *A History of Witchcraft in England from 1558 to 1718* (1911; reprint, New York: Russell and Russell, 1965), 224.

26. Katherine Mary Briggs, *Pale Hecate's Team: An Examination of the Beliefs on Witchcraft and Magic among Shakespeare's Contemporaries and His Immediate Successors* (London: Routledge and Kegan Paul, 1962), 103.

27. Ibid., 103. Stuart Clark, "Witchcraft and Kingship," in *The Damned Art: Essays in the Literature of Witchcraft*, ed. Sydney Anglo (London: Routledge and Kegan Paul, 1977); William Lamont, *Godly Rule: Politics and Religion, 1603–1660* (London: St. Martin's Press, 1969); Notestein, *A History of Witchcraft*, 28–31, 201.

28. Chu, *Neighbors, Friends, or Madmen*, 19–21, 38. Carla Gardina Pestana, "The City Upon a Hill under Siege: The Puritan Perception of the Quaker Threat to Massachusetts Bay, 1656–1661," *New England Quarterly* 56 (1983): 338–39, 344–45, 349, 350–51. BQ, 172.

29. Deposition from the Castle of York, August 24, 1652, reprinted in Ernest E. Taylor, "The Great Revival at Malton in 1652," JFHS 33 (1936): 31.

30. On the perception of Quakers as comparable to scolds and witches, see David Underdown, *Revel, Riot, and Rebellion: Popular Politics and Culture in England 1603–1660* (Oxford: Clarendon Press, 1985), 254; BQ, 284.

That Quakers were perceived as a threat to order comes as no surprise to the modern reader of seventeenth-century texts. Indeed, in the volatile period of the Civil War and Interregnum, fires, wars, food shortages, street crime, and uppity women were all interpreted in the most dire terms as threats to the safety and order of society. In what *specific* ways did Quaker women prophets aggravate contemporary anxieties about impending disorder, and how did those anxieties, in turn, affect the Quakers' own perception of their continued mission?

CROSSING BOUNDARIES

The Quakers appeared on the English public scene at a historical moment when the categories of family, state, religion, and politics and the respective roles of women and men were intensely problematic; when anxiety about social and spiritual boundaries—the rituals and prescribed behavior that distinguished the privileged from the plebeian, the visionary from the rational citizen, the men from the women—dominated popular imagination. Indeed, the condition of women's limited public authority had always been a highly tenuous compartmentalization. Thus, the same individual might preach as a vessel of God and obey as a daughter, but a daughter could not be perceived to preach; likewise, the same individual might rule as a queen or deputy husband and obey as a wife, but a wife could not be perceived to rule. Queen Elizabeth I wore a medallion in the shape of a pelican to symbolize her sacrificial mothering of her people but cleverly avoided confronting her subjects with the sight of a real mother on the throne. Her contemporary, Catherine de Medicis, was far less successful in exploiting maternal imagery to enhance her authority, perhaps because *her* motherhood was all too messy, too concrete.[31]

Quaker women prophets also did more than use maternal *imagery*. They were mothers, neighbors, and workers, ordinary people using ordinary, if inflammatory, language, claiming to be the conscience of their society. Women visionaries walked into prison carrying their babies and their spinning wheels, while those who prophesied in the streets returned home to open their shops, wipe their children's noses, and

31. On Elizabeth's costume, see Louis Adrian Montrose, "Shaping Fantasies: Figurations of Gender and Power in Elizabethan Culture," *Represenations* 2 (1983), 63–64. On Catherine de Medici's maternal imagery, see Rachel Weil, "The Crown Has Fallen to the Distaff: Gender and Politics in the Age of Catherine de Medici, 1560–1589," *Princeton Working Papers in Women's Studies* 1, no. 4 (1985): 1–38.

protect their families' interests. So George Fox and several other Friends rode in an open wagon on the way to jail:

> We passed through the people in the fields at their harvest, and in the towns. And we declared the Truth to them with our open Bibles in our hands; and the two women they carried wheels on their laps to spin in prison. So we rode through the country to Leicester in that manner, five of us, and declared how we were prisoners of the Lord . . . which astonished the country people and it had an effect upon their hearts.[32]

When Anne Curtis was instructed to bar her doors against some Quakers who arrived for a meeting, she replied that the house was her husband's "and bid them judge whether they themselves would look on it as an equal thing for their wives to contradict their [husbands] in what they did require them to do."[33] When Margaret Fell was brought to trial at Lancaster in 1664, she addressed the judges:

> I . . . seek the Ground and Cause wherefore I am indicted, . . . my Question is, what Matter of Fact they did inform of, for I was sent for from my own House, from amongst my Children and Family, when I was about my outward Occasions, when I was in no Meeting . . . therefore I desire to know what this Foundation or Matter of Fact was, for there is no Law against the Innocent and Righteous.[34]

When Margaret Brewster was whipped in Boston, George Fox defended her innocence by emphasizing both her womanly simplicity and her membership in a tradition of male prophecy: "It is a shame for you to feed a company of priests in their burrows, when that a poor simple woman should leave her family, and come some thousands of miles, to be as a *sign* among you. . . . And will not the king of *Nineveh* rise up in judgment against you, . . . who repented at the preaching of *Jonah*"?[35] In short, the Quaker woman visionary displayed the attributes of the solid citizen, the fluid behavior of the religious ecstatic, and the masculine behavior of the aggressive biblical prophet. In a society characterized by a heightened concern about the means of distinguishing divine truth from diabolical illusion, the trustworthy citizen from the usurper of authority, her public persona surely impressed many observers as profoundly threatening.[36]

32. Fox, *Journal*, 431–32.
33. GBS, 1:55–56 (Berkshire, 1665).
34. "Abstract of the Trial of Margaret Fell, at the Assizes Holden at Lancaster, the 29th Day of the 6th Month, 1664," in Besse, 1:312.
35. G[eorge] F[ox], *Something in Answer to a Letter (Which I Have Seen) of John Leverat Governour of Boston* . . . (n.d.), 2, 3.
36. Bernard Capp writes, "Even more alarming [than the mob] was the prospect of

Now the prophets' audiences were undoubtedly ignorant of many of the Quakers' more traditional virtues and habits, but their responses to Quaker preaching indicate that they were aware of some of them. Thus, attacks on Quakers accused them of being holier-than-thou, of saying, among other things, that "they had known as much if they had had no Scripture," despite the fact that they were really just like everyone else.[37] So Marmaduke Lord Langdale reported to a royal official:

> There are in the country a sect of people called Quakers . . . they are persons of most exemplar regular course of life free from all debauchery or almost other offence to their neighbors yet extreme strict to the rules of their profession. . . . I beseech you . . . what I shall do against these people whose course of life being no offence to the government nor fall within His Majesty's last concessions, I am pressed by divers who are not very canonical to interrupt their meetings . . . and desire His Majesty's order.[38]

The Puritan Richard Baxter remarked that the Quakers "were but the Ranters turned from horrid profaneness and blasphemy to a life of extreme austerity on the other side."[39] John Bunyan also believed that Quakers held the same beliefs as Ranters, "only the Ranters made them threadbare in the alehouse, and the Quakers have set a new gloss upon them again, by an outward legal righteousness."[40] The radical sectarian Lodowijk Muggleton could barely contain himself as he ridiculed the Quakers' bodily excesses:

> It was your Principle of Zeal to fall into Witchcraft fits, supposing it was the Spirit of Christ that moved you to foam at the mouth and sigh, and groan, and swell with spiritual Witchcraft, and howl and groan as if hell were like to burst in you; and perhaps a while after your spirit would break forth into a many non-sensical words. . . . [Some] got the Quaker language of "thee" and "thou" but could not attain the Fits. . . . And the cause why these

---

rebellion in the very heart of the social order, the family. Almost every year it was predicted that wives would seek to challenge the subordinate position they held in a patriarchal society." One author even suggested that suttee be adopted in England (Bernard Capp, *Astrology and the Popular Press: English Almanacs, 1500–1800* [London and Boston: Faber and Faber, 1979], 112, 116, 124–25). On the anxiety induced by the crossing of boundaries, see Mary Douglas, *Purity and Danger: An Analysis of Concepts of Pollution and Taboo* (London and Henley: Routledge and Kegan Paul, 1966), 41–57.

37. Elizabeth Atkinson, *A Brief Discovery of the Labourers in Mistery Babylon, Called Quakers* (London, 1669), 1, 6.

38. Marmaduke Lord Langdale to Right Honorable Edward Nicholas principal secretary to His Majesty, London, January 3, 1661, SP 29, vol. 28, London Public Records Office.

39. Richard Baxter, *Reliquae Baxterianae* (1696), quoted in BQ, 22.

40. John Bunyan quoted in Christopher Hill, *A Tinker and a Poor Man: John Bunyan and His Church, 1628–1688* (New York: Alfred A. Knopf, 1989), 81.

persons . . . could have no such Fits, it was because they had talked with me before.[41]

Yet Muggleton was clearly on the defensive when he wrote to the Quaker Susannah Frith, answering her charges that some Muggletonians were disorderly:

> If any do . . . live an intemperate life, it is not my desire they should do so; for I did always love a temperate life from my childhood. . . . Yet you may remember, that it was the practice of Christ himself, to keep company with publicans and sinners. . . . And you, by the light of Christ within you, leading you to a more preciseness of life than others, you have taken upon you to judge and speak evil of the commission of the spirit. . . . Therefore . . . I do pronounce Susannah Frith cursed, and damned.[42]

There was also popular hostility to Quakers from both mobs and people of "the middling sort," who resented Friends' relative prosperity as well as their antisocial behavior.[43]

The Quakers' insistence on using honest, plain language further contributed to their audiences' sense that Quaker prophets were both more incendiary and more self-consciously virtuous than other prophets. Certainly, the tone of Quaker apocalyptic rhetoric was extremely violent; indeed, it was intended to be so. Yet it was often quite alarmingly close to the way ordinary people might express themselves, as in this forthright declarative statement by the prophet Ann Audland: "And whereas I am accused for causing a tumult in the church . . . and likewise to assault the minister: I answer, this is likewise false; liars must be cast into the lake." At such moments, Quaker plain style and verbal exactitude was actually closer to that of Puritans or Baconian scientists than it was to the language of visionaries like Abiezer Coppe or Lady Eleanor Davies.[44]

41. Lodowijk Muggleton, *A Looking-Glass for George Fox the Quaker, and Other Quakers: Wherein They May See Themselves to Be Right Devils* (1667), 36–37.
42. "A Letter Written by the Prophet Lodowicke Muggleton, to One Susannah Frith, a Quaker, Bearing the Date the 28th of Nov. 1662, from London," reprinted in A. Delamaine and T. Terry, eds., *A Volume of Spiritual Epistles . . . by John Reeves and Lodowijk Muggleton* (1755), 80–82.
43. Reay, *Quakers and the English Revolution*, 72–75; Underdown, *Revel, Riot, and Rebellion*, 250.
44. Ann Audland, *A True Declaration of the Suffering of the Innocent . . .* (London, 1655), 29–30. The Quaker Richard Farnsworth wrote, "The people in this generation profess themselves to be the people of God . . . but . . . all their language is corrupt, and if any speak to them in plainness of speech, they are so scornful, that they cannot bear it . . . those that speak in plainness of speech, them they hate" (Richard Farnsworth, *A Call Out of Egypt and Babylon* [1653], 29, quoted in Richard Bauman, *Let Your Words Be Few: Symbolism of Speaking and Silence among Seventeenth-Century Quakers*, Cambridge Studies in Oral and Literate Culture [Cambridge: Cambridge University Press, 1983], 8). Bauman emphasizes the unusual aspects of Quaker plain style, quoting ob-

It was also more irritating to some audiences, as can be seen by Priscilla Cotton's account of her trial in her home town of Plymouth in 1656:

> Said the Judge, "[Plead] guilty or not guilty." I waited what I should say to him and I said "It's false what is on the paper." Then he said often over to me "guilty or not guilty." I was to say still "tis false." Then the judge said to me, "say not guilty then." I was not to say that word, but I said "Tis false, what is laid to my charge." Then the judge was mad and said "Say not guilty." I said to him "Art thou a man to judge for God and canst not rule thy self, but art angry. Be sober man and fear the Lord, and do justice, and let not passion rule thee." Then he raged more and said, "Jailer, have her away, have her away, I can not endure her. I can not abide this people."[45]

"A frugal, plain, silent, yet crafty sect," wrote John Evelyn of the Quakers, "allowing their women to preach, pretending the most primitive simplicity"[46]

Thus, Quaker women prophets aroused hostility not only because they appeared aggressive or hysterical or because they attacked the upholders of privilege and property. They also reinforced the popular notion that women of *all* classes had affinities with men of the lowest class; women might therefore threaten the social order not only from below but from within. When Horred Gardner preached in Boston accompanied by a servant and a nursing infant but without a husband, her behavior surely convinced many magistrates that the disease of lower class rebellion had finally metastasized and was spreading throughout the social body by means of middle class women, finally attacking the basic cellular structure of society itself, the family.[47] When Mary Dyer, wife of the secretary of Rhode Island, stood before the Boston magistrates and defended, with considerable dignity, her right to prophesy, the

---

servers who said they spoke differently from everyone else. I argue that Quaker speech *was* distinctive, but the way in which it differed from ordinary usage was in the opposite direction from other visionaries, who used more convoluted language. Quakers' concern for plain, literally honest language was paralleled in other social groups, including Puritans and scientists (Bauman, *Let Your Words Be Few*, 2–3; see also Barbara J. Shapiro, *Probability and Certainty in Seventeenth-Century England: A Study of the Relationship between Natural Science, Religion, History, Law, and Literature* [Princeton: Princeton University Press, 1983], 12, 238–39).

45. "An Account of the Trial of Priscilla Cotton," Devonshire, August 1656, MS. G4/ORS/1, No. 310 transcpt, (in Horle, "A Listing of the Original Records of Sufferings"). GBS, 3 (Part 1): 174 (Cornwall, 1656).

46. John Evelyn, *History of Religion*, 2 vols. (London: Henry Colburn, 1850), 2: 266.

47. On Horred Gardner, see Jeanetter Carter Gadt, "Women and Protestant Culture: The Quaker Dissent from Puritanism," Ph.D. diss., University of California, Los Angeles, 1974, 128–29. On Quakers as a threat to the family in New England, see Chu, *Neighbors, Friends, or Madmen*, 19–20, 47.

magistrates remembered that the same Mary Dyer had once given birth to a monstrous infant, thereby proving that respectability and matronly virtue were no hedge against the evil potentialities of the female soul.[48]

Certainly, the magistrates' hostility toward respectable women was no less brutal than it was toward poor servants. Margaret Fell *was* immune to the savage physical abuse meted out to other, humbler prophets while her husband continued to protect her, but other women were divested of their property, whipped, pricked for witches' marks, even executed, whether they were servants like Jane Waugh or respectable matrons like Mary Dyer. Margaret Killam was taken from prison by a constable who tied a rope around her and hauled her onto a horse's back, her arms bound behind her, her feet tied under the horse—"a monstrous barbarity," wrote the chronicler, "to a tender woman of good education, and a considerable fortune."[49] Katherine Evans, whose husband was a well-to-do landowner, was shoved into a dungeon kept for madwomen after preaching in her own county. "A Friend did hold me in her arms," wrote the prosperous widow Margaret Newby,

> and I cleared my conscience, and I was moved to sing, and Friends was much broken and the heathen was much astonished. And one of them said that if we were let alone we would destroy the whole town. And the mayor came . . . and took hold on me, and Friends did hold me and strove with him, and at length he tore me from them, and . . . put both my feet in the same stocks.[50]

After being thus confined for seventeen hours in November weather, she was whipped and sent home as a vagrant. She died two years later of the results of exposure.

NEW ENGLAND PURITANS

The confusion that Quaker women prophets inspired in their audiences was nowhere more intense than in New England, among those Puritans

48. Johan Winsser, "Mary Dyer and the 'Monster' Story," QH 79, no. 1 (Spring 1990): 29–31. Two weeks before Dyer was hanged on the Boston gallows, the Reverend John Eliot provided an eyewitness account of the birth in response to a request by the Puritan clergymen Richard Baxter and Thomas Brooks, quoted above, p. 43, and reprinted in Winsser, 30–31. Her letters to the magistrates of Boston are reprinted in Besse 2:202–3, 205–6.

49. Besse, 1:65.

50. Quoted in BQ, 197.

who had attempted to establish a utopian city of God on the shores of Massachusetts Bay.[51]

The early Puritans shared, indeed they probably inspired, the Quaker doctrines of the spiritual equality of the sexes and of the wife as a spiritual, affectionate, and authoritative partner in marriage as well as the custom of informal prophesying by both men and women. In Puritan theology, the image of the bride of Christ was transformed from the virgin of Catholicism into an ardent wife, prepared for sexual union with the bridegroom; Cotton Mather would later speculate on whether the Holy Spirit might not be the maternal member of the Trinity. The Puritans' perception of the ministry, and of divinity itself, was also enriched by the same feminine and bodily symbolism that characterized Quaker language.[52] For New England Puritans in particular, women's roles as helpmeets in the family and pillars of the elect church were absolutely crucial to their sense of themselves as a unified model community, a paradigm of both social and divine justice for the entire world.[53]

51. The complex historiography of Puritanism reflects the confusion of Puritans themselves about the relative importance of church structure, dominated by men, and spontaneous, emotional worship, in which both men and women participated as equals. For an overview of the literature on Puritanism in relation to Quakerism, see Melvin P. Endy, Jr., "Puritanism, Spiritualism, and Quakerism: An Historiographical Essay," in The World of William Penn, ed. Richard S. Dunn and Mary Maples Dunn (Philadelphia: University of Pennsylvania Press, 1986), 281–302. For an interesting discussion of the way this confusion was resolved in Puritan sermons and child-rearing practices, see David Leverenz, The Language of Puritan Feeling: An Exploration in Literature, Psychology, and Social History (New Brunswick, N.J.: Rutgers University Press, 1980). See also Geoffrey F. Nuttall, "Puritan and Quaker Mysticism," Theology 78 (1975): 518–31.

52. On prophesying among Puritans, see Geoffrey F. Nuttall, The Holy Spirit in Puritan Faith and Experience (Oxford: Basil Blackwell, 1946), 75ff. On Puritan feminine symbolism, see Leverenz, The Language of Puritan Feeling, 1ff., 123–25. Leverenz emphasizes the maternal imagery of Puritan preaching (143). See also David D. Hall, The Faithful Shepherd: A History of the New England Ministry in the Seventeenth Century (Williamsburg and Chapel Hill: University of North Carolina Press, 1972), 2; Donald Maltz, "The Bride of Christ Is Filled with His Spirit," in Women in Ritual and Symbolic Roles, ed. Judith Hoch-Smith and Anita Spring (New York and London: Plenum Press, 1978), 36. Peter Stallybrass, "Patriarchial Territories: The Body Enclosed," in Rewriting the Renaissance: The Discourses of Sexual Difference in Early Modern Europe, ed. Margaret W. Ferguson, Maureen Quilligan, and Nancy J. Vickers (Chicago and London: University of Chicago Press, 1986), 127. On Cotton Mather, see Laurel Thatcher Ulhrich, Good Wives: Image and Reality in the Lives of Women in Northern New England, 1650–1750 (New York and Toronto: Oxford University Press, 1980), 153. See also Mary Maples Dunn, "Saints and Sisters: Congregational and Quaker Women in the Early Colonial Period," American Quarterly 30 (1978): 588–92. Dunn emphasizes that, while there was mounting hysteria among Puritans regarding women moving out of their places, there was fluidity on the spiritual plane; men unembarrassedly adopted a feminine role in relation to God.

53. On Puritan values regarding women, see Carol F. Karlsen, The Devil in the Shape of a Woman: Witchcraft in Colonial New England (New York and London: W. W.

However, unlike the early Quakers, who portrayed themselves, in both published and private writings, as resting securely in the light, Puritans never described themselves as restful; Cotton Mather wrote that without the grace of faith, "we should every one of us be a *dog* and a *witch* too."[54] Puritans were especially sensitive to the danger that a member of the Elect might slide into the sin of presumption, falling from there into the worse sin of infallibility, finally hurtling downward into the pit of antinomianism, the heresy for which Anne Hutchinson had been banished in 1637 and with which female visionaries were invariably associated. Finally, Puritans had a particular concern to enforce patriarchal codes of female behavior in a setting in which women's domestic and economic activities were, of necessity, both extremely varied and extremely visible.[55] In short, Puritans strained to achieve, with no little stress, a balance between the spiritual importance of the egalitarian marriage partnership on one hand and the need for a rigid church and family structure on the other.[56]

Not surprisingly, the Puritans' reactions to Quaker women prophets were both ambivalent and violent.[57] Many were impressed by the missionaries who preached and distributed books in their neighborhoods. To those who actually converted, Quaker prophets must have been seen to realize the ideals of sanctified daily life that their ministers had always espoused, for only a very few adopted the Quakers' most extreme ecstatic practices and appeared naked, while a great many preached at Quaker meetings alongside their spouses and children; still others converted as

---

Norton and Co., 1987), 162–81. On women's public confessions, see Charles Lloyd Cohen, *God's Caress: The Psychology of Puritan Religious Experience* (New York and Oxford: Oxford University Press, 1986), 143–44, 150–51; Cohen emphasizes the "unity of discourse" of Puritan women and men (222–23). On the Puritans' development of an ideal of "heroic marriage," which made the family a model for church and state, see Mary Beth Rose, *The Expense of Spirit: Love and Sexuality in English Renaissance Drama* (Ithaca, N.Y., and London: Cornell University Press, 1988), 120ff.

54. Cotton Mather, *Memorable Providences, Relating to Witchcrafts and Possessions* quoted in Michael J. Colacurcio, "Visible Sanctity and Specter Evidence: The Moral World of Hawthorne's 'Young Goodman Brown,'" *Essex Institute Historical Collections* 110, no. 4 (October 1974): 271, n. 19.

55. Gadt, "Women and Protestant Culture," 163–64.

56. Carol Karlsen views the Puritans' silence on the question of female witchcraft, in contrast to prolific Catholic writing on this issue, as an attempt to mask this contradiction. "There was a deep and fundamental split in the Puritan psyche where women were concerned: their two conflicting sets of beliefs about women coexisted, albeit precariously, one on a conscious level, the other layers beneath" (*The Devil in the Shape of a Woman*, 153–81, esp. 178).

57. On the feminine symbolism associated with Hutchinson, see above, chap. 1. David Hall writes that "the logic of Anne Hutchinson's spiritism pointed clearly in the direction of the Baptists and Quakers" (*Faithful Shepherd*, 99, 161).

individuals, but without being reprimanded or disowned by their husbands.[58] Yet Puritans also occupy starring roles as villains in Quaker books of sufferings, whipping, mutilating and hanging Quakers as disturbers of the social order.[59] While the word "witch" was used by all their enemies as a general epithet against Quakers, New England Puritans were the only ones to actually examine Quaker women for witches' marks; indeed, eleven of the twenty-two accusations of witchcraft made in New England between 1656 and 1664 were directed at Quakers.[60] Ann Austin, whose body was stripped and searched for "witches teats," said "she had not suffered so much in the birth of them all [her five children] as she had done under their barbarous and cruel hands."[61]

Other witnesses were less certain that Quakers were monsters, and at least one was driven to despair by confusion over the meaning of Quaker prophecy: "Sometimes she would hate Quakers, sometimes plead for them: sometime, weeping tears, she could of herself, speak not a word to any; sometime [she would] weary others with much speaking."[62] The Puritans in general displayed almost as much vacillation as fanaticism in their treatment of Quaker women. Mary Dyer was actually reprieved by the magistrates just before her execution, probably because of the influence of her son and husband. By her own voluntary reappearance to

58. Chu, *Neighbors, Friends, or Madmen*, 154–57. Chu emphasizes the similarity of women's roles in Puritan and Quaker congregations (155).

59. Pestana, "The City Upon a Hill under Seige," 325. Whipping was applied to Quakers on their second or third offences; others had their ears cut off; still others were hanged (Chu, *Neighbors, Friends, or Madmen*, 40–41, 45). David Hall discusses disagreements among Puritans about proper treatment of Quakers (*Faithful Shepherd*, 229–31).

60. Mary Fisher and Anne Austin were arrested as witches while still on the boat from England and examined for witches' marks in 1656 (Karlsen, *The Devil in the Shape of a Woman*, 122–24); Karlsen notes that 1647–63 was a period of intense witch fear in New England (20). See also Reay, *The Quakers and the English Revolution*, 68. Gadt emphasizes the Puritans' concentration on the terms "infection" and "seduction," thus characterizing the Quaker invasion as essentially female; Increase Mather asserted that two Quaker women and a man were seen dancing naked together; one woman claimed to be Christ and ordered the man to sacrifice a dog ("Women and Protestant Culture," 138, 145–48). The Quaker John Whiting accused the Boston magistrates of being eager to prosecute Quakers for witchcraft while being "cautious and tender" toward other suspected witches. One woman was examined by five or six doctors to make sure she was not just "craz'd in her intellectuals" before condemning her, but Quakers were accused "with being *Madmen*, and with *Phrensie*" (*Persecution Exposed* [London, 1715], 53). See also Pestana, "The City Upon a Hill under Seige," 336–38.

61. Humphrey Norton, *New England's Bloody Ensigne* (London, 1659), 7, quoted in Pestana, "City Upon a Hill under Seige," 323.

62. John Hull, "Memoir and Diaries," 192, quoted in Koehler, *Search for Power*, 253. Five other women fell into violent fits on that occasion. Koehler speculates that the increasing number of female offenders in Puritan courts were inspired by Quaker women preachers (243).

preach in Boston after her release, she virtually forced her own head into the noose.[63]

Indeed, even the Quakers experienced confusion as they attempted to collapse class and gender boundaries while insisting that Friends serve the movement only "in their measure." For women's stature as prophets or mothers in Israel was not predicated on a new conception of womanhood or of the nature of religious and political authority. Rather, it derived from the assumption that all of life was spiritualized; once in the light, the individual's outward behavior would, automatically and spontaneously, answer to universal moral standards as well as the particular standards appropriate to the individual acting "in her measure." During the earliest years of the movement, when apocalyptic expectations were highest, Quakers were sometimes able to approach this ideal of spontaneous perfection in their social and spiritual relationships, but in 1656 the tragedy of James Nayler exposed the inherent fragility of their enterprise. In later years, when internal organization and outward respectability became even more important, Quakers would have a far more difficult time reconciling certain of their "feminine" elements— whether found in the prominence of their female adherents, in the emotive writing and behavior and androgynous religious symbolism of men like George Fox, or in the fluid relationships that characterized the group as a whole—with the constraints of a rationally organized community and church.

As good cultural relativists, we say that almost any mode of expression or behavior is "right" or authentic if it seems organic—that is, in tune with prevailing cultural norms or with the deepest values of the individual writer or actor. On both these counts, the Quakers' language and experiences were unquestionably authentic. The letters of Henry Fell, writing to Margaret Fell from Barbados, achieved an absolute fusion of biblical and personal language:

> In that which comprehends both sea and land which limits and sets bounds thereunto that it cannot pass: which fathoms the deep and shakes the Earth, and brings down the high mountains and makes all plain, in that do I reach unto thee and see thee, and there is my love to thee which tongue nor pen cannot express, where I feed with thee, and rejoice with thee sitting under my

63. On Mary Dyer, see BQ, 404, and Chu, *Neighbors, Friends, or Madmen*, 47. Chu emphasizes the considerable variation in the Massachusetts courts' response to Quakers (59–84).

own vine and drawing water out of my own cistern where none can make me afraid.[64]

Similarly, for women whose thinking had been shaped within a patriarchal society, it was authentic, completely in tune with their own personal and cultural experiences as well as with Quaker doctrine, to express their private spiritual authority as mothers in Israel and their public authority in the language of male prophets. Women woke up at night with the words of Jonah and Jeremiah ringing in their heads. So Katherine Evans asked the Inquisitor at Malta, "'what *representation Daniel* had in the *lion's den*; or *Jonas* in the *whale's belly*; they cried unto the Lord, and he delivered them.' He said, *I talked like a mad woman....* [I replied] 'The Lord did say unto us, *LIFT UP YOUR VOICE LIKE THE NOISE OF A TRUMPET, AND SOUND FORTH MY TRUTH LIKE THE SHOUT OF A KING.'*"[65]

When Katherine Evans addressed the Inquisitors in Malta in the language of the prophet Daniel, she assumed that a statement that expressed her own deepest convictions in terms of traditional biblical imagery was certain to overwhelm her audience by its authenticity. She was wrong. The problem, of course, was that no matter how virtuous her behavior or how heartfelt her preaching, her masculine vocabulary of images and gestures would inevitably appear to many in her audience as inauthentic, for the assertion of prophetic authority by a married woman who utilized her time in jail by knitting was, in the opinion of most contemporaries, simply beyond the bounds of imagination; indeed, Katherine Evans appeared to her Inquisitor not only as a heretic but as a mad woman. Clearly, if Quakers were to achieve permanent stability, the movement would have to change. Some more delineated concept of spiritual service would have to be found for respectable matrons like Katherine Evans or Elizabeth Hooton, traveling and preaching with no husbands or guardians in sight, who spoke with the voice of authority by using the language of a male prophet, "like the shout of a king."

64. Henry Fell to Margaret Fell, Barbados, February 19, 1656, SM 1/68 (II, 111).
65. K[atherine] Evans and S[arah] Cheevers, *A Short Relation of Some of the Cruel Sufferings (For the Truths Sake) of Katharine Evans and Sarah Chevers . . .* (London, 1662), 21, 35, 37, 45, 67.

PART THREE

Visionary Order: Women in the Quaker Movement, 1664–1700

CHAPTER EIGHT

The Snake in the Garden: Quaker Politics and the Origin of the Women's Meeting

Your bawling women come . . . in a wailing manner in
defiance of the army of the living God to cause . . . the
outward enemies to set upon us with persecution. . . . For
you do not only envy George Fox whom god hath set as a
pillar in his temple because he hath stood fast from the
beginning . . . but your enmity is against God . . . and the
evil eye looks out at others, and hath got into prejudice
which hath eaten you up . . . murdering spirits are you all,
and except you repent you will all perish.
Elizabeth Hooton to some Quakers, 1667

I am . . . changing my two maids into Quakers, . . . for if
they prove what they seem to be, lovers of quiet and
retirement, they will fit the circumstances I am in (that
cannot endure any noise) better than others.
Lady Anne Conway to Henry More, 1676

INTRODUCTION

In the summer of 1664, two Quaker men imprisoned in Peel Castle
addressed a long and urgent appeal to Friends outside. One of the men,
William Callow, had asked to be temporarily released from jail in order
to harvest his corn, so that he might pay his rents and provide for his
ailing family. The magistrate responded that the rents might be amply
paid by confiscating the man's estate. "Therefore our dear friends,"
Callow wrote,

> we desire . . . that some of you go to the Earl of Derby to know whether we
> may have the same law that you have or no, and if his answer be nay, send

them or get them sent to some of our friends there to get us the benefit of the Act and laws that you have. . . . We desire you . . . to work in our behalf that we may have as you will have and not be sufferers at every man's pleasure, what you suffer we are willing to suffer the same if it be to the laying down of our bodies. . . . Send us the Act that you suffer by . . . as soon as you can, that we may know what to suffer.[1]

"That we may know what to suffer": Surely no Friend would have dreamed of posing such a problem in the first decade of the movement, when verbal confrontation and physical suffering were automatically greeted, if not actually sought after, as occasions for provoking the unregenerate and bearing witness to the truth. By the 1660s, however, there was a tremendous increase in the systematic, long-term persecution of dissident groups. In 1662 the restored monarchical government, re-acting to the plotting of the radical Fifth Monarchist sect, began issuing a series of acts known as the Clarendon Code, which forbade sectarian meetings and sent Quakers to prison for refusing to pay tithes and take oaths in court. In 1664, it passed the Conventicle Act, increasing the severity of punishments for offenders. Thereafter, Friends were arrested by the thousands and died in jail by the hundreds and continued to do so until the passage of the Toleration Act in 1689.[2]

In this extremity, Friends rose to new dramatic heights in protesting the injustice of their predicaments. The day after one government raid, Solomon Eccles passed through Bartholomew Fair as a sign, "naked, with a pan on his head full of fire and brimstone, flaming up in the sight of the people, crying repentance among them, and bade them remember Sodom." The following Sunday two women appeared at St. Paul's, one "with her face made black, and her hair down with blood poured in it, which run down upon her sackcloth which she had on, and she poured also some blood down upon the altar and spoke some words."[3]

Rather than withdraw to private houses or forests for clandestine worship as many other groups did, many Friends also persisted in re-fusing to swear oaths and in holding public meetings. In the absence of

1. William Callow to Friends, Peel Castle, August 13, 1664, SM 3/117 (I, 317). Prisoners customarily continued working while in prison and paid for their own upkeep. Many had permission to leave the premises for limited periods. On Friends manipulating the law in order to help those in prison, see Craig W. Horle, *The Quakers and the English Legal System, 1660–1688* (Philadelphia: University of Pennsylvania Press, 1988).

2. Hugh Barbour estimates that from 1655 to 1670, 450 Friends died in prison, 15,000 were jailed, and 243 were sentenced to penal colonies (QPE, 53).

3. George Fox, *Journal of George Fox*, 2 vols. (Cambridge: Cambridge University Press, 1911), 2:428; "A brief Relation of the Persecutions . . . since . . . 7th mo . . . 1662," quoted in SPQ, 25.

male leaders, several such meetings were attended only by women; others were sustained only by children, who continued to meet and to be dragged out of meetings and beaten by the authorities while their parents were in prison.[4] In Reading, as four women and three children were arrested by the magistrate, one of the women declared finely:

> This is the place we met in in the beginning, and have ever since. . . . We do not meet here in wilfulness or stubbornness, God is our witness, but we cannot run into corners to meet as some do, but must bear our testimony publicly in this thing, whatever we suffer . . . to us it's a weighty matter, and our case is the same as it was with Daniel in days past.[5]

In London, Rebeckah Travers received a letter from her sister, the visionary Mary Booth, with the news that some constables had broken into the lodgings of her pregnant daughter while her husband was away and taken all their furniture but two beds. "My sister writes me her daughter is contented, and that if they take the beds she has left, she intends to fill a bed with straw to lie on . . . but . . . they are faithful to the Lord in bearing testimony to his name and truth."[6] In Aberdeen, the Scottish leader Lilias Skene addressed the magistrates:

> We feel the old hatred. We see the envy of the people: We hear the cry of *Edom*, crying, *Raze even to the Foundation: Esau's* rough voice has been often heard from your pulpits these thirteen years past, and has caused us to feel rough hands from civil authority. . . . [You have imprisoned] honest men, who have families, wives and children deeply suffering with them, and in these cold, nasty, stinking holes, where ye have shut them up, who have been as neatly handled, and tenderly educated, and as useful in their generations as any amongst you.[7]

In Cirencester, the elderly Theophila Townsend was seized at a meeting and shaken while she was speaking, "but I took no notice of him, but continued until I had eased my spirit."[8]

There was, in short, no diminution of heroic endurance and public testimony during the time of persecution. Nevertheless, Friends were

4. On Friends' sufferings during the period, see SPQ, 21–54. On women and children, see 227.

5. Quoted in SPQ, 227. This was in 1671.

6. Rebeckah Travers to Margaret Fox, n.d., Gibson Manuscripts, 335/119, Library of the Society of Friends, London.

7. Lilias Skene, "A Warning to the Magistrates and Inhabitants of Aberdeen, writ the 31st Day of the the First Month 1677," reprinted in Besse 2:522–23.

8. Theophila Townsend, *A Word of Counsel, in the Love of God, to the Persecuting Magistrates & Clergy, for Them to Read and Consider* (1687), 4.

now constrained to view their imprisonments and loss of property not only as moments of dramatic confrontation and self-transcendence but as a virtual way of life, an interminable succession of ordeals that threatened both their families' material survival and their own integrity as soldiers in the Lamb's war. In Quakerism's early days, the adolescent Elizabeth Farmer had boldly confronted her noble patron, Lord Newport, with the authority of Moses. By 1708, after decades of fines and confiscations of the goods from her drygoods shop, Elizabeth Farmer Andrews was still a minister, but she and her husband had become charity cases. As Friends in Shropshire reported to the London Two Weeks Meeting, "Roger Andrews and his wife [formerly Elizabeth Farmer] . . . being very aged near eighty years each of them and very poor and in distress, and their necessity being more than those few friends in that county is well able to supply [them] . . . requests this meeting to afford them some relief." Two years later the meeting discussed the sale of Elizabeth Andrews's still.[9]

Thus, William Callow, whose letter to Friends was quoted earlier, contemplated the prospect of his own martyrdom not only as a duty to God and an affirmation of his own integrity but as an issue of legality involving his obligations as a tenant and as a husband and father. Mary Penington also scrupled to renounce her property after the imprisonment of her husband Isaac. She argued that she had willingly given up her goods when her husband was fined for preaching in the service of God but that when he was taken prisoner by a fluke, after a chance visit to Friends in jail in Reading, she was entitled to transfer title to her lands and possessions to relatives. "And . . . what I have here asserted to be done by me, was no shift, or carnal hiding from spoil, in that that was a testimony, but a clear acting to disappoint the betrayer of the innocent."[10]

Other Friends' private letters reveal moods of depression and exhaustion, moods that were largely absent from their earlier ecstatic prose. In 1669, the prophet Joseph Nicholson, now somewhat settled in America (living in a borrowed house, two of his four children board-

9. Elizabeth Andrews, "An Account of the Birth, Education and Sufferings for the Truth's Sake of that faithful friend Elizabeth Andrews," reprinted in JFHS 26 (1929): 3. Norris Manuscripts, vol. 9, MS. vol. S. 201/11, Library of the Society of Friends, London. In 1711 she requested a certificate to travel in the ministry; she was buried in 1718 (fol. 72).

10. The account of Mary Penington appears in James Nayler, *Milk for Babes: And Meat for Strong-Men* (London, 1661), 12.

ing with friends), wrote to Margaret Fell about his wife Jane's latest
lying-in:

> My wife . . . hath had a very hard time . . . it was seven weeks wanting but
> one day before she was able to sit up, it is now ten weeks since and now she
> is able to go a little about the house upon a staff . . . the child is living and
> put out to nurse for she had a fever which took away her milk, yet we have
> hopes she may gain her milk yet as she gets strength, it was with me to have
> gone to Maryland this fall and so to have come home at spring for England
> if she had recovered strength as at other times, but to leave her in such a weak
> condition I am not clear. . . . I have had a great desire in my heart this several
> years to come for England.[11]

Even the redoubtable Elizabeth Hooton, who had marched straight
ahead through more than a decade of whippings and imprisonments,
found herself, at one moment, unable to rise to the challenge of bearing
witness. "Friends," she wrote in a private letter,

> I do truly acknowledge that my mind hath been burdened, and oppressed oft
> times more than I can express because I did bring dishonor to the Lord of
> mercy in whom I hope to [be] preserved in the time to come and not to do
> the like again, and I do know that it hath grieved the Lord and you his people
> very much but the Lord in mercy hath in a large measure I hope passed it by,
> and I do desire with my whole heart that you that fear the Lord may do the
> like and I have borne a testimony against baal's priests . . . and [I] hope if the
> Lord do require another testimony from me to bear it.[12]

In the same year 1664, another Quaker prisoner, William Smith,
addressed a letter to Margaret Fell from his jail cell in Nottingham. Some
years earlier, he wrote, an acquaintance of his, one Martha Plats, had
experienced a "motion" toward marriage with another Quaker, Edward
Langford. Langford, however, had experienced no such motion and was
disturbed by her repeated proposals. At first Smith had advised the
woman to wait "in the power":

> And thus it hath been for certain years, and now of late the matter being
> brought up again on her part and he yet finding nothing to answer it, she hath
> sorely judged him, and not only so, but hath judged me also, for not dealing
> plainly with her, as to tell positively whether her motion was right or wrong,

11. Joseph Nicholson to Margaret Fell, Boston, November 8, 1669, SM 1/111 (II,
951). Most of the passage was crossed out.
12. Eliz. Houton to George Fox, January 1677(?), The First Book of the Monthly
Meeting of the People Call'd Quakers, at Horslydown (Later Southwark), London, 1666,
ms. IV, no. 8, Library of the Society of Friends, London.

which thing I never found freedom in, but was rather willing that she might feel the thing in her self, for which cause I did at the first exhort her to mind the power, from which she now draws this conclusion . . . that she had not gone on in the thing, but that I through these words did strengthen her in it. . . . These things was much upon me to lay before thee, that if she should come thou might the more clearly feel into her mind. . . . The man hath been a prisoner in this place a long time, and is an honest man.[13]

"To tell positively whether her motion was right or wrong." During the early years of the movement, Friends did occasionally ponder whether their motions or "leadings" were true divine imperatives or mere personal whimsies, but their doubts about the means of validating individual testimonies multiplied and intensified when they realized that the piety of their most esteemed leaders was no guarantee against those leaders' own "running out." One of those leaders was James Nayler, whose story is told in chapter 5; another was John Perrot, a pious and respected minister who arrived in England in 1661, having spent three years as a prisoner of the Inquisition in Rome. A letter from Perrot had arrived in England in 1661, shortly before his return, in which he suggested that

> if any friend be moved of the Lord god to pray in the congregation of God fallen down with his face to the ground, without taking off the hat, or the shoes, let him do so in the fear and name of the Lord, and if the world be contentious, ask them why take . . . off your hat without precept, and not your shoes, being it was a precept which god commanded Moses, saying take off thy shoe from off thy feet.[14]

Once in England, Perrot amplified this suggestion into an explicit denial of the efficacy of forms in worship, including, finally, that of the meeting itself. He and his followers based their argument on the orthodox Quaker doctrine of the light embedded in each individual soul. So the prophet Dorothy White counseled,

> Dwell everyone in your own light . . . so will every one have an ear kept open . . . to hear the bridegroom's voice. . . . He that is born of god . . . knoweth the deciding betwixt the good motions and the bad, and so cometh to know the word of god in himself, . . . and so he beareth not witness of himself, but of the father who hath sent him, and so it is no more I but the spirit of my father which speaketh in me.[15]

    13. William Smith to Margaret Fell, June 21, 1664, Nottingham County jail, MS no. 861, Quaker Collection, Haverford College Library, Haverford, Pa.
    14. John Perrot to Friends, Edmund Crosse Collection, MS. 12, quoted in Kenneth L. Carroll, "John Perrot, Early Quaker Schismatic," *Journal of the Friends Historical Society* Supp. 33 (1971): 44–45.
    15. Dorothy White to Friends, 1660s, Edmund Crosse Collection, 292/8, Library of the Society of Friends, London.

Perrot took this principle to imply that, since every soul in the light knows the word of God, there can be no occasion for one Friend to judge another or for worship to be constrained by external ritual. "God . . . teaches us to love one another with a pure heart," wrote a follower, Mary Pordage,

> then judging will be at an end; the form and words will cease, . . . the meek nature of the Lamb will rise in his saints . . . purifying the evil flesh, and changing the nature of man, into the nature of god . . . all the outward forms must die. . . . My soul groans for the life that is past through death, to manifest itself in the brotherhood.[16]

If judging was to be at an end, the end could only be antinomianism, the claim of the individual worshiper to be above the law. So wrote another of Perrot's follower's, Robert Rich, the same who had once licked the brand on James Nayler's forehead as he stood in the pillory:

> Where the mind is purified with the love of God, which thinketh no evil; such a one can do [no wrong], and all things are lawful, good, and holy to him; nothing is common or unclean: for all is sanctified by the power of love. So that whether he eats or drinks, feasts or fasteth, whether clothed or naked, in robes or rags, finally, in all actions and in all conditions . . . the eternal God accepts him, as one without spot and blemish: though condemned by G[eorge] F[ox] as a Ranter and as the vilest and worst of sinners.[17]

Preaching to Friends already traumatized by the scandal of James Nayler in 1656 and exhausted by persecution, Perrot was treated with severity by the established leadership. George Fox accused him of writing in Cain's spirit, betraying the children of God to persecution, throwing his "dung and excrements" among Friends.[18] Several women Friends (all of whom, interestingly, came from the northern counties), joined with Fox in condemning Perrot. So Elizabeth Hooton wrote, "your bawling women come reproachfully in a wailing manner in defiance of the army of the living God to cause if it were possible the outward enemies to set upon us with persecution . . . as all other Ranters have done ever since the beginning."[19] The southerner Rebeckah Travers, a supporter of Perrot and a former partisan of James Nayler, wrote more circumspectly,

---

16. Mary Pordage to Friend, n.d., Edmund Crosse Collection, 292/69. Conceivably this is the same Mary Pordage who was the wife of John Pordage, discussed in chapter 2. Mrs. Pordage died in 1668.
17. Robert Rich, *Hidden Things Brought to Light or the Discord of the Grand Quakers among Themselves* (1678), 28.
18. Ibid., 22.
19. Elizabeth Hooton to some Friends, August 13, 1667, Portfolio Manuscripts 3/33.

but with obvious anguish and confusion, about the damage to unity that
Perrot had caused. She also tried to minimize the importance of the issues
involved, perhaps because her own sister, Mary Booth, was one of
Perrot's chief adherents:

> My dear brethren and sisters . . . all drawing from the one breast the milk of
> the Word . . . remember of old what this spirit led to, and what reward it
> met with . . . which I have a more perfect knowledge of than many. . . . I have
> feared nothing more than to lay stumbling blocks in the way of those without,
> who by our good example are to be drawn in, and by our order is all in the
> disorder and confusion to be judged. . . . Now if one come who sees you in
> difference and confusion, will he not be hardened? . . . For the Coat of our
> Lord is seamless, and must not be divided; for though . . . our unity stands
> not in any outside thing, yet it stands and hath its strength in that which doth
> unite . . . though the matter seem never so small, a hat or a hand, these are
> outside things little or nothing, yet they have made so much of it.[20]

Perrot soon emigrated to America and Barbados, where he continued
to preach and write until his death in 1665, but his defeat did little to
resolve the confusion he had wrought in some Friends' minds, for the
controversies that troubled the movement for the next forty years would
revolve around the issue he had posed: the meaning and justification of
outward forms for a people dedicated wholly to the cultivation of the
inner light. Perrot's impact on English Quakerism was especially profound because his personal sincerity and gift for lyrical spiritual expression had always been acknowledged by Friends. Indeed, Perrot's disgrace, coming so soon after that of Nayler, must have caused the ground
to shake, for a moment, under Friends' feet, for if men like these were
capable of misinterpreting God's message, surely an ordinary Friend like
Martha Plats must have been the more ready to doubt the authenticity
of *her* own small testimony. Having been convinced for years that God
intended her to marry Edward Langford, she must have thought to
herself, "If God has really given me a motion to marry, why, in heaven's
name, does He not also inform the man?"

In 1670 another crisis erupted when John Pennyman, a prosperous
London woollen draper and a former adherent of John Perrot, walked
into the London Royal Exchange and attempted to set fire to a load of

20. Rebeckah Travers, *A Testimony concerning the Light and Life of Jesus (the True
Foundation) As It Was Laid Down and Delivered to Us, and Received of Us From the
Beginning* . . . (London, 1663), Introduction, 10, 12. Jane Nicholson, Elizabeth Hooton,
Mary Tompkins, and Alice Ambrose, all northerners, opposed Perrot. His supporters—
Mary Booth, Jane Stokes, Martha Simmonds, and Isabel Harker—were from the south
(Elizabeth Hooton to George Fox, n.d., A. R. Barclay Manuscripts, vol. 324, no. 153,
transcpt. 73–75, Library of the Society of Friends, London; QAC, 276).

books. In earlier days such an action by a convinced Friend would have been instantly intelligible to the community; thus, in 1655 Francis Howgill reported that the wife of an Irish army officer had piled a load of books in the street on market day and set them on fire, "and these things are a good smell."[21] Fifteen years later, John Pennyman's associates were not so sure. Indeed, what most disturbed Friends about Pennyman's action was less the damage he had done to their public image than the realization that the light of God was no longer sufficient to illuminate another's motives. "Perhaps," wrote one confused Friend, "thou intendest only to burn some loose and vain pamphlets, to give public detestation of their vanity; or, perhaps thou didst intend to burn some of thy Friends' books, and other good writings, to show that they are too much idolized."[22] Another Friend supposed that the action must have been acceptable because of Pennyman's good reputation, but William Penn knew better. In a famous polemic, *Judas and the Jews*, he pinpointed the source of the infection in the ailing body of Friends: "In short, *that a man may follow a wrong spirit when he thinks he follows the right; and though he ought to follow the light and spirit, yet is to be judged when he does not act thereby (though he may think he doth) by such as walk thereby.*"[23] Personal reputation and inner conviction were castles in the sand; good Friends could err.

FRIENDS ORGANIZE

In the wake of the crises occasioned by Nayler, Perrot, and Pennyman, and amid the hardships caused by ongoing persecution, the Quakers perceived a need for increased structure and organization in order to ensure both their own spiritual well-being and the material survival of the movement. Thus, they adopted a formal peace testimony, pledging themselves to good behavior as loyal citizens. They adopted a theology in which reason and judgment were to buttress the inspired leadings of the first "publishers of Truth." They altered the shape of the ministry from a loose association of preachers who stood in graveyards, shops,

21. Francis Howgill to Margaret Fell, Bandon (Ireland), 1655, A. R. Barclay Manuscripts vol. 323, no. 65, reprinted in JFHS 37 (1940): 12.
22. The letter was included in an untitled tract by John Pennyman, beginning, "These following words the LORD required a Servant of his to write" (1670), quoted in Lesley H. Higgins, "The Apostatized Apostle, John Pennyman: Heresy and Community in Seventeenth Century Quakerism," QH 69 (1980): 106.
23. William Penn, *Judas and the Jews Combined against Christ and His Followers* (1673), 14.

parlors, and marketplaces and who traveled as they were moved to a formal organization whose members addressed their fellows from raised benches at one end of the meeting-room and who carried certificates permitting them to travel to specified locations. They toned down the style of preaching itself from confrontational prophecy to one that emphasized coherent sermons, delivered by mature, recognized leaders. Finally, they instituted a committee of male worthies who had the authority to pass judgment on every work written for publication by a Quaker and to censor all writings deemed detrimental to the well-being of the community. In short, the history of late seventeenth-century Quakerism presents the observer with a virtual ideal type of radical religious movement: a loose, egalitarian group under charismatic leadership evolving into a tightly knit, bureaucratized, hierarchical church.

Depending on their own predilections and concerns, historians have expressed widely varying responses to these developments. Christopher Hill saw them as elements in the defeat of the authentic, militant radicalism of the 1650s, a radicalism distinguished by the prominence of communal ideologies and experiments.[24] The Quaker historian William Braithwaite lamented a different defeat, that of the charismatic energy of the earliest ecstatic visionaries:

> Quakerism . . . began as a fellowship, thrilling with intense life, with the great purposes of God ringing in its ears and driving it forth to adventurous, if sometimes mistaken service, and later by . . . the accretions of habit, the stereotyping force of tradition, and the pressure of the outside world, it established a strong organization and lost something of its soul.[25]

Others have viewed the end of the period of enthusiasm as the genesis of true, modern Quakerism, whose chief elements are the Friends' peace testimony and the highly developed theology and social activism of Robert Barclay and William Penn.[26]

For this historian, interested primarily in the development of attitudes toward gender relationships, the story of Quakerism in the final forty years of the century seemed, initially, to be both entirely predictable and quite definitely dismal. Tracking the movement's evolution from sect to church, one watched prophetic women, once the bearers of considerable charismatic authority, slowly disappear behind the rising edifice of the

---

24. Christopher Hill, *The Experience of Defeat: Milton and Some Contemporaries* (New York: Faber and Faber, 1984), Chap. 5, "Quakers, 1641–1661."

25. SPQ, 324.

26. Barry Levy, *Quakers and the American Family: British Settlement in the Delaware Valley* (New York and Oxford: Oxford University Press, 1988), Part 1.

new structure, their voices muffled by the clearer discourse of the proponents of new rules and values.[27] Indeed, the Quaker leaders of the 1660s and 1670s appeared to have replicated the pattern exhibited by Gerrard Winstanley and other utopians under siege; once the necessity for structure and rationality became of paramount concern, the "feminine" or liminal aspects of the movement began to be viewed as suspect, if not absolutely vestigial. So the male Quaker who depicted himself as a baby suckled by Christ or a passive vessel of God was now to be transformed into an official minister, while the woman who had engaged in a sort of spiritual cross-dressing by adopting the persona of the rowdy, male, Old Testament prophet was to be metamorphosed into the virtuous and respectable clerk of the women's meeting, notable for piety and restraint rather than charismatic zeal.

As we examine the Quaker experience more closely, however, we realize that the theory of the ideal type of charismatic movement evolving into that of the bureaucratized church, with its attendant polarities of spontaneity/rigidity, democracy/elitism, and freedom/repression, simply cannot be made to fit enough of the facts to make it stick. For it was Fox and his party, the proponents of structure, who affirmed the continued importance of ecstatic prophecy, while their opponents, called Separatists, argued that there was too much singing and groaning in meetings and upbraided Fox for publishing his own fantasies and opinions as night visions sent to him by God.[28] Separatists also expressed their opposition to Fox's meeting system not by leaving on itinerant preaching missions but by establishing their own independent and stable meetings. Moreover, it was the so-called bureaucrats who advocated open attendance at meetings and the importance of communal worship and decision making (albeit limited by the supervision of eminent Friends), while Separatists argued that only selected male delegates be admitted to

27. Phyllis Mack, "Women as Prophets during the English Civil War," *Feminist Studies* 8 (1982): 19–47.
28. SPQ, 313. Fox wrote, "thou sayest how that many of those who are zealous of my orders do in their preaching and praying with the hearers make such a singing and humming noi[se] that many times one can scarce understand what is said, . . . but why do your preachers preach while others sing?" (George Fox to Robert Arch, June 20, 1683, A. R. Barclay Manuscripts vol. 324, no. 198). At a meeting in Reading in 1683, Thomas Curtis said that "singing (or speaking singingly) in prayer or in preaching, or with a vocal voice was abomination" (Reading Monthly Meeting Minutes [orthodox], 8, Library of the Society of Friends, London). Thomas Ellwood defined the Separatists' position as exalting human, "creaturely" wisdom, while he and Fox maintained that spiritual insight is above "natural wisdom" (*An Antidote against the Infection of William Rogers's Book, Mis-called, "The Christian-Quaker Distinguished from the Apostate and Innovator* [London, 1682], 69–70).

business meetings.[29] It was the bureaucrats who insisted on acceptance of martyrdom rather than on capitulation to the government's strictures on public meetings or orders to pay tithes, while the Separatists were relatively indecisive on this issue. Most curious of all, it was the bureaucrats who advocated the protection of the female ministry and the autonomous women's meeting, while the defenders of individual liberty instructed their women to stay home and wash the dishes.

Clearly, the transition from sect to church did not involve anything so simple, or so dismal, as the death of female freedom and the birth of repression. Rather, it changed the setting of women's spiritual creativity from the home and the street to the women's meeting, and, in so doing, it introduced a political dimension into the discussion of the proper vocation of female Friends. Quaker women in the later years of the century *were* often prevented from preaching and writing as they were moved, but they also claimed new authority, albeit very limited authority, as self-conscious actors in the movement's internal political process. The following three chapters tell the story of these actions and emotions and of these gains and losses.

SYSTEM

Walk on your own legs.
    George Fox

Quakers living through the crises of the 1660s and 1670s felt endangered not only by the brutality of the magistrates but by their diminished ability to achieve certain knowledge and a stable order—problems not unlike those faced by contemporaries who struggled to discern the difference between prophecy and witchcraft or between vision and dream. And like the contemporaries described in earlier chapters, Friends perceived their own questions about knowledge, order, and personal integrity to be connected, in more than one sense, with questions about the meaning of gender. At the most superficial level, women's aggressive preaching threatened the physical safety of Friends, because the public actions of even an upright woman like Elizabeth Hooton were perceived as more disorderly—and frequently more ludicrous—than those of her male counterparts. "Now shall the windmill of affection," wrote one satirist,

29. Richard T. Vann, *The Social Development of English Quakerism, 1655–1755* (Cambridge, Mass.: Harvard University Press, 1969), 105–7.

blown by the sails of fancy, turn round the marble of a tender sister's pity, separating the flower of her compassion from the brain of disdain, and kneading it up into a loaf of love. . . . Then shall pride a bound in the outward creature, and the peacocks tail of vanity shall be display'd by the females of the world.[30]

Not only was the prominence of Quaker women both disturbing and amusing to those outside the movement; the specter of emotional excess and spiritual anarchy that Nayler and Perrot had raised up and whose shadows continued to hover over the meeting was seen by many beleaguered and exhausted Friends to wear a decidedly female shape. For like the Ranters discussed in chapter 2, those on the antinomian fringe of Quakerism had invariably expressed their denial of outward forms and categories by means of feminine imagery. "Thou art my sister, and mother," wrote John Perrot to Mary Booth:

> Is it possible for me to mention the remembrance of thee . . . without bathed cheeks, with streamed tears? Surely nay, for thy love overpowers, overpowers, overpowers my tender simple heart and soul. . . . I am as a vessel that is broken which cannot contain waters: Now Mary I must tell thee a secret . . . which is, the lord leads people into divers forms, to witness against other corrupted forms, but when they corrupted themselves also in the latter forms, the lord leads into other forms.[31]

In a more public epistle, Perrot addressed Friends as though his spiritual self had actually been reborn as female: "In this kingdom of the tribulation I am one of you dear *sisters* and bear no other lovers but . . . that which would do his will and . . . salvation reacheth me and I the *damsel* am refreshed, dear *sisters*." He signed still another letter, "I am your sister in our Spouse."[32]

Like the Ranters and some Quakers, Perrot and his followers also expressed their ideal of spiritual unity as an intense bodily identification and sexual release. "Ah feel me," wrote John Browne in a letter to Mary Booth:

> feel me springing in thy breast and it is enough, my love, my love, my unutterable love . . . ah! I am full, I am full of tears, and a soul dropping down blood on your behalfs. . . . [I] embrace thee in mine arms of chastity, and kiss

30. *Yea and Nay Almanack For the People Call'd by the Men of the World Quakers* (London, 1678), April, n.p.
31. John Perrot to Mary Booth, June 6, 1663, Edmund Crosse Collection, 292/13.
32. John Perrot to Friends, May 5, 1660, quoted in Carroll, "John Perrot," 40–41. Carroll speculates that this mode of expression was a sign of mental instability, whereas I argue that crossing gender boundaries was an integral aspect of the attempt to rise beyond formal categories, as it was also for Abiezer Coppe.

thee with those kisses never yet defiled by lust . . . come with me into the garden
of pleasure, and I will give thee the delight of thy soul. . . . I will give thee of
the choicest clusters of the grapes of love. . . . I love my wife so much.[33]

Indeed, Perrot carried the use of sexual metaphor well beyond the bounds
of acceptable Quaker convention. When he was reprimanded by George
Fox for declaring that he was prepared to take a slut for a wife, he
dutifully explained that he was merely adopting the time-honored metaphor of Hosea.

Not only was womanhood a central metaphor of Perrot's self-transcendence (which some Friends translated as airiness and self-exalta-
tion); it was also central in a more concrete sense, for although Perrot
attracted large numbers of eminent male followers, he was perceived by
many of his antagonists as a lone male figure in a landscape of clinging
and aggressive women. One of these was Elizabeth Barnes, who was said
to have torn the scriptures and "in a height of rage . . . [did] offer to burn
them." Another was Jane Stokes, who acted as a missionary for Perrot's
doctrines in America. Still another was Martha Simmonds, who was
thought to have corrupted the soul of James Nayler.[34] George Fox
himself criticized the women who followed Perrot as "deceitful spirits
run up and down among friends, their tongues preaching one thing, and
their lives another"; he also criticized men who kept their hats on in
prayer as being like a company of women.[35]

Yet if the figure of the visionary woman stood near the heart of
Friends' problems, both as a real instigator of disorder and as a symbol
of divisive spiritual energy, women had also to be part of the solution,
for at no time did Quakers abandon their belief in the primacy of inward
revelation and ecstatic communal worship; no one sought to obliterate
the pregnant, amorphous silence of the meeting with the didactic noise
of the sermonizer. Instead, a group of Friends, led by George Fox,
attempted to achieve a fusion of essentially contradictory elements, to
create a harmony between their original spiritual spontaneity and the
new formality of sermon, censorship, and discipline. There was to be no

33. John Browne to Mary Booth, n.d., Edmund Crosse Collection, 292/14. On Isaac
Penington's mysticism, see EQW, 25.
34. Penn, *Judas and the Jews*, quoted in Carroll, "John Perrot," 85. Jane Stokes
settled in Jamaica and had submitted a paper of condemnation before 1672 (SPQ, 238).
35. George Fox, *The Spirit of Envy, Lying, and Persecution, Made Manifest* (London, 1663), 7, 9. Fox also criticized Perrot for sending too much money to Katherine
Evans and Sarah Cheevers when they were imprisoned at Malta (Carroll, "John Perrot,"
51). See also Rich, *Hidden Things Brought to Light*, 34. For explicitly compared Perrot
to James Nayler and the Ranters in an epistle to Friends in 1661 (quoted in Carroll, "John
Perrot," 50).

question of mere coexistence, as in the public obedience and private liberty that would characterize some Enlightenment ideology, but a mutual penetration of opposites. So the individual's prayer and ecstatic worship were to be infused by a new sense of decorum and a sense of one's proper place or office in the world, while public meetings for business and discipline were to be infused by the shared charisma and deep passivity of the original silent meeting. "Forasmuch as not all are called in the same station," wrote Robert Barclay,

> some rich, some poor; some servants, some masters, some married, some unmarried; some widows, and some orphans . . . it is . . . absolutely needful, that there be certain meetings at certain places and times . . . where both those that are to take care may assemble, and those who may need this care, may come and make known their necessities, and receive help . . . according to their respective needs. This doth not at all contradict the principle of being led inwardly and immediately by the Spirit.[36]

This fusion of opposites, this blending of the ideal of orderly thinking and behavior with that of spiritual ecstasy and enlightenment, was most fully articulated in the Friends' peace testimony. Quakers had always endured violent treatment from their persecutors without retaliating physically, but they had also felt free to express anger, both against injustice from outsiders and against improper behavior by one of their own. Now, Friends were enjoined not only to forebear against the use of *physical* violence but to eschew verbal and emotional violence as well. Fox wrote,

> Keep over all that which tends to strife in the seed Christ; in which is peace and life; for that which tends to strife . . . will corrupt you; and therefore live in that which is pure, steadfast, and is not changeable and in that know one another; and lay hands on no man suddenly; for that which is fickle, and changeable will bring people into an unsettled state, and bring them out of their own conditions, and bringeth into a questioning state and therefore keep in the seed . . . in which you may walk on your own legs, and not give

36. Robert Barclay, *The Anarchy of the Ranters and Other Libertines* . . . (1676; reprint, Philadelphia, 1757), 38. Fox imbued the mother in Israel with charismatic healing power: "I believe there is a thousand women that are beyond the wisdom of the world all: yea, and the power of God hath wrought miracles among them" (October 28, 1671, at the house of Thomas Rous, quoted in *George Fox's "Book of Miracles,"* ed. Henry J. Cadbury [New York: Octagon Books, 1973], 46). He also insisted that meeting business was also spiritual business: "So Friends are not to meet like a company of people about town and parish business, neither in their men nor women's meetings, but to wait upon the Lord feeling his power and spirit to lead them" (George Fox to Friends, n.d., Richardson Manuscript, Quaker Collection, Haverford College Library, Haverford, Pa., 102).

away your power . . . be quiet and live; and dwell in the power of truth over all the unruly spirits in peace, love, and unity.[37]

The means by which Quakers were to sustain this state of constancy and unity were twofold. Internally, the individual would rely on universal reason and conscience to interpret the true, uniform meaning of the inner light; externally, he or she would rely on a new system of meetings within which differences would be resolved, the individual encouraged and protected, and where Friends' cooperation would enable them to unite to face a hostile outside world.

REASON AND VISION

The leaders who pondered the theology of the evolving Quaker movement found themselves in a position that was remarkably akin to that of many of their old antagonists, those clergymen and intellectuals who believed in mystical spiritual enlightenment but who had recoiled at the "excessive" visionary enthusiasm of the radical sects. Like the Latitudinarians and Cambridge Platonists described in chapter 2, Quakers continued to believe in the validity of prophecy and visionary insight, but they were also coming to believe in the importance, if not the preeminence, of natural human reason and moral conscience.

This new theological emphasis was enunciated by a largely new group of leaders. While writers like Edward Burrough (who died in prison in 1663) had emphasized the depravity of human reason and the ecstatic experience of the light, newer converts like William Penn and Robert Barclay emphasized the agreement of divine light with the individual's innate rationality and conscience. William Penn wrote that conscience is "a little God sitting in the middle of men's hearts, arraigning them in this life," but he added that conscience can only operate in the mind when the understanding is first able to conceive the truth.[38] Penn also affirmed that "the understanding can never be convinced nor properly submit but by such arguments as are rational, persuasive, and suitable to its own nature."[39] And again, "reason, like the sun, is common to all, and 'tis for want of examining all by the same light and measure that we are not

---

37. G[eorge] F[ox] to Friends, n.d., Richardson Manuscript 127.
38. William Penn, "Skirmisher Defeated" (1676), quoted in M. P. Endy, Jr., *William Penn and Early Quakerism* (Princeton: Princeton University Press, 1973), 247.
39. William Penn, *Great Case of Liberty* (1670), 22, quoted in QPE, 244.

all of the same mind."[40] Reading these passages, it comes as no surprise to learn that Penn, a Whig aristocrat, was invited to become a member of the Royal Society and that he also conducted a friendly correspondence with the Cambridge Platonist Henry More, who rejoiced "that the Quakers have emerged above that low beginning of an heartless and hopeless familism."[41]

Henry More may have been favorably affected by the Quakers' rational theology and increasingly skillful public relations, but he did not fully understand the mind of William Penn. Penn did advertise Quakerism in terms that would have done credit to an eighteenth-century philosophe:

> By revelation we don't mean whimsical raptures, [or] strange and prodigious trances. We disclaim any share or interest in those vain whimsies and idle intoxications, professing our revelation to be solid and necessary discovery from the Lord, of those things that do import and concern our daily conditions; in reference to the honour which is due to him, and care owing to our own souls.[42]

But just one year earlier, in 1670, he had delivered himself of a visionary tract that was not published:

> Wo, Wo, Wo to the murderer and the oppressor, the unclean person and drunkards, the liar and swearer, the prophane; and such as live in vanity. . . . Overturn, overturn, overturn will I by my own outstretched arm. . . . And . . . that harlot, that false Church, that says, she is the Lamb's wife, . . . her brats will I dash against the stones, . . . your faces will smoke to gather paleness, and your hearts shall faint and your hands tremble, and your knees smite together; And I will change your sweet smells into a stink, your girdle into a rent, and instead of well set hair there shall be baldness, and for a stomacher a girding of sackcloth. . . . O come down, come down from every exalted imagination, and be ye separated from that spirit, which having only the form of godliness denyeth the inward feeling of the power of the same, and that ingrafted Word, which like a living hammer breaks in pieces the stony

40. William Penn, *Witness*, 191, from *More Fruits of Solitude*, quoted in QPE, 245.

41. Henry More to William Penn, May 22, 1675, quoted in PWP, 1:305. Melvin P. Endy writes of Penn, "The inner light, which provided an 'infallible Demonstration' of divine truth, was at times indistinguishable in his mind from the Platonic and Stoic principles of a divine Reason permeating the cosmos and linking human minds to God" (*William Penn and Early Quakerism*, 153). In later controversies, Penn used the arguments of the Latitudinarians against dissenters (Hugh Barbour, "The Young Controversialist," in *The World of William Penn*, ed. Richard S. Dunn and Mary Maples Dunn, [Philadelphia: University of Pennsylvania Press, 1986], 26).

42. William Penn, *Serious Apology* (1671), quoted in Endy, *William Penn and Early Quakerism*, 255.

heart . . . and like devouring fire consumes the briars and thorns, that under all your crying Lord, Lord, abounds in you.[43]

Another eminent thinker among this second generation of leaders was the Scotsman Robert Barclay, who became a convinced Friend in 1666. Barclay asserted that the light gave human beings as clear a grasp of divine truths as they had of any natural knowledge: "this divine revelation and inward illumination, is that which is evident and clear of itself, forcing, by its own evidence and clearness, the well-disposed understanding to assent . . . even as the common principles of natural truths do move and incline the mind to a natural assent." For Barclay, the light never contradicts reason, "that noble and excellent faculty of the Mind."[44]

Barclay's theology was characterized by the same blend of rationality and mystical insight as that of William Penn. In his *Apology for the True Christian Divinity,* which became the most widely read defense of Quakerism, Barclay argued for the affinity of reason and revelation, but he was also careful to point out that the light within human beings is not the equivalent of conscience but a totally distinct principle. Similarly, Barclay insisted that, while the spirit does not contradict reason, reason itself will not lead to spiritual knowledge, for "knowledge . . . of Christ, which is not by the revelation of his own spirit in the heart, is no more properly the knowledge of Christ, than the prattling of a *parrot,* which has been taught a few Words, may be said to be the voice of a man."[45] It was said that the words that converted Barclay at his first meeting were "In stillness there is fullness; in fullness there is nothingness; in nothingness there are all things."[46] In 1672, after praying with tears that he might be excused from such an action, Barclay walked through the main streets of Aberdeen in sackcloth and ashes.[47]

In short, the ultimate aim of the new Quaker theology was less to discredit or transcend visionary insight than to contain it within a rational and orderly context. Just as the Cambridge Platonist John Smith maintained that only men with the finest minds and morals might be-

43. William Penn, "Gods Controversy Proclaim'd to the Nation through One of His Servants & Wittnesses W. P." (1670) PWP 1:184–91.

44. Robert Barclay, *An Apology for the True, Christian Divinity as the Same Is Held Forth, and Preached, by the People Called, in Scorn, Quakers,* 6th ed. (London, 1736), quoted in Endy, *William Penn and Early Quakerism,* 152.

45. Barclay, *Apology* (1843), 31. Barclay quoted "Dr. Smith of Cambridge" to the effect that we cannot seek God in books but rather await a "heavenly warmth in our hearts" (23–24).

46. SPQ, 336.

47. SPQ, 339–40.

come true prophets, so William Penn asserted that there was a difference between the ordinary knowledge of truth and the extraordinary inspiration that generates prophecy and that this higher knowledge was experienced only by extraordinary men. Quakers and Cambridge Platonists differed, of course, in their definitions of the word "extraordinary," for Quakers retained an egalitarian belief in the capacity of even unlearned individuals like George Fox to attain the highest levels of visionary insight. So Barclay wrote, "my heart hath been often greatly broken and tender'd by that virtuous life, that proceeded from the powerful ministry of . . . illiterate men."[48] Nevertheless, Quakers sensitized by the prophetic excesses of individuals like James Nayler, Martha Simmonds, or John Perrot had a distinctly narrower view of which individuals were entitled to present themselves as ministering Friends. The project of restricting the Quakers' public activity to these worthy individuals was one of the chief preoccupations of the new system of rules and meetings instituted by the leaders in 1667.

MEETINGS AND CENSORSHIP

Beginning in the mid-1660s, George Fox, William Penn, and others worked to establish a system of local monthly meetings, regional or county quarterly meetings, and larger general meetings, each divided into meetings for men and women; a yearly meeting for ministers, a meeting for sufferings, and a morning meeting, dealing with publication of Quaker works, were also eventually established.[49] This extremely complex organizational system was intended to serve manifold functions.

First, the organization served as a means of censorship. In 1672 the Second Day (i.e., Monday) Morning Meeting appointed ten Friends to a committee that became responsible for reading all Quaker works intended for publication, examining them for diction and rhetoric, ordering revisions, or suppressing them altogether. Henceforth, when collected works were to be published, editors were to omit passages that were written under the Protectorate that expressed loyalty to Cromwell. The committee also favored doctrinal works over prophecies, visions, or reports of healings or fasts, even omitting many of the passages in Fox's own journal in which he claimed that he had accomplished miraculous cures. The meeting also undertook to answer outsiders' attacks on

48. Barclay, *Apology* (1736), 319.
49. QPE, 231.

Friends; William Penn was particularly eminent as a member of the
committee to gather and answer this anti-Quaker literature.[50]

Second, the organization served both to encourage and monitor public
prophecy. In 1675, an epistle of the London Yearly Meeting affirmed
Friends' willingness to encourage ecstatic worship as well as their firm
intention to control it:

> There hath been and is serious sighing (sensible groaning and reverent sing-
> ing,) . . . with the Spirit and . . . in blessed unity with the brethren while they
> are in the public labor and service of the gospel, whether by preaching,
> praying or praising God . . . which therefore is not to be quenched or
> discouraged by any; but where any do or shall abuse the power of God, or
> are immoderate . . . such ought to be (privately) admonished.[51]

Robert Barclay also affirmed the freedom of all Friends to speak and
prophesy as they were moved but maintained "that some are more
particularly called to the work of the *ministry* . . . whose work is more
constantly and particularly to instruct, exhort, admonish, oversee, and
watch over their brethren."[52] Thus, Friends had established not only
distinct parameters of ecstatic behavior but a distinct clergy; an elite
group of public Friends who customarily addressed meetings for worship
from a raised platform at one end of the meeting room. In contrast to
the practice of ordinary Friends, who might testify spontaneously, if
restrainedly, ministers or "public Friends" knew beforehand when and
where they would speak. So ministers arriving in London from the
country noted in a book which of several local meetings for worship they
planned to attend that week.

Third, the meeting system was intended both to provide for social
welfare and to prevent disorderly walking. Local meetings throughout
England were empowered to solicit funds to assist Friends who were
bereaved, impoverished, and imprisoned. Women's and men's meetings
were to find places for young Quaker apprentices, dispense funds to
traveling ministers, provide for the care of children orphaned by persecution, and assist widows in the conduct of their outward businesses.[53]
The women's meetings, in particular, were established in 1671, "so the

---

50. Vann, *Social Development of English Quakerism*, 215; Luella M. Wright, *The
Literary Life of the Early Friends, 1650–1725* (New York: Columbia University Press,
1932), 97–110.

51. Epistle of the London Yearly Meeting, May 27, 1675, in PWP, 1:330.

52. Barclay, *Apology* (1736), 324.

53. Epistle of George Fox, ca. 1668, reprinted in William Beck and T. Frederick Ball,
The London Friends' Meetings: Showing the Rise of the Society of Friends in London
(London: F. Bowyer Kitto, 1869), 48. See also SPQ, 247–48, 251–68, and 269–89.

women may come into the practice of pure religion, which is to visit the widows and fatherless and to see that all be kept from the spots of the world."[54] The women's meetings were also directed to supervise marriages: Those couples who had a desire to marry were to appear on at least two occasions before the meeting, which would then verify their freedom from previous commitments, the consent of their families, and whether provisions had been made for any children of previous marriages. The women would then report to the men's meeting; only when the approval of both meetings had been obtained did the couple have leave to take each other before witnesses in a public meeting.[55] The women's meetings were further to admonish Friends accused of "disorderly walking": being married by an Anglican priest, drunkenness, wearing the hat in prayer, studying astrology, paying tithes, falling in love with more than one woman (or man), using false measures, slandering Friends, incurring excessive debts, playing at ninepins. The ultimate penalty for such behavior was disownment—formal and public rejection from the entire body of Friends.

Clearly, the system of meetings established by Friends was both supportive and repressive, and clearly the two functions were linked; the support of the community was conditional on the individual's willingness to conduct his or her private and public life within the parameters set by the meetings. So in George Fox's many general epistles, disciplinary measures against disorderly walking alternated with injunctions to assist bereaved and indigent Friends:

> If any that profess the truth follow pleasures, drunkenness, gaming; or is not faithful in their dealings, nor honest, nor just, but runs into debt, and so brings

54. George Fox, circular letter of June 16, 1671, quoted in SPQ, 373. The women's meetings evolved from two earlier meetings that had already existed in London and Bristol. The box meeting (which was begun in 1659 by Sarah Blackborow) collected funds for poor relief and kept them in a box. The other meeting worked in conjunction with the two weeks men's meeting, visiting the sick and poor and assisting widows and orphans as well as supervising marriages. The Bristol meeting was apparently in existence well before 1669 (Irene L. Edwards, "The Women Friends of London: The Two-Weeks and Box Meetings," JFHS 47, no. 1 [Spring 1955]: 3–21. See also Beck and Ball, *London Friends' Meetings*, 343–49).

55. R. S. Mortimer, "Marriage Discipline in Early Friends: A Study in Church Administration Illustrated from Bristol Records," JFHS 48, no. 4 (Autumn 1957): 175–95. In 1692 the men's meeting, noting that "the woman many times speaks too low," established a procedure "to ensure them to speaking," whereby both parties would express their intentions at an initial meeting and then be advised to speak clearly when they "consummate" the marriage before invited witnesses (179).

a scandal upon the truth; some may be ordered to go and exhort them. . . .
And also all widows in your several meetings, let them be taken notice of and
informed, and encouraged in their outward business, that there may be no
hindrance in their inward growth; and, so carefully looked after, that they
may be nourished, and cherished.[56]

Thus, in their altered theology and system of meetings, Friends hoped
to cultivate in themselves both the political virtues of the citizen and the
inspired insights of the visionary. In 1678, William Penn wrote to Margaret Fell (now Margaret Fox), in a tone that was itself a fusion of
Friends' earlier ecstatic prose and the newer values and conventions: "I
have been lately very ill oppressed in body and spirit; but . . . am finely
recovered. O! we are bound up together in everlasting love . . . no waters
quench our love and union . . . yea prophecy shall cease and miracles shall
cease, but this more excellent way shall endure for ever."[57]

WOMEN AND "THIS MORE EXCELLENT WAY"

As Quakers strove to contain their impulses and activities within a more
fully articulated church order, how would they achieve the integration
of visionary womanhood, the archetypal symbol of complete *disorder*?
At first or even second glance, Fox's proposals for a system of meetings
appear to be quite explicitly aimed at excluding women from a magisterial role within the movement. In his vision of the newly structured,
ideal community, matters involving charity, marital problems, discipline
of women, and healing were viewed as women's work, while problems
dealing with censorship, business, organization of the ministry, and
debates with non-Quakers were viewed as men's work:

All things must be done in [God's] power and name: and there is many things
that is proper for women to look into both in their families, and concerning
of women which is not so proper for the men, which modesty in women
cannot so well speak of before men as they can do among their sex; and
women are more in their families, and have more of the tuition of their
children and servants than the men, they being always among them either for
the making of them, or the marring of them. . . . And many women are of

56. George Fox, "Friends Fellowship must be in ye Spirit; & all Friends must know
one another in ye Spirit & Power of God," n.d., "Book of Epistles of George Fox,
1666–1682," Richardson Manuscript, 1, Quaker Collection, Haverford College Library,
Haverford, Pa.
57. William Penn to Margaret Fox, Bucks, January 8, 1677, "A Collection of Letters, Dreams, Visions and Other Remarkable Occurrences of Some of the People Called
Quakers," MS. S. 78/2, Library of the Society of Friends, London.

more capacity than others are, and so they must instruct and inform the rest . . . concerning ordering of their children and families.[58]

Far from being an improper elevation of women's independent role, this new segregation was presented as the only proper course for respectable Friends, for "none but Ranters will desire to look into women's matters."[59] In a time when Friends were attempting to present themselves as defenders of the restored monarchy and to manipulate the law rather than repudiate it, Fox also defended the separation of male and female activities as conforming to Adam and Eve's lawful state in Eden:

> And what the women cannot do they may three or four of them go from their Meeting to the Men's, and lay it before them which is more proper for them: And what is more proper for the women than the men, the men may three or four of them go and lay it before the women; so that they may be helps meet together in the restauration, in truth and righteousness as man and woman was before they fell.[60]

Once in authority, the mother in Israel was to behave as a parent toward unruly younger Friends and to instruct the younger women "to be sober, to love their own husbands, to love their children and to be discreet, chaste keepers at home, good and obedient. . . . So let none spoil their families with bad lives and unruly tongues with letting the poison of asps be under their tongues."[61] In short, permission to teach and prophesy in no way negated woman's normal social subordination: "If any have a moving to speak the truth, obey; and then when you have done return to your places again with speed."[62]

Several of George Fox's contemporaries were even more explicit in presenting the women's meeting as a means of keeping women in their place. William Penn advocated separate women's meetings in Pennsylvania by arguing that "women, whose bashfulness will not permit them to say or do as much as to church affairs before the men, when by themselves exercise their gifts of wisdom and understanding, in a discreet

58. George Fox, "To the Men and Womens Monthly and Quarterly Meetings" n.d., Richardson Manuscript, 7.
59. George Fox, Epistle to Friends, n.d., Richardson Manuscript, 47.
60. George Fox, Epistle to Friends, Richardson Manuscript, 7.
61. G[eorge] F[ox] to the men and Womens meetings, Swarthmore, December 1679, to be sent to Bedfordshire, Northamptonshire, and Leicestershire, Portfolio Manuscripts 30/96.
62. George Fox, "The Word of the Lord God to all Families, Masters, and Servants," n.d., Richardson Manuscript, 63.

care for their own sex."[63] Another eminent Quaker, William Loddington, defended women's meetings on the grounds that they actually
prevented the empowerment of women in relation to men:

> Women Friends meeting by themselves, may without the least suspicion of
> usurping authority over the men, confer and reason together, how to serve
> truth in their places, in such things as are most proper and suitable for them,
> still submitting to the wisdom of God in the Men's Meetings: whereas being
> mixed together, if a man should make a motion about any business, and a
> woman should stand up and signify her dislike of it, though in most mild and
> tender words, would not any man, yea, an unbeliever . . . conclude the women
> in such meetings had as much power as the men?[64]

But once having firmly established that women were women and men
were men, Fox proceeded to elaborate what was, in reality, an extremely
radical solution to the problem of reconciling emotion and spirituality
with the new political order. His project was to broaden the accepted
parameters of political discourse by defining parenthood—not mere
fatherhood—as a position of public stature and parental activities and
values as identical to those of the upright citizen of the Quaker community. The informal authority of the earlier mother in Israel was thus
superceded by the female elder's formal decision-making power over
Friends' personal, social, and economic activities. In an epistle that was
to be preserved in every women's meeting record book, Fox wrote:

> In this wisdom you may treat the elder men as fathers, and the elder women
> as mothers, and the younger men as brethren, and the younger women as
> sisters in all purity; so that all may be arrayed with a meek and quiet spirit . . .
> and so that there may [be] no harshness, nor fierceness, or wilfullness appear
> in your meetings; . . . there were mothers in the Church as well as fathers.[65]

Of course, women's jurisdiction over family life and charity was of less
outward importance than men's jurisdiction over public business and
public controversy. Nevertheless, the women's meeting was not a form
of seventeenth-century tokenism, for while women's jurisdiction over
marriage did not belong to the sphere of public policy, it did involve the
authority to instruct and discipline male relatives and neighbors. More-

---

63. William Penn, "Just Measures in an Epistle of Peace and Love," quoted in Linda
Ford, "William Penn's Views on Women: Subjects of Friendship," QH 72, no. 2 (Fall
1983): 83.
64. William Loddington, *The Good Order of Truth Justified; Wherein our Womens
Meetings and Order of Marriage . . . Are Proved Agreeable to Scripture and Sound
Reason* (London, 1685), 5.
65. George Fox to Friends of the Six Weeks Meeting and others, n.d., Richardson
Manuscript, 15.

over, the London Six Weeks Meeting, established by Fox as the prime meeting in the city, was attended by both men and women. In this meeting, beginning in 1671, thirty-five women (and forty-nine men) were to exercise administrative and legislative functions as a court of appeal for other local meetings, with additional authority to regulate and maintain meetings for worship and to dispense funds to traveling ministers.[66]

Like that of the male minister, the authority of the mother in Israel was based on competence and personal integrity as well as passive obedience to the spirit. William Penn once wrote, in response to the Perrot crisis, "To be short, a Christian implies a man; and a man implies conscience and understanding; but he that has no conscience and understanding . . . that has delivered them up to the will of another man, is no man, and therefore no Christian."[67] Fox gave women authority based on *their* conscience and understanding. In this sense, the meeting system and its attendant symbolism reflected Fox's perception of what it meant to "grow up" as a movement. Thus, he sought to transcend the Quakers' antinomian and anarchic spirit, symbolized by the image of the babe in Christ or the passive vessel of God, by the image of the mother in Israel as a mature adult, more like the wife in Proverbs than the ecstatic prophet:

> Now a mother in the Church of Christ, and a mother in Israel is one that gives suck and nourishes, and feeds, and dresses, and washes, and rules, and is a teacher in the Church, . . . and an admonisher, and instructor, and exhorter . . . and [has] the breasts of life that are full of the milk of the word to suckle all the young ones, . . . and has the heavenly flax, and the wheel, and spindle, by which she hath the fine linen to clothe the young ones. . . . So the elder women as mothers are to be teachers of good things. . . . And if the unbelieving husband be sanctified by the believing wife, then where is the speaker, and where is the hearer; surely such a woman is permitted to speak, and to work the works of God, and to make a member in the Church, and then as an elder to oversee that he walk according to the gospel.[68]

It is important to understand the degree to which the positive authority of the mother in Israel as both elder and minister was central to the new theology and values of the movement. During the tidal wave of persecution in the 1660s, the Quakers might well have taken several roads: They might have become like other radical groups of the period and plotted open revolt against the crown. If they had adopted a war

66. Beck and Ball, *London Friends' Meetings*, 91ff.
67. William Penn, "An Address to Protestants of All Persuasions" (1679), quoted in Endy, *William Penn and Early Quakerism*, 247.
68. George Fox to Friends, n.d., Richardson Manuscript, 29.

testimony rather than a peace testimony, they would not have needed the mother in Israel as a symbol of nurture and familial affection. Or they might have become thoroughly rationalized, with a fixed, formal creed and clergy. Then they would not have needed to deal with charismatic preaching or worship, which was still theoretically open even to the least of Friends, including women; indeed, it was in the period of retrenchment, the 1660s and 1670s, that almost every formal defense of women's preaching was published.[69] Or Friends might have adopted a testimony of quietism and asceticism, in which case they would not have needed the image of the mother in Israel as a virtuous and competent businesswoman and hostess of the meeting, having authority over children's apprenticeships, the disbursement of charity, and her own livelihood and property.

The Quakers embarked on none of these roads. On the contrary, despite the changes brought about by their rationalized theology and concern with structure, Friends held fast to that part of their original testimony that affirmed the integration of ecstatic preaching and self-transcendence with life in society and the projection of the domestic values of mutual love and discipline into the public sphere. The establishment of the women's meeting as a mechanism of social expression and social control, and of the mother in Israel as the central female symbol of the movement, were the logical extensions of this commitment. For as Fox said, women were the ones who knew what went on in families, and the family, as the focus of both personal emotion and personal discipline, was the material and metaphorical basis of the new Quakerism. Above all, the Quakers' repudiation of violence accentuated the importance of the familial image of parent and child, coexisting in a stable relationship of benevolent control and loving obedience, as opposed to the earlier, more fluid and egalitarian images of collective friendship and brotherhood. Thus, Fox described the state of aggression and disagreement as a deserted home, overrun by wilderness and rot:

> The truth is above all, and will stand over all them that hate it, who labor in vain against it, and will bring their old house on their own head in great trouble, and in their winter and cold weather when that their house is down, and their religion is frozen, and their rivers dried up, and their husks gone; and the swine begin to cry about their plantations, and the vermin run up and

69. Margaret Fell, *Women's Speaking Justified, Proved and Allowed of by the Scriptures* (London, 1666); John Whitehead, *A Manifestation of Truth* . . . (1662). Barclay, *Apology* (1736), 142–43; George Keith, *The Woman Preacher of Samaria* . . . (London, 1674); Patrick Livingstone, *Truth Owned and Deceit Denied and Witnessed Against* . . . (London, 1667).

down their old rubbish, and their sparks and candles are gone out and hail, and storm lighteth upon the head of the wicked. . . . In Christ you have peace, in the world you have trouble: In Christ you have peace, in the world you have trouble. No Peace with God but in the Light. No peace with God but in the covenant of light, with out is trouble, Amen.[70]

Of course, Fox and his adherents invariably muffled these sharp proposals for reform in a protective blanket of assurances regarding women's subject status in the world, perhaps for their own peace of mind as much as anyone else's. So Friends argued that women's right to preach derived from the fact that they had been restored to the state of Adam and Eve before the Fall and were hence above the law, which subjected them to men, but they invariably coupled statements of this kind with assurances that the true mother in Israel was like a member of the Puritan Elect: Being above the law, she was incapable of acting contrary to the law. "All women," wrote Hugh Wood, "that are apt to usurp authority over their husbands; all women that are under the law, and that have not learned true subjection; and every woman that hearkens to the voice of the serpent . . . while they continue in that state, cannot, nor may not be permitted to speak in the church of God."[71] Likewise, Thomas Ellwood and William Penn, both stellar defenders of the female meeting and ministry, assembled hosts of biblical and classical women as examples of female virtue and obedience; Ellwood observed that "Rachel and Leah . . . readily . . . gave up to leave their kindred and father's house, and with their husband follow the Lord," while Penn contemplated the chastity, prudence, and meekness of Penelope, Lucretia, and Plotina.[72] Yet in the midst of this array of loyal biblical wives and modest matrons stood the newly empowered mother in Israel, a woman of independent conscience and a practitioner of public authority over both men and women. "Is there any reason," wrote another Friend,

but that women (without whom, there can be no marriages) . . . should see into marriages as well as men . . . else how should they set their hands to it? Must they pin their faith on men's sleeves? . . . Are they afraid that the women that are wise orderers of families that they should discover something amiss if they should examine apart? And is it not moral, honest and civil and modest

70. George Fox to Friends, n.d., Richardson Manuscript, 50.
71. Hugh Wood, *A Brief Treatise of Religious Women's Meetings, Services and Testimonies* (1684), 41.
72. Ellwood, *Antidote*, 214; William Penn, *No Cross, No Crown. A Discourse Showing the Nature and Discipline of the Holy Cross of Christ*, in vol. 1 of The Friends Library (Philadelphia, 1837), 296–98.

that women . . . should examine apart and be satisfied before they subscribe?
And so our . . . order is reasonable.[73]

Clearly, the mother in Israel as elder of the meeting was not so much out
of the law as against the laws and customs of seventeenth-century patriarchal culture, for she wielded an authority that was no less innovative
because limited to matters of hearth and home.

The radical nature of the women's meeting appears even more striking
when we remember that, in the matter of female authority, contemporaries were far more concerned with form than with substance. Women
were frequently to be seen running businesses or estates or supervising
the morals of their dependents, but they did these things informally, as
surrogates for a man, either as deputy husbands, bereaved daughters, or
widows. A woman might also enlist the aid of neighbors and female
relatives in emergencies such as childbirth, or in the event she was beaten
by her husband, but these female associations were also temporary and
informal.[74] Even in her public prophecy, the female visionary was understood to be acting as a deputy spokesperson for God on earth. The
Quaker elder and minister, on the other hand, exercised her individual
and collective *formal* authority on the basis of her own reputation for
morality and integrity and in her own person. "It eased me much," Fox
wrote,

> when those Meetings were set up for men and women that are heirs of the
> gospel, have a right to the gospel order, it belongs to them, then take your
> possessions, and be not talkers only; as if a man should sit over a people, and
> tell them of brave gardens, and pearls, and precious stones, . . . and only talk
> of them, and keep talking of them many years, and not to possess none of
> these . . . you must get riches of your own, get wine of your own and vines
> of your own, and to draw water out of your own wells, and know the well
> of salvation in your own hearts . . . the women can do more than men in some
> particulars. . . . This is the word of the Lord God to the Men and Women's
> Meetings, that all them that have felt the power of God, and are heirs of it,
> take your possessions, you have right to the authority and dignity.[75]

Anyone doubting the radical implications of this proclamation has only
to observe the reaction of the Quaker community to the reforms that Fox
proposed, for the project of a meeting system that included women as

73. Reply to one of William Roger's books (probably *The Seventh Part of the
Christian Quaker*), hand unidentified, A. R. Barclay Manuscripts, vol. 324, no. 233.
74. Margaret Hunt, "Wife Beating, Domesticity, and Women's Independence in
Early Eighteenth Century London," forthcoming in *Gender and History*, 1992.
75. George Fox to Friends, n.d., Richardson Manuscript, 98–99.

organizers and overseers was to result in the most serious and extended internal schism of the entire century.

SCHISM

Without spectacles some see your shame
having made yourselves a spectacle, for
team Rogers, Crisp, Pennyman, Bullock and Bug
dark, drivel driven, dungy Gods desperately lug
That are ty'd to ye tail of their separate schism
Pap-Libertin-Heathen-Juda-Athe-ism.

Robert Sandilands(?)

For more than twenty years, from the early 1670s until the close of the century in some places, the issues of order and authority dramatized by John Perrot and elaborated by the proponents of the meeting system exploded in a series of internal battles whose fallout threatened to destroy the movement. And, as had been the case from the earliest years of the crisis, the sticking point of almost every battle was the vexing question of female authority.[76]

The main, "stem" controversy was initiated by "the two Johns," Wilkinson and Story, two northern Quakers who were angered by the leaders' criticism of Friends who protected themselves from arrest by meeting in the woods and fields rather than in public buildings. They also objected to the notion of a fixed clergy and fixed procedure for marriage. Finally, they objected to the establishment of autonomous women's meetings, except as a means of administering poor relief in large towns.

Variations of these same arguments were played out again and again by groups and individuals in all parts of the country. In London, John and Mary Pennyman were married in an ostentatious ceremony, inviting the aldermen of the city and "the whole synagogue of the Jews" to attend, thus deliberately flouting the advice that Friends maintain a sober public profile; both Pennymans continued to wrangle with dominant Quakers

---

76. Most historians list the opposition to women's meetings as the Separatists' chief complaint, but none have gone on to analyze the schism in terms of those complaints. Richard Vann, for example, writes that "wherever the schism made headway, the chief grievance was the composition of the business meetings. The Separatists objected particularly to the establishment of women's meetings for church business." He further points out that there was no schism in Norwich or the rest of Norfolk, where there was also no evidence of women's business meetings. Yet Vann's complex and perceptive analysis of the crisis does not treat the issue of gender (Vann, *Social Development of English Quakerism*, 103–4).

for the next thirty years. In Cambridge, Ann Docwra engaged in a protracted public battle against the leaders of the men's and women's meetings. In Westmoreland, a group of Friends acknowledged that they had been seduced by the Wilkinson/Story party, known as Separatists, into relaxing their vigilance against the payment of tithes. In Reading, Bristol, Buckinghamshire, and Hertfordshire, Thomas Curtis and William Rogers were the instigators of a movement challenging the leadership of Fox and the validity of the women's meeting.[77]

Partisans of Fox and of the Separatists hotly denied the political dimension of their own program, presenting themselves as defenders of the Quakers' original spiritual mission while imputing crass political motives and moral looseness to their opponents. So Thomas Ellwood based the necessity for women's scrutiny over marriages on the bad conduct of some Separatists, one of whom had reportedly committed incest with her own father.[78] William Penn also defended the systemization of worship and discipline as a moral necessity:

> Where doth our apostasy lie? In not suffering loose and libertine spirits to tread down our hedge, under the specious pretense of being left to the Light within? As if the Light were inconsistent with itself, or admitted of unity under not only different but contrary practices in the one family and flock of God.[79]

Separatists, on the other hand, viewed themselves as heroes of an uneven struggle between the juggernaut of bureaucratization and the valiant forces of spiritual charisma and social equality. Thus, William Mucklow criticized the new tendency toward legalism and elitism:

> Such arbitrary courses have an ill operation upon the spirits of men: it weakens their hearts and cools their courage and begets in them a slavish temper and disposition; and where this arbitrary and unlimited power is set up a way is open . . . for the advancement and encouragement of evil and a means to increase flatterers. Such men are aptest to cry up the body in all respects and are the only good Friends; but others, though exemplary in their conversations, who cannot yield and comply against the light in their consciences . . . are subject to jealousy, censure, if not an ejection.[80]

77. On the Pennymans, see Higgins, "The Apostatized Apostle," 102–19; on Docwra, see DQB; on Westmoreland Friends, see "A Testimony of 29 Friends of Preston Patrick Meeting Against that Paper which John Storye's Party gave forth 28th of the 2nd Month, 1678," MS. 975A, Quaker Collection, Haverford College Library, Haverford, Pa.; on Curtis and Rogers, see SPQ, 470–75.

78. Thomas Ellwood, *The Account from Wickham (Lately Published by John Raunce and Charles Harris) Examin'd, and Found False* (1690), 4.

79. William Penn, September 11, 1676, quoted in SPQ, 307.

80. William Mucklow, *The Spirit of the Hat: Or, the Government of the Quakers among Themselves* (London, 1673), quoted in SPQ, 293.

Another Separatist ridiculed a Friend who knelt down to pray: "How canst thou say thy dependency is only upon the Lord when you depend upon the Second Day's Meeting and council table and George Fox, and it may be said of you . . . as it was said of old, according to the number of thy cities so are thy gods oh Israel."[81] Separatists also dismissed Fox's vision of sanctified, familial discipline as a sure sign of his hypocrisy, as a sentimental aura manufactured to obscure the hard light of his own political ambition. So Thomas Curtis compared the yearly meeting to a cabal of Oliver Cromwell's, hatching plots and spreading them abroad through the ministry, while other Separatists, whose souls had resonated with the feminine spiritual imagery of John Perrot, now recoiled at the feminine *political* imagery—the notion of a church ruled by mothers—of George Fox.[82]

Both Fox's party and the Separatists exhibited a distorted and frequently vindictive attitude toward their opponents, but each was entirely correct in pointing to the other group's divided consciousness. As they struggled to protect the integrity of the movement, Friends remembered their original harmonious spiritual utopia, a condition in which the individual had succeeded in moving beyond personal concerns and political relationships and toward a conviction of divine knowledge and a divinely sanctioned union of friends. Power, for these earliest Friends, was everywhere and nowhere. No individual or group "owned" power; on the contrary, one was "in" the power only insofar as one had transcended individual identity or class loyalty. The word "freedom," for them, meant freedom from self and from the bonds between the self and society.

For Fox in the 1660s and 1670s, and for Separatists, the word "freedom" retained this original sense, and phrases like "full of love" and "bowels of compassion" continued to resonate through their writings. However, in the process of responding to outside criticism and attempting to orchestrate Friends' behavior, it was inevitable that each side would resort to some form of organization, to politics. Fox's idea, as we have seen, was to strengthen the original, communal body of Friends by building a skeleton inside it, a structure of authority that would give direction to the limbs' increasingly random and self-destructive movements. The word "freedom" thus acquired added meaning for him and his followers, for the merging of self and other was no longer to be purely

---

81. Reading Monthly Meeting Minutes (orthodox), transcpt. 12. This was in 1683; the speaker was Leonard Key.
82. Ibid., 25.

spontaneous, as in the cacaphony of early Friends' groans and singing, but shaped according to the shared direction or melody of the meeting, as in a symphony.

The Separatists remembered *their* original utopia less as a single body than as a free space for the expression of each Friend's spontaneous leadings. They sought to protect that space by introducing a loose, democratic structure; not the liminal, apolitical utopia of the 1650s, but a religious association in which authority was vested in certain individuals and groups rather than progressively centralized institutions. For them, the word "freedom" as an ideal of self-transcendence had modulated into an ideal of independent conscience and autonomous action. The struggle, in short, was not between bureaucrats and charismatic leaders, or between the forces of structure and those of antistructure, but between each group's hard estimate of the form of political authority best suited to sustain the movement as they saw and valued it. In the garden of Eden that was Friends' infant state of communal ecstasy and harmony, each had helped to introduce the snake.

WOMEN AND POLITICS

To the degree that the religious discourse of Friends had become politicized during the 1660s, so too did the terms of women's authority. In the many arguments for female preaching and leadership that were published during the period, Fox and others endlessly reiterated the principle that women's authority to preach was above the law; Separatists, however, rightly perceived that while religious ecstasy might still exist inside the meeting system, the new women's meeting was unquestionably a political institution. So William Mather, a former supporter of John Perrot, assaulted Fox:

> Can there be greater imposers in the world, than those that judge all people, *not to be of God*, for not submitting to a *female government* in marriage? A thing never heard of . . . except the government of the *Amazons*. . . . And whether such *women-judges* ever did any good, who come into the seat of counsel, rustling in gaudy flowered stuffs, or silks, from top to toe, mincing with their feet. . . . Was not that eminent man, W[illiam] P[enn], ashamed to mention this frivolous government of women . . . fearing . . . the world would laugh at it, as indeed well they might, having never heard before, that a meeting of women must be advised with, before marriage. . . . [We are not] against a woman's declaring in a religious meeting, what God has done for her soul, by silently waiting at the feet of Jesus, as *Mary* did. . . . Nor are we

against women meeting by themselves, upon a particular occasion, but not monthly for government.[83]

Mather argued that women do good by administering charity, "yea its good in rich widows, and also in married women, when their husbands are incapable to do it themselves"; it is the notion that women are to meet on a regular basis that appalls him.[84] Another Friend, Richard Smith, agreed:

> Now it lyeth on your part to prove, that females were ever intrusted to look after the government of the church . . . that women had meetings separate and apart by themselves on purpose, as they have now here once a month, and once a quarter, as men . . . to look after . . . the church's business: for though I grant, those that have received a measure of God's spirit, may as it moves, prophesy, . . . according to their several gifts; yet every member hath not the same office.[85]

Thomas Curtis expressed the same sentiments in cruder terms:"We did not build the [meeting] house for the women to meet in apart from the men . . . we never had unity with such meetings to draw young lasses from their homes to learn to preach."[86]

As the argument progressed, the note of hysteria among Separatists became even higher-pitched; some even accused Fox of a conspiracy to lead unsuspecting Friends into a nightmare world ruled by himself and his fanatic female disciples. In 1678 a group of Hertford Quakers signed a certificate attesting that George Fox had spoken repeatedly in public meetings about "a woman High Sherriff."[87] In *The Christian Quaker*, an angry, extremely diffuse polemic by the Separatist William Rogers, Fox was accused of succumbing to the same appetite for female adulation that had doomed James Nayler. "Hast thou forgotten," wrote Rogers, "how thou hast testified against *James Nayler's* spirit, whose great fall was *his owning*, or at least *not reproving the women*, when they cried

83. William Mather, *A Novelty: Or, a Government of Women, Distinct from Men, Erected among Some of the People Call'd Quakers* (London, 1694), 4–5, 9.

84. Ibid., 19–20.

85. Richard Smith, *The Light Unchangeable: And Truth and Good Order, Justified against Error and Disorder* (London, 1677), 33.

86. A Record Belonging to the Quarterly Meeting of the People of the Lord in Scorne Called Quakers in the County of Berks, transcribed Beatrice Saxon Snell and Nina Saxon Snell, 30, Library of the Society of Friends, London.

87. Edward Perkin, Hartford, February 17, 1678, "Certificates relating to the Passages which passed between G. F. and some at Hartford, 23/12th mo/78/9," A. R. Barclay Manuscripts vol. 324, no. 208: "The false witnesses charge against G. F. by some at Hartford etc., ye 12th mon.1678/9."

with a carnal tongue *Hosanna* to him?"[88] Rogers also accused Fox of
foisting women's rule on unsuspecting Friends under cover of a simple
meeting for the care of the poor:

> And therefore Friends, who in simplicity assented to the . . . meetings, as
> supposing women in some cases fitter to pry into the *necessities of the poor*,
> than *men* . . . did at length begin to be jealous, that the words of the prophet
> *Isaiah* . . . were again fulfilled in our age, *As for my people, children are their*
> *oppressors, and women rule over them.* . . . [Friends are worried] lest instead
> of being servants to the *poor* for truth's sake, and taking the weight and
> burden of that care from the men, they should become *rulers over both men*
> *and women.*[89]

CLASS AND GENDER

Why did the advocates of decentralization and democracy among
Friends also take their stand, and such a passionate stand, against the
extension of that democracy to women? It would be interesting, if it were
possible, to investigate the Separatists' own familial relationships, for
one cannot help but sense, beneath the stridency of their accusations, the
shudder with which they contemplated the image of the lone, innocent
man barred from approaching the marriage bed by a phalanx of hostile
mothers. Such a one must have been

> that unclean fellow of Barthelmew close with whom thee [Margaret Fell] and
> dear George did take so much pains. . . . [He] did come with a lass yester-
> day . . . to the women's meeting to take her to wife, but he was so threshed
> there that he so discovered his spirit amongst them calling them very oft liars,
> but went away not daring to come to the men's meeting.[90]

Indeed, contemporary pamphlet literature contained many humorous
references to the sexual affinities and antipathies between Quaker men

88. William Rogers, *The Fourth Part of the Christian Quaker Distinguished from
the Apostate and Innovator* (London, 1680), 96.
89. William Rogers, *The First Part of the Christian Quaker Distinguished from the
Apostate and Innovator* (London, 1680), 65. Rogers also attacked Fox for basing wom-
en's meetings on assemblies of women found in the time of Judges in Palestine, stating that
the women had gathered only to be purified after childbirth. Ellwood answered, "For
since the time of their purification after child-birth was fixed and appointed by the law,
if you will suppose they came in troops to be purified, you must suppose they were
delivered by troops also" (*Antidote*, 212–13). The belief that Fox had perverted the
original women's meeting, intended strictly for administration of charity, may have influenced Thomas Curtis, who had originally supported the meeting in Reading and later
turned against it (Record of the Quakers in the County of Berks, 1669–1678/9, transcpt.
30).
90. William Dundas to M[argaret] F[ell], London, 1671, Gibson Manuscripts,
336/91.

and their older, obnoxiously righteous Quaker wives and neighbors. In *The Secret Sinners*, an unhappy Quaker husband complained that he had been forced to fornicate with his maidservant because his motherly, ministerial wife was too distant, "by reason she hath kept all her light within, and . . . it has dried her up, nay burnt her to a charcoal."[91]

A more tangible and possibly more fruitful avenue of investigation might lead us to question the material and social conditions of the two parties. The leading supporters of Fox included two general groups of Friends: those of middling, yeomen stock, largely from the north of England, and those few Friends who were also members of the gentry. These gentry leaders were unified not only by class loyalties and personal friendship but by marriage and business interests.[92] Fox also cultivated relations with sympathetic members of the gentry who were not Quakers in order to facilitate negotiations with the authorities and the release of Friends from prison.

The leading Separatists, on the other hand, were, by and large, men of business—city merchants. They were also the most eminent (and frequently the most ostentatious) individuals in their own local meetings, most of which were located in the more prosperous urbanized southern counties. Thomas Curtis was a rich woolen draper and eminent local Friend in Reading. William Rogers was an eminent conservative merchant of Bristol. John Pennyman was a well-to-do London merchant, whose wedding to Mary Boreman was celebrated amid wide publicity in the largest public hall in town ("as I hear," wrote one Friend, "he has provided twenty-seven venison pasties and several pipes of wine, and now at last he will show to all the world what a prophane Quaker he is").[93] John Story and John Wilkinson, though from the north, were also both prosperous and pretentious: "Their great friends have sent them home well-mounted and well-clothed," wrote one Friend, "and J[ohn] St[ory] with his extraordinary broad-brimmed beaver hat and his periwig and broad belt with silver buckles and great hose

91. *The Secret Sinners* (London, 1675), quoted in Levy, *Quakers and the American Family*, 83. Several prominent women *were* older than their husbands. Margaret Fell married George Fox when she was fifty-five and he was forty-five; Ann Downer married George Whitehead when she was forty-six and he thirty-four; Ann Audland married Thomas Camm when she was thirty-nine and he was twenty-five.

92. Robert Barclay, whose mother was a distant cousin of the king, acted as a business agent for William Penn, encouraging wealthy Scotsmen to invest in Pennsylvania (Endy, *William Penn and Early Quakerism*, 136). Penn's wife was Gulielma Springett, daughter of Mary Penington. They in turn were close friends of Thomas Ellwood.

93. Ellis Hooks to Margaret Fell, 21/8th/1671, SM 1/57 (II, 435), quoted in Higgins, "The Apostasized Apostle," 110.

etc. hath great obeisance rendered to him in the country where he comes by those that know him not."[94] In short, the Wilkinson/Story party was both more bourgeois and more status-conscious than the party of George Fox.

Evidently, the secular values of the leaders of Fox's party made it logical for them to defend the spiritual values of women's ministry and meetings. As Barry Levy has shown in gratifying detail, middling farmers from the more impoverished northern counties welcomed the meeting system as an inexpensive means of finding Quaker apprenticeships for their children, who were now to be raised "in the light," apart from non-Quaker kin and neighbors; and the women's meeting was instrumental in carrying out this useful function.[95] Northerners also took understandable pride in the accomplishments of that eminent local heroine Margaret Fell, one of their own, whom many revered as a paragon of spiritual and maternal womanhood.

For those leaders who were also members of the gentry, the hierarchy of the meeting system had the virtue of being a divinely sanctioned improvement on the social hierarchy of which they were an integral part. Fox continued to defend the right of *all* Friends, including even children, to worship aloud in Quaker meetings—as long as they were brief—but he also dictated that the female ministry would be composed of female elders, women in their forties or fifties, with years of service to Quakerism already behind them. The tone of Fox's letter to Elizabeth Hearbey, written in 1687, is that of benevolent parent to erring child:

> I understood by some ancient friends in the ministry and such as were mothers [that] last when thou was at London thou was a little too long in thy testimony and thee must consider when so many ancient friends were gathered . . . which were as fathers and mothers and in Christ long before thee, it is good at such times to be swift to hear and slow to speak, for thou must consider that before such thou art but as a babe in Christ.

94. Hugh Barbour, "Quaker Prophetesses and Mothers in Israel," in *Seeking the Light: Essays in Quaker History in Honor of Edwin B. Bronner*, ed. J. William Frost and John M. Moore (Wallingford and Haverford, Pa.: Pendle Hill Publications and Friends Historical Association, 1986), 53. Thomas Lower to Margaret Fox, February 11, 1675, quoted in SPQ, 297. The Curtis party was more status-conscious than other Friends, referring to those they considered inferiors by surname only, as "the woman Mosdell" or just "Mosdell." The orthodox party rarely did this (The Minute-Book of Reading Monthly Meeting [Curtis Party], 1668–1716, transcribed Nina Saxon Snell, notes Beatrice Saxon Snell, 101n, Library of the Society of Friends, London). John Perrot and Robert Rich were also prosperous and ostentatious merchants. John Perrot wore a satin jacket and carried a sword; he was defended in this by Rich (Carroll, "John Perrot," 77).
95. Levy, *Quakers and the American Family*, 3–85.

One is brought up short by Fox's concluding salutation, "Remember me to thy husband."[96] Certainly, the female eldership was partially a meritocracy, elevating those women noted for integrity, service, and piety rather than birth—but only partially, for many of the most prominent mothers in Israel were socially eminent as well as pious; many were those with the means, education, and personal connections to negotiate for the release of Quakers in prison (rather than harangue the jailers as prophets), publish coherent epistles and tracts (as well as dreams and visions), and open their own houses for the use of the meeting.

Thus, the proposed arena of Quaker women's authority was completely hedged in, not only by moral injunctions that stressed service rather than self-expression but by outward social barriers. William Penn wrote to Margaret Fell, his social equal, in tones of the highest affection and respect: "Truly sweet and precious is the holy fellowship that our dear lord hath given us together . . . that hath made us very near and very dear. . . . I am in endless bonds of heavenly friendship and fellowship."[97] He also allowed for the activity of women in Pennsylvania in meetings and as ministers. But his legislation for the new colony also classed ordinary women, along with infants and idiots, as those with no property rights; women were also gagged and ducked as scolds.[98]

Separatists, on the other hand, committed as they were to the principles and practices of competition and independent action, both social and spiritual, could imagine no such hedges to the political ambition of any and all women. Thus, not for the first or the last time in their history, women found themselves at the center of a fundamental contradiction, in which conservative class relationships were allied with progressive gender relationships. Just so, in our own time, one finds highly stratified and sexist cultures like those of India or Pakistan able to sustain the contradiction of a female prime minister, while the mere possibility of an American woman vice president sends shock waves and titters through the democratic body politic.

The danger of women's grandiose political ambitions was a general concern, though no less disturbing to Separatists for being unsubstan-

96. George Fox to Elizabeth Hearbey, Saffornwallden, Essex, June 13, 1687, Portfolio Manuscripts 36/14.
97. William Penn to Margaret Fox, January 8, 1678, PWP 1:518–19.
98. Ford, "Penn's Views on Women," 89, 91, 93–96. See also Hill, *Experience of Defeat*, 166: "It is interesting to contrast Billynge's constitution [of New Jersey] with William Penn's Frame of Government for Pennsylvania in 1682. There the representative assembly was not sovereign: there was an upper house composed of men of wealth. And even for the elective assembly there was a property qualification."

tiated. The Wilkinson/Story party also expressed a more focused antagonism in its resentment of the particular women who belonged to the aristocratic group that was allied with Fox. One of these gentlewomen was Mary Penington, who, it was said, acted on Fox's advice to secure her own property when her husband was arrested ("neither was G[eorge] F[ox] ever so friendly to me, as to take so much care of me and my family," sulked William Rogers).[99] A far more formidable enemy, and, for Separatists, the surest proof of Quaker women's secret political machinations, was the person of Fox's own *eminence grise*, his new wife Margaret Fell.

MARGARET FELL BECOMES MARGARET FOX

Margaret Fell, we know, had been a pillar of Quakerism since the movement's beginnings. During the 1650s, she organized a communications network among itinerant Friends and established a regional fund to support their travels. She was a prolific and effective polemicist and agitator for the rights of Friends in prison. James Nayler and others appealed to her because of her considerable influence with George Fox. Indeed, she was revered as a minister and mother in Israel by the entire body of Quakers, being addressed by some male Friends as if she had ascended to a stature only slightly less exalted than that of a maternal divinity.

In the later decades of the movement, Friends were led by different men with different ideologies, and some of those men would have argued that Fell herself was different. There was, first of all, her high-handed behavior as a wealthy, landed widow. In one particularly ugly and extended battle during the 1660s, she apparently used the local Quaker meeting as a stick to beat a wealthy Friend, Thomas Rawlinson, whom she had accused of unethical behavior when he was a steward of one of her properties, an iron-smelting forge near Swarthmore.[100] Fell maintained that Rawlinson had mismanaged the business and understated the profits, which he had appropriated for his own use. His position was that *she* had cheated *him* of the money that he had advanced toward running the forge. For many years thereafter, Rawlinson continued to protest his

99. William Rogers, *The Fifth Part of the Christian Quaker Distinguish'd from the Apostate and Innovator* (London, 1680), 44.
100. Bonnelyn Young Kunze, "The Family, Social, and Religious Life of Margaret Fell," Ph.D. diss., University of Rochester, 1986, Chap. 6. Bonnelyn Young Kunze, "Margaret Fell versus Thomas Rawlinson," QH 77 (1988): 52–54.

innocence, accusing Fell of bribing witnesses and falsifying the accounts. He even kept up his attendance at meetings after he had been censured by the monthly meeting in 1669. "You are such a great woman," he wrote to Fell, "that loves to be great in the earth and among friends: to sit as judges and to reign . . . even as a queen upon the people." He also wrote with deep resentment to the meeting, "if the said M. F. spoke but [a] word to you in this matter against me, though never so false you would hear her and believe her, receive her sayings and obey her voice . . . she is such a great, rich woman that hath openly carried such a great sway . . . among friends . . . you are so . . . under her all."[101] Rawlinson was partially disowned by the meeting but kept appearing until 1680, when he was finally reinstated.

Margaret Fell married George Fox in 1669. The union was presented to Friends as an emblem of Adam and Eve's spiritual unity before the Fall; looking back, many Separatists must have felt that the marriage had removed the Quakers' last line of defense against this very formidable Eve's lust for power, for Margaret Fox was the prime female organizer of the women's meeting and the first woman to publish a defense of female preaching. In 1671, after seeing George Fox embark on a voyage to America, she returned immediately to Swarthmore, where she inaugurated the women's meeting there. She then began a tour through the north of England, most probably to do the same in other communities.[102]

Not surprisingly, Margaret Fox locked horns with Wilkinson and Story from the beginning of the separation. After she publicly chastised some Westmoreland Friends for paying tithes, William Rogers accused her of delivering a paper against John Story at a quarterly meeting in 1672, a paper that gave "grievous accusations against our faithful brother John Story . . . from the female."[103] In 1676, William Penn wrote

101. Rawlinson Manuscripts, Bodleian Library, Oxford, quoted in Kunze, "The Family, Social, and Religious Life of Margaret Fell," 309, 323.
102. Fox's proposal for women's meetings was made after his release from Lancaster jail in 1666, where Fell was also incarcerated. Kunze speculates that she was an important architect of the meeting plan and that evidence of her influence on Fox was later suppressed ("'Walking in ye Gospel Order': Margaret Fell and the Establishment of Women's Meetings," paper presented at the Berkshire Conference of Women Historians, Rutgers University, June 1987).
103. Quoted in Kunze, "'Walking in ye Gospel Order,'" 8. Rogers denied that Story had referred to her as "the female," but he also accused George Fox of marrying up in the world and of traveling with a great attendance (Ellwood, *Antidote*, 202–3, referring to Rogers). In a tract called *Anti-Christian Treachery Discovered and Its Way Blocked Up* (1683), John Blaykling and others defended Fell and accused Story of talking against her behind her back (Kunze, "The Family, Social, and Religious Life of Margaret Fell," 8–9). George Fox wrote to Fell in 1674, advising her not to stir up opponents' anger further: "I desire you may be wise and if you do leave Westmorland Women's Meeting to

to George Fox, begging him to attend a meeting, "because Poor Margaret
is so much smit at, and run upon (as I believe never woman was) . . . as
if she was the cause; and of an implacable temper; without bowels, or
the spirit of reconcilication, to show them that she can pass by all that
passed between them that concerns herself."[104] In 1684, Gulielma Penn,
writing to Margaret Fell Fox, recounted a dream she had had during the
height of the Wilkinson/Story crisis:

> I saw thee, and dear George and many Friends in a meeting, and the power
> of the Lord was greatly manifested and methoughts there came dark wicked
> spirits into the meeting and they strove exceedingly against the life that was
> in the meeting, and their chief aim was first at thee and George, but mostly
> at thee, and they strove to hurt thee, but methought thou gottest so over them
> they could not touch thee, but only went to tear some little part of thy clothes,
> but thou escaped unhurt or touched. . . . It was long ago, but it rose now I
> was writing to thee fresh in my mind . . . but thy life reigns over them all, for
> it was thee they began with.[105]

The little part of her clothes her enemies tore was probably of very fine
stuff, for Margaret Fox always defied Quaker convention by wearing the
opulent clothing of her rank.[106] In 1677 she published a tract, *The
Daughter of Sion Awakened, And putting on Strength, She is Arising,
and Shaking her self out of the Dust, and putting on her Beautiful
Garments.*

---

themselves a while and let their spirits cool and not strive for the power, life will arise over
all" (*The Journal of George Fox*, ed. John L. Nickalls [London: Religious Society of
Friends, 1975], 691–92, quoted Kunze, "The Family, Social, and Religious Life of Margaret Fell," 9). Apparently, she did go to the Westmoreland meeting, however.

    104. William Penn to George Fox, Walthamstow, March 4, 1676, reprinted in PWP,
1:360, and 362n.

    105. Gulielma Penn to Margaret Fox, 1684, William Caton Manuscripts III, S. 81
(3/153) 460–62, quoted in Ross, *Margaret Fell*, 287. Gulielma was the wife of William
Penn.

    106. George Fox wrote to Margaret Fox in February 1674 from Worcester jail, "the
three pound[s] thou sent up to me in love, for it I did speak to a Friend to send thee as
much Spanish black cloth as will make thee a gown, and it did cost us a pretty deal of
money." The passage was crossed out (Abraham Manuscripts no. 18, Library of the
Society of Friends, London).

CHAPTER NINE

The Mystical Housewife

Let us keep our Women's Meetings in God's pure fear . . .
[and] allow of nothing whereby the worthy name of the
Lord is blasphemed . . . calling pride decency, covetousness,
carefulness, nicety and curiosity in the forms of meat, drink,
or other things, a point of good housewifery: . . . let us see
every corner, let all that's unclean be rid, and swept out;
. . . for . . . to have this house (to wit, our hearts and
inward parts) clean swept, and all its furniture of
righteousness set in good and comely order, in carefulness,
is very commendable and consistent with good housewifery
too: . . . God . . . hath remembered our many tears, when
we mourned apart for him as silly doves without mates. . . .
He is altogether comely . . . he is amiable in our eye, . . .
yea with our souls have we desired him in the night season.

Katherine Whitton, Epistle, Yorkshire
Women's Quarterly Meeting, 1681

INTRODUCTION

In the introduction to his study of English radical thought in the world
turned rightside up, *The Experience of Defeat: Milton and Some Contemporaries*, Christopher Hill remarked that he was unfortunately unable to include the views of any women. "I was disappointed," he wrote,
"not to be able to find any woman who left adequate evidence of her
experience of defeat. Margaret Fell was . . . [a] possibility, but her main
contribution was in the sphere of Quaker organization rather than of
ideas."[1] While one might quarrel with this estimate of the character and
quality of women's ideas as well as with the very notion of defeat, one
must also agree that Quaker women did not write systematically about

1. Christopher Hill, *The Experience of Defeat: Milton and Some Contemporaries*,
(New York: Faber and Faber, 1984), 21.

the issues that absorbed the movement in the period of its retrenchment. Why was this so?

Quaker women, whether ministers, mothers in Israel, adherents of the meeting system, or Separatists, brought as much concentrated energy to the discussion of the movement's crises as the most concerned and thoughtful of Quaker men. They aligned themselves for or against the parties of John Perrot, John Pennyman, and George Fox, composing both private letters and published treatises. They wrote as theologians, as polemicists, and as visionaries. Some assumed positions of leadership in the new hierarchy, while others left the movement. Yet what strikes the reader most forcibly in these women's declarations are their silences, the omission of any discussion of the role of reason or politics per se or of their own political role in the organization of the new church, and this was true regardless of the personal capacities or political positions of the women involved. The quality of this silence, more than the opinions actually expressed, speaks worlds about the evolving gender roles that had come to characterize the newly established Quaker church.

We have seen that the men who shaped the direction of Quakerism after 1660 believed that their new structuring of the movement was a matter of social control as well as spirituality. They also believed that it was a matter that involved, at its core, the political relations between women and men. Fox and his adherents presented the women's meeting as an emblem of a new kind of sanctified domestic politics, buttressed by an authority that was both law abiding and above the law, just as the new meetings for sufferings, censorship, and discipline were at once meetings for business and for worship. Separatists repudiated the women's meeting as the ultimate expression of inappropriate and un-justified authority—an inversion of every natural political relationship. "This church government," avowed Thomas Curtis, "my soul abhors it and I trample it under my foot."[2]

Indeed, no Quaker ever argued for or against women's aggressive prophetic authority as a vessel of God with anything like the energy that both parties brought to the discussion of women's relatively modest political authority in meetings. In the 1650s, women who traveled across oceans to prophesy had been extolled as heroes; now, the housewife who traveled to a quarterly meeting in her own county was exposed to

2. Reading Monthly Meeting Minutes (orthodox), 25, Library of the Society of Friends, London.

outright personal attacks on her as a bad wife and mother, a virago who had neglected her true domestic vocation. In Wiltshire, the prophet Elizabeth Stirredge spoke to some women who had testified against the Wilkinson and Story separation: "He [John Story] grieved them, bidding them go home about their business, and wash their dishes, and not go about to preach. And said, that Paul did absolutely forbid women to preach; and sent them crying home."[3] At the Reading (Berkshire) Monthly Meeting in October 1681, when the topic of the women's meeting was raised, "Robert Pocock . . . said it was the way for the women to confound their estates, to go from one end of the county to the other, and some to hire horses, and to be out from their families, some having scarce of their own to live on." Another Friend's rejoinder, that women frequently traveled across the county to visit their relatives, apparently cut no ice with Mr. Pocock.[4] In Bristol, Elizabeth Walker felt called upon to present an impassioned testimony in defense of her friend Anne Juxon:

> that she hath been diligent according to that ability the Lord hath given her to promote his work in the truth, but the serpent hath begotten an enmity against her innocent life and labor . . . they in scorn say she cries up order order [sic] and government in the church [yet] governeth not her own family . . . it's a false charge against her for she is a true laborer when she hath liberty from the Lord to come into her family from employment abroad for him when he hath employed her in his great and glorious work. I say and bear my testimony for her that she is a diligent laborer for the prosperity of truth in her own family . . . therefore turn turn you that are not past feeling . . . out of this wallowing like the sow to the mire.[5]

Moreover, the negative feminine symbolism formerly used by women as a metaphorical weapon against the unregenerate, now began to be taken in its concrete meaning, as a slur on women's individual characters. Thus William Penn recounted a heated argument between supporters of

3. Elizabeth Stirredge, *Strength in Weakness Manifest*, . . . 3d ed. (London, 1772), 73.

4. A Record Belonging to the Quarterly Meeting of the People of the Lord in Scorne Called Quakers in the County of Berks, transcribed Beatrice Saxon Snell and Nina Saxon Snell, II, 41n, Library of the Society of Friends, London, referring to the Reading Monthly Meeting (orthodox), October 16, 1681 minutes.

5. Testimony of Elizabeth Walker to Friends, n.d., Portfolio Manuscripts 6/14. In April 1683 a paper was submitted to the morning meeting condemning the "disorderly and scandalous conversation" of Ann Juxon and John Greenwood. They were disowned (The Morning Meeting's Book of Records from the 15th of the 7th Month, 1673, to the 6th of the 4th Month, 1692, Inclusive, I, fol. 73, Library of the Society of Friends, London).

John Pennyman and adherents of the meeting system about the meaning of the word "whore":

> [Elizabeth Barnes] *cried out, while* R[ichard] Farnsworth *was preaching,* "You have whored from the Lord." *Farnsworth . . . replied, "thou art a whore . . . or the Whore;" This* Michael Stanclift *called* unsavory . . . But does he take *E[lizabeth] Barnes'* word *"whore,"* in a spiritual sense, as degenerating; and will he seem to understand R[ichard] F[arnsworth]'s word *"whore,"* only in a *common* and *proper acceptation, as a dishonest woman?* Yes, that he will . . . O monstrous! O partial![6]

Yet even William Penn displayed a vivid imagination on the subject of individual women's capacity to subvert the good intentions of their men. Thus he criticized Mary Pennyman for undermining John Pennyman's spiritual equilibrium because she was besotted by her attractive new husband. "Thou art not so retired, as thou would have us believe," he told her:

> A rich, young, neat, sparkish husband is a certain visible thing . . . and I am of the mind, to speak plainly, that a great part of thy delight is lodged in him. . . . How canst thou admonish me not to be puffed up, that hast so puffed up the poor man [John Pennyman] that he is ever and anon ready to be cracked? . . . I testify in the truth of God that your humility is feigned, and your exaltation high: and thou has entered that poor man, and helped to his being beguiled, by swelling him beyond his place, as if he were some God on Earth.[7]

Many male Friends felt equally suspicious of Anne Curtis, whom they blamed as the guiding force behind her husband Thomas's rejection of the meeting system, calling her "the mother of this mischief."[8]

The historical importance of these and other remarks lies less in the latent misogyny of Robert Pocock or William Penn than in the prominence that every leading male Quaker now assigned to gender roles and gender relationships. During the movement's early days, leading public Friends sought to transcend all particular and limiting modes of social identity, none more so than that of gender. Though George Fox urged Friends to remain in their places while pursuing their daily activities "in the body," he also urged them to view themselves as part of a larger life force, inhabitants of a kind of spiritual fourth dimension where men

6. William Penn, *Judas and the Jews Combined against Christ and His Followers* (1673), 52.

7. William Penn to Mary Pennyman, Rickmansworth, November 22, 1673, in PWP, 1:264.

8. Record Belonging to the People Called Quakers, I, 30 and 30n. Thomas Curtis had originally supported the meeting, and Friends blamed his change of heart on his wife.

might feel themselves transformed into brides and infants and where
women might speak in the sacred language of male prophets. Twenty
years later, Fox was defending the meeting system not as an emblem of
women's *transcendence* of the limits of gender but as a mode of activity
appropriate for women's separate sphere of domestic knowledge and
capacity. Quakerism was to be a family religion, and women, more than
the male leaders of the business meeting or the meeting for censorship,
were held to be natural experts on family life. Women would become like
Sarah, Deborah, Miriam, Dorcas, Priscilla, and the repentant Mary
Magdalene, "to give suck to nurse up the seed and heir of the promise."[9]

I have argued that Fox's presentation of the mother in Israel as a leader
of the meeting was a progressive measure, because it widened the political and moral dimensions of women's traditional role. Yet it was also
a conservative measure inspired by a conservative goal: the desire to
ensure the internal stability of the movement as well as the safety and
prosperity of Friends in the world. Indeed, both Fox's party and Separatists believed that the survival of Quakerism depended upon their
ability not only to organize and discipline their own ranks but to become
more fully integrated into the life of the larger society. Their attitude was
clearly paradoxical, for it was during the period of retrenchment that
Quakerism evolved from a loosely organized group into a full-fledged
church, with its own unique and highly visible modes of dress, marriage,
language, and education. Yet Quakers also insisted on their reliability as
citizens and public servants. They demonstrated respect for the king,
integrity in business relationships, and, most importantly, their adherence to a high moral code of personal interaction. Rather than present
themselves dramatically, as prophets holding up a mirror to a corrupt
nation, they now attempted to stand as high-minded, public-spirited
citizens demonstrating exemplary social behavior and bourgeois moral
values. Adherence to conventional gender roles was obviously a key
element of this new public presence, and so Fox's defense of the meeting
system was based not only on the motherly woman's spiritual equality
with men but on the specifically feminine attributes that made her
socially subordinate to men.

Quaker women concurred wholeheartedly with the concerns of male
leaders to protect the integrity of the movement. In a long, tormented

9. G[eorge] F[ox], "To the men and Womens meetings," Swarthmore, December
1679, to be sent to Bedfordshire, Northamptonshire, and Leicestershire, Portfolio Manuscripts 30/96.

letter to George Fox written in 1676, Rebeckah Travers expressed her
guilt at having inadvertantly damaged the unity of Friends:

> My sorrows and exercises are great and many, in my old age, . . . so that my
> constant course and plain way in which I walked seemeth to be hedged up,
> and I to be thrust into the world again—where there is nothing to be found
> but trouble. . . . Dear G[eorge] F[ox] bear with me in laying my state a little
> open to thee, . . . the ancient love among some of the brethren waxes cold,
> and self love and ye too much love of this world stains our precious glory when
> it was said even by our enemies, they so love one another that we shall never
> be able to break them. . . . My purpose . . . has been all along to clear my self
> of having any hand, word, or thought intentionally . . . to strengthen that spirit
> of gainsaying in the two Johns [Wilkinson and Story], or any of their mind. . . .
> The women's meetings are accompanied with the power and presence of the
> Lord as ever, our service great and our supply faileth not.[10]

One year later, Mary Woolley wrote plaintively to Margaret Fell Fox:

> Oh dear Margaret . . . what shall I say but that I fear and also believe [my
> husband's] righteous soul hath been too much pressed upon: oh the lord in
> his good time rebuke those gainsayers: and that we may be as of old a people
> of one heart and one mind that we may serve the Lord together with one
> consent.[11]

In a more formal epistle to Friends, Elizabeth Hooton meditated on the
dangers of backsliding:

> O dear friends, when the lord hath set you free and brought you into joy, then
> you think you have overcome all, but there is a daily cross to be taken up,
> whilst that the fleshly will remaineth . . . there doth the serpent get in and tells
> the creature of ease, and liberty in the flesh, and say thou needest to take up
> the cross no longer . . . and thus many a poor soul is drowned and runs on
> in lightness and wantonness . . . and cause scandals to arise against the church,
> and so through backsliders we are rendered odious to the world.[12]

Because women shared the anxieties of male leaders regarding persecution from without and disunity from within the movement, they also

10. Rebeckah Travers to G[eorge] F[ox], London, August 17, 1676, Gibson Manuscripts II, 335/119, Library of the Society of Friends, London.
11. Mary Woolley to Margaret Fox, February 23, 1677, Portfolio Manuscripts,
36/44.
12. Elizabeth Hooton to Captain Sothers (Amor Stoddard) and his wife, n.d. (Mrs.
Stoddard died in 1665), Portfolio Manuscripts 3/35A; and see Emily Manners, *Elizabeth
Hooton: First Quaker Woman Preacher (1600–1672)* (London: Headley Bros., 1914),
8–9.

agreed on the necessity for a more stable social organization and more rigid gender roles, and for that very reason they were constrained to write about the issues confronting Quakerism differently from men. When William Penn and Robert Barclay published works addressed to outsiders, they defended Quakerism with the tough-minded, male virtues of rationality and clear argument while privately continuing to seek the kinds of experience accessible only to the visionary. Penn, we have seen, wrote but did not publish an extravagant prophetic tract, while Barclay, who converted during a mystical experience, once appeared in sackcloth and ashes.[13] Conversely, women acted as competent administrators and thinkers within the household and meeting while treating the issues of reason, conscience, church structure, and politics as taboo subjects in their published polemics. Their discussion of women's authority in the meeting system was cast in visionary language and antiformalist arguments. Their stated preoccupations were, above all, the issue of suffering and the need for a meeting system to buttress Friends' mutual love and courage in the face of ongoing persecution. Women also began to embroider their writings with feminine mystical images; unlike the earlier female prophets, who adopted the personae of Daniel or Jonah, the visionary voices of Elizabeth Bathurst and Elizabeth Webb were recognizably and consistently female. Thus, we find a double movement within Quaker women's texts and within the meeting system itself: one a movement of deliberate self-enclosure within a limited and subordinate public role, the other a movement of self-affirmation, an equally deliberate definition of women's writing and public service as part of a new, highly expressive female identity.

---

13. Men's unpublished epistles were also more lyrical than their published theological writings. Richard Smith of the Gloucestershire Quarterly Meeting wrote to the London Yearly Meeting in 1691 asking for more visits from traveling Friends to replace "those many faithful friends that are lately deceased that were as tender nursing fathers in Israel: . . . with, and in whom the heavenly glorious overcoming life (if but in poor contemptible vessels) and ancient eternal power, resides, attends and streams forth" (May 26, 1691, London Yearly Meeting, Epistles Received 1683–1706, I/152, Library of the Society of Friends, London). The Haverford (Wales) Men's Meeting wrote to the London Yearly Meeting the same year, "Dear Friends and Brethren, sons and co-heirs of the same inheritance of life and glory and . . . begotten by the same immortal seed, nourished and sustained by the same breasts, . . . [we are] submissively waiting for further appearance and manifestation of the highest power in his sons and daughters. . . . Oh let the voice of our salutation reach and sound in our ears, that there may be an echoing back again, this is the voice [of] our brother Joseph . . . that [God's] glory filling his temple may stain and overturn all the Dagons and idols of the nations . . . [our] mens and women's meetings duly kept they were set up" (April 14, 1691, London Yearly Meeting, Epistles Received 1683–1706, I/137).

A THEOLOGY OF UNREASON AND UNIVERSAL LOVE

Daily to die unto self, that Christ may live in me, I
becoming a passive creature, and he an active Christ,
in the increase of his government I feel an increase of
my peace.

Lilias Skene

The bridegroom is with his bride, and he opens her
mouth.

Margaret Fell, "Women's Speaking Justified"

Elizabeth Bathurst, a young, unmarried gentlewoman in delicate health,
was convinced along with her brother and sister in 1678, becoming active
as a minister and writer until her premature death seven years later. Her
intellectual gifts were so much admired that George Whitehead, in a
preface to one of her works, accounted it a miracle that the treatise was
produced by a woman, assuring sceptical readers that he had seen the
manuscript in her own handwriting. He further assured those readers of
her feminine modesty and virtue: "She became one of the wise virgins
of the day. . . . Oh! that all young women that read this, may follow that
good example."[14]

Bathurst's extended treatise on Quaker doctrine, *Truth's Vindication*,
reprinted six times by Quaker publishers, was explicitly aimed at con-
vincing outsiders of Friends' theological purity and moral integrity. Yet
rather than emphasize the harmony of reason and revelation and the
necessity for church order, as Penn and Barclay had done, she affirmed
the Quakers' original beliefs in a light beyond reason, in the reality of
universal love, in the saintliness of Friends, and in the ultimate restitution
of prophecy. Thus, she repudiated the doctrines of predestination and the
primacy of scripture:

> [Puritans] are so narrow-spirited as to shut out the greatest number of
> mankind, by absolute predestination; not sticking to affirm, that God nor
> Christ never purposed love nor salvation, to a great part of mankind, and that
> the coming and suffering of Christ never was intended, nor can be useful to
> their justification, but must and will be effectual for their condemnation. So

14. Testimonial by George Whitehead, in Elizabeth Bathurst, *Truth Vindicated by
the Faithful Testimony and Writings of the Innocent Servant and Hand-Maid of the Lord,
Elizabeth Bathurst, Deceased*, n.p.

being void of universal love themselves, they fondly imagine the Lord to be like themselves.[15]

Denying the existence of anger or substantive disagreement among Friends, she described the pliant, almost feminine character of the truly devout Quaker. "Christianity," she wrote,

> doth not consist in the belief of so many doctrines, articles and principles (as some suppose) but in conformity unto that one eternal principle . . . the light of Christ manifest in the conscience. . . . [Friends] have . . . labored to answer their Christian calling, with such a meek, patient, holy, harmless, humble, trembling, self-denying conversation, as may be most conformable to the pattern of Christ Jesus.[16]

Bathurst also published *The Sayings of Women*, a compendium of the words of women as mothers, judges, soothsayers, praise singers, and propheteses from the Old and New Testaments.[17]

Elizabeth Bathurst was among the most notable female exponents of Quaker theology, but she was not alone in basing her defense of Friends on a denial of forms and an affirmation of universal love and free grace. Elizabeth Webb (1663–1727) was a prophet whose exploits were reminiscent of the earliest heroic women Friends. In 1697 she left her husband and children to preach in the American wilderness, traveling on boat and horseback from Virginia to Massachusetts, seeking converts in places like "Great Choptank" and "dragon swamp," holding silent meetings to bring down the pride of men who had got "above their witness," and writing to newly convinced Friends with the authority of an Old Testament patriarch: "The Lord is come to restore unto his people a pure language, yea, and to restore judges as at the first. . . . Therefore I exhort and counsel you as one that have found favor with God that you meet often together and wait for the counsel of the spirit of truth."[18]

15. Elizabeth Bathurst, *Truths Vindication, or, a Gentle Stroke to Wipe off the Foul Aspersions, False Accusations and Misrepresentations, Cast upon the People of God, called Quakers* . . . (London, 1683), 97. Susanna Blandford also wrote about election as the free gift of God (*A Small Account Given forth by One That Hath Been a Traveller for These 40 Years in the Good Old Way* [1698], 8). See also Jane Fearon, *Absolute Predestination Not Scriptural: Or Some Queries upon a Doctrine Which I Heard Preach'd* . . . (London, 1705).

16. Bathurst, *Truths Vindication*, 71, 146–47.

17. Elizabeth Bathurst, *The Sayings of Women, Which were Spoken upon Sundry Occasions in several Places of the Scriptures* (Shoreditch, 1683).

18. Elizabeth Webb, "A Short Account of my Voyage into America with Mary Rogers my Companion," ed. Frederick B. Tolles and John Beverley Riggs, Manuscript. 975B/2, 3, 7, 9, Quaker Collection, Haverford College Library, Haverford, Pa.

   Unlike those earlier prophets, however, Elizabeth Webb presented
readers with a curiously gentle, introspective rendition of biblical theology. In a voluminous manuscript, she explicated the book of Revelation, once the Quakers' prime source of violent apocalyptic imagery,
as a parable of God's loving mercy. Quoting the passage "Repent or else
I will come unto thee quickly and will fight against them with the sword
of my mouth," she commented, "Here we may observe the tender
mercies of God in giving time to repent, he is the same God still."[19] To
the verse "Suppose ye . . . that I am come to give peace on Earth, I tell
you nay, but rather division, for from henceforth there shall be five in
a house divided, three gainst two and two against three," she responded,
"Oh! it is good to observe the operations of the divine power of him who
rules in the kingdom of men, and then we shall see cause to admire his
wisdom, goodness, mercy and just judgments and glorify his excellent
name."[20] Webb also embellished her writing with a brand of feminine
imagery more resonant of the mysticism of Jacob Boehme than Quaker
ethical prophecy:

> The glory of the true church or mystical body, or bride of Christ . . . is made
> up of souls who have entered into covenant with the Lord, . . . her clothing
> is of wrought gold, and the curious needlework of virgin wisdom is upon
> her. . . . Her bridegroom . . . is clothing her with the beautiful garment of his
> salvation . . . she is depending on him for her daily bread: so that she is not
> eating her own bread, nor wearing her own apparel; . . . she is wholly subject
> to him; . . . she hath no will of her own, but the will of her Lord is her will
> in all things. . . . Her steps are comely in the eyes of her beloved.[21]

In another meditation, she portrayed the worshiper's experience of subdued, passive contentment by her repeated use of the word "sweet":

> O my sweet Lord that my soul loveth to wait for thee . . . that so every thing
> may be judged down and done away that is displeasing unto thee, for it is thy
> sweet love and the light of thy countenance, that is the sole comfort of my
> soul by which thou art daily sweetening my passage through this vale of
> tears.[22]

These images of feminine subservience were complemented by an emphasis on Christ, not only as a light diffused within the soul but as a

      19. Elizabeth Webb, "Some Meditations with Some Obserations Upon the Revela-
tions of Jesus Christ," MS. G4.2/38, Quaker Collection, Haverford College Library,
Haverford, Pa.
      20. Ibid., 44.
      21. Elizabeth Webb, *A Letter from Elizabeth Webb, to Anthony William Boehm*
(Philadelphia, 1783), 7–8.
      22. Ibid., 291

historical man and mystical husband: "When I retire inward I find thee O my beloved my bridegroom sitting in the center of my mind giving forth thy royal law. . . . My sweet peaceable saviour . . . take to thyself thy great power and rule and reign in my bosom . . . that my poor simple soul may be thy loyal subject."[23]

A far more eminent public Friend was Isabel Fell Yeamans (ca. 1637–1694). The daughter of Margaret Fell and the widow of a Bristol merchant, she was the only woman minister to accompany George Fox, William Penn, Robert Barclay, and other leading male Friends in 1677 on a mission to Holland and Germany, where she preached to Princess Elizabeth of the Palatinate, the princess admiring her "curious voice and . . . freer way of delivering herself." She also traveled on horseback throughout England and Scotland, where she visited meetings accompanied by Robert Barclay.[24] Her reputation among Friends was as a woman both knowledgeable and accomplished; yet she defined the true believer as one who had transcended intellectual accomplishments. "So look not for [God] in the shadows and forms without the power and substance, nor be satisfied with the hearing of him by the hearing of the ear, or a notional traditional knowledge."[25] Her plea was for a gradual spiritual regeneration, an inward response to wisdom's gentle voice within the soul:

> the small still voice, which calls unto you when you are running to do evil. . . . Return, return, hearken unto the voice of wisdom; for she uttereth her voice in the streets of the world, and in the midst of the concourse of the people. . . . The sheep of Christ's pasture are clothed with the lamb-like, meek, quiet and suffering spirit of Jesus, who makes his followers conformable unto himself.[26]

If Isabel Yeamans was a chief ornament of the emerging Quaker church, Anne Docwra was its chief female gadfly and curmudgeon. An

23. Elizabeth Webb, "An Inward Breathing of a Soul to Almighty God, and some Communication with him Set down in the Spring, and Openings of divine love and in humility," MS. G4.2/292–93. On the man Christ, see also Mary Sandilands, *A Tender Salutation of Endeared Love* (London, 1696).

24. DQB. William Charles Braithwaite, "Payments for Friends' Horses," *Friends' Quarterly Examiner* 46 (1912): 483; in 1677 Yeaman's horse was stabled for three nights at Banbury.

25. Isabel Yeamans, *An Invitation of Love to All Who Hunger and Thirst after Righteousness* (1679), 8.

26. Ibid., 14, 29. Anne Docwra, "True Intelligence to be Read and Considered in the Light," Cambridge, October 12, 1683, A. R. Barclay Manuscripts, vol. 324, no. 236, n.p., Library of the Society of Friends, London.

elderly gentlewoman, widow, and former Royalist living near Cambridge, Docwra accommodated the local meeting and housed traveling
ministers for several years before the public meeting house was built,
acting as a self-appointed guardian of Quaker ethics. "And further I have
to say," she assured readers, "that when I knew of any person among
us, that was blameworthy, in wronging each other, I have not been
wanting . . . to let them know their error."[27]

Docwra's own predilection was clearly for rational argument and
spirited polemic rather than visionary insight. Responding to the attacks
of an opponent (who was also a relative), she wrote:

> And to [Francis Bugg's] report, that I am a she-preacher, that he cannot prove,
> that I ever preached in a public meeting. . . . That is not the office in the Church
> that God hath called me to . . . our preachers have a commission from God,
> and they speak what he requires of them; and they know when to speak, and
> when to be silent.[28]

She herself was an educated woman of the world, and proud of it:

> If he had called me a she-lawyer, he had some grounds for this; for when I
> was about fifteen years of age, my father finding me reading some idle books,
> he took them from me, and told me he would have me read better books, and
> pointed to the great *statute* book that lay upon the *parlour* window, and bid
> me read that, and said it was as proper for a woman as a man to understand
> the laws, because they must live under them as well as men.[29]

Elsewhere she argued that magistrates have no legal right to prosecute
Protestants for heresy:

> But to return to my former discourse concerning those laws that are put in
> execution against *Protestant dissenters*, with a serious consideration of the
> transactions of our magistrates, in putting the statute of the 29th of
> *Elizabeth* in execution against them. . . . Do the laws of this land judge any
> man before he is suffered to speak for himself? Is a felon or murderer
> convicted before his accusers are brought face to face before him? And must

---

27. A[nne] D[ocwra], *An Apostate-Conscience Exposed, and the Miserable Consequences thereof Disclosed, for Information and Caution . . .* (London, 1699), 34, 35.
28. Francis Bugg had joined the Quakers and then repudiated them. He referred to
Docwra as "the old Woman with her Incoherent Fables." He was also Docwra's cousin
(Francis Bugg, *Jezebel Withstood, & Her Daughter Anne Docwra, Publickly Reprov'd*
[1699], 1–2). On Bugg, see SPQ, 487–88.
29. D[ocwra], *Apostate-Conscience*, 24–25.

innocent people deliver their bodies to the sheriff before they have personal notice given them to appear before you, to show a reason why they do not conform?[30]

Repeatedly referring to her own respectable background and education as a daughter of a justice of the peace, Docwra was particularly exercised by allegations that Quakers were of humble origins or engaged in financial fraud. She had even less patience with Friends who covered their heads during the time of persecution, those who "lay still skulking, until the storm of persecution was over, and when the sun shined, then every viper crept out of his hole."[31] She also repeated Francis Bugg's assertion of the rumor that George Fox learned twenty-four languages in one night by divine inspiration and that she believed it for twenty years; she countered by saying that Bugg, an ex-Quaker and an enemy of Friends, was known as a "shatter-headed man" who belonged in Bedlam.[32] "Although I am entered into the seventy-sixth year of my age," she declared, "yet, through mercy, I can walk the streets to visit the sick, and my friends and relations also, and can see without spectacles still, to read *Francis Bugg's* lies and deceit."[33]

Anne Docwra was sceptical of the new-fangled meeting system and described herself riding to London in a stagecoach with her maid, seeking out George Fox in order to interrogate him about the jurisdiction of the women's meeting over marriages.[34] Yet for all her obvious pride in her knowledge of the law and her pleasure in matching wits with her various antagonists, Docwra never discussed the relation of reason and conscience or the political aspects of the meeting system that she opposed. "This I have seen," she wrote, "in my time of understanding things of this nature, which is above forty years, [that] although the Lord Christ hath appeared to people in several forms, yet he died to end shadows and typical forms."[35] Elsewhere, this student of the law disavowed the necessity for laws and prescriptions for the Quaker church: "[Friends] are retired from the world, and the fashions thereof, which pass away; whether they be the *decrees* of Counsels, (*or meetings*) *directories*, or *any*

30. A[nne] D[ocwra], *A Looking-Glass for the Recorder and Justices of the Peace* . . . (Cambridge, 1682), 5, 6.
31. A[nne] D[ocwra], *The Second Part of an Apostate-Conscience Exposed* (London, 1700), 36.
32. D[ocwra], *Apostate-Conscience*, 18.
33. D[ocwra], *Second Part of an Apostate Conscience Exposed*, 40.
34. D[ocwra], *Apostate-Conscience*, 9–10.
35. A[nne] D[ocwra], *An Epistle of Love and Good Advice* . . . (1683), 5.

other *outward rule* or *prescription*."[36] Quoting the French writer Male-
branche, whom she claimed to have read in English translation, she used
her considerable erudition in the service of a resolutely antiintellectual
position: "[Professors'] superficial words have no substance in them, . . .
they are but pictures for the ears, as images are for the eyes, and there
may be as much idolatry in the one as the other."[37] Having vindicated
the reality of visionary insight and the irrelevance of formal worship,
Docwra was careful to defend female prophecy as a traditional privilege
that in no way conflicted with women's traditional subservience toward
their husbands:

> [Paul] speaks concerning women's service in the Church, both of praying and
> prophesying; and in some other places in the Scripture he forbids some
> women's teaching and usurping authority over the man; all which do no ways
> obstruct nor contradict what is formerly declared concerning such women as
> have received power from God to pray, prophesy or declare the glad tidings
> of the Light.[38]

The prophet Rebeckah Travers may stand as a final example of
women's theological writing during the period of Quakerism's long
transition from charismatic movement to established church. As a pillar
of the London Six Weeks Meeting, Travers was completely opposed to
Anne Docwra in her defense of the women's meeting and of an over-
arching church structure, yet, like Docwra, she articulated her beliefs in
terms of a faith that rendered structure obsolete:

> The Light is sufficient to beget, to build up, and to bring into the inheritance
> of life and glory. . . . And the knowledge of this is not attained by words or
> writing. . . . [Faith is] changing you into its own nature of love and mercy,
> kindness and good will to every creature, saving you out of every evil. . . . Yet
> this is not I, nor you, who may still have a place in us for the evil one . . . for
> our unity is in the faith, not in any form whatsoever. . . . [Our enemies act]
> all in the will, voluntary indeed in their lowliness, and in their love. . . . That
> which would comprehend the life, is not life.[39]

Quaker women's doctrinal writings present the reader with a fascinating juxtaposition of style and substance. Unlike the prophets of the

36. A[nne] D[ocwra], *A Brief Discovery of the Work of the Enemy of Sion's
Peace* . . . (Cambridge, 1683), 2.
37. D[ocwra], *Second Part of an Apostate-Conscience*, 46, 47.
38. D[ocwra], *An epistle of love*, 4.
39. Rebeckah Travers, *A Testimony concerning the Light and Life of Jesus* . . .
(London, 1663), 1–3, 7–8.

1650s, these female Friends presented themselves not as ethical prophets but as theologians and moralists, using logic and clear argument, as well as a highly personal idiom, to make their case. Indeed, the women whose writings are summarized above were notable for their independent, even idiosyncratic personalities and behavior. All were educated and prosperous, all enjoyed the respect (in Docwra's case, grudging respect) of eminent male Friends, and almost all were single or widowed for long periods in their careers. (The exception was Elizabeth Webb, who left her family in England to travel with a female companion and whose meetings in New England were so effectual "that had I been a man I thought I could have went into all corners of the land to declare of it."[40]

Yet the *substance* of Quaker women's theological writings reflects virtually nothing of these personal attributes. Eschewing both the violent ecstasies of earlier prophets and the metaphysical energy of male theologians, women acknowledged the gentle murmur of wisdom but not the cool voice of reason, using feminine imagery that was more reminiscent of contemporary mysticism than of their own Puritan roots. Moreover, despite their almost universal support for the new meeting structure, they resolutely and persistently defended Quakerism as a religion of anti-structure. The one theological tenet that was absolutely fundamental to each of them was the denial of predestination and the affirmation of the potential for universal salvation through virtue, love, and the capacity for suffering. Finally, their affirmation of feminine wisdom was now complemented by an emphasis on the historical Jesus, their true judge and spouse. Each of these themes fell well within the lines of argument advanced by male Friends. Yet their increased emphasis in women's theological writings marked a subtle bifurcation, a recognition of the need to present themselves not simply as Friends, but as females.

WOMEN DEFEND THE WOMEN'S MEETING

If the most eminent women writers of the period were chary of discussing issues of reason and politics, we should not be surprised to learn that female advocates of the women's meeting were less eager to analyze their political position than to disavow their own political ambitions. "And for what they say of me," wrote Rebeckah Travers, a leader of the

40. Isabel Fell married the Bristol merchant William Yeamans in 1664. He died ten years later; she remained a widow until 1689 (Isabel Ross, *Margaret Fell: Mother of Quakerism* [London: Longmans and Green, 1949], 178). Elizabeth Webb, "A Short Account of My Voyage into America," MS. 975B/7.

London meeting, "as being a *great mother and governess among these people*, is but to set me on high, that the dirt they sling, may the more come upon me. . . . I have gladly and long been a servant to this people of the Lord, and no more government have I coveted or gained, but by love."[41] Women also attempted to direct the focus of the discussion away from issues of gender, and from the general questions of church structure and politics, and toward the practical necessity for unity and discipline among Friends. So Travers defended the Fox party because it affirmed the importance of maintaining a united front in the face of "justices and mayors who are ready to tear us in pieces," while Separatist women claimed that the Fox party was to blame for endangering the safety of Friends: "Their separate Men's Meetings have been the nurseries of contention," wrote Anne Docwra, "and I believe the chief cause of this long-grinding persecution . . . more dangerous to the peace of the nation, than our public meetings (with doors open) where men and women meet altogether."[42]

In their eagerness to defend themselves against charges of personal ambition, women readily adopted images of female evil as a contrast to their own virtue and modesty. Ann Whitehead attacked Anne Docwra as a "mother agent," busily preaching false liberty, but described herself as

> a simple woman . . . encouraged with my small measure of light and divine grace. . . . I pray . . . that I may not be found exercising myself in things too high for me. . . . Ann [Docwra], . . . do not glory in showing thy wits and parts and speaking great words . . . and stop the current of thy own working brain . . . [but] attend upon the teachings of the Lord in silent subjection as become us.[43]

Docwra, in turn, accused the women's meetings as being of little purpose "but to shelter great bellies" (illicit pregnancies).[44]

41. Rebeckah Travers, "A *Testimony* in the Spirit of Love, against that Malitious Spirit That in Certain *Apostates* and Their Abettors Exercises *Tyranny* and *Hypocrisie*, Everywhere," in Penn, *Judas and the Jews*, 97. Travers had been accused of following her and her son's interest by encouraging a couple to marry without license.
42. R[ebeckah] T[ravers], *A Testimony for God's Everlasting Truth* (London, 1669). On Docwra, see Bugg, *Jezebel Withstood*, 9–10.
43. Ann Whitehead to Anne Docwra, London, June 4, 1683, A. R. Barclay Manuscripts, vol. 324, 195. An unknown reader of Docwra's tract noted in the margin, "Thou hadst better have studied to be quiet and have kept down that unruly, willfull, ravenous sp[iri]t and have . . . power over that before thou had set up thyself . . . in print and usurped authority" (Docwra, *A Brief Discovery*, copy in A. R. Barclay Manuscripts, vol. 324, no. 237, transcript).
44. Whitehead to Docwra, A. R. Barclay Manuscripts, vol. 324, no. 195. Bugg, *Jezebel Withstood*, 10. Docwra also defended the women's meeting against the attacks of

Those women who ventured to defend the women's meeting in more positive terms often did so with their hands over their mouths. Ann Whitehead reassured male Friends that the women's meeting would do only what was proper to women, "as visiting and relieving the sick, [and] the poor . . . and fatherless orphans, that the distressed in all things be rightly answered, the children at nurse be rightly educated, and well brought up." Elder women would also teach the younger to love their husbands and children and be good housekeepers. Indeed, women's jurisdiction over marriages was necessary in order to teach these young women "that Christ's yoke be not cast off by either, nor any false liberty of the flesh set up, encouraged or soothed among us."[45] Mary Penington went even farther, portraying the women's meeting as both domestic and subordinate:

> Our place in the creation is to bring forth and nurse up, to keep things orderly, sweet and clean in a family, to preserve from waste and putrefaction, and to provide things necessary for food and rainment; . . . to cleanse out what is unsavoury and unclean, and to cast out evil doers out of the home and . . . to preserve and keep wholesome and orderly things in this house. The men need not grudge us this place in the body, wherein we are meet helps, and usurp not authority over them, and act as the inferior parts of the body, being members, though but a finger or a toe.[46]

Penington argued that women were more suitable for overseeing marriages than men:

> It being more modest and comely, and more suitable to the bashfulness of a woman, to lay her intention before those of her own sex, for the laying it in the first place before the men puts a force on their bashfulness more than is right . . . [moreover] it is more seemly for [women] to take notice of inconvenient familiarities, through the letting up the affectionate part. And women having thus brought it to the men, it is left with them to determine of, to set by or reject, or to give certificate or permit, as they feel.

Francis Bugg, arguing that they were useful where Friends were numerous, as a support to the men, to tell them what services were needed for the poor and so on (D[ocwra], *Apostate-Conscience*, 28).

45. Mary Forster, Mary Elson, Anne Travers, Ruth Crouch, Susannah Dew, and Mary Plumstead, *A Living Testimony from the Power and Spirit of Our Lord J. C. in Our Faithful Women's Meeting and Christian Socity [sic]* (London, 1685), 2–3; Ann Whitehead and Mary Elson, *An Epistle for True Love, Unity and Order in the Church of Christ* (London, 1680), 6–11.

46. M[ary] P[enington], "ffor those Women friends yt are dissatisfied at present wth the Womens meeting distinct from the Men, & having Collections & severall businesses apart," Amschot, Sept. 7, 1678, John Penington Manuscripts, IV/160, Library of the Society of Friends, London.

Women might also dispense charity and visit orphans or children "who have a weak mother, either in respect of understanding or weakness of body."[47]

Yet if women were skittish about contributing to a rational discussion of their position as administrators and organizers, their eloquence was released in full force as they defended the meeting system with the voice of the visionary. In London, Mary Elson addressed an epistle to women Friends:

> I do declare . . . that it was the same everlasting quickening power that first visited us by the spirit of judgment and of burning, and wrought in our inward parts mightily . . . to purify and to cleanse, to purge out and put under all that was contrary to the Lord . . . that gathered us and made us a Meeting. . . . And I can truly say, I had true breathings to the Lord in the behalf of our younger women. . . . And . . . I have felt the zeal of the Lord to arise in my heart . . . sometimes upon my bed against this wicked Spirit, that hath sought to lay waste . . . our blessed Meeting.[48]

In Oxfordshire, women Friends took the restoration of the drunkard Edward Green as proof that God's work had been manifested through the miraculous healing properties of the women's meeting:

> One Edward Green of Farringdon . . . a very bad living man much given to drunkenness . . . could (not) be satisfied (as he said) but must come to this meeting . . . and the said Edward Green . . . was so reached that he broke in confession of his iniquity . . . having some brokenness of heart . . . at that time upon him much more than ever was observed in him before although he have come among us . . . *this twenty years.* . . . This . . . may . . . be sufficient to convince *all questioners and opposers*: that the Lord do own and justify our Godly care and Christian endeavors as well in our women's as in our men's meetings by the example aforsaid of this man who never was at such a meeting in all his life before.[49]

In Buckinghamshire, the women attached to the Upperside Monthly Meeting informed the men's meeting that they had met together "to wait

47. Ibid., fol. 159.
48. Whitehead and Elson, *An Epistle for True Love*, 13, 14–15.
49. The Vale of the White Horse Monthly Meeting, Women's Monthly Minute-Book, 1676–1730, transcribed Beatrice Saxon Snell and Nina Saxon Snell, Monthly Women's Meeting at Charney, April 25, 1681, 13–14, Library of the Society of Friends, London (original at Oxfordshire Record Office). George Fox wrote to the women of Barbados, "I believe there is a thousand women that are beyond the wisdom of the world all: yea, and the power of God hath wrought miracles among them" (George Fox, *George Fox's Book of Miracles,* ed. Henry J. Cadbury [New York: Octagon Books, 1973], Introduction, 46).

upon the Lord," after which they delivered a message to the men "that they have a sense that their Meeting is of the Lord, and that they cannot go back, and therefore desire that they may go on with the encouragement and unity of the men." The men, in this instance, agreed that they were "willing to encourage them, and do not desire they should go back, but go on in the name of the Lord."[50]

Given the general temper of the movement during the period of crisis and restructuring, it should not be difficult to understand why women writers would choose to ignore the rational and political aspects of the meeting system, defending their proposed authority in terms that were visionary and conservative rather than rational and socially progressive. For as women undoubtedly understood all too well, it was one thing to display a thorough knowledge of the Bible and the capacity for reasonable behavior in one's own shop or home or religious meeting, as many women certainly did, and quite another to extend Penn's or Barclay's analysis of reason and conscience to an analysis of the rational female nature or the abstract rights of womanhood, subjects that no male Quaker ever thought to broach, and that were indeed revolutionary when Mary Wollstonecraft discussed them more than a century later. Thus, the opening that Elizabeth Stirredge found to express her defense of the women's meeting was, on reflection, the only one she could have found at this historical moment. In a journal composed for the instruction of her children, she described how the controversy had forced her to become a chastiser of her own people:

> My exercise increased, my inward pains grew stronger and stronger, my heart was troubled within me, my eyes were as a fountain of tears, and I cried out, "Woe is me, that ever I was born. Oh! what is the matter that all my bowels seem to be displaced? . . . And seeing they despise the service of women so much, . . . make use of them that are more worthy. . . . Oh! how unfit am I for such service!" . . . I dreaded to go to a meeting, for fear that testimony

50. Beatrice Saxon Snell, ed., *The Minute Book of the Monthly Meeting of the Society of Friends for the Upperside of Buckinghamshire, 1669–1690*, Records Branch of the Buckinghamshire Archaeological Society (High Wycombe: Hague and Gill, 1937), 37 (September 1, 1675). In other cases the women's meetings were set up by the men. The Gainsborough (Lincolnshire) Monthly Meeting ordered that women Friends attend a meeting in 1675 to set up a women's meeting (Harold W. Brace, ed., *The First Minute Book of the Gainsborough Monthly Meeting of the Society of Friends, 1669–1719*, 2 vols., vol. 38 of the Lincoln Record Society [Hereford: The Hereford Times, 1948], 1:41). The same happened in Herefordshire in 1673 (Herefordshire Quarterly Meeting, Temp. Manuscripts, fol. 1, Library of the Society of Friends, London).

would be required of me . . . [then] the power of the Lord seized on me, which
made me to tremble; insomuch that my bones were shaken, and my teeth
chattered . . . and standing up with a dreadful testimony, . . . [I] proclaimed
God's controversy with the exalted and high amongst the professors of
truth.[51]

Returning home in great relief, she was visited by John Story and three
men, who told her she had no business accusing him in public, whereupon she reared up and admonished him to go back where he belonged,
to his own people in the north. Soon afterward, hearing Story preach at
a meeting, she was moved to interrupt him, crying, "Woe to that spirit
that dimneth the glory of the Lord, and woe to that pot whose scum
remains in it, for in it is the broth of abominable things."

> It ran through me again and again. . . . I would fain have foreborn till he had
> done, but I durst not; for I was afraid to speak, and afraid to keep silent. . . .
> I strove against it by reasoning, and saying, "Oh, that the Lord would be
> pleased to excuse me this day. . . ." But all this reasoning, would not do that
> service that God had for me to do that day. But when I found no way to pass
> it by, I stood up to clear my conscience, and discharge my duty in the sight
> of God.[52]

In all this account of intimidation, inward struggle, and heroic expression, Stirredge never mentioned the issues of structure, authority, or
politics, portraying the schism as a simple argument about the necessity
to meet in public and endure persecution.

Surely the silences of these prophets and writers resulted in a skewed
expression of many women's actual capacities, for Quaker female leaders were not adolescent girls or illiterate prophets but the most esteemed,
educated, and practical of mature women Friends. Rebeckah Travers
was a prolific author and the only woman who regularly attended the
London Meeting of Ministers. Mary Penington was a highly educated
gentlewoman who stood with her husband Isaac at the very center of the
new Quaker church. Sarah Fell taught herself Hebrew in order to pursue
her own biblical studies and served as clerk of both the Swarthmore and
London Meetings. Ann Downer, now Ann Whitehead, had acted as
George Fox's secretary in the 1650s and was the most highly respected
woman Friend in London.[53]

51. Stirredge, *Strength in Weakness Manifest*, 69–70, 75, 82.
52. Ibid., 91, 92.
53. On Penington, see DQB; on Travers, see DQB and the Morning Meeting's Book
of Records, I; on Whitehead, see *Piety Promoted by Faithfulness, Manifested by Several
Testimonies concerning That True Servant of God Ann Whitehead* (1686).

However, to interpret women's visionary writing in wholly negative and derivative terms, as shaped by the policies and prejudices of the male leaders or of society at large, would be both one-sided and overly cynical, for from their own perspective these older visionaries were desperately trying to hold on to what, for them, was best in their movement: their capacity to be collectively touched and ennobled by divine light. They were also sensitive to the timidity of many women Friends, who, while they might have been ready to prophesy in an ecstatic state, might well have been terrified to take on a more public role "in the body." Mary Penington therefore assured them that their new meeting was innocuous:

> We come together and sit down solemnly to wait on the Lord . . . to favour us and fit us for his service; and in this weighty frame, if prayer or praises arise in our hearts, we give up unto it. . . . But we do not find that it is our work and service there to spend our time in declaration one to another in an instructive way, as to make known truth, but only what is suitable to our present service . . . speaking but one at a time; . . . [our] enquiries and reproofs and admonitions are only to those of our own sex. . . . Friends, I seeing your discouragements . . . hope it is not in opposition but in a sense of that you know not, that makes you so shy of this kind of assembling yourselves together.[54]

Moreover, while the female defenders of the meeting system may have repressed their own capacity to be analytical or clever, they also introduced a new and more personalized prophetic voice, for the minister of the 1650s, who had engaged her audience by speaking the language of Amos or Daniel, was a far cry from the visionary mother in Israel, who proudly invoked the biblical figures of Deborah and Miriam, as well as her own domestic expertise, to justify her position. "Sisters," wrote Sarah Fell to women Friends everywhere:

> [T]ithe . . . belongs to women to pay, as well as the men, not only for widows, but them that have husbands, as pigs, and geese, hens and eggs, hemp and flax, wool and lamb; all which women may have a hand in: So it concerns the women's meetings. . . . [God] can make us good and bold, and valiant soldiers of Jesus Christ, if he . . . arm us with his armour of light . . . and cover our hearts with the breast-plate of righteousness . . . if he shoe our feet, with the preparation of the gospel of peace, and set our feet upon the mountains, so

---

54. Mary Penington, "ffor those Women friends," 160.

that we stand there, and publish glad tidings of great joy. . . . This is given
for information, instruction, and direction.[55]

These leaders of the new ministry and meeting system were defending
their authority not as souls who had transcended their humanity but as
women who had proven their worth.

IN THE UPPER ROOM: THE WORK OF
THE WOMEN'S MEETING

They were all gathered together in an upper room . . .
with the women and Mary the mother of Jesus . . .
and the holy ghost was poured upon them, so
plentifully, that the multitude were all amazed. . . .
Therefore let all mouths be stopped, which would
limit the spirit of the Lord God in male or female,
which he hath not limited; but the Lord hath regard
unto and takes notice of the women, and despises
them not.
  Lancashire Women's Meeting, 1689, Sarah Fell, clerk

By me paid Jane Hawthornethwaite for five young
  ducks, mother's account . . . . 1 shilling
By me paid of the Women's Meeting stock . . . to be
  given to Mabel Gunson of Hawkshead Meeting
  towards her journey for Ireland with three
  children . . . . 10 shillings
By me given towards building Lancaster Meeting
  House . . . . 10 shillings
By me paid Ja. Lang to buy a pair of shoes with,
  which is part of his wages . . . . 3 shillings
      Sarah Fell's Account Book, 1676, 1677, 1678

The women's meeting survived the controversies of the 1670s and 1680s
intact, albeit with an authority somewhat less awesome than that en-

55. "From our Country Women's meeting in Lancashire to be Dispersed abroad,
among the Women's meetings every where," Nottinghamshire Record Office Q618,
handwritten copy in Temporary Manuscripts 394. This document was edited by Milton
D. Spiezman and Jane C. Kronick and published: "A Seventeenth-Century Quaker
Women's Declaration," *Signs* 1, no. 1 (Autumn 1975): 231–45. The LSF document is
dated June 25, 1689, while Spiezman and Kronick put the composition (most likely by
Sarah Fell, clerk of the meeting) at 1675–80.

visioned by George and Margaret Fell Fox. Chiefly, the meetings protected Friends and their families during times of persecution, which continued almost unabated for the three decades after 1660. They collected and distributed funds for projects as minute as the provision of underclothes for indigent Friends and as grand as the building of meeting houses. They set up children in apprenticeships and widows in private businesses. They buttressed women's (and men's) adherence to the Quaker doctrine of perfection by monitoring sexual morality and collecting public testimonies against the payment of tithes.[56]

The oldest and preeminent organization of women was the network of meetings settled in London. London women Friends attended two-week, quarterly and yearly meetings as well as the so-called box meeting (named for the box in which funds were originally kept).[57] The yearly and box meetings received books and epistles from monthly and quarterly meetings throughout England as well as from Ireland, America, and the Caribbean. One such epistle urged them to scrutinize seamen, merchants, and passengers on ships and chastise them for improper language or trading practices.[58] They also lent money to individuals (including William Penn), donated funds to poor Friends and to other meetings, and circulated epistles that directed the conduct of newer meetings else-

---

56. I make no claim to understand or explain the full complexity of the meeting system. Meetings differed in different locations: In Yorkshire the women's quarterly meeting actually met three times a year, while in Surrey and Sussex it did not meet at all (W. Pearson Thistlethwaite, *Yorkshire Quarterly Meeting [of the Society of Friends] 1665–1966* [Harrogate: by the author, 1979], and Thomas W. Marsh, ed., *Some Records of the Early Friends in Surrey and Sussex from the Original Minute-Books and other Sources* [London: S. Harris and Co., 1886]). In the Vale of the White Horse (Oxfordshire) the women's meeting was autonomous; in Bristol it was not. In 1684 George Fox wrote a letter to Friends about "some jumble concerning a meeting out of your three meetings lately erected" in London. This "flying" meeting was originally to meet quarterly in order to help other meetings in reproving slackness, but the meeting began dealing with marriages, taking jurisdiction from the monthly meeting, and disturbing Friends (G[eorge] F[ox] to Friends, April 8, 1684, Ford's Greene, Middlesex, A. R. Barclay Manuscripts 217, no. 193). For an overview of the meeting system, see SPQ, Chaps. 10–12.

57. On the box meeting, see William Beck and T. Frederick Ball, *The London Friends' Meetings: Showing the Rise of the Society of Friends in London* (London: F. Bowyer Kitto, 1869), 344–50, and Irene L. Edwards, "The Women Friends of London: The Two-Weeks and Box Meetings," JFHS 47, no. 1 (Spring 1955): 2–21. The meeting was established in 1659 at the instigation of Sarah Blackborow. Women from any of the six London monthly meetings (attended by both women and men) might attend the box meeting, which was beholden to no other meeting in its expenditures. Originally the members dropped money into the box, but the meeting later acquired funds and property for this use.

58. Ross, *Margaret Fell*, 300–1. Rebeckah Travers sent books to the meeting (Letter to Rebeckah Travers, December 30, 1677, London Women's Box Meeting Manuscripts, Sr1/127, fol. 35, Library of the Society of Friends, London).

where.[59] The document, signed by Ann Travers and Ann Downer White-head in 1674, may serve as a blueprint of the women's meeting's intended functions:

[These services] have been and are: to visit the sick and the prisoners . . . making provision for the needy, aged and weak, that are incapable of work: a due consideration for the widows . . . and poor orphans . . . for their education and bringing up in good nurture and in the fear of the Lord: and putting them out to trades in the wholesome order of the creation. Also the elder women exhorting the younger in all sobriety, modesty in apparel . . . and to stop tatlers and false reports. . . . Also admonishing such maids and widows as may be in danger . . . either to marry with unbelievers, or to go to the priest to be married. . . . And that maid servants that profess truth and want places, be orderly disposed of. . . . But chiefly our work is, to help the helpless in all cases.[60]

Such epistles provided inspiration to such far-flung communities as this one in Virginia, which appealed to the London Meeting for guidance:

Ordered of our women's meeting in the western branch of Nancimund in Virginia . . . we could gladly receive advertisement from you that are ancient, and have been long experienced in the work of the Lord and the wisdom of God. But we are a poor and contemptible people, in the estimation of the world, and have our being, as some say, where the off-scouring of nations do inhabit. . . . [We desire] that you would have us in remembrance when you meet together before the Lord.[61]

The women's meeting in Aberdeen, Scotland, also wrote to the London Meeting in 1675, "O Dear friends travail with us . . . [that] we may not fail through discouragement, . . . [we have] never any occasion to repent our turning our backs upon the fleshpots of Egypt." Likewise the Women's Monthly Meeting in Settle, Yorkshire, wrote to the London Yearly Meeting in 1680, "we have cause to bless the Lord which hath called us weak ones into a spiritual exercise . . . and we find it our duty in our several meetings to exhort one another to be faithful and to be

59. For example, the Nottingham Women's Meeting thanked them for receipt of seventeen pounds to distribute (Sarah Watson and Elizabeth Smith to Ann Whitehead in London, December 1677, London Women's Box Meeting Manuscripts 36a). On Penn, see Edwards, "Women Friends of London," 9.

60. "from the Women Friends in London to the Women Friends in the Country, also elsewhere, about the service of a Women's Meeting," 1674, quoted in Mabel R. Brailsford, *Quaker Women, 1650–1690* (London: Duckworth and Co., 1915), 285.

61. SM transcpt. (V, 33), quoted in Brailsford, *Quaker Women*, 284.

steadfast."[62] Thus, the London meetings stood at the center of an invisible web, made tangible by exchanges of money, epistles, and gifts (like the two hogsheads of tobacco sent to the women of London by the women of Maryland in 1678), by which women from the tiniest rural communities in Lancashire or Yorkshire might feel themselves linked to women in meetings as remote as Ireland, Barbados, and Virginia.[63]

The women's quarterly meetings throughout England were largely concerned with the distribution of funds and the collection of written testimonies affirming the refusal to pay tithes; in the words of the Lancashire Quarterly Meeting, "so . . . everyone may give in a true account, how it is with them; and how they feel the testimony of the Lord settled in their hearts, which is able to abide the suffering, and to resist the temptation."[64] In cases where the husband was an unbeliever, the wife was expected to testify against his wishes. Thus, in 1678 the Lancashire Quarterly Meeting remonstrated with Mary Proctor, who wrote from the Rossendale Meeting that her unbelieving husband made a bargain with an official to pay tithes, which she opposed. (She acknowledged the meeting's advice but said she could not withstand the bargain of her husband, "yet hath let her mind, so much into the Earth, and weakness is so far come over her, being under the power of the Enemy to mankind.")[65] Two years later the Gisbrough (Yorkshire) Monthly Meeting received this testimony from a Friend: "I Jane Carhal do put in my testimony with the rest of my sisters that I never did pay no tithe neither to priest nor to any thing belonging to their worship or the serpent's followers but in obedience to the Lord hath borne my testimony against it, and shall through god's assistance as long as I remain in this

62. Epistle from the Women's Meeting Aberdeen to London, April 15, 1675 (signed by Lilias Skein among others), Portfolio Manuscripts 2/34. Yorkshire Women's Quarterly Meeting Book, 1678–1745, Epistle from Settle Monthly Meeting to Yearly Meeting, October 12, 1680, fol. 35, Friends Historical Library, Swarthmore College, Swarthmore, Pa.

63. QAC, 314.

64. Lancashire Women's Quarterly Meeting Minute Book, 1675–1777, June 22, 1676, September 27, 1677 (no fol. numbers), Preston Public Record Office. Quarterly meetings did not always meet four times a year; often they met three times; in some years they did not meet at all. The Yorkshire Women's Quarterly Meeting was held irregularly during the final quarter of the century; they were often referred to as yearly meetings (Thistlethwaite, *Yorkshire*, 23, 24). Thistlethwaite believes the meetings started in 1677. On tithe testimonies, see Beatrice Carre, "Early Quaker Women in Lancaster and Lancashire," in *Early Lancaster Friends*, ed. Michael Mullet, Centre for North-West Regional Studies, University of Lancaster, Occasional Paper no. 5 (Leeds: W. S. Maney and Son, 1978), 44–45. Women's monthly and quarterly meetings did not exist in all counties.

65. Lancashire Women's Quarterly Meeting Minute Book, 1675–1777, September 18, 1678, July 2, 1679.

life."[66] In 1708 Mary Tarbuck submitted a paper to the Lancashire Meeting, stating that her neighbor and cousin borrowed fifteen pence, which she paid as tithes on her account without her knowledge, "and I can never account her or any other my friend, who pay any such thing for me."[67]

The monthly and quarterly meetings not only stiffened the spines of Friends who were persecuted for violating civil procedures; as overseers of marriage, education, and charity, Quaker women sought to defend themselves and their families against the more insidious danger of assimilation to the loose morality and customs of Restoration society. In the process they adopted a siege mentality, an obsession with the imagined scrutiny of the hostile and decadent outside world and with the need to affirm and display an unfaltering moral superiority. In Lancashire, where persecution was unusually severe, the women's meetings were particularly aggressive in monitoring the individual's behavior and competence. In 1671 the monthly meeting received the testimony of Persilla Pye, who had committed fornication, "not minding the measure or manifestation of God in my own heart . . . [I] have been advised by my father whom also I have been very disobedient and stubborn unto, and so let out my mind."[68] In 1675 the same meeting chastised Mabel Brittaine, midwife, accused of killing babies by incompetence; she was not allowed to practice without the supervision of another midwife.[69] In 1678 the quarterly meeting warned Isaac Mosse to instruct his daughter to condemn her marriage by a priest (she was disowned three months later). The meeting also received a paper of Mary Rothell, confessing to "wickedness" with her master, whom she later married. "And it's our desire, that she may truly feel God's judgment heavy upon her, for this great wickedness."[70] The following year they rejected a paper of self-condemnation by Isabel Bikerstaff, who "hath run into the world, for a

66. Yorkshire Women's Quarterly Meeting Minute Book, 1678–1745, September 25 and 26, 1745, I/36: Testimony from Gisbrough Monthly Meeting July 4, 1680.

67. Testimony of Mary Tarbuck, November 15, 1708, Lancaster Monthly Meeting Papers on Discipline and Tithe Testimony, 1671–1803, FRL 2BXV, Preston Public Record Office, Lancashire.

68. Testimony of Persilla Pye, September 19, 1671, Lancaster Monthly Meeting Papers on Discipline and Tithe testimony 1671–1803, FRL 2 BXV.

69. Ross, *Margaret Fell*, 292.

70. Lancashire Women's Quarterly Meeting Minute Book, 1675–1777, June 18, 1678, September 18, 1678, no fol. numbers, Preston Public Record Office, Lancashire. And see Michael Mullett, "'The Assembly of the People of God': The Social Organisation of Lancashire Friends," in *Early Lancaster Friends*, ed. Michael Mullett, 15–16.

husband . . . [because it was not] written from the plainness of her heart, nor from a true sense of that dark spirit, that led her to this wicked action."[71] In 1689 the quarterly meeting at Lancaster issued a testimony of denial against Phoebe Baines:

> Whereas Phoebe Baines . . . widow hath for several years made profession of the truth and now through the enticements of the enemy of her soul . . . she hath committed adultery . . . with a neighbor and servant in her house, And is thereby conceived with child, some neighbors that were Friends having labored with her and admonished her several times to put the said servant man from her house before she run into this wicked action, yet she persisting in this her wicked ungodly practice . . . to the great grief of those who fear the Lord . . . we who are called Quakers do deny the said Phoebe Baines to be one of us.[72]

Lancaster Friends also instituted the practice of home visits to monitor the behavior of family members. If parents had failed to train their children properly, the children were removed from the house and placed in service and the parents instructed to take in other servants who were Friends.[73]

Local meetings also gave economic assistance to impoverished women Friends, not all of whom were gracious in accepting the discipline that accompanied the material gifts. Jane Woodell received cloth for a petticoat, which was to be returned to the meeting if she died before she wore it out. (She did, and the garment went to Jane Fisher; again, to be returned to the meeting if she did not live to wear it out.)[74] The peddlar Jane Coulton, who sold manure, baked goods, and stockings to the Fell family, received an iron pot from the Swarthmore Meeting, which also apprenticed Colton's twelve-year-old daughter Isabel in a Quaker household, "less she mix with the world." The girl soon returned to her mother "in a stubborn unservantlike state . . . notwithstanding Friends' trouble and care touching her at our last meeting"; the mother also showed "an ungrateful spirit" but later confessed her

71. Lancashire Women's Quarterly Meeting Minute Book, 1675–1777, July 2, 1679.
72. Ibid. October 3, 1689.
73. Mullett, "'The Assembly of the People of God,'" 17. The meeting at Leeds (Yorkshire) also conducted family visits about every two years (Jean Mortimer and Russell Mortimer, eds., *Leeds Friends' Minute Book, 1692 to 1712*, Yorkshire Archaeological Society, Record Series 139, 1977 and 1978 [Leeds: Yorkshire Archaeological Society, 1980], xxxvi).
74. Ross, *Margaret Fell*, 292–94.

bad behavior.[75] Ann Birkett "let up a cross peevish spirit of prejudice in her against Friends without a cause." The meeting still awarded her small sums from the women's stock and paid her house rent, exhorting her "to cast out that cross wicked spirit (which hurts herself) and come to that, in which we can distribute to her necessity in love." (The following month she was reported "rather more tender and sensible of Friends' love.") Margaret Fell's biographer finds a consistent pattern of charity here, consisting of small gifts to poor women over an extended period of time; she contrasts this with the patterns of men like Daniel Fleming and William Penn, who were generous but sporadic in their gifts, and to the Catholic gentlewoman Anne, Countess of Pembroke, whose gifts were likewise generous but indiscriminate.[76]

If the Lancashire meetings were heavy-handed in inculcating virtue, they also displayed considerable sensitivity to the needs and limitations of individual Friends. The quarterly meeting noted in 1677 that some women were suffering for refusing to pay tithes but were reluctant to submit written testimonies; they were requested to come to the meeting, "and friends will endeavor . . . to give them satisfaction, in anything that may seem to obstruct, or be in their minds against it."[77] In 1679 the meeting noted that the women of Chipping Meeting had not been attending their monthly meeting, concluding that it was because the women were impoverished "and not well fitted to travel so far . . . and so they are kept ignorant of truth's concerns, and their own service." They decided to rotate the meeting to make attendance easier, "that they have a helping hand held out to them: . . . that [the strong] perform their duty, and do not desire to eat their Morsel alone: And this edifies the body, and all is kept in good order."[78]

Thus the Yorkshire and Lancashire meetings were instrumental, on all levels, in bolstering northern women's sense of personal and collective identity both as neighbors and as moral crusaders. In 1678 Joan Killam, whose sister had been a prophet during the 1650s, wrote to the general yearly meeting at York, "which gathered us in the beginning which knit

75. Bonnelyn Young Kunze, "The Family, Social, and Religious Life of Margaret Fell," Ph.D diss., University of Rochester, 1986, 125, 128, 154. The arrangement failed, and Isabel returned home "in a stubborn state."

76. Ibid., 150.

77. Women's Quarterly Meeting Lancashire, Lancaster, September 27, 1677 (no folio numbers). Michael Mullett discusses the "tension in Friends' thought between censure and solicitude" ("'The Assembly of the People of God," 15).

78. Lancashire Women's Quarterly Meeting Minute Book, 1675–1777, September 19, 1679.

our hearts to god and one toward another to feel the good of one another."[79] Isabel Yeamans and Mary Waite responded on behalf of the yearly meeting:

> We understand that although there was a women's meeting set up about Balby yet it is now lost which we are concerned for that the evil spirit, hath so far prevailed as to disunite the meeting, but our desire . . . is that for as much as thou art sensible with us of the service thereof that thou endeavor with all diligence to be helpful in setting up the meeting again . . . and to look over and see where things are wrong and amiss amongst you . . . and though you be but few in number and may meet with great opposition you being found waiting upon the lord in the patience of the lamb's spirit you shall know an overcoming and a breaking down of that spirit that hath set it self against you.[80]

In 1693, the prophet Judith Boulbie again encouraged the women of Yorkshire to hold firm against outward ridicule:

> And [you] . . . scoffers [who say] those silly Quakers . . . setting up men and women's meeting their prescribing laws and statutes . . . and decrees to what purpose is women's meetings the men can do the business the women must be subject to their husbands, but . . . there is a little remnant which is one with our brethren and is entered into the work and service and feels that heavenly reward in their bosoms which all that world . . . can[not] . . . take it from us. Therefore my dear sisters let nothing discompose your minds . . . but go on in that name and power of the Lord and all come to Deborah's spirit for though she was but a woman she served the Lord . . . the chaff must be blown away by the whirlwind of God's destruction.[81]

Typical of local women's meetings in the southern counties was that of the Vale of the White Horse, in Oxfordshire. The meeting was sustained in large part by the work of two sisters. Jane Sansom, the treasurer, also ran her husband's drapery business during his absences in prison or

79. Joan Killam, to the general yearly meeting in York, June 12, 1678, Yorkshire Women's Quarterly Meeting Book, 1678–1745, fol. 15.

80. Isabel Yeamans, Mary Waite, etc., Yearly Women's Meeting, to Joan Killam, June 13, 1678, Yorkshire Women's Quarterly Meeting Book, 1675–1777, fol. 16. Compare the women's letter with this entry by the men's meeting of Upperside (Buckinghamshire), July 7, 1675: "The Meeting being informed that friends of Chesham are of late grown more negligent in Meeting together, so as that that Meeting is in danger to be lost; It is ordered that John Raunce and Nicholas Noy do shortly visit them and upon inquiry into the business, admonish and advise them as need shall require" (Snell, ed., *The Minute Book of the Society of Friends for the Upperside of Buckinghamsire*, 36).

81. Judith Boulbie to Women's Monthly Meeting and Quarterly Meeting, York, May 22, 1693, Yorkshire Women's Quarterly Meeting Book, 1678–1745, fols. 87, 89.

the ministry and brought up their several children. Joan Vokins, an itinerant minister, wife, and mother, once turned back from a journey to America to assist the meeting in its struggle against the Separatist Thomas Curtis. "Though *Amalek* lay in wait by the way, and the opposite spirit did strongly strive, yet our good shepherd did visit his handmaids, and . . . filled us with his overcoming power, when the mothers in Israel were so dismayed, as we were likely to have lost our Women's Meeting."[82]

Unlike the Lancashire women described above, these southern Friends were rarely engaged in reproving sexual misconduct.[83] Chiefly, they approved marriages and assisted impoverished Friends, many of them widows with young children. The minute book is replete with entries like these: "Agreed that Ann Lawrence shall go to Spashalt and speak with the woman that tended Joan Thrupp lately deceased: and to give something to the said nurse to gratify for her kindness and care"; "Agreed that twenty shillings shall be given to the widow Wightwick for the cherishing [of] her children which are both visited with sickness"; "An account was given concerning the widow White that her ague hath left her and at present all is well"; "Joan Newman did give an account . . . that the widow Wightwick is not in much want at present but the meeting thought fit to send 5 s[hillings] to pay for her children's schooling this quarter that she may have her liberty to go abroad to work the harvest time", "Mention was made of a friend belonging to Oar meeting who hath the use of his limbs taken from him and lies in a very sad weak condition and it is agreed to send him a box of ointment hoping it may do him good the charge deducted out of the stock two shillings"; "Mention was made of the weakness and sickliness of the poor widow Weethers and agreed to send her 5 s[hillings] by Jane Sansom who is desired to lay it out to buy something to comfort and cherish her as she shall think convenient"; "Mention was made of the poverty of the widow Wightwick's children and agreed to send them 5 s[hillings]";

---

82. Joan Vokins, *God's Mighty Power Magnified, as Manifested and Revealed in His Faithful Handmaid, Joan Vokins* (London, 1691), Foreword, and 14, n. 28.
83. An exception was their admonishing of a Friend who received an unmarried mother into her house. (The editors of the Vale of White Horse Monthly Meeting records point out that since Friends eschewed conventional marriage ceremonies, they had to be particularly careful to observe *their* own procedures to avoid any appearance of scandal; The Vale of the White Horse Women's Monthly Meeting Minute-Book, 1676–1730, Foreword, 3 and n. 7.) The meeting at Lewes (Sussex) was also far less concerned with disciplinary questions, dealing mainly with marriages and charity for needy Friends (Quaker Women's Monthly Meeting in Lewes 1677–1709, MSS. vol. 235, Library of the Society of Friends, London).

"Agreed to send the widow Weethers of Farringdon 3 s[hillings] for her pains in sweeping the meeting house and . . . Jane Sansom having received from the widow Waterhouse one s[hilling] gave that also to the said widow Weethers."[84] The meeting also counseled patience to Elizabeth Hickman, who could not handle her "stubborn rebellious son," and paid several visits to Elizabeth Morse and Katherine Koomber, who expressed "much bitterness in both of them one against the other."[85]

Even more illustrative of these women's patience (and doggedness) in dispensing both virtue and charity was their fourteen-year relationship with one Jane Coules: In May 1678 Joan Vokins and another Friend visited the woman for an unknown offence. "With many words [the woman] did endeavor to cover her self and vindicate her clearness from what have been reported of her; but the two Friends . . . have a sense that she is not altogether clear: Wherefore it is agreed that . . . [they] shall visit her again."[86] She was visited three more times, each time promising to reform. Then in March 1679, "Mention was made that scandalous reports of Jane Coules is much spread about of being accused of drunkenness and the like: wherefore . . . she shall be visited, examined, and admonished by Ann Willis, Mary Slade and Joan Vokins or any two of them." The women were then instructed to inform men Friends "how uncapable Jane Coules is (in their judgment) to manage her shopkeeping trade. To the end that upon weighty consideration she may be advised by them and set in some way for a livelihood that she have a capacity to manage." In July she was visited by a delegation of men and women Friends, who could not determine whether her "disordered senses" were the result of illness or alcohol; they exhorted her to good behavior "and so at present left her to the Lord . . . believing he will give a more open discovery of her in his time." In November 1679, two Friends were again appointed to visit her "to see if they can bring her to a sense of her state and if possible to bring her to tenderness." She was again admonished "and left to the witness of God in her own conscience." In January 1681, Jane Coules applied for assistance to visit a physician in order to recover her sight; the matter was shelved. A year later (February 1682) the issue of her poverty was again mentioned, and Friends agreed "it shall be let

84. Vale of the White Horse Women's Monthly Meeting Minute-Book, 1676–1730, November 27, 1677, 4; November 24, 1679, 9; the widow Wightwick later requested funds to emigrate to Pennsylvania (May 22, 1682, 18); October 23, 1682, 20; July 24, 1682, 19; February 24, 1683, 25; June 24, 1686, 33; February 23, 1687, 38; November 29, 1688, 41.

85. Ibid., August 23, 1680, 11; October 24, 1681, 16; November 21, 1681, December 26, 1681, 16.

86. Ibid., May 27, 1678, 5.

alone and passed by." Eleven years later (January 1693), the meeting
agreed to send Jane Coules some money to relieve her poverty.[87]

WOMEN AND MEN, TOGETHER AND APART

Quakers portrayed the men's and women's meetings as complementary
bodies. In practice the meetings did function with varying degrees of
complementarity, more so in Cumberland or Yorkshire than in Surrey
or Sussex. In all cases, however, this mutuality was accompanied by a
(sometimes grudging) acknowledgement of the men's meetings' greater
administrative and moral authority.[88]

In some counties women were protected and encouraged by individual
male advocates. Thus, Margaret Fawcett, reporting on the activities of
the women's meeting in Cumberland, was thankful that John Banks was
assisting them in their proceedings "and hath done all along." When the
women delivered their testimonies against the payment of tithes, "J[ohn]
B[anks] took their testimonies one by one from their own mouth, . . .
which are all ready gathered up and recorded in a book." Fawcett was
disturbed because the ministers took up too much time in the quarterly
meeting and because the book, containing testimonies of 109 women,
was not read out loud (John Banks, their advocate, being away); Fawcett
wanted the book copied and sent throughout the county.[89]

The Vale of the White Horse Women's Meeting, although formed
despite aggressive opposition from local Separatists, also enjoyed excellent relations with the men's meeting. Unlike meetings in Bristol and
elsewhere, it was an autonomous institution, and there were no instances
of engaged couples refusing to submit to the scrutiny of women as well
as men. In Westmoreland, home of the Separatists Wilkinson and Story,

87. Ibid., July 22, 1678, November 25, 1678, 6; January 27, 1678, March 24, 1679,
7; May 26, 1679, 8; November 24, 1679, January 26, 1679, 9; January 24, 1680, 13;
February 20, 1681, 17; January 26, 1692, 51. The Vale of the White Horse Monthly
Meeting Minutes 1673–1722, 31, June 27, 1679, 31, July 25, 1679, 32.

88. In Surrey and Sussex, women's monthly meetings were set up in the 1670s; in
1694 Ambrose Rigge proposed a women's quarterly meeting as in other counties, but the
men's meeting refused to consider it (Thomas W. Marsh, ed., Some Records of the Early
Friends in Surrey and Sussex from the Original Minute-Books and Other Sources (London: S. Harris and Co., 1886).

89. Margaret Fawcett to Margaret Fox, October 5, 1677, Abraham Manuscripts no.
22, Library of the Society of Friends, London. Fawcett was also disturbed about a proposal to record the meeting's disbursements in writing, fearing that needy Friends would
go without rather than receive public charity. John Banks was a noted defender of
women's meetings, arguing, among other things, that women might feel less constrained
in a single-sex environment (Carre, "Early Quaker Women," 43).

women struggled harder for credibility among male Friends, as witnessed by this passage from an epistle from the Kendall Women's Meeting to the London Box Meeting in 1675: "And though our meetings be lightly looked upon and of little esteem among some who should have strengthened us." The women had an epistle from London read at the men's meeting in order to bolster their official status.[90]

In most instances, however, men's and women's meetings worked in tandem, with women delegated to make disciplinary visits to male as well as female Friends. Much of their joint activity consisted in overseeing marriages, a process involving multiple visits of engaged couples to both meetings and the submission of written testimonies of the parents' approval as well as the couple's freedom from previous attachments. In 1685 the Lancashire Women's Meeting opposed Mary Carr's engagement; the men's meeting found her paper of condemnation inadequate and appointed two men to help her compose a better testimony.[91] In 1681 the Bristol (Gloucestershire) men and women together disowned Katherine Henbury and her daughter for conniving in the marriage of the daughter by a priest.[92] Twelve years later the men's meeting requested that the women admonish Mary Hort, "who we fear is inclinable to marry her late husband's brother." That same year they asked the

90. Vale of the White Horse Women's Monthly Meeting Minute-Book, 1676–1730, Introduction. London Women's Box Meeting Manuscripts, fol. 23, Library of the Society of Friends, London. The epistle from Kendall was signed by Ann Camm, formerly the prophet Ann Audland, among others.

91. Lancashire Men's Quarterly Meeting Minute Book, January 7, 1685, fol. 59, Preston Public Record Office, Lancashire. William Grant submitted a paper of contrition to a Lancashire women's meeting, apologizing for his bad conversation: "Dear Margaret [Fox] after the acknowledgement of the great obligation that lyeth upon me to respect thee for thy care and Christian zeal I do acknowledge that I have been so weak in my duty towards god which I have been often sorry for and I pray god help my infirmity and I am glad of your Care" (Dix Manuscripts, G14 I, Library of the Society of Friends, London).

92. Men's meeting minutes, May 13, 1681, in Dix Manuscripts 294, G.7.B. Russell Mortimer, ed., *Minute Book of the Society of Friends in Bristol, 1667–1686*, Bristol Record Society's Publications no. 26 (Gateshead: Northumberland Press, 1971), September 15, 1673, November 10, 1673, XXVI, 78, 80. The meetings dealing with Hanbury began in 1673. The meeting also wanted to know why Katherine herself was living apart from her husband (November 10, 1673, 81). There was some discussion in meetings about proper procedure for Friends who had lived together before marriage. The meeting ruled that they should marry and live together decently but without the ritualized sanction and meeting prescribed for more orderly Friends. The Bristol Women's Meeting minutes have not survived. See also R. S. Mortimer, "Marriage Discipline in Early Friends: A Study in Church Administration Illustrated from Bristol Records," JFHS 48, no. 4 (Autumn 1957): 175–95. On several occasions women were requested to keep a register of all births (Mortimer, ed., *Minute Book of Friends in Bristol*, XXVI, October 21, 1669, 24, May 1, 1671, 46, May 15, 1671, 47, March 3, 1672, 71). On October 31, 1670, the men's meeting refused to approve Joel Gibson's marriage until the women's meeting was satisfied (Ibid., 34).

338   Visionary Order

women's meeting to deal with a woman, reputed to be a harlot, who had
taken shelter in Friends' public meetings, "to quit us of the reproach her
frequenting our meeting may cause."[93] The Upperside (Buckinghamshire) Meeting also asked women Friends to visit wayward individuals,
such as Mary Mitchell, married by a priest, or Elizabeth Crouch, who
was accused of behaving "immodestly" with her father.[94] The men also
supported the women's meeting's jurisdiction over marriage against
critics, though with varying degrees of resolution. In one case an engaged
couple had refused to make the requisite two appearances before the
women's meeting, and the man had insulted a woman Friend; the men's
meeting refused to condone their marriage until they had given satisfaction to the women's meeting.[95] In another case a couple refused
altogether to visit the women's meeting, the man stating that women
must not speak in the church and opposing the women's meeting as a
separate institution. "This was manifested to be insincere as being utterly
inconsistent with his allegation . . . against women's speaking in the
Church: for to what end should women be with the men in meetings for
business, where matters are to be examined and spoken to, if they are
not permitted to speak there, but must be silent, as he ignorantly inti-
mates." After this spirited defense, the men's meeting sidestepped the
issue altogether, stating that their objection to the man was not that he
refused to visit the women's meeting but that his refusal was not in good
conscience:

> there can be no just cause for a conscientious scruple in this case, yet so tender
> a regard is had to conscience, that where any through weakness, shortsight-
> edness or misinformation, have made it really matter of conscience not to go
> to the women's meetings, in such cases this Meeting always hath been, and
> still is ready to exercise a condescension.[96]

As every women's meeting existed in conjunction with the local (or
preparative) men's meeting, and subordinate to the monthly, quarterly,
and yearly meetings above it, so the persona of the new mother in Israel
was actively shaped by male influence. The records of men's meetings,

93. Ibid. 68–69, 72.
94. Snell, ed., *Minute Book of Friends of Buckinghamshire*, April 4, 1677, 49, 53;
December 5, 1677, 56–58. Mary Mitchell prevaricated; Elizabeth repented, stating that
she had lodged with her aged and ill father out of simple affection. She was also reported
to have been married by a priest (December 4, 1678, 65).
95. Ibid., May 26, 1680, 83.
96. Ibid., April 3, 1682, 107. In a third case, where the man had objected to a
separate women's meeting, the men's meeting responded that he was not a true Friend
"but one whose mind was roving and at liberty," and he was advised to delay his marriage
until he should obey the Truth (ibid., July 3, 1682, 108–9).

and of the larger meetings in which men and women worked (and sometimes sat) together, show us an image of the goodwife similar to but less vibrant and certainly less visionary than that conveyed by meetings where women sat apart. In general, the discipline imposed by the men's meetings was stricter for both women and men than that imposed by women's meetings.[97] Women were also censured for a narrower range of misdeeds than men. Male delinquency or "disorderly walking" consisted of drunkenness, fornication, physical violence, indebtedness and gambling, or improper marriage (i.e., marriage to a non-Friend or marriage by a priest), while women were overwhelmingly cited for only two kinds of crimes: sexual misdeeds (fornication or improper marriage) and bad language and deportment, the archetypal sins of the scolding, unfaithful wife.[98]

These were some of the women cited by London meetings from 1668 to 1687: Susan Atkins was "Ranter-like," seducing another woman's husband "and did say it was a revelation from the Lord . . . she still persists in the matter and will not condemn it." Catherine Cleaton was denied for her "evil conversation and bad doings." Mary Bett apologized for her "forward and hasty" spirit, but the meeting was not satisfied, and she was instructed to remain absent "till she appear to be more serious and savory." Margaret Waters was visited by two men "about her forward speaking in friends' meetings out of that spirit that ministers life . . . therefore we . . . would have her to be silent." Martha Brickhill was accused of speaking scandalous words against Will Spouter's wife; she denied it. Ann Wyett's life and conversation were approved but she was criticized for forwardness in contracting a marriage before asking her father's consent.[99]

97. In Leeds (Yorkshire), few initiatives in disciplinary matters came from women Friends (Mortimer and Mortimer, eds., *Leeds Friends' Minute Book, 1692 to 1712*, xxxvii).
98. I have examined the Reading (Berkshire), Somerset, Herefordshire, Bristol (Gloucestershire), Vale of the White Horse (Oxfordshire), and Leeds (Yorkshire) monthly and/or quarterly minutes. See also Thistlethwaite, *Yorkshire Quarterly Meeting*, 161–62, and Carre, "Early Quaker Women," 50–51. The Vale of the White Horse Meeting condemned one man for speaking with "an unbridled tongue in a rash heady willfull spirit" (The Vale of the White Horse Women's Monthly Meeting Minute-Book, 1676–1730, January 26, 1681, 50).
99. The First Book of the Monthly Meeting of the People Call'd Quakers, at Horsly-down (Later Southwark), London, 1666, I, no folio numbers, Library of the Society of Friends, London: October 7, 1668, November 4, 1668, November 3, 1670, December 22, 1675. A Book for the Business of the Monthly Meeting at the Peel in the County of Middlesex, vol. 1, 1668–1683/4, Library of the Society of Friends, London: July 30, 1673, and April 29, 1674. The First Book of the Monthly Meeting at Horslydown, I, February 18, 1687.

In Bristol in 1687, several men were appointed to keep Katherine Welch from causing disturbances in public meetings, while in 1694 they refused to countenance the marriage of Mary Forrest because of her mother's "scandalous conversation."[100] In 1685 the Upperside Men's and Women's Meetings closed ranks against Susanna Aldridge, who had publicly attacked Friends. The men described her as confident, obstinate, and resolute in her position and published a testimony of denial: "And we do solemnly declare . . . that we bear not this testimony against the said Susanna Aldridge out of any personal ill-will, or prejudice against her as a woman; but . . . that all concerned herein may know, that we have no fellowship . . . with her unfruitful works of darkness." The women published their own tract alleging that Susanna Aldridge was insane.[101]

In Leeds (Yorkshire) in 1696, Margaret Lapage defended her daughter's improper marriage, "appearing in the meeting very boistrous"; the next year she behaved again "in a boistrous manner . . . and when being dealt with by Friends did . . . give such abusive language as did fully demonstrate the spirit she was of." In 1702, Elizabeth Merry "fell into extravagant reflections and uncomely speeches, wholly refusing the advice of this Meeting." Mary Harrison, a schoolteacher, was also denied for refusing to behave, "which if she had done, it would have stayed her uneasy mind, and bridled her unruly tongue, and quelled her fury, and passion (which frequently got over her)." When the meeting reproached her, "she rather grew harder, and was more at a distance from us, and made excuses and lies her refuge."[102]

In Somerset in 1669, the Ilchester Monthly Meeting cited the widow Joan Gundry, who "refuseth to perform her husband's will and will not refer the matters in difference to the judgment of Friends." The same meeting reproved Mary Webber for "hard speeches against friends and their meetings." In 1670 another single woman, Elizabeth Douch, was admonished "to beware of that spirit that sows discord amongst friends, and of a self exalting spirit . . . touching her service at Taunton." In 1684

100. Mortimer, ed., *Minute Book of Friends in Bristol*, Monthly Meeting, November 7, 1687, May 13–14, 1694, XXX, 13, 83.

101. Snell, ed., *Minute Book of Friends of Buckinghamshire*, March 2, 1685, 146; May 4, 1685, 150; June 1, 1685, 153; July 6, 1685, August 3, 1685, 154–56. The tract was *The Spirit That Works Abomination and its Abominable Work Discovered*, by Mary Ellwood and Margery Clipsham (London, 1685).

102. Mortimer and Mortimer, eds., *Leeds Friends' Minute Book, 1692 to 1712*, xxxv, 20, 30, 122–23. Elizabeth Merry's husband Jonathan was also censured for drunkenness and having left his wife.

the meeting disowned Hester Cousins. A widow, she had been advised
not to marry Edward Cousins, "considering that he was not a fit husband
for her nor she a fit wife for him, in regard of his family of children, she
being not of so mild, and gentle a spirit as was necessary for the well
discharging of the duty of such a place . . . or [to] be a meet helper to
her said husband." She was obdurate, further refusing to settle a portion
of her late husband's estate on her daughter "and followed the evil
counsel of her own heart." In 1685 the meeting issued a testimony
against Isaac Bryan and his wife. Isaac had abandoned her and all their
children but one, alleging that she had wasted his estate during his
absence. The meeting disagreed, finding that she was in fact industrious,
discreet, and a good parent "but do also find that she hath too much
given up her self to a contentious spirit, and many times given her
husband great provocation, not behaving her self as a wife ought to do
towards him."[103]

None of these criticisms was intended to stifle women's capacity for
travel or for service in the ministry; in Bristol, where the women's
meeting had very limited authority, the widow Elizabeth Walker felt free
to ask the men's meeting to keep an eye on her children while she traveled
with her oldest son to Barbados.[104] Nor was the men's discipline intended to undermine women's independent economic activities. Indeed,
it was essential to men that women be competent in business and have
sufficient moral authority to sustain family life, if only to enable husbands to uphold *their* own testimony by paying fines and going to prison
with a clear conscience. Thus, Anthony Tompkins submitted a paper to
the Horslydown (London) Monthly Meeting in 1668 condemning his
own fear of persecution: "When Friends was taken to prison, the Enemy
began subtly with me, laying before me the weak capacity of my wife,
who could not manage the concerns I had in the world . . . the Enemy

103. Stephen C. Morland, ed., *The Somersetshire Quarterly Meeting of the Society of Friends, 1668–1699* (Old Woking, Surrey: Somerset Record Society, 1978), 83; Webber was reproved again in 1673 (ibid., 104). (Joan Gundry's husband died in 1668; the matter may have referred to the handling of his estate.) Ibid., 87, 95; 162. (Gundry was later disowned; ibid., 167.)

104. Mortimer, ed., *Minute Book of Friends in Bristol*, XXVI, July 20, 1674, 87–88, 219. (Walker settled in Barbados.) In Bristol, the men's meeting wanted to know why the women had published their own monthly meeting (the preparatory meeting already existed). Margaret Heale responded that she herself had done it after reading a letter from George Fox. The men responded that they had not intended that letter to be read by the women. They advised the women not to hold a monthly meeting until they had unity among themselves and with the men. This advice was delivered to Isabel Yeamans and other women (ibid., November 27, 1671, December 11, 1671, 54, 55).

signified to me that the infidels took care of their families . . . [and] if I took up the cross . . . I should be worse than them."[105]

It was therefore in men's own moral interest, as well as a part of their communal ideology, to scrutinize the women's financial records and advise them on business matters. In 1676 the Southwark (London) Meeting resolved a dispute between a husband and wife, hoping that "they can continue in two different trades and give each other full understanding of all things relating to it and help and assist each other."[106] In 1677 the Upperside Meeting gave Mary Tod money to set up as a weaver of silk laces after she had given up making bone lace, in accordance with Friends' testimony against finery.[107] In 1679 the Vale of the White Horse Monthly Meeting reported that the widow Wightwick "did not appear . . . willing to be ruled nor to receive counsel from Friends" as to the ordering of her husband's affairs. They would admonish her again; "if she refuse to hear, friends will be clear: and she left without excuse." A month later they accused her of dealing "very doubly," promising to follow their advice and going her own way.[108] In 1689 the Bristol Men's Meeting lent Elizabeth Wheaton money, "she being industrious and in a hopeful way to improve the same for her livelihood."[109]

The need for the practical and moral contribution of women Friends was surely one reason that men's meetings repeatedly urged the establishment of additional women's meetings as time went on. In Bristol, the men's meeting had originally opposed the formation of a women's monthly meeting even though George Fox had advised it. Yet in 1681 the men's meeting announced that all care of the poor would be handled by the preparatory women's meeting from its own funds, with additional money to be contributed by the men's meeting when needed.[110] In 1684 the monthly meeting stated that too few women were attending the women's meeting to handle the charge of poor relief; the men's meeting would give them five pounds and advise them to urge greater attendance

105. The First Book of the Monthly Meeting at Horslydown, Letter of condemnation, Anthony Tompkins, December 30, 1668.

106. The Friends were Peter and Alice Cornelius. The First Book of the Monthly Meeting at Horslydown, June 14, 1676, fol. 111.

107. Snell, ed., *Minute Book of Friends of Buckinghamshire*, April 4, 1677, 52.

108. Vale of the White Horse Monthly Meeting Minutes, 1673–1722, October 31, 1679, 33, November 28, 1679, 34. In 1684 the same group of women helped the local men's meeting with its own expenses (The Vale of the White Horse Women's Monthly Meeting Minute-Book, 1676–1730, Foreword, and November 24, 1684, 28).

109. Mortimer, ed., *Minute Book of Friends in Bristol*, XXX, Introduction, xxvii.

110. Ibid., April 18, 1681, XXVI, 156. This policy was still in effect during the 1690s (ibid., XXX, Introduction, xxvii).

on women and greater charitable contributions.[111] In 1693 they desired "that the Friends of our Women's Meeting be stirred up to assist us in reproving and preventing disorders amongst friends especially in their own sex," and by 1698 women were active participants in investigations for clearness in marriage, being advised to appoint a woman Friend "as the center of their intelligence to certify what they discover to the next Men's Meeting."[112]

Thus, we observe Quaker men encouraging women's material and moral independence while simultaneously attempting to promote an image of the ideal matron as modest, selfless, and obedient, a task that must have seemed all the more necessary (and all the more difficult) since so many leading Quaker women were widows effectively beholden to no one. In 1697, the Bristol Men's Meeting admonished Rebecca Russell for leaving her husband and children in Dublin without Friends' consent, "which this meeting do hold disorderly and not to be encouraged or countenanced; wherefore . . . tis her place and duty to return to her husband and children, and with diligence use her endeavors honestly to provide for them, teaching them also to work and provide for themselves."[113]

WAS THE WOMEN'S MEETING GOOD FOR WOMEN?

We shall not forget our times and hours to wait for
the seasons of the Lord, for they are so sweet to the
thirsty soul that it cannot be satisfied without them,
and therefore many times thinks it long ere the
meeting day come, that it might be replenished.

> *Joan Vokins to the Vale of the*
> *White Horse Monthly Meeting*

Should we interpret Quaker women's experience as Christopher Hill interpreted the decline of the radical Civil War sects? Did the meeting

111. Ibid., July 7, 1684, XXVI, 179–80.
112. Ibid., March 6, 1693, XXX, 68–69; Introduction, xviii. On three occasions the Somerset Quarterly Meeting also worried about the neglect of women's monthly meetings (Morland, ed., *The Somersetshire Quarterly Meeting*, December 19, 1678, 124; December 23, 1686, 190; December 24, 1691, 218). In 1703 the Leeds Men's Meeting encouraged the women to keep their own quarterly meetings regularly and ordered that a book be purchased for them to record charitable transactions (Mortimer and Mortimer, eds., *Leeds Friends' Minute Book, 1692 to 1712*, xxxvii, 90).
113. Mortimer, ed., *Minute Book of Friends in Bristol*, May 24, 1697, XXX, 118–19.

system mark the defeat of Friends' struggle for human perfectability and spiritual equality? There is no question that the new theology and meeting system had ambiguous results for both women and men. Both gained a public identity in which traditional gender roles were acknowledged and enhanced as never before; both lost the opportunity to be writers and actors in a universe where gender itself, and every other limiting social attribute, was happily laid aside.

In pleading for support for the women's meeting among male Friends, women never failed to emphasize the essential unity of the two sexes. Friends of the London Box Meeting wrote that they were chosen "distinct, as we may say, in some sense, yet in perfect unity with our brethren . . . only distinct as to our places, and in those particular things which most properly appertains unto us as women, still eying our Universal head, in whom Male and Female are one, where no division can be admitted of."[114]

Yet if the ethos of men's and women's meetings was one of unity, of a community without secrets or divisions, the atmosphere inside the women's meeting was surely rather special. For within its purview, groups of women worshiped, traveled, published testimonies and epistles, delivered judgments on the morals of both men and women, and shaped the education of the next generation, and they did all of this collectively and in an explicitly female capacity. In terms of their purely social functions, the meeting system and other, non-Quaker institutions differed merely in degree, for the distribution of charity, disciplining of delinquent workers and family members, and supervision of marriages and of the activities of ministers were all to be found in the wider neighborhood, church, and municipality. In establishing a formal, collective identity for women as women, however, the meeting system was unique within Protestantism.[115]

Within the shelter and authority of their meetings, women not only suffered for tithes and dispensed counseling and charity on behalf of themselves and their men; they also defended the interests of individual women *against* men. In a tract called *The Sad Effects of Cruelty De-*

---

114. London Women's Box Meeting Manuscripts fol. 17, undated, unsigned.
115. Michael Mullett discusses Quaker institutions and practices in light of municipal functions ("'The Assembly of the People of God,'" 12–21). Susan Amussen discusses the collective character of family and neighborhood life during the period ("Running the Country, Running the Household, and Running Amok: Violence, Force, and Power in Early Modern England," paper presented at the Davis Center, Princeton University, 1989).

tected, several women of the Westminster (London) Meeting defended themselves against a man's accusations that his wife had been driven mad by attending Friends' meetings. They, in turn, blamed the husband for abusing his wife,

> sometimes beating her with a cudgel or cane, . . . that no good man would so beat his dog, . . . dragging her forth (from our meetings) and driving her home, as butchers do their beasts. . . . He would so beat her with his fist, that her eyes and face would be so swelled and black and blue, that it was often visible to the neighborhood; . . . when he hath come home in drink, he hath pulled her out of the bed, in her shift, and so beaten her . . . for above a year, hath he kept her . . . a close prisoner, locked up in one room in his house. . . . (Let him deny these things if he can, before his neighbors, who know his behavior towards his wife.)[116]

The authors closed by admonishing all upstanding men to "take warning hereby, not to be cruel to their wives . . . for differences in judgment or opinion."[117] At a Vale of the White Horse Monthly Meeting, Friends were appointed to assist Mary Thatcher of Uffington, who was "much cast down in her mind partly by reason of necessity of outward things occasioned by her husband's idleness and bad carriage towards her." (She kindly received their love "but was not free to receive any relief.") Some years later, "mention was made of Katherine Koomber's weakness in letting her unkind son have her house and goods and she her self ready to want bread so Mary Reynolds was [ap]pointed to speak to her and advise her to take her goods and sell them rather than to suffer so much want."[118] While assuring readers of the limited ambitions of the women's meeting, Mary Penington also defended Quaker women's rights to a portion of their husbands' property, to be dispersed at their discretion for the larger family of Friends.[119]

Yet the meeting also demanded the sacrifice of other female networks. Women were encouraged in the experience of communal worship but not that of communal festivity or ritual. An epistle from the women's meet-

116. *The Sad Effects of Cruelty Detected; Being an Impartial Account of the Poor Woman near Temple-Barr* . . . (1675), 4–5.
117. Ibid., 7.
118. The Vale of the White Horse Women's Monthly Meeting Minute-Book, 1676–1730, monthly meeting at Apleton, June 21, 1680, 10; July 26, 1680, 11; April 30, 1696, 57.
119. P[enington], "ffor those Women Friends," fol. 160. On rituals of childbirth, see Adrian Wilson, "The Ceremony of Childbirth and Its Interpretation," in *Women as Mothers in Pre-Industrial England: Essays in Memory of Dorothy McLaren* (London and New York: Routledge, 1990), 68–107.

ing at York to "all Friends and sisters" inveighed against the collective
rituals and feasting associated with childbirth:

> Put your hands to the Lord's plow, make his business your business . . . and
> none look back . . . after the profits, pleasures, or preferments of this world,
> for thither the Enemy . . . is drawing the minds of many as Lot's wife back
> again. . . . We do . . . entreat all childbearing women to wait upon God for
> his wisdom to order you in the time of your lying in, that out of all the needless
> customs and feasting in the world you may be gathered . . . be fed in the fresh
> and green pastures where your bread will be sure and your water never fail,
> yea and lie down in the fold of rest where none can make afraid.[120]

In 1677 the midwives of Barbados, writing to the women of Dublin,
Ireland, and elsewhere, affirmed their resolution to hold a worship
meeting immediately after a birth to testify "against the world and their
ways, who as soon as the woman is delivered, do run into eating and
drinking and foolish talking and jesting . . . instead of returning praise
to God." They also resolved not to ask non-Quaker women for help in
difficult deliveries.[121] In 1694 the monthly meeting of Hardshaw chastised a Friend for bringing "provision or banqueting stuff" to a woman
in childbed; the woman had as yet refused to confess her weakness.[122]

The collective authority of women was also linked to the advocacy of
traditional social values. Thus, the York Women's Meeting also reminded mothers that the family was not an egalitarian community: "You
that are mothers of children, and rulers of families, be good examples
to your children and servants in all things . . . for if children rule over
parents, it is not comely . . . and will not tend to truth's honor, their good,
nor parents' comfort."[123] In 1672 the London Six Weeks Meeting (consisting of women and men) issued a statement that no maidservant may
leave her position to live by her own work without the monthly meeting's consent.[124] In 1693 the women's monthly meeting at Hardshaw

120. "From Women's Meeting at York June 23 and 24, 1680 to all Friends and
Sisters," Portfolio Manuscripts 8/168.
121. "At a Meeting of the Midwives in Barbadoes, February 11, 1677," reprinted in
JFHS 37 (1940): 22–24. The women also resolved to help slave women without charge
and to refuse to wrap the child in lace-trimmed linen.
122. Minutes of the Women's Monthly Meeting of Hardshaw 1693–1694, September 18, 1694, Portfolio Manuscripts 31/32.
123. Catherine Whitton et al., "A Testimony for the Lord and his Truth: Given forth
by the Women Friends at their Yearly-Meeting at York," 1688, London Women's Box
Meeting Manuscripts (printed and inserted in MSS.), 1688. "From our Women's yearly
Meetng held at York the 6th and 7th dayes of the 5th Month 1698," ibid. (printed), 2–3.
124. London and Middlesex Six Weeks Meeting, 4 vols., MSS. 11 a 2, Library of the
Society of Friends, London. For an account of the meeting's activities, see Beck and Ball,
London Friends' Meetings, 91–131. The original meeting included, among others, Rebec-
kah Travers, Ann Whitehead, Mary Elson, Mary Forster, and Mary Woolley.

reported that Mary Gore's daughter had refused to take service with James Laithwaite as instructed. She was ordered to return to her place, "and if she refuse to take friends' advice in the matter, her mother is not to entertain her, but to turn her out and let her fend for herself."[125]

As children, servants, and apprentices were to remain fixed in their places, so places at the top of the meeting hierarchy were reserved for socially and economically prominent women Friends. The many widows whose names appear in meeting records were invariably women of property. In Lancashire, some women engaged in retail trade or shop-keeping or worked as milleners, but most were farmers, some with quite large estates; in Lancaster itself, some Quaker widows were actually named freemen of the borough. The meeting records also reveal that Lancashire women had better skills in grammar and handwriting than their men.[126]

Related to this social stratification was the linkage between female activism and feminine self-effacement; indeed, the stress laid on women's modesty in clothing and deportment was in direct proportion to their enlarged sphere of public activity as wives and mothers. Take, for example, the following epistle, which begins with an assertive, even aggressive attack on men who oppose women's meetings:

> These men should be convinced, that they themselves are out of the Authority in the Usurpation, . . . and their opposing of . . . mothers that be God's servants is but an effect thereof. . . . Read the authority that was in Sarah when she spake to Abraham the word of God, . . . what do you think of Abigail when she took 200 loaves and five sheep . . . and carried them to David, contrary to her churlish husband's mind. . . . And whereas it is objected against women that their husbands and Parents have power to . . . annul and make void all their vows or resolutions, this was under the law and under the curse, but who comes to Christ Jesus the end of the law . . . to speak and do that which is right and true . . . no man hath power, neither father nor husband, to [dis]annul it or make it void.[127]

The writer continues, in a passage that was crossed out:

> Neither men nor women . . . cannot take out the evil weeds, but as we take them out at home first, . . . for there is too many women professing godliness in this day, with whom many . . . upbraid us, saying . . . they are as proud as any other people, and were there not some truth in the thing, I would not

125. Minutes of the Women's Monthly Meeting of Hardshaw, 1693–1694, April 18, 1693.

126. Carre, "Early Quaker Women," 45, 46, 47.

127. "Concerning the Authority and Dominion in the Church and in the outward Creation, whether it be in the Male or ffemale, or in Christ Jesus the power of God only, both in the male and female," n.d. Portfolio Manuscripts 1/140.

[speak]. . . . I am greatly oppressed, and grieved in spirit to see so many as
I do, with their sett-hoods, their new-fashioned whisks, and short sleeves with
other things that many women be gone into. . . . So all you women friends
that have a mind to work for God . . . as we begin [at home] we may go to
do it abroad, and in that that condemns an evil in our selves we may condemn
it in others.[128]

In equally urgent tones, Theophila Townsend cautioned women in London about their children's clothes:

Judge down pride and vanity, especially in your own families, and give no
liberty to your children to please them in any thing that is contrary to truth:
when they shall say to you such a one have a chain of gold, why may not I?
. . . that may give occasion to the enemies of truth, to point at it, and say the
Quakers are as ready to run into any new fashion as we . . . away with the
naked necks and backs, the needless pinches and ruffles the high dresses upon
the head . . . wanton Eyes walking and mincing as they go . . . you are the
chosen vessels of the Lord, stand up in the strength of the Lord . . . against
all such which would destroy your comely order.[129]

Margaret Fell Fox, who always insisted on dressing according to her
taste and rank, criticized Friends' obsession with plain clothing as a new
fetishism with outward things.[130] Perhaps so; yet women's concern with
dress was also the result of clear-sighted realism, for their increased
visibility in meetings *did* make them personally vulnerable to attack as
both prideful and lascivious, exposing the movement as a whole to
criticism both from within and from without.[131] Indeed, Margaret Fox
herself was criticized by Gulielma Penn, though in the most delicate
terms, for spending so much time away from her family: "Me thinks if
thou foundest a clearness and freedom in the Lord it would be happy
thou wert nearer thy dear husband and children but that I leave [to] the
Lord's ordering and thy freedom."[132]

128. Ibid.
129. Theophila Townsend, "An Epistle of Love to Friends in the Womens Meetings
in London, etc. To Be Read among Them in the Fear of God" (1680), 3–4.
130. Margaret Fell, Epistles, 1698, 1700, in A *Brief Collection* . . . (London, 1710),
534–35. "Christ Jesus saith, that we must take no thought what we shall eat, or what we
shall drink, or what we shall put on; . . . But . . . they say we must look at no colors, nor
make anything that is changeable colors as the hills are, nor sell them nor wear them. But
we must be all in one dress, and one color. This is a silly poor Gospel." On the Fell
women's clothing, see Ross, *Margaret Fell*, 261, 378.
131. Men were also chastised for overdressing; George Fox once defended William
Penn's wearing of a wig. However, men's clothing was of far less importance to Friends
than women's.
132. Guli Penn to M[argaret] F[ox], Worminghurst, August 2, 1684, Thirnbeck
Manuscript 368/18, Library of the Society of Friends, London.

On balance, and in the long run, I believe that the separate women's meeting was good for women; indeed, it may be said to have been a cradle not only of modern feminism but of the movements of abolitionism, women's suffrage, and peace activism, all of which were, and are, enlivened by the presence (even predominance) of Quaker female leaders.[133] Even in the short run, the smaller, segregated women's meetings appear to have sustained more vitality than those larger administrative bodies in which women and men worked together.

The London Six Weeks Meeting, established in 1671, comprised forty-nine men and thirty-five women, "grave and ancient Friends," chosen from all the meetings in the city and district; it was described by George Fox in 1671 as "the prime meeting of the city," a final court of appeal for difficult cases. However, the minutes lack the color and fervor of the provincial meeting records. They also concerned matters that were progressively more mundane until, by the 1690s, the meeting operated chiefly as an accounting office, collecting ar.d disbursing money bequeathed to Friends.[134] During the 1670s, assembling frequently at the home of Rebeckah Travers, the meeting settled personal disputes and dealt with cases of marriage procedure. In 1674 Travers offered funds collected by the women's meeting to help start a school, to which the women might send as many children of impoverished Friends as they judged suitable. In 1678, to prevent young men crowding against the women under the gallery of the meeting house, a paper was sent to each monthly meeting, advising Friends "that the women do sit on one side of the Public Meeting place apart from the men." The same year the women proposed that Margery Browne be appointed to sort flax and deliver it to spinners and oversee their work; a male Friend would sell the goods. In 1679 the care of poor children was referred to the women's meeting, the charges to be defrayed from the public stock by a male subcommittee for finance (called the Meeting of Twelve). In 1680 the subcommittee held a series of discussions on the "houses of easement" (outhouses) owned by two women living adjacent to the meeting house; these were to be stopped up and new ones built, to keep the meeting

133. Margaret Hope Bacon, *Mothers of Feminism: The Story of Quaker Women in America* (San Francisco: Harper and Row, 1986), Chaps. 7–14. Elizabeth Potts Brown and Susan Stuard, eds., *Witnesses for Change: Quaker Women over Three Centuries* (New Brunswick, N.J.: Rutgers University Press, 1989).

134. London and Middlesex Six Weeks Meeting 11 a 2 I/55, 56, 58, 127; II/31, 56, 64–65, 177; III/157. Frequently women bequeathed money and houses to Friends but were allowed to use them for their lifetime. Today the meeting, composed of about thirty men, acts as a cash committee of the quarterly meeting in charge of meeting houses, burial grounds, and so forth (Beck and Ball, *London Friends' Meetings*, 91).

house "sweet." In 1685 monthly meetings were instructed to prevent
Friends from crowding around the meeting house door or talking in the
street. In 1698 the meeting considered the need to avoid giving gloves
and other gifts after marriages and births and the wearing of black at
burials, in imitation of the world. Friends were also cautioned to eat and
drink sparingly before meetings to prevent their falling asleep.[135]

One paper of advice by the six weeks meeting called for "ancient
women to visit the young faithful women, and stir them up to frequent
the Monthly Meetings and the Women's Meetings . . . and the Friends
employed in the said meetings and the business not to be kept among a
few ancient women Friends."[136] Their concern reflected the fact that the
new mother in Israel was a much older person than the young servant
or matron who had helped shape the movement in earlier days. Indeed,
she was often the very same person, molded by experience into a being
who was competent, trustworthy, courageous, unbending, and frequently dictatorial. Yet if these leading Quakers were sometimes viewed
by outsiders as guardians of a petty, conventional morality, they themselves understood the value of their own legacy. In 1695 Margaret Fell
Fox, aged eighty-one, received a letter from the London Women's Meeting, signed by four of her daughters and by Ruth Crouch, Mary Elson,
Mary Penington, Mary Woolley (in a shaky hand), and many others:

> Well beloved and honored mother . . . we are truly comforted in our
> meetings . . . in the renewing of that ancient love which was raised amongst
> us in the dawning of the day . . . through which the seed did spring and
> grow and to this day remains fresh and green in many who are as living
> branches of the heavenly vine and receive their sap and nourishment from
> the root of life Christ Jesus.[137]

In these venerable women, and in many other Friends of both sexes, the
strict outward behavior dictated by the meeting system often masked a
complex and volatile inner life. It is to that inner life, the formation of
a new subjectivity within Quaker thought and worship, that we turn in
the following chapter.

135. Six Weeks Meeting, I/9–10, 19–21, 25, 78–79, 82, 121, 132–36; II/36, 49, 96,
98, 141, 226–27; III/339–40.
136. Beck and Pall, *London Friends' Meetings*, 125–26.
137. Women's Quarterly Meeting in London to Margaret Fox, September 30, 1695,
Spence Manuscripts III, nos. 195–96, Library of the Society of Friends, London.

CHAPTER TEN

Selfhood and Enlightenment: Quaker Preaching and Discipline, 1664–1700

INTRODUCTION

"It hath been in my heart for many years, to leave behind me a brief relation concerning the way and manner of the Lord's dealings with me, from my youth up to this day, for the encouragement of the young in years to faithfulness."[1] So began Alice Hayes's account of her spiritual education from the year of her birth, 1657, until 1708, twelve years before her death. Born in Hertfordshire of Anglican parents, raised by her father and the "sharp government" of a stepmother, she languished, and her conscience was troubled for the sins of gossiping, singing, and dancing. "Oh! that I had had but parents that could have informed me . . . that those reproofs I often felt in secret, was of the spirit of the Lord!" At age sixteen she escaped into service with another family, hoping for a more peaceful life, "and I was very glad that I was from my father's house, because of the quietness I enjoyed."[2] Some time later, she heard reports of a Quaker woman preacher who was visiting the area and was expected to appear at a public meeting. Some neighbors who planned to attend out of curiosity invited her to accompany them.

---

1. Alice Hayes, *A Legacy, or Widow's Mite: Left by Alice Hayes, to Her Children and Others. With an Account of Some of Her Dying Sayings* (London, 1723), 13. On Quaker autobiographies, see Felicity A. Nussbaum, *The Autobiographical Subject: Gender and Ideology in Eighteenth-Century England* (Baltimore: Johns Hopkins University Press, 1989), 154–77.
2. Hayes, *A Legacy*, 15, 17.

When I came to the meeting, it had made a great impression upon my mind, beholding the solidity of the people, and the weighty frame of spirit they were under, occasioned many deep thoughts to pass through my heart. . . . After some time of silence, a woman stood up and spoke, whose testimony affected my heart, . . . so that I could not refrain from weeping: but alas! alas! after meeting was over, the enemy soon prevailed again, . . . so that I went no more to any such meeting for several years.[3]

Alice moved on to service in two other households. In the first, a family of a justice of the peace, her piety was encouraged; at the second she lost her spiritual momentum through listening to vain conversation. She also wrenched her ankle and for two years walked on crutches and prayed for a miracle, which materialized in the shape of a handsome young farmer who had also served in the magistrate's house and who courted and married her despite her disfigurement. She recovered, was happy and full of life, and again slid backward, "for being recovered of my lameness, and grown strong, lived at heart's content with a loving and tender husband, and outward things prospered . . . I forgot the tender dealings . . . of so gracious a God . . . and gave myself what liberty my unstable mind desired."[4] She was saved from perdition only through a near-mortal illness, which moved her to commence a regimen of prayer, meditation, and righteous action, hoping thereby to attain true serenity. Instead, she was consumed by temptations and self-hatred.

I searched the Scriptures from one end to the other, and read several books, but I thought none reached my state to the full. . . . And Oh! the bitter whisperings of Satan, and the thoughts that passed through my mind, such as my very soul hated; yet such was the suggestions of the Enemy, that he would charge them upon me, as if they were my own. I looked for some fruits of sobriety, [in church] . . . but . . . [I saw] actions of pride; others rude and wanton; and some asleeping; and so little solidity, that I was often ready to say to myself, "Is there no people that serves the Lord better than these?"[5]

There *was* such a people, she knew, for an inner voice whispered, "Go to the Quakers," until she at last inquired after a meeting, where she heard another woman preach words that she knew to be true to her own condition. When her husband learned of her attendance at meetings, however, "his love all turned into hatred and contempt of me."[6] When she prepared to leave for a meeting, he hid her clothes, and when she

3. Ibid., 19. This was in 1680; the preacher was Elizabeth Stamper.
4. Ibid., 23–24. Her husband was Daniel Smith. She married Thomas Hayes, a mealman, in 1697; he died in 1699.
5. Ibid., 29, 32.
6. Ibid., 35, 39.

avowed her loyalty to Friends, he threatened to sell his property, move away, and leave her. This was the greatest trial of Alice's young life:

> I could not let go this interest in my Saviour, for the love of a husband, though nothing in this world was so dear to me as my husband . . . all in this world, that was near and dear to me, was turned against me: yea, father and mother, brothers and sisters; but nothing came so near me as my husband. . . . We had not then been married above two years, so that if God had not upheld me, I had fainted.[7]

Relatives and acquaintances continued to plague her and were vanquished. Her former patron maligned her but soon fell ill in London "and was brought home dead." Her mother-in-law accused her of trying to destroy her husband; "She went home, where she soon fell sick and died, and was buried in less than a week's time." Her husband and father-in-law sat her down and lectured her, and when she tried to leave the room, her husband blocked the door. "Do not *thee* and *thou* me," shouted her father-in-law when she turned and rebuked him, "If you will not turn, I will buy a chain, and chain you to that maple-tree that stands in the green; and there you shall be glad to turn for hunger."[8] In the end, she tells us, both men succumbed and apologized, and her husband affirmed the truth of her convictions.

Alice then recounted her call to make a public testimony before the local parish priest. After long deliberation, she sought the company of a male Friend, and the two appeared at the church, where she addressed the congregation after the service, affirming the Quakers' faith in Christ and the scriptures. Before she was accosted and thrown out of the building, she climbed on a seat and announced a forthcoming Quaker meeting, attracting several new converts to the movement.

Some time later, now a widow with five children, she became involved in a dilemma about the payment of tithes. She had signed a contract to pay an annual tax or "impropriation" on her farm, belonging to the dowry of the lady of Essex, as her husband had done during his lifetime. Now, wondering whether she had in fact agreed to pay a form of tithes "in the ground," and so disobey God, she became ill with worry. "To suffer for suffering sake I never desired, and to suffer for well-doing, the Lord knew my heart to be wholly given up to his will: only 'Lord, let be fully satisfied that I suffer for well-doing.'"[9] She resolved her confusion by holding a debate:

7. Ibid., 41, 42, 46–47.
8. Ibid., 45, 46, 48.
9. Ibid., 63.

It opened in my mind to get a few Friends together to have the matter of
impropriation fully discoursed upon, and there were two sensible Friends that
discoursed the matter, the one for paying it, the other against it. . . . He that
was for paying . . . did not then see it to be the same with tithe, because it
paid no priest, nor any part of it belonged to the church; . . . but the other
Friend so plainly proved it to be the same in the ground, that I was fully
satisfied, and so were all the rest that was at the meeting.[10]

Here the account broke off, to be resumed some years later, in 1708,
when, in great weakness of body, she attained a deeper insight into "the
wonders of the Lord in the deep." Her counsel was one of patience,
humility, and suffering, given as an encouragement both for her own
children "and for all the babes and lambs of God, and for the mourners
in Sion, who go heavily on . . . when the time of weakness takes hold
on your outward man, and no worldly means will avail you, . . . he will
give you power to tread on scorpions, and to keep under every foul
spirit."[11] In 1720, lying on her deathbed, all her children but one living
far away, she told Friends, "all that I desire is, that the Lord's presence
may be continued to me, and then I fear not the pinching time, the hour
of death. . . . Dear God, make my passage easy." Days later, as Friends
prayed by the bedside, she broke forth, "Oh! Love; this is love that may
be felt; my God, thy goodness is wonderful large." And again, just before
death, "All will be well; I am going home, I am going home."[12]

Turning from the writings of early Quaker prophets to the autobiography of Alice Hayes, we soon realize that we have encountered a new
and highly complex emotional vocabulary. Alice Hayes is reticent where
earlier Friends were eloquent and expressive where earlier Friends were
silent. Her inner life and personal relationships are far more central to
this story than they were in accounts of prophets such as Elizabeth
Hooton, while her public activities are less so. She withholds from the
reader what the archival sources and posthumous testimonials reveal:
that she was imprisoned for nonpayment of tithes, that she preached for
years in many parts of England, that she traveled as a minister in Holland
and Germany, and that she was a respected member of the local women's
meeting, which recorded her gift of "cordial water" to an ailing Friend

10. Ibid., 64.
11. Ibid., 65, 70–71.
12. "A Testimony from our Monthly Meeting at Tottenham, Held the 25th Day of
the Eleventh Month, 1720, concerning our Deceased Friend, Alice Hayes; With an Account of Some of Her Dying Sayings," in Hayes, *A Legacy*, 6, 8, 9, 10.

in 1702. Her one account of public prophecy in a church occupies a paragraph; her moments of spiritual fragility and self-analysis are recounted in page after page. On her deathbed she celebrated her unity with Friends. "Oh! what comfortable times we have had often in our week-day meetings; how have our cups overflowed with the love of our heavenly Father."[13] Yet for the most part she presents herself as isolated, at a distance from others, passionate in specific personal relationships yet ultimately struggling alone.

Her spiritual growth is described in terms of predominantly negative *emotions*, not physical sensations. She does not melt with love or breathe toward Friends or feed upon God. Although she suggests an experience of physical pleasure in relation to her young husband, she clearly grew to believe that all pleasure was treacherous and that her spirit could flourish only within a sick body, a negated body. Indeed, in Hayes's autobiography, bodily metaphors have meaning only in relation to the conditions of suffering and damnation. Thus, souls who are distanced from God "have great reason to cry out, and say, they are full of putrefied sores, and that they have no soundness in them."[14]

Her desire for self-abasement is total and continual. "And I may say, in the bowedness of my spirit," she affirmed at age fifty-one, "that I have no might of my own, nor power, nor ability, but what he shall be pleased to give me: and let nothing be attributed to that monster self, which too often appears both in preachers and in writers, which proves like the 'fly in the ointment of the apothecary.'"[15] Yet she also presents her life story as a fairy tale in which the heroine triumphs over wicked stepmothers and the evil monsters who oppose her pursuit of truth and where the adult, independent Alice organizes public debates and oversees an extensive farm and household (the wheat, straw, and barley seized by tax collectors in only one year of her widowhood, 1707, was valued at over forty-three pounds).[16]

She communicates an experience of subdued insight rather than prophetic zeal. Unlike earlier prophets, whose writings pulsate with spiritual energy, her speech to the local Anglican congregation is not ecstatic but

13. "A Testimony concerning Alice Hayes," 9. Women's Monthly Meeting, Hungerford Hill, November 3, 1701, and December 7, 1702. My thanks to Catherine Blecki, who shared archival material on Alice Hayes with me. (Hungerford Hill Meeting Manuscripts, Aylesbury Public Record Office.)

14. Hayes, *A Legacy*, 84.

15. Ibid., 65.

16. Catherine La Courreye Blecki, "Alice Hayes and Mary Penington: Personal Identity Within the Traditions of Quaker Spiritual Autobiography," OH, 65 (1976): 21.

explanatory. She is unable to recount her one great epiphany. "What I have seen and felt, this year, [1708] is unutterable," she writes, "being a year wherein I was led into the deeps, and beheld much of the wonders of the Lord, more abundantly than I am able to express."[17] Yet Friends remembered that "her ministry [was] very plain and powerful: but oh! to the disconsolate, it often dropped like rain, and run like oil to the wounded. . . . And often in our week-day meetings, oh! how her advice hath dropped from her like dew."[18]

How are we to decipher this new emotional vocabulary in the context of the broader social and spiritual developments of eighteenth-century Quakerism? In discussing Friends' earlier history, I have interpreted their concept of prophecy both as an expression of complete passivity—an involuntary utterance of the divine word—and as an expression of the integrity or conscience of the speaker, the light within the individual merging with divine universal truth. I have also emphasized Friends' integration of ecstasy and everyday life, what historian Luella Wright called their "practical and basic mysticism."[19]

By the closing decades of the century, these two strains, the practical and the mystical, seem to have begun a process of bifurcation. The most pious of eighteenth-century Friends underwent a process of spiritual implosion. They were quietists, defining the light as emanating from a being utterly outside the self. They were obsessed with their own personal nullity—a hatred of the creature—and with the cultivation of extreme passivity both in outward gesture and inward contemplation. Alongside this increased inwardness went a diminution of Friends' collective vitality, their evangelical energy sapped both by persecution and by the imposed discipline of the meeting system. The loose fluidity of their early communal experience was thus transformed into a rigid uniformity of dress, thinking, and behavior. Public prophets were muzzled, women more than men.

From an outsider's point of view, these quietist Friends must have seemed increasingly irrelevant to the dynamics of the new Enlightenment. They were a sect, a peculiar people, emotionally and physically repressed, looking, indeed, as though they would have liked to make themselves physically invisible, dressing in plain grey clothing, eternally watchful for signs of vanity and frivolity. Thus, an eminent female

17. Hayes, *A Legacy*, 66.
18. "A Testimony concerning Alice Hayes," 11.
19. Luella M. Wright, *The Literary Life of the Early Friends, 1650–1725* (New York: Columbia University Press, 1932), 32.

minister preached against the use of starch in white aprons, calling it "devil's water."[20]

Yet eighteenth- and nineteenth-century Friends were also social and intellectual innovators. They cannot be classified alongside their spiritual descendants, the Shakers, whose tasteful furniture and advanced agricultural technology evolved in conjunction with noisy dancing, a repressive, celibate culture, and ghostly visitations from George Washington and Napoleon Bonaparte. Quite the opposite; far from being a peculiar people, many prominent Friends demonstrated an affinity for making and managing money as well as an apparently limitless energy in the arena of social reorganization. They were centrally involved in the development of a capitalist economy and the affective nuclear family and in such social reform movements as the abolition of slavery and the treatment of mental illness, all of which set a high value on the principle of the worth and autonomy of the individual.[21]

These two strains in modern Quakerism are clearly reflected in two distinct historiographical traditions. The quietist has been described by Rufus Jones and others as a mystic: uneducated, simple-minded in the best sense, utterly detached from the worldliness and inward dryness of more worldly and socially active Friends.[22] The capitalist has been described by Frederic Tolles and others as a puritan: zealous, self-disciplined, and gifted in the practice of frugality, prudence, and a spirit of order that ultimately generated a rationalized economy, scientific inquiry, and social reform.[23] Historians of Quakerism as a force for modernity take the movement's original religious impulse as a given, but their explanation of the Quakers' effect on society is made in terms of purely social factors. Thus, Frederick Tolles described the Quakers' Puritan roots but emphasized an inherent contradiction between their spiritual ideals and their social energy. More recently, Barry Levy has pointed to the link between Friends' domesticity and their economic

20. James Jenkins, *Records and Recollections* (1764), 1:88, 89, quoted in Lucia K. Beamish, *Quaker Ministry, 1691–1834* (Oxford: by the author, 1967), 89. The minister was Sophia Hume.

21. On capitalism, see Frederick B. Tolles, *Meeting House and Counting House: The Quaker Merchants of Colonial Philadelphia, 1682–1763* (Chapel Hill: University of North Carolina Press, 1948). On the family, see Barry Levy, *Quakers and the American Family: British Settlement in the Delaware Valley* (New York and Oxford: Oxford University Press, 1988). On mental illness, see Charles Cherry, *A Quiet Haven: Quakers, Moral Treatment, and Asylum Reform* (Rutherford, N.J.: Fairleigh Dickinson University Press, 1989).

22. Rufus M. Jones, *The Later Periods of Quakerism*, 2 vols. (London: MacMillan and Co., 1921), 1:57–103.

23. Tolles, *Meeting House and Counting House*, 52f., 80.

success. He observes repeatedly that the modern family was created by a group of "religious fanatics" but analyzes that process in wholly material terms, discussing the cheapness of Quaker preaching (as opposed to the paid Anglican clergy) and the monetary expense of finding apprenticeships for Quaker children.

Alice Hayes was surely a quietist and possibly a mystic, yet, when considering the ethics of paying taxes on her farm, she organized a debate rather than await a revelation. Like other prominent female ministers of the period, she was a practitioner of both solitary meditation and the robust domesticity that Barry Levy correctly views as central to the development of modern Western society. Taking Alice Hayes's writings and those of other Quaker leaders as a starting point, I want to explore the relationship between the self-negation of these premodern Friends and the evolution of a concept of individual selfhood that is familiar to modern eyes.

Quakers of the late seventeenth and early eighteenth centuries did not invent introspection. The notion of the "inward man" was intrinsic to the thinking of the earliest Friends, as it was to the mentality of Puritans, poets, and many ordinary people. However, the loneliness and uncertainty of early Quakers opened directly onto a wide vista of collective, not individual, experience. Once convinced, they tended to give weight to their own passions and uncertainties only insofar as they resonated with biblical themes or with the dynamic of the group as a whole. Yet those individual passions and uncertainties existed. We may catch glimpses of them by reading the journals of later Friends, composed in a period when the probing of the individual's emotional life was more widely encouraged. Thus, William Edmundson, recalling his early travels in the ministry during the 1650s, described two women prophets who came traveling on foot through Ireland and Scotland during a bleak winter: "Anne Gould, being a tender woman, was much spent . . . the enemy persuading her, that God had forsaken her, and that she was there to be destroyed: So that she fell into despair . . . in bed overwhelmed under trouble of mind." After Edmundson went to her under a divine call, she revived and he escorted the women to his house. Since they were afraid to ride alone, "when we came in very foul way, I set them both on horseback, and waded myself through dirt and mire in my boots, holding them both on horseback with my hands."[24] In writings of the

24. William Edmundson, *Journal of the Life, Travels, Sufferings, and Labour of Love in the Work of the Ministry* . . . (London, 1715), 18, 20.

1650s, respected women prophets did not collapse in depression, and they did not shrink from the challenge of sitting on their horses alone.

Later Friends, in contrast, were far more concerned to monitor their inward spiritual progress than to publicize their uninhibited verbal and physical behavior. We are therefore more apt to encounter a woman chastising her own moral weakness than descriptions of the collective ecstasies of earlier times. Yet those ecstasies still existed, as we learn from reading Friends' unpublished letters. Here is an epistle of Mary Amye to Friends, read aloud in the women's box meeting in London:

> How doth my soul even breathe to the lord my god night and day . . . his love his love, wherewith he hath loved me, never did mother more tender the babe of her womb . . . he hath encompassed me about within his arms of pity and compassion . . . and my hand hath handled, and I have also tasted of the good word of life, and my heart is even overcome at this time . . . nothing of my own, nothing of my own self saith my soul, but of him, and to him, be all praise. . . . Oh our little sister that hath no breast to suck consolation from . . . he chooses the contemptible and the foolish. . . . Let us the despised ones . . . praise him.[25]

In examining the records of later Friends, we are also apt to encounter the public advocacy of strict, even brutal treatment of children by mothers concerned for the purity of the next generation; yet affection and tenderness continued to be expressed in private letters. Thus Mary Gullson, a minister who wrote and spoke against the Baptists in her home town of Coventry, sent an epistle to the women's meeting at Devonshire House, London, in 1697: "Keep [your children] under your eye as much as may be, and always at your command, begin betimes to bow them to the yoke, keep them employed in some employment that may suit with truth . . . my soul is grieved . . . for the backslidings . . . of the daughters of Sion." Yet years later she wrote to one of her own children,

> It has been for your sakes I have borne many a burden, and love made it easy, although hard in itself, and now I feel the same love to thee . . . as I did when I dandled thee upon my knees, and sweetly hugged thee in my bosom, I have the same tender affections to thee as ever, . . . Betsy I love thee much more than I can express![26]

25. Mary Amye to Friends, letter read in the London Box Meeting, November 19, 1674, Box Meeting Manuscripts, Library of the Society of Friends, London, fol. 27.
26. Mary Gullson to the women's meeting, Devonshire House, London, June 1, 1697; letter of Mary Gullson to E. M., Coventry, August 15, 1715, Gullson Manuscripts, 2, 42–43, Library of the Society of Friends, London.

What the sources allow us to construct, in short, is not a history of inner life or emotion per se; it is the history of a body of writing in which the description of particular emotions appears as a moral priority and a literary convention. It is in that limited sense that we may speak of the developing subjectivity of English Quakers, as they entered the period of the Enlightenment.

KILLING THE CREATURE: MODES OF REPRESSION AND SELF-DISCIPLINE

Friends keep clear from the superfluous part in
drinking tea.
   York Women's Quarterly Meeting Epistle,
                                   1714

In 1706 a group of French Huguenot prophets known as Camisards, victims of the draconian policies of King Louis XIV, appeared in the drawing rooms and meeting houses of London.[27] They included individuals of both sexes and all ages, and, like the Friends who had arrived in that city nearly fifty years earlier, they held public meetings that culminated in ecstatic prophesying and bodily contortions. George Keith, an Anglican minister and lapsed Quaker, commented on the event, ridiculing both Camisards and Quakers for denigrating the importance of an ordained ministry, producing false miracles "done in corners," indulging in bodily agitations more appropriate to hysterical heathens than to good Christians, and allowing women to preach.

> [The Camisards'] whole superstructure stands upon a precarious foundation; both their men and women, and some children have had these extraordinary inspirations, for which they cannot give the least instance of proof more than Quakers have offered to give; for in Quaker's meetings, not only some very ignorant women have seemed to speak with great readiness and fluency . . . but even some boys and girls have been greatly agitated in their bodies . . . the wildest enthusiasts have had as equal and fair pretences, and as seemingly good morals.[28]

Keith charged that it was impossible to prove whether such extraordinary inspirations or claims about the "light within" were valid or invalid, for "as the Quakers themselves will acknowledge . . . it is not every light

    27. Hillel Schwartz, *The French Prophets: The History of a Millenarian Group in Eighteenth-Century England* (Berkeley: University of California Press, 1980).
    28. George Keith, *The Magick of Quakerism, Or, the Chief Mysteries of Quakerism Laid Open* . . . (London, 1707), 81–85, 86–87.

or spirit in men, that is the true divine light or spirit . . . for when differences have risen among the Quakers themselves . . . they have contradicted one another, and severely judged one another."[29] This cut to the heart of the Quaker experience. Indeed, London Friends had recently disowned one Elizabeth Nicholls for slandering several respectable Friends "under pretense of having visions and hearing voices that speak locally to her."[30] Quakers were by no means immune to the excitement produced by the new prophets' ecstatic preaching and mysterious healing powers; in Bristol the men's meeting offered financial assistance to the refugees in their town. Nevertheless, the position of official Quakerism with regard to the Camisards was unbending: Friends were not to associate themselves with the French prophets or their mode of public worship.[31]

Three decades of persecution and internal controversy, and the aging or demise of the first generation of evangelists, had radically changed the mentality, if not the ultimate spiritual goals, of most Quaker leaders. Like the Puritans, Quakers had always had an ambiguous conception of selfhood. Individual personality and social identity were considered crucial to the proper exercise of God's intentions but ultimately irrelevant to the experience of the light within the soul. During the millennial excitement of the Interregnum, that light had seemed to make all things clear: the workings of the body, the colors of nature, the right and proper action required at any given moment. Now, in quieter times, it had become evident that all these things were *not* clear. While Friends still trusted in the light's spontaneous appearance to those who waited with pure hearts, they now emphasized the ease with which the individual's inborn goodness might be squandered. "The great danger," warned Mary Forster,

> lies here in little things . . . taking liberty in little matters in *decency*, till *pride* sits in the chair, in excessive *merriment*, which some call *cheerfulness*, till it come to such *vain* and *immoderate laughter* as the wise men call *madness*. . . . [Some may say] *we may be Angry and sin not*; which is true; but letting themselves loose, here the Enemy takes an advantage, and in the night sows

29. Ibid., 13.
30. Testimony of Denial, Monthly Meeting at Devonshire House, May 2, 1698, reprinted in William Beck and T. Frederick Ball, eds., *London Friends' Meetings: Showing the Rise of the Society of Friends in London* (London: F. Bowyer Kitto, 1869), 90.
31. Russell Mortimer, ed., *Minute Book of the Men's Meeting of the Society of Friends in Bristol, 1667–1686*, Bristol Record Society's Publications, no. 26 (Gateshead: Northumberland Press, 1971), March 26, 1688, 18. And see Schwartz, *French Prophets*, 52, 117, 175, 280.

his evil seed, and the wrathful hasty spirit gets up, grows strong, till that which
is tender, meek and lowly in themselves, and others they converse with, is
grieved.[32]

While they still affirmed their collective unity and mutual understanding,
Friends now admitted to a sense of spiritual isolation. "I well remember,"
wrote Elizabeth Webb,

> that I told a friend in *London* I felt the divine extendings of the love of God,
> so to flow to the people, as I walked in the streets of the city, that I could have
> freely published the salvation of God . . . in the public places of concourse:
> the friend said he hoped it would not be required of me, this I mention to
> convince thee that universal love prevails in the hearts of some who are
> unknown to the world, and hardly known to their own brethren, . . . so now
> unless the Lord be pleased to reveal things to us, we are liable to mistake.[33]

While Quakers were still open to the unconventional and flamboyant
behavior of Friends in a state of spiritual ecstasy, emphasis was now
laid on the consistent exercise of virtue and self-control. Thus, George
Fox criticized Friends who remarried too soon after the death of a
spouse: "Before twelve months be expired they are not cold in the grave
and surely Friends should have a little more chastity and dominion over
their spirits than the people of the world, for Friends professing a faith,
light, and life beyond them therefore should show more virtue than
they."[34] In short, Quakers had come to believe that a life lived in a
condition of perfection had also to be a life of conscious and continuous
mental effort.

All good Friends continued to remind each other that the mind was
a mere physical organ, devouring information and ideas as the eye
devours beauty and the stomach food, in danger of being made bloated
and insensible by the unhealthy aroma of its own self-esteem. Thus,
Elizabeth Hendricks counseled Friends to "[keep] single and clean of all
incumbrances; and reasonings, and consultations about things which
you cannot discern. . . . Watch against that which would be striving to
comprehend, and know, and understand."[35] Friends also continued to
celebrate the body's capacity to express the soul's knowledge in that

---

32. Mary Forster, *Some Seasonable Considerations to the Young Men and Women
Who in This Day of Tryal, Are Made Willing to Offer up Themselves* . . . (London, 1684).
33. Elizabeth Webb, *A Letter from Elizabeth Webb to Anthony William Boehm,
with His Answer* (Philadelphia, 1783), 6.
34. George Fox to Christopher Holder in Rhode Island, London, June 15, 1677,
reprinted in JFHS 47, no. 1 (Spring 1955): 79.
35. Elizabeth Hendricks, *An Epistle to Friends in England* . . . (London, 1672), 4–6.

moment when all selves were shed and the worshiper collapsed in a union with God that was at once both blissful and righteous. Nevertheless, their concern for a more sustained experience of walking (as well as resting) in the light meant that the mind must inevitably become more important and the body less so, for the attainment of a perfection that would stand both the test of time and the world's scrutiny depended more on the capacity for self-analysis than it did on the capacity to shed inhibitions.[36] William Loddington directed an epistle "To the Young Friends that have a Public Testimony for Truth who meet on the First day Mornings at E[llis] H[ook]'s chamber." Loddington cautioned them "first when you feel any meeting opened . . . to receive your testimony. . . . O thou, even then take heed of letting in any thought that lifteth up self. Ah the Enemy I know is very busy at such a time." He also counseled what to do in case of failure:

> When you feel a meeting so shut up from you or you from them, that your testimony maketh little or no impression upon their spirit, or that you feel . . . a cloud upon your own tabernacles that you cannot move towards them . . . beware of reflecting upon the meeting. . . . This very trial a vain glorious spirit . . . cannot bear, especially if another friend be there that speaks more powerfully than himself. Saul was a figure of this . . . when the women preferred David before him.[37]

The analysis of one's own hidden motives was necessary not only to keep the mind pure; it was also needed to monitor virtue itself, for even righteous action might become thoughtlessly automatic or, what was worse, conducive to pride. So Mary Forster warned young people in the ministry:

> 'Tis possible you may speak the *plain language* without interruption, if you will but use it in *foolish talking* and *Idle jesting*; and although you do not appear in the *superfluities* of this wanton age in your *apparel*, but in *plain clothing*, yet if you do suffer your hearts to be in the *niceties, costliness* and *curiosities* . . . you may for a time possibly, . . . *come frequently to meetings, stand in the streets, bear the gain-saying of scoffers* . . . but if any of you indulge in a loose careless spirit, such *make void their suffering, invalidate*

36. On introspection among Quakers, and in nonconformist writing in general, see N. H. Keeble, *The Literary Culture of Nonconformity in Later Seventeenth-Century England* (Leicester, England: Leicester University Press, 1987), esp. Chap. 6, "A Paradise Within."

37. William Loddington, "To the young Friends that have a Publique Testimony for Truth who meet on the First day Mornings at E.H.'s Chamber," January 1687, Portfolio Manuscripts 4/8, Library of the Society of Friends, London.

their testimony, and fall short of the reward and comfort of the upright, and so will not hold out to the end.[38]

The elderly Margaret Fell Fox worried that suffering itself had been turned by some into a fetish. In 1698 she wrote an epistle chiding Friends who refused to use the word "God" (e.g., "as God is my witness") as a substitute for swearing oaths.

> Must we turn God out of the earth? Is he not the God of the whole earth? . . . I am sorry that Friends should be so weak, and so childish in the truth. . . . I write this because I perceive that some Friends' scruples to make use of these words, which the King and Parliament hath granted them instead of an oath, and so hinders themselves of the benefit and ease, it would bring Friends unto. . . . So I desire Friends generally, let not this false blind doctrine prevail upon you, but make use of the mercy that God hath granted you.[39]

However, while introspection was encouraged as an aid in sustaining true righteousness, it was possible that the techniques designed to facilitate that introspection would themselves work to inflate the ego. Certainly, no form of writing was to be undertaken as a mere intellectual or aesthetic exercise. A poem, just as much as a prophecy, was to be composed "in the light," as a vehicle for *God's* voice, not the writer's. Yet an autobiography or sermon or poem required considerably more mediation by the speaker or writer, more attention to craft, than the prophetic repetition of a single biblical phrase. Indeed, many personal journals and autobiographies were intended to be read as formal epistles or to be published at or soon after death for the encouragement of other Friends. Thus, Friends were encouraged to engage in more elaborate forms of self-expression in the pursuit of self-denial, and they were not unaware of the danger that the means used to achieve the spirit's liberation might become the means of choking it.

DISCIPLINE AND CENSORSHIP

The Quakers' increasingly complicated struggle for self-transcendence was assisted by a system of civilized but comprehensive repression. Ministers who had once wandered freely, celebrating their liberation from the constraints of a fixed address, were now to establish official

38. Forster, *Some Seasonable Considerations,* 4–5.
39. M[argaret] F[ox] to Friends, January 19, 1698, Miller Manuscripts, vol. 295, transcpt. 1–3. Library of the Society of Friends, London.

residences, both in order to maintain their subjection to the local meeting and to clarify responsibility for their financial support. London Friends were forbidden to leave the city on Sundays without acquainting the Morning Meeting of Ministers, while ministers everywhere were urged not to travel without certificates from their home meeting. Unsavory preaching was to be admonished by that meeting and then by public testimony. Should delinquent ministers persist in traveling, other meetings would be warned not to assist them.[40] When Mary Knight disturbed Suffolk Friends by her itinerant preaching, several men were delegated to obtain a testimony against her from her home meeting in London, while another was instructed to write a letter to Friends in Suffolk, two others being "desired to speak to her husband about her rambling about the country to use his endeavor to restrain her."[41]

Ministers whose forebears had preached in a mode that was openly irrational and emotional were now vulnerable to disownment, particularly when their sermons implied a criticism of the government or of other Quakers. In 1695 Elizabeth Redford preached in Wandsworth, encouraging Friends to withhold taxes that would be used to support the coming war. The morning meeting hoped she would become sensible of her mistake and so avoid disownment.[42] Ten years earlier, two female Friends had published a diatribe against Susanna Aldridge, who had traveled from meeting to meeting while pregnant and in a supposedly unstable emotional condition. After childbirth, "being weak, and disordered in her head, . . . she came forth again with a pretense of visions and revelations," accusing herself and Friends of dryness and deadness. Later she appeared at a local meeting in Buckinghamshire, "in so great a disorder of spirit, and disturbance of mind (with so strange a voice and gesture) that many, who had better hopes of her, went away grieved, fearing lest she should be distracted." The writers acknowledged that her charges against Friends might have been correct in individual cases, "but her thundering is from an unholy mountain, and her trumpet gives an uncertain sound . . . and yet, so strong is the delusion . . . that she fathers

40. The Morning Meeting's Book of Records from the 15th of the 7th Month, 1673, to the 6th of the 4th Month 1692, Inclusive," 3 vols., I/103, August 1689, Library of the Society of Friends, London. Epistle of the London Yearly Meeting to the Monthly and Quarterly Meetings in England, Wales, and elsewhere, May 20, 21, 22, 1689, reprinted in *Epistles from the Yearly Meeting of Friends, Held in London, to the Quarterly and Monthly Meetings in Great Britain, Ireland, and Elsewhere, from 1681 to 1817, Inclusive* (London, 1818), 47.
41. Morning Meeting's Book of Records, July, 1689, I/101.
42. Ibid., II/92, July 1695. A paper of Redford's was rejected in December 1694 (II/74).

all this upon the Lord, and pretends to have received it *immediately from his mouth.*"[43]

Women felt the brunt of these restrictions on movement and behavior more than men. Some irregular monthly meetings of public Friends were held with men and women together, and women were given permission to attend the yearly meeting of ministers. Nevertheless, in 1700 the morning meeting cautioned against women's excessive speaking and refused to countenance a separate meeting of women ministers:[44]

> There being several women Friends in and about this city that have a public testimony for the Truth and have sometimes met on the Seventh day [i.e., Saturday]. This Meeting . . . do declare they do not understand that ever this Meeting gave direction for the setting up of the said Meeting, neither do they judge there is any necessity for it . . . and therefore do advise that when any public approved women friends have a concern of service upon them to go to any particular public meeting in or about this City, they may leave their names at the chamber, . . . and . . . have an opportunity to clear themselves, and yet be careful not to interfere with the brethren in their public mixed meetings.[45]

In 1701 the London Morning Meeting of Ministers, an exclusively male body,

> finding that it is a hurt to truth for women Friends to take up so much time as some do in our public meetings, when several public and serviceable men friends are present and are by them prevented in their services. It is therefore advised that the women friends should be tenderly cautioned against taking up so much time in our mixed public meetings.[46]

In 1706 Mary Elson announced at the Peel Monthly Meeting that women Friends had no place to stand when they wanted to speak. A "conveniency" was provided, facing away from the men, and female ministers now addressed the women, whose seats were located under the men's gallery.[47]

43. Mary Ellwood and Margery Clipsham, *The Spirit That Works Abomination and Its Abominable Work Discovered* . . . (London, 1685), 4, 5, 7, 8. For an example of similar reactions to a man's disorderly preaching, see Stephen C. Morland, ed., *The Somersetshire Quarterly Meeting of the Society of Friends, 1668–1699* (Old Woking, Surrey: Somerset Record Society, 1978), 222.
44. SPQ, 286. The morning meeting had approved a meeting of London women ministers and visitors from out of town in May 1697 (Morning Meeting's Book of Records, II/172–73).
45. Morning Meeting's Book of Records, January 6, 1701, III/10. On the composition of the meeting, see Beck and Ball, eds., *London Friends' Meetings*, 336.
46. Morning Meeting's Book of Records, March 4, 1700, III/17.
47. Beck and Ball, eds., *London Friends' Meetings*, 192–94.

Leading Quakers were particularly exercised about the activities of young women. An undated letter from the London Box Meeting and signed by five of Margaret Fox's daughters, gave advice to sisters who received "some measure and show of the dispensation of the Gospel, so as to publish it to others, and go forth in the Works of the Ministry." They were exhorted to humility,

> that no sinister ends might creep in to precipitate any young ones either to popularity or to be seen or heard of men . . . when we have seen young women lately come forth in a testimony, they are for going to visit London, Bristol or Norwich when alas they are not qualified, fitted nor furnished for such a weighty work in these populous places where so many carping contrary spirits are. . . . On the other hand if such tender and young ones (unto whom we have a special regard that nothing may be stopped or quenched, that comes from motion of life, to be delivered to others) could satisfy themselves with visiting meetings in adjacent counties they belong to, their services would be more acceptable.[48]

Young women were also advised not to travel when pregnant, while servants should be watchful when going abroad, that they not feel themselves risen above their station. The London Box Meeting issued a further epistle concerning visionary children, the language of which was nearly identical to that used in its epistle to young women:

> As on the one hand we would not have anything . . . crushed that proceeds from the gift of God in either young or old, So, on the other hand we would not have children . . . encouraged to go beyond their measure or gift . . . for we must consider the tender capacities of children, that they may be soon drawn aside or lifted up, and think they must be doing something when their mouths is opened in a meeting . . . [so] it is both good and safe for such children to be kept close to their employment, and to their meetings at home . . . for we have seen sad effects, that hath happened to some in the beginning of our day that has been set up and admired in the affectionate part, . . . that has brought them into a bewildered state, and the Enemy has prevailed, so to darken them that they lost their conditions and never regained them.[49]

Beginning in 1672, all Friends' writings, including those of George and Margaret Fox, were scrutinized by the Second Day Morning Meeting of Ministers, a body consisting exclusively of male Friends but

---

48. Proceedings of the Yearly Meeting, Letter to be read in Meetings, London Women's Box Meeting Manuscripts, fol. 15, Library of the Society of Friends, London. Eighteen other women also signed the document.

49. Letter of yearly meeting to be read to Friends, n.d., London Women's Box Meeting Manuscripts, fol. 15.

frequently meeting at the homes of Rebeckah Travers and Ann Travers. Through a process of censorship and extensive editing, the meeting attempted to redirect Friends' creative expression away from political and apocalyptic works and toward the personal genres of autobiography, works of instruction or consolation, and testimonies to deceased Friends. The autobiography of Alice Hayes was reprinted six times in England and America.[50] Theological and doctrinal works like those of Anne Docwra and Elizabeth Bathurst (submitted to a committee of six editors), or Dorcas Dole's "Salutation to Children," were fairly readily accepted, while the letters to the king by Susanna Sparke and Dorcas Dole were delayed or rejected.[51] In 1675 a tract on the war in New England was ordered to be collected and used for waste paper and its author instructed not to print anything else without prior approval.[52] In 1677 the meeting objected to Margaret Fell Fox's tract, *The Daughter of Zion awakened*, and two Friends were delegated to explain to her why it could not be printed without changes.[53] In 1683 Anne Docwra's *Epistle to the Royalists* was referred to George Whitehead, "with her to review such places as may be safely exposed to print."[54] In 1687 and again in in 1689, Judith Boulbie's *Lamentation* was judged not safe to print, "several severe ancient prophesies applied to England too general and absolute . . . they think it meet to be laid by here at present, not knowing whether she will admit of the alterations they think fit." Three years later a paper of hers was accepted, the political portions excised.[55] In 1700 Alice Hayes was instructed to omit passages on her husband from her autobiography. She had also announced plans to publish some writings addressed to women and was informed that she might circulate the work in manuscript.[56]

50. Joseph Smith, ed., *A Descriptive Catalogue of Friends' Books, or Books Written by Members of the Society of Friends, Commonly Called Quakers, from Their First Rise to the Present Time*, 4 vols. (London: Joseph Smith, 1867), 927–28. On new genres in Quaker literature, see Wright, *Literary Life*, Chaps. 9–13.

51. Morning Meeting's Book of Records, I: Docwra in May 1682, fol. 63; Bathurst in October 1678, fol. 21; July 1679, fol. 27; July 1683, fol. 76; Sparke in April 1675, fol. 5; Dole in January 1682/3, fol. 70, and April 1684, fol. 79. For a general account of censorship see Wright, *Literary Life*, Chap. 8, "Quaker Censorship."

52. Morning Meeting's Book of Records, December 1675, I/10.

53. Ibid., July 1677, I/17.

54. Ibid., April 1683, I/74.

55. Ibid., January 1687, I/89; January 1689, I/98; June 1690, I/122. Another paper was tabled in June 1693 (II/28). In May 1695 Boulbie agreed to withdraw her paper (II/86).

56. Ibid., March 1700, II/326.

In erecting the apparatus of the morning meeting and propounding new strictures on authorship and preaching, Quakers never intended to create a spiritual dictatorship. On the contrary, their attempt to monitor their own movement and expression was as much the result of sensitivity about outside opinion as it was a restatement of fundamental beliefs and goals. Political works were apt to be censored because they were indiscreet or inappropriate, not because they were wrong. Prophetic writings were often abridged or allowed to be circulated in manuscript, not placed on an index and burned. Theophila Townsend composed a testimony to the deceased Jane Waugh Whitehead in language that would surely have been censored as public prophecy:

> No peace to the wicked . . . no peace to the persecutors of the Lord's people, no peace to the despisers of the true light of Christ within, no peace to the blind seers, nor sleepy watchmen, nor false hireling priests, that oppress the poor, and live by the sweat of other men's brows; . . . who pull the sheaf from the hungry, and the fatherless from the breast.[57]

Barbara Blaugdone's visionary work "Thus saith the Lord" was rejected by the morning meeting in 1689, and her letter to the Prince of Orange laid by, yet the meeting did accept her autobiography, which recounted the most hair-raising details of her prophetic career during the 1650s:

> They whipped me till the blood ran down my back, and I never startled at a blow: but the Lord made me to rejoice that I was counted worthy to suffer for his name's sake and I sung aloud. . . . I shall never forget the large experience of the love and power of God which I had . . . for if he had whipped me to death in that state which then I was in, I should not have been terrified or dismayed at it.[58]

Visionary preaching continued to be encouraged in closed meetings, at burials, and, on at least one occasion, at the new Quaker school at Waltham Abbey, where children of twelve engaged in ecstatic prophecy.[59] An epistle from several women of the Yorkshire Meeting to the London Box Meeting exulted, "Sons and daughters are opening their mouths in our assemblies and publishing [the] day of redemption and

---

57. Theophila Townsend, *A Testimony concerning the Life and Death of Jane Whitehead* (London, 1676), 23–24. On the importance of circulating works in manuscript for seventeenth-century female writers, see Margaret J. M. Ezell, *The Patriarch's Wife: Literary Evidence and the History of the Family* (Chapel Hill and London: University of North Carolina Press, 1987), 62–100.

58. Morning Meeting's Book of Records, January 1689, I/99. Blaugdone's autobiography (*An Account of the Travels, Sufferings & Persecutions of Barbara Blaugdone* [Shoreditch, 1691]) was printed with corrections in November 1691 (fol. 155). The quotation is from page 15 of her autobiography.

59. John Matern, *A Testimony to the Everlasting Power of God* (1679), 3–4.

witnessing against [a] sinful generation. God's power runs as a river and
the shout of a king is amongst us."[60] The meeting responsible for the
repression of Friends' visionary writings met at the home of Rebeckah
Travers, a pillar of the London Women's Meeting. Yet when William
Penn preached a sermon at her funeral in 1688, he celebrated her life as
an exemplum of Friends' original ecstatic experience:

> Our deceased Friend . . . received the truth in early days, the days of the
> dawning of God's power in this land, and in this city, [and] the remembrance
> of it was sweet to her soul; let us remember the love of God, and the power
> and glory . . . that shined then, that we may be encouraged to keep together
> as a *peculiar people to the praise of him that hath called us out of darkness
> into his marvelous Light.*[61]

Yet if Friends continued to cherish these moments of individual and
communal ecstasy, they also sought to reconstitute the public ministry
as a closed body with a relatively fixed agenda. Women and men who
embarked on extended preaching missions were generally sent *by* meetings in order to preach *to* meetings. Their frame of mind was to be zealous
but not impetuous, in the manner of Elizabeth Collard, who submitted
a petition to Friends in 1687:

> It hath been pretty much before me, and several times in my mind, for some
> months past, to visit friends in some of the western counties and north-
> ward . . . which thing I was desirous to acquaint friends with: that if upon
> their weighty consideration, any thing might be in any friend's mind to say
> concerning the thing it would be exceptably received by me who with un-
> feigned love presents these lines unto you and am willing to have your council
> herein.

The letter was accompanied by a note from her husband: "Friends, I
having for some months past understood that a concern have been upon
my wife to visit friends in the places aforementioned so this is to satisfy
friends that I am freely willing to give up that she may go: as the Lord
may order it."[62] Thus would God's message be conveyed, not in a hot

---

60. Isabel Sutton, Margaret Breckon, and other women of the Scarborough, Whitby,
and Bridlington Meetings to the London Box Meeting, June 3, 1691, London Women's
Box Meeting Manuscripts fol. 40 r. and v.

61. "A Sermon Preached by Mr. William Penn, upon Occasion of the Death of Mrs.
Rebecca Travers, an Aged Servant of God, June 19, 1688," in *The Concurrence and
Unanimity of the People Called Quakers* (London, 1694), 76.

62. Elizabeth Collard to Friends, May 26, 1687, Portfolio Manuscripts 16/38. All
Friends traveling in the ministry had to satisfy Friends as to their health, family duties, and
the soundness of their ministry. Friends wishing merely to visit meetings, but not to
preach, required a different sort of traveling "minute" (Margaret Hope Bacon, *Mothers*

gush of spontaneous revelation but in the steady drip of a measured, moderate, and entirely virtuous piety, intoned and explicated by a lady holding a certificate.

DIVIDING THE WORD: THE SELF-CONSCIOUS VISIONARY AND THE IDEAL WOMAN

The women are taking your crowns from off your
heads, O ye boobies and earthlings of men!
John Rutty, Ireland, 1766

In 1699 Friends of the morning meeting received an epistle from Mary Ellerton of Yorkshire, who challenged the authority of the elite ministry:

> I have something rests upon my spirit to deliver to you that are as elders, and as I may say of the foremost rank . . . sink down. . . . Consider where you are, least any should be found preaching and not in the cross. . . . Those amongst you that are . . . still growing at the root . . . they have not such need of these cautions, but [there are] those that are methinks to be compared to great trees that are full of branches and great leaves at the top, but the root dry and decayed, and therefore yields not fruit. . . . Quench not the spirit neither despise prophesying, least you be found fighting or striving against the work of God. . . . I have had some days and nights of exercise, before I was willing to give up to this concern.[63]

If old men and women had turned inward to cultivate their own gardens, Mary Ellerton saw a fresh new ministry straining to be released. Many of these young Friends, "still growing at the root," were second-generation Quakers, brought up to emulate or surpass their parents in the practices of self-denial and meditation. Unlike the prophets of the 1650s, whose authority derived from the belief in universal perfectability rather than individual gifts, these new ministers were spiritual commandos, virtuosos in self-discipline and aggressive piety. "My very soul mourns for [the sinners]," wrote Elizabeth Webb, "but we must press forwards and leave them if they will not arise out of their false rest."[64]

The new prophets' language interspersed descriptions of mystical rapture with counsels of asceticism and extravagant feminine imagery

---

of Feminism: The Story of Quaker Women in America [San Francisco: Harper and Row, 1986], 33–34).

63. Epistle of Mary Ellerton to the Morning Meeting, September 23, 1699, Portfolio Manuscripts 1/100.

64. Webb, *A Letter from Elizabeth Webb*, 31.

with (often harsh) pastoral advice to parents and children. Thus, Eleanor
Haydock, whom Friends described as "open-hearted and free to her
friends, her house as well as heart open to receive and entertain them . . .
careful over her family and household," conflated the good mother and
the true church:

> Come consider your little ones, and think how it may fare with their seed, if
> you . . . example them in error, . . . she that was termed barren and unfruit-
> ful . . . should bring forth in abundance of all virtue; . . . neither doth any
> defilement come from her, for she openeth her mouth in Wisdom, so that the
> moving of her lips showeth forth knowledge clearly; yea there is prudence in
> all her ways, for she still looketh well to the ways of her household. . . . Is
> this not the true Church?[65]

Gertruyd Niesen, in an epistle sent to Friends from Holland, chided
parents for hesitating to beat their children, "fearing lest the child should
be grieved and vexed, and perhaps grow sick, yea, perhaps die . . . and
what is this but unbelief and self-love in such parents? . . . When *fleshly
affection* rules, what miserable *disorder* doth it bring forth, even among
them that profess *truth?*"[66]

While the new generation of female ministers expressed their prophetic and pastoral authority as virtuous wives and mothers, they were
also highly visible as daughters. Barbara Bevan traveled through West
and East Jersey at age sixteen and later accompanied her father from
America to Wales, where she rode on horseback over six hundred miles,
dying at age twenty-three. (Welsh Friends recommended publishing her
papers, but the morning meeting decided that they needed too much
correction.) Mercy Johnson, daughter of Quaker parents, became a
minister at twenty-seven, while still unmarried, and traveled with Jennet
Stow through southern England and Wales, then with her father to
Scotland; afterward she married and died at thirty-four. Elizabeth Huntington used her father's house in Cumberland as a base, returning there
between trips in north England and Scotland, dying at twenty-three.
Mary Stubs, raised by Quaker parents, became a minister at twenty-six,
traveling in northern England and Ireland. She died unmarried in her
parents' house at thirty-three.[67]

---

65. Eleanor Haydock, *A Visitation of Love*, 15–18. Testimony to Eleanor Haydock,
Portfolio Manuscripts 13/34. She died in 1723, having preached for about twenty-six years.
66. Gertruyd Dieriks Niesen, *An Epistle to Be Communicated to Friends . . .*
(Colchester, 1677), 4–5.
67. On Bevan, see PP, 2:24–26. Morning Meeting's Book of Records, III/236, August 12, 1706; III/356, December 11, 1710. On Johnson, see PP 1:252–57. On Huntington, see PP 1:346–47. On Stubs, see PP 1:367.

Thus, the ideal woman of late seventeenth-century Quakerism presented herself in two clear aspects, the venerable matriarch and the
ardent virgin.[68] In the eldership of those who had nurtured the movement
in its beginnings, and in the activities of the girls and women who were
the architects of a strict morality and an orderly family life, women both
mothered and energized a movement exhausted and demoralized by
suffering. The following abridged account of a single mission undertaken
by Margaret Fell and her daughter Rachel from April 16 to May 27,
1669, probably on horseback, allows us a glimpse of the vigor and
doggedness with which leading women Friends worked to sustain every
tiny local community:

> We came out of London the 16th of [April], 1669, the 6th day of the week,
> about the 11th hour and then came to Gravesend 20 miles and debated there
> and from thence to the widow Clemon's at Frindsbury 6 miles that night and
> there had a meeting in the morning . . . from thence, went that night to
> Canterbury 26 miles and had a meeting there on [Sunday] . . . from thence,
> to Wingham 6 miles . . . and stayed there all night; . . . [the next] night went
> to Deal 8 miles and there had a meeting the 21st day in the town; from
> thence that night went to Dover 6 miles and there had a meeting the 22nd
> day in Luke Howard's house; from thence went the next day to Sandwich 10
> miles and there had a meeting; the next day to . . . Edward Noakes', 1 mile
> and from thence to Walmestone 6 miles . . . and there had a very great
> meeting [Sunday]; . . . [In May we went] to Maidstone 12 miles to see
> William Gibson; from thence to Sutton Valance 7 miles and there had a
> meeting [Tuesday]; from thence to Staplehurst 4 miles and lay at John Grin-
> sted's that night; from thence to Cranbrook 5 miles and lay at John Ben-
> nett's; from thence to Otham Farm . . . in Sussex 20 miles; from thence to
> Alciston 4 miles and there had a meeting; from thence to Rottingdean 8
> miles to Nicholas Beard's; from thence to Blatchington 5 miles and there had
> a meeting the first day of the week being the 23rd day of [May]; from thence
> to Hurstpierpoint 5 miles to Thomas Luxford's; from thence to Horsham 10
> miles and had there a meeting in the prison; from thence to Ifield Mill 5 miles
> and there had a meeting; from thence to Red Hill by Reigate 8 miles and
> there had a meeting the 27th day of [May]; from thence to Reigate that night
> 1 mile and from thence to London 18 miles.[69]

68. It is unclear from testimonies how often ministers stopped traveling during the
early years of marriage. Alice Curwen felt a call to prophesy while a mother with young
children, but she did not begin to travel until her husband was released from prison and
her children grown (A Relation of the Labour, Travail and Suffering of That Faithful
Servant of the Lord Alice Curwen [1680], 2–3). Other women are described as continuing
to preach after marriage. On the preaching in England of eighteenth-century American
women who were generally either unmarried or past childbearing years, see Bacon, Mothers of Feminism, 35–36.
69. An Account or Journell of M[argaret] F[ell]'s Travaile with Her Daughter Ra-

Remembering his early years as a poor apprentice the minister Samuel Bownas described himself as a boy "given to jesting, and turns of wit to provoke mirth," even though his mother had worked hard to instill a proper gravity in his nature; "my mother kept me very strict . . . and would frequently in winter evenings . . . tell me sundry passages of my dear father's sufferings, admonishing me so to live, that I might be worthy to bear the name of so good a man's son." Not surprisingly, it was another stern woman, Anne Wilson, who succeeded in rousing Bownas's spirit as he sat literally dozing at a meeting:

> Fixing my eye upon her, she with a great zeal pointed her finger at me, uttering these words with much power, "A traditional *Quaker*, thou comest to meeting as thou went from it (the last time) and goes from it as thou came to it, but art no better for thy coming, what wilt thou do in the end?" This was so pat to my then condition, that, like *Saul*, I was smitten to the ground.[70]

LAMENTATIONS

If Friends felt themselves energized by the zeal of the new ministry, they were also chastened by the subdued quality of women's pastoral and autobiographical writings. The Quakers' original tone combining anger and exultation had evolved into an attitude that was sacrificial, lonely, and pessimistic, far closer in spirit to that of Jeremiah or Ecclesiastes than to Amos or Daniel. So Eleanor Haydock lamented:

> Oh! who can but mourn . . . to see the Church as in her sable weeds, because of the unfaithfulness and backslidings of many; . . . sitteth she not as in the dust, covered with sackcloth? . . . Will not dogs lick the blood of those who are joined unto her, and eat her flesh. . . . Come, consider, look upon the face of the times, . . . is it not altogether so in this very age of ours?[71]

Virtually every epistle and sermon addressed to Friends drove home the need for inward contemplation and self-condemnation. "Do you not desire to be of that number that quakes and trembles at the word of the Lord?" asked Abigail Fisher. "[This] you can never do, except you retire,

---

chell Fell into Kent, Sussex and Surrey (Recorded by Rachel Fell), William Caton Manuscripts III, 37/173, listing and index by Craig Horle, 135, Library of the Society of Friends, London.

70. Samuel Bownas, *An Account of the Life, Travels, and Christian Experiences in the Work of the Ministry of Samuel Bownas*, 2d ed. (London, 1761), 4, 5. An Ann Wilson was chided by the morning meeting for preaching and required to appear in July 1699; after a period of resistance, she did appear and was contrite (Morning Meeting's Book of Records, July 1699, II/293–94, 295).

71. Haydock, *A Visitation of Love*, 3–4, 7–9.

consider and hearken to the voice of the Lord at home in your selves, every one apart."[72] A new phrase, "dividing the word," appeared in Quaker writings, referring to the minister's ability to address Friends as individuals rather than as a single body. The minister John Banks was praised after his death as one who *"divided the word aright,* according to their several *states* and *conditions,* of which he had a good *discerning."*[73] John Furly, mourning the death of his thirteen-year-old daughter, praised her behavior on the grounds that she had preached separately to each of her brothers on her deathbed; "The spirit of her heavenly Father . . . spake in her, and . . . enabled her rightly to divide the word of truth, and to give to each of her brothers their portion in due season."[74]

Visionary insights were often perceived as dreams or as injunctions to silent meditation rather than as external voices or calls to action. In 1700 a woman wrote down a dream, the memory of which she had cherished for many years, of a great flood threatening the world and her attempt to reach the safety of a city across a narrow bridge. Aided by an invisible hand, she removed her sodden clothes and climbed naked out of the rising water to the bridge. There she saw many other people, all naked, all crowned by God and filled with the power that descended on Friends in "good meetings," no one of them in sorrow or pain.[75] Martha Betterton heard God's voice while walking in the streets of London. "It opened in my mind in this wise: Wo! wo! to the crown of pride!" Rather than speak the words aloud, however, she began to meditate on whether she would be one of the sheep God spared. "Then a cry was raised in me, 'Cause me to hear thy voice; and not only so, but enable me to obey the same.'"[76]

Clearly, many such individuals, inculcated with stories of the straightforward physical heroism of the earliest Friends, experienced their own more circumspect behavior as both a practical necessity and a psycho-

72. Abigail Fisher, *A Few Lines in True Love to Such That Frequent the Meetings of the People Called Quakers* . . . (London, 1694), 2.

73. John Banks, *A Journal of the Life, Labours, Travels, and Sufferings (in and for the Gospel) of That Ancient Servant, and Faithful Minister of Jesus Christ, John Banks* (London, 1712), "Testimony of John Whiting," n.p.

74. John Furly, *A Testimony to the True Light . . . More Especially Intended for the Inhabitants of the Town of Colchester* . . . , 2d ed. (1670), 27.

75. "A dream of Mary Cumberford's, 1700," A Collection of Letters, Dreams, Visions, and Other Remarkable Occurrences of Some of the People Called Quakers, fols. 71–72, Library of the Society of Friends, London.

76. Thomas Chalkley, "An Account of the Exercise of Martha Betterton," in *The Journal of Thomas Chalkley*, 13. Martha Betterton was the wife of the minister Thomas Chalkley. She died around 1710.

logical burden. "I can truly say," wrote Catherine Whitton, "many a time when I have viewed in my mind their sufferings . . . in the beginning, my heart hath been broken, and I have secretly said . . . what can I now do, or suffer for the truth? Am not I as one born out of due time?"[77] Even when the individual did feel impelled to deliver a public testimony, she or he almost invariably did so not as a representative of the group but as one set apart from the group, as a critic or counselor of other Friends. Thus, while ministers no longer needed to fear that their audiences might attack them physically as witches or vagrants, they *were* vulnerable to the insidious and possibly more inhibiting emotions of timidity and embarrassment. In 1703 Thomas Gwin, of Cornwall, wrote in his diary (which he did not intend to publish), "when I had said a few words in the Yearly Meeting, I sat down very fearful least I had been too forward, which brought me greatly down, while many of my friends seemed to me to enjoy great satisfaction and comfort." At another meeting, Gwin was disappointed by another Friend's sermon:"I expected some other of those friends who were young in testimony might have [spoken] but D[orcas] Dole took up the time, and the end seemed not [to] answer the beginning."[78] Those individuals who did feel moved to address outsiders were not buoyed up by the collective exultation of other Friends; on the contrary, they frequently felt themselves to be going against the grain of their own movement. In 1686 Barbara Blaugdone wrote bitterly to George Fox:

> I have not received one line from thee this great while though I writ to thee twice, now this thing was with me to lay before the King . . . I leave it with thee as thou shalt order it, I have not showed it to anyone here because that they see not themselves there joining it. . . . I have been and am still a great sufferer . . . I believe thou art not insensible of it. . . . Jone Elie is gone from all good and turned sottish. . . . I am sorry for her . . . a rich friend told me he would do more good then ever I would do but he lied the more.[79]

Eight years later, Margaret Fell Fox worried about her son-in-law, who had left home under a concern for the city of London. She hoped that

---

77. Catharine Whitton, *An Epistle to Friends Everywhere: To Be Distinctly Read in Their Meetings, When Assembled together in the Fear of the Lord* (London, 1681), 6–7.

78. The Journal of Thomas Gwin, of Falmouth, A Minister of the Society of Friends, MS. vol. 214 (transcribed 1837 and copied 1904–05, S. 74/49, 65–66, 78, Library of the Society of Friends, London. "And seeing this is written only for my own remembrance, I know no cause why I may not be so bold with myself as to note my dream the night foregoing said first day" (55). Gwin was a merchant; he lived from 1656 to 1720.

79. Barbara Blaugdone to George Fox, ca. 1686, Portfolio Manuscripts 1/41. Fox had written to her in 1676, but the letter does not survive (Henry J. Cadbury, *Annual Catalogue of George Fox's Papers Compiled in 1694–1697* (Philadelphia and London: Friends Book Store, 1939), 142.

he would feel free to write down his words rather than preach them aloud. "I desire much your kindness with respect to his present state and condition," she told a relative, "for thou knows he is young and so easily hurt. I perceive he has a desire to lodge at thy house."[80]

The isolation and personal deprivation in many writings of the period also reflected the fact that their authors were female. In published journals composed by men, the subject was invariably presented as courageous and resolute, if not actually heroic.[81] Women's self-presentation as prophets was equally resolute, yet women insisted on their own humility and physical incapacity to a far greater extent than men did. Margaret Brewster justified her appearance in sackcloth and ashes by the sickness that preceded it and that left her as soon as she had finished speaking, while Joan Vokins confronted a group of Ranters in Long Island in 1681:

> The night before the general Meeting, I was near unto death, and many *Friends* were with me, who did not expect my life, and I was so weak when I came there, that two *women-Friends* led me into the meeting, and there was a great meeting of several sorts of people, and in a little time the God of wisdom, life and power, filled me with the word of his power, and I stood up in the strength thereof, and it was so prevailing over the meeting . . . that the opposing *Ranters* and *apostates* could not show their antic tricks.[82]

Women's autobiographical writing was by no means stereotyped. On the contrary, we find a wide range of voices: the easy confidentiality of the upper class Mary Penington, the mystical ardor of Elizabeth Webb, the intellectualism of Elizabeth Bathurst, and the contemplative poetry of Mary Mollineux, who described her weak eyes—both physical and spiritual—in these lines:

> Have mercy on me, ease me from my grief,
> And grant unto thy hand-maid some relief;
> . . . Ah, heal my feeble eyes,
> Of soul and body, Lord, that I may see
> Thy heavenly light, and learn to follow thee![83]

80. Margaret Fell Fox to Thomas Lower, Swarthmore, December 24, 1694, Miller Manuscripts, no. 85.
81. See, for example, the journals of John Banks, William Edmundson, and William Dewsbury, reprinted in vol. 2 of The Friends Library (Philadelphia, 1842).
82. Besse, 2:262. Joan Vokins, *God's Mighty Power Magnified, as Manifested and Revealed in His Faithful Handmaid, Joan Vokins* (London, 1691), 34.
83. Mary Mollineux, "A Meditation in Affliction" (1668), in *Fruits of Retirement: Or, Miscellaneous Poems, Moral and Divine* (London, 1702), 24.

Yet the link between sacrifice and spiritual power is central to every story. Joan Vokins converted her entire family and then left her seven children in the care of her husband and traveled to America to preach. She bade farewell to her women's meeting, which she had helped organize, without asking their permission to travel. She dominated a harassed ship's captain en route to the Caribbean, prophesied in the streets, and resettled meetings that had foundered. Yet in an autobiographical testimony, written from her sickbed and presented with corroborative testimonies from family, friends, and neighbors, she constructed a fragmented private persona that justified and complemented the public one. Thus, she described herself as literally flung from one place to another, as each divine summons was interrupted by a new, contradictory summons. Following her mission to New England and West Jersey, she went to New York to take passage for England but was suddenly called to visit Barbados. En route to Barbados, "the Lord put it into [her] heart to visit Friends in the leeward islands," and the boat reached there despite the efforts of the captain to steer toward Barbados. There she preached and reembarked for Barbados but suddenly felt another call to visit Friends at Nevis, and the ship duly changed direction and sailed there against the captain's will. Vokins was finally allowed to leave the boat at a deserted, mountainous spot,

> with my clothes so wet, that I could wring water out of them, and so dried them upon my weakly body, which cast me into such a feverish condition, that I was very dry, and I sat down on the shore . . . and then I swooned, and lay some time; but the arising of the life of Jesus set me on my feet again, and . . . I went to inquire for a passage for *Barbados*, . . . but I was not clear of Nevis, but hearing of a leaking vessel to go to *Antigua*, took my passage in that.[84]

Vokins's physical weakness and (as she thought) mental incapacity were not merely impediments that she had to surmount; they were, in her rendition, the very ground of her ministry, the proof that God was the sole agent of her accomplishments. Recounting her voyage to America, she wrote:

> I traveled by sea and land in the strength of the supporting power to many places . . . and [God] fitted me, who was the most unfit, and the poorest and most helpless that ever I did see concerned in such a service . . . and many *Friends* were tendered thereby (in many places in the sense of my

84. Vokins, *God's Mighty Power*, 38–40.

weakness) . . . and in the sense of God's great love to his tender Seed, I encouraged his children to suffer.[85]

The poet and preacher Lilias Skene comforted Lady Anne Conway, who suffered from chronic and excruciating headaches: "My desires are that more and more that eye may be opened in thee that looks beyond the things that are seen, and . . . live above the desire of temporary satisfactions, crying secretly in thy heart that by all thy present sufferings thy inquietness may be purged away and sensitive nature be crucified."[86] Conway's ultimate conversion to Quakerism, against the objections of family and her intellectual companion, the Cambridge Platonist Henry More, was inspired by her sense of the Quakers' deep calm in the midst of suffering, which she had witnessed in the Quaker female servants who attended her.[87]

For male writers, the terrors of self-doubt and the material deprivations caused by persecution were often mitigated by the solace of a good wife. Indeed, men perceived the finding of a helpmeet as essential to their effectiveness as itinerant preachers, and the discussion of courtship and marriage was a centerpiece of their published autobiographies.[88] Richard Davies vowed that he would travel to Wales only after God had promised to provide him with a wife.[89] John Banks's published journal is laden with nineteen letters to his wife, expressing his solicitude and describing his travels in the ministry (in the only printed letter she wrote to him, she described the details of her recent illness).[90] Women writers, however, tended either to ignore the existence of husbands or to describe their convincement in the face of a husband's opposition. Jane Atkinson Biles was so persistent in declaring her intention to travel in the ministry that her meeting approved her request over the refusal of her husband.[91]

85. Ibid., 36–37.
86. Ibid., 22. Lilias Skene to Anne Conway, August 16, 1677, reprinted in Marjorie Hope Nicholson, ed., *Conway Letters: The Correspondence of Anne, Viscountess Conway, Henry More, and Their Friends, 1642–1684* (New Haven: Yale University Press, 1930), 439.
87. Lady Conway to Henry More, Ragley, February 4, 1676, in Nicholson, ed., *Conway Letters*, 421–22.
88. Wright, *Literary Life*, 174. See the journals of Thomas Elwood (*The History of the Life of Thomas Ellwood: Written by Himself*, in vol. 7 of the Friends Library [Philadelphia, 1843], 399f.) and Thomas Chalkley (*The Journal of Thomas Chalkley*, 30).
89. Richard Davies, *An Account of the Convincement, Exercises, Services, and Travels, of That Ancient Servant of the Lord, Richard Davies* . . . (London, 1710).
90. Banks, *Journal of John Banks*, 14.
91. Bacon, *Mothers of Feminism*, 38. The next day Biles's husband announced that he was ready to "give up" his wife; finally he accompanied her on her voyage. Her first request to travel from America to England (her birthplace) was in 1699; the couple finally left in 1701.

Joan Vokins was convinced alone and converted father, husband, and children by her good example.[92]

> And I was, even as *Israel* at the *Red sea*, compassed all round on every hand . . . that [the Enemy's] proud waves of temptations, buffetings, and false accusations had almost sunk me under. . . . [Then God] did rebuke the Enemy . . . and overturned the mountains that were on each hand, and dismayed *Pharoah* and his host (which I may compare my relations and the professors unto,) for they pursued me and made my suffering great . . . and now when my husband, and children, and relations are with me in a good meeting, . . . it is a blessed reward for all.[93]

Regardless of her husband's newfound faith, Vokins clearly saw herself as the person responsible for keeping the family on the straight path, writing to him from Rhode Island, "it is my fear, now I am from them, that if you do not supply my place in my absence, that the spirit of this world will prevail, and hinder the work of the Lord in their hearts, and in thine too, and that will be to all our sorrow."[94] Elizabeth Webb told her husband of her call to travel to America, avowing that she would not go without his free consent. When he withheld it, she became ill and begged to be carried on board the ship as the only means of restoring her life. He relented, and she recovered.[95]

Unlike women's journals and autobiographies, formal testimonies to deceased husbands did affirm a strong emotional bond, yet even here, emphasis was laid on the wife's ability to sacrifice the bond for the good of the Lord, while children were mentioned only when they died or the mother had to leave them. As Ann Whitehead lay dying she said (in words later recorded by her husband), "this I shall leave behind me, as that which is satisfaction to me, that I never did detain [my husband] one quarter of an hour out of the Lord's service. . . . I have nothing desirable to me in this world save my husband."[96] The testimony of Eleanor Haydock to her husband described another ideal Quaker marriage. At the first Quaker meeting she attended, she saw him, and, "although I cannot say I was begotten into the faith by him as a father, yet can say, he was to me a faithful instructor." The two traveled with another Friend

92. PP, 1:109.
93. Vokins, *God's Mighty Power*, 20–21.
94. Joan Vokins, "A Letter to Her Husband, Richard Vokins, Sent from Road Island," June 14, 1680, in, *God's Mighty Power*, 52.
95. Webb, *A Letter from Elizabeth Webb*, 36.
96. Testimony to Ann Whitehead by George Whitehead, 1686, in *Piety Promoted by Faithfulness, Manifested by Several Testimonies concerning That True servant of God Anne Whitehead* (1686), 8, 9–10.

to meetings in Cheshire during the early 1670s, and then she continued traveling in Yorkshire with her female cousin. For five years they loved each other but took no action, each continuing separately in the ministry. They met again at the yearly meeting in London, after which she and Mary Worrel traveled in western England. They were finally married in 1682. "My dear husband often expressing his great love to me, above all visibles, as the best of enjoyment he had in this world; yet would say, I was not too dear to give up to serve the truth." When he died she was far away, he having come part way with her on her journey.[97]

In short, what the modern reader might recognize as an increasing self-awareness and rationality, what the modern feminist reader might applaud as a new, gendered self-confidence and assertiveness in a public forum, women themselves portrayed as an ever-present and potentially crippling loneliness and self-consciousness. The more they succeeded in presenting themselves as ministers who were also women (rather than as visionaries claiming to be out of the body), the more they depicted their bodies as burdensome or insignificant. The more they conflated their vocation as ministers with the exercise of a virtuous domesticity, the more they portrayed their own domestic happiness as threatened or nonexistent. Paradoxically, these assertive Quaker women drew their justification for personal authority from a long tradition of passive female visionaries who, Christ-like, became spiritual exemplars by embracing and enacting both their own suffering and that of others. Yet if women were sufferers, they also viewed their sacrifices as gestures that enabled them to achieve independence from social and emotional obligations as well as from an ancient tradition of female guilt. "And as for my husband and children," wrote Joan Vokins,

> my true and tender love was so great, that I could have done or suffered much for them: But if I had disobeyed the Lord, to please them, I might have provoked him to have withholden his mercies from us all . . . and none that disobeys the Lord can be excused, no more than *Adam* was, when he said, that the woman gave him the forbidden fruit, and he did eat. . . . And though man and wife should be helpful one to another in righteousness, yet too many there are, since the fall, that hinder and hurt each other.[98]

Was the tone of these women's writings a response to an actual lack of encouragement from men? Most male Friends gave their full respect,

97. Eleanor Haydock, "Testimony to Roger Haydock," in Roger Haydock, *A Collection of the Christian Writings . . . of . . . Roger Haydock* (London, 1710), B2–B4.
98. Vokins, *God's Mighty Power*, 23.

even adulation, to women as prophets. The physician who attended the dying Jennet Stow in 1702 recalled:

> The first time I cast my eye upon her was in a meeting, and though she spoke no words in that meeting, yet the very sight of her preached aloud to me. . . . In meetings she was valiant to fetch water for others. Her dwelling was deep, and the water she brought up was living to all whose senses were lively. The sound of her voice was beyond all the music I ever heard, and the least sound that dropped from her . . . with words, or if only a sigh or sound of any sort, I thought it always brought my mind nearer to the Lord, from whence everything of hers had its sweetness. . . . I am loth to say she was pure gold, yet never saw anything more like it.[99]

Another male Friend delivered this testimony to Jane Fearon: "She was at the first meeting of Friends, which it was my lot, more by accident than design, to drop into, and was the first minister I ever heard who preached up life and salvation, and perfect redemption. . . . I ever after highly esteemed and valued her as a messenger of glad tidings."[100] Indeed, several men's journals suggest that they took the ministry of women entirely for granted. "[I] got home," wrote Thomas Gwin in his (unpublished) diary, "to a meeting at Falmouth where our friend Mary Roak only was concerned, so as to preach in public a very good opportunity, and she rode to Marazion meeting next day." A few days later, "our friend Sarah Ellan and her companion were here: this Sarah had a serviceable gift and substantial ministry." A few days later again, "I had some service after Sarah Ellan had largely spoken." And again, "The next day I was at Looe with Dorcas Dole, where I had a short time after her, and in the evening we had another meeting in which I was much larger to the people."[101]

Several men also affirmed their support for the ministry of their own wives. So Thomas Whitehead testified of his wife Jane Waugh, "when the Lord has laid a necessity upon her to travel she have had freely of me and the Lord has blessed us so that we never wanted anything. . . . Now he has taken her from me again who was so near and dear unto me."[102] Alice Curwen was remembered by her husband in 1680:

> She was a dread and a terror to the wicked wherever she came: . . . and she would have stooped for the least grain for the gathering of the seed . . . her children and many more were convinced by her wise walking before them. . . .

99. "Testimony of Dr. Heathcot," PP, 2:271.
100. PP, 2:329.
101. Journal of Thomas Gwin, vol. S. 74/50, 54, 60. This was in 1703.
102. Testimony of Thomas Whitehead to Jane Waugh Whitehead, 1675, Dix Manuscripts 294, O.2.S., 3, Library of the Society of Friends, London.

And [let] this little testimony . . . be upon record for ages and generations to come, and that every testimony that is from the right seed may be kept, and that not one grain be lost.[103]

John Bowne's testimony to his wife Hannah reveals the complex attitude of a man eager to protect his spouse's (and his own) reputation by defending her wifely subservience and motherly care of her seven children, while at the same time attempting to convey his genuine awe of her superior vocation as a prophet: "She hath been truly faithful unto me until her last minute," he wrote, "as I have often heard her say: The resolution of her heart, and the bent of her spirit was altogether to be subject unto me in all things."[104] Bowne described Hannah's voyage from America to England and her return home:

But in a little time she declared unto me, that when she was upon the seas, it was in her [mind] that she must say, "Husband, I am come to see thee, but I must not tarry." . . . I could freely have given up all to have accompanied her [back to England]; but not daring to stir without the leading of the Lord, I was made freely willing to part with her, and remain at home with my little ones.

Bowne eventually sought his wife in Ireland, "but it was much with me to press her (so far as I durst) to haste away to her children; and when I durst proceed no farther, I gave up to accompany her . . . which hath been through Holland, Friesland, and . . . Emden."[105] Hannah Bowne died in London without seeing her children again. Bowne's closing testimony celebrated his wife's virtues:

Her garments are clean, and were clean without spot: a tender mother to her children, and faithful wife to her husband: and that which passeth all, truly resigned up to serve the Lord to the utmost of her power. . . . And now it's the breathing of my soul . . . that the residue of my time here I may live her life; and not only perform the faithful and true care of a loving father, but also keep the diligent watch of a tender mother unto and over our dear children.[106]

103. "Thomas Curwen his Testimony," in Alice Curwen, A Relation, B2, C1, C3.
104. "The Testimony of John Bowne Concerning his Innocent Wife and faithful yokefellow Hannah Bowne, as in the Simplicity of Truth it arose and was spoken amongst Friends, when met together to Accompany her body to the ground, at the house of their dear friends John and Mary Elson at the Peel-meeting-place London, ye 2nd of ye 12th month 1677," Luke Howard Collection, MS. 150, no. 15, Library of the Society of Friends, London. My thanks to Kenneth Carroll for directing me to this and other sources.
105. Ibid. Alice Curwen's husband Thomas had a similar experience, following his wife into the itinerant ministry after much hesitation (Curwen, A Relation, 2–3).
106. "The Testimony of John Bowne," MS. 150, Luke Howard Collection, no. 15.

Yet in several men's journals, and, indeed, in women's writings as well, we find the expectation that when the husband was a minister, the wife would readily defer to his vocation. William Dewsbury counseled "handmaids, whom the Lord hath counted worthy to part with your dear, and tender husbands" but had no parallel counsel for the husbands of female ministers.[107] After Mrs. John Banks died in 1691, her husband paid her this tribute: "She was a careful industrious woman, bringing up her children in good order . . . a meet-help and a good support to me in my travels, . . . and was never known to murmur, though I often had to leave her with a weak family."[108] The Dutch Quaker Gertruyd Niesen counseled women never to forget their wifely subordination. Nor should women think that, because they were more successful in business than their husbands, their subordinate status was thereby nullified: "And if any should say, I earn as well as my husband, and more, if it be so, that things so fall out that the wife has more opportunity to earn than the husband, yet know, that thou art the wife in the ordinance of God, and thy husband is thy head and thy Crown."[109]

Clearly, Friends' appreciation of female elders and ministers was based as much on notions of traditional femininity as on women's eloquence and capacity for leadership. The testimony to Ann Camm, wife of the minister Thomas Camm, shows the change in priorities, if not in basic values. The accounts of her career during her first marriage, when she prophesied as Ann Audland during the 1650s, described her independent travels in the ministry, her assertive self-defense at her public trial (attended by several eminent male Friends), and her establishment of new meetings. During her second marriage, she was separated from her husband only during *his* imprisonments or travels in the ministry:

> She participated with him as a faithful helpmeet, sympathizing with, and encouraging him, . . . supplying his place . . . in his family and business, and exerting a prudent care to keep their outward concerns in commendable

107. William Dewsbury, "Epistle from Warwick jail," 1664, in *The Life of William Dewsbury*, vol. 2 of The Friends Library (Philadelphia, 1842), 277.

108. John Banks, *A Journal of the Labours, Travels, and Sufferings of That Faithful Minister of Jesus Christ, John Banks*, vol. 2 of The Friends Library (Philadelphia, 1842), 40. See also the journal of James Dickinson, *A Journal of the Life and Labour of Love in the Work . . . of James Dickinson* (London, 1745), 384, and of Thomas Chalkley (*A Journal*, 26).

109. Gertruyd Niesen, "An Epistle to Friends in Holland, Friesland, the Palatinate, Crevelt, Frederickstad, Dantzik etc. to be read among them in the fear of the Lord," Rotterdam, September 15, 1682, A Collection of Letters, Dreams, Visions, and Other Remarkable Occurrences, fols. 45–46.

order. When he was at liberty, and believed himself called to go from home
in the work of the ministry, she not only freely resigned him to the Lord's
service . . . but was also at times a powerful fellow-laborer with him.[110]

Another version of Friends' testimony applauded her feminine reticence:

> She was . . . a pattern to ministers of her own sex in her wisdom and care to
> observe the proper season for her service; for without extraordinary impulse
> and concern, it was rare for her to preach in large meetings where she knew
> there were brethren qualified for the service, . . . and she was grieved when
> any, especially of her own sex, should be too . . . forward . . . and she would
> give advice to such.[111]

Moreover, while strong Quaker housewives and businesswomen
were viewed by male ministers as an essential and highly valued support
system, it was apparently crucial to men that women as ministers be
physically weak. Unlike testimonies written for men, which do not
mention the subject's health until the depiction of the last illness, public
women Friends were almost invariably described in terms of their
bodily afflictions. Joan Vokins, who led a women's meeting in Berkshire
and traveled in America and the Caribbean, was described as frail:
"Although her bodily presence and speech did seem weak, yet her testimony and writing was weighty and powerful." Elizabeth Stirredge had
a weak body but great eloquence. Mercy Johnson seemed strong only
when she was preaching. Agnes Penquite, when old, her nature almost
spent, seemed more divinely favored. Mary Mollineux was afflicted
with weak eyes and, being unfit for any other employment, was given a
good education by her father. The virtuous Barbara Bevan succumbed
to "delight in vain objects," but a severe illness at age sixteen taught her
that her soul was truly weak and "in need of a saviour." Elizabeth
Bathurst was so weak as a child that she was four years old before she
could walk.[112] These women's ability to surmount their own physical
weakness was clearly viewed as proof of their perfection, of their having
"killed the creature." And it is surely not too far-fetched to suggest that

110. Ann Camm, *A Short Account of the Life of Anne Camm, a Minister of the
Gospel, in the Society of Friends*, vol. 1 of the Friends Library (Philadelphia, 1837),
474–77.
111. Robson Manuscripts, H.R. N.1, 37, Library of the Society of Friends, London.
112. On Vokins, see "Testimony of Mary Drewet," in Vokins, *God's Mighty Power*,
n.p.; on Stirredge, see FL, 2:186; on Johnson, see PP, 1:252; on Penquite, see PP, 4:416;
on Mollineux, see PP, 1:154; on Bevan, see PP, 2:25; on Bathurst, see "Elizabeth
Bathurst," *The Friend* 52, no. 28 (April 22, 1879): 217.

for their male congregations and traveling companions, physical weakness was also an unconscious euphemism for sexual passivity.

WOMEN DEFECT

Not surprisingly, the Quakers' disciplinary apparatus and their new standards of self-scrutiny and public virtue engendered various forms of revolt. Joan Whitrow, who had composed a tract and put on sackcloth after the deaths of her two children in 1675, was instructed by the morning meeting to submit the tract to them for editing, "and tis desired by this meeting that what is chiefly to her own praise be left out."[113] By 1689 Whitrow had apparently defected, claiming that she was "one that is of no sect or gathered people whatsoever, . . . so I walk alone as a woman forsaken; I have fellowship with them that lived in caves, and in dens, and desolate places of the Earth, of whom the world was not worthy."[114] Her mystical and political writings of the 1690s would surely have been censored by the morning meeting had she remained a Friend. Addressing the king and Parliament in 1697, she wrote:

> The superior by his craft and subtlety gets the estate of the inferior to himself, by his oppression and extortion, and so constraineth the poor silly souls to labor hard, to maintain the pride and luxury of the rich . . . when, at the same time, the rich man's dogs fares better than the needy soul, and all this must be counted equal, just, and right, although it be contrary to nature it self . . . and then another sort of inferior learns of the superior to maintain a luxurious life, by covetous cozening, cheating, lying, over-reaching the simple, and so robbing one another of their rights, measures, and weights, without pity or compassion to their poor distressed neighbor.[115]

In language that was reminiscent of the radical prophecy of the Interregnum, Whitrow urged the government to stop taxing the poor and start taxing "paintings, all sorts of sports, perfumes, packs of dogs, costly furniture in houses, jewels, rings, necklaces . . . and all taverns . . . and the cursed playhouses to be severely taxed . . . and every particular person, men, women, and children, that goes to them."[116] She further urged readers not to cower in fear of an impending apocalypse, nor to

113. Morning Meeting's Book of Records, July 1677, fols. 17–18.
114. Joan Whitrow, *The Humble Address of the Widow Whitrowe to King William* (1689), 11–13.
115. Joan Whitrow, *Faithful Warning . . . to the Several Professors of Christianity in England, as Well Those of the Highest as the Lowest Quality* (London, 1697), Preface, "To the King and Parliament," n.p.
116. Ibid., n.p.

submit to any earthly authority, but to change their own lives through their own effort:

> I have seen the harvest ripe, the grapes and fruit just ready to drop . . . and say not in your hearts, "Who shall ascend to fetch it from above," . . . because it is in you; the word of faith is in you, the power to do the will of GOD is in you, . . . so that you need not go to the universities for it, or travel beyond the seas in far countries to seek for wisdom in remote places, for she standeth at the door of your hearts knocking, saying, "Open to me my beloved;" . . . if the soul yield it self to her for a full possession, then she penetrateth through it with her inflaming fire of love.[117]

This was dazzling prose, yet in Whitrow's own mind, the self-centeredness that Friends had observed and criticized twenty years earlier had made her unable to communicate a state of ecstasy directly. Instead, she narrated her own experience and mourned its passing:

> I was so inflamed with the burning love of God to all mankind, that I had poured it forth in the streets as I went along. . . . For Oh! the . . . melting bowels that I have had to poor orphans, as they have lain in the streets, almost eaten up of the evil and other distempers, which I have cried to the Lord to heal them: I thought, if I had had a little more faith, it would have been done.[118]

Whitrow's ecstatic moments invariably dissolved under an onslaught of self-doubt. Inspired, as she said, by the works of the mystic Johan Tauler, she recalled her own mystical experience:

> If ever any enjoyed a heaven upon earth, I enjoyed it then; . . . I withdrew my self out of the city and towns, into the fields and woods, where I spent my time from morning till night, in contemplating His glorious power. . . . I sat in the fields with the roaring bulls as with lambs, and with the birds I sang melodious praises; . . . visions and revelations attended me night and day; . . . I was as innocent in reality as a young child, and it was impossible to move me to anger.[119]

However, hearing of rumors circulating against her in London, she lost the vision; it was "as if I had never gone through it, which was the travail of my soul in watching, prayer and fasting, which hath been my exercise ever since."[120]

Abigail Abbott had an allied experience. She had been a much admired minister in Ireland and England but was, in the words of a Friend, "not strong enough to bear praise." After being married by a priest and

117. Ibid., n.p.
118. Whitrow, *Faithful Warning*, 76–77.
119. Ibid., 69–70, 103.
120. Ibid., 73.

disowned by Friends, she used her letter of condemnation as an opportunity for one last burst of self-flagellation:

> Which of you could think that such an one as I, whom God so evidently and graciously visited with exceeding kindness . . . should fall away? . . . I thought [Friends] were too severe with me, from whence a prejudice arose in my vile heart against them, . . . and so, rashly and resolutely, I rushed into the congregation of the dead, as a dog returns to his vomit. . . . Oh how can I now but wax hot against my self, and be contented to be trodden under foot by all, as mire in the streets! . . . I know none can parallel me in this our age; surely none so wicked as I . . . my crown is fallen from my head which once covered it, by which I had knowledge and skill how to behave myself: I am stripped naked.[121]

Other women felt entitled to greater freedom of movement and expression than the movement could or would tolerate, while still others apparently wanted less. Nine defected and joined the Camisards, five of them as prophets. Anne Steed, who had prophesied in London in 1705 and was disciplined by Friends, later preached and cohabited with another Camisard prophet. Sarah Wiltshire joined the mystical Philadelphian Society and in 1710 helped to inaugurate the Polemica Sacro-Prophetica, intended as a new synthesis of the Philadelphians and the French prophets. After she became the first woman to engage in miraculous healing, she and the mystic Richard Roach came into conflict with the Camisards, during which she was once actually pummeled by a male prophet.[122]

A greater number of women remained within the Quaker fold but ignored attempts by the meeting to curtail their activities. Mary Scott was admonished for preaching at Westminster Meeting, "pronouncing of divers judgments from God to come upon the people, which is cause of much disatisfaction to the Meeting." Summoned before Friends, she was reprimanded for being too long away from her family and ordered to stop preaching and return home to Wiltshire to clear herself of scandalous reports made against her there. Three months later the Wiltshire Meeting of Ministers also wrote, instructing her to come home. She

121. Abigail Abbot, letter of condemnation, reprinted in Thomas Wight, *History of the Rise and Progress of the People Called Quakers in Ireland, from the Year 1653 to 1700* (Dublin, 1751), 275–78. Abbott died in 1717.

122. Schwartz, *The French Prophets*, 117n, 142–43, 146n, 195. The other women were Ann Topham, Mary Turner, and Mary Parks. Wiltshire spoke her last prophecies in 1722–23. Marie Sterrill, a Frenchwoman, attended Quaker meetings in London before becoming a Camisard prophet. Beata Tovey, her husband, and Rachel East hosted Camisard meetings. Ann Finkley also had some connection to the group. Thirteen male Quakers joined the Camisards. The total number of English people who joined was 404. (Schwartz, *The French Prophets*, Appendix I).

acknowledged this, adding, "that her husband hath also commanded her home, notwithstanding all which she doth not incline to go as yet."[123] Alice Leake had traveled and preached for several years before 1692, when the Yorkshire Quarterly Meeting discussed her case:

> She has been cautioned and advised . . . [not] to wander about as she had done . . . and endeavor to settle herself in some place or other; to labor for her living: (as others are willing to do who have not otherwise in outward substance sufficient for their maintenance). But . . . [as she] after an idle unsettled manner continues to be both troublesome and burdensome to friends . . . we do advise . . . that until there be some manifestation of reformation and willingness in her to settle herself to some employment as aforesaid, and to take the advice of friends therein; . . . friends do not take notice of her appointment of meetings, nor yield her any assistance in her idle or wandering inclinations, for as to put her forth with horses or otherwise, from place to place.[124]

Two years later, Friends were still attempting to force her to adhere to one meeting; six months after that she was granted sixty-five pence, provided she stayed put; six months later again she was threatened with disownment and prosecution for vagrancy. In 1694 the prophet Esther Biddle, who had been imprisoned fourteen times since the 1650s, sought an audience with King Louis XIV of France in order to plead for peace. The contemporary Quaker historian William Sewel purposely omitted the fact from his new work, for although Biddle had been granted permission by Friends to make the trip, her mission was ill-advised and not to be imputed to the general policy of Friends.[125]

A number of women also pushed against the constraints on religious writing. When Elizabeth Redford's papers were repeatedly tabled or rejected by the meeting, she published them outside England and sent the printed work to one of the members.[126] Abigail Fisher's papers were returned to her because of her "hard expressions . . . [for] she suggests that some laws made by this meeting do stop the passage of the spirit, which is an undue reflection on the said Meeting. And her directing the Meeting to make her papers fit for the press this Meeting is not satisfied in nor cannot safely undertake." Fisher duly appeared before the meeting

    123. Morning Meeting's Book of Records, April 19, 1703, III/111–12; July 19, 1703, III/122; July 26, 1703, III/123. Scott had submitted a paper with Mary Bucket on January 6, 1700, III/9.
    124. Yorkshire Quarterly Meeting Minute of January 1, 1690, quoted in W. Pearson Thistlethwaite, *Yorkshire Quarterly Meeting (of the Society of Friends) 1665–1966* (Harrowgate: by the author, 1979), 163–64.
    125. Lydia L. Rickman, "Esther Biddle and Her Mission to Louis XIV," QH 47, (1955): 38.
    126. Morning Meeting's Book of Records, May 1695, II/83.

and affirmed both her unity with her own monthly meeting and her continued intention to publish her work. Judith Boulbie had been active as a writer and member of the Yorkshire Women's Meeting since the 1670s. In 1686 she submitted a paper on the impending judgment and a "Warning and Lamentation over England." After repeated submissions, publication was refused, but she was allowed to circulate it in manuscript.[127] Twelve years later the Yorkshire Quarterly Meeting of Ministers and Elders considered a paper that they had already rejected,

> which she desired might go forth to the magistrates and the like having formerly been presented to this meeting and she being desired to acquiesce in the matter, but still remaining under exercise it is consented to by friends that this paper may be laid before friends in the ministry of the second day morning meeting at London for them to . . . give their sense whether it may be expedient to publish it.[128]

Of those women who demanded more freedom of movement as prophets, many were poor, and some may have actually been homeless. In 1694 the York Quarterly Meeting gave the Balby Monthly Meeting five pounds toward the support of Alice Leake and asked to be kept informed of her needs, "she being now weak, and not in a capacity of being removed to Holderness Monthly Meeting, where her right settlement ought to be."[129] In 1697 Judith Boulbie was given nearly ten pounds "in regard of her great necessity," the fourth time she had been so helped. (In 1701 the meeting recorded that Boulbie, "an ancient friend," wanted to travel to Ireland. They referred her to the monthly meeting for a certificate.)[130] Thirteen years after Abigail Fisher tangled

127. Wright, *Literary Life*, 105 and 252 n. 18.
128. Yorkshire Quarterly Meeting of Ministers and Elders, Minute Book June 21, 1689–August 26, 1798, October 6, 1698, reel 4, fol. 25, Friends Historical Library, Swarthmore College, Swarthmore, Pa.
129. Thistlethwaite, *Yorkshire Quarterly Meeting*, 164. In 1676 Margery Ffan came to Whitby (Yorkshire) from London as a minister and was supported by the Scarborough monthly and the quarterly meetings. Nine months later the monthly meeting wrote to London, inquiring whether they had approved her move to the north, "for it is the general sense of this Q[uarterly] M[eeting] that she ought to have a settled abode that she may not be necessitated to travel continually which may both draw beyond a true motion and is also beyond her ability." Six months later the meeting recorded that London Friends had little knowledge of her movements and that Friends at Whitby were urged to assume responsibility for her (155). Margaret Phillips was cited by the quarterly meeting at Stafford as "a poor woman void of habitation" who "desert[ed] her honest employment to wander about from country to country under pretence of the service of truth" (QM at Stafford vs. Margret Phillips, July 8, 1689, Leek Manuscripts, Crosfield Collection, fols. 157–58, Library of the Society of Friends, London.
130. Thistlethwaite, *Yorkshire Quarterly Meeting*, 50, 56, 62. Boulbie had already received funds in 1679, 1689, and 1695 (Yorkshire Quarterly Meeting of Ministers and Elders, April 3, 1701, reel 4).

with the authorities, she submitted another paper and was advised "to be quiet and neither trouble her self nor friends with her papers, but study to be a good example of peace and industry in the house where she is placed." She died shortly thereafter in the London Friends' work house.[131] Esther Biddle had once been married to a prosperous London cordwainer, whose business had suffered after the Great Fire of 1665. She later lived behind the Peel meeting house in a room given over to poor widows and received a regular pension of five shillings from Friends.[132]

In contrast, women who were privileged by wealth or education often evinced less interest in freedom of the spirit than in personal agency. Indeed, several were clearly relieved to have the burden of their own leadings lifted off their shoulders. In 1681 Mary Hampton, active in the Bristol Women's Meeting, informed George Fox that the Lord had visited her while in bed and instructed her to write the king a letter that began, "Hear O King and live for ever, for the lord requires it of thee that thou wilt take this great oppression that is put upon the tender consciences of his tender people." Terrified to do so, and even more terrified of divine wrath if she did nothing, she finally delivered the prophecy to two men Friends to submit to Fox's own judgment; it was not published.[133]

Mary Rogers would have envied her. The former traveling companion of Elizabeth Webb, she informed the Burlington Meeting of Ministers in 1698 that the Lord had called her to travel to the Caribbean, "and though she had tried several ways to have evaded it . . . yet every way, except that, seemed as darkness to her." She asked the advice of Friends, who gave testimonies of their satisfaction in her, and "in much love and brokenness, the meeting gave her up to the will of the Lord. (She died the following year en route to Jamaica.)[134] Frances Danson of Virginia confided to George Fox after being forbidden to preach:

> When they were angry and did watch over me maliciously for evil . . . if I had not had so great consolation from god . . . I think I could readily have set my hand to any paper of condemnation that friends in London should have

131. Morning Meeting's Book of Records, May 1700, II/337; February 10, 1700, III/14; August 9, 1703, III/124; August 16 and 23, 1703, III/126, 127; September 20, 1703, III/128, 129; May 7, 1716, IV/102.

132. Rickman, "Esther Biddle's Mission," 39.

133. Mary Hampton to George Fox, Bristol, 1681, A. R. Barclay Manuscripts, Library of the Society of Friends, London, reprinted in JFHS 46, no. 2 (Autumn 1954): 87–88.

134. Burlington Meeting, July 22, 1698, quoted in James Bowden, The History of the Society of Friends in America, 2 vols. (London: Charles Gilpin, 1850), 2:43, 45.

required of me, though I knew not wherein I had done wrong. So I was at a
great strait: fearing to sin against god by condemning that which god had not
condemned: and fearing to give offence to friends.[135]

Affirming her loyalty and love for Friends, Danson went on to present
a proposal to act as a broker in the purchase of large tracts of land from
the Indians for transfer to Quaker owners. Her success in negotiating
with the Indians was, she claimed, a feat that others marveled at:

I being but a woman and of a weak capacity. Many wise men have sought
to have this and could not prevail, for they had not the Indians' free consent.
The Indians' kings, they will sell my friends any land they have. I have given
many of the kings and princes a coat in ernest for the land and some further
debts they owe me. . . . One of the kings said I did well that I was not hasty
for my debt, for if I had not the land, never *no Englishman* should.[136]

Margaret Everard had been a successful preacher. Later she published
a tract in which she defended her preaching of a Christ outside humanity
and the doctrine of the resurrection and original sin and accused Friends
of laying too much emphasis on the doctrine of the light within:

And Friends, least any should imagine or say, this is not her inditing, nor
would she have put to print, without being put on or advised by some; In
answer, I tell you, it was my own act, without the persuasion of any; and if
it were needful, I could produce sufficient witnesses, who have heard me say
often, I shall not be easy, until I have written something, that all that have
any true love to me, might understand how it is with me.[137]

Convinced that her work would be censored, she refused to submit it to
the morning meeting: "I was not willing to give them trouble, or myself
the disappointment. Well I have done it, and am satisfied. . . . And as for
those, or such as will not be satisfied, I cannot help it, it is no disappointment to me."[138] Susanna Blandford, an opponent of the meeting
system who called herself a dissenting Quaker, composed a polemic that
criticized promiscuous preaching and urged a renewal of traditional
female subordination:

I am of the apostle's mind, ". . . Women . . . keep silence in the church, and
give place to man, to whom God hath given preeminency, and made fit for

135. Frances Danson (in Virginia) to George Fox in London, n.d., A. R. Barclay
Manuscripts, reprinted in JFHS 50, no. 3 (1963): 173.
136. Ibid., 174, 175.
137. Margaret Everard, *An Epistle of Margaret Everard To the People Called Quakers and the Ministry among Them* (London, 1699), 7. See William Mather, *An Instrument
from That Little Stone . . .* (London, 1694).
138. Everard, *An Epistle*, 7.

that great work." . . . Not but that I know there is many good and virtuous *women*, who are appointed for good examples in their families, who in *modesty*, *sobriety*, *charity*, and *good works*, a *good life*, and *conversation*; with these I join, and in that life I desire to preach to my children, friends, neighbors and servants. . . . I have also by my experience learned that in sights and visions, without watchfulness, there is a temptation near, there being a readiness in man to cast that on others, which God intends for our selves, if we could patiently wait till the vision speaks.[139]

In support of her argument that women keep out of the public ministry, Blandford composed a poem, recounted a prophetical dream in which she put her hands into the mouth of a wild dog who had no power to bite, and shared her reservations on a controversial work by George Keith, inferring that Keith should, like Mary, have sat silently at Christ's feet.[140]

Not one of these confused or delinquent women was a good soldier in the mold of the new ministry described earlier. Yet each of them was the product of a mentality that put the ideal of passivity and selflessness in tension with that of independent action and self-scrutiny. For those who did embrace an orthodox Quaker identity, that tension would be resolved only during the final moments of life, when they would be able to demonstrate, both to themselves and to others, that they had permanently killed the creature.

THE ART OF DYING

Seeing us sorrowful, she said, "Be quiet, for I am as
comfortable, and as well in my spirit, as ever I was."
And a little before she departed, she called [her
daughter] Rachel, saying, "Take me in thy arms;" and
then said, "I am in peace."
        The death of Margaret Fell Fox, 1702

They saw . . . that the way to life was through death.
    Charles Marshall's testimony to Elizabeth Bathurst

One spring day in 1677, Susanna Whitrow, a fifteen-year-old girl living with her parents near London, suddenly fell ill. Her mother's first

139. S[usanna] B[landford], *A Small Account Given Forth by One That Hath Been a Traveller for These 40 Years in the Good Old Way* (1698), 22.
140. Ibid., 29–30, 39–40; S[usanna] B[landford], *A Small Treatise Writ by One of the True Christian Faith; Who Believes in God and in His Son Jesus Christ* (London, 1700), 5.

thought was that Susanna was depressed about a romance, because the girl's father had recently been abusive toward her about a young man she seemed to fancy. However, Susanna did not want to marry, she said, though she acknowledged that her father *had* been harsh to her, to the whole family, in fact. "Oh my bowed down and broken-hearted mother! What have been thy sufferings in this family! . . . How often hast thou told my father . . . [to] repent and turn from the evil of his ways? . . . Now the day is come thou hast so long warned us of, now the Lord is broke in upon us."[141] Far from suffering the pangs of mere lovesickness, Susanna felt herself locked in mortal combat with a fiend she called "the tempter." If the girl prevailed against her own (and her father's) sinfulness, if she fully overcame her own vain will to live, she would fulfill an earlier vision of her mother, the prophet Joan Whitrow, that she herself would one day have the power to prophesy.

> O Lord, the Enemy has wounded my heart, he has wounded my head, and he has wounded my heel; Come, Lord, I make room, I make room, my heart is open: O rip me up, and set me in thy bosom. . . . O, I feel the Enemy coming in like a flood; Lord, drive him out. . . . I am poor, I am needy, I need thy strength continually to withstand the tempter. O Lord, stand by me, move not from me; for if thou go, the tempter will come.[142]

Susanna asked her mother to fetch another minister, the elderly Rebeckah Travers, to come and pray at the bedside. Then she begged for a reprieve: "O Lord, be pleased to restore me to my former health, then I will wait diligently upon thee; I will sit on the ground, with my head in the dunghill; I will never lift up my soul to vanity; my heart shall never go after the sight of my eyes. My dear mother pray for me."[143]

Susanna's own sin, which "stood like mountains" between herself and God, was that she had disobeyed her mother by attending an Anglican service in Covent Garden, where her companions mocked her for her unfashionable Quaker clothing.

> Then I have come home . . . and have gone immediately up into my chamber and locked the door, and altered all my laces, and so I have gone to their worship in the afternoon dressed in their mode, and then I have pleased them. . . . Oh! if they had ever tasted the [life of Jesus] . . . they would not

141. Joan Whitrow, *The Work of God in a Dying Maid, Being a Short Account of the Dealings of the Lord with one Susannah Whitrow, About the Age of Fifteen* (London, 1677), 18.
142. Whitrow, *The Work of God in a Dying Maid*, 13.
143. Ibid, 21.

dare to spend their precious time in adorning themselves like *Jezebel's* patching and painting, and curling their monstrous heads.[144]

For a time, Susanna was able to identify with the great prophets of history. "Come all ye holy prophets, who were Quakers and tremblers at the word of the Lord; come Moses, come Jeremiah, come holy Habbakuk, now I am one with thee, now my belly trembles, my lips quiver, and my heart droops, because of the Lord." But the terror came back, and the wretched girl refused to let her head be moved on the pillow; it had to be "nailed" there to help her concentration until she had overcome the tempter. "I would not suffer a thought to wander, if I move, I shall be drawn off my watch, and then the tempter will prevail."

At last, after four days and nights of struggle, her cries taken down by several women witnesses, including the maid, Susanna embraced her own death. "I have overcome, my Saviour hath bound him." Now began her great ecstasy. For several days and nights she hardly slept, but woke herself up to pray, oblivious of the neighbors who passed in and out of the room to listen: "Be contented with mean things; . . . remember him that sat on the ground . . . that withdrew into gardens and desolate places of the earth, my soul hath fellowship with him." Then she faltered, unable to let go of life.

> O my dear mother, if it please our . . . Father to spare me this time, we will get us into the country to some little remote place, amongst the woods, where none can hear us; O there shall our cries pierce through the heavens, which shall make the earth to ring, and the birds shall hear the echo thereof. Oh there my blessed mother, will we sing praises praises praises with rended hearts, and our mouths in the dust.[145]

Susanna asked, if she were really to die, for one whole day in which to pray without ceasing, in order to ensure her place in heaven, and for that day she prophesied continuously to audiences who had come to hear her preach: "What shall we do for the daughters of Jerusalem, who are haughty and go with outstretched necks and wanton eyes." Her final words were for her mother, whom she prayed would die also: "My dear mother, I shall be as a new born babe. I shall be very simple, but bear me, for the Lord is with me. . . . O come away, why dost thou stay? I am ready, I am ready." Then she died, "without either sigh or groan," the miraculous event witnessed and recorded by Joan Whitrow, Rebeckah Travers, and another woman Quaker and published in two versions

144. Ibid, 26, 30 (page misprinted as 14).
145. Ibid., 36.

by Friends. "So I felt and know in these sudden and renewing trials there was judgment," Travers wrote, "and none but a tender mother can tell what it is to have hopeful children so soon taken from them, and see the Lord is righteous in what he doth, and I . . . have drunk into this cup, and a more bitter one."[146]

Joan Whitrow also recorded the recent death of her other child, a boy named Jason, who studied at the local Latin school. Before he became ill Jason told his mother:

> Mother, the next time I go to the tavern they will bid me preach a sermon to them in Latin; then I will say unto them, "I will preach you a sermon in English" . . . then I will say, "Wo to the proud persons, wo to the scoffers, wo to the drunkards of England. . . . What will you do in the dreadful day of the Lord, that is coming upon England?" . . . Mother, sometimes I have such a trouble in me, that I am not so good as I would be, that I play so much, and do not everything as you would have me; [I pray] yet for all this, the Devil will come in, and take my mind off the Lord.

Weeping, Jason often told his mother that he wanted to die and be out of this wicked world. "Oh, that I did enjoy that that you enjoy . . . that my heart might be made glad as yours is." "He departed this life," his mother wrote, "not being six and a half years old."[147]

For Friends of the second and third generations, the apocalypse was no longer envisioned as a world turned upside down. It was that moment at the end of each person's life when the triumph over "the creature" was put to its final test. When Rebeckah Travers was asked to add some words to a testimony written for the minister Alice Curwen, since she had been present at the death, Travers at first laid it aside.

> In my mind I had not much for printing it, there being not much prophecy in it . . . but upon my bed that night or towards morning, . . . was set before me the blessing of Abraham . . . "and his portion was to die in peace, and this thou art a witness this good woman did; and dost thou think it small to be testified to when thou seest so many restless impatient ones tossed, and crying for help to physicians of no value, and can find no rest?" Then said I, "Let me die as she had done . . . for prophecy has and must cease, and tongues fail, but the peace that is given us of Christ Jesus is everlasting."[148]

146. Ibid., 5.
147. Ibid., 51.
148. R[ebeckah] T[ravers], "A Testimony concerning Alice Curwen," in Curwen, *A Relation*, n.p.

If death was a more individualized experience than public prophecy, it was by no means a private experience for Quakers or virtually any seventeenth-century person. Death, like childbirth, was a communal ritual, attended by relatives, neighbors, and fellow church members, who rejoiced at a "good" or peaceful death as proof that the soul was on its way to paradise. When the little daughter of the prophet Ann Audland Camm lay suffering, her father asked those sitting on the bed (including servants) to leave the room, but the child soon called them back in order to preach to them.[149]

Quakers immortalized the good deaths of Friends by composing and publishing formal testimonies. After Jane Waugh Whitehead died in 1675, her friend Theophila Townsend wrote to Whitehead's husband requesting a letter:

> For she is worthy for her uprightness to be had in remembrance because she kept her garments clean and never lost her integrity to the end of her days . . . and it often lives in my heart that her uprightness must not be forgotten though the lord hath taken her . . . out of the midst of a crooked and perverse generation that were not worthy of her, so desiring thee to be careful to answer my desire with all the speed thee can and send it to me by some trusty messenger.[150]

Whitehead has also written to Friends on his own account. His own testimony described his wife's final epiphany:

> [The] morning before death [she] told friends she was going. . . . All along she still desired my company. . . . John Anderdon held her hand and I held her up about her neck and she manifested her sensibleness and her faithful constant love unto me. . . . So they that are wise shall shine as the brightness of the firmament and they that turn many to righteousness as the stars for ever and ever.[151]

Clearly, the written testimony was far more personalized and introspective than earlier tracts or books of sufferings, yet it was just as much a literary genre with its own literary conventions. Friends' private letters are replete with detailed descriptions of illnesses and suggestions for

149. Thomas and Ann [Audland] Camm, *The Admirable and Glorious Appearance of the Eternal God* . . . (London, 1684), 4. Sarah died in 1682. On the social experience of dying, see Lucinda McCray Beier, *Sufferers and Healers: The Experience of Illness in Seventeenth-Century England* (London and New York: Routledge and Kegan Paul, 1987), 247.

150. "A letter of Theophila Townsend of Cirencester to Thomas Whitehead of South Cadbury requesting an account of his late wife by way of testimony," September 22, 1675, Dix Manuscripts, O.1.S.

151. Thomas Whitehead's testimony to Jane Waugh Whitehead, 1675 Dix Manuscripts 294, O.2.S., 3.

cures. So in 1686, John Rous wrote to his mother-in-law, Margaret Fell
Fox, about his son Nathaniel, who had taken sick while at boarding
school: "We presently sent for a doctor who gave him a vomit that
afternoon, which gave him near twenty vomits and four stools, and next
day gave him a purge which wrought five or six times with him and
cleared his body very finely. The next day after that, he was pretty well
and came down stairs."[152] In testimonies, however, attempts to cure or
nurse the patient were mentioned only to demonstrate the futility of
earthly intervention, while the family's expressions of grief were presented only to set the stage for the protagonists' triumph over their own
and others' egoistic sentiments. We find no displays of passion like that
of Mary Penington, describing the death of her first husband years before
her convincement:

> At last he called to me—"come my dear, let me kiss thee before I die!" which
> he did with that heartiness, as if he would have left his breath in me . . . which
> having done, he fell into a very great agony . . . [and] snapped his arms and
> legs with such a force that the veins seemed to sound like catgut tighted upon
> an instrument of music . . . upon which [the doctors] came to me and desired
> me to go from the bedside to the fire . . . for while I stayed there he could not
> die; which word was so great, so much too big to enter into me; that I like
> an astonished amazed creature, stamped with my foot, and cried, die! die!
> must he die! I cannot go from him.[153]

Nor do we find instances of personal meanness or spite, such as this
passage from an unpublished letter by Mary Lovell to a woman Friend,
written on her deathbed in 1680: "I am moved of the lord to write to
thee, to let thee know, that thou hast not had the true love of god in thy
heart towards me . . . but a feigned love of thy own making, and thou
didst show it to me, in thy own will at thy own time, and for thy own
ends, so it did me, none or any good."[154] Nor, finally do we find any hint
of self-regard, as in this unpublished passage by Joan Whitrow, probably
censored by the morning meeting: "Out of the willingness of my heart
have I offered my children unto the Lord, although my children were as
dear to me as my life, and I could have laid down my life for theirs, . . .

152. John Rous to Margaret Fell Fox, Kingston, March 20, 1686, Abraham Manu-
scripts no. 29A, transcript, Library of the Society of Friends, London, and Ross, *Margaret Fell*, 342–43.
153. Mary Penington, *A Brief Account of My Exercises from My Childhood* (Philadelphia, 1848), 33.
154. Mary Lovell to Mercy Atey, May 24, 1680, Temp. Manuscripts 10/45, Library
of the Society of Friends, London.

yet I durst not ask their life, although my dear child so much desired it: but I said unto the Lord . . . let thy will be done."[155]

Nevertheless, the raw emotional force of the deathbed ritual makes the formalized expressions of piety and resignation come alive for the modern reader. "I have all my days had a great sense of death . . . that is, the state after death is removed. But there remaineth still a deep sense of the passage; how strait, hard and difficult it is. . . . My . . . husband [Isaac Penington] . . . was constantly with the Lord in his sickness, yet when the last breath was breathing out, his groans were dreadful. I may call them roarings . . . through the disquiet of his soul at that moment."[156] The minister Sarah Padley, "much through her husband's great affection to her and his earnest desire for her life, . . . seemed a little to desire life, but presently checked herself for it, and returned to her former resignation of spirit . . . a little time after she said, 'In a few days, in a few days, they will say, Sarah Padley is dead.'" Her audience marveled. She was thirty-four.[157] Mary Sam, who lived with her grandfather William Dewsbury during his long imprisonment in Warwick jail, told him, "I shall die today, and a grave shall be made, and my body put into a hole, . . . and I am very willing to die, because I know it is better for me to die than to live." She was twelve.[158] In this way every good death—and there were hundreds recorded in collections of testimonies—reminded other Friends of their original convincement and reaffirmed the group's solidarity by the new evidence of God's presence among them in the hearts of the afflicted. For it was surely easier to identify with these ordinary people dying ordinary deaths than with the superhuman figures who had suffered earlier. In the frightened eyes of Susanna Whitrow, a girl who liked pretty clothes and the admiration of friends, every bystander could read his or her own destiny and final apotheosis.

Indeed, the passage of certain Friends, as recorded in their testimonies, must have appeared so transcendent as to make witnesses and readers almost long for death. Alice Curwen refused to take any medicine, "not choosing anything but the will of God . . . though she seemed not very aged, and but a few days before appeared a healthy strong woman." Curwen herself avowed, "I am freely given up to [God's] will, whether it be life or death; I am as clear as a child." When Grace Watson became

155. "Joan Whitrowe's testimony concerning the loving kindness of the Lord," MS. vol. S. 462/86, Library of the Society of Friends, London.

156. Mary Penington, *Experiences in the Life of Mary Penington*, 3d ed. (Philadelphia, 1848), 23.

157. PP, 1:201–2.

158. Dewsbury, *Life of William Dewsbury*, 287. PP, 1:86. Sam died in 1680.

ill at age nineteen, "it was not perceived in all the time of her sickness that she desired to live." Ann Whitehead achieved a pinnacle of detachment before her own death: "I am in peace and have nothing to do." To her husband she said, "It may be you are afraid . . . my dear, go to bed, go to rest, and if I should speak no more words to thee, thou knowest the everlasting love of God . . . though I am in a dying condition it is a living death." Gulielma Penn avowed on her deathbed, "I never did, to my knowledge, a wicked thing in all my life." Mercy Johnson affirmed, "I have nothing to do but to die. Keep you near to the Lord, that so when you come to lay down your heads you may have nothing to do but to die. . . . I would not live if I might choose to have the whole world."[159]

The public dying of Friends was also important in attracting new converts, since non-Quakers often visited the afflicted and attended the funerals, where they witnessed Quaker sermons preached at the graveside. Elizabeth Stirredge's imprisonment came about because she testified a day of mortality to some non-Quakers surrounding the deathbed of a neighbor. When several of the group died soon afterward, the local priest, perceiving a threat to his authority, went after her. Stirredge described a crowd of onlookers at the Quaker graveyard and herself trembling "that I could hardly stand on my feet," preaching repentence. "I saw the tears running down many faces, and many said, they would never be again as they had been." She was haled off to the magistrates, one of whom spat out, "You are an old prophetess, I know you of old . . . you are a troublesome woman, parson Cross complains of you; you scatter his flock . . . you made an oration at the daughter's grave last week, and now at the father's also: you shall certainly go to prison, that shall be the least I will do to you."[160]

If the spiritual *meaning* of this public dying was to reaffirm the Quakers' direct connection to God's word and power, its therapeutic *function* was to bring both the dying person and the family to an acceptance of death, often over a prolonged period, by placing the patient in the role of minister. Indeed, it often happened that the patient could not die until he or she had counseled the family about their own morality and led them to an acceptance of their impending loss. From the time of her earliest fits, Judith Fell, age twenty-four, began exhorting

159. On Curwen, see Travers, "Testimony concerning Alice Curwen," n.p. On Watson, see PP, 1:163. On Whitehead, see PP, 1:100. On Penn, see PP, 1:113; On Johnson, see PP, 1:253, 255.

160. Elizabeth Stirredge, *Strength in Weakness Manifest* . . . 3d ed. (London, 1772), 115, 116, 117.

her visitors. "I am well every way. . . . If I should live never so long, it can never be better; for my heart is fully satisfied, and my soul magnifies God. . . . thou has cast me on this bed of sickness for the glory of thy Name; therefore Father, glorify thy self in me." As her father cradled her in his arms, her mother asked how she was; "All is well," she said, "I am in my Father's Arms every way." Her illness increasing, she asked to see Friends and began preaching to them:

> And always after thus exercised, she was very sweet in her spirit, and had great room in her heart to speak to any that came in. . . . So that the third day in the Morning we [her parents] were made willing to give her up to the Lord . . . and she was glad and embraced us with much love. And . . . [her] sister . . . was made willing to come to her, and giver her up to the Lord, though it was very hard to part with her willingly; for they greatly loved one the other. . . . And so on the third day she said, 'Father, I have long waited for you all, but now it's well.' And after she had some very violent fits . . . yet return'd again with high praises in her joy; Oh! the streams of his love runs over all, even to the skirt of the garment. Oh! the now is the fountain set open for . . . Jerusalem to bathe in! . . . And so, within a little time after, she drew her last breath and so ended comfortably.[161]

Ruth Middleton was sick with consumption for seven months in 1701. Seeing her mother in distress, she advised her to remember Abraham's willingness to sacrifice Isaac and let her die. "O dear mother! I would be glad if thou couldst freely give me up." Asking to see her father and brother, "feeling for her brother's face, she stroked it and said, 'Farewell, be a good boy.'" She died, wrote her father, "being eleven years, two months, and four days old."[162] The prophet Ann Audland Camm's daughter Sarah kissed her weeping mother and then recited the Lord's Prayer three times, "and the third time till she came to that petition, 'Thy will be done . . . ' which she spoke deliberately, signifying to those about her, that they were all to mind that." Lying in her father's arms, she comforted him, "thou art tender and careful over me, and hath taken great pains with me in my sickness, but . . . it is the Lord that is my health and physician. . . . She died; wanting eleven days of nine years old."[163]

For children, a perfect death might have canceled out guilt at having fallen short of their parents' high expectations. Susanna Whitrow knew

161. *A Short Testimony concerning the Death . . . of Judith Fell* (London, 1682), 3–4.

162. PP, 1:194. Middleton died in 1701.

163. Miscellanous Manuscripts, Dying Words of Children, 1675–1709, n.p., Friends Historical Library, Swarthmore College, Swarthmore, Pa. Two other versions exist, one in PP, 1:88–90. The other, *The Admirable and Glorious Appearance*, is by Thomas and Ann Camm (5, 8).

that her mother saw in her the germ of prophecy, but she had never been
ready to endure that humiliation. "Oh! how have I been against a
woman's speaking in a meeting? but now, whether it comes from man,
woman, or child, it is precious indeed."[164] For parents, the deathbed was
a place where the tenderness that had been repressed in the interests of
good child-rearing might be freely and safely expressed, for the calmness
and miraculous resignation of the dying child proved that the triumph
over the creature was at last complete. When David Barclay, the nine-
year-old grandson of Robert Barclay, lay dying, Friends remembered,
"he spoke not as a child but a man of weighty experience."[165] Thus, in
a curious reversal of values, the Quakers' earlier vision of the adult as
a metaphoric child, shedding the encumbrances of his or her identity in
an ocean of infantilized bliss, was replaced by that of the child as a
metaphoric adult, shedding the trivial joys and sins of childhood in an
acceptance of his or her own final dissolution. Death may have been a
social ritual, but, unlike the ecstatic meetings of earlier times, it was a
ritual not of bonding but of individuation and separation.

164. Whitrow, *Work of God in a Dying Maid*, 20.
165. Manuscripts by Robert Barclay, son of R. Barclay, Urie, February 20, 1691, A
Collection of Letters, Dreams, Visions, and Other Remarkable Occurrences, MSS. S. 78,
fol. 27. On the ideal of the child's adult behavior see Jerry W. Frost, "As the Twig Is Bent:
Quaker Ideas of Childhood," QH, 60, no. 2 (Autumn 1971): 81–82.

Epilogue

Sometime in the early eighteenth century, two elderly Quaker ministers sat down with Sarah Taylor, an eighteen-year-old Friend, and passed on the tale of an adventure they once had when they too were young.[1] The storytellers were Jane Fearon and James Dickinson, recounting a visit to Scotland during the early years of their ministry. On a night when it was late and raining and Jane was very tired, they passed a commodious house and decided to ask for shelter, but their guide was chary of going in, and when they insisted he announced they had no further need of him and disappeared. The two ventured inside and were taken to a small, inviting room, provided with a posset and a cold meat pie, and left alone. After a time they began to grow uneasy, until Jane confided that she mistrusted their hosts so much, she believed the pie might be made of human flesh. James ate the pie, counseled caution, and wedged the door shut with a bench while they waited for divine guidance. "His mind," he assured her, "had been favored by that which never had deceived him, to believe if they carefully minded its pointings they should be directed how to escape."

The two sat perfectly still for some considerable time, until James announced that the moment had come to flee for their lives. They found

1. "A memorable instance of divine guidance and Protection in an account of some extraordinary circumstances which attended James Dickinson and Jane Fearon, ..." A Collection of Letters, Dreams, Visions, and Other Remarkable Occurrences of Some of the People Called Quakers, fols. 77–80, Library of the Society of Friends, London. Jane Fearon died in 1737. The adventure probably occurred in the 1680s.

a second door leading to a stone stairway, slipped through it and, taking off their shoes, silently escaped from the house past an old woman who sat sharpening a knife. Once outdoors, they ran through the rain to a bridge "but felt a restraint when they had got to the middle of it, on which James said that was not their way." He soon became convinced that they must wade or swim across the river, and when Jane cried that they would surely be drowned, as the river was full, he assured her they would be preserved, "if they kept a steady eye to best direction." They struggled across, trudged on, and sat down under a sand bank, but James, still uneasy, insisted they go farther, "upon which Jane said, 'Well! I must go by thy faith, I know not what to do.'" Finally, crawling under another sand bank, James allowed them to rest; "I am now easy and believe we are perfectly safe and feel in my heart a song of thanksgiving and praise." Jane, exhausted, replied, "I am so far from that I cannot so much as say the Lord have mercy upon us."

Some minutes later a group of men holding torches and leading a dog appeared on the other side of the river. "Seek'em Keeper!" they cried, but the dog refused to cross the bridge. The Quakers lay low and safe until morning, when they saw clearly that, had they remained under the first sand bank, they would have been spied by their attackers. Jane was afraid to return to the house for their baggage, but James was clear; "thou mayst Jane safely for I have seen it in that, that never failed me." They ventured back and found their horses saddled and the old woman gone.

Nearly two years later, James passed by on another preaching mission and found the house destroyed. The townspeople told him they believed the inhabitants were indeed murderers, for they had found bodies in different states of decay with some body parts missing. Five people had been executed.

Quakers of the seventeenth and early eighteenth centuries wrote many autobiographical accounts of their experiences among hostile magistrates and countryfolk, nearly all of them steeped in an aura of occult power, divine miracle, and personal heroism. This particular story is similar, in many respects, to the eighteenth-century folk tale "Hansel and Gretel." We see the inviting house, the seductive offer of food and comfort, the hint of cannibalism, and the innocent young hero and heroine far from home, running through the woods to safety, watched by a divine presence. The similarity ends, however, in the story's depiction of its heroine, waiting in terrified passivity while her companion attuned himself to the divine forces that would direct his attempts to save them both.

What is the story's truth? As a rendition of the couple's exciting exploits and religious faith (and allowing for the inevitable distortion of nostalgia and fading memory), the story as it stands may be taken as literally true, and one whose memory both hero and heroine apparently treasured. Interestingly, James Dickinson did not include it in his published journal, perhaps because he felt he should have succeeded in subduing and converting his attackers, as other Friends had reportedly done, instead of merely escaping from them.[2]

As a rendition of Quaker women's experience, the problem of interpretation is far more complex. Female ministers did defer to the male leadership in matters of general policy, though not always in matters of visionary insight. Moreover, Jane's reticence actually reflected a persona that was both more modern and more rational than James' visionary hero. For James remained a traditional prophet, one of the dying breed who preached in the streets of London during the 1690s: "Woe . . . woe . . . woe . . . from the Lord to the crown of pride in this place . . . for the viols of his wrath will be poured down upon it."[3] Jane Fearon, on the other hand, became the New Woman, an educated pastor and author of theological treatises. In 1698, attempting to preach about universal love in a Baptist meeting in Cumberland, she was put out of the room, the minister refusing to allow a woman to speak. She then offered to engage in a public dispute on this and other subjects "but was denied, . . . except on these terms, that only one man of my friends should dispute with him in my stead, and neither I nor any other should be suffered to speak a word." We may imagine the words she would have spoken in debate by reading the tract that she published

2. James Dickinson, *A Journal of the Life and Labour of Love in the Work of . . . James Dickinson . . .* (London, 1745). Dickinson recounted several trips to Scotland but did not provide many specific details. Leonard Fell, on a visit to Scotland during the same period, was robbed by a highwayman of his horse and money. He began to preach to the robber, who threatened to blow out his brains. Fell said, "Though I would not give my life for my money or my horse, I would give it to save thy soul," upon which the man returned both horse and money (SPQ, 370; see also 446). Typical of Dickinson's own journal accounts of visits to Scotland is the following, in 1701: "The inhabitants came running out of their houses and crowded about me, I opened unto them *how they might come to the true knowledge of God* . . . and the hearts of several were reached" (Dickinson, *A Journal*, 133–34).

3. James Dickinson, "A Message and warning I delivered in the streets of London from Whitechapell to Westminster ye 5 of ye 11 month 1694," Gibson Manuscripts 334/79, Library of the Society of Friends, London.

as a substitute: "It is to no purpose to allege that the death of CHRIST was effectual enough to have saved all mankind, if in effect its virtue be not so far extended as to put all mankind in a capacity of salvation. . . . Neither doth [God] require of any man that which is impossible, but is a principle of truth engraven in every just man's mind."[4] Crudely put, James Dickinson walked in the light, while Jane was enlightened.

Yet we have also learned that many of these new women presented themselves as fragmented, isolated, and fragile, both physically and emotionally. As Jane herself tells us, she was not imbued with any special insight or courage; indeed, she became so terrified and disoriented that she could not even say "The Lord have mercy upon us." Whether we take women's humility and insecurity as an expression of their real inner consciousness or as a narrative strategy—an attempt to deflect readers' attention away from the fact that they were crossing all kinds of physical, social, and literary frontiers—we must admit that at some level Jane Fearon had a less integrated sense of self than James Dickinson.

The reader of seventeenth-century Quaker texts observes a group of individuals undergoing a transition in which the attentiveness to external voices and visions was redirected toward the voices that speak inside the mind. Later Friends continued to seek and to experience visionary ecstasy; indeed, their writings, particularly those epistles addressed to Friends, are replete with mystical imagery and feminine spiritual symbolism. Yet Friends also displayed a more active interest in personal motivation, a readiness to analyze and reanalyze their own thought processes and emotions. We may observe both old and new modes of attention or perception at work in this testimony by Sarah Fell, addressed to the monthly meeting at Hawkshead, Lancashire, in 1688, expressing contrition for her impulsive behavior in a meeting:

> Friends . . . the last time that I was amongst you . . . in the latter end of the meeting by the rehearsing of things . . . concerning my sister [I] did fall into a passion or hastiness in which I did speak something . . . which was thought did touch the meeting generally though I did not think so when I spoke it, yet because I spoke it so publicly I am willing to give you satisfaction hereby for I do acknowledge that it was not right in me to speak such a thing . . . but it was *a hasty spirit that was up in me* upon which I own my condemnation

4. Jane Fearon, *Universal Redemption Offered in Jesus Christ, in Opposition to That Pernicious and Destructive Doctrine of Election and Reprobation of Persons from Everlasting* (1698), n.p., 4, 11, 17.

and am willing if this will not give you satisfaction to do what more you may require of me who is your friend.[5]

The Quakers' developing subjectivity involved not only an increased attentiveness toward personal motivation and emotion but a self-censoring process that rendered aspects of bodily experience as forbidden territory. The earliest Friends' capacity to achieve physical ecstasy had been predicated on a concept of self-transcendence, a casting-off of their individual social bodies as wives, husbands, servants, or gentlewomen. Friends thus experienced intense physical sensations while feeling themselves to be in a partially disembodied state. However, once women's attention was refocused on those social bodies, once their authority as prophets or elders was understood to rest on their identities as virtuous daughters or female heads of families, their bodies' potential range of expression inevitably became tied to notions of appropriate daughterly or matronly behavior. Thus, Alice Hayes's autobiography revealed both a new openness about personal emotion and a new negativity about physical sensation. Her intense passion for her husband was presented as a challenge to be surmounted, ("nothing came so near me as my husband"), not the ecstatic experience of earlier Friends (as in Francis Howgill's letter to George Fox, written in 1655, "I am melted I am melted with thy love").[6] The fact that Alice Hayes was presumably referring to an actual physical relationship, while that of Francis Howgill and George Fox was purely spiritual, negates neither her attempt to distance herself from her own passionate attachment nor Howgill's earlier attempt to achieve a sensation of total merger with his soulmate.

Certainly, earlier Friends had displayed an aptitude for suffering equal to that of the next generation, yet Quakers of the 1650s also perceived their spiritual salvation as the ability to cure physical illness. For later Friends the reverse was true: Their spiritual epiphany was accompanied not by a state of heightened sense perception or physical well-being but by physical dissolution. Indeed, the only passages that match the intensity of earlier Friends' physical experience are accounts of bodily negation: Joan Vokins lying panting and exhausted on a Caribbean beach,

5. "Letter from Sarah Fell to Mo Mtg of Hawkshead expressing contrition for hasty conduct in Mtg, 1st/88," Dix Manuscripts, G13 I, Vol. 294, Library of the Society of Friends, London (emphasis added). Margaret Fell's daughter Sarah was married to William Meade in 1681, so this may have been a different Sarah Fell.

6. Francis Howgill to George Fox, 1655, A. R. Barclay Manuscripts, vol. 323, no. 117, reprinted in JFHS 48, no. 2 (Autumn 1956): 93.

letting the sun dry out her sodden clothing; eleven-year-old Ruth Middleton stroking her brother's face as she calmly prepared herself to die.

As leading Friends came to identify the condition of walking in the light with the exercise of conventional social virtues, they, like many of their contemporaries, became progressively less committed to the goal of universal social transformation and progressively more concerned with internal organization, the ordering of families, competence in business, and the good opinion of the world. Their visionary expression was generally restricted to closed meetings of Friends, and their evangelizing was frequently conducted in America or Wales or Scotland, far from the scrutiny of their own close neighbors. The ideal of collapsing class and gender boundaries, expressed in women prophets traveling together in pairs of young and old, mistress and servant, evolved into an ideal of benevolent charity, accompanied by massive doses of business advice and moral counsel.

To be a new woman, then, was not to identify oneself with the poor and deprived of this world, as earlier female prophets had done, nor was it to affirm those qualities that were considered generic to all females. Later women writers celebrated not simply nurturing motherhood but strict, moralistic, competent motherhood. They celebrated not simply loving charity and compassion but tutelage, helping the poor and deprived of this world to strive toward a condition of self-sufficiency and respectability. In short, for later Quakers to affirm the rights of women was also to affirm, explicitly or implicitly, the importance of bourgeois values.

In this respect, the Quaker experience paralleled developments in the wider society, for the most systematic feminist thinker of the 1690s was Mary Astell (1666–1731), who combined a passionate belief in women's capacity for mature judgment and independence with an equally passionate attachment to conservative social values. Astell's own vision of utopia, "such a paradise as your mother Eve forfeited," was centered on the formation of a residential college for women, whose inmates would enjoy both the leisure and the seclusion necessary to develop their full intellectual and moral capacities, embracing a life of noble friendship, sustained scholarship, and Christian philanthropy.[7] This intellectual and

7. Mary Astell, *A Serious Proposal to the Ladies* (n.d.), 40. On Astell, see Ruth Perry, *The Celebrated Mary Astell: An Early English Feminist* (Chicago: University of Chicago Press, 1986). Hilda L. Smith discusses Astell's systematic feminism and conservative politics in *Reason's Disciples: Seventeenth-Century English Feminists* (Urbana: University of Illinois Press, 1982), x–xi, 117. Astell was a gentlewoman whose adult life was spent in London as an independent writer. She never married.

moral discipline required freedom from the body as much as freedom from the demands of society, for "she who is swayed by her affections more than by her judgment, owes the happiness of her soul in a great measure to the temper of her body; her piety may perhaps blaze high but will not last long."[8] Astell's world view was clearly aristocratic, as she defended the high-church principles and Tory politics of her class. It was also bourgeois, for her advocacy of gender equality was based not on a recitation of high-born woman worthies, nor on the opportunities for queens and noblewomen inherent in dynastic government, but on the role of education in shaping character and on the potential for talented middle and upper class women to develop those characters by rejecting a life of triviality and acquiring habits of bodily restraint and voluntary self-discipline.[9]

The most eminent female visionary of the 1690s was a blind, elderly, middle class widow, whose writings spoke eloquently for female autonomy and women's education yet were silent on the political and social issues that had engaged the prophets of the Civil War period.[10] Jane Lead (1624–1704) was the central figure of the Philadelphian Society for the Advancement of Piety and Philosophy, a community of intellectuals and mystics in London who adhered to the theosophy of Jacob Boehme.[11] Lead's first important vision revealed

> an overshadowing bright cloud, and in the midst of it the figure of a woman, most richly adorned with transparent gold, her hair hanging down, and her face as terrible as crystal for brightness, but her countenance was sweet and mild. . . . Immediately this voice came, saying, Behold, I am God's eternal virgin, Wisdom, whom thou hast been enquiring after. I am to unseal the treasures of God's deep wisdom unto thee. . . . I felt myself transmuted into one pure flame.[12]

8. Astell, *A Serious Proposal*, 33.
9. Smith, *Reason's Disciples*, 125, 127.
10. DBR 2:181. Lead came from a respectable family in Norfolk and was married to a London merchant. Impoverished after her husband's death in 1670, she joined the household of John Pordage, and the two established an Independent congregation. After Pordage's death in 1681, and another period of poverty, she became the inspiration for the Philadelphian Society, a group that included Richard Roach and Francis Lee, both Oxford scholars, and the mystic Ann Bathurst, a gentlewoman. D. P. Walker writes that "the . . . Philadelphians were all middle or upper class, well educated, comfortable people who, until they went in for chiliasm, enjoyed social and financial security" (*The Decline of Hell* [Chicago: University of Chicago Press, 1964], 255). Asking God what he would do for the nation, Bathurst was advised to attend to her inward teaching "and not to look out after national concerns, or the public affairs of the world" (The Diaries of Ann Bathurst, Rawlinson Manuscripts D. 1262/15, Bodleian Library, Oxford).
11. Désirée Hirst, *Hidden Riches: Traditional Symbolism from the Renaissance to Blake* (New York: Barnes and Noble, 1964), 103–9.
12. Jane Lead, *A Fountain of Gardens* (London, 1697–1701), 1:18.

Lead totally transformed Boehme's rendition of feminine wisdom as a
passive receptacle for God's revelation:

> Great Heros yet must now give way,
> And learn a *Female* General to obey;
> Led on to mighty Deeds and vast Renown,
> [By] The High-born Beauteous *Amazonian* Queen,
> Immortal Heroine:
> Of all the Virgin Train most dazling fair.
> Mother of All, and All compriz'd in Her.[13]

As an outspoken advocate of female prophecy (conditional on the
prophet's modest and sober behavior), she recorded a vision of a Tree
of Life with an eagle's nest in its branches: the nest of Eve. "For, as of
old, Eve will now come forth as a mighty, strong, terrible Eagle."[14] Her
spiritual symbolism also included metaphors of money and credit, metaphors that lent an added material dimension to her vision of female
autonomy:

> Being dead wherein we were held fast, we should serve in the newness of spirit;
> as being discharged from the law of the first husband, to which we were
> married, after the law of a carnal command: whence we are now free to be
> married unto him that is raised from the dead, and so shall become the Lamb's
> wife, jointured unto all the lands and possessions that he hath. The eternal
> revenues are belonging to her, whether invisible or visible; all power in heaven
> and earth is committed to her . . . whether it be gifts of prophecy, or of
> revelation, or of manifestation, . . . or that high tongue of the learned.[15]

Thus, the ongoing tradition of female mysticism and nascent feminism
was increasingly detached from any vision of social solidarity or broad
social transformation. In this respect, the true inheritors of the radical
tradition of early Quakerism were the eighteenth-century Shakers, a

13. Lead, *Solomon's Porch*, Preface to *A Fountain of Gardens*, n.p. Internal evidence suggests that Lead, who was then blind, may have written this poem in collaboration with her disciple Richard Roach. My thanks to Pat Sommers for this insight. Lead
was criticized for calling her Virgin Wisdom a goddess and the mother of the eternal son
of God (Letter of Henry Dodwell to Francis Lee, Aug. 23, 1698, reprinted in Christopher
Walton, *Notes and Materials for an Adequate Biography of the Celebrated Divine and
Theosopher, William Law* [London: printed for private circulation, 1854], 191–94, esp.
193).
14. Lead, *A Fountain of Gardens* 2:106, quoted in Hirst, *Hidden Riches*, 171.
Lead's injunction to prophets to behave soberly and modestly is quoted in Nils Thune,
*The Behmenists and the Philadelphians: A Contribution to the Study of English Mysti-
cism in the Seventeenth and Eighteenth Centuries*. (Uppsala: Almquist & Wiksells Bok-
tryckeri AB, 1948), 91–92.
15. Lead, *A Fountain of Gardens*, 1:69–71, and see Catherine F. Smith, "Jane
Lead's Wisdom: Women, Property, and Prophecy in Sevententh Century England," in
Poetic Prophecy in Western Literature, ed. Jan Wojcik and Raymond-Jean Frontain
(Rutherford, N.J.: Fairleigh Dickinson University Press, 1984), 55–63.

movement of artisans and workers whose worship was characterized by social egalitarianism, the leadership of female visionaries, and an attitude toward the body that combined celibacy and uninhibited physical worship.[16]

Quaker women ministers and elders occupied a social environment that was considerably more spacious than that of most of their contemporaries. Unlike earlier visionaries, dying Friends were not attended and counseled by male confessors or ministers, for they themselves were ministers. Unlike Puritan goodwives (who ruled their children but sat silent in their congregations), or members of John Bunyan's church at Bedford (which completely disavowed women's speaking), or women in Baptist congregations (who might vote but could not pray or hold church office), Quaker women traveled widely and independently, expressing moral and doctrinal insights as well as visions. And unlike the housewife of eighteenth-century bourgeois society, Quaker matrons were encouraged not only to work and earn but to control the funds set aside for Friends' charitable operations.[17] Nevertheless, Quaker women's increased authority was conditional on a number of important sacrifices: an abrogation of their original commitment to universal social transformation, a gradual renunciation of the ecstatic, bodily knowledge experienced by earlier prophets, and the cultivation of a painful double consciousness: the denigration of one part of the mind, called "the creature," by another part of the mind, which watched and subdued it.

Quaker women of a much later period, those who inspired and organized the movements of abolition and women's suffrage, appear to have drawn on both the early tradition of egalitarian worship and the later tradition of formal organization and bourgeois womanhood. Certainly, the experience of the women's meeting (transported to America) was a training ground for women who became social and political activists. Yet the most prominent of those activists—Susan B. Anthony, Lucretia Mott, Florence Kelley, Alice Paul, Jane Addams—were associated with a faction within nineteenth-century Quakerism known as

16. Edward Deming Andrews, *The People Called Shakers: A Search for the Perfect Society* (New York: Dover Publications, 1963). On the influence of Quakerism on the early Shakers, see Clarke Garrett, *Spirit Possession and Popular Religion from the Camisards to the Shakers* (Baltimore and London: Johns Hopkins University Press, 1987), 140–42.

17. Michael R. Watts, *The Dissenters: From the Reformation to the French Revolution* (Oxford: Clarendon Press, 1978), 319–20. Sheila Wright, "Quakerism and Its Implications for Quaker Women: The Women Itinerant Ministers of York Meeting, 1780–1840," in *Women in the Church*, ed. W. J. Sheils and Diana Wood, Studies in Church History, no. 27 (Oxford: Basil Blackwell, 1990), 403–14.

Hicksites. Named after Elias Hicks, a rural Friend from Long Island, the Hicksites separated from the orthodox Quaker establishment in defense of the original principle of Christ within the believer (as opposed to the emphasis on the historical Christ) and as opponents of slavery. In some ways these rural Hicksites, largely farmers and small shopkeepers, recalled the original communities of Friends from the northern counties of Yorkshire and Lancashire, for both groups subscribed to a kind of cooperative asceticism that stressed social justice and deemphasized social compartmentalization, particularly the notion of separate roles for men and women, rich or poor.[18]

It is as automatic for feminists to point to a decline for women in the early modern period as it is for Whig historians to see progress. Indeed, the two are evidently interrelated, for the evolution of the modern nation-state and expanding capitalist economy was linked to a restriction of women's economic activities and to a conception of citizenship and public service that was emphatically masculine. Yet the experience of Quaker women visionaries, and of other religious women of the seventeenth century, makes plain the inadequacy of words like "advance" or "decline" for historians of gender. Women's prophecy during the Civil War period was wide-ranging and utopian; yet it also entailed a denial of womanhood as a source of public power and expressiveness. By the end of the century, women mystics, theologians, poets, mothers in Israel, clerks of meetings, and itinerant ministers, all based their public authority on a conception of womanhood that narrowed their physical and intellectual horizons as it opened up new avenues of intellectual expression and public action. Women had thus placed themselves on a trajectory that moved them to claim progressively greater authority and feel progressively greater anxiety; for the freedom of the earliest Quakers, the liberation from the customs and contradictions of a hierarchical society, had been transformed into another set of customs and contradictions, against which modern feminist thinkers would brace as they mobilized their own new energy.

18. Margaret Hope Bacon, *Mothers of Feminism: The Story of Quaker Women in America* (San Francisco: Harper and Row, 1986), 90–97. Nancy A. Hewitt argues that it was the schism itself, rather than the specific views of the Hicksites, that opened a space for Quaker women activists ("The Fragmentation of Friends: The Consequences for Quaker Women in Antebellum America," in *Witnesses for Change: Quaker Women over Three Centuries*, ed. Elizabeth Potts Brown and Susan Stuard [New Brunswick, N.J., and London: Rutgers University Press, 1989], 93–119).

Well-Known Women Visionaries
of the 1640s and Early 1650s

Name	Sect or Group	Location
Adams, Mary	Baptist, Familist, Ranter	Essex
Attaway, Mrs.	General Baptist	London
Avery, Elizabeth	Fifth Monarchist	
Bancroft, Elizabeth	preached against Laudian ritual	Cambridgeshire
Bauford, Joan		Kent
Bilbrowe, Mary		
Burch, Dorothy		
Cary, Grace	Puritan Royalist	Bristol
Cary, Mary	Fifth Monarchist	London
Channel, Elinor	Royalist	Surrey, London
Chidley, Katherine	Brownist, Leveler	London
Davies, Eleanor		London
Gadbury, Mary	Ranter	London, Southampton
Gray, Elizabeth		
Griffin, Anne		
Hall, Anne	Baptist	Suffolk, Scotland
Hazzard, Dorothy	Puritan, then Particular Baptist	London
Hempstall, Anne		London
James, Christian	Royalist	Cornwall
Johnson, Katherine	prophesied Charles's death	
Jones, Sarah	Independent	
Kent, Mrs. Robert		
Lee, Lydia		
"Major's wife"		London
May, Susan	Puritan	Kent
Parr, Susannah	Independent/Presbyterian	Exeter
Pocock, Mary	mystic, follower of John Pordage	Reading
Pod, Ann		
Poole, Elizabeth	Particular Baptist	London

SOURCES: DBR; *Discoverie of Six Women Preachers;* Ludlow, "'Arise and Be Doing'"; Edwards, *Gangraena; Calendar of State Papers*, D. S., Charles I.

Name	Sect or Group	Location
Pope, Mary	Puritan	London
Pordage, Mary	mystic, wife of John Pordage	Reading
Robins, Mrs. John	wife of John Robins, "the Shakers' God"	
Sutton, Katherine	Baptist	
Thomas, Arabella		Salisbury
Trapnel, Anna	Baptist, Fifth Monarchist	London
Turner, Jane	Independent, Baptist	
Warren, Elizabeth	moderate Independent/Presbyterian	Suffolk
Wight, Sarah	Independent, Baptist	London

"First Publishers of Truth":

Women Active as Prophets, Missionaries, and Writers, 1650–1665

Name	Location	Prophet	Missionary	Writer[2]	Married[3]	Quaker after 1665
NORTHERN AND MIDLANDS COUNTIES[1]						
Aldam, Mary*	Yorkshire	x			MF	x
Ambrose, Alice*	Lancashire	x	x			
Audland, Ann, then Camm	Westmoreland	x	x	x	MF	x
Backhouse, Sarah*	Lancashire	x			MF	x
Barwick, Grace*	Yorkshire	x		x	MF	
Benson, Dorothy*	Yorkshire	x	x		MF	d. by 1660
Benson, Mabel Camm*	Westmoreland	x	x		MF	x
Birkett, Alice	Westmoreland	x	x			
Blaykling, Anne	Yorkshire	x	x	x	S	x
Braidley, Margaret	Westmoreland	x	x	x	M	x
Brooksop, Joan*	Derbyshire	x	x	x	MF	x
Buttery, Isabel	Yorkshire	x	x		S	
Cleaton, Ann	Lancashire	x	x	x	S	x
Clement, Mary		x	x		MF	d. 1659
Cowart (Court), Elizabeth	Westmoreland	x	x		S	

SOURCES: DQB; SM; GBS; BQ; FPT; Besse; Morning Meeting's Book of Records, Library of the Society of Friends, London.

*Signed petition against tithes, 1659.

[1]The North/South division is taken from the maps in BQ.

[2]Includes women who wrote works addressed to the public, either individually or cooperatively.

[3]M = married at time of conversion. MF = married to a Friend at time of conversion. S = single at time of conversion. Most single women later married Friends.

Name	Location	Prophet	Missionary	Writer	Married	Quaker after 1665
NORTHERN AND MIDLANDS COUNTIES (*continued*)						
Crackenthorp, Grace*	Lancashire	x				
Farmer, Elizabeth, then Yarkley, then Andrews	Salop	x		x	S	x
Fell, Margaret, then Fox*	Lancashire	x	x	x	M	x
Fisher, Mary*	Yorkshire	x	x	x	S	x
Fletcher, Elizabeth	Westmoreland	x	x	x	S	d. 1658
Frith, Susanna*	Derbyshire	x		x	MF	x
Holmes, Jane	Yorkshire	x		x		x?
Hooton, Elizabeth	Nottinghamshire	x	x	x	M	x
Howgill, Mary	Westmoreland	x	x	x	S	x
Killam, Margaret*	Yorkshire	x	x	x	MF	x
Latchett, Sarah	Cheshire	x	x			
Leake, Ann	Yorkshire	x				x
Leavens, Elizabeth, then Holme	Westmoreland	x	x	x	S	d. 1665
Milner, Jane, then Simcock	Cheshire	x	x		S	x
Morgan, Elizabeth*	Cheshire	x	x		MF	d. 1666
Newby, Margaret	Westmoreland	x	x	x	MF	d. 1657
Nicholson, Jane	Cumberland	x	x		MF	x
Pattison, Barbara	Yorkshire	x	x	x		
Robinson, Ann*	Cumberland	x	x			d. 1662
Routh, Elizabeth	Yorkshire	x				
Smith, Mary	Yorkshire Cheshire	x		x	S	x

Name	Location	Prophet	Missionary	Writer	Married	Quaker after 1665

NORTHERN AND MIDLANDS COUNTIES (continued)

Name	Location	Prophet	Missionary	Writer	Married	Quaker after 1665
Stokes, Jane	Derbyshire	x	x		MF	x
Sutton, Margaret	Westmoreland	x	x	x		x
Tickell, Bridget (?)		x	x		MF	d. 1650s
Tomlinson, Elizabeth	Yorkshire	x			MF	x
Tompkins, Mary	Lancashire	x	x			x
Ward, Rebecca*		x	x		S	
Waugh, Dorothy,* then Lotherington	Westmoreland	x	x	x	S	x
Waugh, Jane,* then Whitehead	Westmoreland	x	x	x	S	x
Wheatley, Elizabeth	Durham	x	x		S	x
Wilkinson, Agnes	Yorkshire	x				
Wilkinson, Jane*	Yorkshire	x	x			
Williams, Elizabeth		x	x			x
Wilson, Ann		x	x			x
Wilson, Margaret*	Durham	x	x			x
Wood, Margaret*	Cheshire	x	x			

SOUTHERN COUNTIES

Name	Location	Prophet	Missionary	Writer	Married	Quaker after 1665
Adams, Elizabeth*	Kent	x			M	x
Anderdon, Mary	Devonshire			x	S	
Austin, Ann*	London	x	x		M	d. 1665
Bennet, Sarah*	Bristol	x	x		M	x
Bettris, Jane*	Oxford	x	x	x	M	x
Biddle, Esther	Oxfordshire, London	x	x	x	MF	x

Name	Location	Prophet	Missionary	Writer	Married	Quaker after 1665
SOUTHERN COUNTIES (*continued*)						
Blackborow (Blackbury), Sara	London	x		x	MF	d. 1665
Blaugdone, Barbara*	Bristol	x	x	x	Widow	x
Booth, Mary*	London			x	M	x
Brown, Ruth, later Crouch*	London	x			S	x
Burden, Ann,* then Richardson	Bristol	x	x	x	M	x
Burges, Grace	Cornwall	x	x			
Cannings, Eleanor	Gloucestershire	x			M	x
Chattam, Katherine, then Chamberlain	London	x	x		S	
Cheevers, Sarah	Wiltshire	x	x	x	M(F?)	
Clark, Mary	London	x	x		MF	d. 1658
Coleman, Ann	Dorset	x	x			x
Cook, Mary	Colchester	x				
Cotton, Priscilla	Plymouth	x	x	x	MF	d. 1664
Cox, Elizabeth*	London	x	x		S	
Davies, Tacy*	London, Wales	x			MF	x
Desborow, Joan	Colchester	x				
Downer, Ann, then Whitehead	Oxfordshire, London	x	x	x	S	x
Dyer, Mary	Essex	x	x	x	M	d. 1660
Erbury, Dorcas*	London	x	x	x	S	
Erbury, Mary		x	x			
Evans, Katherine	Somerset	x	x	x	MF	x
Fairman, Lydia	London			x		
Gargill, Anne	London	x	x	x		
Gibbons, Sarah	Bristol	x	x			d. 1659
Gilman, Anne	Reading			x		x

Name	Location	Prophet	Missionary	Writer	Married	Quaker after 1665

SOUTHERN COUNTIES (continued)

Name	Location	Prophet	Missionary	Writer	Married	Quaker after 1665
Gold, Ann	London	x	x	x		x
Gotherson, Dorothea Scott*	Kent	x		x	MF	x
Gouldney, Mary*	Bristol	x				
Gove, Jane	Kent	x	x			
Greenway, Margaret*	London			x		
Grey, Margaret	Colchester	x				
Harding, Deborah	Gloucester- shire	x	x		M	d. 1665
Harris, Elizabeth*	London	x	x		MF	x
Hignell, Temperance	Bristol	x		x		d. 1656
Hunt, Elizabeth*	Welling- borough	x				
Jones, Sarah*	Bristol?			x	M	
Juxon, Anne	Leicester- shire	x	x		M	x
Langley, Ann	Colchester	x				x
Marshall, Elizabeth	Bristol	x	x		MF	x
Morry, Dewens		x		x	S	x
Oades, Lydia	London	x	x	x		x
Page, Mary	Welling- borough	x			MF	d. in jail
Peake, Rebecca	Welling- borough	x			MF	x
Penington, Mary	London			x	MF	x
Prince (Pierce), Mary*	Bristol	x	x		MF	x
Raunce, Frances	Oxfordshire	x	x		MF	d. 1665
Simmonds, Martha*	Essex, London	x	x	x	M	x
Smith, Elizabeth, then Hubbersty*	Gloucester- shire	x	x		S	d. 1668

Name	Location	Prophet	Missionary	Writer	Married	Quaker after 1665

SOUTHERN COUNTIES (continued)

Name	Location	Prophet	Missionary	Writer	Married	Quaker after 1665
Stammage, Anne	Colchester	x				
Stirredge, Elizabeth	Gloucester-shire	x		x	MF	x
Stranger, Hannah, then Salter	London	x	x	x	MF	x
Travers, Rebeckah	London	x		x	MF	x
Webb, Mary*	London			x	Widow	x
Wetherhead, Mary	Bristol	x	x		S	d. 1658
White, Dorothy*	Weymouth	x	x	x		x

OUTSIDE ENGLAND OR UNKNOWN

Name	Location	Prophet	Missionary	Writer	Married	Quaker after 1665
Bateman, Susanna				x		
Beckly, Beatrice		x	x			
Cooke, Lucretia	Ireland	x			M	x
Eedes, Judith				x		
Lynam, Margaret	Ireland	x	x	x	MF	x
Mallins, Mary	Ireland	x	x			
Withers, Mary		x	x			
Zinspinning, Judith	Holland	x	x	x		

Prophets Appearing Once or Twice, 1650–1665

Name	Location	Known to Be Active after 1665
NORTHERN AND MIDLANDS COUNTIES		
Adgit, Sarah	Cheshire	
Airey, Anne (Agnes)	Westmoreland	
Arnell, Elizabeth	Derbyshire	
Arnold, Susanna*	Yorkshire	x
Ashburner, Jane	Lancashire	
Beck, Anne	Lancashire, Yorkshire	
Clayton, Margaret (Mary)*	Lancashire	
Dawney, Susanna*	Yorkshire	x
Endon, Mary*	Cheshire	
Fara, Anne	Cheshire	
Fell, Katherine*	Cumberland	x
Fell, Mary*	Lancashire	x
Fricknall, Ann*	Nottinghamshire	
Garnet, Widow		
Gilpin, Margaret	Westmoreland	
Grones, Isabel		
Howgill, Mary	Lancashire	
Kennebie, Anne*	Lancashire	
Leadbetter, Mary*	Nottinghamshire	x
Liddall, Barbara	Yorkshire	
Makreth, Agnes*	Lancashire	
Morley, Bathia	Yorkshire	
Nicholson, Anne*	Yorkshire	
Ramsey, Margaret	Durham	
Scaif, Mary*	Lancashire	
Siddall, Barbery*	Yorkshire	
Simcock, Elizabeth	Cheshire	
Veery, Anne	Westmoreland	
Wilkinson, Jane		
Wilkinson, Margaret	Horsham?	

SOURCES: GBS; Besse; FPT; SM.
*Signed petition against tithes, 1659.

Name	Location	Known to Be Active after 1665

NORTHERN AND MIDLANDS COUNTIES (*continued*)

Williamson, Mrs.		
Withers, Jane	Yorkshire	
Wood, Mary*	Cheshire	
Woolhead, Alice	Derbyshire	

SOUTHERN COUNTIES

Akehurst, Mary	Lewes, Sussex	x
Alcock, Hannah	Oxfordshire	
Atkins, Elizabeth	Dorset	x
Baker, Elizabeth	London	
Baker, Sarah	Bedfordshire	x
Botham, Mary	Wellingborough	
Bourne, Mary	Essex	
Bowman, Alice	Staffordshire	
Braddy, Mary	Essex	
Burges, Grace	Cornwall	
Caustock, Margery	Sussex	
Child, Ann*	Essex	
Coates, Elizabeth?		
Coates, Mary	Oxfordshire	
Cocks, Ann	Cambridge	
Cole, Margaret (Mary)	Plymouth	
Corbey, Ann*	Northamptonshire	
Cox (Cocke), Ann*	Northamptonshire	x
Crooke, Katherine	Herefordshire	
Crouch, Judah (Judy?)	London	
Crouch, Mildred	London	
Curtis, Anne*	Reading	x
Daniel, Susan	Truro	
Day, Alice*	Norwich	
Deane, Elizabeth	Worcester	
Doore, Dorothy*	London	
Edwards, Joan	Cornwall	
Embree, Ellen*	Hampshire	x
Ferris, Susanna*	Wiltshire	
Fowler, Elizabeth	Kent	

Name	Location	Known to Be Active after 1665

SOUTHERN COUNTIES (continued)

Name	Location	Known to Be Active after 1665
Freebody, Margaret	Northamptonshire	
Goldsmith, Sarah	Gloucestershire	
Goodman, Mary	Wiltshire	
Hartley, Ellen	Surrey	
Hasell, Mary*	Somerset	
Haselwood, Bathia	Oxfordshire	
Hatch, Widow	Sussex	
Hersent, Anne	Hampshire	d. 1666
Hibbs, Joane	Gloucestershire	
Hickes, Jane*	Worcestershire	
Hiley, Joan	Bristol	x
Hill, Ruth	London	
Horne, Mary	Northamptonshire	
Humphrey, Ann	Essex	
Kendall, Susan	London	
Lamprey, Mary	Oxfordshire	
Lockwood, Elizabeth	Suffolk	x
Loe, Mary*	Oxfordshire, Wiltshire	
Marner, Sarah	Sussex	
Martindale, Katherine	Cornwall	
Mills, Hannah	Berkshire	x
Mitchell, Edith	Somerset	
Morris, Ann	Devonshire	x
Naithe, Eleanor	London	
Newman, Winifred*	Winchester?	
Norris, Anne	Cambridgeshire	
Parlour, Isabel	Bedfordshire	
Peacock, Elizabeth*	London	
Pearson, Susanna	Worcestershire	x
Pell, Anne*	Northamptonshire	x
Plant, Mary	Gloucestershire	
Poole, Agnes*	London	
Powel, Mary*	London	
Richardson, Anne*	Wellingborough	
Rickman, Frances	Sussex	
Russell, Mary	Dorsetshire	

Name	Location	Known to Be Active after 1665

SOUTHERN COUNTIES (continued)

Name	Location	Known to Be Active after 1665
Saunders, Dorothy*	Dorsetshire	
Spier, Mary	Hampshire	
Streater, Elizabeth*	Hampshire	x
Summers, Ginevra*	Wiltshire	
Thomas, Margaret	Bristol	x
Thorne, Mary	Cornwall	
Thrift, Mary	London	
Tibbots, Anne*	Wiltshire	
Tilsley, Mary	Worcestershire	
Timms, Sarah	Oxfordshire	
Tizard, Edith*	Southampton	
Tucker, Elizabeth	Somerset	
Upcott, Anne	Cornwall	x
Vivers, Margaret	Banbury	
West, Alice	Sussex	
White, Ruth	Surrey	

OUTSIDE ENGLAND OR UNKNOWN

Name	Location	Known to Be Active after 1665
Hamilton, Lady Margaret	Scotland	
Jones, Jennet*	Wales	
Moss, Mary	Wales	
Richard, Elizabeth*	Wales	
Richard, Mary	Wales	
Thomas, Margaret*	Wales	
Thomas, Rebecca	Wales	
Tompson, Anne		

Bibliography

MANUSCRIPT SOURCES

LIBRARY OF THE SOCIETY OF FRIENDS, LONDON

Abraham Manuscripts. MSS. vol. 364. Listing and Index, Craig W. Horle, 1977.

A. R. B[arclay] Collection. MSS. vols. 323 (1–125), 324 (126–249). Partially transcribed by Craig W. Horle. (Nos. 1–157 published in JFHS, 1930–1963.)

Book of Ministering Friends: London First Days' Meetings Supplied by Friends in the Ministry in and about London. 1682, MSS. vol. 40.

A Collection of Letters, Dreams, Visions, and Other Remarkable Occurrences of Some of the People Called Quakers. 1788. MSS. vol. S. 78.

Dictionary of Quaker Biography. Typescript.

Dix Manuscripts. MSS. vol. 294.

Edmund Crosse Collection. MSS. vol. 292.

Elizabeth Hooton. A Testemony of elesebeth hoton before she dyde by Ja, Lancaster, 1672. MSS. vol 366.

Gibson Manuscripts. MSS. vol. 336.

Great Book of Sufferings.

Gullson Manuscripts. Box E 1/1.

T. E. Harvey Manuscripts. MSS. vol. 214.

Craig W. Horle. "A Listing of the Original Records of Sufferings." Nos. 1–500 (vols. 1–4) compiled for the Library of the Society of Friends.

Joan Whitrowe's Testimony concerning the Loving Kindness of the Lord. MSS. vol. S. 462.

John Penington Manuscripts. MSS. vol. 344.

The Journal of Thomas Gwin, of Falmouth, a Minister of the Society of Friends. Vols. S. 74–S. 75. MSS. vol. 214 (transcribed 1837 and copied 1904–5).

Leek Manuscripts. Crosfield Collection. MSS. vol. 330.

Luke Howard Collection.
Markey Manuscripts. Box C 4/1.
Meeting Records (listed alphabetically by location)
   A Record Belonging to the Quarterly Meeting of the People of the Lord in
      Scorne Called Quakers in the County of Berks. Transcribed by Beatrice
      Saxon Snell and Nina Saxon Snell.
   Herefordshire Quarterly Meeting. Temp. Manuscripts 9/6.
   Quaker Women's Monthly Meeting in Lewes, 1677–1709. MSS. vol. 235.
   London and Middlesex
      A Book for the Business of the Monthly Meeting at the Peel in the County
         of Middlesex. Vol. 1, 1668–1683/4.
      The First Book of the Monthly Meeting of the People Call'd Quakers, at
         Horslydown (Later Southwark), London, 1666.
      London Women's Box Meeting Manuscripts. Sr1/127.
      London Yearly Meeting, Epistles Received 1683–1706.
      Men's Meeting (1690–1701), 11 a 1.
      The Morning Meeting's Book of Records from the 15th of the 7th Month,
         1673, to the 6th of the 4th Month 1692, Inclusive. 3 vols. (1: 1673–
         1692 (typescript); 2: 1692–1700 (typescript); 3: 1700–1711).
      The Second Book of the Monthly Meeting of the People Call'd Quakers
         at Horslydown, 1677.
      Six Weeks Meeting (1671–), 11 a 2.
      Two Weeks Meeting (1672–), 11 a 3.
      Women's Two Weeks Meeting, 1659–, 11 a 4.
   The Minute-Book of Reading Monthly Meeting (Curtis Party), 1668–1716.
      Transcribed Nina Saxon Snell, notes by Beatrice Saxon Snell.
   Reading Monthly Meeting (orthodox), 1685. Transcript.
   The Vale of the White Horse Monthly Meeting Minutes 1673–1722. Tran-
      scribed by Nina Saxon Snell. Typescript.
   The Vale of the White Horse Women's Monthly Meeting Minute-Book,
      1676–1730. Transcribed by Beatrice Saxon Snell and Nina Saxon Snell,
      vol. 2b4 (original at Oxfordshire Record Office).
Miller Manuscripts. Seventeen Letters from and to the Fell or Abraham families.
   (Typescript index; original collection destroyed.)
Norris Manuscripts. MSS. vol. S. 201.
Portfolio Manuscripts. Multi-volume collection of letters and other documents.
Robson Manuscripts. Testimonies, T.R.1 (Temp. MSS. 745/1); T.R.2 (Temp.
   MSS. 745/2); T.R.3 (Temp. MSS. 745/3).
Spence Manuscripts. Vol. III.
Swarthmore Manuscripts. I–IV, letters of early Friends. Transcript, "Letters and
   Documents of Early Friends. Copied from the Originals Which Were pre-
   served at Swarthmore Hall."
Temp. Manuscripts. MSS. vol. 394.
Thirnbeck Manuscripts. MSS. vol. 368.
Toft Manuscripts. vol. 332.
Watson Manuscripts. MSS. vol. 41.

William Caton Manuscripts. Vol. S. 81. MSS. vols. 320, 321. Index of vol. III
by Craig Horle.

BODLEIAN LIBRARY, OXFORD

The Diaries of Ann Bathurst. 3 vols., MSS Bodleian Rawlinson D. 1262, 1263,
1238.

BRITISH LIBRARY, LONDON

Muggletonian Archives. British Library, Add. MSS. 60168–60256.

HAVERFORD COLLEGE LIBRARY: QUAKER COLLECTION

A Catalogue of the Names of Friends Who Have Visited New England. MS.
975C.
Dictionary of Quaker Biography. Typescript.
Elizabeth Webb. A Short Account of My Voyage into America with Mary Rogers
My Companion. Edited by Frederick B. Tolles and John Beverley Riggs. MS.
975B.
———. Some Meditations with Some Observations upon the Revelations of
Jesus Christ.
MSS. 861. Letters.
Richardson Manuscript. Writings of George Fox.

LONDON PUBLIC RECORD OFFICE

Conway Papers. SP14/130/135.

PRESTON PUBLIC RECORD OFFICE, LANCASHIRE

Alphabetical List of Deceased Ministers in Lancashire Quarterly Meeting, 1669–
1686.
Lancashire Men's Quarterly Meeting Minute Book.
Lancashire Women's Quarterly Meeting Minute Book, 1675–1777.
Lancaster Monthly Meeting Papers on Discipline and Tithe Testimony, 1671–
1803. FRL 2 BXV.

FRIENDS HISTORICAL LIBRARY, SWARTHMORE
COLLEGE, SWARTHMORE, PA.

Miscellaneous Manuscripts, Dying Words of Children, A.D. 1675–1709.
Yorkshire meeting records on microfilm, originals originals at the Brotherton
Library, University of Leeds:

York Monthly Meeting, Applications for Membership, Disownments, Documents of Discipline, Etc., 1672–1797.
Yorkshire Quarterly Meeting of Ministers and Elders, Minute Book June 21, 1689–August 26, 1798.
Yorkshire Women's Monthly Meeting, August 4, 1674–August 5, 1767.
Yorkshire Women's Quarterly Meeting Book, June 12, 1678–September 26, 1745.

PRINTED PRIMARY SOURCES

WORKS BY QUAKER AND EX-QUAKER WOMEN

Andrews, Elizabeth. "An Account of the Birth, Education and Sufferings for the Truth's Sake of That Faithful Friend Elizabeth Andrews." *Journal of the Friends Historical Society* 26 (1929): 3–8.
Atkinson, Elizabeth. *A Brief Discovery of the Labourers in Mistery Babylon, Called Quakers.* London, 1669.
Audland, Ann. *A Testimony against False Prophets, and False Teachers: And Also the Objection Answered, concerning the Woman Forbidden to Speak in the Church.* In *The Saints Testimony Finishing through Sufferings.* London, 1655.
———. *A True Declaration of the Suffering of the Innocent. . . .* In *The Saints Testimony Finishing through Sufferings.* London, 1655.
———. *A Warning from the Spirit of the Lord (in His Handmaid) Anne Audland, to the Priest and Persecuting People in Banbury, and All Such as May Be Found in Their Nature, Falsly Accusing and Imprisoning the Servants of the Lord Jesus.* In *The Saints Testimony Finishing through Sufferings.* London, 1655.
Barwick, Grace. *To All Present Rulers, Whether Parliament, or Whomsoever of England.* London, 1659.
Bathurst, Elizabeth. *An Expostulatory Appeal to the Professors of Christianity, Joyned in Community with Samuel Ansley.* London, 1680.
———. *The Sayings of Women. Which Were Spoken upon Sundry Occasions in Several Places of the Scriptures.* Shoreditch, 1683.
———. *Truths Vindication, Or, A Gentle Stroke to Wipe Off the Foul Aspersions, False Accusations and Misrepresentations, Cast upon the People of God, Called Quakers. . . .* London, 1683.
Biddle, Esther. *The Trumpet of the Lord God Sounded Forth unto these Three Nations.* London, 1662.
Blackborow, Sarah. *A Testimony concerning Richard Hubberthorne.* In *A Collection of the Several Books and Writings of That Faithful Servant of God Richard Hubberthorne Who Finished His Testimony (Being a Prisoner in Newgate for the Truth's Sake) the 17th of the 6th Month 1662.* London, 1663.
———. *A Visit to the Spirit in Prison; And an Invitation to All People to Come to Christ the Light of the World, in Whom Is Life, and Doth Enlighten Every One That Cometh into the World.* London, 1658.

B[landford], S[usanna]. *A Small Account Given forth by One That Hath Been a Traveller for These 40 Years in the Good Old Way.* 1698.

Blaugdone, Barbara. *An Account of the Travels, Sufferings and Persecutions of Barbara Blaugdone, Given forth as a Testimony to the Lord's Power, and for the Encouragement of Friends.* Shoreditch, 1691.

Boulbie, Judith. *A Few Words as a Warning from the Lord to the Inhabitants of Londonderry, and Also to the Whole Nation of Ireland.* 1679.

Braidley, Margaret. *Certain Papers Which Is the Word of the Lord, as Was Moved from the Lord, by His Servants, to Several Places, and Persons, That They May Be Left without Excuse, and God May Be Cleared When He Judges, and Justified in His Judgements.* n.d.

Brooksop, Joan. *An Invitation of Love unto the Seed of God, throughout the World, with a Word to the Wise in Heart, and a Lamentation for New England.* London, 1662.

Cotton, Mrs. Priscilla, and Mary Cole. *To the Priests and People of England, We Discharge Our Consciences, and Give Them Warning.* London, 1655.

Curwen, Alice. *A Relation of the Labour, Travail and Suffering of That Faithful Servant of the Lord Alice Curwen.* 1680.

D[ocwra], A[nne]. *An Apostate-Conscience Exposed, and the Miserable Consequences thereof Disclosed, for Information and Caution. By an Ancient Woman, and Lover of Truth, and the Sincere Friends thereof.* London, 1699.

——. *A Brief Discovery of the Work of the Enemy of Sion's Peace; Written in True Love, to the End That All May Return to the Inward Teaching of the Blessed Light and Grace of God in Their Own Hearts and Consciences.* Cambridge, 1683.

——. *An Epistle of Love and Good Advice, to My Old Friends and Fellow-Sufferers in the Late Times, the Old Royalists and Their Posterity, and to All Others That Have Any Sincere Desire towards God.* 1683.

——. *A Looking-Glass for the Recorder and Justices of the Peace, and Grand Juries for the Town and County of Cambridge.* Cambridge, 1682.

——. *The Second Part of An Apostate-Conscience Exposed.* London, 1700.

Eedes, Judith. *A Warning to All the Inhabitants of the Earth . . . but Especially to Those That Are Called Magistrates or Rulers.* 1659.

Ellwood, Mary, and Margery Clipsham. *The Spirit that Works Abomination.* London, 1685.

Evans, Katherine. *A Brief Discovery of God's Eternal Truth: And, a Way Opened to the Simple Hearted, Whereby They May Come to Know Christ and His Ministers, from Antichrist and His Ministers, Written in the Inquisition at Malta.* London, 1663.

Evans, K[atherine], and S[arah] Cheevers. *A Short Relation of Some of the Cruel Sufferings (for the Truths Sake) of Katherine Evans and Sarah Chevers, in the Inquisition in the Isle of Malta.* London, 1662.

——. *A True Account of the Great Tryals and Cruel Sufferings Undergone by Those Two Faithful Servants of God, Katherine Evans and Sarah Cheevers, in the Time of Their above Three Years and a Halfs Confinement in the Island Malta.* London, 1663.

Everard, Margaret. *An Epistle of Margaret Everard to the People Called Quakers and the Ministry among Them.* 1699.

Fearon, Jane. *Absolute Predestination Not Scriptural: Or Some Queries upon a Doctrine Which I Heard Preach'd. . . .* London, 1705.

———. *Universal Redemption Offered in Jesus Christ, in Opposition to That Pernicious and Destructive Doctrine of Election and Reprobation of Persons from Everlasting.* 1698.

Fell, Margaret. *A Brief Collection of Remarkable Passages and Occurences Relating to the Birth, Education, Life, Conversion, Travels, Services and Deep Sufferings of That Ancient, Eminent and Faithful Servant of the Lord, Margaret Fell, but by Her Second Marriage, Margaret Fox.* London, 1710.

Fell, Sarah. *Household Account Book of Sarah Fell of Swarthmoor Hall.* Cambridge: Cambridge University Press, 1920.

Fisher, Abigail. *A Few Lines in True Love to Such That Frequent the Meetings of the People Called Quakers, and Love to Hear the Sound of Truth, but Are Not Yet Come to Obey the Testimony of It, That They May Also Hear and Learn to Read at Home.* London, 1694.

Forster, Mary. *Some Seasonable Considerations to the Young Men and Women Who in This Day of Tryal, Are Made Willing to Offer up Themselves, Estates or Liberty, and Suffer Reproaches, with Other Hard Usages in the Streets of This City, and Elsewhere.* London, 1684.

Forster, Mary, Mary Elson, Anne Travers, Ruth Crouch, Susannah Dew, and Mary Plumstead. *A Living Testimony from the Power and Spirit of Our Lord J.C. in our Faithful Women's Meeting and Christian Society.* London, 1685.

Gilman, Anne. *An Epistle to Friends: Being a Tender Salutation to the Faithful in God Everywhere. Also a Letter to Charles, King of England.* London, 1662.

Gotherson, Dorothea. *To All That Are Unregenerated: A Call to Repentance.* London, 1661. Reprinted in G. D. Scull, *Dorothea Scott, Otherwise Gotherson and Hogben, of Egerton House, Kent, 1611–1680.* Oxford: Parker and Co., 1883.

Gould, Ann, Mary Webb, Robert Hasle, Humphrey Bache, and Daniel Baker. *An Epistle to All the Christian Magistrates and Powers in the Whole Christendom.* London, 1659.

Haydock, Eleanor. *A Visitation of Love.*

Hayes, Alice. *A Legacy, or Widow's Mite: Left by Alice Hayes, to Her Children and Others, with an Account of Some of Her Dying Sayings.* London, 1723.

Hendricks, Elizabeth. *An Epistle to Friends in England, to Be Read in Their Assemblies in the Fear of the Lord.* London, 1672.

Howgill, Mary. *A Remarkable Letter of Mary Howgill to Oliver Cromwell, Called Protector, a Copy Whereof Was Delivered by Herself to His Own Hands Some Moneths Ago, with Whom She Had Face to Face a Large Discourse Thereupon.* London, 1657.

———. *The Vision of the Lord of Hosts, Faithfully Declared in His Own Time; and the Decree of the Lord God Also Recorded, Which Is Nigh to Be Fulfilled, Written at Colchester.* 1662.

Killin, Margaret, and Barbara Patison. *A Warning from the Lord to the Teachers and People of Plimouth. With a Few Queries to the Parish Teachers of This Nation, That Have Great Sums of Money for Teaching the People.* London, 1656.

Lynam, Margaret. *Extracts from Letters by Margaret Lynam Written about the Year 1660.* Gloucester, n.d.

Martin, Ann. *A Short Account of the Dealings of the Lord with Susanna Whitrow, about the Age of Fifteen, Daughter of Robert and Joan Whitrow in Covent Garden, County of Middlesex.* Philadelphia, 1804.

Mollineux, Mary. *Fruits of Retirement: Or, Miscellaneous Poems, Moral and Divine.* London, 1702.

Morey, Dewance. *A True and Faithful Warning from the Lord God, Sounded through Me, a Poor Despised Earthen Vessel, unto All the Inhabitants of England, Who Are Yet in Their Sins.* n.d.

Nicholson, Marjorie Hope, ed. *Conway Letters: The Correspondence of Anne, Viscountess Conway, Henry More, and Their Friends, 1642–1684.* New Haven: Yale University Press, 1930.

Niesen, Gertruyd Dieriks. *An Epistle to Be Communicated to Friends, and to Be Read in the Fear of the Lord in Their Men and Womens Meetings, and Other Meetings; Only among Friends, As They in the Wisdom of God Shall See Meet and Serviceable.* Colchester, 1677.

Penington, Mary. *A Brief Account of My Exercises from My Childhood: Left with My Dear Daughter Gulielma Maria Penn.* Philadelphia, 1848.

The Sad Effects of Cruelty Detected; Being an Impartial Account of the Por Woman near Temple-Barr, Lately Tempted in Her Distraction to Make Away Her Self, Whose Temptation . . . Proceeded Not from Her Owning the Quakers . . . but From the Devil and a Wicked Husband. 1675.

Sandilands, Mary. *A Tender Salutation of Endeared Love.* London, 1696.

Simmonds, Martha. *A Lamentation for the Lost Sheep of the House of Israel.* London, 1655.

Simmonds, Martha, Hannah Stranger, James Nayler, William Tomlinson, *O England; Thy Time Is Come.* London, n.d.

Smith, Rebecca. *The Foundation of True Preaching Asserted.* London, 1687.

Spiezman, Milton D., and Jane C. Kronick, eds. "A Seventeenth-Century Quaker Women's Declaration," *Signs* 1, no. 1 (Autumn 1975): 231–45.

Stirredge, Elizabeth. *Strength in Weakness Manifest: In the Life, Various Trials, and Christian Testimony of That Faithful Servant and Handmaid of the Lord, Elizabeth Stirredge, Who Departed This Life, at Her House at Hempstead in Hertfordshire, in the 72nd Year of Her Age.* 3d ed. London, 1772.

These Several Papers Were Sent to the Parliament the 20th Day of the 5th Moneth, 1659. Being above 7000 of the Names of the Hand-Maids and Daughters of the Lord, and Such As Feels the Oppression of Tithes. . . . Preface by Mary Forster. London, 1659.

Townsend, Theophila. *A Testimony concerning the Life and Death of Jane Whitehead.* London, 1676.

Travers, Rebeckah. *For Those That Meet to Worship at the Steeplehouse, Called John Evangelist in London.* London, 1659.

———. *Of That Eternal Breath Begotten and Brought Forth Not of Flesh and Blood, Nor of the Will of Man, but by the Father of Spirits, Which According to His Own Wil Worketh to Wil and to Do of His Good Pleasure, When, or in Whom He Pleaseth.* n.d.

———. *A Testimony concerning the Light and Life of Jesus (the True Foundation) As It Was Laid Down and Delivered to Us, and Received of Us from the Beginning, (Etc.).* London, 1663.

———. *A Testimony for God's Everlasting Truth.* London, 1669.

Vokins, Joan. *God's Mighty Power Magnified, as Manifested and Revealed in His Faithful Handmaid, Joan Vokins.* London, 1691.

Webb, Elizabeth. *A Letter from Elizabeth Webb, to Anthony William Boehm with His Answer.* Philadelphia, 1783.

White, Dorothy. *A Call from God out of Egypt, by His Son Christ the Light of Life.* London, 1662.

———. *A Diligent Search amongst Rulers, Priests, Professors, and People; And a Warning to All Sorts High and Low, That Are out of the Doctrine of Christ, and Fear not God.* 1659.

———. *An Epistle of Love, and of Consolation unto Israel.* London, 1661.

———. *This to Be Delivered to the Counsellors That Are Sitting in Counsel.* London, 1659.

———. *A Trumpet of the Lord of Hosts, Blown unto the City of London.* 1662.

Whitehead, Ann, and Mary Elson. *An Epistle for True Love, Unity and Order in the Church of Christ.* London, 1680.

Whitrow, Joan. *Faithful Warning . . . to the Several Professors of Christianity in England, as Well Those of the Highest as the Lowest Quality.* London, 1697.

———. *The Humble Address of the Widow Whitrowe to King William.* 1689.

———. *The Work of God in a Dying Maid, Being a Short Account of the Dealings of the Lord with One Susannah Whitrow, about the Age of Fifteen.* London, 1677.

Whitton, Catherine. *An Epistle to Friends Everywhere; To Be Distinctly Read in Their Meetings, When Assembled together in the Fear of the Lord.* London, 1681.

Yeamans, Isabel. *An Invitation of Love to All Who Hunger and Thirst after Righteousness.* Swarthmore, 1679.

GENERAL WORKS BY QUAKERS AND EX-QUAKERS

Banks, John. *A Journal of the Labours, Travels, and Sufferings (in and for the Gospel) of That Ancient Servant, and Faithful Minister of Jesus Christ, John Banks.* London, 1712.

Barbour, Hugh, and Arthur O. Roberts, eds. *Early Quaker Writings, 1650–1700.* Grand Rapids: William B. Eerdmans Publishing Co., 1973.

Barclay, Abram Rawlinson, ed. *Letters, etc. of Early Friends, Illustrative of the*

History of the Society. London, 1841. Reprint. In vol. 11 of The Friends Library. Philadelphia, 1847.

Barclay, Robert. *The Anarchy of the Ranters and Other Libertines, the Hierarchy of the Romanists, and Other Pretended Churches, Equally Refused and Refuted, in a Two-Fold Apology for the Church and People of God Called in Derision Quakers*. 1676. Reprint. Philadelphia, 1757.

————. *An Apology for the True, Christian Divinity as the Same Is Held Forth, and Preached, by the People Called, in Scorn, Quakers*. 8th ed. London, 1843.

Bayly, Charles. *A True and Faithful Warning unto the People and Inhabitants of Bristol*. London, 1663.

Besse, Joseph. *A Collection of the Sufferings of the People Called Quakers for the Testimony of a Good Conscience, from 1650–1689, Taken from Original Records and Other Authentick Accounts by Joseph Besse*. 2 vols. London, 1753.

Bishop, George. *New England Judged, Not by Man's, but by the Spirit of the Lord*. London, 1661.

Bownas, Samuel. *An Account of the Life, Travels, and Christian Experiences in the Work of the Ministry of Samuel Bownas*. 2d ed. London, 1761.

Brace, Harold W., ed. *The First Minute Book of the Gainsborough Monthly Meeting of the Society of Friends 1669–1719*. 2 vols. Vol. 38 of the Lincoln Record Society. Hereford: The Hereford Times, 1948.

Bugg, Francis. *Jezebel Withstood, and Her Daughter Anne Docwra, Publickly Reprov'd*. 1699.

Burrough, Edward. *An Alarm to All Flesh; With an Invitation to the True Seeker, Forthwith to Flye for His Life (Clearly) out of the Short-Lived Babylon, into the Life; Out of words, into the Word; Out of the Many and Changeable Likenesses, into Him, the Same Yesterday, Today, for Ever and Ever*. London, 1660.

————. *A Warning from the Lord to the Inhabitants of Underbarrow, and So to All the Inhabitants of England*. London, 1654.

Camm, Thomas, and Ann [Audland] Camm. *The Admirable and Glorious Appearance of the Eternal God, in his Glorious Power, in and through a Child, of the Age of betwixt Eight and Nine Years, upon Her Dying Bed. . . .* London, 1684.

Camm, Thomas, and Charles Marshall, eds. *The Memory of the Righteous Revived. Being a Brief Collection of the Books and Written Epistles of John Camm and John Audland*. London, 1689.

Chalkley, Thomas. *Journal of Thomas Chalkley*. Vol. 6 of the Friends Library. Philadelphia, 1842.

The Concurrence and Unanimity of the People Called Quakers: In Owning and Asserting the Principle Doctrines of the Christian Religion; Demonstrated in the Sermons or, Declarations, of Several of Their Publick Preachers. . . . London, 1694.

Davies, Richard. *An Account of the Convincement, Exercises, Services and Travels of That Ancient Servant of the Lord, Richard Davies; With Some*

Relation of Ancient Friends, and the Spreading of the Truth in North Wales. London, 1710.

Dewsbury, William. *The Life of William Dewsbury.* In vol. 2 of the Friends Library. Philadelphia, 1842.

Dickinson, James. *A Journal of the Life and Labour of Love in the Work of the Ministry, of That Worthy Elder, and Faithful Servant of Jesus Christ, James Dickinson, Who Departed This Life on the 6th of the 3rd Month 1741, in the 83rd Year of his Age.* London, 1745.

Eccles, Solomon. *In the Year 1659 . . . the Presence of the Lord God Was Felt within Me.* 1659.

Edmundson, William. *Journal of the Life, Travels, Sufferings, and Labour of Love in the Work of the Ministry, of That Worthy Elder, and Faithful Servant of Jesus Christ, William Edmundson, Who Departed This Life, the Thirty First of the Sixth Month, 1712.* London, 1715.

Ellwood, Thomas. *The Account from Wickham (Lately Published by John Raunce and Charles Harris) Examin'd, and Found False.* 1690.

———. *An Antidote against the Infection of William Rogers's Book, Mis-called, "The Christian-Quaker Distinguished from the Apostate and Innovator."* London, 1682.

———. *The History of the Life of Thomas Ellwood: Written by Himself.* In vol. 7 of The Friends Library. Philadelphia, 1843.

Epistles from the Yearly Meeting of Friends, Held in London, to the Quarterly and Monthly Meetings in Great Britain, Ireland, and Elsewhere, from 1681 to 1817, Inclusive. London, 1818.

Farnsworth, Richard. *A Woman Forbidden to Speak in the Church, the Grounds Examined, the Mystery Opened, the Truth Cleared, and the Ignorance Both of Priests, and People Discovered.* London, 1654.

Fox, George. *Concerning Sons and Daughters, and Prophetesses speaking and Prophesying, in the Law and in the Gospel.* London, n.d.

———. *George Fox's "Book of Miracles."* Edited by Henry J. Cadbury. New York: Octagon Books, 1973.

———. *The Great Mistery of the Great Whore Unfolded.* London, 1659.

———. *The Journal of George Fox.* Edited by John L. Nickalls. London: Religious Society of Friends, 1975.

———. *Something in Answer to a Letter (Which I Have Seen) of John Leverat Governour of Boston, to William Coddington Governour of Rode-Island, Dated 1677, Wherein He Mentions My Name, and Also Wherein John Leverat Justifies Roger William's Book of Lyes.* n.d.

———. *The Spirit of Envy, Lying, and Persecution, Made Manifest.* London, 1663.

Furly, John. *A Testimony to the True Light . . . More Especially Intended for the Inhabitants of the Town of Colchester. . . .* 2d ed. 1670.

Haydock, Roger. *A Collection of the Christian Writings, Labours, Travels and Sufferings, of That Faithful and Approved Minister of Jesus Christ, Roger Haydock.* London, 1700.

H[owgill], F[rancis]. *A Testimony concerning the Life, Death, Trials, Travels and Labours of Edward Burrough That Worthy Prophet of the Lord Who Dyed a Prisoner for the Testimony of Jesus, and the Word of God, in the City of London, the 14th of the 12th Month, 1662*. London, 1662.

Hubberthorne, Richard. *A Collection of the Several Books and Writings of That Faithful Servant of God Richard Hubberthorne Who Finished His Testimony (Being a Prisoner in Newgate for the Truth's Sake) the 17th of the 6th Month 1662*. London, 1663.

Keith, George. *The Magick of Quakerism, or, the Chief Mysteries of Quakerism Laid Open. To Which Are Added, a Preface and Postscript Relating to the Camisars, in Answer to Mr. Lacy's Preface to the "Cry from the Desart."* London, 1707.

———. *The Woman Preacher of Samaria: A Better Preacher, and More Sufficiently Qualified to Preach Than Any of the Men-Preachers of the Man-Made-Ministry in These Three Nations*. London, 1674.

Livingston, Patrick. *Truth Owned and Deceit Denyed and Witnessed Against: . . . Some Queries Touching Women's Speaking in the Church*. London, 1667.

Loddington, William. *The Good Order of Truth Justified; Wherein our Womens Meetings and Order of Marriage . . . Are Proved Agreeable to Scripture and Sound Reason*. London, 1685.

Marsh, Thomas W., ed. *Minute-Books and Other Sources*. London: S. Harris and Co., 1886.

Matern, John. *A Testimony to the Everlasting Power of God*. 1679.

Mather, William. *An Instrument from That Little Stone Cut out of the Mountain without Hands, to Help to Break in Pieces, That Great Image Which Daniel Mentions, . . . to Satisfie the Chief Preacher in the Independent Church in Bedford, Who Desired the Author to Write unto Him, What Proofs He Had for a Woman's Speaking in the Church. He Being Concerned That So Many of His Hearers Should Leave Him to Go to Hear Margaret Everard Declare What God Had Done for Her Soul, the 17th Day of June Last, at My Dwelling in Bedford*. London, 1694.

———. *A Novelty: Or, a Government of Women, Distinct from Men, Erected among Some of the People Call'd Quakers*. London, 1694.

Morland, Stephen C., ed. *The Somersetshire Quarterly Meeting of the Society of Friends 1668–1699*. Old Woking, Surrey: Somerset Record Society, 1978.

Mortimer, Jean, and Russell Mortimer, eds. *Leeds Friends' Minute Book 1692 to 1712*. Yorkshire Archaeological Society Record Series, vol. 139. Leeds: Yorkshire Archaeological Society, 1980.

Mortimer, Russell, ed. *Minute Book of the Men's Meeting of the Society of Friends in Bristol 1667–1686*. Bristol Record Society's Publications, no. 26. Gateshead: Northumberland Press, 1971.

Mucklow, William. *The Spirit of the Hat: Or, the Government of the Quakers among Themselves*. London, 1673.

Nayler, James. *A Collection of Sundry Books, Epistles and Papers Written by James Nayler, Some of Which Were Never before Printed, with an Impartial Relation of the Most Remarkable Transactions Relating to His Life*. London, 1716.

———. *How Sin Is Strengthened, and How It Is Overcome*. London, 1657.

————. *A Message from the Spirit of Truth unto the Holy Seed*. London, 1658.

————. *Milk for Babes; And Meat for Strong-Men*. London, 1661.

Penn, William. *Judas and the Jews Combined against Christ and His Followers*. 1673.

————. *No Cross, No Crown, a Discourse Showing the Nature and Discipline of the Holy Cross of Christ*. In vol. 1 of the Friends Library. Philadelphia, 1837.

————. *The Papers of William Penn*. Edited by Mary Maples Dunn and Richard S. Dunn. Vol. 1, *1644–1679*. Philadelphia: University of Pennsylvania, 1981.

Penney, Norman, ed. *Extracts from State Papers Relating to Friends, 1654 to 1672*. London: Headley Bros., 1913.

————. *The First Publishers of Truth: Being Early Records (Now First Printed) of the Introduction of Quakerism into the Counties of England and Wales*. London, Philadelphia, and New York: Headley Bros., 1907.

Piety Promoted by Faithfulness, Manifested by Several Testimonies concerning That True Servant of God Ann Whitehead. 1686.

Piety Promoted, in a Collection of Dying Sayings of Many of the People Called Quakers. 4 vols. Philadelphia: Friends' Book Store, 1854.

Rogers, William. *The Christian Quaker Distinguished from the Apostate and Innovator in Five Parts*. London, 1680.

The Saints Testimony Finishing through Sufferings: Or, the Proceedings of the Court against the Servants of Jesus . . . Held in the County of Oxon, the 26 Day of the Seventh Moneth, 1655. London, 1655.

Sewel, William. *The History of the Rise, Increase, and Progress, of the Christian People Called Quakers*. 2 vols. 1722. Reprint, Philadelphia, 1823.

A Short Account of the Life of Anne Camm, a Minister of the Gospel, in the Society of Friends. In vol. 1 of the Friends Library. Philadelphia, 1837.

A Short Testimony concerning the Death and Finishing of Judieth Fell, Daughter of Thomas Fell, Who Finished Her Course and Gave up to the Lord, the Twenty-fourth Year of Her Age, in the Year 1682. London, 1682.

Smith, Joseph, ed. *A Descriptive Catalogue of Friends' Books, or Books Written by Members of the Society of Friends, Commonly Called Quakers, from Their First Rise to the Present Time*. 4 vols. London: Joseph Smith, 1867.

Smith, Richard. *The Light Unchangeable: And Truth and Good Order, Justified against Error and Disorder*. London, 1677.

Snell, Beatrice Saxon, ed. *The Minute Book of the Monthly Meeting of the Society of Friends for the Upperside of Buckinghamshire 1669–1690*. Records Branch of the Buckinghamshire Archeological Society. High Wycombe: Hague and Gill, 1937.

A Testimony concerning the Life and Death of Jane Whitehead, That Faithful Servant and Handmaid of the Lord. . . . 1676.

Toldervy, John. *The Foot out of the Snare Being a Brief Declaration of His Entrance into That Sect Called Quakers*. 1656.

Whitehead, John. *A Manifestation of Truth . . . Writ in Answer to a Book Which a Nameless Author Hath Written against the People called Quakers*. 1662.

Whiting, John. *Persecution Exposed*. London, 1715.

Wood, Hugh. *A Brief Treatise of Religious Women's Meetings, Services and Testimonies. According to the Scriptures of Truth. Also, Something concerning Women's Prophesying and Teaching.* 1684.

WORKS BY NON-QUAKER WOMEN

Allen, Hannah. *Satan His Methods and Malice Baffled.* London, 1683.

Astell, Mary. *A Serious Proposal to the Ladies.* n.d.

Audeley, Eleanor. [Eleanor (Davies).] *Bethlehem Signifying the House of Bread: Or War, Whereof Informs, Whoso Takes a Small Roul to Taste . . . Distraction in the Supreamest Nature; with Such Vertue indu'd.* 1652.

———. [Lady Eleanor.] *The Everlasting Gospel.* 1649.

———. [Eleanor Davies.] *Her Blessing to Her Beloved Daughter.* London, 1644.

———. *The Lady Eleanor Her Appeal. Present This to Mr. Mace the Prophet of the Most High, His Messenger.* 1646.

———. [Lady Eleanor.] *The Restitution of Prophecy; That Buried Talent to Be revived.* 1651.

———. [Eleanor Davies.] *To Parliament.* 1641.

———. *A warning to the dragon and all his angels.* 1625.

Avery, E[lizabeth]. *Scripture-Prophecies Opened, Which Are to Be Accomplished in These Last Times, Which Do Attend the Second Coming of Christ; . . . In several Letters Written to Christian Friends.* London, 1647.

Burch, Dorothy. *A Catechism of the Several Heads of the Christian Religion . . . Intended Only for Private Use, but Now Published for the Good and Benefit of Others, by the Importunitie of Some Friends.* London, 1646.

Cary, Mary. *The Little Horn's Doom and Downfall: Or a Scripture-Prophesie of King James, and King Charles, and of This Present Parliament, Unfolded.* London, 1651.

———. *A New and More Exact Mappe or Description of New Jerusalems Glory, When Jesus Christ and His Saints with Him Shall Reign on Earth a Thousand Years, and Possess All Kingdoms.* London, 1651.

———. *The Resurrection of the Witness; And Englands Fall from (the Mystical Babylon) Rome.* London, 1648.

———. [Mary Rande.] *Twelve Proposals to the Supreme Governours of the Three Nations Now Assembled at Westminster.* London, 1653.

Channel, Elinor. *A Message from God, By a Dumb Woman to His Highness the Lord Protector.* Edited by Arise Evans. London, 1653.

Chidley, Katherine. "Good Counsell, to the Petitioners for Presbyterian Government That They May Declare Their Faith before They Build Their Church." Broadside. London, 1645.

———. *The Justification of the Independent Churches of Christ. Being an Answer to Mr. Edwards His Booke, Which Hee Hath Written against the Government of Christ's Church, and Toleration of Christs Publike Worship.* London, 1641.

———. *A New-Yeares-Gift, or a Brief Exhortation to Mr. Thomas Edwards.* London, 1645.

Davies, Eleanor. See Eleanor Audeley.

Eleanor, Lady. See Eleanor Audeley.

Jinner, Sarah. *An Almanack and Prognostication for the Year of Our Lord 1659*. London, 1659.

Jones, Mrs. Sarah. *This Is the Light's Appearance*. 1650.

Lead, Jane. *A Fountain of Gardens. Watered by the River of Divine Pleasure, and Springing Up in All Variety of Spiritual Plants*. 2 vols. London, 1697–1701.

Parr, Susanna. *Susanna's Apology against the Elders: Or a Vindication of Susanna Parr; One of Those Two Women Lately Excommunicated by Mr. Lewis Stucley and His church in Exeter*. Oxford, 1659.

Pocock, Mary. *The Mystery of the Deity in the Humanity*. 1649.

Poole, Elizabeth. *An(other) Alarum of War, Given to the Army*. London, 1649.

———. *A Prophecie Touching the Death of King Charles*. 1649.

———. *A Vision: Wherein Is Manifested the Disease and Cure of the Kingdome*. London, 1648.

Pope, Mary. *Behold Here Is a Word or, an Answer to the Late Remonstrance of the Army*. London, 1649.

———. *A Treatise of Magistracy, Shewing the Magistrate Hath Beene, and for Ever Is to Be the Chiefe Officer in the Church, out of the Church, and over the Church: And That the Two Testaments Hold Forth*. 1647.

Rande, Mary. See Mary Cary.

Trapnel, Anna. *Anna Trapnel's Report and Plea, or, A Narrative of Her Journey from London into Cornwal*. London, 1654.

———. *The Cry of a Stone: Or a Relation of Something Spoken in Whitehall, by Anna Trapnel, Being in the Visions of God*. London, 1654.

———. *A Legacy for Saints, Being Several Experiences of the Dealings of God with Anna Trapnel, in, and after Her Conversion*. London, 1654.

Turner, Jane. *Choice Experiences of the Kind Dealings of God before, in, and after Conversion*. London, 1653.

Warren, Elizabeth. *Spiritual Thrift, or, Meditations, Wherein Humble Christians (as in a Mirrour) May View the Verity of Their Saving Graces, and May See How to Make a Spirituall Improvement of All Opportunities and Advantages of a Pious Proficiencie (or a Holy Growth) in Grace and Goodnesse*. London, 1647.

"Wonderful Prophecie, Declared by Christian James." Broadside. n.d.

MISCELLANEOUS CONTEMPORARY WORKS

The Account Audited, Or the Date of the Resurrection of the Witnesses, Pretended to Be Demonstrated by M. Cary a Minister. London, 1649.

An Account of Mary Adams, the Ranters Monster. London, 1652.

Ballard, George. *Memoirs of Several Ladies of Great Britain Who Have Been Celebrated for Their Writings or Skill in the Learned Languages, Arts and Sciences*. 1775. Edited by Ruth Perry. Detroit: Wayne State University Press, 1985.

Bishop, R. *Trodden Down Strength, by the God of Strength. Or, Mrs. Drake Revived.* London, 1647.

Bloody News from Dover. Being a True Relation of the Great and Bloudy Murder, Committed by Mary Champion (an Anabaptist) Who Cut off Her Childs Head. . . . 1647.

Bower, Edmund. *Doctor Lamb Revived, or, Witchcraft Condemn'd in Anne Bodenham.* London, 1653.

The Brownist Haeresies Confuted . . . Their Knavery Anatomized, and Their Fleshly Spirits Painted at Full, in a True History of One Mistris Sarah Miller of Banbury in Oxfordshire. 1641.

Bunyan, John. *A Case of Conscience Resolved; viz., Whether, Where a Church of Christ Is Situate, It Is the Duty of the Women of That Congregation, Ordinarily, and by Appointment, to Separate Themselves from Their Brethren, and So to Assemble Together, to Perform Some Parts of Divine Worship, As Prayer, etc. without Their Men?* 1683. In *The Complete Works of John Bunyan, Author of "The Pilgrim's Progress."* 4 vols. Edited by Henry Stebbing. Hildesheim and New York: George Olms Verlag and Johnson Reprint Corp., 1970.

Calendar of State Papers: Domestic Series of the Reign of Charles I, 1628–29. London: Longman, Brown, Green, Longmans, and Roberts, 1859.

The Copy of a Letter Written by Mr. Thomas Parker, Pastor of the Church of Newbury in New England to His Sister, Mrs. Elizabeth Avery, Sometimes of Newbury in the County of Berks, Touching Sundry Opinions by Her Professed and Maintained. London, 1650.

The Declaration of John Robins, the Shakers God. London, 1651.

Delamaine, A., and T. Terry, eds. *A Volume of Spiritual Epistles . . . by John Reeve and Lodowijk Muggleton.* 1755.

A Description of the Sect Called the Familie of Love: With Their Common Place of Residence. Being Discovered by Mrs. Susannah Snow of Pirford near Chersey in the County of Surrey, Who Was Vainly Led Away for a Time through Their Base Allurements. London, 1641.

A Discoverie of Six Women Preachers, in Middlesex, Kent, Cambridgshire, and Salisbury, with a Relation of Their Names, Manners, Life, and Doctrine, Pleasant to Be Read, but Horrid to Be Judged Of. 1641.

Dr. Lamb's Darling: Or, Strange and Terrible News from Salisbury. London, 1653.

Edwards, Thomas. *Gangraena, or a Catalogue and Discovery of Many of the Errours, Heresies, Blasphemies and Pernicious Practices of the Sectaries of This Time, Vented and Acted in England in These Four Last Years.* London, 1645.

Ellis, H[umphrey]. *Pseudochristus: Or, a True and Faithful Relation of the Grand Impostures, Abominable Practises, Horrid Blasphemies, Gross Deceits, Lately Spread abroad and Acted in the County of Southampton, by William Franklin and Mary Gadbury, and Their Companions.* London, 1650.

Evelyn, John. *History of Religion.* 2 vols. London: Henry Colburn, 1850.

Fairfax, Edward. *A Discourse of Witchcraft. As It Was Acted in the Family of*

Mr. Edward Fairfax of Fuystone in the County of York, in the Year 1621. Harrogate: R. Ackrill, 1882.

Farmer, Ralph. *Sathan Enthron'd in His Chair of Pestilence, or Quakerism in Its Exaltation. Being a True Narrative and Relation of the Manner of James Nailer (That Eminent Quaker's) Entrance into the City of Bristoll the 24 Day of October, 1656.* London, 1657.

Firth, C. H., ed. *The Clarke Papers: Selections from the Papers of William Clarke.* 4 vols. Westminster: Nichols and Sons, 1894.

Fisher, James. *The Wise Virgin, or, a Wonderfull Narration of the Hand of God, Wherein His Severity and Goodness Hath Appeared in Afflicting a Childe of Eleven Years of Age.* London, 1653.

Fowler, Christopher. *Daemonium Meridianum. Sathan at Noon . . . the Second Part. . . . This Now Discovereth the Slanders and Calumnies Cast upon Some Corporations, with Forged and False Articles upon the Author in a Pamphlet Intituled, The Case of Reading Rightly Stated, by the Adherents and Abettors of the said J[ohn] P[ordage].* London, 1656.

Frost, Joseph, and Isaac Frost, eds. *The Works of John Reeve and Lodowicke Muggleton, the Two Last Prophets of the Only True God, Our Lord Jesus Christ.* 3 vols. London, 1832.

Garden, George. *Apology for M. Antonia Bourignon.* London, 1699.

Gilpin, John. *The Quakers Shaken: Or, a Fire-Brand Snatch'd out of the Fire.* London, 1653.

H. I., *A Strange Wonder or a Wonder in a Woman, Wherein Is Plainely Expressed the True Nature of Most Women.* London, 1642.

Hart, John. *The Firebrand Taken out of the Fire, or, the Wonderfull History, Case, and Cure of Mis(tress) Drake Sometimes the Wife of Francis Drake of Esher in the County of Surrey Esq.* London, 1654.

Henderson, Katherine Usher, and Barbara F. McManus, eds. *Half Humankind: Contexts and Texts of the Controversy about Women in England, 1540–1640.* Urbana and Chicago: University of Illinois Press, 1985.

Heywood, Thomas. *The Exemplary Lives and Memorable Acts of Nine of the Most Worthy Women of the World.* London, 1640.

Higginson, Francis. *A Brief Relation of the Irreligion of the Northern Quakers.* London, 1653.

The Holy Sisters Conspiracy against Their Husbands, and the City of London. 1661.

Irwin, Joyce L., ed. *Womanhood in Radical Protestantism, 1525–1675.* New York and Toronto: The Edwin Mellen Press, 1979.

J. T., *A Brief Representation and Discovery of the Notorious Falshood and Dissimulation Contained in a Book Styled, The Gospel-Way Confirmed by Miracles.* London, 1649.

Jeaffreson, John Cordy, ed. *Middlesex County Records.* Vol. 3, *Indictments, Recognizances, Coroners' Inquisitions-Post-Mortem . . . 1 Charles I to 18 Charles II.* London: County Record Society, 1888.

Jessey, Henry. *The Exceeding Riches of Grace Advanced.* 7th ed. 1658.

Jordan, Edward. *A Briefe Discourse of a Disease Called the Suffocation of the Mother.* London, 1603.

Lilly, William. *Astrological Almanac*. 1680.

———. *Merlinus Anglicus Junior: The English Merlin Revived, or, His Prediction upon the Affaires of the English Common-wealth, and of All or Most Kingdomes of Christendome This Present Yeare, 1644*. London, 1644.

———. *A Prophecy of the White King: And Dreadfull Dead-man Explained. To Which Is Added the Prophecie of Sibylla Tiburtina & Prediction of John Kepler: All of Especiall Concernment for These Times*. London, 1644.

Livingston, Patrick. *Truth Owned and Deceit Denyed*. London, 1667.

Montelion 1661, Or, the Prophetical Almanack. 1661.

Moore, Mary. *Wonderfull News from the North: Or, a True Relation of the Sad and Grievous Torments, Inflicted upon the Bodies of Three Children . . . by Witchcraft*. London, 1650.

More, Henry. *Enthusiasmus Triumphatus: Or, a Brief Discourse of the Nature, Causes, Kinds, and Cure of Enthusiam*. William Andrews Clark Memorial Library, no. 118. Los Angeles: University of California Press, 1966.

Mother Shipton. *The End of the World*. London, n.d.

Muggleton, Lodowijk. *A Looking-Glass for George Fox the Quaker, and Other Quakers: Wherein They May See Themselves to Be Right Devils*. 1667.

Norton, Humphrey. *New England's Bloody Ensigne*. London, 1659.

Paget, John. *An Arrow against the Separation of the Brownists*. Amsterdam, 1618.

Poor Robin. 1664. An Almanack after a New Fashion. London, 1664.

Pordage, John. *Innocencie Appearing, through the Dark Mists of Pretended Guilt. Or, a Full and True Narration of the Unjust and Illegal Proceedings of the Commissioners of Berks*. London, 1654.

———. *Theological Mystica, or the Mystic Divinitie of the Aeternal Invisibles*. London, 1683.

———. *Truth Appearing through the Clouds of Undeserved Scandal*. London, 1665.

Prynne, William, Esq. *A Fresh Discovery of Prodigious New Wandring-Blasing-Stars and Fire-Brands, Stiling Themselves "New-Lights:" Firing Our Church and State into New Combustions*. London, 1645.

———. *The Quakers Unmasked, and Clearly Detected to Be But the Spawn of Romish Frogs, Jesuits, and Franciscan Fryers, Sent from Rome to Seduce the Intoxicated Giddy-headed English Nation by an Information Newly Taken upon Oath in the City of Bristol. . . . 2d ed*. London, 1655.

Quakers Are Inchanters, and Dangerous Seducers, Appearing in Their Enchantment of One Mary White at Wickham-Skeyth in Suffolk, 1655. London, 1655.

Rich, Robert. *Hidden Things Brought to Light or the Discord of the Grand Quakers among Themselves*. 1678.

R[ogers], D[aniel]. *Matrimoniall Honour: Or, the Mutuall Crowne and Comfort of Godly, Loyall, and Chaste Marriage*. London, 1642.

Rogers, John. *Ohel or Beth-shemesh: A Tabernacle for the Sun*. London, 1653.

Rollins, Hyder Edward, ed. *The Pack of Autolycus, or Strange and Terrible News of Ghosts, Apparations . . . as Told in the Broadside Ballads of the Years 1624–1693*. Cambridge, Mass.: Harvard University Press, 1927.

Rose, William, ed. *The Historie of the Damnable Life, and Deserved Death of Doctor John Faustus and the Second Report of Faustus, Containing His Appearances and the Deeds of Wagner*. 1592. Reprint. London, n.d.

Rump, or an Exact Collection of the Choycest Poems and Songs. 2 vols. London, 1662.

Satan His Methods and Malice Baffled. A Narrative of God's Gracious Dealings with That Choice Christian Mrs. Hannah Allen, (afterwards Married to Mr. Hat). London, 1683.

Scott, Reginald. *The Discoverie of Witchcraft*. 1886.

Smith, John. "Of Prophecy." In *Select Discourses*. 1660. Reprint. Delmar, N.Y.: Scholars' Facsimiles and Reprints, 1979.

Smith, Nigel, ed. *A Collection of Ranter Writings from the Seventeenth Century*. London: Junction Books, 1983.

Smith, Thomas. *A Gagg for the Quakers, Speaking by the Inspiration of the Papists*. London, 1659.

A Strange Accident That Happened Lately at Mears-Ashby in Northamptonshire of One Mary Wilmore, Wife of John Wilmore, Rough Mason, Who Was Delivered of a Childe without a Head and Credibly Reported to Have a Firme Crosse on the Brest. London, 1642.

Strange and Terrible Newes from Cambridge, Being a True Relation of the Quakers Bewitching of Mary Philips out of the Bed from Her Husband in the Night, and Transformed Her into the Shape of a Bay Mare, Riding Her from Dinton, towards the University. London, 1659.

Tilley, M. P., ed. *A Dictionary of the Proverbs in England in the Sixteenth and Seventeenth Centuries*. Ann Arbor: University of Michigan Press, 1950.

Toxander, Theophilus Philaleihes. *Vox Coeli to England, or England's Fore-warning from heaven*. London, 1646.

The Virgin Mary. A Sermon Preach'd in St. Mary's College (Vulgo New-College) Oxon, March the 25th, 1641. London, 1710.

Wade, William. *Arcandam, or Alcandrin, to Finde the Fatall Destiny, Constellation, Complexion, and Naturall Inclination of Every Man and Childe by His Birth*. London, 1652.

Wheelwright, John. *Mercurius Americanus, Thomas Welds His Antitype, or Massachusetts Great Apologie Examined....* 1645. In *John Wheelwright His Writings, Including His Fast-Day Sermon, 1637, and His Mercurius Americanus 1645; With a Paper upon the Genuineness of the Indian Deed of 1629*. Burt Franklin Research and Source Work Series no. 131, The Prince Society, vol. 9. New York: Burt Franklin, n.d.

Winstanley, Gerrard. *Fire in the Bush: The Spirit Burning Not Consuming, but Purging Mankinde*. 1650. In *The Works of Gerrard Winstanley*, edited by George H. Sabine. Ithaca, N.Y.: Cornell University Press, 1941.

———. *The Law of Freedom in a Platform or True Magistracy Restored*. 1651. In *The Works of Gerrard Winstanley*, edited George H. Sabine. Ithaca, N.Y.: Cornell University Press, 1941.

———. "Letter to Eleanor Davies, Pirton, Hertfordshire, 1650," ed. Paul H. Hardacre, *Huntington Library Quarterly* 22 (1959): 345–49.

Winstanley, William. *Poor Robin's Almanac (An Almanack after a New Fashion)*. London, 1662.

———. *Poor Robin's Visions: Wherein Is Described, the Present Humours of the Times; the Vices and Fashionable Fopperies thereof; and after What Manner Men Are Punished for Them Hereafter, Discovered in a Dream*. London, 1677.

The Wonderfull Works of God, Declared by a Strange Prophecie of a Maid in Nottingham-shire, Who Departed This Life 21 Nov. 1641.

A Yea and Nay Almanack for the People Call'd by the Men of the World Quakers. London, 1678, 1679, 1680.

SECONDARY WORKS ON QUAKERS

Bacon, Margaret Hope. *Mothers of Feminism: The Story of Quaker Women in America*. San Francisco: Harper and Row Publishers, 1986.

Barbour, Hugh. "Quaker Prophetesses and Mothers in Israel." In *Seeking the Light: Essays in Quaker History in Honor of Edwin B. Bronner*, ed. J. William Frost and John M. Moore. Wallingford and Haverford, Pa.: Pendle Hill Publications and Friends Historical Association, 1986.

———. *The Quakers in Puritan England*. New Haven and London: Yale University Press, 1964.

Barclay, Robert. *The Inner Life of the Religious Societies of the Commonwealth*. London: Hodder and Stoughton, 1876.

Bauman, Richard. *Let Your Words Be Few: Symbolism of Speaking and Silence among Seventeenth-Century Quakers*. Cambridge Studies in Oral and Literate Culture. Cambridge: Cambridge University Press, 1983.

Beamish, Lucia K. *Quaker Ministry, 1691–1834*. Oxford: by the author, 1967.

Beck, William, and T. Frederick Ball. *The London Friends' Meetings: Showing the Rise of the Society of Friends in London*. London: F. Bowyer Kitto, 1869.

Biddle, Henry D. *Notes on the Genealogy of the Biddle Family*. Philadelphia: W. S. Fortescue and Co., 1895.

Bittle, William G. *James Nayler, 1618–1660: The Quaker Indicted by Parliament*. York: William Sessions, 1986.

Blecki, Catherine La Courreye. "Alice Hayes and Mary Penington: Personal Identity within the Traditions of Quaker Spiritual Autobiography." *Quaker History* 65, no. 1 (Spring 1976): 19–31.

Bowden, James. *The History of the Society of Friends in America*. 2 vols. London: Charles Gilpin, 1850.

Brailsford, Mabel R. *Quaker Women, 1650–1690*. London: Duckworth and Co., 1915.

Braithwaite, William C. *The Beginnings of Quakerism*. 2d ed. Cambridge: Cambridge University Press, 1955.

———. "Payments for Friends' Horses." *Friends Quarterly Examiner* 46 (1912): 482–88.

———. *The Second Period of Quakerism*. York: William Sessions, 1979.

Brinton, Howard H. *Friends for 300 Years: The History and Beliefs of the Society of Friends since George Fox Started the Quaker Movement.* Wallingford, Pa.: Pendle Hill Publications and Philadelphia Yearly Meeting of the Religious Society of Friends, 1983.

Brown, Elizabeth Potts, and Susan Stuard, eds. *Witnesses for Change: Quaker Women over Three Centuries.* New Brunswick, N.J.: Rutgers University Press, 1989.

Cadbury, Henry J., ed. *Annual Catalogue of George Fox's Papers Compiled in 1694–1697.* Philadelphia and London: Friends Book Store and Friends Book Centre, 1939.

Carre, Beatrice. "Early Quaker Women in Lancaster and Lancashire." In *Early Lancaster Friends,* edited Michael Mullet. Centre for North-West Regional Studies, University of Lancaster, Occasional Paper no. 5. Leeds: W. S. Maney and Son, 1978.

Carroll, Kenneth L. "The Anatomy of a Separation: The Lynam Countroversy." *Quaker History* 55 (1966): 67–78.

———. "Early Quakers and 'Going Naked As a Sign.'" *Quaker History* 67 (1978): 69–87.

———. "Elizabeth Harris, the Founder of American Quakerism." *Quaker History* 55 (1968): 96–111.

———. "John Perrot, Early Quaker Schismatic." *Journal of the Friends Historical Society* Supp. 33 (1971).

———. "A Look at James Milner and His 'False Prophecy.'" *Quaker History* 74 (1985): 18–26.

———. "Martha Simmonds, a Quaker Enigma." *Journal of the Friends Historical Society* 53 (1972): 31–52.

Cherry, Charles. *A Quiet Haven: Quakers, Moral Treatment, and Asylum Reform.* Rutherford, N.J.: Fairleigh Dickinson University Press, 1989.

Chu, Jonathan M. *Neighbors, Friends, or Madmen: The Puritan Adjustment to Quakerism in Seventeenth-Century Massachusetts Bay.* Westport, Conn., and London: Greenwood Press, 1985.

Coudert, Alison. "A Quaker-Kabbalist Controversy: George Fox's Reaction to Francis Mercury van Helmont." *Journal of the Warburg and Courtauld Institutes* (1976): 171–89.

Douglas, Mary. *Purity and Danger: An Analysis of Concepts of Pollution and Taboo.* London and Henley: Routledge and Kegan Paul, 1966.

Dunn, Mary Maples. "Saints and Sisters: Congregational and Quaker Women in the Early Colonial Period," *American Quarterly* 30 (1978): 582–601.

Dunn, Richard S., and Mary Maples Dunn, eds. *The World of William Penn.* Philadelphia: University of Pennsylvania Press, 1986.

Edwards, Irene L. "The Women Friends of London: The Two-Weeks and Box Meetings." *Journal of the Friends Historical Society* 47 (1955): 2–21.

Endy, Melvin P. Jr. *William Penn and Early Quakerism.* Princeton: Princeton University Press, 1973.

Evans, Charles. *Friends in the Seventeenth Century.* Philadelphia: 1876.

Fogelklou, Emelia. *James Nayler, the Rebel Saint 1618–1660: An Attempt to Reconstruct the Chequered Life History of a Singular Personality from the*

Age of the Commonwealth. Translated by Lajla Yapp. London: E. Benn, 1931.

Gadt, Jeannette Carter. "Women and Protestant Culture: The Quaker Dissent from Puritanism." Ph.D. diss., University of California, Los Angeles, 1974.

Gardner, Judith Kegan. "Re-Gendering Individualism: Margaret Fell Fox and Quaker Rhetoric." In *Privileging Gender in Early Modern Britain,* edited by Jean R. Brink. Kirksville, Missouri: Sixteenth Century Journal Publications, forthcoming.

Gummere, Amelia M. *Witchcraft and Quakerism: A Study in Social History.* Philadelphia: The Biddle Press, 1908.

Gwyn, Douglas. *Apocalypse of the Word: The Life and Message of George Fox (1624–1691).* Richmond, Ind.: Friends United Press, 1986.

Higgins, Lesley H. "The Apostatized Apostle, John Pennyman: Heresy and Community in Seventeenth Century Quakerism," *Quaker History* 69 (1980): 102–108.

Hodgkin, Lucy V. *Gulielma: Wife of William Penn.* London, New York, and Toronto: Longmans, Green, and Co., 1947.

———. *A Quaker Saint of Cornwall: Loveday Hambly and Her Guests.* London: Longmans, Green, and Co., 1927.

Horle, Craig W. "John Camm: Profile of a Quaker Minister during the Interregnum." *Quaker History* 70, no. 2 (Fall 1981): 69–83, and 71, no. 1 (Spring–Summer 1982): 3–15.

———. *The Quakers and the English Legal System, 1660–1688.* Philadelphia: University of Pennsylvania Press, 1988.

Hull, William. *The Rise of Quakerism in Amsterdam, 1655–1685.* Swarthmore College Monographs on Quaker History, no. 4. Philadelphia: Patterson and White Co., 1938.

Jones, Rufus M. *The Later Periods of Quakerism.* 2 vols. London: MacMillan and Co., 1921.

———. *The Quakers in the American Colonies.* London: MacMillan and Co., 1911.

Jones, T. Canby. *George Fox's Attitude toward War.* Richmond, Ind.: Friends United Press, 1972.

Keiser, G. Melvin. "From Dark Christian to Fullness of Life: Isaac Penington's Journey from Puritanism to Quakerism." *Guilford Review* 23 (1986): 44–63.

Kunze, Bonnelyn Young. "The Family, Social, and Religious Life of Margaret Fell." Ph.D. diss., University of Rochester, 1986.

Leach, Robert J. *Women Ministers: A Quaker Contribution.* Pendle Hill Pamphlet no. 227. Wallingford, Pa.: Pendle Hill Publications, 1979.

Levy, Barry. *Quakers and the American Family: British Settlement in the Delaware Valley.* New York and Oxford: Oxford University Press, 1988.

Luder, Hope Elizabeth. *Women and Quakerism.* Pendle Hill Pamphlet no. 196. Wallingford, Pa.: Pendle Hill Publications, 1974.

Manners, Emily. *Elizabeth Hooton: First Quaker Woman Preacher (1600–1672).* London: Headley Brothers, 1914.

Mortimer, R. S. "Marriage Discipline in Early Friends: A Study in Church

Administration Illustrated from Bristol Records." *Journal of the Friends Historical Society* 48 (1957): 175–95.

Mullett, Michael. "'The Assembly of the People of God': The Social Organization of Lancashire Friends." In *Early Lancaster Friends,* edited Michael Mullett. Centre for North-West Regional Studies, University of Lancaster, Occasional Paper, no. 5. Leeds: W. S. Maney and Son., 1978.

Nicholson, Marjorie Hope. "George Keith and the Cambridge Platonists." *Philosophical Review* 39 (1930): 36–55.

Nuttall, Geoffrey F. "James Nayler: A Fresh Approach." *Journal of the Friends Historical Society.* Supp 26 (1954): 1–20.

———. "Puritan and Quaker Mysticism." *Theology* 78 (1975): 518–31.

———. *Studies in Christian Enthusiasm: Illustrated from Early Quakerism.* Wallingford, Pa.: Pendle Hill Publications, 1948.

———. "Unity with the Creation: George Fox and the Hermetic Philosophy." *Friends Quarterly* 1 (1947): 134–43.

Pestana, Carla Gardina. "The City upon a Hill under Siege: The Puritan Perception of the Quaker Threat to Massachusetts Bay, 1656–1661." *New England Quarterly* 56 (1983): 323–53.

Reay, Barry. *The Quakers and the English Revolution.* London: Temple Smith, 1985.

Rickman, Lydia L. "Esther Biddle and Her Mission to Louis XIV." *Quaker History* 47 (1955): 38–45.

Ross, Isabel. *Margaret Fell: Mother of Quakerism.* London: Longmans, Green, and Co., 1949.

Scull, G. D. *Dorothea Scott, Otherwise Gotherson and Hogben, of Egerton House, Kent, 1611–1680.* Oxford: Parker and Co., 1883.

Smith, Joseph. *A Descriptive Catalogue of Friends' Books . . . from their first Rise to the Present Time.* 2 vols. London: Joseph Smith, 1867.

Spurrier, William Wayne. "The Persecution of the Quakers in England: 1650–1714." Ph.D. diss., University of North Carolina, 1976.

Stoneburner, Carol, O. Theodor Benfey, and Robert Kraus, eds. "Perspectives on the Seventeenth-Century World of Viscountess Anne Conway." *Guilford Review* 23 (Spring 1986).

Taylor, Ernest E. "The Great Revival at Malton in 1652." *Journal of the Friends Historical Society* 33 (1936): 29–31.

———. *The Valiant Sixty.* London: The Bannisdale Press, 1947.

Thistlethwaite, W. Pearson. *Yorkshire Quarterly Meeting (of the Society of Friends) 1665–1966.* Harrowgate: by the author, 1979.

Tolles, Frederick B. *Meeting House and Counting House: The Quaker Merchants of Colonial Philadelphia, 1682–1763.* Chapel Hill: University of North Carolina Press, 1948.

Underwood, T. L. "Early Quaker Eschatology." In *Puritans, the Millennium, and the Future of Israel: Puritan Eschatology, 1600 to 1660,* edited by Peter Toon. Cambridge and London: James Clarke, 1970.

Vann, Richard T. *The Social Development of English Quakerism, 1655–1755.* Cambridge, Mass.: Harvard University Press, 1969.

Vipont, Elfrida. *George Fox and the Valiant Sixty.* London: Hamish Hamilton, 1975.

Whitbeck, Caroline. "Friends Historical Testimony on the Marriage Relationship." *Quaker Thought and Life Today,* 35, no. 6 (June 1989): 13–15.

Wight, Thomas. *History of the Rise and Progress of the People Called Quakers in Ireland, from the Year 1653 to 1700.* Dublin, 1751.

Willauer, G. J., Jr. "Notes and Documents—First Publishers of Truth in New England: A Composite List, 1656–1775." *Quaker History* 65 (1976): 35–44.

Winsser, Johan. "Mary Dyer and the 'Monster' Story." *Quaker History* 79 (1990): 20–34.

Worrall, Arthur J. *Quakers in the Colonial Northeast.* Hanover, N.H.: University Press of New England, 1980.

Wright, Luella M. *The Literary Life of the Early Friends, 1650–1725.* New York: Columbia University Press, 1932.

Wright, Sheila. "Quakerism and Its Implications for Quaker Women: The Women Itinerant Ministers of York Meeting, 1780–1840." In *Women in the Church,* edited by W. J. Sheils and Diana Wood. Vol. 27 of Studies in Church History. Oxford: Basil Blackwell, 1990.

SELECTED GENERAL SECONDARY SOURCES

Amussen, Susan Dwyer. *An Ordered Society: Family and Village in England, 1560–1725.* Oxford, New York: Basil Blackwell, 1988.

Anglo, Sidney, ed. *The Damned Art: Essays in the Literature of Witchcraft.* London: Routledge and Kegan Paul, 1977.

Beier, Lucinda McCray. *Sufferers and Healers: The Experience of Illness in Seventeenth-Century England.* London and New York: Routledge and Kegan Paul, 1987.

Belsey, Catherine. *The Subject of Tragedy: Identity and Difference in Renaissance Drama.* London and New York: Methuen, 1985.

Berg, Christina, and Philippa Berry. "Spiritual Whoredom: An Essay on Female Prophets in the Seventeenth Century." In *1642: Literature and Power in the Seventeenth Century,* edited by Francis Barker et al. Proceedings of the Essex Conference on the Sociology of Literature, July 1980. Colchester: University of Essex Press, 1981.

Briggs, Katharine Mary. *Pale Hecate's Team: An Examination of the Beliefs on Witchcraft and Magic among Shakespeare's Contemporaries and His Immediate Successors.* London: Routledge and Kegan Paul, 1962.

Burke, Peter. *Popular Culture in Early Modern Europe.* New York and London: Harper and Row, 1978.

Burnham, Frederic B. "The More-Vaughan Controversy: The Revolt against Philosophical Enthusiasm." *Journal of the History of Ideas* 35 (1974): 33–49.

Bynum, Caroline Walker. *Jesus as Mother: Studies in the Spirituality of the High Middle Ages.* Berkeley: University of California Press, 1982.

———. "Women's Stories, Women's Symbols: A Critique of Victor Turner's Theory of Liminality." In *Anthropology and the Study of Religion,* edited by Robert L. Moore and Frank E. Reynolds. Chicago: Center for the Scientific Study of Religion, 1984.

Bynum, Caroline Walker, Stevan Harrell, and Paula Richman, eds. *Gender and Religion: On the Complexity of Symbols.* Boston: Beacon Press, 1986.

Capp, Bernard S. *Astrology and the Popular Press: English Almanacs, 1500–1800.* London and Boston: Faber and Faber, 1979.

———. *The Fifth Monarchy Men: A Study in Seventeenth-Century English Millenarianism.* London: Faber and Faber, 1972.

Christianson, Paul. *Reformers and Babylon: English Apocalyptic Visions from the Reformation to the Eye of the Civil War.* Toronto: University of Toronto Press, 1978.

Clark, Stuart. "Inversion, Misrule, and the Meaning of Witchcraft." *Past and Present* 87 (1980): 98–127.

Cohen, Alfred. "Prophecy and Madness: Women Visionaries during the Puritan Revolution." *Journal of Psychohistory* 11 (1984): 411–30.

Colie, Rosalie L. *Paradoxica Epidemica: The Renaissance Tradition of Paradox.* Princeton: Princeton University Press, 1966.

Cope, Esther S. "Dame Eleanor Davies Never Soe Mad a Ladie?" *Huntingdon Library Quarterly* 50, no. 2 (Spring 1987) 133–44.

Coudert, Alison. "A Cambridge Platonist's Kabbalist Nightmare." *Journal of the History of Ideas* 35 (1975): 633–52.

Crawford, Patricia. "The Construction and Experience of Maternity in Seventeenth-Century England." In *Women as Mothers in Pre-Industrial England: Essays in Memory of Dorothy McClaren,* edited by Valerie Fildes. London and New York: Routledge, 1990.

———. "'The Sucking Child': Adult Attitudes to Child Care in the First Year of Life in Seventeenth-Century England." *Continuity and Change* 1 (1986): 23–52.

———. "Women's Published Writings, 1600–1700." In *Women in English Society, 1500–1800,* edited by Mary Prior. London and New York: Methuen, 1985.

Cross, Claire. "The Church in England, 1646–1660." In *The Interregnum: The Quest for Settlement, 1640–1660,* edited by G. E. Aylmer. Hamden: Archon Books, 1972.

———. "'He-Goats Before the Flocks': A Note on the Part Played by Women in the Founding of Some Civil War Churches." in *Popular Belief and Practice,* edited by G. J. Cuming and Derek Baker. Cambridge: Cambridge University Press, 1972.

Dailey, Barbara Ritter. "The Itinerant Preacher and the Social Network in Seventeenth-Century New England." In *Itinerancy in New England and New York,* The Dublin Seminar for New England Folklife: Annual Proceedings, edited by Peter Benes. Boston: Boston University Press, 1984.

———. "The Visitation of Sarah Wight: Holy Carnival and the Revolution of the Saints in Civil War London." *Church History* 55 (1986): 438–55.

Davis, J. C. *Fear, Myth, and History: The Ranters and the Historians.* Cambridge and New York: Cambridge University Press, 1986.

Debus, Allen G. *The Chemical Philosophy: Paracelsian Science and Medicine in the Sixteenth and Seventeenth Centuries.* 2 vols. New York: Science History Publications, 1977.

———. *The English Paracelsians.* New York: F. Watts, 1966.

Dow, Frances D. *Radicalism in the English Revolution, 1640–1660.* Oxford: Basil Blackwell, 1985.

Eccles, Audrey. *Obstetrics and Gynecology in Tudor and Stuart England.* Kent, Ohio: Kent State University Press, 1982.

Ewen, G. L'Estrange. *Witchcraft and Demonianism.* London: Heath, Cranton, 1933.

Ezell, Margaret J. M. *The Patriarch's Wife: Literary Evidence and the History of the Family.* Chapel Hill and London: University of North Carolina Press, 1987.

Friedman, Jerome. *Blasphemy, Immorality, and Anarchy: The Ranters and the English Revolution.* Athens, Ohio, and London: Ohio University Press, 1987.

Garrett, Clarke. *Spirit Possession and Popular Religion from the Camisards to the Shakers.* Baltimore and London: Johns Hopkins University Press, 1987.

George, Margaret. *Women in the First Capitalist Society: Experiences in Seventeenth-Century England.* Urbana and Chicago: University of Illinois Press, 1988.

Greaves, Richard L. *Deliver Us from Evil: The Radical Underground in Britain, 1660–1663.* New York: Oxford University Press, 1986.

Greaves, Richard L., and Robert Zaller, eds. *Biographical Dictionary of British Radicals in the Seventeenth Century.* 3 vols. Brighton, Sussex: Harvester Press, 1982.

Greven, Philip. *The Protestant Temperament: Patterns of Child-Rearing, Religious Experience, and the Self in Early America.* New York: Alfred A. Knopf, 1980.

Hall, David D. *The Antinomian Controversy, 1636–1638.* Middletown, Conn.: Wesleyan University Press, 1968.

———. "A World of Wonders: The Mentality of the Supernatural in Seventeenth-Century New England." In *Seventeenth-Century New England,* edited by David D. Hall and David Grayson Allen. The Colonial Society of Massachusetts, vol. 63. Charlottesville: University Press of Virginia, 1984.

Hayes, T. Wilson. *Winstanley the Digger: A Literary Analysis of Radical Ideas in the English Revolution.* Cambridge, Mass.: Harvard University Press, 1979.

Henson, Linda Draper. "The Witch in Eve: Milton's Use of Witchcraft in *Paradise Lost.*" In *Milton Reconsidered: Essays in Honor of Arthur E. Barker,* edited by John Karl Franson. Salzburg Studies in English Literature, Elizabethan and Renaissance Studies, no. 49. Salzburg: Institut für Englische Sprache und Literatur, Universität Salzburg, 1976.

Higgins, Patricia. "The Reaction of Women." In *Politics, Religion and the English Civil War*, edited by Brian Manning. New York: St. Martin's Press, 1973.

Hill, Christopher. "Abolishing the Ranters." In *A Nation of Change and Novelty: Radical Politics, Religion, and Literature in Seventeenth-Century England*. London and New York: Routledge, 1990.

———. *The Experience of Defeat: Milton and Some Contemporaries*. New York: Viking, 1984.

———. "The Poor and the People in Seventeenth-Century England." In *History from Below: Studies in Popular Protest and Popular Ideology in Honour of George Rude*, edited by Frederick Krantz. Montreal: Concordia University Press, 1986.

———. "The Religion of Gerrard Winstanley." In *Collected Essays of Christopher Hill*. Vol. 2, *Religion and Politics in Seventeenth-Century England*. Amherst: University of Massachusetts Press, 1986.

———. *A Tinker and a Poor Man; John Bunyan and His Church, 1628–1688*. New York: Alfred A. Knopf, 1989.

———. *The World Turned Upside Down: Radical Ideas during the English Revolution*. New York: Viking Press, 1972.

Hill, Christopher, Barry Reay, and William Lamont. *The World of the Muggletonians*. London: Temple Smith Huehns, 1983.

Hirst, Desiree. *Hidden Riches: Traditional Symbolism from the Renaissance to Blake*. New York: Barnes and Noble, 1964.

Hobby, Elaine. *Virtue of Necessity: English Women's Writing, 1649–88*. London: Virago Press, 1988.

Howard, Jean E. "Crossdressing, the Theatre, and Gender Struggle in Early Modern England." *Shakespeare Quarterly* 39 (1988): 418–40.

Huehns, Gertrude. *Antinomianism in English History: With Special Reference to the Period 1640–1660*. London: Cresset Press, 1951.

Hunt, Margaret. "Wife Beating, Domesticity and Women's Independence in Early Eighteenth-Century London." *Gender and History*, 1992. Forthcoming.

Ingram, Martin. "Ridings, Rough Music, and Mocking Rhymes in Early Modern England." In *Popular Culture in Seventeenth-Century England*, edited by Barry Reay. London and Sydney: Croom Helm, 1985.

Johnson, William C. "The Family of Love in Stuart Literature: A Chronology of Name-Crossed Lovers." *Journal of Medieval and Renaissance Studies* 7 (1977): 95–112.

Jones, Rufus M. *Spiritual Reformers in the Sixteenth and Seventeenth Centuries*. London: MacMillan and Co., 1914.

Jordan, W. K. *The Charities of London 1480–1660: The Aspirations and the Achievements of the Urban Society*. London: Geo. Allen and Unwin Ltd., 1960.

Karlsen, Carol F. *The Devil in the Shape of a Woman: Witchcraft in Colonial New England*. New York and London: W. W. Norton and Co., 1987.

Keeble, N. H. *The Literary Culture of Nonconformity in Later Seventeenth-Century England*. Leicester, England: Leicester University Press, 1987.

Kittredge, G. L. "English Witchcraft and James I." In *Studies in the History of Religions Presented to Crawford Howell Toy by Pupils, Colleagues, and Friends*, edited by D. Lyon and G. Moore. New York: Macmillan, 1912.

Koehler, Lyle. *A Search for Power: The "Weaker Sex" in Seventeenth-Century New England*. Urbana, Chicago, and London: University of Illinois Press, 1980.

Lake, Peter. "Feminine Piety and Personal Potency: The 'Emancipation' of Mrs. Jane Ratcliffe." *The Seventeenth Century* 2 (1987): 143–65.

Lang, Amy Schrager. *Prophetic Woman: Anne Hutchinson and the Problem of Dissent in the Literature of New England*. Berkeley: University of California Press, 1987.

Laqueur, Thomas. "Orgasm, Generation, and the Politics of Reproductive Biology." In *The Making of the Modern Body: Sexuality and Society in the Nineteenth Century*, edited by Catherine Gallagher and Thomas Laqueur. Berkeley: University of California Press, 1987.

Laurence, Anne. "A Priesthood of She-Believers: Women and Congregations in Mid-Seventeenth-Century England." In *Women in the Church*, edited by W. J. Sheils and Diana Wood. Vol. 27 of Studies in Church History. Oxford: Basil Blackwell, 1990.

Leverenz, David. *The Language of Puritan Feeling: An Exploration in Literature, Psychology, and Social History*. New Brunswick, N.J.: Rutgers University Press, 1980.

Lichtenstein, Aharon. *Henry More: The Rational Theology of a Cambridge Platonist*. Cambridge, Mass.: Harvard University Press, 1962.

Ludlow, Dorothy P. "'Arise and Be Doing': English 'Preaching' Women, 1640–1660." Ph.D. diss., Indiana University, 1978.

McArthur, Ellen. "Women Petitioners and the Long Parliament." *English Historical Review* 29 (1909): 698–709.

McClaren, Angus. *Reproductive Rituals: Perceptions of Fertility in Britain from the Sixteenth Century to the Nineteenth Century*. London and New York: Methuen, 1984.

McClaren, Dorothy. "Marital Fertility and Lactation, 1570–1720." In *Women in English Society, 1500–1800*, edited by Mary Prior. London and New York: Methuen, 1985.

MacClean, Ian. *Woman Triumphant: Feminism in French Literature 1610–1652*. Oxford: Clarendon Press, 1977.

MacDonald, Michael. *Mystical Bedlam: Madness, Anxiety, and Healing in Seventeenth-Century England*. Cambridge: Cambridge University Press, 1981.

McGregor, J. F., and B. Reay, eds. *Radical Religion in the English Revolution* New York: Oxford University Press, 1984.

Mack, Phyllis. "Feminine Behavior and Radical Action: Franciscans, Quakers, and the Followers of Gandhi." *Signs: Journal of Women in Culture and Society* 11 (1986): 457–77.

———. "Women as Prophets during the English Civil War." *Feminist Studies* 8 (1982): 19–47.

Maltz, Donald. "The Bride of Christ Is Filled with His Spirit." In *Women in Ritual and Symbolic Roles*, edited by Judith Hoch-Smith and Anita Spring. New York and London: Plenum Press, 1978.

Marcus, Leah Sinanoglou. "Shakespeare's Comic Heroines, Elizabeth I, and the Political Uses of Androgyny." In *Women in the Middle Ages and the Renaissance: Literary and Historical Perspectives*, edited by Mary Beth Rose. Syracuse: Syracuse University Press, 1986.

Masson, Margaret. "The Typology of the Female as a Model for the Regenerate: Puritan Preaching, 1690–1730." *Signs: A Journal of Women in Culture and Society* 2 (1976): 304–15.

Mendelson, Sara Heller. *The Mental World of Stuart Women: Three Studies*. Amherst: University of Massachusetts Press, 1987.

———. "Stuart Women's Diaries and Occasional Memoirs." In *Women in English Society, 1500–1800*, edited by Mary Prior. London and New York: Methuen, 1985.

Montrose, Louis Adrian. "Shaping Fantasies: Figurations of Gender and Power in Elizabethan Culture." *Representations* 2 (1983): 61–89.

Morton, A. L. *The World of the Ranters: Religious Radicalism in the English Revolution*. London: Lawrence and Wishart, 1970.

Mulligan, Lotte. "'Reason,' 'Right Reason,' and 'Revelation' in Mid-Seventeenth-Century England." In *Occult and Scientific Mentalities in the Renaissance*, edited by Brian Vickers. Cambridge: Cambridge University Press, 1984.

Notestein, Wallace. *A History of Witchcraft in England from 1558 to 1718*. 1911. Reprint. New York: Russell and Russell, 1965.

Nussbaum, Felicity A. *The Autobiographical Subject: Gender and Ideology in Eighteenth-Century England*. Baltimore and London: The Johns Hopkins University Press, 1989.

Nuttall, Geoffrey F. *The Holy Spirit in Puritan Faith and Experience*. Oxford: Basil Blackwell, 1946.

Ortner, Sherry. "Is Female to Male as Nature Is to Culture?" In *Women, Culture, and Society*. edited by Michelle Z. Rosaldo and Louise Lamphere. Stanford: Stanford University Press, 1974.

Park, Katherine, and Lorraine Daston. "Unnatural Conceptions: The Study of Monsters in France and England." *Past and Present* 92 (1981): 20–54.

Porter, Roy, ed. *Patients and Practitioners: Lay Perceptions of Medicine in Pre-Industrial Society*. Cambridge: Cambridge University Press, 1985.

Radizinowicz, M. A. N. "Eve and Delila: Renovation and the Hardening of the Heart." In *Reason and the Imagination: Studies in the History of Ideas, 1600–1800*, edited by J. A. Mazzeo. New York: Columbia University Press, 1962.

Rattansi, P. M. "Paracelsus and the Puritan Revolution." *Ambix* 2 (1964): 24–32.

Reay, Barry, ed. *Popular Culture in Seventeenth-Century England*. London and Sydney: Croom Helm, 1985.

Riley, Denise. *Am I That Name? Feminism and the Category of "Women" in History*. Minneapolis: University of Minnesota Press, 1988.

Rose, Mary Beth. *The Expense of Spirit: Love and Sexuality in English Renaissance Drama*. Ithaca and London: Cornell University Press, 1988.

St. George, Robert. "'Heated' Speech and Literacy in Seventeenth-Century New England." In *Seventeenth-Century New England*, edited by David D. Hall and David Grayson Allen. The Colonial Society of Massachusetts, vol. 63. Charlottesville: University Press of Virginia, 1984.

Schwartz, Hillel. *The French Prophets: The History of a Millenarian Group in Eighteenth-Century England*. Berkeley: University of California Press, 1980.

Shammas, Carole. "The World Women Knew: Women Workers in the North of England during the Late Seventeenth Century." In *The World of William Penn*, edited by Richard S. Dunn and Mary Maples Dunn. Philadelphia: University of Pennsylvania Press, 1986.

Shapiro, Barbara. *Probability and Certainty in Seventeenth-Century England: A Study of the Relationship between Natural Science, Religion, History, Law, and Literature*. Princeton: Princeton University Press, 1983.

Shulman, George M. *Radicalism and Reverence: The Political Thought of Gerrard Winstanley*. Berkeley, Los Angeles, and London: University of California Press, 1984.

Slater, Miriam. *Family Life in the Seventeenth Century: The Verneys of Claydon House*. London: Routledge and Kegan Paul, 1984.

Smith, Catherine F. "Jane Lead: Mysticism and the Woman Cloathed with the Sun." In *Shakespeare's Sisters: Feminist Essays on Women Poets*, edited by Sandra M. Gilbert and Susan Gubar. Bloomington and London: Indiana University Press, 1979.

———. "Jane Lead's Wisdom: Women and Prophecy in Seventeenth-Century England." In *Poetic Prophecy in Western Literature*, edited by Jan Wojcik and Raymond-Jean Frontain. Rutherford, Madison, Teaneck: Fairleigh Dickinson University Press, 1984.

Smith, Hilda. "Gynecology and Ideology in Seventeenth-Century England." In *Liberating Women's History: Theoretical and Critical Essays*, edited by Berenice A. Carroll. Urbana, Chicago, and London: University of Illinois Press, 1976.

———. *Reasons's Disciples: Seventeenth-Century English Feminists*. Urbana: University of Illinois Press, 1982.

Smith, Nigel. *Perfection Proclaimed: Language and Literature in English Radical Religion, 1640–1660*. Oxford: Clarendon Press, 1989.

Spargo, John Webster. *Juridical Folklore in England, Illustrated by the Cucking-Stool*. Durham, N.C.: Duke University Press, 1944.

Spencer, Theodore. "The History of an Unfortunate Lady." *Harvard Studies and Notes in Philology and Literature* 20 (1938): 43–59.

Stallybrass, Peter. "Patriarchal Territories: The Body Enclosed." In *Rewriting the Renaissance: The Discourses of Sexual Difference in Early Modern Europe*, edited by Margaret W. Ferguson, Maureen Quilligan, and Nancy J. Vickers. Chicago and London: University of Chicago Press, 1986.

Staudenbaur, C. A. "Platonism, Theosophy, and Immaterialism: Recent Views of the Cambridge Platonists." *Journal of the History of Ideas* 35 (1974): 157–69.

Stoneburner, John H. "Henry More and Anne Conway." *Guilford Review* 23 (1986): 24–35.

Thomas, Keith. *Man and the Natural World: A History of the Modern Sensibility.* New York: Pantheon Books, 1983.

———. *Religion and the Decline of Magic.* New York: Scribner's, 1971.

———. "Women and the Civil War Sects." *Past and Present* 13 (1958): 42–62.

Thune, Nils. *The Behmenists and the Philadelphians: A Contribution to the Study of English Mysticism in the Seventeenth and Eighteenth Centuries.* Uppsala: Almquist & Wiksells Boktryckeri AB, 1948.

Trevett, Christine. *Women and Quakerism in the Seventeenth Century.* York: Ebor Press and William Sessions, 1991.

Turner, Victor. *The Ritual Process: Structure and Anti-Structure.* Ithaca, N.Y.: Cornell University Press, 1977.

Ulrich, Laurel Thatcher. *Good Wives: Image and Reality in the Lives of Women in Northern New England, 1650–1750.* New York and Toronto: Oxford University Press, 1980.

Underdown, David. *Revel, Riot, and Rebellion: Popular Politics and Culture in England, 1603–1660.* Oxford: Clarendon Press, 1985.

———. "The Taming of the Scold: The Enforcement of Patriarchal Authority in Early Modern England." In *Order and Disorder in Early Modern England,* edited by Anthony Fletcher and John Stevenson. Cambridge: Cambridge University Press, 1985.

Watkins, Owen. *The Puritan Experiment: Studies in Spiritual Autobiography.* New York: Schocken Press, 1972.

Watts, Michael R. *The Dissenters: From the Reformation to the French Revolution.* Oxford: Clarendon Press, 1978.

Webster, Charles. *The Great Instauration: Science, Medicine, and Reform, 1626–1660.* New York: Holmes and Meier Publishers, 1976.

Wells, Robin Headlam. *Spenser's "Faerie Queene" and the Cult of Elizabeth.* London and Totowa, N.J.: Barnes and Noble Books, 1983.

Williams, George Huntston. "Called by Thy Name, Leave Us Not: The Case of Mrs. Joan Drake, A Formative Episode in the Pastoral Career of Thomas Hooker in England." *Harvard Library Bulletin* 16 (1968): 111–28, 278–300.

Wilson, Adrian. "The Ceremony of Childbirth and Its Interpretation." In *Women as Mothers in Pre-Industrial England,* edited by Valerie Fildes. London and New York: Routledge, 1990.

Woodbridge, Linda. *Women and the English Renaissance: Literature and the Nature of Womankind, 1540–1620.* Urbana and Chicago: University of Illinois Press, 1984.

Yates, Frances A. *The Occult Philosophy in the Elizabethan Age.* London, Boston, and Henley: Routledge and Kegan Paul, 1979.

———. *The Rosicrucian Enlightenment.* London and Boston: Routledge and Kegan Paul, 1972.

Index

Abbott, Abigail, 387–88
Adamites, 99
Adams, Elizabeth, 167, 193, 417
Adams, Mary, 41, 117n, 413
Addams, Jane, 411
Adgit, Sarah, 421
Airey, Agnes, 421
Akehurst, Mary, 146n, 196, 422
Alcock, Hannah, 422
Aldam, Mary, 415
Aldam, Thomas, 156, 168, 182, 233–34
Aldridge, Susanna, 340, 365–66
Allen, Hannah, 82
Ambrose, Alice, 415
Amye, Mary, 358
Anabaptists, 82, 99, 249
Anderdon, John, 397
Anderdon, Mary, 417
Andrews, Elizabeth. *See* Farmer, Elizabeth
Andrews, Roger, 268
Anglicans, 58, 77; criticism of, 57, 80, 91, 104; and Quakers, 1, 3, 10, 131, 139, 143, 161n, 176, 285, 351, 355, 358, 360; and women, 79, 95, 100, 112n, 118, 138
Anne, Countess of Pembroke, 332
Anthony, Susan B., 411
Anti-formalism, 3–4, 241–45, 270–72, 277–78, 293–98, 311–19
Antinomianism, 42, 88, 99, 258; and Quakers, 133, 155, 157, 271, 277, 289

Anti-Quaker writings, 29, 65, 161n, 249, 253, 276–77, 283–84, 298–99, 360–61
Arminianism, 99
Arnell, Elizabeth, 421
Arnold, Susanna, 194n, 212, 421
Asceticism, 129, 151, 160
Ashburner, Jane, 2, 421
Ashmole, Elias, 58
Astell, Mary, 408–9
Astrology, 51, 58, 60n, 64, 76; and Quakers, 29, 285; and women, 17, 26, 31, 52, 65–66, 84 & n
Atkins, Elizabeth, 422
Atkins, Susan, 339
Attaway, Mrs., 56, 98, 112, 413
Audeley, Eleanor. *See* Davies, Eleanor
Audland, Ann (later Camm), 145n, 153–54, 158, 174–75, 189, 190, 192, 194n, 204, 222, 224–25, 228, 229, 231, 232n, 233, 240, 254, 299n, 337n, 384–85, 397, 401, 415
Audland, John, 148, 154, 214, 224–25, 228–29, 231
Austin, Ann, 131, 146n, 169, 259, 417
Avery, Elizabeth, 92–93, 95, 101, 116, 118–19, 122, 413
Ayrey, Agnes, 203n

Backhouse, Sarah, 415
Baines, Phoebe, 331
Baker, Daniel, 172
Baker, Elizabeth, 180, 422
Baker, Sarah, 422

Compositor:	Braun-Brumfield, Inc.
Printer:	Braun-Brumfield, Inc.
Binder:	Braun-Brumfield, Inc.
Text:	10/13 Sabon
Display:	Sabon